P

"Hamilton, … isted
any attempt … cep-
tional (best … oice.
Although H … t we
can imagine … em-
bodies at … most
ambiguous … read
Powell in re…

…ooks

"Hamilton'… ogant
champion o… within
a prism of … basic
American v…
Essential f… civil
rights, or p…

…urnal

"The first f… e one
for years to… as lib-
ertine, exe… s and
practices. … nt, an
admirably … d any-
thing but o…

—*Kirkus Reviews*

ALSO BY CHARLES V. HAMILTON

American Government

The Black Preacher in America

The Bench and the Ballot: Southern Federal Judges and Black Voters

The Black Experience in American Politics

Black Power (with Stokely Carmichael)

Adam Clayton Powell Jr.

The Political Biography of an American Dilemma

Charles V. Hamilton

Cooper Square Press

First Cooper Square Press edition 2002

This Cooper Square Press paperback edition of *Adam Clayton Powell Jr.* is an unabridged republication of the edition first published in New York in 1991. It is reprinted by arrangement with Scribner, an imprint of Simon & Schuster Inc.

Published by Cooper Square Press
An Imprint of the Rowman & Littlefield Publishing Group
150 Fifth Avenue, Suite 817
New York, New York 10011

Distributed by National Book Network

Library of Congress has catalogued the hardcover edition as follows:

Hamilton, Charles V.
Adam Clayton Powell, Jr. : the political biography of an American dilemma / Charles V. Hamilton.
p. cm.
Includes bibliographical references and index.
1. Powell, Adam Clayton, 1908–1972. 2. Legislators—United States—Biography. 3. United States. Congress. House—Biography. 4. Afro-Americans—Civil rights. 5. United States—Moral conditions. 6. United States—Politics and government—1945–
I. Title.
E748.P86H35 1991
973.92092—dc20
[B] 90-28505 CIP

ISBN 0-689-12062-1 (cloth : alk. paper)
ISBN: 0-8154-1184-7 (pbk. : alk. paper)

™ The paper used in this publication meets the minimum requirements of American National Standard for Information Sciences—Permanence of Paper for Printed Library Materials, ANSI/NISO Z39.48–1992.
Manufactured in the United States of America.

To Owen and Bea; Lyna and Albert . . . and Christopher

Contents

Power and Paradox, 1960s

Acknowledgments

Most authors say it; they all have their particular reasons to believe it, and I am no exception. This book benefited from the help of many individuals and institutions for which I am grateful. In addition to those interviewed and cited in the text, I appreciate the many discussions (they could hardly be called interviews in many cases) I had with others who provided insights into the times and terrain of Adam Clayton Powell, Jr. Certainly, these included James Herbert, James L. Watson, the late Andrew Tyler, Edward Costikyan, J. Herbert Cameron. M. Moran Weston, all knowledgeable in their own ways. Richard Kilberg, producer of the deservedly widely acclaimed television documentary, "Adam Clayton Powell, Jr." has my appreciation for permission to use the many interviews conducted by him and the RKB Productions with the assistance of Yvonne Smith. Likewise, I thank Norman Hill of the A. Philip Randolph Institute for permission to quote from the oral history of A. Philip Randolph in the Columbia University Oral History Project. The professional staffs of the several archival libraries I consulted were enormously helpful: Schomburg Research Center of the New York Public Library, Lyndon B. Johnson Library, Dwight D. Eisenhower Library, John F. Kennedy Library, the Library of Congress, the Fiorello H. La Guardia Papers in the New York Municipal Archives and Research Center, and the Columbia University Oral History Project, which also granted permission to quote from the several oral histories cited in the text. Inasmuch as Congressman Powell left no systematic collection of papers of his own readily available for research and study, these rich archival sources were invaluable. Two of my students at Columbia College, Anthony Fletcher and Jeffrey Klein, performed research tasks for which I owe them more than the usual professorial nod of thanks. To Aida Llabaly, I am grateful for the many secretarial tasks she performed. All authors should be fortunate to have the editorial attention provided by Barbara Campo at Atheneum. As for my Publisher, Lee Goerner, I am sure any author will understand when

I say what a delight it is to work with a professional who combines constructive commentary with caring as much about the book as the author does. He has mastered the art: an astute, gentle suggestion which leaves you reflecting—of course, makes eminent sense. My wife, Dona, knows of my longstanding interest in writing about the Congressman. And she should also know that her continued encouragement and confidence have been more important to me than any other single factor over the years. If I have not presented this biography precisely as all these would have it, at least they should know that they had an enormous influence. The strengths of the book are their to share; the weaknesses are mine alone.

Charles V. Hamilton

ADAM CLAYTON POWELL, JR.

Prologue: An American Dilemma and a Political Career

Adam Clayton Powell, Jr., was elected to Congress from Harlem, New York City, the same year, 1944, that *An American Dilemma,* the classic book by Gunnar Myrdal, was published. The Swedish scholar spent several years studying the condition of black Americans and concluded that one fundamental problem was the discrepancy between what Americans *believed* and how they *acted* in regard to the treatment of blacks in the society. He labeled these beliefs "the American Creed." They encompassed a reasonably clear set of ideas and ideals that included liberty, equality, respect for law, and democracy. These basic tenets were set forth in the Declaration of Independence, declaring that all men are created equal, and they received their nurturing in the countless and continuing speeches and tracts throughout American history. And yet, from the beginning of the new nation, slavery was sanctioned, then racial segregation and discrimination were enshrined in law. There was no denying that the American society said one thing and practiced another in regard to blacks. Thus the "dilemma."

As Myrdal put it:

> These ideals of the essential dignity of the individual human being, of the fundamental equality of all men, and of certain inalienable rights to freedom, justice, and a fair opportunity represent to the American people the essential meaning of the nation's early struggle for independence. In the clarity and intellectual boldness of the Enlightenment period these tenets were written into the Declaration of Independence, the Preamble of the Constitution, the Bill of Rights and into the constitutions of the several states. The ideals of the American Creed have thus become the highest law of the land.[1]

America fought wars articulating the moral precepts of the "Creed." These beliefs were—and are—taken seriously. They were not simply pious pronouncements intended only as empty political rhetoric. Human beings are entitled, by nature, to certain basic rights that respect their dignity and relieve them from arbitrary oppression by government or any other societal forces. The majority rules, but the minorities must have rights. The law must not operate in a discriminatory way to favor one person or group over another in matters not perceived ultimately in the common good and certainly not on criteria perceived as irrelevant, indeed antagonistic, to the basic purposes of democracy and egalitarianism. And no person should be denied the opportunity to realize her or his fullest potential.

Hardly any American school child has not been exposed to these elemental propositions:

> ". . . all Men are created equal, . . . they are endowed by their Creator with certain unalienable Rights, that among these are Life, Liberty and the Pursuit of Happiness." —Declaration of Independence.
>
> ". . . one nation under God with liberty and justice for all." —Pledge of Allegiance to the flag.
>
> "We the people . . . in order to . . . establish Justice . . . secure the blessings of liberty to ourselves and our posterity . . ." —Preamble to the United States Constitution.
>
> ". . . nor shall any State deprive any person of life, liberty, or property, without due process of law; nor deny to any person within its jurisdiction the equal protection of the laws." —Fourteenth Amendment to the United States Constitution.

And yet these seriously articulated propositions were not realized fully in practice. Inequalities and undemocratic practices persisted—not accidentally, but deliberately. Therein lies the dilemma. Myrdal pinpointed this contradiction and insisted that it posed a major moral problem for "the great majority of white Americans." It was "embarrassing." It was morally discomforting. He concluded:

> The American Negro problem is a problem in the heart of the American. It is there that the interracial tension has its focus. It is there that the decisive struggle goes on. . . . Though our study includes economic, social, and political race relations, at bottom our problem is

> the moral dilemma of the American—the conflict between his moral valuations on various levels of consciousness and generality.[2]

The blatant contradiction in American society between the Creed and reality was constantly highlighted by white and black advocates of civil rights. It permitted them the advantage of taking the moral high ground, of being righteously indignant, of accusing their opponents of being hypocritical and insincere. They pointed to segregation laws and discriminatory practices, as well as the persistence of economic inequality. And surely they called attention to the denial of the right to vote to blacks in the South—such denial hardly being a laudable practice for a society that put so much theoretical emphasis on the value of political freedom.

Adam Clayton Powell, Jr., was coming to maturity at the time Myrdal was doing his research in the late 1930s. He took over the large Abyssinian Baptist Church as its pastor following in his father's footsteps, and he turned the church into a veritable command post for his many civic protest and subsequent political activities. For over thirty years, Powell the preacher and Powell the politician were wrapped into one with Abyssinian as his base of mobilization—to preach the gospel and save souls, or to file petitions and win elections. Powell also understood all too well the "dilemma" that Myrdal talked about, and from the beginning of his career Powell made that dilemma the main issue of his public life.

Myrdal noted the rise of Powell, who had already served one term in the New York City Council, in a footnote in *An American Dilemma*:

> The young, popular, and ambitious minister, Rev. A. Clayton Powell, has not only taken a lead in sponsoring community welfare work, but has helped the workers' side in several strikes, has succeeded in getting jobs for Negroes, and has become a publisher of a Negro newspaper and a member of the New York City Council.[3]

The moral dilemma facing America was ready-made for Powell's brand of leadership. During World War II, he called attention to the fight for freedom abroad *and* at home. "Abroad, the United States was preaching 'the century of the common man' and the 'Four Freedoms,' yet it was denying any of these freedoms at home, even in the nation's capital. America was talking about the creation of a new world while its conscience was filled with guilt."[4]

He used his Christian background and theological training as argumentative weapons against civil rights opponents:

> . . . America is not a Christian country. It is a country of pretensions, of "churchianity," where the institution of Christianity has been perverted into an instrument to perpetuate if not to propagate, directly and indirectly, anti-christian doctrines of segregation and discrimination. The only Christian churches in the United States are those churches that, at all levels, welcome and encourage the participation of all the sons of man.[5]

This was hardly language aimed at soothing consciences already perplexed by the American Dilemma. And for those blacks who believed him, Powell could even be understood as asserting a special religious brand of moral superiority over white segregationists. This was not a minor matter when it is understood how strong the forces were for instilling attitudes of inferiority within blacks. A people *legally* shunted aside and oppressed would understandably come to question their own worthiness and abilities. Thus many blacks hid behind the wall of segregation, never venturing out to challenge whites or competing with them, even, on the rare occasions, when they could. The message that Powell preached at least made them feel some sense of worth, if not complete self-confidence. And he did this by referring to the one thing he knew most of his followers possessed—namely, a close attachment to their religion.

Powell understood this as he also recognized the delicacy—to many whites and some blacks—of the issue of race. Such an explosive and potentially embarrassing issue is frequently best dealt with, if at all, subtly or, at least, politely. Myrdal described this as "the etiquette of discussion."[6] "I have come to understand," Myrdal wrote, "how a whole system of moral escape has become polite form in the South. [He could well have included the North.] This form is applicable even to scientific writings and, definitely, to public discussion and teaching on all levels. . . . It is contrary to the aims of raising issues and facing problems; it makes difficult an effective choice of words. . . . There is nearly common agreement in the South that reforms in interracial relations should be introduced with as little discussion about them as possible. It is actually assumed that the race issue is a half dormant, but easily awakened, beast. It is a complex which is irrational and uncomfortable, laden with emotions, and to be touched as little as possible."[7]

Therefore, there was a preference for the covert, quiet, subtle approach to racial problems. But Powell was nothing if he was not openly, loudly condemnatory of America's racial dilemma. He went to Congress shouting and protesting. His adversaries hated him for it; his admirers loved him precisely because of it. Given such inclinations he could hardly be anything but extremely controversial. The combination of his fiery persona and the touchy racial problem were the ingredients of an inevitably stormy political career. It is as if he consciously decided to make Americans as blatantly uncomfortable as possible with the discrepancy between creed and practice. His aim in race relations was *not* to be polite, but rather deliberately to raise the discomfort level as high as possible on this subject. And, it should be noted, whites were not his only targets. If blacks disagreed with him, as many often did at least over his style if not his substance, he shrugged them off with a scathing charge of "Uncle Tomism." His career was constantly one of positioning himself on the "militant" wing of the racial protest movement. In Powell, this was a complex mixture of sincere temperament and astute tactics. His friends preferred to conclude the former; his adversaries were convinced the major motivation was the latter.

Almost four decades after Myrdal, political scientist Samuel P. Huntington picked up the dilemma theme in his book *American Politics, The Promise of Disharmony*. Huntington agreed that there was a peculiarly American creed based on liberty, equality, individualism, and the rule of law under a constitution. These constitute widely held goals and values, and it is recognized that they can be in conflict with one another from time to time. This is so because

> [t]he unsystematic and unideological character of this Creed is reflected in the fact that no theory exists for ordering these values in relation to one another and for resolving on a theoretical level the conflicts that inherently exist among them. Conflicts easily materialize when any one value is taken to an extreme: majority rule versus minority rights; higher law versus popular sovereignty; liberty versus equality; individualism versus democracy. In other societies, ideologies give priority to one value or the other, but in American society all these values coexist together in theory, even as they may conflict with each other when applied in practice. They coexist, indeed, not only within American society, but also within individual citizens.[8]

These values are, as noted, commonly shared, and therein lies the basis for periodic disharmony and instability. On the one hand,

Americans sincerely adopt and believe in those values; on the other, their institutions and practices—à la Myrdal—do not measure up to them. This leads to a gap between ideals and institutions; Huntington calls this the "I v. I Gap." This gap exists because it is impossible to achieve in practice what the ideals call for. "Therein," Huntington concludes, "lies the dilemma. In the United States, government is legitimate to the extent to which it reflects the basic principles of the American Creed. Government can never, however, reflect those principles perfectly, and it is therefore illegitimate to the extent to which people take seriously the principles of the American Creed."[9]

So what happens? Americans strive to cope with this phenomenon Huntington identifies as "cognitive dissonance"—namely, the situation whereby a person simultaneously accepts opposing, conflicting beliefs, attitudes, or conditions. He suggests four types of responses: moralism (eliminate the gap); cynicism (tolerate the gap); complacency (ignore the gap); and hypocrisy (deny the existence of the gap).

At times, although not often, many Americans have been very perplexed about the "gap" between ideals and institutions and have acted to overcome or eliminate it. This is a time of "creedal passion" politics. This brings about a situation of rather intense political instability, such as the heightened activity over civil rights in the 1960s. But the cause of this, it should be remembered, is not a disagreement over the goals and values of the society, but the opposite. That is, the *consensus* on such matters is so strong that that very consensus is the source of the emotional, political upheaval. People become angry and frustrated that the gap exists, and they try to do something about it.

Some Americans simply try to tolerate the gap. Nothing really can be done about it, they rationalize; it has to be accepted as an uncomfortable, albeit unfortunate, way of life. There is a cynical feeling of "moral helplessness."

Others opt for a different response: ignore the gap. This leads to "creedal passivity." "During such periods of creedal passivity and perceptual opaqueness, Americans may, if compelled to do so, admit the existence of a gap between ideal and reality—*as they did for years with respect to the role of black people in American life*—but then shunt it off into a back corner of their consciousness and simply not become terribly concerned about it."[10]

A final response is to deny that a gap exists. This effort attempts to read reality as being in conformity with the ideals, to redefine the actual situation in a way that makes it consistent with values and goals. "The discrepancies are strained out and avoided. The United States not only *should* be the land of liberty, equality, and justice for all; it actually *is*."[11]

An important point for understanding Adam Powell's leadership role lies in Huntington's accurate characterization of the *infrequency* of the moral response. Most people cannot live constantly or indefinitely in a turbulent state of high creedal passion. Thus there are prolonged periods of moral latency. Herein lies the rub. When Powell came on the scene, he immediately began championing the civil rights cause and seldom let up. In doing so, he was reflecting the clear desires of large numbers of people, especially, but by no means exclusively, his black constituents. Those people could not (or chose not to) accept the more comfortable responses of complacency, hypocrisy, or cynicism. Thus what was latent in many Americans was constantly manifest in others. And, of course, blacks have had far *fewer* moments of "creedal passivity" (and more of creedal passion) than their fellow citizens on the subject of racial segregation and discrimination.

This experiential fact alone makes a political biography of Adam Clayton Powell, Jr., understandable as one that portrays him as a mirror, as a reflection of what others saw and understood to be the state of the American Dilemma Myrdal and many others so aptly described. Powell's leadership was singularly focused on that issue—America's treatment of the downtrodden, especially black people. These were the people who elected him; these were the people to whom he turned when he needed political protection, as was often the case. His official policy positions were never absent of attention to this issue. This is so whether the particular concern was civil rights and racial segregation, as it was earlier in his career, or broader socioeconomic issues in the 1960s. How one responded to Adam Powell reflected how one responded to the American Dilemma. His personal eccentricities made the response more difficult, but in a sense this made it more meaningful. This is so because friend and foe alike had to jump through many ad hominem hoops to get at the essence—the dilemma—of the race issues Powell was raising. (In this sense, Powell's leadership was different from that of Martin Luther King, Jr., who also came on the scene challenging the "gap." King's total style as well as the message of "redemptive suffering" he constantly preached made him a much easier person to accept as one who chided Americans on their dilemma. Both men preached the need for reconciliation. But somehow or other, it was easier to believe the words sincere when they came from

King rather than Powell.) Powell always required that everyone—again, friend or foe—question whether his being black was the *real* reason he was attacked so often or indicted for income tax problems or refused his seat in Congress toward the end of his career. More often than not, his supporters had to take an "in-spite-of-Adam" stance in order to defend what he "stood for." In other words, they had to engage the American Dilemma that Powell exposed, notwithstanding the source of the exposure. And even then, there were more than a few who loved him totally—warts and all.

The political career of Adam Clayton Powell, Jr., spanned three distinct periods: the Great Depression and World War II years of the 1930s to mid–1940s; the post–World War II years from 1945 to 1960; and the decade of the 1960s. In each, he had a different role on the American scene, and that role coincided with very different manifestations of the "dilemma" he and the country were grappling with. This was expected since we are talking about the four decades following 1930, when he graduated from college and became assistant pastor of his father's church in Harlem, to 1970, when he was finally defeated in a reelection bid to Congress.

America had changed drastically during that time, but amazingly "the dilemma" persisted, albeit in different forms. Those changes, new responses, and new issues with Powell as the constant referent constitute the story of this book.

Importantly, and some said unfortunately, Powell, especially after he became chairperson of a major congressional committee in 1961, flaunted his power. He boasted of his influence and taunted his detractors. Always, his issue was race prejudice and economic oppression of the poor. He used the weapons of ridicule to put down the segregationists, and this made him that much more objectionable to friend and foe alike. His friends wished he would be less of a show-off, less openly arrogant, and less obviously opportunistic. But these were traits of a lifetime. Others saw him as a defiant hero, self-confident, a relentless fighter against injustice. He had a way of dismissing criticism that was at once infuriating and peevish. When some congressional colleagues accused him, a married man, of taking two beautiful women congressional staff members to Europe alone with him, one white and one black, he quipped: "What was all the fuss about? Did they want me to take an all-black staff?"[12]

He kept his third wife on his congressional payroll long after she ceased performing any work to earn her salary, apparently having no qualms about having her checks sent to him for deposit in his own bank account. He misused congressional travel funds, using innumerable airline tickets made out to staff members to pay for vacation trips to the Bahamas for himself and his woman companion. He shrugged off criticism of his behavior and dared his colleagues to challenge him. They were a bunch of hypocrites, he charged, accusing some of attacking him simply because he was a staunch advocate of civil rights.

He had the American Dilemma tiger by the tail, and he knew precisely how vulnerable the country was to the charge of hypocrisy and moral deceit. In all likelihood this was one of the major objections to him. In a sense, one who would raise the credibility issue of America's Creed should, himself, be above reproach. He should come into court, as it were, with clean hands. (This apparently weighed heavily on Martin Luther King, Jr., in terms of his own personal life and the suspected evidence obtained by the FBI.)[13] But Adam Powell was having none of what he assumed was a "double standard." "I do not do any more than any other member of Congress, and by the grace of God, I'll not do less," he said on more than one occasion in defending his various questionable sallies.

Perhaps so. But apparently he should have known, and if he did he seemed not to care, that if there were forces as sinister and as devoted to his downfall and the defeat of the causes he championed as he constantly claimed, the resentment of him would be boundless. And above all, there was little escaping the conclusion that one who would raise the moral issue of America's dilemma—and do it so forcefully and effectively—would himself be under intense scrutiny. The dilemma is so serious and painful to many Americans that there would be resentment against anyone who rubbed America's face in the problem and who himself exhibited seemingly aberrant and, at times, morally and legally questionable behavior.

Such was the dynamic intersection of the American Dilemma and Powell's political career. And when Americans looked at him and responded to him, they saw reflected their own varied, complex responses to society's gap between ideals and practices. That the mirror itself contained cracks made the viewing that much more difficult, and the reflection that much more confusing and hard to read.

Introduction

1

The Fall from Power: Double Standard or Due Punishment?

The President of the United States, Lyndon B. Johnson, had told his staff that he wanted to be kept informed of the vote in the House of Representatives that afternoon on the Adam Clayton Powell matter.

At 3:32 P.M. on January 10, 1967, a secretary put the following memo on the President's desk:

> Mr. President:
>
> Henry Wilson just called to report the following: The House of Representatives just defeated by 305–126 the Democratic motion which provided that Powell be seated but a blue ribbon committee to determine if he remained seated. The House is now considering a Republican motion for Powell to stand aside for five (5) weeks while a committee of 5 Democrats and 4 Republicans investigate.[1]

One hour later, the secretary put another memo on the President's desk:

> Mr. President:
>
> The Republican motion to unseat Powell was adopted on roll call.
> The vote is 354–64
> Henry Wilson/mf
> 4:30 p[2]

Now the President knew, and soon the country would hear the

results of the three-hour discussion conducted in the House of Representatives the afternoon of January 10, 1967. The citizens of a congressional district in Harlem in New York City would be, for the time being, without a representative. The black candidate, the Reverend Adam Clayton Powell, Jr., Democrat, they had reelected the previous November and had been electing to Congress since 1944 had been ordered to "step aside."

The atmosphere inside the chamber during the debate was tense and somber, lightened only momentarily when Democratic Majority Leader Carl Albert, from Oklahoma, pleading that Powell should first be seated and then investigated, inadvertently said: "The American way is first give a man a trial and then convict him." This brought a ripple of nervous laughter from the legislators and even amused Powell, who was standing in the rear of the chamber, puffing his cigarillo and waiting his turn to use the four and one-half minutes allotted him to defend himself.

But several hundred ardent Powell supporters, mostly come by chartered buses from New York, who had assembled outside the Capitol, were in no mood for levity. With rarely granted special permission to hold a rally on the Capitol steps, they began assembling at eighty-thirty that morning, making angry speeches challenging the impending House action and generally charging Powell's colleagues with racism and with pursuing a vendetta against Powell for his years of strong advocacy of civil rights generally, and of "Black Power" specifically.

But the congressional action inside the chamber would not be influenced by the protesters outside. Whatever the legislators felt about Powell, they were keenly aware, from public opinion polls and from hundreds if not thousands of letters from constituents around the country, that the supporters outside had their counterparts in those around the country who wanted to see Adam Powell out of Congress.

Around noon, as the swearing-in ceremony began, Representative-elect Lionel Van Deerlin, Democrat from California, made the first move against Powell.[3] He rose to be recognized.

Mr. Van Deerlin: Mr. Speaker.

The Speaker: For what purpose does the gentleman from California rise?

Mr. Van Deerlin: Mr. Speaker, upon my responsibility as a Member-Elect of the 90th Congress, I object to the oath being administered at this time to the gentleman from New York, Mr. Powell.

> I base this upon facts and statements which I consider reliable. I intend at the proper time to offer a resolution providing that the question of eligibility of Mr. Powell to a seat in this House be referred to a special committee.
>
> *The Speaker:* Does the gentleman demand that the gentleman from New York step aside?
>
> *Mr. Van Deerlin:* Yes, Mr. Speaker.
>
> *The Speaker:* The gentleman has performed his duties and has taken the action he desires to take under the rule. The gentleman from New York, Mr. Powell, will be requested to be seated during the further proceedings.

The motion was not subject to debate or challenge at that time. The person so challenged had to remain seated while the others stood and took the oath of office. Powell so obliged.

Then, after the 433 other elected representatives were sworn in, the Speaker of the House recognized Congressman Morris K. Udall, Democrat from Arizona, who moved that Powell be sworn in and then an investigation of his future status as a member be determined. This motion had the support of the leadership of the Majority Party, Powell's party, but it was defeated—305–126. (At that point the first call was made to the White House.) This set the stage for the decisive vote against Powell on a motion by the Republican Minority Leader, Gerald R. Ford of Michigan, that Powell not be sworn in at that time, and that a special bipartisan committee be appointed to determine what ultimately should happen to him. The committee was to report within five weeks after its appointment. This, in effect, was a motion to exclude Powell; it was not an expulsion since Powell would not be sworn in. An expulsion would require a two-thirds vote; exclusion, only a simple majority. The Ford motion provided, however, that Powell be paid his congressional salary, allowed to keep his congressional staff, and use his offices pending the investigation—all rather unique concessions to one who was not, in fact, a sworn-in member of Congress. He would not, of course, be allowed to vote. No one questioned the rather odd pieces of the motion; the entire Powell affair was complicated and uncomfortable enough.

While the Van Deerlin, Udall, and Ford motions did not specify the reasons for the various moves, there was likely no one in the country who had been only slightly following the events—and certainly no one in the House chamber, legislators or spectators who jammed the galleries—who was unaware of the "Powell matter" that had developed over the years. He had been embroiled in a protracted, complex five-year court battle in New York, defending against a defamation-of-character lawsuit brought by a Harlem resident he had accused on television of being a "bag woman" (handler of payoff money from gamblers to the police). After several judgments against him he had been charged with criminal contempt of the New York courts for failing to cooperate with the state courts or to appear when subpoenaed. His handling of travel vouchers for his staff and family had been investigated by another House subcommittee and a report raised serious questions of improper use of funds on his part. He had his wife on the payroll although she performed no business for him either in Washington, D.C., or in his Harlem congressional district office, as required by law of one so employed. And he had angered more than a few colleagues on the powerful House Committee on Education and Labor, which he chaired since 1961, for what some of them felt to be a cavalier handling of the powers and perks of the chairmanship. A few months before, in the fall of 1966, his committee had revolted against him and voted to seriously curtail his powers as chairman. In addition, throughout the previous year, he had held up committee consideration of antipoverty and labor union legislation that President Johnson, organized labor, and many Democrats sorely wanted passed. In doing so, he was accused of holding the bill hostage for his own political patronage purposes, especially relating to funds going to Harlem.

All these things were known to be part of the various motivations behind the exclusion move on the part of his colleagues. Many of them were beginning to say out loud what they had been muttering softly for years: enough is enough. Powell was constantly stepping beyond the bounds of acceptable congressional behavior. His frequent European trips under questionable financial circumstances and accompanied by beautiful female congressional staff members were proving embarrassing to his colleagues, who resented the fact that such action was calling attention to similar behavior by others in Congress.

But to the hundreds outside, it was a different story. Adam Clayton Powell, Jr., the Baptist preacher, was the black congressman who had, since first being elected to Congress in 1944, spoken and acted vigorously against racial segregation and discrimination. He had constantly challenged segregation over the years by attempting to withhold federal funds from racially segregated facilities. For more than a decade, he was preeminently "Mr. Civil Rights." To be sure, he had taken extravagant European junkets in the company of attractive female staff companions (leaving his wife behind), but his supporters felt this was no worse than what some other congressmen had done, and continued to do. Without question, he was arrogant and flamboyant, but his supporters looked with pride on his jaunty air, calculated, they believed, to antagonize and intimidate his white racist detractors. He was a proud, defiant black congressman, and his constituents loved him for it.

Thus, to the Powell supporters on the Capitol steps that chilly January day, the issue was clear. If the people inside would vote against Powell, it would be a sure sign that they were applying a double standard—a standard aimed at bringing down Adam Clayton Powell, Jr., the outspoken and controversial black congressman from Harlem.

And for hours, as they waited, they chanted and yelled the words of their champion inside: "Keep the faith, baby." Speaker after speaker fired up the crowd. The mood was belligerent, the words threatening. They shouted at the white policemen, almost taunting them. They wanted to make clear their support for their besieged hero inside the hostile halls of Congress. Reflecting the range of ideological views that constituted his support base, the protesters appeared in dress from mink coats to African dashikis to plain simple working clothes to menacing black masks. There was a mixture of the young and old, and a large contingency of middle-age parishioners down from his Abyssinian Baptist Church and the other churches in Harlem.

Inside, the debate continued.

Answering the charge that Powell had not had his "day in court," Van Deerlin, alluding to the protracted New York State court case where Powell had refused to appear time and again, stated:

> Nearly a dozen judges in New York State will tell you where the fault lies. We who are charged with helping write the laws of the land must show respect for those laws, and more particularly, for the other branch of government. . . . if the election to the House of Representatives carries a license for scofflaws, if this chamber is to become a haven for fugitives, then, before the bar of public opinion, I say God help the Congress of the United States.

Van Deerlin was referring to one of Powell's claims that he was not subject to contempt of court proceedings pending against him in New York while going to, attending, or returning from congressional sessions.

Congressman Udall, however, felt that stripping Powell of his chairmanship was punishment enough. Powell's abuses stemmed mainly from his conduct of the committee he chaired. Those powers had been denied him the previous day by a vote of the Democratic Party Caucus, thus completing the process of denying him the important powers of chairman initiated the previous fall. "This story is done," Udall said. "The public has won. He is no longer chairman of this committee and probably never will be again. He is no longer in control of the staff. Are we going to kick a man when he is down?"

Then Udall put his finger on what everyone knew to be a major concern in the Powell matter, and what the hundreds outside represented by their presence and support of Powell: "Race is not involved but the cold fact is that 20 million fellow citizens [the approximate number of black Americans in the country] will think it is if we act in haste." Of course, not all black Americans held such a view, but the nature of political oratory and the general circumstances made this statement less challengeable than otherwise would be the case. Public opinion polls did show that most blacks felt Powell was being singled out for particular treatment, that he was being dealt with in a way not experienced by his white colleagues who were equally vulnerable to charges of misbehavior. In other words, a double standard. Surely, he was not the only committee chairman who had held up legislation—the most notorious example being the treatment of civil rights legislation for years by Southern committee chairmen—and he was hardly the only congressman to have a spouse or relative on the payroll in a questionable capacity. And how many would seriously claim that his was the only face on European junkets at taxpayers' expense? Therefore, it was rather easy for his supporters to argue that whatever his particular transgressions, he was clearly being subjected to standards of behavior not applied across the board.

Powell stood behind the rail in the rear, listening, not smiling. Then his time came to speak. Only Alabama Republican William L. Dickinson had objected to permitting him to speak, but he quickly withdrew his objection when his Republican colleagues quietly but audibly murmured "no" to his move.

Powell strode to the podium. Neatly dressed in a dark blue suit, yellow shirt, and knitted blue tie, he struck an imposing figure as he laid aside his notes. The first thing one always noticed about this black preacher-politician from Abyssinian Baptist Church in Harlem was that in physical appearance he looked like a white man. Tall, six feet three inches, wavy black hair, light-skinned, now suntanned after weeks of fishing on his yacht off the Bahamian island of Bimini, neatly trimmed mustache, he was more the figure of a movie star than any of his congressional colleagues. In the lexicon of American race relations, he could have "passed" for white—and for a brief few months in college at Colgate University in the late 1920s, he did. He was a black man, but unless one knew this, he would have to tell them. He was well aware, obviously, of his reputation as a playboy and womanizer, and this did not seriously threaten his pastorship of the Harlem church which he continued to lead while in Congress. The wide latitude given him by his parishioners and his political constituents must have been, so he and others frequently mused over the years, a source of envy for some of his congressional colleagues who could not afford to be so flagrant and open in their questionable personal activities. Many of them were kept on much shorter moral leashes by their followers, which was another reason why they resented Powell's flaunting his nightclub visits with other women and other eyebrow raising acts. Powell had been married three times, and he made no secret of pursuing a prospective bride before he had divorced the current wife.

Now, standing at the podium, fifty-eight years old, after twenty-one years in the Congress, and more than three decades of front-line civil rights activity, Powell clearly knew he was facing the most serious political challenge of his stormy career. But because he had survived so many controversies before, he must have harbored deep feelings that this particular confrontation likewise could be met successfully. He had never been publicly deferential, and he would not be now. At the same time, he knew that he ought to appear cooperative or at least somewhat conciliatory, certainly not overly defiant. It was not in him to capitulate, however. There were, after all, those hundreds of supporters outside and thousands more back home and around the country who had come to expect a fighting Adam Clayton Powell, Jr., one who would continue to represent the resistance to racial injustice they associated with his leadership. For so long he had been the symbol of noncompromise with racial segregation and discrimination and bigotry, and many felt this latest move against him was so motivated. He knew that to disappoint them now, even with his congressional status on the line, would be a blow too difficult, perhaps, to sustain—for his followers' vicarious sense of identification, and for his own ego. At the same time, he had to survive, and Adam Powell *was* a survivor. Thus, once again, Powell had to balance between righteous, pompous indignation and respectful acquiescence to the Congress that would decide his political future.

He began with the customary felicitous greetings of the Congress,

"My beloved colleagues . . ." But the old defiant Adam Powell took over. *He* would excuse *them* for what they were doing! He told them that he understood the pressures on them to vote the harshest punishment possible. "I know that if you could vote by secret ballot you would vote differently." He admonished in a most accusatory way those other members who had "skeletons in their closet"; he knew "the names of every one of them." For weeks there had been rumors, some fed by Powell himself, that he would blow the whistle on other congressmen who were guilty of at least as many transgressions as he was charged with. He could not be contrite, and he ended his brief comments by telling his colleagues: "My conscience is clear. I am in God's hands and your hands. All I hope is that you have a good sleep tonight."

No apology. No attempt to explain. Perhaps it was because he concluded that anything he said in the way of attempting to win support would be useless. He certainly had seen enough discussions on the floor of the House to know that few votes are changed by what gets said *at that point* in the political process.

The House of Representatives then voted. Powell lost 363 to 65 on a roll-call vote. (The second telephone call was made to the White House.) He left the chamber before the final tally, and immediately was swept into the arms of his waiting supporters outside.

"You are looking at the first black man who was ever lynched by Congress!" he shouted to the throng. It was shortly after 4:00 P.M. and they had waited all day. They shouted words of support and agreement to Powell, and raised clenched fists in the manner of the militant Black Power salute. He characteristically overdrew the implications of the congressional exclusion action against him. This vote, he charged, would do "irreparable damage to the U.S.A. in international relations. The Arabs and the black people, the Latin Americans and the West Indians will look twice before they vote with us again."

As he had done many times before, he posed himself as the measuring rod for subsequent potential action against minorities. "If they can do this to me after twenty-four years of excellence . . . then you know what they can do to you." The crowd constantly shouted support and anger. The mood was feverish. Television and news reporters pressed around him to get every word and arrogant gesture.

Powell was doing what he had been required to do for years, namely, go home to his constituents for protective cover, and to raise the charge of racism. The crowd was predominantly black, but there were noticeably some white supporters present. In spite of the general air of antiwhite sentiment that pervaded the gathering, Powell assured the whites that he welcomed their support. Throughout his political career, he had frequently occupied a balancing position between more nationalist-oriented black constituents and those, white and black, who leaned more in the direction of cooperative-integrated activity. His inclinations were always clearly with the latter. This afternoon, sensitive to the Black Power of the time, he stated to the whites in the crowd: "March with us. We won't reject you if you take our orders." Again, there were loud cheers of approval from the crowd. Powell's demeanor alternated between a contemptuous scowl and a peevish grin. He showed no signs of worry or of political insecurity.

He concluded by turning contemptuously toward the building he had just left and giving his parting shot. Perhaps now was the time to think of withholding taxes on the basis of no taxation without representation. Perhaps now there should be a third party—this drew particular approval from the black nationalists in the crowd who were disenchanted with both the Democrats and the Republicans, and a chant started: "Powell for President."

Finally, he stated, "Behind me in this Congress is the biggest bunch of elected hypocrites the world has ever known." More cheers of agreement.

Now, smiling and pleased, but not surprised, with the response on the steps, he made his way to a waiting car, acknowledging congratulatory waves and shouts. He had made two speeches that day, and clearly this second one was his kind of action. The crowd surged around the car. It had to be pushed slowly at first, lest some enthusiastic admirers be crushed under the wheels. White policemen who offered to help were yelled off by angry blacks.

The car drove off, leaving men and women running after it. Powell, in the front seat, turned and waved, smiled broadly, and gave the Black Power salute.

An hour later he was back in the congressional halls, out of sight of his supporters outside, surrounded only by a few aides and a few reporters, talking quietly with some of the congressmen who had just decided his fate. As always, he was touching various bases, taking his own astute reading of the situation. He had returned, he said, because he had heard that his salary would continue and he could keep his offices while the Special Committee investigated him over the next five weeks. He spoke to a few congressmen passing in the hall, mostly sarcastic banter. "Thanks for everything," he said to Congressman Wayne Hays of Ohio, who was *not* a supporter. "Do the same for you some day." Hays grinned; Powell smiled back.[4]

He told a reporter that he was not angry. "When you've been in here twenty-four years [it had actually been twenty-one years, since January 1945], and you have this feeling, you really can't be mad."

Also, he was sure that he was not finished. "I'm not through here yet. There are judicial processes. If there is another election, I'll win by the greatest majority ever received by any candidate, except in Mississippi, of course."

Boasting, outwardly confident, he conceded that he really did not think he would be excluded. "I thought that in an off year and because of twenty-four years that they, well, they might vote differently."

He had miscalculated, but being Adam Clayton Powell, Jr., this was only a temporary setback. He probably honestly believed that he would eventually be seated. There would be political maneuvers and new elections and court battles, but he was buoyed by the response of the crowd on the Capitol steps earlier. He really did not see how that kind of fervent support and what it represented in the many Harlems across the country could ultimately be denied. Did he really mean it about withholding taxes, and possibly starting a third party? Would he really carry out his threat to reveal the names of other congressmen who had engaged in questionable conduct? When asked these questions, he just smiled and puffed his cigarillo. How could one tell? Least of all Adam Powell, who was never known in his political life to lock any doors behind him, though he had closed more than a few in his time.

The months leading to the opening of that congressional session were filled with controversy for Powell personally and politically. In fact, throughout 1966 at least six important phenomena came to fruition and set him on a collision course with various political and legal authorities and adversaries. The year saw continued political battles over the two-year-old antipoverty programs, and Powell had angered President Lyndon Johnson and many congressmen by holding up legislative action. An important civil rights measure was before Congress, but Powell's influence was minimal, due to his frequent absences. The civil rights movement was growing increasingly vexing on the heels of the cry for Black Power, which caused a serious division in the ranks of the major black leaders. Powell had cast his lot with the younger, more strident advocates of mass militancy. But even in doing so, he was not completely accepted by that contingency. As a result of his delaying tactics over the antipoverty bill, a majority of the members on the Education and Labor Committee, in July, began a move to circumvent his authority. This culminated in September with a committee agreement (which Powell attempted to portray as *his* initiative) to curtail his powers as chairman. All the time, he was involved with running battles on the local Harlem front with the longtime political leader, J. Raymond Jones, who was the first black leader of Tammany Hall. Control of the Harlem-based antipoverty organization HARYOU-ACT was one source of the tension. And finally, Powell was wracked constantly by his continuing court battle in New York with the lady he had called a "bag woman" back in 1960, Mrs. Esther James. She had relentlessly pursued her defamation lawsuit against him, and in 1966 the various legal processes were beginning to run out for him as he faced several contempt citations, including one for criminal contempt. The year ended with a congressional subcommittee, led by Representative Wayne Hays of Ohio, investigating his use of committee funds.

Early in 1966, while new funds were being sought for the antipoverty programs, Powell made it known that he felt that the Johnson administration was asking for too little money. He would ask for $7 billion instead of the "timid," "wrist-tapping" amount of $1.75 billion. He also wanted to prevent local officials from having the power to veto local programs.[5]

"Mayors cannot veto Social Security, mayors cannot veto Medicare, mayors cannot veto unemployment compensation. I intend to see that they cannot veto programs of 90 percent Federal funds when their cities only supply 10 percent matching funds," he said at a news conference on March 30, 1966. This was aimed, he pointed out, at those local officials around the country who wanted to control the program for their own political purposes. This, of course, was one of the main charges leveled against him in his battles with opponents in New York City.

But into the summer of 1966, Powell was still important enough to the White House to get a meeting with the President to discuss the legislative agenda as it pertained to the various poverty programs. On a particular occasion in July, however, after President Johnson had scheduled a meeting with him three weeks in advance, Powell called up at the last minute to cancel it because, as he advised the White House, he had to attend a rally in his behalf back in Harlem. Could the President possibly reschedule the meeting? This was done, and they met five days later. So he was still considered someone to try to accommodate, but the White House and many people on Capitol Hill were having their patience tested.[6]

He further angered the Johnson administration by bringing up the Vietnam War. While the country spent "uncountable billions of dollars to pursue a victory-less war" in Vietnam, we were "short-changing our own citizens with a heartless stinginess."[7] He knew this would incur the wrath of the White House, even as it was sure to enlist the support of many who, even then, were beginning to question the administration's policies in South East Asia.

This Powell blast came just ten days after he had received a letter from President Johnson praising him for his work as chairman:

> The White House March 18, 1966
>
> Dear Adam:
>
> The fifth anniversary of your Chairmanship of the House Education and Labor Committee reflects a brilliant record of accomplishment.
>
> It represents the successful reporting to the Congress of 49 pieces of bedrock legislation. And the passage of every one of these bills attests to your ability to get things done.
>
> Even now, these laws which you so effectively guided through the House are finding abundant reward in the lives of our people.
>
> The poverty program is rapidly paving new pathways to progress for those whom the economic vitality of this land had previously bypassed.
>
> The education measures are being translated into fuller opportunities for all our citizens to develop their God-given talents to their fullest potential.
>
> Minimum wage, long a guarantee of a fair return for an honest day's work, has been increased and greatly extended.
>
> And the problems of juvenile delinquency are being met and curtailed by positive and determined action.
>
> Only with progressive leadership could so much have been accomplished by one Committee in so short a time. I speak for the millions of Americans who benefit from these laws when I say that I am truly grateful.
>
> Sincerely yours,
>
> Lyndon B. Johnson[8]

The White House surely hoped that such a letter would elicit cooperation from the chairman. Politicians often exchange such public commendations in expectation of reciprocal response of support. But not Powell. He constantly cited the letter as evidence of his good work and proceeded to pursue his own course of caustic criticism. A few months later he called for the resignation of the director of the Office of Economic Opportunity (OEO), R. Sargent Shriver. And testifying before a Senate committee on August 31, 1966, he said that antipoverty programs were not coordinated and that "maybe both" the President and Shriver were to blame for this situation. So much for mutual praise. When Senator Robert F. Kennedy reminded him of a report in June 1966 from Powell's own committee praising the OEO, Powell casually dismissed it as "campaign oratory."

Powell's committee reported the antipoverty bill in June, but Powell took off for an International Labor Conference in Geneva and returned later to his vacation home in Bimini. Still no action on the bill. The House Rules Committee proceeded to act without Powell's cooperation, criticizing him for his absence. All the time, several members of his own committee were becoming increasingly frustrated with his leadership. One of these, Sam Gibbons from Florida, was beginning to think of ways to render the chairman powerless or at least less capable of being obstructive in the face of a majority of the committee's wishes.

Powell was not oblivious to the undercurrents of dissatisfaction against him. He had spent more than two decades in the political trenches, and he was keenly sensitive to nuances of favor and disfavor, likes and dislikes. Years later, he wrote:

> I had realized that there had been some realignment of power when, in September of 1966, I had attended the signing of the War on Poverty Bill in President Johnson's office. The President refused to shake my hand when I arrived, and his entire attitude toward me was one of complete detachment—as if I were already a dead man and he would have preferred not to have a corpse in his office. At the same time he warmly embraced Gibbons, so I knew that whatever Gibbons was planning, he obviously had strong Democratic backing—all the way to the White House, in fact.[9]

Of course, Powell could hardly have expected red carpet treatment after having strongly criticized the President personally just three weeks earlier. He recognized the obviously awkward position he had put the White House in by his outspoken criticism. In a letter to President Johnson on September 9, marked "Personal and

Confidential," he wrote: "I can appreciate that my public call for Sargent Shriver's resignation may have caused you some concern, particularly as it can affect the continued success of the administration of the War on Poverty." He indicated that he had investigative results that showed gross racist practices in some programs. He then continued: "Thus, as you can appreciate, I have been caught in the bind between vigorously supporting you and your Administration and the component programs such as the War on Poverty—on the one hand—and on the other hand, attempting to develop a more effective War on Poverty without exposing many of its weaknesses." He gratuitously suggested that Johnson might consider replacing Shriver with someone with "the talents of an Abe Fortas, a Bob McNamara or a Bill Wirtz directing" the antipoverty program.[10]

At any rate, there was no avoiding the conclusion that Adam Clayton Powell, Jr., was trying the political patience of some of his colleagues—indeed, an increasing number. In addition to the chilly reception he perceived from President Johnson, the President's advisers were now cautioning the President not to get too close to the congressman. They simply did not trust him. On September 10, as committee sentiments were building against Powell, a White House aide, Henry Wilson, sent the following memo to President Johnson:

September 10, 1966

10:20 a.m.

For the President
From: Henry H. Wilson, Jr.

Adam Powell is telling any Members of Congress who happen to be standing around, and doubtless also members of the press, that you called him at 11:25 in the evening and asked his help on the Frank Roosevelt problem in New York State.

I don't know that there is much to be done about it, but I thought you ought to know that this can be the anticipated result any time you talk with him. And sometimes when you don't talk with him.[11]

He was still a man to be dealt with, however. There was no denying him his popular support in many segments of American society, particularly among black Americans. Notwithstanding successful efforts to curtail his power as chairman, he *was* still the chairman. And he still had the general reputation of being a staunch fighter for civil rights, a reputation based more on his past record than on his current personal involvement.

The summer of 1966 was also a time of intense civil rights activity. Congress was debating a civil rights housing bill, but Powell was not a major participant in that discussion. In fact, in five votes taken in the House on August 9, he was absent on three, and "paired" for or against on two. Substantively, he was more attentive to the antipoverty measures coming from his own committee, which was understandable. There were other participants (Clarence Mitchell of the NAACP, Congressman John Conyers, among others) to turn to for leadership in the legislative civil rights battles. Powell, when available, was always good for a press-conference statement of support, but few expected his involved hand in the housing antidiscrimination bill. In a sense, the "Mr. Civil Rights" of a prior decade had now shifted his attention to social and economic issues, a shift he began signaling in his speeches as early as 1963.

But there was still a dynamic civil rights movement in the country.

Dr. Martin Luther King, Jr., was preparing to take his Southern drive against segregation and discrimination north to Chicago in the summer of 1966.

In June, James Meredith, who had integrated the University of Mississippi in 1962, launched a one-man March Against Fear from Memphis into Mississippi. He was shot on the second day, and the top civil rights leaders in the country took up the march. It was on this venture that the cry of Black Power was raised by the youthful participants of the Student Nonviolent Coordinating Committee (SNCC) led by Stokely Carmichael. The cry swept the country, kicking off a groundswell of debate and controversy within the civil rights movement and in the media. This was accompanied by continuing rioting in several northern urban areas, and many people interpreted the developing violence and new language as signs of growing disaffection with traditional civil rights goals of integration and desegregation.

Powell immediately aligned himself with the "new militants." It was language he sensed was appealing to the more defiant in the poor urban communities. It was less compromising; it was more threatening. It was, to many, decidedly more dramatic. At a news conference on July 19, he warned of an "endless cycle of violence and destruction" if Black Power was ignored. He said there was a "new breed of cats" now taking over the civil rights movement, and accused the "self-righteous, old-fashioned leaders and opinion makers, black and white" of not understanding the new mood. Black Power, he insisted, was not antiwhite or advocating "black supremacy" or kicking whites out of the civil rights movement. He, along with countless others, attempted to put *his* interpretation on the term. "Black Power is a new philosophy for the tough, proud young Negroes who categorically refuse to compromise or negotiate any longer for their rights." He must have had reminiscences of his earlier days in Harlem in the 1930s when he was leading protest marches and picket lines, and balancing the ideological calls for black nationalism with black and white insistence on integration. This cry of "Black Power" was not new to him. He had, he constantly asserted, really introduced the term years ago when he called for "audacious Black Power."

Many saw him now, in 1966, as attempting to ride a crest of rising resentment and racial determination. The Black Power that Powell articulated was nothing more than concerted black voting strength, working in the mode of earlier ethnic bloc voting to cause the established political forces to deal with blacks. He met with Stokely Carmichael and announced a national Black Power conference to be held in Washington over the Labor Day weekend. Various civil rights leaders and organizations would be invited.

But Powell's definition of Black Power seemed to satisfy neither the critics of the term nor the proponents. A few weeks later, SNCC leaders became disenchanted with Powell's involvement, and they decided not to participate in the projected conference. Carmichael is reported as saying: "Powell is talking about stopping the throwing of Molotov cocktails and not about stopping the causes that bring about the throwing of the cocktails." Carmichael believed that Powell was more interested in bringing more blacks into the Democratic Party in a bloc than in the possibility of "independent politics."[12] This was a debate within SNCC itself, with some members certainly agreeing with the Powell position. Under the circumstances, there was little agreement about what could be gained from allying at that time with Adam Powell.

On the other hand, Powell was perceived by some civil rights leaders as definitely aligned with the Carmichael–Black Power forces. He had invited several civil rights leaders, including Roy Wilkins of the NAACP, to a planning conference on Black Power. But Wilkins, the cautious veteran civil rights integrationist, was having none of the current furor, and clearly had no intention of letting a crafty Powell draw the NAACP into a meeting with radicals. He wrote Powell reminding him of the NAACP's long-standing commitment to the principles of integration and interracial cooperation and seriously questioning whether the Black Power advocates subscribed to those principles. "We of the NAACP do not believe that integration is 'irrelevant,' that white persons should be excluded from participation in the civil rights movement (they created and help maintain the problem and owe it to themselves and to the nation to help rectify racial wrongs), that civil rights legislation is a 'sham,' or that Negroes cannot successfully compete with non-Negroes given an equal opportunity." He followed this the next day with a letter to Powell calling attention to inflammatory language used by Carmichael and others.[13]

Powell held his closed meeting on Black Power in the hearing room of the House Education and Labor Committee. Reporters were barred, and he stated that Roy Wilkins of the NAACP could not attend because of a previous engagement, but had sent a "very fine letter." Powell, of course, did not mention the contents of the Wilkins letters.

Later in the year, in November, Powell preached a sermon at Abyssinian Baptist Church that drew praise from Wilkins and likely did not please Stokely Carmichael and the Black Power advocates. This, of course, was vintage Powell. His association with Carmichael in the summer did not necessarily suggest support for him a few months later in the winter. In addition, Powell had for some time made his position on violence clear. He never openly counseled such action, even in his most fiery moments. In November 1966, Wilkins wrote:

> A lot of people have been speaking out on the damage done by the so-called militants but the last word was said recently by no less an authority than Congressman Adam Clayton Powell. For this unexpected pronouncement he put on his preacher's hat and denounced violence. He did not call names in his sermon, but afterwards he did disassociate himself from Stokely Carmichael, the "black power" prophet.
>
> With typical Powell flair, the preacher called the "black power" concept "a fuse for rebellions in America's cities." . . .
>
> On very solid ground, Reverend Powell admonished his congregation to "exercise a massive responsibility for their fate." . . .
>
> For his own unfathomable reasons, Adam has raised his voice to call us back from the hi-de-ho road to the high road.[14]

A few weeks from then, however, Powell and Carmichael would be photographed walking down a road in Bimini where Carmichael, along with several others over a period of weeks, had gone to give Powell moral support in his battle against the ouster effort shaping up in Congress.

Thus 1966 was a vexing, ideologically turbulent year for the civil rights movement, and, characteristically, Powell was found in many camps sometimes simultaneously. It had always been his political style to defy any particular labeling of him in terms of tactics or broad ideological categorization. He was too unpredictable in that sense. Some saw this as the most negative manifestation of opportunism. He preferred to see himself as tactically flexible. He enjoyed keeping friend and foe off-balance, knowing that with each latest salvo he could attract attention and speculation. He always appeared to be having fun, which irritated some who wanted him to be more consistent, more reliable, more trustworthy, indeed, more serious than he sometimes seemed to be. Such characteristics seemed almost to bore him, and caused more than a few supporters to conclude in frustration that he could not be depended on as a loyal ally.

His digressions did, in fact, have boundaries. Throughout his long political career, he seldom put himself in a position of having his commitment to the civil rights struggle questioned. Every move he made was done in such a way as to position himself as *more*, not less, committed to the cause of racial justice. Thus in 1956, when he supported Eisenhower over Adlai Stevenson for President, he explained it was because the latter was weaker on the issue of civil rights than the Republican President, although most civil rights advocates at the time disagreed with this assessment. When he became chairman of the House Education and Labor Committee in 1961, he decided to stop introducing the "Powell Amendment" to legislation forbidding the use of federal funds for segregated facilities. He explained:

> Instead of fighting to attach the "Powell Amendment" to legislation to bring about equality, I evolved the tactic of getting a *written* promise from the Cabinet Secretary concerned that fair employment practices and standards would be maintained in the implementation of each program. This guaranteed that minority groups would have their civil rights protected, while avoiding the long battles that sometimes were occasioned by my not so popular amendment.[15]

Perhaps so, but some civil rights advocates believed that such a promise would not have the force and effect of a statutory enactment, and would not be nearly as extensive and effective in coverage.

But as chairman of a major congressional committee, Powell

had achieved unquestionably the strongest position a black person had ever attained in the United States government. And he cherished it. "I'm the only black man in the white power structure," he was fond of saying to appreciative Harlem audiences. And in that position, he could do far more, he felt, than any of his annoying, irritating tactics had accomplished the previous fifteen years in Congress.

Therefore, in 1966, when several members of his committee began a move to curtail his powers, he knew clearly that this was serious. They were striking at the core of what made him—in the 1960s—more than a rhetorical, symbolic black leader. He had *institutional* power as the chairman of an important congressional committee. This was not only civil rights leadership; this was political leadership in the fullest sense. It had taken him fifteen years to get to that point through the seniority system in Congress. This was not to be dismissed lightly, and he knew that. *Chairman* Powell had legitimate political power. He understood the American political system, and he knew what constituted respected positions of bargaining and influence in that system. Therefore, a successful effort to undercut his role as chairman was not simply one more temporary political fracas he could casually dismiss.

He began to plot his defense. On August 24, 1966, he had a letter hand-delivered to the Speaker of the House, John W. McCormack.

> My dear Mr. Speaker:
>
> I am sick and tired of being picked on solely because I am a Negro.
>
> In the opinion of our late and beloved President Kennedy, and our present beloved President Johnson and your distinguished self, I am one of the most effective Chairmen on the Hill. . . .

He then proceeded to complain of specific acts to undermine his chairmanship, and stated: "Under these conditions, Mr. Speaker, regardless of the high esteem and warm affection which I hold for you and always will, I do not think it wise to bring up the 1966 amendments to the Economic Opportunity Act next week until we have had a summit meeting of the minds and hearts." He had to let it be known to the top leadership of his party and Congress that he would not stand for tampering with his power. He was, after all, still the chairman of a powerful committee. And by this letter, he hoped that the Speaker would intervene to head off the mutiny within his committee that was, by then, clearly under way. The problem, of course, and surely he must have known this, was that in the nature of power and its exercise, if he had to resort to such blatant statements of defense, in many ways the situation had already deteriorated beyond repair.

The move to weaken his chairmanship began to take shape in the summer, led by Representative Sam Gibbons, Democrat of Florida, and it surfaced in early September. There was a news story that indicated that Powell's wife, who had been living in her native Puerto Rico for several years, was not receiving her paychecks as a member of his congressional staff. The checks, apparently, were being deposited in Powell's bank account, and it was suspected that his wife had not performed any work for his office to warrant the pay. In fact, there was widespread knowledge that Powell and his wife were estranged. Since shortly after their marriage in 1960, Mrs. Powell had been staying in San Juan and constantly asked her husband to let her return to Washington with their young son, Adam Clayton Powell IV. Powell preferred that she remain in Puerto Rico. He refused to see her when she came to Washington in August 1966. Clearly, he had lost interest in this third marriage, but not the income his wife received as a staff member.

The House Rules Committee had launched a legislative move in July to bring the antipoverty bill to the floor of the House in spite of Powell's lack of cooperation. His continued stalling had frustrated the White House and many congressional antipoverty supporters. Powell was continuing to receive negative publicity for his refusal to cooperate with the courts in New York City over the defamation suit against him. He blocked the labor union–supported common situs picketing bill, because, he stated, unions were still racially discriminatory. His absentee record on congressional roll-call votes continued to be one of the worst in Congress. (Gibbons noted that from February 24 through September 12, not including the three weeks in June while he was in Geneva, Powell missed 164 roll calls and quorum calls out of 218.) Gibbons also stated that Powell's overall actions "contributed to worsening race relations." Likewise, there were complaints that he had arbitrarily dismissed committee staff members.

Armed with this mounting record of vulnerabilities, Gibbons, a junior two-term member of the House, relentlessly pursued the goal of stripping Powell of his powers. He needed sixteen votes on the thirty-one-member committee, and there was strong indication that these were available. Powell's response to Gibbons was predictable: "Next week, when Sam offers his incredible proposals, I want the American people to watch the anti-Negro termites crawl out of the woodwork of hate." Gibbons countered with the defense of his own voting record on civil rights, supporting the Voting Rights Act of 1965 and the 1966 fair housing measure. "I suppose I could have asked him [Powell] how the fishing was down in Bimini when I was here voting for the civil rights bill," Gibbons responded.

An agreement was reached in Powell's office one afternoon in September between the chairman and five Northern Democrats on the committee. Essentially, Powell was required to consult with and seek approval of a committee majority on staffing, budget, meetings, referral of bills, and creation of subcommittees. Although Powell attempted to put the new rules in the best face-saving light, there was little doubt that his committee's revolt was successful. The full committee met and by a 27–1 vote (Powell voted "present," and Republican William H. Ayres of Ohio "no") seriously curtailed the chairman's powers. Powell *appeared* undaunted as he told news reporters and constituents who crowded the committee room: "I consider this a very progressive step forward." The changes, he said, were the kind he had advocated for some time, namely, to give more power to the majority on the committee over that of subcommittees. In addition, he asserted, he planned to introduce similar proposals for all the House committees at the opening of the next session of Congress. His committee, he boasted, was simply taking the lead in much needed congressional reforms.

But his public explanation that day differed from his account a few years later after he was no longer in Congress. Later, he wrote: "Even in the watered-down version it was obvious that I had lost. And it was becoming even more obvious to me that this was merely the first round in what must certainly be a new 'get Adam' vendetta."[16]

Again, varying reactions followed the committee's action.

The *New York Times* concluded that "in the end it was his arrogant utterances, his open contempt, his absenteeism, his looseness with committee finances, and finally the flaunting of his private life in public that finally brought him down."[17] But the newspaper also felt that Powell should not be the only chairman restricted: "The restraints that have been put upon him represent a healthy precedent for similar curbs on other committee chairmen. Mr. Powell is not alone in stalling bills that the committee majority favors, packing the staff with his own retainers and spending committee funds in a high-handed manner. The House has an obligation to run all of its committees democratically, rather than yield to the arbitrariness of individual oligarchs."[18]

The "double standard" issue was raised by major civil rights leaders. Roy Wilkins this time, as so often before, felt compelled to raise the point reluctantly in defense of Powell: "Unless members of Congress proceed with a complete reorganization of committee structure and procedures in both houses, they will give substance to Adam Clayton Powell's charge that he is a victim of racism."[19]

Whitney M. Young, Jr., of the National Urban League issued a one-sentence press release: "Unless the action of the House Committee on Education and Labor, stripping Congressman Powell of his authority as Chairman, is followed immediately by similar action against other chairmen who have obstructed the will of Congress and abused the privileges of their offices, then this action will be interpreted by many citizens, white and Negro, as a move which is racially inspired."[20]

The head of the Congress of Racial Equality (CORE), Floyd B. McKissick, was even more blunt: "CORE contends that the singling out of Congressman Adam Clayton Powell is a denial and rejection of the needs and wishes of Negro communities throughout the country. It will set the civil rights movement backward."[21]

These were representative of the "double standard" comments one would hear a few months later on the vote to exclude Powell from Congress. They were also similar to reactions over the previous decade when various moves were made, political and legal, against the controversial congressman. In every case, Powell was subject to political reprimand or legal action of questionable activity on his part. His supporters recognized his tendencies for flamboyant, aberrant behavior, but always they felt inclined to give him the benefit of the doubt. His identification with civil rights was so prominent that it made the countercharge of racism or "double standard" at least initially plausible.

This made liberal civil rights advocates wary of attacking him, even when they were infuriated by some of his antics.

Arthur Spingarn, the president of the NAACP for twenty-six years, expressed the frustration felt by some civil rights leaders in his characterization of Powell:

> Now, I can't understand him. He introduces me as one of his oldest and best friends. He attacked me by name for a year on the radio, and then he had a big dinner of 3,500 and asked me to be honorary chairman. I can't understand that. If a man is your enemy, he's your enemy. Of course, I had to say yes because we couldn't afford to turn him down. Today, I could say no. But then when I was President [of the NAACP] I couldn't say no. He's too influential. But he's a tragedy. If he had character he'd be a great man.[22]

But Powell's opponents were not all vulnerable to the charge of racism or anti–civil rights. While his own congressional seat from Harlem was as safe as any politician could reasonably hope it to be, he nonetheless had political forces in that community not allied with him. J. Raymond Jones, the first black leader of Tammany Hall (New York–Manhattan County Democratic Party) had an off-again, on-again relationship with Powell.

In 1966, Jones (known affectionately in Harlem politics as "the Fox") was feuding with Powell. Their fight centered mainly on control of the Harlem-based antipoverty program (HARYOU-ACT), but it also focused on such perennial political issues as patronage and political appointments. In August 1966—the month that Powell was fighting with the White House over antipoverty legislation; planning to defend himself against the growing revolt among his committee as well as figuring out how to position himself with the Black Power movement; consulting with his lawyers on the New York court case and a pending criminal contempt citation against him; and refusing to see his wife, who had come from Puerto Rico to have a face-to-face meeting with him about the future of their marriage—he was engaged in a public dispute with Jones over judgeships in New York City.

Powell was angry that the county Democratic Party under Jones's leadership failed to nominate one black or Puerto Rican candidate for a city court judgeship on a slate of four. "I do not believe in violence," Powell's statement to the press read. "Therefore from now on, when a black man in Harlem sees Ray Jones in the street, he ought to spit on him." Using characteristically biting language, he equated Jones's action to "the combined treason of Judas, Benedict Arnold and Quisling."[23]

Jones, however, was hardly cowed by Powell, whom he knew well as both friend and foe. Eight years earlier, the two had been allied in a dramatic, successful battle against Tammany Hall when the party attempted to defeat Powell in a primary race for reelection. And for a very brief time, the two had led the United Democratic Leadership Team in Harlem, constituting a formidable but short-lived political force. (A few years later, Jones would recall this temporary alliance as the "beginning" of "basic black political power in New York City." When he and Powell "formed the team, that was the beginning and Harlem had to be reckoned with." However, as Jones saw it, "personalities and differences of concepts" kept them from working together. "I would not accept Powell's style and beliefs and he surely would not accept mine."[24])

Now, in 1966, the two crafty, strong-willed politicians, both nurtured in the streets of Harlem, were locked in open political battle. Jones responded to Powell's statement in terms he knew the frequently absent congressman would find at least uncomfortable if not embarrassing. "I can well understand Congressman Powell's need to get a Supreme Court justiceship for one of the lawyers in his club. But I am concerned more with the thousands of young Negroes who are out of work in Harlem. Congressman Powell ought to be devoting himself to straightening out the problems in HARYOU-ACT so that these young men and women can get to work. I would say to Mr. Powell that I am not afraid of the violence that he attempts to create, and I would suggest that if he would spend more time in Harlem that he might be the subject of more violence than he is attempting to create."

Jones knew, of course, that one reason Powell was away from his Harlem district so much was because of his legal problems involving the lawsuit against him. He was staying out of New York on weekdays to avoid being served a court warrant for his arrest. This case, indeed, was very likely Adam Powell's Achilles' heel.

In 1960, Powell had called a Mrs. Esther James, a sixty-two-year-old widow, a "bag woman." In the language of gambling circles, this meant she was one who carried money from gamblers to the police as payoff to permit the continuance of illegal activities in the community. She sued for defamation of character. Powell repeatedly ignored the several subpoenas, and a judgment was entered against him. This led to further court maneuvers and several civil contempt citations. By mid-1966, the protracted case, which had then become two lawsuits, consumed an inordinate amount of court time and legal paperwork. The second suit developed when Mrs. James complained that Powell had transferred some property in Puerto Rico and New York to his wife's relatives to avoid paying the original judgment. The legal maneuvers, by one estimate, had involved as many as seventy-five judges, three juries totaling forty-seven people, "and all the papers over the past six years add up to a stack more than twenty-feet high."[25]

The two civil contempt citations against Powell meant that he could not appear in New York City except on Sunday without running the risk of being arrested. Thus, for almost a year, he was in his Harlem base only on that day. This made the J. Raymond Jones comment that much more stinging and pertinent. To add to his problems, Powell was cited for *criminal* contempt in August. The third week in September, he was hit with the simultaneous challenge of his committee's successful revolt against him and an order to appear in court to answer the criminal citation.

"This is the reward I get for excellence," he told his Abyssinian congregation in a Sunday sermon on September 18, referring to the committee action.[26] He was less vocal on his legal problems with Mrs. James. He continued to fail to appear in court. Finally, the string ran out. On November 28, 1966, a court order was issued to arrest him "on any day of the week including Sunday" for criminal contempt.

There was likely no public official anywhere in the country faced with so many legal and political problems at the same time. And there were more to come.

The Committee on House Administration, following the September revolt of his own committee against him, began to inquire into his handling of expenditures, especially in relation to his wife's employment on his staff, and a series of highly questionable airline tickets issued for flights to Miami and Bimini. Apparently, tickets were issued in names of persons on his staff but not used by those persons. The obvious inference, and the subcommittee so concluded, was that these airline tickets were used by Powell, his friends, and family for personal purposes, not committee business. On October 5, 1966, a House Resolution authorized the investigation into Powell's dealings. The Special Subcommittee on Contracts was led by Congressman Wayne L. Hays of Ohio. Public and closed hearings were held. The committee concluded that there were many irregularities connected with travel of Powell and his staff members. Travel vouchers were not filed or were incomplete. At least one person appeared to have been hired by Powell for his personal housekeeping needs for a brief period. Mrs. Powell did not appear before the committee and it recommended that her employment be terminated. Powell refused to appear before the committee. The Hays committee submitted its report in early January, 1967, a few days before the fateful move to exclude him from Congress. That report and the wide publicity it received, were, in fact, important considerations in the minds of many of his colleagues as they prepared to deliberate his future.

The tide was building against Adam Clayton Powell, Jr., as 1967 began and Congress convened. He was a man besieged, and even his strongest defenders had to wonder just how many of his wounds were self-inflicted. He made advocacy of his cause difficult under the best of circumstances because of his flagrant deviant behavior. But also his supporters wondered how much of the negative reaction was to Powell, the black congressman, and how much simply to one who had overstepped the bounds of personal and political propriety.

After the exclusion vote, the bipartisan committee deliberated for five weeks under the leadership of a Northern liberal from New York City, Emanuel Celler. Powell made one appearance before the committee, claiming only that he was constitutionally entitled to his seat to which he had been elected, because he met the specific requirements of age, citizenship, and inhabitancy. He was accompanied by eight lawyers.

Media attention to the case was intense, and the perennial arguments on all sides surfaced again.

In January 1967, a Louis Harris poll asked:

> [As you know] Congress is now holding an investigation over whether or not Congressman Powell should be seated in Congress. Do you think Rep. Powell should or should not be given his seat in Congress?

Should	18.1%
Should not	56.5%
Not sure	25.2%

The Gallup poll in February 1967 asked:

> A Congressional committee is now investigating the question of whether Representative Adam Clayton Powell should be allowed to keep his seat in Congress. Have you heard or read about this?

Yes	84.8%
No	15.1%

> How do you, yourself, feel? Do you think Powell should be allowed to keep his seat, or not?

Yes	20.5%
No	60.6%
Don't know	18.8%

Powell's supporters, as we have seen, often charged that he was being singled out for special treatment, that he was hardly alone in his congressional transgressions. Therefore, any move against him could only be interpreted as imposing a "double standard" of behavior and punishment based on Powell's race and his anti-racism struggles. In late January, 1967, a Gallup poll reported:

> Representative Powell is charged with misusing Government funds for personal reasons. Just from your own feelings or impressions, do you think that the misuse of Government funds by congressmen is fairly common, or not?

Yes, fairly common	60%
No	21%
No opinion	19%

A Louis Harris survey addressed the "double standard" issue directly in January 1967:

> Congressman Powell claims that the action taken by Congress was mainly because he is a Negro. Do you agree or disagree that a major reason why Rep. Powell was unseated as Chairman was that he is a Negro?

Agree	7%
Disagree	80.1%
Not sure	12.7%

Thus survey respondents generally believed that Powell was not alone in behaving in a questionable way, but they overwhelmingly did not believe that he was being singled out for harsh treatment because of his race. Presumably, these respondents, then, would support similar action against others.

The Celler committee finally recommended that Powell be seated, and then censured. It also recommended that forty thousand dollars be repaid by Powell as funds he inappropriately expended. He was, in addition, to be denied his twenty-one years of seniority, and be required to start again as a freshman legislator. Several observers recognized the unprecedented nature of the recommended punishment. The black member of the committee, John Conyers, Jr., made this point in his "additional views" appended to the report. "A review of all cases of alleged misconduct brought before the House and Senate indicates that punishment has never exceeded censure. There is no precedent for the removal of accumulated seniority combined with a monetary assessment, as is proposed in the instant case."[27]

But once again the House was in no mood to be the least bit lenient with Powell. On March 1, 1967, the full body rejected the Celler committee's recommendations, and voted by 307–116 roll-call vote to exclude Powell and to notify the governor of New York of the vacancy so that a special election could be held in the Harlem district. Powell's exclusion was the third in the twentieth century, and the first since 1921.

The Harlem voters, as they had been doing for over two decades, gave their electoral vote of confidence to Powell. But the general public was still not prepared to accept their choice. In April 1967, a Harris survey told the story:

> [As you know] Rep. Adam Clayton Powell has been reelected to Congress from Harlem in New York City. The House of Representatives refused to give him his seat after he was elected last November. But now that he has been reelected, do you think the House should seat him or still refuse to seat him?

Should seat him	26.1%
Refuse to seat him	59.1%
Not sure	14.6%

Adam Clayton Powell, Jr., continued to be the source of intense controversy and disagreement as he entered the final stages of a long stormy career. He was by no means finished. He would go to the U.S. Supreme Court, being the first one ever to challenge such a move by either chamber of Congress. He would continue to go to Bimini and the alluring fishing waters which he loved so much. He would return to the streets and rallies of Harlem after finally resolving his legal battles with Mrs. Esther James. He would continue to be a sought-after speaker especially on the college lecture circuit around the country, taking aim as much at America's Vietnam War as at racial injustice at home. He would continue to be, for a while at least, what he always was, a bellwether of sorts on the American political scene.

Politically, Powell was a problem because he was so closely identified with one of America's major problems: racial segregation and discrimination. Whether he was subjected to a "double standard" by his congressional colleagues or whether he received the punishment his conduct warranted depended essentially on how one viewed the issue of race in the United States—an issue clearly recognized then and now as a genuine American dilemma.

2

Born to Privilege and Pampering

Adam Clayton Powell, Jr., was born on November 29, 1908, in New Haven, Connecticut, the second child of the Reverend Adam Clayton Powell and Mattie Fletcher Powell. The first child was a daughter, Blanche, ten years old when Adam Jr. was born.

Within one month of his birth, his father accepted the post as pastor of the Abyssinian Baptist Church in New York City. The family followed the elder Powell to New York in six months, and the church and Harlem, where they lived henceforth except for a very brief time, became the grooming ground for the future minister and congressman.

Adam Jr.'s genealogy was typical of very many blacks at that time, because slavery and scanty family records made it difficult to trace with any degree of reasonable accuracy. Powell contributed to the confusion by engaging in concocted stories, again not uncommon, of his lineage.[1] His father's mother is reasonably established as nineteen-year-old Sally (Dunnings). His father's father is not known. Sally was a light-complexioned young woman in a family of free tenant farmers in Virginia's Franklin County, where she gave birth to Adam Clayton Powell on May 4, 1865.

Adam Jr.'s mother, Mattie, was born in 1872 in Fayette County, West Virginia. Her parents were Samuel and Eliza Wilson Buster, farm laborers, who separated shortly after her birth. Her mother took the last name of Shaffer and became Mattie Fletcher Shaffer.

All of Powell Jr.'s grandparents were "mulattos," Americans of mixed—white, Negro, Indian—heritage. And as far as is known, there were no slaves in their immediate background. They were all sharecropppers, tenant farmers, and domestic servants. This meant, of course, that they were all poor. They were not part of that small class of free black artisans in the pre– and post–Civil War period who were able to acquire some education and skills and a modicum of property and status in the Negro community. Their light skin was an indication that they descended from a mixture of blacks and whites, but it did not carry the *relative* higher incomes or education occasionally associated with such lineage. The whites in the lineage were either poor themselves or left no inheritance to the black offspring, as was sometimes the case.

(Adam Jr. tried to improve upon this account years later when he wrote that his mother, Mattie, was, in fact, a daughter of the Schaefer Brewing Company family. He asserted that, as such, she was entitled to a substantial inheritance that she never claimed. No one else in the Powell family or any authenticated records documented this story.)[2]

The name of Powell came into being rather unceremoniously. Sally (Dunnings) began living with one Anthony Bush, a mulatto farmer. The household consisted of Sally, Anthony, Sally's mother, Mildred, Adam, and several cousins. In November 1867, Sally and Anthony married, and Anthony decided to take the name of Powell as a new identity. In 1875, the entire nine-member extended family moved to West Virginia, where, it was advertised, better opportunities existed. They worked as tenant farmers and domestics. Here, Adam Powell spent his adolescence—from ten to nineteen years of age—and characterized the time and place as a "mental and moral disaster."[3] Schooling was limited, and he became involved with a raucous, hard-drinking, pistol-packing crowd that eventually led him into violence and trouble. He shot a thief trying to steal from the farm one night and was advised to flee before he became the victim of the revenge of the wounded man's accomplices.

During this traumatic period, however, he met Mattie Fletcher Shaffer on their daily trips to school. They would be married in 1889, and the relationship lasted until her death in 1945.

Powell fled West Virginia in 1884 for Rendville, Ohio, an equally tough but more economically rewarding town. Working in the coal mines, he earned as much as a hundred dollars per month. But virtually all of this was dissipated through gambling, liquor, and generally "loose living." This lasted only a short time when in 1885 he came under the religious spell of a week-long revival meeting and became converted to Christianity. His wayward, reckless days were over, and he devoted himself to school, work, and being a stalwart citizen of the town. His educational ambitions took him, in 1887, to Washington, D.C., to attend the Howard University Law School, but his academic record was not good enough for admission. He had envisioned a legal career as a means ultimately of going to Congress, even though black congressmen in the post-Reconstruction era were a diminishing breed.

He enrolled instead in Wayland Seminary and College, preparing himself for the ministry. Succeeding in this, he also married Mattie Fletcher Shaffer, and then began his ministerial career. Brief stints at churches in St. Paul and in Philadelphia finally led him to the Immanuel Baptist Church in New Haven in 1893. For the next fifteen years, the Powells built the church, had their first child, Blanche, in 1898, and became an established presence in the college town. Powell also attended classes at Yale Divinity School. In New Haven, he met a Dr. George Barton Cutten of the Baptist Ministers Conference, who was later to be president of Colgate University when Adam Jr. enrolled there years afterward.

The New Haven years at the turn of the century apparently were good ones, and relatively prosperous for the black preacher. He lectured around the country, and became noted as a forceful, articulate, and respected Christian spokesman. Black clergymen played the major leadership role in the various black communities around the country. There was no established political leadership class and no significant business class that were automatically recognized as obvious spokesmen. A few black weekly newspapers certainly played an important role as did some individual educational leaders and a handful of professional men, but for the most part, the bulk of the black articulated leadership came from the community's pulpits. Such was the case with the senior Powell operating out of New Haven. Apparently, the years of abject poverty were behind him, and he could now provide his family the extra amenities denied him and his wife in their younger years, when he had to take side jobs as a waiter, and his wife as a seamstress, to supplement his meager pastor's salary.

New Haven was the site of the rather comfortable black middle-class home into which Adam Jr. was born in 1908. When his father was extended the invitation to lead the prestigious Abyssinian Baptist Church in New York City, Powell Sr. did not hesitate to accept the offer. He was growing bored in small-town New Haven, and longed for the bigger city and bigger challenges. It was a quite well-off Powell family that moved to New York with a full-time maid, Josephine, who took care of the roomy house in Harlem (the church was at that time still in what is now called midtown Manhattan on West Fortieth Street), and above all cared for the infant Adam Powell, Jr.

Under such protective circumstances, it would have been difficult for Adam Jr. to be anything but pampered—or "spoiled." His mother and Josephine doted over him, curled his long blondish hair, dressed him in Little Lord Fauntleroy suits, and saw to his every need. His sister was older enough not to suffer from sibling rivalry and lavished him with big-sister attention. The church members outdid themselves in heaping accolades on the pastor's beautiful baby boy.

This pampering intensified when, at the age of six, Adam Jr. became seriously ill with a lung ailment and required even more constant care for the next six years. His contacts with other boys his age were limited during this period, but he nonetheless was able to develop some playmates, after overcoming the devastating stigma of being a "sissy" or a "momma's boy." His father's position in the church and community grew, as did Adam Jr.'s adulation of him. It was easily apparent to the young son that he was a privileged member of an important family, and he took every advantage of it. All the hardships experienced by his father and mother earlier were completely absent from his childhood from the day of his birth. Although the condition of Negroes in New York City (and the country) was one of subordination, segregation, and denial, this was substantially not a part of the daily life of Adam Jr. as a young boy. To the extent that Negroes could carve out a relatively luxurious life within a segregated society and develop a social class system behind the racial barrier, the Powells enjoyed Negro upper-class status. This was facilitated by the family skin color. They *looked* white.

One of the anomalies of race in the United States has been the preference that both blacks and whites attach to lighter skin color. Black Americans with lighter skin have always been associated with higher status. This dated from slavery when those slaves who worked in the master's house, and were subject to greater contacts (sexual and master-servant) with whites, were accorded better treatment than the "field slaves." They were thought to be better mannered, more attractive in physical appearance, obviously better clothed, and most often afforded better educational opportunities. Whites preferred those Negroes around them who had such characteristics. Blacks, not surprisingly, assimilated these preferences, and saw such lighter-skinned blacks in a more favorable light. They were "more beautiful" with their light skin, thinner lips, straight (not "kinky") hair, and generally Anglo features. A not-so-subtle class distinction developed within the race based on these kinds of characteristics. The Powells exhibited all these features to go along with their commanding role in an influential black church—undoubtedly the most important institution in the Negro community at that time.

In fact, the Powells, in physical appearance, were so indistinguishable from whites that they could, in the lexicon of race relations, "pass." That is, it was not likely that any one would, upon simply seeing them in a crowd, conclude that they were *not* white. And in some circles in the black community, those blacks who deliberately chose (and that is precisely what they would have to do) to be identified as "colored" or "Negro" were that much more admired. After all, they did not *have* to subject themselves to the degradation and insults experienced by other American Negroes.

But such a position also had its potential drawbacks as illustrated by a story Powell often told of his youth. (Like so many of Powell's anecdotes, this too could be apocryphal, but it makes the point of confused racial identity often experienced by some blacks of his complexion.) In the Harlem his family moved to in the second decade of the century, there were ethnic and racial gangs: Negro, Irish, Italian. They had all the stereotypical language common among the adults; Irish, for example, were "Micks." Once when Adam Jr. was accosted by Negroes and asked "What are you?" he answered innocently "white." They pounced on him. The next evening, he was met by whites and required to identify his race. He said, "Colored," and got another beating. A third time, some Negroes challenged him, and in his confusion, he blurted out "Mixed." The gang thought he said "Mick," and he was beaten again.

Years later, he wrote, "That was my first real brush with racism. It sowed the seeds of my belief that it's not the color of your skin but the way you think that makes you what you are."[4]

As much as he probably believed this, he also had to face the fact that his skin color *would* be a factor in how others related to him in this society. If he were considered white, he would be accorded certain advantages not enjoyed by blacks. Any sensitive white-looking black person would be negatively effected by this preferential treatment. It was not a function of his own choosing; it was society's response. If he chose to be black, he knew there were many advantages denied him, and the resentment had to exist. He had to resent this obvious gap between the ideal and the actual, this dilemma, not in his own mind, but in society's.

As far as is known, Powell's mother and father never chose to be other than Negroes, but as was so often the case, they might not have seen it necessary to make known their race if the circumstance did not call for it—as on vacations or in daily transactions in stores downtown, the countless times in casual contact when instant identification can mean the difference between cordial or hostile treatment. His sister, however, whom he adored, did "pass" for white for a time when she worked downtown in a Wall Street firm. Powell only mentioned this briefly and without evaluation: "Blanche was well educated and worked for a member of the Stock Exchange downtown, where she passed for white."[5] There is no indication how he personally felt about such a delusion. Among black Americans generally this is not (nor was it then) a subject of extensive discussion. Some blacks simply saw it as a rational means of improving one's social and economic condition, and thus as a defensible individual choice for which one should not be required to explain or apologize. To others, it was a denial of one's racial group, and capitulation to a system of unfairness and even evil. It furthered the hypocrisy. Essentially, however, as with ethnics who change their names, have facial operations, and seek to be more *Anglo-Saxon*, the phenomenon was perceived more as one individual's decision to deal with a societally imposed dilemma. It was a means of coping.

Powell would face this choice a few years later when he attended Colgate University.

The Powell household of his early youth was dominated by the presence of his father, reading the Bible at mealtimes, and an abundance of food and clothing. What was not a part of that household or family gatherings was a discussion of race. There is no evidence that the father, as involved with and committed to the rights of Negroes as he was, discussed civil rights at the dinner table or on any other occasions with his young son. This is not particularly exceptional among some black families, especially middle-class ones, who feel that mentioning the subject and drawing attention to the subordinate status of their fellow blacks might have negative reactions from the children. It might instill a sense of guilt based on their own relative advantage. It might lead to feelings of inferiority for being a member of a subordinated group, which could lead to self-hate. At times, the silence, or avoidance, is attributed to the desire to raise one's children in a "color-blind" manner, as if race were not an important factor in determining one's ability, external societal forces notwithstanding. Essentially, it was a manifestation of the "avoidance" response mechanism, calculated to shield the child from the harsh realities of the outside world. Slavery was seen as an *embarrassing* experience, one best not discussed. Some blacks even believed that their fellow black citizens did, in fact, need to be "civilized" by exposure to a more modern higher Western culture. For whatever reasons, Powell Sr. and his wife did not put race or color on the agenda for explicit family discussion with their son. This was something he would have to discover and experience outside the home, with the hope that whatever other personal strengths he gained from the family—psychological, religious, and material—would stand him in good stead to deal with the issue of race when he faced it.

In the meantime, Powell spent his adolescent years at P.S. 5 (where he was a good student), and at Townsend Harris High School (where his academic performance was lackluster).[6] He was beginning to grow physically (the illness was behind him), and his interest in an active social life, especially with girls, blossomed. He was set on a road of enjoying the attention that female pursuers lavished on him—as if they had replaced the pampering he had received from his parents, sister, and maid earlier—while he did nothing, he later noted, to discourage them. He played basketball for the high school team, and the church team, but mostly because of his height rather than because of any obvious superb athletic talent.

This continued into his first year at City College of New York where clearly he spent more time indulging in his pleasures than developing his intellectual abilities. His parents grew increasingly disappointed in him, and he spent much of his time with his sister and her second husband. It was Blanche and her husband who provided the sympathetic understanding and knowledge he wanted as he was making his way to manhood. But the pampering continued, now from them more than anyone else. It was in their home where he would learn to play cards, dance, drink, and bring his many girlfriends. His sister's home permitted him the personal freedom he had not known, notwithstanding the pampering, with his parents. Here he could smoke and do things absolutely prohibited in his parent's home.

This was the mid-1920s, the time of the flourishing Harlem Renaissance—flowing liquor, in violation of Prohibition, of course; swinging nightclubs; new dances; new, exciting literary artists.

Powell described his young and exploratory life then. From his sister and brother-in-law he acquired a love for five-card stud poker, learned all the latest dances—the shimmy, the Black Bottom, the Charleston—and was provided a haven for his rebellious nature. His dependence on his sister, as he later described, "became almost absolute."[7]

Then, in his first year at CCNY, with his grades reflecting the woeful neglect of his studies, his main lifeline, Blanche, died. "She died of a ruptured appendix while stupid doctors," Powell wrote bitterly later, "diagnosed her as suffering from 'female trouble.' "[8]

This was unquestionably the first and most painful blow in his life. More so than his parents, his older sister was the most important person in his fast and young life. He immediately gave up on school, church, parents, and very likely any sense of responsible relationship with other human beings. Already a carefree spirit, he now became a careless and reckless one. Unaware at the time of his father's earlier escapades in West Virginia and Ohio, Adam Jr. was now on a similar path. His mother, who *did* know of her husband's past, came back into her son's life, praying with him and trying to help. "This bored me," Powell later wrote, "but because I had nowhere to go any more—Blanche was dead—I had to come back to Mother."[9]

He got jobs as an errand boy, busboy at a restaurant, and as hotel bellboy. He made money, gambled, had many women, drank, and generally frolicked. All the while, his mother prayed for him. And his father, while thoroughly disgusted with him, sought ways to intervene in what he knew from personal experience was a self-destructive path.

He had flunked out of CCNY, but this was believed by his parents to be the result of refusal to apply himself to his studies rather than from inability to do the work. Aware that a college education was a major advantage to anyone, but especially a young Negro then, they persisted in their view that their son should at least give himself another try at college. They sought counsel from an old family friend, who bluntly told them that Adam Jr. would likely benefit from time out of the overly protective and excessively religious environment of their home. He advised them to enroll their son in Colgate University where, apparently, special allowance could be made to overlook his existing poor academic record. Colgate was approximately 160 miles from Harlem in the semirural setting of upstate New York, and virtually all-white. Only five (at the most) black students were among the total of 1,000 students at the all-male college.

Reverend and Mrs. Powell agreed and made their wishes known to their son, who had no objection. Why not go off to college? Powell Jr. clearly recognized that college at that time was just as acceptable as the seemingly aimless life he was then living. In addition, he was aware that the distance was short enough to permit weekend trips back to his old social stomping grounds. The family packed their son, and the hopeful Reverend Powell drove him to Colgate for the opening of the 1926 fall term. The president of the college was the senior Powell's old friend from New Haven, George Barton Cutten. The conversation between them was warm and cordial, and apparently Cutten had no intention of making Powell's race known to other members of the college, faculty or students.

Adam was assigned to a freshman dormitory with a white roommate, and the school year began comfortably enough. His old social habits continued, however, and Adam and his buddies had a grand collegiate time of weekend frolicking and beer drinking. This time, unlike the situation at CCNY, he devoted more attention to his studies and his grades improved considerably. At first he planned on becoming a medical doctor and enrolled in a premedical curriculum.

The first year at Colgate presented Powell with his first serious confrontation with the color problem and racism (discounting the earlier anecdote with the street gangs in Harlem). When he enrolled it was assumed that he was white, and he made no effort to inform anyone otherwise. Even the few Negro students did not suspect he was a Negro. To say that he was "passing" for white would imply a deliberate intent to conceal his racial identity, but it is clear that he knew that he was being treated differently than the other black students who, for example, were never housed with whites. The final stroke came when Powell attempted to join an all-white fraternity. As was customary, the fraternity checked the family background of each prospective member, and his race became known. The fraternity immediately dropped him, and his white roommate insisted that he be required to move. The university, of course, consented and told Powell he would have to find other living arrangements. The incident became widely known, and Powell was ostracized by most white and Negro students.

He went to one Negro student, Ray Vaughn, and sought help. "I think I've made a mistake," Vaughn reports Powell as saying.[10] When Powell entered the room, another black student (who, according to Vaughn, "looked even whiter than Powell,") was so angry with Powell that he walked out and refused to speak to him. Vaughn helped him join a Negro fraternity, Alpha Phi Alpha, in New York City that accepted members from other college campuses. As far as is known, from that point on, Powell did not attempt to cross the color line overtly or covertly. There were times, when he worked during the summers as a bellboy at resort hotels in New England, that he kept quiet about his race (his employers and fellow workers knew, however) when guests preferred not to be served by the black staff. Powell saw such incidents as humorous, and enjoyed the extra income that came his way as a result.

One episode involved the son of President Abraham Lincoln, Robert Todd Lincoln. Powell was working at the summer hotel, the Equinox House, in Manchester, Vermont, and Lincoln came there each night for dinner. Powell wrote:

> He hated Negroes and whenever a Negro put his hand on the car door to open it, Mr. Lincoln took his cane and cracked him across the knuckles. The manager asked me if, at a special increase in salary, I would take care of Mr. Lincoln's car each night when it arrived. So promptly every day, when Robert Todd Lincoln's chauffeured car rolled up with the son of the former President of the United States, I . . . would open his door. And Mr. Lincoln, looking at my white hand, was satisfied. For this service I received $1 a day from him and $10 a week from the inn's management.[11]

This sort of "passing" was acceptable, in the nature of playing a trick on an unsuspecting prejudiced white America—and turning a profit in the process.

While he was pampered throughout his childhood and did not have to work to earn his tuition and college expenses, Powell was required by his father to find a job every summer. The income apparently was less important to his father than the character-building experience of working for an honest day's pay. Powell continued to use his money for support of a very active social life. He and his friend, Ray Vaughn, bought a used Model T Ford for $425, and drove to New York City many weekends to continue their partying. On more than a few occasions, he would return to Colgate with suitcases full of bootleg whiskey and gin, which he sold on campus for a neat profit.

It was during this period on one of his trips to New York City that he met and fell in love with a nightclub dancer and Broadway actress, Isabel Washington. She was a member of the chorus line at the famed Harlem Cotton Club. She was also married (but separated at the time) and had a two-year-old son. They were introduced by Isabel's aunt when Adam came into town one weekend. At the time, she was in a show on Broadway called *Harlem*, which Adam had seen. He asked if he could see her again. When he returned to Colgate, he wrote and asked if he could call her "bunny girl," since it was the Easter weekend they had met. Isabel replied: "Yes, if I can call you bunny-boy."[12] Apparently, she was not overwhelmed with him at first. He was nice enough, but nothing spectacular. She recalled her first impressions: "I didn't think too much of him then. After all, I was on Broadway, and I was a show girl. I had many eyes looking at me." She remembered him as "skinny, gangly, tall—very thin." She and Powell began to see each other as often as possible either in New York City or when she visited him at Colgate. It became evident that the relationship was something more than one of Powell's many temporary flings. They fell in love. And Powell's parents, especially his father, once again registered their strong disapproval of their son's actions. The senior Powell for some time had hoped his son would follow him into the ministry and eventually take the helm of Abyssinian Baptist Church, although this was not made a matter of open pronouncement. A preacher with a showgirl wife—divorced, and with a child—was not the proper reputation for such a projected role. He made this clear to Adam Jr., but with no success. The romance flourished.

Although Powell insisted that his decision to give up a possible medical career and become a minister had nothing to do with his father and was the result of a "divine revelation" one evening in his dormitory room, Ray Vaughn told a different story.

Vaughn indicated that on one trip to Harlem with Adam, the senior Powell asked him to speak to Adam about becoming a minister. Driving back to Colgate, Vaughn raised the subject, and Adam, sensing the ready-made opportunities awaiting him upon graduation, thought about it and soon agreed. When he telephoned his parents, they were overjoyed at the decision. Perhaps their son was, indeed, on his way out of the wilderness. But there was still the matter of That Woman.

In the spring of his senior year, 1930, on Good Friday night, Adam Jr. preached his first trial sermon at Abyssinian. The pastor's young son would draw a large turnout from the congregation under any circumstance, but the attendance was swelled by Adam's many nightlife friends who saw the entire affair as slightly less than hilarious. This was their playboy buddy, one with whom they had gambled, danced, drank, and who had "slept with more women than anyone could count"[13] about to mount the pulpit and preach the Word of God. Nothing in their many times together hinted that he would succeed. But he did, giving a rousing sermon in the truest fashion of the black baptist preaching style—obviously drawing on the many years he had listened to his father in that same pulpit—and convincing many that he had at least the oratorical skills necessary to be a good preacher.

A few months later, in June 1930, he graduated from Colgate University and was poised to pursue a career in the ministry, having been licensed to preach by the Board of Deacons of Abyssinian Baptist Church. But first there would be a three-month interlude of a graduation present from his parents—a trip to Europe, Egypt, and Jerusaleum—the crowning act of relief and gratitude from Reverend and Mrs. Powell. Clearly this was an exceptional opportunity for the young graduate that indicated his privileged status at that time of economic doldrums in the country following the stock market crash of the previous October. Powell set sail fully aware that part of the motivation for his parents' generosity was to take his heart and mind off Isabel. His father made him promise that he would not contact her while he was away, a promise Adam immediately broke on the first night at sea when he cabled his love to her. The communications continued throughout the trip.

When he returned on October 1, 1930, Harlem's Abyssinian Baptist Church and a new life awaited him. He was appointed business manager of the church, a new position created by the Board of Deacons, and director of the church's community center. Now, at age twenty-two, he had a purpose, a platform, and a passion to make his own name as a distinct entity on the local Harlem scene. At the same time it was clear that he was not prepared to give up the fun-loving social life he enjoyed with Isabel and their friends. He continued to see her in all their old familiar places, and he enrolled as a part-time student at Union Theological Seminary in New York City.

Adam was fashioning the pastoral and personal life that would characterize his enigmatic career from that Harlem base for the next forty years. From a background of privilege and pampering, he was now launched.

The Pulpit and Protest, 1930s–1940s

3

Harlem: A Report to the Mayor and Advice from a Columnist

Adam Powell's Harlem in the 1930s was a dynamic mixture of pathos and pleasure. Still a playground at night for whites who came "slumming," it was the permanent home of approximately 200,000 who were caught in the throes of the economic depression. People laughed and cried, played and worked (and, as often, looked for work), cursed and prayed—Harlem contained at once in the area bounded by 110th, 155th, Park Avenue, and St. Nicholas Avenue all the emotions and experiences one could expect from a racially segregated ghetto at that time. Some very spacious town houses for the more fortunate Negroes were surrounded by slum tenements. Churches existed next to saloons. Community newspapers were read with avid attention to the crime, dances, church life, sports, and general social club life of the teeming neighborhoods. Street-corner orators mounted makeshift platforms day and evening and offered anyone taking time to stop and listen a menu of opinion and commentary ranging from far-left politics to religious salvation to general folklore advice on how to survive and even prosper. Mostly, however, people kept walking and kept struggling. Children played hopscotch on the sidewalks, and stickball in the streets. On Sundays, even in the depths of the economic depression, people put on their best Sunday clothes and strolled along Seventh Avenue after church. This was all part of the normal scheme of things in that congested community.

But things changed for several tense hours beginning Tuesday afternoon, March 19, 1935, when central Harlem erupted in violence. Around 2:30 P.M., shoppers in the S. H. Kress Five-and-Dime store on 125th Street witnessed a commotion between a sixteen-year-old Puerto Rican boy and the store's employees. The boy, Lino Rivera, had been apprehended stealing a ten-cent pocket knife, and in the scuffle that followed, he bit the hand of one of the white clerks. The police were summoned, and the screaming lad was led to the back of the store and to the basement. Black shoppers crowded around to see what was happening, but were told by the police to disperse. Angry words passed between the police and onlookers, and hostile suspicion grew that the boy was being beaten in the basement of the store. An ambulance came to treat the clerk's bloodied hand, and this further flamed the rumors of brutality against the boy. No one had seen Rivera since he was rushed out of sight. Word spread outside the store that a "Negro boy had been beaten" in the store. Soon this general allegation became "store clerks killed a boy." Emotions got out of control. People throughout the community spilled into the streets, receiving increasing rumored details of a gory murder. The driver of a hearse coincidentally parked in front of the store on a personal errand, and immediately, the growing, angry, shouting crowd assumed the car had come to get the murdered boy.

A group of young Negroes and whites started assembling on the corner to protest the treatment of the boy. Hastily printed leaflets were being distributed. Before they began speaking, a rock was hurled through the plate-glass window of the Kress store. The police immediately pulled the rally leaders off their makeshift stand and arrested them. More loud protests followed, and a major riot was under way.

Kress closed its doors at five-thirty. Unknown to most people, and unlikely to be believed if known, was that Rivera had been released and sent home without charges. Now it was too late. The Rivera incident was only the igniting spark; it no longer mattered to many rioters in the streets what had actually transpired earlier that afternoon. Hundreds roamed the streets, breaking store windows, looting, and yelling at the police and merchants. The local police force was reinforced and police sirens and gunshots could be heard along with crashing windows. Buses were attacked as they sped through the community. By early morning, the melee subsided, but flared up again the following afternoon with more looting. An organization of white store owners, the Harlem Merchants Association, asked Governor Herbert Lehman to send state troopers, but he refused.

Mayor Fiorello La Guardia appealed for calm and charged that the trouble was started by "a few irresponsible individuals" who had spread false rumors and distributed misleading leaflets about what had happened. He was referring to the group known as the Young Liberators that attempted to hold the rally. In addition, a few hours after the violence erupted, the Young Communist League also distributed protest leaflets. La Guardia's statement, which he asked storekeepers to post in their windows the next day, read:

> . . . Malice and viciousness of the instigators are betrayed by the false statements contained in mimeographed hand bills and placards. Attempts may be made to repeat the spreading of false gossip, of misinformation and distributing misinformation in handbills or other printed matter. I appeal to the law abiding element of Harlem to carefully scrutinize any charge, rumor or gossip of racial discrimination being made at this time. Every agency of the city is available to assist in investigating all such charges. I expect a complete report from several sources, giving me details of everything that occurred. As soon as I receive these reports they will be made public. . . .

In the meantime, La Guardia appointed a biracial commission of thirteen persons "to make a thorough investigation of the causes of the disorder and a study of the necessary plans to prevent a repetition of the spread of malicious rumors, racial animosities and the inciting of disorder."[1]

One suspected looter had been killed and more than a hundred were wounded. District Attorney William C. Dodge sought grand jury indictments against those captured in the rioting and looting, and he asserted that much of the trouble was caused by "Reds" who had stirred up the crowds. The Communists, he concluded, were basically responsible for the trouble. He also asked that all rioters on the relief rolls be dropped, and that any aliens be deported. He ordered the Harlem headquarters of the Communist Party, and the Young Liberators, which he claimed was influenced by the communists, closed.

"The Reds have been boring into our institutions for a long time," Dodge said. "When they begin to incite riots, it is time to stop them. We are all sticklers for free speech, but when that speech undermines our laws and causes riots, drastic action must be taken."[2]

As expected, media commentary on the violent events was swift and prolific. Two days after the Tuesday incident, the *New York Post* editorialized:

> . . . A criminal responsibility rests on those who circulated the false reports that led to the worst outbreak New York has seen in a quarter century. . . . Here . . . is a clear-cut case of false rumors which definitely incited to riot, and which is clearly punishable under the law. . . .
>
> . . . [But] it would have been impossible to inflame Harlem residents if there had not been discrimination in employment and on relief, and justifiable complaints of high rents and evil living conditions.
>
> The demand for equal rights for Negroes and greater employment opportunities is a legitimate one, and agitation for it by peaceable means is legitimate. . . .

The *New York Sun* also tended to discount the Communists' influence in the riots:

> Seeing red is an official privilege, diversion and avocation at the moment; no disorder can occur without being attributed to those terror-inspiring Communists whose shadows darken the sky at noonday. . . .
>
> Actually, the communists are more likely to have been passengers on the ebullience of a volatile population than the authors of its effervescence.[3]

And the *New York Herald Tribune* felt obliged to comment on the Communist factor:

> . . . A fine explosive mixture of Red-baiting and race prejudice might have been compounded from it [the rioting].
>
> . . . The Communists have long regarded [Harlem] as an ideal ground for agitation. They easily set down the American Negro as the Achilles' heel of our social system and they have been unwearied in their efforts, both in Harlem and elsewhere, to exploit him to their own ends. Their success has been almost nil. In the depression, as in the World War, the country's Negro citizens have shown themselves as loyal, as patient, and as sensible as those of any other group, and often much more so than some groups.[4]

While the focus on the Communists was not entirely unexpected, neither was it, even in the depths of the Depression, entirely convincing. (This, incidentally, would be an issue raised in every period covered by this political biography—the 1940s, 1950s, and 1960s—and Adam Powell, like most black leaders, was fully aware of the implications.) Because the "Red-baiting" was such a prominent response from some official sources, the *New York Post* immediately asked the young Adam Clayton Powell, Jr., to write a series of three articles commenting on the rioting. Even at that early stage in his career—twenty-six years old and only four years as an assistant pastor of Abyssinian—the *Post* recognized his already prominent, emerging role in the black community. The editor introduced him to the readers as one capable of presenting "the Negro's point of view on the recent disturbances in Harlem," and as writing a book, *Religion Faces a Challenging World*, "the substance of a course he is giving in Columbia University."[5] (The last item must have been quite a revelation to officials at Columbia University.)

At any rate, Powell Jr. accepted the assignment and lived up to his billing. On three successive days ten days after the riots, his articles were prominently published. The headlines to each article indicated his emphasis, and focused on what would be his major political themes for the next several years.

March 27, 1935: "A. Clayton Powell, Jr. Says Men Can't Get Jobs, Relief Is Discriminatory—Hits Fusion Administration."

March 28, 1935: "Powell Says Rent Too High."

March 29, 1935: "Harlem Demands Jobs for Starving—A. Clayton Powell Says Negroes, Idle and Without Aid, Dig in Refuse for Food—Police Brutality Charged."

He peppered his pieces with a few statistics on relative rents charged to Harlem tenants and other sections of the city. He cited anecdotes, with names and addresses, of Negroes denied employment or ill-treated by the relief agency, private companies, and the public utilities. He vividly described filthy living conditions, hungry people eating garbage, and several families living in one room, sharing one bath. He did not spare the city officials, especially the mayor and the commissioner of hospitals, saying: "The entire Fusion administration of Mayor La Guardia is a fusion for Fascism." He sarcastically identified the mayor as the "liberal" La Guardia. And he noted the gerrymandering that denied Negroes representation in the State Senate and in Congress. These were topics and themes he would espouse for much of his political career, always taking aim at the gap between ideals and institutions, between the rhetoric of democracy and the reality of people's lives. "This situation is no different," he wrote in the first article, "in Harlem than in any other locality in this 'land of the free and home of the brave.' "

And he was having none of the argument that laid the disturbances in the laps of the Communists. Citing the litany of wrongs and discrimination, he wrote:

> This is what the man and the woman of Harlem knows, and this knowledge is the fundamental cause of what has been erroneously called New York's worst riot in twenty-five years. It was not a riot; it was an open, unorganized protest against empty stomachs, overcrowded tenements, filthy sanitation, rotten foodstuffs, chiseling landlords and merchants, discrimination on relief, disfranchisement, and against a disinterested administration. It was not caused by Communists.

He struck none of the conciliatory tones of some of the editorials, and paid no attention to pleas for patience. His uncompromising challenge of the weaknesses of America's economic and political systems gained him additional credibility in the eyes of many in Harlem and the city as an effective spokesman for the people he would lead for the next thirty years. His tongue and pen were sharp, sometimes sarcastic. "White folks in the lead" is how he began the first article, using the colloquial speech of the black community. And he constantly emphasized the need for an end to racial discrimination and the need for jobs with decent pay based on merit.

The biracial commission appointed by the mayor set to work. It gathered testimony on what happened on March 19, 1935, and it quickly decided that it had to delve into the entire array of social and economic conditions facing the residents of Harlem. The black sociologist Dr. E. Franklin Frazier of Howard University was selected as staff director and given a staff of thirty researchers to assist him. Data were gathered on employment, housing, health, relief, education, and law enforcement. Public hearings were held for several months where people talked about specific and general experiences. At times the open sessions were volatile, with witnesses being challenged by members of the audience. Much of the work was done in subcommittees of six, dealing with the specific subjects around which data were gathered and the ultimate report organized. One hundred and sixty witnesses appeared. Powell, of course, was one.

The report that was presented to the mayor one year to the day after the Kress/Rivera incident—March 19, 1936—essentially was a seventy-six-page, single-spaced elaboration of the themes and points made by Powell in his *New York Post* articles. The report was not, however, condemnatory of the mayor, as Powell had been, but it did note the lack of cooperation of some city officials, especially

Commissioner of Police Louis W. Valentine, who "was either too busy, unsympathetic or uninterested as to not cooperate with the Commission." Likewise: "Commissioner Goldwater of the Department of Hospitals finally consented to give testimony of a general nature but refused to direct his subordinate, the Superintendent of Harlem Hospital, to submit to questioning by the Commission, thus handicapping the study of Hospitals and Health."

A significant conclusion of the report was that the incident never really turned into "a clash between whites and Negroes." It was, indeed, an attack against property—which was mostly owned by whites—and some of the "young radicals" who distributed leaflets were whites. The presence of the white protesters helped in keeping the incident from becoming a true "race riot." Some were Communists, to be sure, but their leaflets appeared on the streets at 7:30 P.M., several hours after the initial conflagration. The report stated:

> The young white men who mounted the ladder and lamppost on 125th Street and were beaten and arrested because they took the part of the indignant Negro crowds certainly changed the complexion of the outbreak. It was probably due in some measure to the activities of these radical leaders, both white and black, that the crowds attacked property rather than persons.

The important conclusion of the report followed the line set forth earlier by Powell: "The very susceptibility which the people in the community showed towards [the] rumor—which was more or less vague, depending upon the circumstances under which it was communicated—was due to the feeling of insecurity produced by years of unemployment and a deep-seated resentment against the many forms of discrimination which they had suffered as a racial minority."

And then in excrutiating detail the report outlined discrimination in employment by public utilities, private enterprises, and labor unions. "For example, Mr. R. N. Boggs, Vice-President in charge of personnel of the New York Telephone Company did not regard the exclusion of Negroes from all positions, except a few jobs as laborers, as discrimination but only as a customary practice."[6] Other officials frankly admitted that the reason for the failure to employ Negroes was that whites and Negroes could not work in harmony.[7] Figures on employment of blacks in private businesses in Harlem were cited. Most were employed, if at all, in menial or low-paying positions. "The Kress store on 125th Street where the outburst started adopted the subterfuge of employing Negro girls at the lunch counter claiming that it had thereby placed Negro girls on the sales force."[8]

The situation with the New Deal relief agencies was little better. Negroes were seldom employed in professional positions, even when their qualifications were evident; most were laborers. They were more likely to have success, however, in receiving "home relief" on a nondiscriminatory basis. But in the "work-relief" programs—WPA, PWA—the report found "systematic discrimination." Case studies of applicants denied jobs were presented. The agencies' records indicated the reasons for not hiring more blacks: "Quota for colored work filled"; or rejected because of "overquota."[9] The report concluded:

> Thus the Negro worker finds himself in a vicious circle. Discrimination on the part of private and public enterprises causes large numbers of Negroes to become dependent upon relief, but when the relief administration sets up work projects, they are denied the work for which their training and experience fit them. It appears . . . that justice has only been done the Negro when he has been a recipient of direct relief; since both as a member of the staff of the Home Relief Bureau and as a relief client seeking work, he has been systematically discriminated against.

Harlem in the mid-1930s was a community of approximately three and one-half square miles, with roughly 200,000 Negroes. The black population had increased over 800 percent since 1910. Using census tracts, the report outlined the crowded housing conditions and discussed in detail rentals paid for family quarters. The findings were as Powell indicated in his *Post* articles. Some landlords openly testified that they had no interest in or intention of renting to Negroes, and restrictive covenants were readily respected.

Educational and health facilities, likewise, were condemned. Discriminatory hiring, poor equipment, and less experienced personnel were all documented by the Mayor's Commission. Most of the schools were in bad repair, and in some cases presented serious fire hazards. While New York City was seeking federal funds for 168 new school buildings in the amount of $120,747,000 only $400,000 was earmarked for "schools attended by the vast majority of colored children."[10] In addition, Negro students were seldom found in the college preparatory high school courses. And at the Manhattan

Trade School for Boys, which was located in Central Harlem and offered valuable market-needed vocational training, nearly three-fourths of the day students came from the Bronx and were not black. Likewise, the Manhattan Industrial school for girls had only 14 percent Negro students. Some principals and guidance counselors blamed the trade unions for the discrimination. Since they were not generally open to blacks, it would be useless to train black students for such vocations. The report duly noted the paradox that Gunnar Myrdal and countless others would identify for years to come: "Discrimination in one field has its ramifications in all other fields of Negro life."

The health status of Harlemites had long been an issue, and one in which Adam Powell, Jr., would become involved shortly after he took up his duties at Abyssinian. The report was openly skeptical about the commitment of the commissioner of health, Dr. Goldwater. When charges of discrimination against black doctors were raised, he denied that such practice existed after his appointment on January 1, 1934, but he caused the Mayor's Commission to cast doubt on just how forceful he would be in guarding against discrimination:

> . . . his subsequent remark that every minority group is a victim of race prejudice and has been for all time leaves the Mayor's Commission unconvinced that he will take a definite stand against discrimination against Negro doctors. Of the same nature was his observation that, "it is the most natural thing in the world for a man who belongs to a minority group that has received unfair treatment, to attribute it to prevalent prejudice."[11]

The commission felt that this response to America's racial dilemma came dangerously close to "taking a cavalier attitude towards such evils."

This difference in perspectives is at the heart of the American dilemma as articulated by Myrdal and Huntington. The dispute lies not in commitment to the ultimate goals, but in an assessment of what is required *and* feasible in achieving those goals. (This was mainfested sharply in the running battle between Powell and Mayor La Guardia, discussed in Chapter 6.) Different historical experiences lead people to respond in various ways. Different responses, given the nature and difficulty of the issue, *can* be the source of suspicion about another's veracity. This was the nature of the tension constantly presented by the political career of Adam Powell. His own experiences (and presumably that of many of the members of the Mayor's Commission) led him to take forceful, righteously indignant positions against racial discrimination. While not entirely denying such discrimination, others might conceivably conclude either that the reality was overstated (denial response) or that as much as possible was being done *in the circumstances* to deal with the gap (toleration response). In addition, when one such as Powell persisted in raising the issue, his own credibility would be called into question. Thus, when he was under attack for personal aberrant behavior or for political positions he took, he would raise the charge of racism. And this, in turn, could be countered with denial or at least something less than the moral outrage he demanded.

Mutual suspicion builds and the distance between antagonists grows larger. This was evident in the Rivera case. When the police photographed the boy afterwards in the presence of a Negro police lieutenant, this did not convince the angry black community. The commission's report noted:[12]

> The final dramatic attempt on the part of the police to placate the populace by having the unharmed Lino Rivera photographed with the Negro police lieutenant, Samuel Battle, only furnished the basis for the rumor that Rivera, who was on probation for having placed a slug in a subway turnstile, was being used as a substitute to deceive the people.
>
> Lack of confidence in the police and even hostility towards these representatives of the law were evident at every stage of the riot. This attitude of the people of Harlem has been built up over many years of experience with the police in this section.

When the commission's report was delivered to the mayor one year after the riot, it did not get the public attention the commission's appointment received the year before.

The recommendations were predictable enough. Striking a note of moderation and patience, the report stated that "the Commission fully realizes that the economic and social ills of Harlem which are deeply rooted in the very nature of our economic and social system, can not be corrected forthwith. The process must of necessity be gradual and patiently dealt with."[13]

Nonetheless, it specifically recommended, among other things, that no city funds be spent with contractors who discriminated; that discriminatory officials be fired; that the Home Relief and Work

Relief agencies be closely monitored to guard against discrimination. It urged stronger enforcement of housing codes (but did not call for integrated housing.) It called for new schools in Harlem and an increased teaching staff. Appointments to the city hospitals were to be without regard to race, creed or color, especially at Harlem Hospital, which would be enlarged and improved. Finally, the report asked for a civilian committee to hear and investigate complaints alleging police brutality.

Mayor La Guardia received the report on April 3, but he did not release it to the press. His aides stated that he wanted to study it first. After three months, with still no mayoral response, rumors circulated that he wanted the commission to resubmit a toned-down, less controversial version.[14] This was denied by the committee and the mayor's office, but speculation continued on its exact contents and what was planned in reference to the recommendations.

In the meantime, the report's section on health and hospitals was received and printed in the Communist newspaper, the *Daily Worker*.

Finally, on June 30, 1936, the mayor met with members of the commission for two hours to review the report and to tell them, and later the press, what steps he had taken to implement some of the recommendations.[15] Pay for subway porters would be immediately raised. A new playground was soon to be built in Harlem, as was a new Harlem health center to be operated by a black physician, Dr. John West. Plans were under way for two new schools in Harlem; and the Reverend John H. Johnson of St. Martin's Episcopal Church in Harlem was appointed to the Emergency Relief Bureau. "Police abuses will not be tolerated in Harlem, any more than they will be tolerated in any other part of the city," the mayor said.[16] He admitted that facilities at Harlem Hospital were "inadequate," "but the same condition exists in all sections of the city. The new Harlem Hospital will be considered in the general hospital program for next year."

Six weeks later, the full report still not having been officially released, the Harlem newspaper, the *Amsterdam News*, obtained a copy and published it in full.[17] Implicitly criticizing La Guardia for not revealing the text, the newspaper said that the report contained "no facts that Harlemites have not known, or could not have known long before the riots of March 19." But the newspaper felt it was useful to hear from the ordinary Harlem citizens whom the report interviewed about discriminatory conditions.

Finally, in late July, the mayor met with a delegation from

Harlem representing thirty organizations, and outlined again some steps he was taking to alleviate the deplorable economic conditions.[18] But he cautioned that the problems were city- and nationwide. "I can't control that situation. After all, the city is just a municipal government, and I am as helpless in handling a large-scale economic problem as the League of Nations was in preventing the war between Italy and Ethiopia." (He knew that that war was a source of recent violent clashes between Italians and Negroes in New York City.)

On the issue of racial discrimination in employment, he seemed to accept the fact that this presented a knotty problem. While still maintaining that the city hired on the basis of merit, not color, he nonetheless had to grapple with reality.[19] "On discrimination against Negroes in employment, complaints would arise if too many of that race were employed at a given location. If [he] tried to strike a balance between Negro and white workers . . . other complaints would be made."[20]

Adam Powell, following his highly visible and apparently well-received articles in the *New York Post* the previous year, had now taken on an additional role. He began a weekly column in the *Amsterdam News* in February 1936, entitled "The Soap Box." Harlem's readers, as well as Abyssinian's parishioners and the episodic band of local activists he associated with, now would have his words coming to them on a regular basis. Clearly, after only six active years out of college, he was becoming one of the identifiable young leaders in a community seething with social controversy and suffering from no lack of self-appointed and organized groups claiming to point the way for the residents to alleviate their problems. Harlem had two community weeklies in addition to the nationally oriented *Pittsburgh Courier* to bring them news and commentary on race issues. There were innumerable social clubs, lodges, and fraternities, along with countless church-affiliated clubs. In good weather, the streets were lined with soapbox speakers holding forth on political, racial, and assorted other issues day and evening. The economic depression continued to take its toll, leaving the community a mixture of pathos and pain to go along with the night-life pleasures characteristic of the "Negro Renaissance" of the 1920s.

Powell was in the middle of this melange as preacher, pundit, and political activist, while, of course, maintaining his reputation as playboy. He gave every indication of thoroughly enjoying himself in each role.

The editor of the *Amsterdam News* introduced the new columnist as one whose "liberal column will cover a wide range of social and economic subjects." And Powell proceeded exactly in that fashion. He attacked the New Deal in caustic, witty, critical terms, suggesting to President Roosevelt and his advisers that the way to balance the budget was by becoming Negroes and trying to live off the relief rolls.[21] Give "house rent parties on Saturday nights," serve "chitterlings and pig feet," buy clothes and furniture on the installment plan. Forget about decent housing or good schools or trying to get a WPA job.

> If you protest you will be called a Communist. You'll spend your pennies in stores that have one Negro employee at inferior wages in the front, and all the rest white.
>
> ... You'll ride on subways and busses and never see a Negro employee. In other words, you'll be black. *But the Budget will be balanced.*
>
> "My country 'tis of thee"
> Hurrah for America.
> "Land of the free and home
> of the brave."

He was critical of his fellow Harlemites for spending too much time talking—"gum-beating"—and not enough time acting against discrimination. His columns were a mixture of street slang and Baptist preacher homily. He had nothing good to say of the mayor, whom he frequently identified only as the "Little Flower" (an affectionate term when used by some, but clearly intended by Powell to be dismissive) and not caring about the fate of blacks: ". . . the Little Flower has thoroughly wilted. A consistent strike-breaker and foe of labor in general, La Guardia has further distinguished himself as just a 'campaign friend' of the Negro."[22]

He never lost an opportunity to point up the discrepancy between the ideal language of the American Constitution and the reality of American social and economic conditions. "The most liberal written documents of human history are the French and American constitutions, yet we know today they could not pass as such."[23] And in an open letter to Republican congressman Hamilton Fish, Jr., of New York, he wrote: "Yes, the constitution may well be the civil bible, but it is lived up to about the same as the majority of white Christians live up to the Holy Bible. . . .

> Brother, the Thirteenth, Fourteenth and Fifteenth amendments were scrapped long ago. They were scrapped when the first black vote was

> refused at the poll, when the first colored person was kicked out of a white restaurant, when the first jim crow car was built, when the first Negro woman was raped by a white assailant who went unpunished and when the first brown boy was burned at the stake like a piece of barbecue."[24]

When he took vacations for several weeks at Martha's Vineyard in Massachusetts, his mood seemed to change to match the relaxed, serene environment, and he wrote more laughingly, less bitterly, about the quiet idyllic life where jaybirds chirping were considered too noisy. Not bothered by the obvious contrast in life-styles between himself and most of his Harlem readers, he wrote of escaping from the noise and congestion of the city. In taunting delight, he sent one piece back to his readers: "I sneak down to the harbor each day and row out a couple of miles into the ocean. After anchoring, with an evil leer on my face, I let out two good Baptist shouts and thereupon sing, 'I'se a Muggin' at the top of my voice and to my heart's content."[25]

He must have known that many of his readers back home were grinning and shaking their heads in vicarious glee at Adam Powell at play.

One theme in his early columns emerged clear and often. He was an advocate of the political left, and he took great care in telling his readers that what was needed was an alliance of *all* poor people—black and white. Keenly aware of the political ideological disputes ringing from the street-corner speakers, he decidedly came down against the black nationalists:

> It would be foolish and ignorant to try to prove that even the majority of Southerners are sympathetic toward the Negro, but I do say, remove the unemployment, the substandard wages, the inhuman hours and in one generation a new attitude will be evidenced toward the Negro. . . . We've got to stop this blind hatred toward all whites. Our future will be decided not by ourselves, but by a union of all working class forces, white and black. Blind hatred will ultimately destroy only those who hate.[26]

He condemned those Negroes who considered all Italian Americans as followers of Mussolini, and who destroyed the property of Italian store owners in Harlem. "Just like we think all Southerners are lynchers, so we believe all Italians in America are Fascists. . . . There is a strong Italian anti-Fascist organization right here in New York."

"Capitalist oppression" was the evil, he asserted. Blacks had to go into the trade unions and work with their fellow white workers. Eschewing labels of party and race, he urged:

> Party labels no longer mean anything. There is no such thing as Democratic, Republican, Communist and Socialist parties. . . . Boys and girls, political party days are over. All groups are rapidly concentrating at the two opposite poles—Laborers and Leisurers. . . . We must go left with the laborers. We must cast our voting power to those who offer the laboring class most.[27]

As could be expected, the outspoken young minister would not spare his own profession—the ministry. There was too much trivia and irrelevancy, he warned, in the black churches, especially coming from the preachers. The mass of churchgoers, he concluded, especially the younger ones, were much more interested in a civic-minded church, one that organized against community ills. "Harlem has sixty-eight churches, excluding the fly-by-nighters. You can count on your fingers all of them that are worth keeping open."[28] A few months later, he wrote: "Our ministry is composed of a bunch of spiritual sissies. The hour has struck also for a purging of the church. Away with theological twisters, ministerial montebanks, pulpit pounders, clerical clowns. The masses want men who will teach them and lead them into a just way of life."[29]

These were Powell's sentiments on the issues in the mid-to-late 1930s. He was fully on the scene, now, blasting with all the force he felt when the spirit moved him. The social, economic, and political problems of the Harlem community were fully revealed. He was clearly planning to settle in at Abyssinian Baptist Church, leading an active civic life and not letting all his public doings get in the way of a continuingly active social life. With a wife of three years, an adopted son, and multiple community involvements, he prepared to take over as Abyssinian's senior pastor upon the retirement of his father, which would come in 1937.

At that point, Adam, at age twenty-nine, would be in a position to lead one of the largest churches in the country. He had already signaled what kind of leadership he felt that ought to be.

4

Abyssinian Baptist Church: A Symbiotic Relationship

After a number of years—thirteen to be exact, from 1909 when he first arrived in New York to 1922—the Reverend Adam Clayton Powell, Sr., realized his dream of moving Abyssinian Baptist Church to Harlem from its midtown location on West Fortieth Street. On April 9, 1922, an elaborate ground-breaking ceremony was held that would lead to the construction of a hugh Gothic-and-Tudor-style church, the largest such structure owned by blacks in America. Powell Sr. had wanted to move the church because Harlem was fast becoming a community filling up with black migrants from the South and the West Indies. This was the place to find new parishioners. This was the post–World War I future of black New Yorkers. But, as popular as he was as their minister, the energetic pastor down from New Haven, Connecticut, at first met stiff opposition from some influential members of the church. They felt the costs of relocating were too high, the risk of selling the Fortieth Street building and getting equal value in Harlem too great. Powell persisted. He cajoled, argued, and even threatened to resign if he did not get his way. He lambasted his critics for being too narrow-minded and too timid.

He finally convinced them that the move was worth the effort, and the church purchased several lots on West 138th Street in Harlem for $15,000. The Fortieth Street property was sold for $190,000, and after paying off outstanding debts and final transactions, the church had $100,000 toward its new building fund.

Initial estimates for the new building were $200,000, but this quickly became too low when quicksand was discovered on the Harlem land. Meanwhile, Powell mobilized his followers, getting them to launch an intensive building fund drive. Ultimately the total cost would reach $334,881.86. Through diligent fund-raising and careful financial management, the church was able to break ground and pay off all the indebtedness except for a $60,000 twelve-year mortgage received from the Dry Dock Savings Bank. One year later on May 20, 1923, amidst much fanfare, celebrating, and many dignitaries, the new structure was dedicated. Powell Sr. was in his glory. He was hailed as a forward-looking, dynamic religious leader who was capable of taking bold steps, managing a vast financial enterprise, and keeping the confidence of the Abyssinian parishioners that their decision to make the investment was a sound one.

The building by all descriptions was impressive, if, to some, unnecessarily excessive. Constructed of New York bluestone, the windows had stained European and American art glass. In addition to the 2,000-seat horseshoe-shaped sanctuary with full balcony, there were several adjacent lecture rooms, and a six-story community building that housed a gymnasium, several smaller meeting rooms, and a penthouse parsonage with a roof garden. Clearly, a major attraction and pride for Powell Sr. was the massive all-Italian white marble pulpit reputedly costing $6,000. Visitors came—foreign and local—to admire this new monument, and the membership steadily grew.

Powell Sr. understood the enormous commitment he had assumed, and he knew the importance of meeting the financial obligation on time. There had always been criticism from various sources that blacks spent too much money on big church buildings when the money could better be used for economic improvement. These elaborate edifices, more than a few charged, were really testimonies to the pastors' egos and to the misplaced values of their relatively poor parishioners. This was a perennial debate in the black community, and, over time, indeed, some churches overextended themselves financially, could not support their material aspirations, and saw their mortgages foreclosed.

Always the shrewd businessman, however, Powell Sr., who had already been engaged in some profitable personal real estate deals, devoted considerable time to securing the financial base of this new venture. Through national fund-raising drives, advertisements in the press, coaxing his members to "tithe," and meticulous bookkeeping practices—a point he constantly made with special pride—the twelve-year, $60,000 mortgage was paid off four years and five months later in 1928.

When the senior Powell accepted the call to go to Abyssinian Baptist Church twenty years earlier, it was already a well-established, widely known black church that had moved to the West Fortieth Street property from previous locations in lower Manhattan, first on Worth Street, then to Greenwich Village on Waverly Place. The church was founded in 1808 by a handful of merchants from Ethiopia (hence the name Abyssinian) who had attempted to worship in a local white Baptist church and were insulted by being herded to the back upstairs. They immediately left and formed their own church.

When Powell took over, one hundred years later, he was the seventeenth pastor the church had had. When he arrived, the church had approximately 1,600 members of whom only 762 were active contributors, a debt of $146,354, and a checking account overdrawn by $300. Located then in the heart of a notorious "red-light" district, prostitutes lived and worked all around the church, soliciting before, during, and immediately after church services, corralling and enticing worshipers. Some of the best-known solicitors were also members of the church.

Reverend Powell had three goals to achieve: First, to get the church on a sound financial footing. Then to wage a relentless campaign to rid the neighborhood of the prostitutes. Finally, it soon became evident, to convince his followers to move the church three miles (ninety-eight city blocks) north to Harlem. He succeeded in all three.

Immediately upon his arrival, he began nightly services throughout the week, preaching and convincing the few reluctant parishioners who had not looked kindly on his coming (they had preferred to keep the previous pastor, who apparently left out of frustration over financial matters) that they had not made a mistake in inviting him. His reputation as a dynamic speaker was upheld. He established an expert accounting system for the church, hiring two black college-trained accountants (who were also members of the church) to oversee the church's bookkeeping.

His campaign against the prostitutes took him to the mayor and other city officials and to the local police, all of whom, at first, were less than fully cooperative. He persisted and slowly was able to get some satisfaction when most of the more blatant offenders withdrew to other places. This was not without some moments of touchy confrontations—threats mostly—with some of the more aggressive women and their companions. Once a bag of human feces aimed at the Reverend Powell was dropped from a rooftop, narrowly missing him and splattering on the shoes of his young son as they walked by. Such actions only stiffened his resolve to keep up his campaign while simultaneously laying the groundwork to move the church. Some of his neighbors could not have been more happy to see him succeed in the latter goal.

His congregation had purchased a parsonage in Harlem for the pastor's family, and Powell had already dabbled in some real estate deals up there that brought him an added measure of profit and comfort. He continued to lecture and preach around the country, and his sermons were printed and sold, supplementing his church salary and giving him, in time, a measure of reasonable economic independence that permitted him to be even more assertive with his congregation. If they did not support his plans to move, he threatened, he could easily do other things. Recognizing the peculiarly symbiotic relationship between the pastor and his flock, Powell knew that in time he would prevail. When he tendered his resignation out of disgust and frustration, he calculated correctly that it would not be accepted, and he would get his way. And Abyssinian, trusting in its now-revered leader, reconciled to his obvious astute talents, and, some must have concluded, "Divine Providence," prepared to move once again to the home and community many now felt was the church's ultimate destiny.

As could be expected, there are many different kinds of black churches and ministers, although as often as not one hears descriptions and analyses of "the" black church and "the" black preacher. The predominant denomination is Protestant, and within that category the largest groups are the Baptists and Methodists, respectively. Abyssinian Baptist Church under Powell Sr.'s leadership was seen as a church of the working class with more than a few professional blacks: teachers and civil servants, mostly. Powell was highly visible nationally in black church circles. He was perceived as one who believed the church should be involved in ministering as much to the social and economic needs of the congregants as to their spiritual needs. This was by no means a view shared by all ministers, many of whom concentrated their ministry on matters of morality and life after death. With Powell, however, it was expected that there would be many programs in the church aimed at social, economic, and educational activities. The church had over fifty clubs—for youth, the illiterate, those seeking to upgrade their skills or find new jobs, for the elderly. Powell's preaching style matched his exuberance. He believed in and encouraged "shouting" services, where the parishioners would "get happy" and express their emotions in open, often frenzied ways. Such displays of religious fervor were frowned on by some of the more sedate Negro churches, but not Abyssinian, where, in fact, at times, the effectiveness of the minister was as often measured in terms of the amount of noise and jubilation the preacher's sermons could arouse as in the number of converts and members attracted. The latter, of course, was never discounted.

Powell Sr., from the beginning, preached against the consumption of liquor, against dancing and excessive nightclubbing. He was strongly condemnatory of those Negroes who spent more time indulging their pleasures than in devoting their energies to personal development and race-oriented self-help economic ventures. And just as often over the years, as with his son who would follow him into the ministry, he would strongly criticize his fellow black ministers who preached one way of life of piety while leading a private life of promiscuity.

Such charges were perennial. Frequently, from within the clergy and church community and without, complaints were raised about those black preachers who neglected the daily lives and needs of the masses, and emphasized only the "hereafter" aspects of their faith. Failing to deal with the physical needs of the people was seen as just as great a fault as failing to tend to matters of the soul.[1]

In Abyssinian Baptist Church, it was, therefore, expected that there would be Bible classes but also classes throughout the week devoted to sewing, cooking, cosmetology, and reading. It was expected that church club activity would include care for the elderly as well as insurance burial societies. In order to counter the lure of a licentious nightclub, whiskey-drinking life, the church organized social events. Here, "nice" girls could come and meet "proper" prospective spouses. Powell Sr.'s wife, Mattie, spent considerable time with the clubs organizing care for the elderly, as well as the Lyceum, a once-per-month book discussion group. And, of course, much effort was put into developing the several—senior, gospel, junior—choirs of the church. A church's music was often as big an attraction as the pastor's stirring sermons in many black communities. Churches throughout the black community competed for the reputation of having "the best" choirs. They exchanged visits to other churches, and grand galas were often planned around such events. The local community newspapers played up these activities extensively.

Powell Sr. understood all this as an intimate part of the life of the church he wanted to lead. It was part of that black religious experience he knew to be an important part of black American life. He eschewed a "Sunday-morning-only" black church, and both before and after the move to Harlem, he put this stamp of leadership on Abyssinian. The church supported a missionary to the French Congo, West Africa. It contributed to black colleges, establishing a chair in religious education at Virginia Union University in Richmond.[2] The black New York press reported weekly of the many activities taking place in the various churches, especially Abyssinian—basically printing the releases sent out from the various church secretaries, occasionally with pictures.

In the mid-1920s, shortly after his daughter's death, Powell had the church buy a large white stone house in upper Harlem for $40,000.[3] This became the A. Clayton Powell Home for the Elderly with accommodations for seventeen elderly parishioners. One qualified after five years of Abyssinian membership and agreement to have the church manage the person's assets, if any. The $14,000 mortgage was paid off in 1932.

These social and economic activities of the church continued throughout the decade of the 1920s, and the parishioners rewarded their pastor handsomely. He was given a car, free housing, extended vacations, and a salary of $5,000, which was considerably above the average annual income (roughly $1,000) of Negroes in New York at that time. The Powells lived well. Some other black preachers did also, and they were recognized as part of the elite of the community. It was a mark of success for the church, many of whose members could only live vicariously through the minister, to treat the minister in such a comfortable fashion. One's pastor could hardly be seen attending National Baptist Convention meetings in less than the finest attire. It was an outward sign that the church was doing well and appreciated the leadership of the man in the pulpit. This was certainly not true of all or most black preachers, many of whom ministered to very small and very poor congregations and had to be especially attentive to the fact that they simply were unable to afford the lavish buildings and relatively luxurious life-style of persons like Adam C. Powell, Sr.

Therefore, in the bleak winter of 1930, at the beginning of the Depression, when Powell blasted his fellow clergy for not doing enough personally to relieve suffering, he was soundly attacked by some black ministers with bitter resentment. Engaging in one of the endless rounds of debates over (and among) black preachers, Powell conceded that there were vast weaknesses among his brethren and that many of them failed to sacrifice their relatively lavish and comfortable enjoyments. He had donated $1,000 of his salary to the church's welfare programs, as well as turning gifts to him over to the needy. He had refused a new car from his parishioners. He felt his colleagues around the city and country, likewise, could do more. He preached a sermon on the subject that received wide distribution in the Negro press. In it he urged Negro preachers to donate sizable amounts of their monthly salaries to aid the "starving brothers and sisters." He bitingly charged that the Negro ministry had "robbed" these people "under the guise of religion, friendship, love, truth and charity," therefore it was hardly too much to ask that they now give something back to their flock. Otherwise they should be ignored.[4]

This blunt and hard-hitting challenge was received with indignation and resentment by many black preachers around the country.[5] They resented Powell's assumption that most other black preachers were as well off as he was, that he enjoyed a large reasonably generous congregation with a huge magnificent building, and they especially resented his seemingly duplicitous life of comfort even though he had, indeed, done some charitable things. How sincere was he? they questioned: ". . . we call upon you to preach the whole gospel and practice what you preach. . . . Our prayer for you is that God will touch your heart sufficiently to make you more liberal in the gift of human kindness for your weak brother. . . . Let not your ambition for a cheap notoriety spoil your real worth."

Such charges and countercharges raged over the years. They were not new, and they would continue. Gunnar Myrdal drew some generally pessimistic conclusions from his research: "The [Negro] church has been relatively inefficient and uninfluential." Without question, the institution had great potential for mobilizing the masses, but this had not occurred. The overall "prestige and influence" of the ministry was declining, and this seemed likely to continue. The ministers were simply not in the vanguard of the black community leadership ranks.[6]

No other institution in the black community has been subjected to as much scrutiny, and for obvious reasons—the church is the oldest, largest, and most consistently supported institution in the community. It has been praised and condemned. And in a particular way, the black churches and their black pastors present a kind of black American parallel to the larger society's American dilemma. Here is a plethora of groups and individuals constituting many different styles and outlooks, hardly coherent in structure, and reflecting at any given time the dominant personality of the minister and a few leading parishioners. For the most part, especially in the Baptist church, they are free-standing, highly individualized, essentially entrepreneurial enterprises. And yet they profess a theology, an ideology of love and compassion and caring. They stand for high moral values in every aspect of life. What the perennial critics complain about is precisely the sort of complaint levied against America's racial injustice—namely, the failure to close the gap between ideals and reality. All too often one finds ministers and particular churches falling too far short of their pronouncements about what they are or ought to be.

Both Powells and Abyssinian Baptist did not escape harsh criticism, even in the early years of the Great Depression when the church organized soup kitchens and gave clothes to the needy. When the church attempted to find jobs for the unemployed, complaints of favoritism were heard. (The senior Powell was more inclined than his son to favor members of Abyssinian when it came to job referrals or even giving out meal tickets or using the church's community center facilities for recreation.) And the fact that the efforts could hardly be totally sufficient simply aggravated the complaints: those big churches with their rich preachers living off the backs (and shallow pocketbooks) of their poor members. And, as indicated, as often as not the criticisms were internal, which added even greater fervency to the debates and created more tension within the religious ranks. Later, when he succeeded his father as head of Abyssinian, Adam Jr. would be, from time to time, almost vitriolic in his attacks on some of his fellow clergymen. The difference between Junior and Senior was that the latter always aimed his charges generally; the son, in a style that he maintained throughout his later political life, frequently named names and engaged in personal acrimony, using the strongest language of castigation and charges of illegality and immorality.[7]

The irony of this, especially with Powell Jr., was that both Powells clearly enjoyed the extra material benefits their roles provided them, and they relinquished just so much. Powell Sr. continued to receive gifts and paid vacations[8]—albeit fewer and cheaper as the Depression wore on—and while he did cut back his salary (from $5,000 to $3,600) for a time, it was still well above what most Harlemites, even the most educated, earned. Powell Jr., as noted in Chapter 3, felt no need to apologize to anyone in the austere summer of 1936 when he lolled on the beaches and fishing waters of Martha's Vineyard. Indeed, he sent back articles for his "Soap Box" column vividly describing the luxurious life at that summer resort, fully aware that most of his readers and parishioners hardly had extra money for a once-a-week movie or ice cream cone, not to mention summer vacations.

When Powell Sr. talked of his gifts and trips paid for by the church, he did so as the beneficiary of a grateful congregation that wanted to reward him for years of devoted service to his flock, and often as a respite from hectic, round-the-clock, church-serving duties, and to protect his health.

Of his 1924 trip to Europe and Egypt, Powell Sr. wrote:

> When I was informed that the members of the Abyssinian Church were planning to give me a three months' trip abroad as an expression of their appreciation of my leadership, my first reaction was not that of joy or even gratitude, but of tremendous responsibility. I said to myself: "If these loyal people are going to spend three thousand dollars on me, I must see that they get every dollar back in information and increased efficiency."[9]

He did take copious notes on his trip and came back and turned them into fruitful material for speaking engagements around the country for which he was handsomely compensated.

In 1935, at age seventy, clearly tired and aging, Powell Sr. tendered his resignation (in 1924 he had been made pastor-for-life) and looked forward to his remaining years in retirement with the church securely in the hands of his son. The church leaders, however, were not ready for the change. Powell Sr. recorded:

> At a special church meeting where all available standing space was occupied, it was unanimously voted not to accept my resignation. This vote, coupled with a protest from both races outside of the church against my giving up the active pastorate, made me decide to withdraw my resignation. This was made easy because the church voted me a six months' leave of absence with pay.

Thus, in the middle of the Depression, with his followers in the deepest throes of economic deprivation, he and his wife spent the time traveling leisurely as tourists in Cuba and Panama, and pursuing his major pastime—fishing.

Powell Jr., however, presumably had not yet earned such an obvious show of appreciation, but he was soon to inherit the pulpit built by his father. And then he would immediately become benefactor of all a large black church could bestow on its leader. Two things were clear from the beginning when Adam Jr. returned from Colgate University in 1930. First, his father wanted the son to succeed him, and second, this presented some problems for some of the older parishioners. Dissatisfaction stemmed first from the young Powell's insistence on marrying a divorced nightclub singer and dancer in 1933. Although Isabel had given up her career and virtually made Abyssinian her complete home outside her husband and child—organizing young people's choirs, and actively engaging in the many social welfare functions of the church during the Depression—she was still looked upon by some as not having the proper background to be a minister's wife. This, notwithstanding the fact that Adam Jr.'s inclinations for the continued nightclub life never waned, while Isabel seemed more than content to become the model minister's wife. And it was she who apparently was more willing, almost eager, to forgo the old nightclub days and extensive partying.

The second concern was that Adam Jr. was certainly more "radical" in his political views than his father. His "Soap Box" articles as well as sermons had placed him well in the militant political camp. And his theological views were not the doctrinaire life-after-death version the congregation had received from his father. Adam Jr. did not preach the Virgin Birth. He did not adopt the simplistic interpretation of the Bible often associated with his father and preferred by some, if not many, of the congregation. He was much less predictable. To be sure, he had the attractive physical appearance and speaking style of his father, but there was concern about the substance and where that leadership would take the church. Powell Jr. had already, before his father's retirement, established himself as one quite capable of attracting and working with the younger people in the community and the church. And that was a plus. He was fast gaining a reputation as one willing to get involved in community affairs—and to an extent that was likely a plus, if not carried too far. And he was surely becoming known downtown, if not yet too much outside New York, with city and business figures. If handled correctly, that could be an enormous benefit politically and, if needed, economically for the church.

There were bigger, better-known personalities in the black ministry around the country who would have leaped at an offer to head Abyssinian Baptist Church. But somehow it was just assumed that

that leap would have to be too high—over the bodies of both Powells, at least. When Powell Sr. tried to retire in 1935, his intention was rejected by some in the church because they simply were not ready for Powell Jr., and there might be a way to circumvent his succession if there were more time. Rumors circulated throughout Harlem that some Abyssinians were so set against the son that the church would erupt in an open "split."[11] But ultimately this did not happen. The father wanted to retire; he wanted the son to succeed him. And on November 1, 1937, Adam Clayton Powell, Jr., became the new senior minister of Abyssinian Baptist Church.

The old man had gotten his way once again with his flock, as he had throughout his years of leading the church. He and the church had fused into one in a way so characteristic of many independent Protestant churches in the black community. The relationship was almost familial; there was virtually total mutual dependence. A strong pastor could likely command any response of acquiescence from the members. Those who disagreed would drift away and join other churches; they would not stay around for years and attempt to undermine the pastor or the will of the majority. While intra-church battles were rather frequent in some black churches, they were not by any means long-lasting. And Powell Sr., although he rather unconvincingly denied having a hand in the decision,[12] definitely wanted Powell Jr. to succeed him. And in a short time, the same symbiotic relationship with the church enjoyed by the father came to characterize Abyssinian Baptist Church and the father's son.

5

Preaching and Picketing

Many important changes took place in the country in the brief five-month period from November 1932 through March 1933. Franklin Delano Roosevelt was elected President and launched his historic "First 100 days" and the New Deal, beginning with the dramatic closing of the nation's banks on March 6, 1933. The country was in the grips of a deep, dire economic depression. "The Great Depression was one of the turning points of American history," historian William E. Leuchtenburg concluded. "The six years from 1933 through 1938 marked a greater upheaval in American institutions than in any similar period in our history, save perhaps for the impact on the South of the Civil War."[1]

These same months and years were the beginning of Adam Powell, Jr.'s, long public career. When he returned from Colgate University in 1930 and began working in Abyssinian Baptist Church, he had a brief stint as a student at Union Theological Seminary in New York City. This was not a fruitful experience, his work and personal life likely being too much to accommodate the demands of a graduate divinity school. He quickly dropped out. In his own account, he was dissatisfied with what he described as the rather doctrinaire religious teachings of the school and felt that a confined theological curriculum was not for him.[2] His ministry was not going to be based mainly on a philosophical understanding of the Bible, and he saw no need to pursue advanced studies that led in that direction. As he tells it, one indication of his unease was a prayer he had written for a class taught by Professor (and President) William Sloane Coffin which was returned marked "of no value." This irritated Powell, who asked himself "how any man could decide on what was or was not of value concerning another man's conversation with his God. . . . I felt that my studies there were not equipping me for the job the church required of me."[3]

Instead, in the fall of 1931 he enrolled part-time at Columbia University Teachers College to study toward a master's degree in religious education. This was a much more rewarding exposure, as he saw his needs, one that would better prepare him for his role at Abyssinian and in the Harlem community. There, he concentrated on the studies of many religions, and attended lectures by anthropologist Margaret Mead and educator John Dewey. In December 1932, one month after FDR was elected, Powell received his M.A. degree.

Earlier that year, Isabel Washington had been divorced, and she and Powell began serious preparations to be married.

Powell Sr. remained staunchly opposed to the marriage and insisted that his son seek the approval of the church's Board of Deacons. Adam agreed to this, but it is hardly likely that he would have been bound by a negative vote of that group. He knew all along how his father felt about his relationship with the showgirl, and that made no difference. He had no intention of being influenced by others in this matter—family or church. He had also withstood the disapproval of his father several times before—especially in his rollicking days at City College and after his sister's death. His father was certainly aware of his son's night life even after joining Abyssinian as assistant pastor. And the father's annoyance was only tempered by the fact that at least his son was doing good work in the church and going to graduate school. He also likely understood that, try as he might, he could not dissuade his son from doing what he had set his mind to do. In this they were much alike.

Therefore, the decision of the deacons to raise no objection to their assistant pastor marrying this particular woman served to save face for the father and the church. It clearly had nothing to do with whether that marriage would or would not take place. As an apparent concession to the senior Powell, Isabel agreed to be baptized in the Abyssinian Church (she was a Catholic) before the marriage took place. Years later she remembered that ceremony vividly—and humorously. Baptism in the Baptist faith meant total immersion, and Powell Sr. was doing the honors that morning. Isabel recalled: "I was already nervous. Then he put his hand over my nose and mouth [as is the custom] and he dunked me. And I came up fighting, and I thought, 'Oh my goodness, this old man is going to get rid of me now.' "[4]

As things developed, the marriage occurred on a rain-soaked Wednesday, March 8, 1933—the day before Congress passed FDR's emergency banking measure.[5] While the country was anxiously waiting and watching to see what first steps the new President would take to recover from the Depression, many thousands filled Abyssinian to see the young Negro preacher take a bride. Thousands more, despite the rain, jammed the streets outside to get a glimpse of the young couple. Isabel knew that many onlookers had rented standing space in apartments across the street from which they could view the festivities. It was a grand affair, with the Reverend Powell Sr. and two other ministers officiating. "With all that fanfare, and three ministers, I thought I would be married for life," Isabel quipped over fifty years later. Her mother baked a seven-tier fruitcake, and each guest at the reception received a little box containing a piece of cake and tied with a ribbon. Isabel remembers shaking 2,000 hands in the receiving line. They immediately left for a two-week honeymoon, first for a few days to the farm of a friend in Virginia, then to one of their favorite vacation spots, Oak Bluffs on Martha's Vineyard in Massachusetts.

The young pastor's preaching duties combined with running the church's community center kept him busy enough the first few years, and he was pretty much absorbed by the activities of the church. His father was finding it necessary, because of advancing age and occasional spells of illness, to cut back on the number of his own sermons, and Adam filled the gap. He had not yet achieved the speaking brilliance of the old man, of course, but there was enough there in style and substance, to keep the parishioners happy and reasonably satisfied that they were not being too short-changed.

Early on it was apparent, however, that the son's theology did not follow the exact mold of the father's. Adam Jr. rejected the concept of a "hereafter," quite a departure for a traditional black Baptist congregation. Later, he wrote: "There is no heaven or hell in the sense that they are places to which one goes after death. The heaven or hell to which one goes is right here in the span of years that we spend in this body on this earth. That is the life I believe in."[6] Likewise, he did not "believe in the Bible as the word of God. It is too filled with contradictions."[7] He accepted only the words of Jesus Christ as recorded in the books of Matthew, Mark, Luke, and John.

To Adam, Jr. the first thing was to recognize human weaknesses and the "predilection to sin." Then it was necessary to struggle to overcome these "frailties." This could be accomplished only by "an awareness of God."[8]

He let it be known that one need not attend church in one's finest clothes or even with a coat and tie (truly radical views for such a Sunday-morning black congregation), but only that the attire be "decent."

Thus he preached a message that emphasized the difference between right and wrong, and that stressed admitting the temptation to sin, but emphasized ways to combat it. A centerpiece of his sermons was the moral dilemma in American society.

> . . . I am critical of those who claim to be Christian but do not carry out in their daily life this kind of religion.
>
> Next to our foreign policy no institution in our American life is more hypocritical and therefore does more to hurt the cause of God and the cause of democracy than our so-called Christian church. Next to our lack of an adequate foreign policy stands our lack of Christianity, twins of hypocrisy walking hand in hand.[9]

His personal life was a bundle of ironies and contradictions. It was not merely that he frequented nightclubs and drank liquor with obvious relish and enormous capacity. These things were debatable, to some, as sinful. But his continuing to see other women shortly after he was married, arranging rendezvous with the aid of friends—such activities could hardly be condoned. He lived, in other words, the hypocritical, dilemma-filled life he so forcefully condemned in America's racial system. He constantly raised the race-dilemma theme, linking Southern racists to Hitler and, later, Stalin. Surely he saw the contradiction in his own life, as he saw it in American democracy.

As America was preparing to change political regimes in the winter of 1932–33, Powell Jr. was becoming increasingly involved in community protest activities. He had been involved in a small way with one group, the Harlem Citizens' Committee for More and Better Jobs, formed by his father and a few other ministers in 1930. This organization had attempted to persuade merchants in Harlem to hire Negro sales clerks, but to no avail. Their tactics essentially were polite entreaties to employers to change their discriminatory practices, and these simply elicited no sympathetic response from the white merchants. The emphasis of the group was to encourage Negroes to patronize Negro businesses and those white businesses that employed Negroes. No effort was made to organize picket lines in front of the white stores.

The most notable protest issue to occupy Adam Jr.'s energies first centered on the Harlem Hospital. For over a decade, black doctors and nurses had complained about employment practices and working conditions at the municipal hospital that served the majority of blacks in the city. Charges were made that racial discrimination existed in hiring and promotion, and that the hospital administration was run essentially as a political appendage of the local Tammany Hall–Democratic Party. In 1920, a prominent black doctor, Louis T. Wright, was hired on the staff and made a member of the executive committee. Although a respected member of the board of directors of the National Association for the Advancement of Colored People (NAACP), Wright was considered by some black doctors as merely a pawn in the hands of the white political authorities and their Harlem appendage, the United Colored Democracy. Harvard-trained, he was often accused of denigrating the medical education received by most other blacks at that time from the two black medical schools—Howard University in Washington, D.C., and Meharry Medical College in Nashville, Tennessee.

In his privileged position, Wright was frequently charged with catering to the white and black Democratic Party officials to whom he owed his job. Complaints persisted. Several black doctors attempted to air their grievances with the commissioner of hospitals, William Greeff, and with the city's mayors, first Jimmy Walker and then John P. O'Brien. These protests were essentially fruitless.

The NAACP appointed an interracial committee of fourteen people to study the situation. The group consisted of three blacks: Professor Ernest Just, Howard University biologist; a Harlem minister, the Reverend Ethelred Brown; and the Reverend Adam Clayton Powell, Sr., who had rejoined the national board of the NAACP in 1931. Socialist and prominent journalist Heywood Broun and NAACP vice president Arthur Spingarn were also asked to serve. The two doctors who were to devote themselves full-time to preparing the study were white, non–New Yorkers. The fact that Dr. Wright was a member of the NAACP Board of Directors as well as a central figure at Harlem Hospital created doubts in some quarters about how objective and thorough the committee's work would be.

At this juncture, the distrusting and complaining black doctors asked Powell Jr. to enter the controversy as their main spokesman.

Aware that his father had agreed to serve on the NAACP-appointed committee and unhappy about that, he readily accepted. For the first time, their public lives promised to clash. Adam Jr. lost no time in making Abyssinian Baptist available for mass meetings and strategy sessions aimed at pressuring the city officials to hire more black doctors and nurses and to remedy discriminatory practices at Harlem Hospital. For a time, the episode occupied the intense attention of many in the community, with Powell Jr. and his colleagues forming a Citizens' Committee on Conditions at Harlem Hospital. Meanwhile, the Communist Party in Harlem formed another group, the People's Committee. Initially, Powell Jr. invited participation of the Communists, as well as black nationalists, and socialists—a difficult mixture of ideological strands in the black community.

During those tension-filled weeks of meetings, speeches, letters to officials, charges, and denunciations in the local black press, Adam and Isabel found time to get married and go on their two-week honeymoon.[10]

On his return, Powell immediately took up the community leadership in the fight against the hospital. His Citizens' Committee planned a mass demonstration rally at City Hall during a meeting of the Board of Estimate. They would put their demands in person before the public officials. It would be the young preacher's first major effort at such mass mobilization and protest leadership.

On the morning of April 21, 1933, several hundred people began assembling in front of City Hall.[11] Powell Jr. arrived with his delegation of doctors and Harlem activists. Speeches were made on the City Hall steps. Then Powell and his smaller designated group attempted to enter the Board of Estimate meeting. At first, Mayor O'Brien refused, but when the aldermanic president, Joseph McKee, insisted, the group was permitted to enter and make its presentation. Powell spoke for the group in forceful, eloquent terms. He blasted the hospital commissioner, accusing him of being incompetent and prejudiced. He wanted several members of the Harlem Hospital governing board, including Dr. Wright, removed, and he called for a board selected by the black medical professionals in the Harlem community.[12] The delegation was proud of its young spokesman. He had done what they expected—delivered a stinging, eloquently phrased speech face-to-face with those responsible for Harlem's poor health care. From that point on, it was clear that Harlem had not only an attractive young leader of a major church, but one willing and able to play a mass civic leadership role outside the church as well.

In virtually all accounts of Powell's career, this Harlem Hospital episode in 1933 is listed most often as his inaugural as a community leader. To be sure, it did not lead to the immediate results that he later claimed—namely, reinstatement of five Negro doctors who had been fired.[13] In fact, the situation at the hospital lingered, became the focus of the Mayor's Commission report after the 1935 riots, and was still being debated into the early 1940s.

There is no reliable source to report on how the father and son personally fared over this incident. Powell Sr. continued on the NAACP-appointed interracial committee, but he disassociated himself from the final report, calling it an ineffective document that failed to deal with the core of the racial and professional problems facing the hospital.[14] His son called the report a "white-wash." What the episode showed, however, was that the son was not averse to taking a public position potentially at variance with that of his father. This would not happen often, but it would happen. There was never a *public* dispute between the two, and Junior never attacked Senior personally the way he was prone to name other persons he disagreed with. But the juxtaposition of the two every Sunday in the same pulpit, before the same congregation, yet appearing on opposite or contending sides in a community matter surely presented an anomaly for many Abyssinians and Harlemites. The old and the young, one blood, so much alike in physical appearance and demeanor, both proud and independent—and yet clearly at odds on some fundamental things, the son's personal life being likely the most obvious. The father clearly was resigned to the fact that his son would carve out a ministerial leadership role of his own and that role would likely not be, in all instances, what the father would have preferred. The father was very probably satisfied that at least the son had chosen the ministry and would probably succeed him some day as Abyssinian's leader. He could ask for little else.

In 1933 at age twenty-four, Adam Jr., now launched on a public leadership role, very likely assumed nothing else.

Jobs. These were a major concern of the New Deal in the 1930s. Millions, somehow, had to be put back to work and given some means of income earnings and stability before the society could be considered on the road to recovery. Emergency relief measures were followed by work programs. Policies were adopted to stimulate industries. In 1935 labor unions were given the legal right to organize and bargain collectively, but not until after a wave of strikes by employees shook the country. Roosevelt and many of his top advisers were slow to recognize the plight and demands of labor unions.[15] The President apparently felt more inclined to pursue a business recovery route first as a spur to increased employment. "Neither politically nor intellectually was the New Deal much interested in the labor movement during Roosevelt's first years," historian Arthur M. Schlesinger, Jr. concluded.[16]

But thanks to New York Senator Robert Wagner, things began to change. In March 1935 (the same month of the Harlem riot discussed in Chapter 3), Senate hearings were held that would lead to the historic labor union legislation. Four months later, FDR signed the bill that some came to call the "Magna Carta of Labor."

At that precise time, during the very months that the national government was setting the stage for an important new day for America's organized workers, Negroes in Harlem were mounting their own mass-action drive against local merchants for jobs. If there has been one issue aside from voting and segregated facilities that has occupied the attention of blacks (nationally and locally) throughout the post–Civil War civil rights struggle, it has been jobs. That issue has always been on the civil rights agenda in some form or another: early on as a persistent campaign against racial discrimination in hiring; for equalization of wages; against discrimination in directing blacks into menial job classifications, especially in the New Deal programs; for equal access to jobs in the war industries; even as military recruits into fighting units, as opposed to service units. "Jobs" has been a perennial economic battle cry of the black American struggle with the American Dilemma.[17]

There had been some successful local campaigns in Northern cities in the early thirties—Chicago, Detroit, St. Louis—to get reluctant local merchants to hire Negroes as sales clerks, not just as janitors and porters. Picketing and boycotting tactics had worked to a certain extent to force store owners in the black communities to change their policies.

In 1934 and 1935, the campaign reached Harlem. "Don't buy where you can't work" became a rallying slogan for pickets and boycotts organized by sundry groups. As noted, a few years earlier, the Reverend Powell Sr. and a few other ministers had attempted to encourage their parishioners to spend their money with those merchants who were more sympathetic to their employment demands. Such oblique appeals were not very successful, and the ministers did not favor at that time mass picketing tactics. One tactic was to collect the sales slips from consumers and present them to the merchants to show them, as if they were unaware of it, the purchasing power of the Negroes in the community. But in the mid-thirties, spurred on by successful reports from other cities, increasingly deplorable unemployment rates, and blatant evidence of insult and humiliation of Negro shoppers, the New York community seemed ready to mount a sustained protest against employment discrimination by the white merchants on Harlem's main commercial thoroughfare—125th Street.

That such discrimination existed was not denied. Some merchants openly admitted that they had no intention of hiring Negroes as sales people. Although, in some instances, blacks constituted as much as 75 percent of the purchasing power, the owners asserted that white shoppers would be offended by being served by blacks. Others insisted that blacks simply were less qualified than whites for such positions. The owners of the largest department store in Harlem, Blumstein's, saw no need to alter what they considered an already progressive employment policy of hiring blacks as janitors and even one, a graduate of City College, as an elevator operator.[18] In addition, the owners pointed to their support of the National Urban League and other charities to help Negroes.

The polite Harlem campaign for better local community jobs was going nowhere until a peculiar, unlikely figure, fresh from a successful jobs struggle in Chicago, arrived on the scene sometime in 1932. He called himself Sufi Abdul Hamid, certainly the most recent of several aliases he had adopted in a checkered, questionable past. Later, because of his tactics and anti-Semitic speeches, others, black and white, would call him the "Black Hitler." A tall man with a brightly colored cape draped over his shoulders and wearing a Hindu-type turban and long brown boots, he held forth on Harlem street corners, calling all who would listen and follow—mostly young unemployed Negro males attracted by his flamboyant dress and strident language—to walk picket lines and support boycotts of white (he often said Jewish) racist employers.[19]

For about two and a half years, Harlem was a scene of constant protest activity from various groups demanding the end to job discrimination on the part of the merchants. Groups representing quite different ideological views—nationalists, integrationists, Communists, and some not particularly identifiable beyond a self-proclaimed ad hoc platform such as Sufi's—mounted picket lines in front of major stores as well as small "mom and pop" enterprises. Occasionally, the leadership of the groups would coalesce for a brief time, then break up. Mass rallies were held on street corners and in churches, quite frequently in Abyssinian Baptist. One organization, the Citizens' League for Fair Play (CLFP) started by a highly respected black minister, the Reverend John H. Johnson, was viewed by some observers as a counter in style and composition at least to Sufi's more anti-Semitic group. Adam Powell Jr. marched with all of them. While his sentiments were with the CLFP, he was not completely trusted by that group because of his willingness at times to associate with Sufi's crowd. But it was clear that he was one of the few young ministers willing to walk the picket lines and raise his voice in loud condemnation of discriminatory practices. While the demands were often similar, there were distinct variations. The black nationalists were much more interested in getting virtually all the jobs in the stores for blacks, even to the point of insisting that white employees be dismissed. The CLFP was willing to bargain more, accepting a certain number of new hires as positions became available, and not insisting that whites be dismissed. The Communists, forming their own protest group, always felt uncomfortable with, and indeed rejected, the demand that pitted black workers against white workers.

Still other bones of intracommunity tension were introduced into the protest—namely, the "color" problem, and who should be the source of employment referrals. The black nationalists, led by adherents of Marcus Garvey's UNIA (Universal Negro Improvement Association) movement, had organized the African Patriotic League, and were intensely interested in pursuing their long-standing goals of self-help and building a "black economy" within the Negro community. They saw the "Jobs for Negroes" protests as one step in that direction. This obviously did not sit well with the CLFP, and more often than not, any alliance or "popular front" that developed was of short duration.

But the "color" problem was even more vexing and divisive. As a few store owners capitulated and agreed to negotiate the demand of some hiring of Negroes, in many cases the new sales clerks turned out to be very light skinned, white-looking Negro women. This infuriated Sufi and the African Patriotic League, led by Ira Kemp and Arthur Reid. They blasted both the store owners and the CLFP for further discriminating against darker-skinned Negroes, and charged that the women hired were in any case not even the ones who had walked the picket lines. That such skin-color preference prevailed is not generally disputed. One CLFP leader all but admitted that his group and the National Urban League did, in fact, refer lighter-skinned women to the employers for the new jobs.[20] Understandably, given his own physical appearance, this was not an issue Adam Jr. cared to take up. He felt far more comfortable playing the role of reconciler among the contentious groups, inviting various speakers to appear together at rallies at Abyssinian Baptist Church, and generally focusing attention on the racism of the Harlem merchants.

Throughout this phase of the "Jobs for Negroes" protest in Harlem, the campaigns were often confused and muddled by intergroup battles vying for leadership and prominence as well as attempting to establish one particular group as the major, if not only, employment agency. In this quagmire, Adam Jr. never sided with any particular organization for any length of time. And this decision at times caused him to be attacked by one group or another. One week he would be seen picketing with Sufi's loud, raucous followers. Then he would make comments denouncing their more extreme anti-Semitic slogans. This, in turn, made him the target of Sufi in a street corner rally held near Abyssinian. Another time he would announce his alliance with the picketers organized by the local Communist Party, and then later withdraw an invitation to that party to meet at his church—drawing their ire, of course. When negotiations with store owners were conducted by the CLFP, Adam was not included in the executive committee, largely because he was not fully trusted by them.

This record led to an image of vacillation and untrustworthiness. Certainly, he could be counted on to give a flaming speech condemning employment discrimination. And more often than not he could well show up on a picket line while some of his more restrained ministerial colleagues preferred to remain away—in some circles in Harlem, picketing, even for such a commendable goal as ending job discrimination, was seen as less than dignified; it was what the lower classes did. Adam had no such hang-ups or constraints. In fact, he gave every evidence of thoroughly enjoying himself on the picket line, and he could at times be heard to comment that his fellow brethren of the cloth were conspicuously absent.

But essentially the protest campaign against the Harlem merchants was a movement of several different groups contending with one another as well as against the prejudiced merchants. A court injunction late in 1934 sought by a local shoe store—A. S. Beck's—temporarily ended the campaign.[21] A court ruled that since the protesters were not an organized labor union, but were making demands for a distinctive racial group, they could not mount their pickets and boycotts. This court ruling effectively ended the protests until it was overturned a few years later, when Adam would emerge more in a clear leadership role, heading his own group.

What was reasonably clear from the Harlem Hospital and 1933–34 "Jobs for Negroes" struggles was that Adam C. Powell Jr. functioned best when he was the recognized leader. He was willing to lend his name to different groups, show up at their rallies, march on their picket lines, attend their strategy sessions. But basically he was not a follower, and there is little evidence that he worked well as part of a "team leadership" that required collegial consultation and consensus before acting. In the helter-skelter frenzied days of community activity in the Harlem of the 1930s, there is little wonder that anyone's ability to belong to a group and persist over time would indeed be taxed. Emotions ran high precisely because the issues were intense, conditions were so desperate, feelings at times quite raw. Loyalties could be strained by a suggested compromise, a questioned tactic, a less-than-fervent response, misunderstanding of motives, and, of course, attention from the press. Adam Jr. did not function well under such collegial constraints. He could sit in strategy meetings for hours, but he was as likely to improvise on his own later as to go along with the agreed plan. He functioned best when he was free to read the situation himself and act spontaneously. This would characterize his entire political career, at times serving him well, at other times getting him into trouble and calling into question his reliability. In the early days in Harlem, it got him the reputation of being not so much a loner, but fickle and self-promoting, perhaps overly ambitious. At any rate, his compatriots knew that working with Adam would bring you pluses and minuses. He had, indeed, a "flaming tongue"; he *could* state the case against racial oppression in the most vivid, indicting terms. But he was also eminently unpredictable. How long he would be with you was problematic. Whether he would deliver as precisely agreed was frequently questionable. Whether he was operating in more than one camp at the same time could never be certain. But he had the basic requirements of an effective community leader at that time and for that place—a big church behind him, superb oratorical skills, a clear commitment to fighting racial problems—and these could not be denied. Thus, when Adam called or came, it was rather certain that he would get a very good response and bring a large following with him.

That time did come in the late 1930s—1938—when he became the leading force behind the formation of yet another organization, the Greater New York Coordinating Committee for Employment (GNYCC). In association with an older, and highly respected, minister, the Reverend William Lloyd Imes, who, incidentally, had been one of the three ministers officiating at Adam and Isabel's wedding, Powell decided that the time was ripe for another major assault on discriminatory employment practices throughout the city, not just against the merchants in Harlem. The organization would set its sights not only on the local stores, but also take on the blatantly discriminatory public utilities, especially the light and telephone companies. Powell obviously liked Imes, who seemed to complement him perfectly. Powell himself recognized the mutually reenforcing differences:

> The co-chairman of our committee was the brilliant Reverend Dr. William Lloyd Imes, minister of St. James Presbyterian Church and President of the Alumni Association of Union Theological Seminary, later to be President of Knoxville College in Tennessee. I was young and Dr. Imes was mature. I acted before I thought and he thought before he moved. I was impetuous and impatient, but Dr. Imes always paused to reason. He was a great man, with the mind of a scholar, the soul of a saint, the heart of a brother, the tongue of a prophet, and the hand of a militant.[22]

It probably took all those qualities to presume to be able to work with one as unpredictable and impetuous as Adam Jr. But the organization, composed not of individuals but of organizational membership, was launched. It became Adam's major institutional vehicle outside Abyssinian Baptist Church for his public life, and he would work with it until he transformed it a few years later into the People's Committee, an entity to serve his move into city electoral politics.

In the meantime, the GNYCC became his group. Housed in Abyssinian, it claimed "more than 200" member organizations, consisting of an assortment that included social clubs, fraternities, sororities, churches, professional groups, black nationalists, Communist Party adherents, socialists, and integrationists. It was the kind of political constituency—of varied left-leaning and liberal political tendencies—that Powell always felt more comfortable with. It was also obvious that most of the organizations were there simply to fill out the letterhead. One could hardly expect this to be a cohesive, smooth-running outfit that was geared to anything approaching democratic decision-making. It was too wide a mixture of elements, but that was fine with Powell. As long as they followed his lead and kept their attacks focused on the discriminatory targets and not on the ideological differences among them, he was in his milieu. In a sense, the GNYCC represented the eclectic maxim he often quoted (but which made him appear to some as simply an opportunist): Negroes ought to belong permanently to no particular party, but feel comfortable, at the moment, to be "nationally Republicans, locally Democrats, theoretically Socialist, and practically Communists."

A major U.S. Supreme Court decision in March 1938 was the catalyst for GNYCC's formation and gave impetus to its plans. In *New Negro Alliance* vs. *Sanitary Grocery Company*, the Court overruled the earlier Beck case, and now Negroes could engage in boycott activities against racial discrimination. In its early weeks of protests against utilities, the GNYCC had experimented with such relatively ineffective tactics as having people turn out their lights for several hours once a week, and jamming the circuits of the telephone company by asking for operator service. Dramatic-sounding though they were, these activities did not have wide appeal, nor were they particularly effective in arousing the companies to respond. After several well-attended mass meetings at Abyssinian where enthusiasm was high but where Adam offered little but flaming rhetoric and relatively weak action, the decision was made once again to hit the streets with mass picketing.

Again a rival group was formed, the Harlem Job Committee (HJC), formed by several prominent leaders, among them A. Philip Randolph, the black union leader, and the Reverend John H. Johnson of the earlier CLFP, who denounced GNYCC as too much dominated by the Communists. And again a "jurisdictional" battle of sorts developed. The newer group felt that Powell's GNYCC should focus on the public utilities, and leave the protest against the Harlem stores to the HJC. Powell, of course, was having none of that, and the protests proceeded—against the discriminatory employers—locally and downtown, and against the competitive protest groups. Throughout the entire decade, there appears never to have been a time when the Harlem community was completely united behind one single organized protest group. This rather remarkable fact was the result of a number of factors: ideological differences intensely felt; personality clashes; leadership rivalries; petty jealousies, to name only a few. This division among black protest groups was a phenomenon Powell came to understand and live with throughout his political life. And it is likely a factor in understanding his own attitude about organizational loyalty and personal political commitment. The battleground in which he was nurtured in the 1930s presented a heavy dose of backbiting, sniping, ideological challenging, and the questioning of one's veracity. Powell was groomed in that intense atmosphere and he survived it. He also very likely absorbed it as part of his own political life-style.

For several months in 1938, both groups, plus another holdover from the Marcus Garvey black nationalist days, the Harlem Labor Union, mounted picket lines in front of stores and at the midtown headquarters of the utilities. Powell was able to engage several Negro celebrities and Broadway entertainers to march occasionally with him, such as Duke Ellington and the actor Canada Lee. In Harlem, there were picket lines virtually six days a week for several hours at a time. Powell called strategy meetings and held rallies. First, some Harlem stores relented and agreed to hire a few Negro clerks. Then the Consolidated Edison Light Company came to terms around an agreement to hire a few trainees. Powell and Mayor Fiorello La Guardia hailed the agreement as a major victory for democracy and the city. But others complained that the agreement was vague; it did not specify how long the training period would last, or how many would ultimately be hired. In addition, the light company replaced promoted Negroes with whites, which caused some blacks to accuse Powell of not really achieving a substantial increase in Negro employment. He had been one-upped, his critics complained.[23]

But the protests continued. The interest of the GNYCC followers waxed and waned, as leaders vied with each other to be *the* most effective ones to deliver real benefits to the community. Some groups insisted that the merchants hire all black employees. Others were content to accept an agreement for a reasonable proportion. At times the various demands included assurance that the new Negro employees would be allowed to join a labor union.

Meanwhile, Powell spent some of his time filling speaking engagements around the country, as news of his GNYCC efforts began to spread. He spoke at Negro colleges, at other churches, and often at conventions of national Negro organizations. His reputation as an active, dynamic, young minister was growing as he added his own style and message to the name his father had already established in such circles. (In many regards, he was an earlier-day Martin Luther King, Jr., without the benefit of national television. The major publicity about Powell and his activities beyond Harlem came through the national Negro newspapers: the *Pittsburgh Courier*, the

Chicago Defender, the *Baltimore Afro-American*, the *Kansas City Call*.) His basic message never varied: condemning racial segregation and discrimination, imploring the black churches to lead the fight, and always lining up with liberal social forces on the political spectrum. He seized every opportunity to capitalize on press attention. When the White House in 1940 asked him to join a large committee celebrating President Roosevelt's birthday by supporting the fight against infantile paralysis, he shot back a not-too-polite refusal:

> Many thanks for your kind invitation to become a member of the distinguished group to be known as the Church Council. I would gladly pledge full cooperation of not only myself but all the members of this, the largest Protestant Church in America, if it were not for the rigid practice of discrimination against crippled Negro children and youth now being practiced at Warm Springs, Georgia. If your organization has arrived at any practical plan to include the Negro victims of infantile paralysis, I shall be only too glad to serve.[24]

A symbolic gesture, to be sure. But many in the Negro community loved it. Although Negroes had switched to FDR from the Republican Party in 1936, they felt pleased that one of their spokesmen lost no opportunity to tell the administration of their continuing disappointment with the civil rights record of the Democrats who now so overwhelmingly controlled the national government. Actions such as the rejection of a White House invitation further served to portray Powell as being one not likely to "sell out," not likely to curry favor with prominent sources for his own personal advantage. He was, indeed, piling up political points where he would need and use them the most in years to come—in the black community, and especially at home in Harlem. The honorary doctor of divinity degree he received in 1938 from a Negro college in North Carolina, Shaw University, recognized him as a "militant preacher of a strong gospel message," "dynamic leader of youth," and "courageous spokesman of racial justice and good will."[25] He lent his name to a number of causes, local and national. He spoke at a rally of the Consolidated Tenants League, along with Vito Marcantonio, the liberal-progressive congressman from East Harlem, supporting rent strikes against landlords raising rents.[26] He was a member of the National Committee to Boycott German Products, and urged his parishioners to donate money to help Jewish refugees.[27] "I personally feel that it is significant when the Negro people, as poverty stricken and oppressed as they are, are yet willing to gladly make this contribution."

Throughout this period, he paid careful attention to the administrative and financial needs of Abyssinian Baptist Church. The congregation grew steadily, several hundred each year. He reorganized the staff, rehired several persons previously laid off during the worst months and years of the Depression, and expanded the community center programs, especially those focusing on the youth. The church's board of trustees agreed with his proposal to sell the excessively expensive Home for the Elderly and restructure the day-care center. With an eye to economy, he, Isabel, her son, Preston, whom Powell had adopted, and the Reverend and Mrs. Powell Sr. moved from the old parsonage to new, less expensive quarters. The church was refurbished, and it was clear that the young pastor was not only a popular, attractive preacher who could fill the pews every Sunday, but also a sound administrator. Again, he was following the example set for twenty years by his father. As long as the spiritual and economic needs of the church were being well tended, there was no likelihood that Powell would receive criticism internally for his many activities beyond the pulpit. In fact, many saw these now as complementary. The more publicity he received in the press and around the city and country, the more this would redound to the prominence and prestige of the church.

As the decade ended, Powell's GNYCC took on the officials of the 1939 New York World's Fair. Again, the goal was to break down employment barriers. The officials admitted that they had no plans to hire more than a few Negroes as menials in the enterprise advertised as "Building for a better tomorrow." Powell immediately launched picket lines in front of the Empire State Building in midtown Manhattan, the headquarters of the World's Fair. Earlier appeals to Grover Whelan, the fair's president, were to no avail. Negroes had been making the case for more Negro employees on the World's Fair projects since 1936. But in 1939, with the fair scheduled to open in late April, the GNYCC led by Powell mounted daily pickets and even Thursday all-night vigils. Powell was now *the* recognized leader, and support flocked to him. He laid plans to picket at the fair on opening day. While fair officials hired more Negroes—from forty, out of a total work force of 2,000 to approximately three hundred—these were virtually all in menial jobs, and included no exhibitors, guides, or cashiers. Powell admonished his followers not to let up. His Sunday sermons were virtual calls to action, and the Negro weekly press gave him all the coverage he wanted. Even those Negroes less inclined toward mass demonstrations were supportive—in words of encouragement even if they could not see their way to joining the picket lines.

Now Powell was operating outside Harlem and, indeed, in an arena that would definitely attract worldwide attention. President Roosevelt was even scheduled to attend the opening of the fair. A mass protest demonstration against employment discrimination could only be extremely embarrassing to the city and national officials—so felt Mayor La Guardia. This was not a Harlem-confined affair. The mayor attempted to forestall the protest by meeting with Walter White of the NAACP and the Reverend John H. Johnson from Harlem. These two hoped to persuade Powell to desist. But when they informed Powell that the mayor and Whelan were prepared to hire ten black cashiers, Powell rejected the compromise. On opening day, April 30, 1939, President Roosevelt, Governor Herbert H. Lehman, and thousands of fair-goers were greeted by five hundred Powell-led protesters. Little came of the encounter, and Powell later switched tactics and tried to bring pressure on selected exhibitors at the fair. A selective boycott was organized. It was hardly effective.

One victory did result from the episode, however. An Abyssinian member who worked at the exhibit of the Standard Brands Company informed Powell that the company maintained segregated toilet facilities for its employees. Powell immediately seized on this affront and called for a boycott of the company's several products. He chided publicly: "I don't like Chase and Sanborn coffee, anyway; Tenderleaf Tea sounds fruity; Fleischman's Yeast doesn't streamline your figure; I have always associated Royal Gelatin with sick people and Blue Ribbon Mayonnaise costs too much."[28] With the intervention of the NAACP, the company changed its segregation practice, and rehired the black employee it had fired for informing Powell. At least this much was accomplished.

The NAACP was quite aware of the different roles in the civil rights struggle. Powell clearly was the out-front, loud agitator, who could be relied on to stir up mass audiences to bring pressure. The NAACP was more prone to resort to quiet negotiating, but certainly willing to benefit from Powell's threats. The Standard Brands case is an example. The NAACP had established contact with the company over its segregation practices, and the company, after hesitating, agreed to relent. The company's attorney, Richard L. Fruchterman, expressed sympathy with the NAACP's position, agreed to change the policy, and hoped the NAACP would issue a press release to that effect. The NAACP consented, and an internal NAACP memo from Roy Wilkins to Walter White told the rest of the story. Wilkins said that Fruchterman was critical of the company's "stupid" practice of segregation and was "greatly disturbed" that the black employee had been fired against his [Fruchterman's] advice. Wilkins assured the company that the NAACP was not making "an official issue" of the firing, but he gently reminded the executive that the fired employee was a member of Adam Powell's church. Surely, Wilkins prompted, Powell would more than likely "make dismissal of Mr. Gillespie the subject of a short talk to his congregation." And the NAACP officer also reminded Fruchterman that Abyssinian had a "large membership" and no small amount of "influence." Fruchterman got the message. He was so pleased, in fact, to be able to work in such a harmonious manner with the NAACP that he took out a $25.00 membership then and there in the civil rights organization.[29]

Thus Powell, the lightning rod, could be used by more moderate civil rights advocates to accomplish certain goals. Protests and the threat of protests complemented softer forms of approaches. And the two roles could seldom be conducted by the same groups or individuals. This was a classic example of division of labor, not uncommon in social movements. This was an informal style that would operate throughout the period of the 1960s civil rights movement. And there is every indication that Powell was temperamentally more suited to the image and role of protest catalyst than to that of quiet negotiator, at least at this stage of his public career.

Overall, approximately seven hundred Negroes were hired (mostly in menial jobs) at the World's Fair out of an ultimate fair work force of 7,000. The fair's president, Whelan, insisted throughout, however, that racial discrimination was not the policy. Whether one were hired or not depended on "experience, efficiency, and intelligence" as well as "youth, neat appearance, education, and good character."[30] This is a classic illustration of Huntington's classification of the "denial" response to the gap between ideals and institutions, between theory and practice. What *seems* to be a gap is not that at all; other legitimate factors explain the low employment record of blacks on the fair's payrolls.

Powell and his followers were having none of this, of course, but neither were they able to sustain the protest beyond a few months. Already, their forces were growing weary and, sensing this, Powell let the World's Fair episode fade away, choosing, instead, to pursue some halfhearted attempts at selective boycotting of certain discriminatory stores and a bread company and a dairy company. He and the dwindling GNYCC ranks achieved some success, but not much. Some establishments in Harlem relented during the Christmas shopping season, and the GNYCC was able to reach an agreement with several stores on 125th Street that they would alter their policies. These stores—displaying blue and orange signs in their windows (likely a takeoff from the earlier Blue Eagle signs indicating support for the NRA)—were to be preferred by the Harlem shoppers.[31]

Little else that was even mildly successful could be chalked up on the protest agenda as the decade came to an end and as Powell was finishing his tenth year of preaching and picketing. He continued his column, the "Soap Box," in the *Amsterdam News*, and he devoted considerable time to the affairs of Abyssinian. His trusted ally, the Reverend Imes, had grown weary of GNYCC activity and would soon resign from the organization, later his church, and become the president of Knoxville College in Tennessee. Powell remained at the helm of GNYCC, and he had one more major fight in him in that role—one which did, in fact, yield probably the most discernibly positive results of his ten-year record to date. He would join with others to take on the two local bus companies and the Transport Workers Union led by the popular and liberal Michael Quill. Once again the ideological spectrum in Harlem was in evidence. Communists, nationalists, and the Powell-led GNYCC would link up one more time.

Like most issues of segregation and discrimination in Harlem, the employment practices of the bus companies—the New York City Omnibus Corporation, and the Fifth Avenue Coach Company—were old sore points with the community. The residents relied heavily on the buses as means of transportation, and rolling through the streets of Harlem they were daily reminders of the insult of job discrimination. Only positions as porters were open to Negroes—fourteen out of a total work force of 3,202—and the companies simply refused to consider hiring them as drivers and mechanics. The liberal union spoke good words but was not on record as leading the fight to end job discrimination. The local black nationalists were the ones who decided to resume the struggle once again, and they saw the opportune time when Quill's TWU struck the companies for higher wages in March 1941. The Harlem nationalists calculated that they should organize Harlem to support the white workers in anticipation that when the strike was settled successfully, the union would then support the black demands for jobs as drivers and mechanics. The plan seemed sound enough, but the nationalists figured that they could use Adam Clayton Powell, Jr., in their ranks to mobilize the masses when the strike was over and time came to apply black community pressure. At first the Abyssinian pastor was reluctant. He had not initiated this fight; it could be another case of his being an appendage and not in the sole leadership position. In addition, he was aware of the criticisms of the World's Fair protest movement, namely that little was gained from all the effort. And in the spring and summer of 1941 he was already beginning to think about running for the City Council. This bus protest could be too much of a distraction. But he was finally convinced by the nationalists, his ego surely having something to do with his decision, that he was the one person in Harlem who could make the strategy work. He had the mass following and the protest skills. Whether the nationalists believed every word of their pleas to him, Powell very likely did, and he agreed to take his GNYCC into the fight. He and his colleagues formed a coalition of the GNYCC, the Communist-influenced National Negro Congress, and the nationalist-oriented Harlem Labor Union, and called themselves the United Negro Bus Strike Committee (UNBSC).

When the TWU and the bus companies agreed to arbitration, the UNBSC went into action behind Powell. Harlemites were urged to stay off the buses until an agreement was reached on hiring Negro drivers and mechanics. The union leaders were primarily concerned about protecting their members, and did not want to be caught supporting a policy that favored hiring Negroes over white workers with seniority. This position was quite acceptable to the Communist members of the UNBSC coalition, who always were suspicious of any protest that seemed to pit black and white workers against each other. Worker solidarity was their rallying cry, and they wanted the Harlem bus protest to manifest this unity. The black nationalists in the group were, as expected, not that interested in what they considered to be a useless effort to make common cause with white workers whom they considered to be more interested in white supremacy than in working-class unity. After all, they argued, these white workers gained seniority precisely because they were hired in a racially restricted labor market; they were the beneficiaries of employment discrimination against Negroes. Why should they be protected now? Once again, Powell played mediator.

In the interim, protests became periodically violent as some people harassed bus riders and, in a few instances, stoned the buses as they rolled through the Harlem streets. Negotiating sessions were held with the bus companies, the TWU, and the UNBSC, led by Powell. Weeks and months dragged by into the summer of 1941. (This was the same period when, on the national scene, Negroes led by A. Philip Randolph of the Brotherhood of Sleeping Car Porters, pressured FDR to issue Executive Order 8802 in June

1941, prohibiting employment discrimination in defense industries doing business with the federal government. Eleanor Roosevelt and Mayor La Guardia were involved in those negotiations. The efficacy of a mass protest march in Washington while the country was on the verge of going to war against fascism was the American dilemma debate that received wide attention. Powell, who was a member of Randolph's group, also attempted to make the same dilemma argument on the local scene.)

Clearly the local protesters were becoming frustrated and short-tempered, and Powell sensed that yet another major community protest effort could simply wither and die out. The episodic violence continued, encouraged mainly by the nationalists who could see that any settlement would likely leave the blacks with far less than was acceptable to them. Powell, who was by now an experienced veteran in the subtleties of Harlem community protests and was able to assess a following as well as anyone, knew that a settlement of some kind was important to reach, even if it meant a compromise on less than the full demand of immediate hiring of hundreds of Negro drivers and mechanics. While playing the role of protest leader, he was also becoming adept at seizing the right moment to strike a compromise—thus attempting to combine the two roles. This was, at best, always a precarious leadership tactic, but at times unavoidable. (Years later Dr. Martin Luther King, Jr., would often find himself in the same predicament on the civil rights scene.)

Rumors surfaced of different sorts of deals and proposed agreements. An article in the July 5, 1941, *Amsterdam News* reported that the Fifth Avenue Coach Company agreed to place ten Negro high school graduates as apprentices. Little in a concrete way materialized.

Finally, after further negotiations and wrangling, Powell and his colleagues were able to announce a "victory." In the fall, they told mass rallies that at least thirty-two trainees were to be hired as permanent drivers and mechanics. Others would be hired when the older white TWU workers were called back to work. A quota system was established, and eventually, at the beginning of 1942, with the country now fully engaged in a war against fascism in Europe and Asia, Negro Americans were permitted, for the first time, to drive buses on the streets of New York City. Powell was jubilant. The community celebrated as if World War II itself had been successfully ended. At last here was a clear-cut victory, visible for all to see, and Adam Clayton Powell, Jr., had to be recognized as a major figure to receive much of the credit.

* * *

But as these turbulent, delicate events unfolded throughout the fall of 1941, Powell was gearing up to move into a new phase of his career. He had been involved in pressuring the local city colleges to hire Negro faculty, and he successfully convinced the Interboro News Company, in December 1941, the same month of Pearl Harbor, to hire eight blacks as operators of local newsstands in Harlem. Other local companies fell into line: Negroes as motion picture operators in community theaters; as employees with the Silvercup Bread Company, and at Macy's and Gimbels. Each breakthrough was promptly reported and hailed as significant, major achievements in a country already launched on a battle against fascism abroad. Meanwhile, Powell had decided that summer and fall of 1941 to enter a new arena—he declared for a seat in the City Council as the first black to be a member of that body.

The years of preaching and picketing had now prepared him to move to a larger stage. And all he had learned would now be practiced before a larger audience. His picketing days were pretty much behind him, but his preaching and protesting would certainly continue.

When many people think about the early career of Adam Clayton Powell, Jr., they invariably refer to his activities on the picket lines in Harlem. He is remembered as one who led the protests, even though often enough he did not initiate actions, and his particular roles were frequently questioned as negotiations proceeded and strategies developed. Clearly he was perceived as an activist, willing to lend his name and the influence of Abyssinian Baptist Church to innumerable causes. Years later, in 1981, in an introduction to a new edition of his classic novel, *Invisible Man*, Ralph Ellison reminisced: "I had reported the riot of 1943 for the *New York Post* and had agitated earlier for the release of Angelo Herndon and the Scottsboro Boys, had marched behind Adam Clayton Powell, Jr., in his effort to desegregate the stores along 125th Street."[32]

Powell's interests were reflected in many areas. He vehemently denounced the Hitler-Stalin Pact in September 1939, concluding, to the chagrin of his sometime collaborators in the Communist Party: "Frankly, to an impartial observer of the scene, American communism is just about finished."[33] (A few years later, in February 1942, he would, however, start a weekly newspaper, *The People's Voice*, and call it the "Lenox Avenue edition of the *Daily Worker*." By then, of course, there was a new wartime alliance between the U.S. and the U.S.S.R.) Operating as cochairman of the Greater New York

Coordinating Committee for Employment, he called meetings to protest "the recent series of wanton and unprecipitated beatings of Negro residents in upper Harlem and Washington Heights by white residents,"[34] sought meetings with the mayor, and generally made the Community Center at Abyssinian available for various kinds of protest planning meetings. His value as a spokesman was recognized by a range of interest groups in the community. As early as 1935, he was one of three Negroes recommended by the New York branch of the NAACP to the mayor as a "promising candidate" for the Board of Education.[35] He was then only twenty-six years old and not yet senior pastor of Abyssinian.

He was fast gaining a reputation as an outspoken, energetic preacher, noted more so for his civic activities than, like his father, for his role as a strictly theological figure. But through all his days of protesting and picketing, he paid close attention to the affairs of his church. The church was, after all, what made the rest possible. Adam Clayton Powell, Jr., never forgot that. When the internecine community battles got especially rough and contentious, he could always go home to Abyssinian's pulpit and deliver a blistering self-serving sermon defending his position and issuing more challenges, sometimes as much against his black community adversaries as against the racist structures they were fighting. In this sense, he enjoyed an enormous advantage over the other local, unaffiliated smaller groups—both the black nationalists and the Harlem Communists. Abyssinian provided relative financial and psychological security and stability—a built-in sustained constituency—that several of the other leaders did not have. And this fact alone gave him a competitive advantage in the many community leadership tiffs that erupted from time to time. To be sure, there were other large churches with activist-minded ministers, but Powell's personality and style made the difference. Frequently, as with the response to the FDR/infantile paralysis invitation, he invoked his leadership of the "largest Protestant Church in the nation." The black nationalists on the one hand, and the Communists on the other had no such ongoing base in the community. They were required to rely on the fervor of episodic issues to project their leadership. But with the church, it met every Sunday and there were always various meetings throughout the week—choir practice, youth groups, senior citizen clubs. The church's constituency was always around in some form or other. It did not need a heightened political event to call it together. And in the Harlem of the 1930s and into the 1940s this fact gave one like Adam Powell with his inclinations and talents a considerable advantage over other contenders to community leadership.

Many other leaders had to rely on ideology; Powell could rely also on an institution. The church was and would always be his main base. And there is every indication that this son of Abyssinian understood and appreciated that fact.

In the hectic years following his ascendancy as senior pastor and as leader in the various racial struggles, he continued his active social life. On many occasions, the various protests attracted the big-name Negro celebrities—Duke Ellington, bandleader Jimmy Lunceford, tap dancer Bill Robinson, boxing champion Henry Armstrong, chorus girls from Isabel's days in show business, Isabel herself. Adam liked being around these celebrities and socializing with them. During the World's Fair episode he met a particularly attractive twenty-four-year-old Trinidad-born jazz pianist, Hazel Scott, who was rapidly becoming famous in the supper clubs of downtown New York. Powell was definitely interested and delighted that she joined the picket lines. They began to spend considerable time together, and more than a few close associates of both knew that Adam's marriage was in jeopardy. By 1941, he was decidedly interested in an expanded career as an elected politician, and as he turned his attention to City Council politics, he also was looking beyond his eight-year marriage to another woman and an eventual divorce. In a few short years, he would change his public and private life.

Years later, he wrote that his first marriage was "a grave injustice" to Isabel. When he was fresh out of college with hardly any achievements of note, she had given up her very promising career in show business to be the pastor's supportive wife.[36] And the young pastor kept moving and growing. In the seemingly callous reaction to personal relations that would characterize much of his life, he bluntly summed up his first marriage as a mistake. But not, he concluded, for the reasons raised by his father, namely, her show business life or previous marriage or that she was slightly older than he. The marriage could not last, he stated, "because one day I caught up with her and then passed her."[37]

6

The City Council and Mayor La Guardia

Picketing and protesting were Powell's major political activities in the 1930s, but he also participated occasionally in electoral politics. For a time he disavowed any personal interest in running for public office,[1] but he did take part in Presidential and local election campaigns. In President Roosevelt's bid for reelection in 1936, Powell agreed to act as campaign manager in Harlem for the candidate, but under the American Labor Party, which had also endorsed Roosevelt. Powell did not feel comfortable with the Democratic Party label.[2] At the time, he was more interested in the possibilities of a political party more identified with organized labor, and he saw the American Labor Party as the better vehicle for this purpose. "Organized labor," he wrote, "must take its first step in founding its own permanent political party in the present election under the emblem of the American Labor Party. After we have defeated the forces of reaction this time, we will immediately push our organization for work in future political campaigns in which we will name and elect our own candidates."[3] This Powell effort with Presidential politics was not particularly rewarding. President Roosevelt won overwhelming Harlem support—84 percent, but the Harlem voters preferred him as a Democratic candidate, not on the ALP ticket. Roosevelt got only 4 percent of his Harlem support on the ALP line. Thus Powell could not convince his neighbors to follow his labor party strategy.

A few years earlier, in the 1933 mayoral election, Powell had been mildly involved in electoral politics for the first time. He backed the candidacy of Joseph V. McKee on the Recovery Party ticket, against Fiorello La Guardia (Fusion Party), and John P. O'Brien (Democrat). This was the McKee who, as president of the Board of Aldermen, had insisted that Powell be permitted to speak to the board on the Harlem Hospital protest earlier that year. La Guardia's people had made slight overtures to Powell, but not in the direct manner of McKee.[4] Powell was introduced at a rally as McKee's Harlem campaign manager. He told the rally that his role would be to obtain a "larger share of patronage to the Negroes of the city."[5] In spite of a few speeches to Harlem groups and his own clearly growing popularity, he was not able to help his candidate very much. McKee had little connection with the masses of Harlem, while La Guardia was known as a congressman with a reasonably liberal voting record. La Guardia was elected, and Harlem preferred him over the other candidates, contributing to the eventual downfall of the powerful Tammany Hall machine in the city.

Personally, Powell's popular standing in the community did not suffer from his backing a political loser. A leadership popularity contest conducted in 1934–35 by the *Amsterdam News* indicated that the young preacher was well thought of by Harlemites. He ranked fifth, and led all ministers on the list.[6] This personal attraction, however, apparently was not transferable to others whom Powell supported politically. Electoral politics was another game in Harlem, unlike protest politics which was more adaptable to dramatic issues and dynamic oratorical leaders. Mobilizing voters required other kinds of organizational skills and contacts. Political party structures and ballot requirements had to be mastered, along with certain kinds of bargaining techniques and skills.

Powell, in time, would develop all these, but in the 1920s, 1930s, and early 1940s there was another set of political operatives on the scene who had devoted their efforts to gaining party positions as district leaders and to obtaining elective offices. Powell was not a part of those groups.

As far back as the 1890s, Negroes in New York City were devising strategies to increase their political influence. Out of loyalty to the party of Abraham Lincoln, most Negroes voted Republican in Presidential and local elections. This loyalty, however, was wearing thin. When several New York blacks were disappointed in their efforts to gain patronage jobs in return for their support for President McKinley in 1896, they decided to make overtures to the local

Democratic Party, Tammany Hall. Forming the United Colored Democracy, they hoped to convince Tammany leader Richard Croker that the Democrats could benefit from the support of black voters willing to consider options to the Republicans. Harvard-trained lawyer James C. Carr, and a hotel bellman, Edward "Chief" Lee, were the main movers in this venture. Always open to new opportunities for enlarging its base, Tammany seemed more receptive than the Republicans. The deal was worked out, and the United Colored Democracy (UCD) proceeded to campaign in local elections for the Democrats. Croker was cautiously willing to test the relationship, but it was clear that Tammany Hall was not going to go too far in altering the prevailing political relationships in the city.

Local party structures were organized around the units of state assembly districts. Political clubs were associated with such geographical designations. Out of these came district leaders and operations that led to slating candidates for local and state offices, as well as the basis for making political appointments to office. Always, of course, the arrangement was based on the ability of the clubs to deliver votes for the party. The United Colored Democracy envisioned such a role for New York Negroes. But there was a difference. Croker was, indeed, interested in the UCD, but not on the same basis as with the other clubs. The UCD would speak for and serve as the patronage funnel for all Negroes in the city, not on the basis of assembly district boundaries. Thus the UCD would be a separate, segregated organization "for the colored," and it was not to concern itself with white voters. This meant, of course, that the Negroes would not initially have a shot at becoming party district leaders or election district (precinct) captains. They would be outside the normal political party mainstream, an appendage. Carr and Lee accepted this arrangement as long as they could occupy the position of political bosses for the Negroes. In the circumstance, they concluded that this was the best deal they could get. And out of this "parallel" structure did, in fact, come a few jobs for individual blacks—a handful of patronage appointments—and Carr became assistant district attorney.[7] Ferdinand Q. Morton succeeded Carr and Lee in 1915, and the UCD solidified its position with Tammany. Negroes increased their local support for Democratic mayors from 27 percent for John Hylan in 1917 to 73 percent for him in his reelection in 1921. In turn, Morton, also a lawyer, was rewarded with appointment to the three-member Civil Service Commission. A few other patronage appointments came UCD's way, including that of Dr. Louis

T. Wright to the Harlem Hospital staff and executive board. Throughout the 1920s, this political arrangement prevailed, with blacks willing to support the Democrats locally while still giving their votes to the Republicans in Presidential elections. But with the election of Fiorello La Guardia as mayor in 1933 as a Reform-Fusion candidate, it was clear that the old party machine structure in the city was weakening. Morton himself switched and became a La Guardia supporter.

The groundwork was laid nonetheless for black political organizing, and even in the World War I years there was evidence that Negroes wanted to be considered for candidacies to elective office in the state legislature as well as to seats on the city Board of Aldermen.

Two State Assembly districts—the Nineteenth and Twenty-first—were sufficiently black to permit both the Republican and Democratic parties to put up Negro candidates. Another group started by Negroes around 1914, the United Civic League, deliberately aimed at "elective representation," not "simply appointive recognition."[8] Although officially nonpartisan, the bulk of the members leaned in the Republican direction. The founder of the organization, Negro realtor John M. Royall, tried unsuccessfully for a seat on the Board of Aldermen, but in 1917, Edward A. Johnson, supported by the league, was elected to the State Assembly from the Nineteenth A.D. He was the first Negro elected to the state legislature in the state's history. Ironically, the league's success convinced the regular Republican Party that it should run a Negro—which it did in 1918—and the league as a separate racial entity was no longer needed. A black, John C. Hawkins, was the regular candidate from the adjoining Twenty-first Assembly District.

Throughout the 1920s, black candidates from Harlem won seats in the state legislature—as Democrats (Henri W. Shields in 1922 and 1923), and as Republicans.

Attention was also paid to winning positions in the regular party councils as assembly district leaders (what would be known as ward leaders in many other cities). These positions were the ones coveted by the party activists, black and white, who understood that it was the party county committee, made up of the district leaders, that selected people to run under the party's banner and exercised considerable control over patronage jobs.

A student of that period concluded that Negroes knew they were unlikely to be able to run successful campaigns as independents, thus they needed a major party designation, Republican or Democrat. The Republican Party at that time was the best bet for two reasons: there were more Negro Republicans, and the Republicans needed the Negroes more than the Democrats did. The Democrats were in control of the "patronage and power." Therefore, if Negroes could work their way into the Republican Party, presumably this would both benefit the race and strengthen the party.[9]

In 1929 the first Negro to become a district leader was Colonel Charles W. Fillmore—in the Republican Party. The Democrats got their first black, Herbert L. Bruce, a businessman, as a district leader in 1935.

In time, as this election politics activity continued, several Negroes in a group called the Beavers decided it was time to make a move to become a more important part of the Democratic Party machinery. Why not take over an entire district? Why simply be satisfied either with an appendage role or being selected occasionally by the white leaders downtown? The members of the Beavers decided to mount a struggle that would contest the whites for full control of the party apparatus in Harlem. They were able to ally with some unhappy whites in another group, the Ramapo Club.[10] This coalition insured Herbert Bruce's election, and now blacks were in a position to have much more influence over patronage jobs in the Harlem district. The old ways of relying mainly on a few handpicked leaders to intervene downtown—outside regular party channels—were coming to an end. Harlem, in both parties, was getting its own self-sustaining elective party structures, and developing its own recognized party operatives.

One such person was J. Raymond Jones, up from St.Thomas, the Virgin Islands, who had rejected the appendage structure of the UCD. The place of the Negro, he maintained, was in the regular party structure, not parallel to it. He became a master of the techniques of grass-roots organizing for elections, taking care of constituency needs in the truest manner of a ward leader, and paying meticulous attention to the intricacies of such technicalities as getting and filing candidate petitions. Jones knew that corruption and election fraud could turn around many elections, and his talents in guarding against such practices became, over the years, legendary in the Harlem community, so much so that in later years, he would become known as "the Fox."

In later years, Jones and Powell would become the two most powerful and effective political operators on the Harlem scene. They were perfect complements to each other, but it was a relationship fraught with personal and political acrimony. Each had skills the other needed, and in subsequent years they would coalesce, and then break up. One, Jones, would become, in the 1960s, the first black leader of Tammany Hall, while Powell would become the first black chairman of a major congressional committee.

In the meantime, in the late 1930s, each was honing his skills in different political vineyards: Jones as the skilled clubhouse organizer, Powell as the flamboyant mass orator.

It was not often that the two different types of political operatives—election politics and protest politics—overlapped. On rare occasions a black election official would appear on the platform at one of the many protest rallies, or lend his name to a particular ad hoc protest letterhead. Virtually never, however, were the protest leaders involved in the local struggles for strictly party positions. The few Communist activists in Harlem in the 1930s did, indeed, attempt to span both worlds, but their influence was minimal. They were mostly effective in one wing of the American Labor Party,[11] and not at all in the local Democratic and Republican parties. As we have seen, many protest leaders kept them at arm's length or, as with Powell, formed temporary alliances with them for mutual convenience.

It was Powell, however, who in 1941 was able to put together an operation that would effectively combine protest and election politics in the Harlem community. In 1938, the city revised its charter, abolishing the Board of Aldermen and instituting a City Council that was to have seats filled through the voting mechanism known as proportional representation (PR). There would be five districts corresponding to the city's five boroughs. Exactly how many people would be elected would depend on how many total votes were cast, except that each borough had to have at least one member. A seat was guaranteed to every candidate who received at least 75,000 votes. And in order to get on the ballot, a person needed to file petitions containing at least 2,000 signatures. While candidates ran in the borough in which they lived, they were voted for citywide. Proportional representation permitted the voter to designate first choice, second choice, third choice—and so on until all candidates received a marking. But—and this was an important political strategy—a voter could engage in "bullet voting," that is, vote only for one candidate, and not indicate a second or subsequent choice. This was important because after each round of counting, for those candidates who did not receive the required 75,000, his or her second and subsequent choices were added to the candidate's first-choice votes. Finally, in subsequent rounds, those candidates receiving the lowest number of votes would be eliminated.

The theoretical purpose behind this elaborate electoral scheme was to provide lesser candidates and their followers an opportunity to have at least a chance of being elected. The Negroes of Harlem saw their opportunity, then, to elect one of their own to the new City Council, provided, of course, that they could marshal their forces and enter coalitions behind one candidate. Adam Clayton Powell, Jr., decided in 1941 that he wanted to be that person. Reconstituting his older Greater New York Coordinating Committee into a new People's Committee as his main electoral organization, he and his Abyssinian-based supporters set out to move into election politics. They easily obtained the necessary 2,000 petition signatures. Clearly, he was the choice of the American Labor Party. The Communists in Harlem, however, preferred one of their own black members, Max Yergan. Neither were the Democrats, Republicans, or Fusionists particularly enthusiastic for him. Tammany Hall wanted a more loyal Harlem lawyer, Herman C. Stoute. The Republicans settled on a respectable black official of the YMCA, Channing Tobias. An Abyssinian parishioner, Joseph Ford, managed Powell's campaign. With his petitions secured, Powell received the endorsement of the United City Party and City Fusion.

Powell's old friends from the picketing days swung into action under the banner of the People's Committee, and he was now launched on his electoral career. His father remained skeptical of his chances, but wished him well. His wife, Isabel, was sorely disappointed that he had made the decision.

"I didn't like his entering politics at all," she stated years later.[12] "I said you sell your integrity. In the pulpit, he was his own boss. But in politics you cannot be your own man." And she concluded ruefully, "I believe this was the beginning of my downfall." She knew that her husband had sniffed the tantalizing aroma of elective office, and there was no turning him around.

The People's Committee immediately set up a genuine grass-roots campaign, opening storefront headquarters in various neighborhoods, blanketing the community with leaflets, and holding small street-corner rallies day and evening. Abyssinian Baptist Church became the hub of this frenzied activity. Loudspeakers mounted on trucks canvassed the community. Powell spoke wherever he was invited—churches, social and civic clubs, street corners, barber shops, taverns. Not confining his appearances to black Harlem, he addressed liberal white groups, fully aware that he would need their support if he were to gain the necessary votes in the PR system. Harlem alone could not send a candidate to the Council. He linked "Hitlerism" abroad with antidemocratic forces at home. He made peace with the popular Mayor La Guardia, praising him for his appointment of some blacks to judgeships and for reform of the civil service. La Guardia then strongly endorsed Powell at a meeting of the New York State Baptist Association.

Powell had gone to Yergan and Tobias and persuaded them to drop out of the race, which left only Herman Stoute and Powell as the two blacks running in Manhattan. Important endorsements followed for Powell: the CIO Trade Union Council, and most of the daily press (*Daily News, World Telegram, Herald Tribune, New York Times, PM, Daily Mirror*).

The People's Committee shrewdly printed 200,000 sample ballots highlighting Powell's name (PR listed candidates in alphabetical order) and encouraging voters to "bullet vote" for him.

This first effort to present himself as a candidate was a resounding success. Based on the total votes cast, Manhattan would be entitled to six council members out of a City Council of twenty-six. Powell gained a cumulative 64,000 votes, enough for him to come in third in Manhattan. The other black, Herman Stoute, received an insufficient 29,000 votes on the thirteenth count. Powell clearly was helped by La Guardia's endorsement, which brought him the white support necessary to compete citywide. (And, of course, in the process, La Guardia was reelected to a third term as mayor.)

Thus, in November 1941, two very popular New York political figures went to City Hall—one as mayor for the third and last time, the other as councilman at the beginning of a political career that would last twenty-nine years. For Powell, this was indeed only the beginning. At age thirty-three, he surely had no intention, even then, of settling in permanently on the City Council, but for now it would do. It was a start. He was a proven winner in a new arena, and all indications pointed to the conclusion that he liked the experience. The only black on the Council, he was considered neither Democrat nor Republican, but an ALP-Fusionist. At the beginning, he obviously relished the role of political independent. He had successfully combined protest politics and election politics. And immediately after his election and before he was sworn in, he gave the public a hint of how he intended to pursue those two forms of action.

One week after his election, Powell held an interview in his study at Abyssinian Baptist Church with the *New York Times*. The People's Committee he had put together for his campaign, he said, would be maintained as a protest organization to secure more economic gains for Harlem. The focus especially would be jobs with the telephone company and on the faculties of the city's universities. He had definitely set his sights on the Board of Higher Education. He was proud of the work the People's Committee had done in instructing Harlemites on how to mark their PR ballots. Only 12 percent of the ballots in Harlem were declared void for being improperly cast, while the citywide percentage was 19. Harlem voters effectively pursued the strategy of "bullet" voting.

"Bullet" voting for him? a reporter asked.[13]

"Of course," he replied. "The next time we'll teach them to vote for two or three persons, maybe. It's a matter of education." He leaned back and smiled.

Political-electoral education and organizing would be combined with protest. And the city colleges would be an early target.

"The day after I'm sworn in at the Council there are going to be pickets outside the offices of the Board of Higher Education," Powell promised.

A reporter asked, "Aren't you going to discuss the matter at the Council?"

"Naturally," Powell calmly and shrewdly responded. "I'll raise a ruckus in the Council, but I think it will look better with two or three thousand people crowding around Park Avenue and Sixty-eighth Street [Board of Education headquarters]."

This was to be the Powell style. He was on the inside now, but he saw his role as being strengthened by mass protest on the outside. It was a style he would pursue for the rest of his public career.

At the same time, he was anxious to receive the political rewards, in the form of patronage jobs and political favors, that came with his new insider status. Shortly after being sworn in, he wrote to La Guardia reminding the mayor of a preelection understanding. "You promised to look into the appointment of four or five key workers in our campaign in Harlem."[14] La Guardia was not inclined to follow up. Powell wanted jobs for some members of the People's Committee, but La Guardia believed that such patronage appointments would "encourage a permanent headache."[15] Powell also lost no time in making known to the mayor his interest in being selected as leader of the minority party representatives in the Council. He wanted the mayor's endorsement, but La Guardia, sensing the unpredictable ambitions of this young politician from Harlem, felt the move was "terrible and n.g. (no good)"—sentiments he scribbled in the margins of a note from Powell.

It was clear from the beginning that these two politicians, notwithstanding their earlier electoral alliance in the campaign, would keep each other at a respectable, wary distance. La Guardia had seen young, brash politicians before; indeed, he had been one himself a couple of decades earlier. But he was not about to tie himself too closely to this thirty-three-year-old volatile rising political star from Harlem who had given every indication that he had his own personal and political agenda. In addition, Powell was clearly going to push the race issue in a manner that would likely conflict with La Guardia's timetable, if not with his ultimate goals on that issue. The two simply had different priorities.

Powell was a prominent participant at the many mass rallies held at that time on behalf of the war effort, sharing, for instance, the platform with Eleanor Roosevelt and movie stars and entertainers such as George Jessel, Danny Kaye, Sophie Tucker, Paul Robeson, Helen Hayes, and Burgess Meredith.[16] In one such event, "Salute to Negro Troops," he blasted segregation in the armed forces, one of his constant, favorite topics.

His first major act as councilman was to introduce a series of resolutions dealing with racial discrimination in various city agencies, especially in the city colleges. Aware that the Board of Higher Education was appointed by the mayor, Powell knew that charges of discrimination against the board would reflect negatively on La Guardia. He wanted the City Council to investigate the board and to question the presidents of the four major colleges. There were 2,282 faculty positions and not one was held by a full-time black professor.[17] On the day he introduced these resolutions, the temperature outside hit a low of 5 degrees. Inside the Council chambers, Powell was heating up the political atmosphere. Essentially, he could accomplish little else but to call attention to certain conditions, and to cause officials to explain and justify their actions. The Council's Rules Committee held hearings with the college presidents who, predictably, denied any discrimination in faculty hiring. Powell kept up the pressure, denouncing the schools from his church pulpit and presenting the applications of at least four blacks who had been denied teaching positions. (One of the four was psychologist Dr. Kenneth B. Clark, who later would join the faculty of City College, but who also, twenty years later, would become a bitter foe of Powell's over control of the HARYOU-ACT antipoverty program in Harlem. See Chapter 18.) The Council found no evidence of discrimination, but this result neither surprised nor deterred Powell. While he was convinced that the colleges practiced discrimination, he knew that they would deny it, and it would be very difficult to get hard proof. In the North, such practices in some realms were not so overt as they were in the South at that time.

In February 1942, Powell joined with Harlem businessman Charles Buchanan to found a new weekly newspaper, *The People's Voice.* He continued his "Soap Box" column in this journal and, as editor-in-chief, wrote most of the editorials. He contended that he and Buchanan were the sole financiers of the paper, but rumors circulated that Marshall Field, publisher of (New York) *PM*, had supplied the funds. The *Voice* was printed by the *PM* presses. The rival *Amsterdam News*, where Powell's column had appeared for years, was especially biting in its attack on *The People's Voice.*[18] In an editorial entitled "Look Out for 'Surrender,'" the charge was leveled:

> We have been authoritatively informed that a new weekly is projected for appearance in the near future. Upon equal authority we are told that the paper is to be edited and managed in front by certain ambitious mercenary colored political newcomers—that it is to be backed from behind by certain designing white capital.
>
> These facts speak for themselves. White capital is simply seeking to further exploit the race. The politicians willy-nilly will simply be their pawns to that end. The politicians seek to ride to glory at the price of their people's continued progress and independence.

The first issue of *The People's Voice*, launched on Frederick Douglass's birthday, asserted in its editorial policy that the newspaper "is 100% owned and operated by Negroes." Characterizing itself as "a working class paper," because "we are a working class race," the *Voice* essentially championed the platform Powell had laid out in his Council campaign and what he was saying in speeches from every rostrum on which he appeared: better housing, an end to racial discrimination in all forms, better schools, full job opportunities in the private sector, support of Negro businesses "or companies that employ Negroes with opportunities for advancement." And the editorial policy bluntly called for "a just quota of jobs in all city, state and federal agencies."[19] Each week, the pages of the newspaper would highlight the activity of its editor-in-chief, speeches he made in and out of town, and his resolutions in the City Council. Powell's own "Soap Box" column, as earlier, covered a range of subjects: championing Mahatma Gandhi's struggle for independence for India, condemning American policy of relocation of Japanese-Americans on the West Coast, blasting Fascist treatment of Jews in Poland, condemning the Red Cross for its practice of segregating blood donations. The newspaper held its own mass "symposium for the one billion people of the darker races."[20] Speakers were listed: on behalf of "a free India," on behalf of a "free China," "a free Africa," and Adam Clayton Powell, Jr., "on behalf of free Negroes of the Western Hemisphere." The paper took up the cause of the Communist Party leader, Earl Browder, who was convicted for a passport violation. Continuously, the editorials, many signed by Powell, linked the war in Europe against "Hitlerism and Fascism" with the struggle in the United States against segregation and discrimination.

> There are lots of people in America, born here, who call themselves Americans and yet they believe only in a partial democracy. These people believe only in partial truth, partial freedom, partial justice. Whether they be Daughters of the American Revolution or men who can trace their blood back to Plymouth Rock, they are not Americans. It is just as important to see that these people and their brand of Americanism be crushed as it is to recapture Singapore.[21]

Simultaneously, in the City Council, Powell kept up his "ruckus raising." He introduced resolutions calling for the end to media designation of the race of persons accused of crimes,[22] and demanding that streets in Harlem be renamed for historic Negro figures, especially abolitionist leaders. His charges of discrimination in the city's hospitals led to the hospital commissioner's appearance before the Council's Rules Committee to deny the charges—similar in result to the episode with the city college presidents. But all this was typical Adam Powell action during his tenure in the City Council. He raised issues, required officials to testify, gave publicity in the pages of the *Voice*, and lost no opportunity to prod the city administrators when race issues were involved. Pursuing such a course of action, it was inevitable that Powell would have more tense moments than relaxed ones in his relationship with the voluble and sensitive Mayor Fiorello La Guardia.

This relationship was the first of several over the years that Powell would have with powerful public officials as he conducted his own brand of race politics. Presidents and congressional leaders would be exposed to his charges of racial and economic injustice, and, for varying reasons, would have to respond. In each instance, the response was an insightful glance at the way some major segments of America in turn responded to the American Dilemma that

Powell was constantly holding up before them. In each case—La Guardia, Harry S Truman, Dwight D. Eisenhower, Sam Rayburn, John F. Kennedy, Lyndon B. Johnson, and others discussed in this book—the persons were not the diehard segregationalists Powell found as easy and obvious targets. Each, in varying degrees, was considered liberal or moderate on the issue of race. Each was viewed, again in degrees, by certain segments of the civil rights community as sympathetic to the cause. And each grappled with the American Dilemma in ways that positioned them always on the side of advocates of change and progress rather than as defenders of the status quo. This made their relationship with Powell that much more difficult, because he was always pushing them to go faster and further than they, at the particular time, felt feasible.

At the same time, La Guardia knew that he need not be unnecessarily intimidated by Powell. The new city councilman was not the only source of mayoral contact with the black community. La Guardia did have his own many black supporters, cultivated over the years. He had no hesitancy in appearing before mass audiences in Harlem and elsewhere calling for equal treatment and the end to racial injustice. On more than a few occasions, he was cheered by such audiences, and a 1940 editorial in the *Amsterdam News* praised him for appointing "more Negroes to big responsible jobs in the city government . . . than all the other mayors of the city combined."[23] In addition, La Guardia had played a major role in getting President Roosevelt to issue Executive Order 8802 prohibiting employment discrimination in defense industries. In this, he gained the respect of such black leaders as A. Philip Randolph, who had proposed the mass march on Washington in 1941 if such an order were not forthcoming. Randolph also urged Roosevelt, without success, to appoint La Guardia to the newly created Fair Employment Practices Commission (FEPC) set up to oversee the Executive Order. From time to time, the mayor consulted with prominent civil rights leaders, especially Walter White of the NAACP, and these leaders, in turn, often took care to drop him notes of gratitude or support for certain actions.

In the summer of 1943, as race riots erupted in several cities, most notably in Detroit, white and Negro leaders in New York sought to mobilize to avoid a conflict. Walter White was asked by La Guardia to send a letter to every Negro minister and to the presidents of all Negro community organizations in Harlem and Brooklyn calling for calm and restraint. White's letter read, in part: "Unlike the spineless Mayor of Detroit, Mayor La Guardia is taking every precaution to avert trouble here. We need have no fear that the police here will act as they did in Detroit."[24]

This and other efforts notwithstanding, Harlem exploded in violence on August 1, 1943. The incident started when a white policeman attempted to arrest a Negro woman for disorderly conduct outside a hotel in Harlem. The policeman was confronted by a Negro soldier who resented the way the cop was treating the woman. In the melee, the policeman wounded the soldier. Once again, as they had eight years earlier, rumors spread and rioting broke out. La Guardia immediately sped to Harlem and set up a command post in the local police precinct. He toured the community periodically with a loudspeaker urging calm and reporting that the soldier was not killed. He remained on the scene throughout the night, insisting that the police apprehend looters, but to use restraint in arresting people. He was joined by Walter White and other black community leaders. Powell was out of town.

La Guardia's personal attention drew appreciative comments from black leaders, even from Powell, who sent him a telegram describing his performance as "wise and effective."[25] Only a few weeks earlier, Powell had blasted La Guardia for not appointing a biracial committee to try to head off a possible racial conflagration. In June, Powell told the City Council that he had urged such action:

> If any riot breaks out here in New York, the blood of innocent people, white and Negro, will rest upon the hands of Mayor Fiorello La Guardia and Police Commissioner Lewis Valentine, who have refused to see representative citizens to discuss means of combatting outbreaks in New York. The Mayor says that he is ready. Ready for what? Ready after it is too late? We want to be ready now, beforehand.[26]

Thus Powell and La Guardia had an off-again, on-again relationship. The mayor clearly suspected the motives and political reliability of the black councilman. Powell could always be counted on to attack the mayor, and the words of praise would be few indeed.

In the spring of 1942, a particularly volatile incident occurred that angered the mayor and his aides and caused them even further to distrust Powell. A black man, Wallace Armstrong, had been killed by a white policeman. Powell immediately called for an investigation of the police department, using the pages of *The People's Voice* to arouse interest in the case. He scheduled a mass meeting for May 17, 1942, and had a stridently worded leaflet circulated throughout Harlem:

ONE MORE NEGRO BRUTALLY BEATEN AND KILLED!
SHOT DOWN LIKE A DOG BY THE POLICE
ALL OUT HARLEM
LET'S PACK THE GOLDEN GATE AT 5 P.M.
142ND STREET AND LENOX AVENUE
THIS SUNDAY, MAY 17
"I AM AN AMERICAN DAY"
FREE ADMISSION REAL SPEAKERS
. . . HEAR THE EYE WITNESSES . . .
COUNCILMAN ADAM CLAYTON POWELL, JR. CHAIRMAN

Police Commissioner Lewis J. Valentine sent the circular to La Guardia with a covering letter: "Councilman Adam Clayton Powell knows that this matter is going to be presented to the Grand Jury and he also knows that this type of rabble-rousing is dangerous and might result in serious disorders and he should be advised to cancel this proposed Mass Meeting in the public interest and await the action and decision of the New York County Grand Jury."[27]

La Guardia was in Washington, D.C., on civil defense business, but he received a report from his assistant, Lester Stone, on the latter's efforts to dissuade Powell. Powell would not cancel the meeting. He felt that to do so, without proper response from the officials, would be even more detrimental. He told Stone as much in a telephone conversation:

Powell: . . . it is impossible to cancel the meeting. As soon as the incident happened I sent a wire to the Mayor and Commissioner Valentine. Received no reply from the wire to the Mayor . . . Got a letter from Commissioner Valentine yesterday afternoon—which was 48 hours after the wire was sent. That was pretty slow timing. And the wire to the Mayor was absolutely ignored. After all, I am responsible to the people up here.
. . . I have witnesses, names, addresses, affidavits they have signed. I have all this—sitting tight on it. I don't want the witnesses contacted and threatened. Some of them have been beaten . . .

Stone: You understand the Mayor's message is that if there are disorders it is your responsibility.

Powell: It will be a peaceful meeting. You can send anybody you desire to see that it is peaceful.[28]

The police did have informants at the meeting on May 17, and a detailed five-page report was filed by the local police investigator.[29] The report listed the speakers as follows:

1. Councilman Adam Clayton Powell (colored) chairman
2. Joseph Gavagan, Congressman (white)
3. Harold Brightman, Republican 23 A.D. (colored)
4. Odel Clark, Pres. A.L.P., Right Wing (colored)
5. Danny Burrows, Assemblyman 19 A.D. (colored)
6. Charles Farrell, A.L.P. (Left wing) (colored)
7. Roy [*sic*] Jones, Dem. 22nd Con. Dist. (colored)
8. Louise Streat, attorney (colored)
9. Hughlan [*sic*] Jack, Assemblyman 17 A.D. (colored)
10. James Pendelton, famous basketball player, and Y.M.C.A. worker (colored)
11. William T. Andrews, Assemblyman 19 A.D. (colored)
12. Herbert L. Bruce, Leader Dem. 21 A.D. (colored)

The comments of each speaker were digested in the report. Powell opened the meeting by reporting his efforts to contact the mayor and the discussions with Stone, stating: "If the mayor would have acknowledged our wire, this meeting would not have been held. All the political leaders of Harlem are now united behind this cause. We will elect a citizens committee to demand an investigation and we will sit on the steps of City Hall until the mayor agrees to meet the representatives of Harlem." Each speaker supported Powell's leadership of this latest crusade and expressed confidence in his judgment about what action to take. Congressman Gavagan stated that he knew nothing "about this frightful incident but that Dr. Powell is the man to take charge of this investigation." Assemblyman Burrows "started by stating he cannot pass judgment as he does not know the facts of the case, but he can rely on Rev. Powell, right or wrong."

The informant's report concluded: "Meeting adjourned at 7:15 p.m., there was in attendance about 4,000 persons, no disorder or police action necessary. . . . Detectives Carrington, Necas, Isengard, and '104' also were assigned to this meeting." (*The People's Voice* reported attendance at between 6,000 and 7,000.)

Nothing came of the incident, but Powell's role once again enhanced his leadership in the community. He was perceived as one who would stand up to the authorities and not equivocate. And there were a number of opportunities for him to demonstrate this, although little in the way of positive achievements resulted. This did not deter him. He continued his open criticism of racist policies in local affairs, frequently catching the mayor in his line of fire.

When the city leased buildings of Hunter College to the U.S. Navy to house women recruits for the WAVES and SPARs, Powell criticized this move because those wartime training units excluded Negro women. La Guardia maintained that he had no control over the policies of the United States Navy.

Powell challenged the mayor at a public ceremony laying the cornerstone for a new building at Harlem Hospital. He charged that there was still discrimination in the city's hospital system. Obviously angered by this public confrontation, La Guardia maintained: "I tell you, Dr. Powell, there is no discrimination and a Negro doctor who can qualify can be appointed to any New York City hospital."[30] Powell brushed aside the reply, and called for more mass, direct action. In his "Soap Box" column, he wrote: "Maybe at some future date when the world returns to sanity we can return to educational processes, long-range planning and the conference table, but this day and this hour demand direct action. Whatever gains have been made by the Negro people in New York have been made either by direct action or the threat of direct action."[31]

In the midst of the police shooting of Wallace Armstrong, Powell stepped up his attack on the mayor. There would be future moments of attempted reconciliation, but his editorial on May 23, 1942, was clearly the crowning blow. Entitled "Mickey Mouse vs. Mayor La Guardia—The Winner, Mickey!," the hard-hitting editorial took the mayor on with full force:

> The Mayor of the City of New York is one of the most pathetic figures on the current American scene. Never has a public figure disintegrated so thoroughly as has Fiorello La Guardia. . . . Here is one who was a champion of labor, a liberal, an anti-machine politician and an exalter of the common people. . . . He was the first Italian to sit in the House of Congress. . . . The anti-machine politician now works in the City Council with no one else but the machine politicians. . . . And there he stands . . . once a friend of the Negro people. Now that his political future is finished, we are no longer potential votes for him. We are therefore ignored. When we pressed for Negroes to be appointed to the colleges of the City of New York, he would not see us. He said "What can I do?" When the Negro doctors wired for an appointment concerning his slur upon them at the cornerstone laying of the Harlem Hospital dispensary, he refused to see them. When every elected political leader of all parties desired an appointment concerning the brutal slaying of Wallace Armstrong, he not only refused to see them, but did not have the decency to

> acknowledge the telegram . . . If the Mayor ran against Mickey Mouse tomorrow for Mayor of the City of New York, he would be defeated.[32]

After such a blistering attack, there could be no political amity between these two proud, flamboyant leaders. But Powell apparently could not have cared less.

Surely the final straw for Powell was La Guardia's acquiescence in the building of a major apartment development—Stuyvesant Town—on the Lower East Side. In the spring of 1943, the city, under the leadership of the powerful city parks commissioner, Robert Moses, entered into an agreement with the Metropolitan Life Insurance Company whereby the company would build a $50 million apartment complex in exchange for city tax exemption for several years, 504,449 square feet of land, and the city exercising its power of eminent domain in obtaining the property for the insurance company. Moses maintained that this kind of arrangement was an excellent means of getting the private financial sector in the business of providing much needed housing after the war. The problem, however, was that Metropolitan Life definitely intended to exclude Negroes from renting in the new facilities. Frederick H. Ecker, chairman of the company's board of directors, bluntly stated: "Negroes and whites don't mix. If we brought them into this development, it would be to the detriment of the city, too, because it would depress (the value) of all surrounding property." In a letter to the black state legislator, William T. Andrews, George Gove, the project's manager, wrote:

> Your letter of April 20 to Mr. Frederick H. Ecker, Chairman of the Board, has been referred to me for reply.
>
> The proposed post-war housing development on the East Side of Manhattan will occupy the entire area between 14th Street, 20th Street, First Avenue and Avenue C, and has been planned to accommodate approximately 9,000 families of moderate income similar to those now predominantly resident in that section and the surrounding area of the city. Accordingly no provision will be made in this development for negro families.[33]

When Andrews inquired what exactly was meant by "no provision will be made in this development for negro families,"[34] Gove simply responded: "I believe my letter was direct and explicit and requires no further explanation."[35]

That did it. Liberal forces throughout the city swung into action, bombarding the mayor with letters urging him not to support the project when it came up for a vote before the Board of Estimate.[36] For one of the few times during this period there appeared to be substantial liberal support in favor of a major civil rights issue. Arguments focused on the blatant contradiction of fighting Fascism abroad while sanctioning racial segregation at home. Many sounded, for once, as if they came right out of the pages of Adam Powell's editorials.

The lineup was impressive: the NAACP; Greater New York Industrial Union Council (CIO); American Labor Party (New York County); New York City League of Women Voters; the Jewish Center of Forest Hills West; National Maritime Union of America (CIO); Religious Society of Friends (Quakers); Hotel Front Service Union Local 144; YWCA (Harlem Branch); Victory Council of Williamsburg; State, County, and Municipal Workers of America (Chapter 65, Local 1); International Federation of Architects, Engineers, Chemists, & Technicians (CIO); United Office and Professional Workers of America; Citywide Citizens Committee on Harlem (Algernon D. Black, cochairman); National Council of Negro Women, Inc.,; United Federal Workers (CIO); Permanent Committee for Better Schools in Harlem; National Council of Negro Youth; Communist Party (21st A.D.); Harlem Committee Teachers Union. The Williamsburg (Brooklyn) group reminded the mayor; "It is on account of this and similar restrictions that we are in this war." This group was composed largely of Jews. One union wrote: "With many of our members both Negro and white now fighting and dying on many battlefields for democracy and freedom for all we feel it is an insult to allow a project with City backing to discriminate against Negro tenants." A Jewish organization in Queens felt that "New York City should be the last place where a contemplated fascist measure should be tolerated." The Citywide Citizens Committee on Harlem urged support for a proposed ordinance introduced by councilmen Powell and Stanley M. Isaacs forbidding discrimination in tax-exempt redevelopment projects. And Powell, on behalf of the People's Committee, wrote: "This group strongly urges that you do not vote for Hitler in New York."[37]

Powell corresponded with Robert Moses, but obviously received no satisfaction. Moses claimed: "Those who insist on making projects of this kind a battleground for the vindication of social objectives, however desirable, and who persist in claiming that a private project is in fact a public project, obviously are looking for a political issue and not for results in the form of actual slum clearance."

In August 1943, after the vote of approval, Powell wrote to Moses: "Thank you for your letter. There is no point in my prolonging the discussion between us concerning Stuyvesant Town by the way of written correspondence. Sometime in September or October I am going to give you a ring and maybe we can sit down and talk it over face to face.[38]

The vote of acceptance of the Stuyvesant Town project was taken at the Board of Estimate meeting of June 3, 1943. The project was approved eleven to five, with Council President Morris and Manhattan Borough President Nathan opposing. Mayor La Guardia voted to approve the segregated housing. Morris vainly argued that the treatment of American Negroes was "a very sordid chapter in the history of our country."[39]

The *New York Times* agreed with Robert Moses, "who has a habit of going to the heart of a good many things. Do we want to enlist private capital in behalf of slum removal and rehousing or don't we?"[40]

Likewise, the *New York Herald Tribune* came down in favor of the project, concluding: "The criticism emphasized at Thursday's hearings before the Estimate Board turned on a social issue—the management's right to select its prospective tenants, a right universally conceded to private management. Nothing, plainly, could be gained by further debate."[41]

But Harlem's *Amsterdam News* disagreed, and so did Harlem's city councilman. At a mass Freedom Rally in Madison Square Garden a week later, Adam Powell called for the impeachment of Mayor La Guardia. The audience roared its thunderous approval.

Meanwhile, Walter White of the NAACP, a longtime supporter of and adviser to La Guardia, sought to reach the mayor in a quieter way. Obviously personally hurt by the mayor's vote, White sent a "personal and confidential" letter to La Guardia on June 16, pleading:

> Dear Mayor La Guardia:
>
> I wonder if you would let me know your reasons for approving the Stuyvesant Town project? I am sure they must be good ones and I know personally they are honest ones.
>
> Deputy Mayor McGahen's casting of your three votes announcing your approval of the project, which, as you know proposes to exclude Negroes, puzzles me. Knowing of the long-time friendship which you and I have enjoyed, a number of people have asked me about your position on this project. I have refrained from expressing any opin-

> ion until I could first learn from you your reasons for approval. If you would rather I come in to talk with you, let me know and I will arrange my schedule accordingly.
>
> That was a swell party you and Mrs. La Guardia gave yesterday. I enjoyed it as did Gladys.[42]

He sent a cover note to Miss Betty Cohen, secretary to the mayor: "Dear Betty: I would like to have you put the enclosed letter into Mayor La Guardia's hands not as an official, but as a personal document."

Walter White, unlike Powell, was willing to give La Guardia every benefit of the doubt about the mayor's stand on civil rights, and willing to protect him from making an uncomfortable public record of his views, if the mayor wished. Powell's brand of leadership, at least on this point at this time, did not call for such tactfulness. He did not perceive La Guardia as a personal, social friend, and if he had known of any effort to shield the mayor from public attack, he likely would have loudly condemned that action also. Clearly, this style suited him. La Guardia, more so than the staunch Southern segregationists, was a much more vulnerable target for Powell. After all, the Southerners did not profess to favor any form of civil rights. There was nothing hypocritical about them on this score. But the Northern liberal La Guardia was another matter. "Phony" and "hypocritical" were the terms Powell often used to characterize people like the mayor. And in a sense, because they talked one way and acted another—manifesting the gap between theory and practice—Powell could identify them as just as detrimental, if not more so, to the civil rights cause.

La Guardia's experience with the Stuyvesant Town episode is a quintessential example of the "liberal's dilemma." Neither was the situation made less vexing by the fact that Metropolitan Life proceeded to develop housing in Harlem—Riverton Apartments—for Negroes, a plan initiated by Robert Moses. Again, Walter White and other civil rights advocates saw this as "segregated housing," as it was, of course. But La Guardia weighed the opposing views and opted for support of segregation as a price to pay for enticing private capital to build much-needed housing and to become involved in slum clearance. Council president Morris stated later that La Guardia "felt that since he had the Negroes in his camp anyway, he could get away with it."[43] One historian flatly concluded: "Perhaps the price was higher than La Guardia had anticipated, for clearly he compromised his beliefs in racial justice."[44]

Certainly La Guardia recognized his dilemma. A lawsuit was filed challenging the selection of tenants on a racially discriminatory basis. In a curious, dilemma-laden letter to Frederick Ecker at Metropolitan Life after the agreement was signed, La Guardia attempted to close the "I v. I gap" as much as possible. He wanted the Stuyvesant Town project to be a success, he began.[45] He also believed that tenants should not be excluded on the basis of race, although he had voted for the agreement, fully aware of Metropolitan's policy in this regard. Granted that the project would go forward, La Guardia wanted the insurance company to know where he stood and what he planned to do if he became involved in a lawsuit over the matter. He informed Ecker in carefully measured language:

> I deem it proper at this time also, because of discussion, statements and even gossip during the course of the consideration of this project, and at hearings and even in judicial proceedings, to say that I consider this particular project as having certain public obligations different from and greater than a like project financed entirely by private funds without any tax exemption or right of condemnation or other privileges. The standards or conditions or requirements for tenancy in a housing unit aided by the city through statutory authorization as is the case in Stuyvesant Town, must be applicable to all. In other words, any person meeting all of the requirements should not be barred because of belonging to any particular racial group. There can be no discrimination in tenant selection based on prejudice or contrary to any provisions of our State Constitution or State law. If, after operation of Stuyvesant Town is started, there should be any litigation on the question of barring tenants who are otherwise fully qualified solely because of discrimination or solely because of racial prejudice, you should know now that I will take a position as above indicated.

The letter was dated July 31, 1943, and signed by La Guardia. It obviously represented the mayor's complex stance on this thorny issue. He would rely on the courts to do the job of desegregating the housing project. But he would aid, presumably through testifying, the undoing of what his political vote on the Board of Estimate had helped to create. Following this route, he apparently reasoned, would get the housing needed *and* an integrated project. The final piece to this rather puzzling saga was the handwritten notation on a copy of the letter in the La Guardia files. It simply indicated: "Not Sent."[46]

As indicated, many liberal progressive elements in the city came out against the Stuyvesant Town project. In this instance, the more moderate civil rights advocates did not need to rely on others, such as Powell, to carry the fight. They would not go as far as Powell and call for the mayor's impeachment, but to some this was not an issue that needed to be soft-pedaled or compromised.

At the same time, La Guardia could be consoled somewhat by the open support he received from some quarters against the more harsh attacks from Powell. The editor of the *Brooklyn Tribune*, Brooklyn's "Only Colored Newspaper," wrote to La Guardia:

> I trust that a statement made by Councilman Powell on June 7, 1943 relative to your impeachment, did not disturb you. Political aspirations can at times cause certain persons to say things they later regret. You are the first Mayor in this city, to appoint a Colored Magistrate and later a Justice of the Court of Special Sessions Court. My newspaper has very little power, in comparison with other Colored newspapers to mold public opinion. But the little power it has is one hundred per cent in back of real friends of my Race.
>
> [Signed] Hannibal G. Parsons, Editor.[47]

The mayor sent an appreciative acknowledgment of the letter.

La Guardia surely was aware that his overall record on race issues was one that had gained him many Negro friends and supporters. His role in getting President Roosevelt to issue Executive Order 8802 would be remembered by many highly respected black leaders such as A. Philip Randolph. He was seen in the same light as Eleanor Roosevelt—clearly a friend of the race—especially in times when staunch civil rights enemies such as Senator Theodore Bilbo from Mississippi were making openly racist remarks on the floor of Congress, and when the entire South was characterized by a race-baiting politics that pitted candidates against each other largely on the basis of which ones could denounce the Negro more convincingly. At times, then, this would have to be the measuring stick—La Guardia in comparison with Bilbo or Congressman John Rankin (D.-Miss.). In addition, the mayor and his staff were always appreciative of and alert to those blacks who would support him publicly against critics such as Powell. White support in such circumstance meant less for obvious reasons. One black, Warren Brown, the director of race relations of a group called the Council for Democracy, had written an article published in the *Reader's Digest* entitled "A Negro Warns the Negro Press." He was severely critical of Negro editors, mentioning Powell specifically, who "foster segregation by being race-conscious first and American second."[48] Such people, "living by agitation, aim to capitalize on the war," and are basically irresponsible. Referring to the police shooting of Wallace Armstrong and Powell's handling of the incident, Brown wrote: "The Rev. Mr. Powell called for 'mass action.' The kind of language he used made it plain that what he was asking for was mob action."

The mayor's assistant, Lester Stone, who had tried to talk Powell out of holding the Armstrong protest meeting, was delighted to see this article. He sent it to the mayor with an attached memo, saying:

> This is one of the most lucid, fair-minded, unprejudiced and sensible articles I have ever seen by a member of any race about his own race. It completely debunks, by a mere reference, the Rev. A. Clayton Powell and his newspaper "The People's Voice," and it indicates a man who is really big.
>
> I think we should make an effort to build him up and keep in touch with him for future race problems, as he appears to me from his article, to be miles ahead of even Walter White.

Such a memo in Powell's hands would have been dynamite for Powell. It made the point he would constantly articulate throughout his career: This was what you could expect of leaders of blacks who were handpicked and supported by whites. He, too, in his editorship of the *Voice* had been accused of being such a tool, but he was always able to fend off such accusations by his willingness to go further than most in his public condemnations of officials such as La Guardia. He was always less willing to concede good intentions and good works from those liberal white leaders. This covered him and provided him more legitimacy in the eyes of his black Harlem constituents. This was important, because Powell knew that in the frenetic political scene of Harlem, there were always those willing to wrench the leadership mantle in the name of greater claim to militancy. He knew, because he had played that game himself. For him, there would be no memos lying around in files of downtown white officials planning to "build him up"; friends such as those he did not need.

At the same time, there would always be attacks from another vantage point by those blacks who saw his strident leadership as unproductive of any real gains, and perhaps as even detrimental to the Negro cause. Certainly, such buffeting back and forth was to be expected in the political arena. But it was even more predictable for one, like Powell, who deliberately strove to combine protest politics and electoral politics. These were quite distinct styles of action, and sometimes they required decisions and actions that were not mutually supportive. Powell, however, always felt that protest served well to support electoral politics, feeling that protest strengthened the hand of elected officials and gave them more bargaining chips. Votes were fine, but limited. Mass action had a tantalizing way of being unpredictable in outcome, and in a way required much greater leadership skills. In this sense, it would not have entered Powell's mind to call off that mass protest rally that La Guardia's assistant urged him to do. Powell was an elected politician who preferred the noise of the thousands rather than the whispered tones of a few heads negotiating, but above all, he wanted both—simultaneously.

As Fiorello H. La Guardia was no racial segregationist, neither was Adam C. Powell, Jr., an antiwhite demagogue. Both subscribed to the basic tenets of racial equality, nondiscrimination, nonsegregation, interracial organization, and the necessity for working to achieve mutually respectful relations among various racial and ethnic groups. But that these two politicians—situated as they were in the political terrain of New York City—should have a continuing contentious and problematic relationship is not surprising. One major cause for this, aside from simply having different styles and personalities, was that these two men responded very differently to the serious American Dilemma facing society. They differed over what was necessary at any given time to close the gap between ideals and institutions, between agreed-upon theory and admitted practice.

La Guardia firmly believed that improvement in race relations had to come "from the heart not the head," that is, through the process of people, especially the majority whites, coming to know and respect all others as decent human beings the same as themselves. This was a matter of "education" more than it was of coercive legal statutes. To be sure, this promised an approach identified as "gradualism," precisely because this learning-knowing process was, by its nature, slow. In addition, as the mayor constantly admonished his Negro constituents, blacks were not the only ones who were (or had been) victims of discrimination and segregation. His own experience as an Italian American, and his close association earlier in his legal career with ethnic immigrant problems, made him especially sensitive to the evils and disadvantages of prejudice against ethnic groups. It is also clear that he suspected that some black leaders, Powell being a good example, were prone to use the race issue opportunistically, to strengthen their own leadership, coming very close to exhibiting demagogic behavior.

His impatience with some black demands was also manifested in his frustration at times in explaining that many of the problems encountered in New York City could only be dealt with through action by the national government. This was particularly the case, he argued, with economic problems of widespread unemployment and inadequate housing. And the private economic sector had to be courted tactfully to obtain its cooperation, as in the painful decision to accommodate the segregationist policies of the Metropolitan Life Insurance Company. Sometimes, in other words, one good (namely, integrated housing) had to be sacrificed in order to achieve another good (namely, slum clearance and better affordable housing). Political decision-making always required this kind of difficult balancing of equally desirable interests. Above all, the fact that both Powell and La Guardia were in office during the country's complete mobilization and involvement in a major world war presented a clear distinguishing feature between these two men. To La Guardia, without question, winning the war against the Axis powers was top priority without any qualification. *Everything* had to be subordinated to that goal, even the forceful effort to end legal segregation. The goal of winning the war first could not be shared because it had the preeminent call on the country's resources and attention.

Ultimately, Mayor La Guardia exhibited a form of "toleration" of the American Dilemma. This was not, in the best of worlds, the way he would prefer things, but it was, all circumstances considered, the best likely possible. Progress would take place, but it would, of necessity, be very slow.

Adam Powell, on the other hand, was the epitome of the black political figure in a state of constant moral outrage over America's dilemma. To him, the war in which this country was engaged against the Axis powers abroad needed to be seen as one struggle with the segregationist forces at home. Thus he saw World War II as the opportunity to expose the contradictions of the domestic dilemma, to push the campaign for a "double victory." There was no question with Powell of disloyalty, but he made speeches during the war equating the struggle against Hitler on the same level with that against Bilbo that a La Guardia, however much he despised Bilbo, would never accept. In addition, Powell was impatient with calls for gradualism and the emphasis on persuasion. To him, there was nothing to debate about whether and when segregation should be ended. The Constitution was clear on this. Delay only fed notions of the possible legitimacy of the status quo, which, of course, he could not accept. And he often labeled those like La Guardia who were more willing to tolerate conditions for the time as hypocrites whose basic allegiance to the American Creed had to be questioned. Therefore, where La Guardia sometimes saw in Powell opportunism and demagogy, Powell saw in La Guardia insincerity and hypocrisy.

Ultimately, for Powell, there was no reason to be perplexed over what decision to make regarding Stuyvesant Town. There was no choice between two equally valid, competing interests. One, housing with integration, was good; the other, housing with discrimination, was bad. And he did not accept the argument that Stuyvesant Town would be doomed unless the insurance company got its way. And *if* that were the case, then a segregated Stuyvesant Town should not be built. This episode would be representative of the kinds of issues that would characterize Powell's evolving political career. After a year and a half on the City Council, he was ready to move on. He was headed to Congress, and the Stuyvesant Town tradeoff decision was a preview of the kinds of issues Powell would put on the national political table in post–World War II America.

Congressional Irritant, 1940s–1950s

7

Election to Congress and the Roosevelts

If Adam Clayton Powell, Jr., was to go to Congress, there first had to be a congressional district in which he could run and stand a reasonable chance of winning. And this meant, frankly, a congressional district with a majority of black voters. At the beginning of the 1940s, such a district did not exist. Harlem, his political base, was divided geographically among three congressional seats. But after the 1940 census, the state legislature, once again, was under intense pressure to abide by the federal and state constitutions to redraw district lines to conform more legitimately to population shifts. This was not new. Many state legislatures, dominated by rural legislators, feared the increasing political strength of urban areas, and simply refused to reapportion after the decennial censuses. The last congressional redistricting in New York State had occurred in 1911. Redrawing of *state* legislative boundaries was also long overdue, the last having been in 1917.

In 1941, New York had a liberal Democratic governor, Herbert Lehman, and a Republican-controlled State Assembly and State Senate. Immediately following the 1940 census, Lehman began to put pressure on the politicians in Albany to reapportion the state's legislative congressional districts. The population figures clearly indicated the need for this action. In the state legislature, some upstate rural districts were represented by legislators with as few as 20,000 constituents, while some in New York City had 350,000 citizens. This meant, of course, that the rural areas were disproportionately overrepresented, a common problem throughout the country at that time.[1]

New York City itself stood to gain seats if the legislative and congressional districts were reapportioned properly. But within the city's five boroughs, Manhattan would lose some seats because residents were moving from that borough to others, especially to Brooklyn, Queens, and the Bronx.

The business of redrawing political boundaries was inevitably a zero-sum game: what some gained, others lost. There was no way to avoid this, and the politicians and political parties knew this. They also knew that communities were identified by political party and race and ethnicity. Thus one community was known to be traditionally Republican or Democrat; another was predominantly Italian or Irish or black, etc. And these characteristics were known to have political significance. These characteristics, along with the census figures furnished by the U.S. Department of Commerce, became the grist of the work that involved the delicate process of reappointment.

Governor Lehman, in January 1941, sent a tart message to the state legislators demanding immediate attention to this situation. Three decades of delay and avoidance were enough. He stated:

> I recommend that you immediately create a joint legislative committee, with equal representation of both major parties, to prepare reapportionment bills for our legislative and Congressional districts. Such a committee should be set up now, not at the end of this legislative session. . . . Reapportionment should be made on a true and accurate basis without regard to local or party advantage. . . . I wish to make it absolutely clear that I will not countenance any attempt longer to withhold from any locality its just representation in the Legislature at Albany—or at Washington—no matter how difficult or objectionable it may be for any section now having more than its proper number of representatives to reduce that number.[2]

The Republicans resented the demanding, "dictatorial" tone of the governor's message, asserting in so many words that "no one had even hinted that the legislature did not intend to start work on reapportionment this year."[3]

Of course, there were other targets, not only the Republicans, of the governor's charge. Tammany Hall (Manhattan's Democratic Party organization) was not keen on reapportionment because, given Manhattan's decrease in population, that would mean fewer seats for that borough. Neither was it lost on the Tammany "Tigers" that up in Harlem where there could well be carved out a new congressional seat, the local political forces there were not securely in the pockets of the downtown political machine.

Thus the stakes were not simply between rural and urban, and Democrats and Republicans. There were intraparty factors to take into account, and the likelihood that new district lines would create new opportunities for new potential rivals for office. Reapportionment always opened this can of worms. It unsettled the status quo. And in this complex, cross-party quagmire, one could often find strange political bedfellows. The *New York Times* editorialized in support of Lehman, and recognized the political alliances that would be challenged.

> Nothing has been done by either party because apparently neither party wants an honest reapportionment. . . . A Republican alliance with Tammany to continue its failing political power has been the rule. Urban and rural politicians have combined to maintain an unreasonable status quo.[4]

If Tammany Hall and others recognized the potential for new forces, surely there were those in Harlem watching and waiting—including the inimitable rising star, Adam Clayton Powell, Jr., who then was sharpening his tools to prepare for a race for the City Council. That would be a decent start and stopover while the state legislature grappled with the knotty problems of reapportionment—the final results of which few expected to occur that year (1941) at least. But the ball was rolling, and it would be difficult—possible, but difficult—to deny a congressional district eventually to Harlem. Perhaps not for the next (1942) congressional election, but certainly not too soon after. So Harlem was poised.

The ensuing reapportionment debates did not focus overtly on the consequences for Harlem, but few political observers and activists were naïve about this.

For the next year and a half, the state legislature, dominated by upstate Republicans, wrestled with the issue. Funds were appropriated to obtain and study the intricate census data. Precisely how much had the population shifted? How many were U.S. citizens? How many were aliens? State districts were based on the former. Congressional lines included the latter. A Commission was appointed. Various proposals affecting state assembly and state senatorial seats began to emerge. The state constitution was studied.

Did it permit increasing the number of seats? Should the New York City Council be permitted to have a role? The legislative committee[5] received an appropriation of $50,000 and started its work, instructed to report a plan by February 1, 1942. Block-by-block analyses of the population had to be made in several cities in addition to New York City: Yonkers, Albany, Utica, Syracuse, Rochester, Buffalo, and Binghamton. The work was intricate and tedious. It was also delicately and decidedly political.

Harlem waited and watched.

More money was sought and received (an additional $52,500) to buy more new 1940 census maps from the federal government. The committee asked for and received an extension of its deadline to April 15, 1942.

As deliberations proceeded, the major snag centered on the allocation of state senatorial seats. Manhattan was destined to lose. That borough, in 1917 (when the last state redistricting took place), had two fifths of the city's population. In 1942 there were 400,000 fewer people in the borough. This meant, clearly, that some senatorial districts would be eliminated. But other city boroughs stood to gain a total of five seats. Manhattan had nine state senatorial seats. In the proposal emerging from the committee there would be six. What communities would be sacrificed? In addition, interpreting the state constitution in a way to enlarge the entire state senate, the Republicans hoped to increase that body from fifty-one to fifty-six. This would permit the Republicans to retain their party control, even in the face of New York City (strongly Democratic) gaining some seats. Democrats objected, of course.

In late March, 1942, a stalemate seemed likely. Once again the state appeared to have come to the threshold of reapportionment without crossing over. "Reports from up-state points," the *New York Times* reported, "are that the Congressional reapportionment measure is viewed as upsetting the political balance north of New York City much more than does the legislative reapportionment plan."[6]

The state had forty-three congressional districts and two representatives-at-large.[7] The joint committee was proposing forty-five seats to be elected by districts only. While Manhattan would lose three seats, it was expected that "one of the six probably would have a Negro as Representative, as it contains all of Harlem."[8]

The legislative session was rapidly coming to a close with little time left to consider the many other issues on the agenda. The

Democrats objected to the Republican plan to enlarge the state senate. The argument centered on language in the state constitution that was ambiguous about the circumstances under which the upper chamber could be increased in actual size.[9] Governor Lehman admonished the legislators again to report out a reapportionment bill.[10] Time was running out, with little more than a week to go before adjournment. At one point it appeared that only a congressional redistricting bill would survive; then, both a congressional and state legislative bill. Lehman, repeating the language he had used almost a year and a half earlier, urged action on both. But on April 17, 1942, the State Senate by vote failed to support *any* apportionment plan. The *New York Times* summed up:

> Arguments as to constitutionality, equity and necessity dominated two hours of debate, but the defeat lay in matters not mentioned, such as the feeling among up-state Republicans that the urban areas would control their party as well as the Legislature; the hesitancy to vote to unseat a friend, if the legislator himself were not affected; fear of loss of Republican control of the Assembly in a bad year and similar intangibles.[11]

Conspicuously quiet throughout the several months during the political maneuverings in Albany, Adam Powell now broke his silence with a strong attack on reapportionment rejection in his "Soap Box" column. As expected, he highlighted the race angle. "The refusal of the State legislature to pass the congressional reapportionment bill was a direct insult to the Negro people. Fifteen million Negro people and only one Congressman[12]—sounds like 'taxation without representation.' "[13] Powell noted that the bill would "guarantee a Negro congressman and *this Bill Must Be Passed.*" He bluntly stated that the issue over state senatorial seats was not too important.

> Of course there are up for consideration reapportionment bills giving new Senatorial and Assembly District lines, but these are not important. Whether the new Senatorial lines are passed or not, we are going to have a Negro Senator this year from Harlem. The passing of the assembly district reapportionment bill will probably cut down our present three representatives to two. It will also decrease the number of district leaders in Harlem. However, it is just a question of time before we take over the 22nd assembly district from the standpoint of Negro leadership.[14]

Then Powell warned both the Democrats and the Republicans that if reapportionment failed, they might have to deal with his efforts to organize a new party.

> If we meet with rebuffs from both parties, then we'll organize and launch our own party, the People's Party. This will not be a new party, but a party line on the machine through which all Negroes—Republicans, Democrats, American Laborites—can register a protest vote. We will not be interested in local candidates. We will be in a position to vote solidly as Negro people, with whatever whites who believe in taxation WITH representation, on state and national issues.[15]

His strategy seemed to indicate that he was willing to make no fuss over the loss of seats in Albany in exchange for a Harlem congressional district. One can image that he already had a potential candidate in mind. Failure to achieve this, he appeared to be suggesting, meant that a political party could be organized to get on the ballot as a swing party—pretty much as the American Labor Party was doing, endorsing those candidates from the major parties who were more amenable to its policies. His reference—"we will not be interested in local candidates"—was a strange one, probably intended to appease citywide allies with whom he was working from his position in the City Council. At any rate, his threat seemed especially narrow and tailored to the state legislative situation in Albany. It was reasonably clear that Powell did not want to tamper with his New York City Council base, was willing to sacrifice the seats of a few in the state legislature, and wanted badly to have the option of running for Congress from Harlem as soon as possible. As with all politicians, he was assessing the reapportionment issue in terms of its impact on his own political plans.

A new dimension was introduced into the deliberations shortly afterwards. Word came up from congressional sources in Washington that Congress might intervene and impose redistricting on congressional boundaries if the state did not act. Whether this questionable move would be made or not,[16] this tentative threat seemed enough to spur New York Republicans to action. The remaining issue was whether the reapportionment would become effective in 1942 or two years later, in 1944.

On the evening of April 24, 1942, the state legislature passed a congressional reapportionment bill to take effect in 1944. A new congressional district—the twenty-second—was confined almost exclusively to Harlem, and every commentary assumed, accurately, that this new seat would provide the opportunity for the first Negro to be elected to Congress in the state's history.

Obviously such a development would immediately generate lively speculation and lists of probable contenders. This was a prize too enticing to ignore. Certainly on everyone's "likely" (if not, preferred) list of contenders was the energetic, dynamic young minister–city councilman, Adam Clayton Powell, Jr. Very much in the community spotlight, in the midst of the inflammatory debate over the police shooting of Wallace Armstrong, getting press attention almost weekly for his vehement attacks on segregation and discrimination, preaching each week before thousands at Abyssinian in the middle of Harlem itself, Powell may not have been the *only* viable potential candidate, but he had to be on everyone's (friend's or foe's) shortlist.

By the spring of 1943, Powell's interest in going to Congress was unquestioned, and he began to cultivate potential supporters. Knowing full well that his chances were initially very good, he nonetheless also knew that careful groundwork had to be laid. There were more than a few activists and influential voices in Harlem who either wanted the job for themselves or certainly not for Powell. The widely read *Amsterdam News* sounded out A. Philip Randolph, the nationally popular union leader of the Brotherhood of Sleeping Car Porters. Randolph was deservedly well respected as a protest leader who had forced President Roosevelt in June 1941 to issue Executive Order 8802. His leadership was perceived as militant but dignified, and then (and years later) his reputation as one who spoke forcefully and uncompromisingly was well established. Randolph, however, had never shown interest in local clubhouse politics, and he clearly did not have the church base or local party contacts and organizations Powell enjoyed and was constantly nurturing. Randolph recorded his own recollection of the congressional possibility.

> The *Amsterdam News* wanted me to run for Congress, but of course I had the Brotherhood on my hands, had no time for anything except this particular thing, and I didn't want it ever to be said that I ran away from a job because of opposition or because of failure to get wealth all of a sudden. . . . So I told the *Amsterdam News* that I couldn't run for Congress because I had this organization on my hands and so forth.[17]

Powell Sr. approached Randolph to solicit support for his son. Randolph, who knew the father well and respected him, was receptive. The Brotherhood was planning a mass meeting at

Madison Square Garden to push its own programs of jobs and fair employment practices. Powell Jr. wanted to speak at the rally. It would be good exposure, and likely scare off others who were looking, if not for Randolph to oppose him, for an alternative candidate to support. Appearing on Randolph's platform would indeed be a major boost, an implicit endorsement if nothing more. In spite of Randolph's decision, there were still those who felt, or at least hoped, that the union leader would change his mind and announce his own candidacy at the Madison Square Garden rally. He apparently meant what he said, and this, incidentally, was one of the qualities that made him an almost universally respected leader in civil rights and labor union struggles. Randolph, years later, told of the episode with slight amusement (and understanding) at the aggressiveness of the young preacher-politician.

> So he [Powell Jr.] came to us and wanted to know whether he could get on the program. We said, "Yes." Going to Congress; we were interested in that. So he did. He came and the place was crowded. I told him how much time he could take, but of course he went far above and over that time, because people were applauding him you know and so forth.
>
> So I pulled his coattail and told him the time was up, that we had others [on the] program.
>
> So he said, "Well, Phil, if there is any problem of money over my time of speaking here, don't have any fear about it because I'll see to it that you get the money."[18]

(The program ran longer than anticipated, thanks to Powell's overly long but enthusiastically received speech. The union had to pay overtime costs, and, of course, it did not receive any help in this from the soon-to-be congressional candidate.)

Randolph remembered it fondly, however: "I pulled his coattails again and he finally stopped, and we carried on our movement. It may be said that this was perhaps the first big meeting that he got in the interest of his congressional fight, and he was appreciative of it. Many of the politicians around . . . [were] always trying to get into our meetings for a hearing. We didn't bother with many of them, but of course we liked Powell. He was a radical too, you know."[19]

To be sure, Powell was making the rounds, touching bases, consolidating his support. In March 1944, the still important Tammany Hall endorsed him, even as he announced that he would also seek the endorsements of the Republican and American Labor parties. The Democratic district leaders in Harlem were lining up behind what clearly appeared to be a winner. Powell's campaign organization, the People's Committee, under the tutelage of his political mentor, Joseph E. Ford, called a big meeting in Harlem with the theme "What Do Negroes Want?" Powell invited Roy Wilkins of the NAACP to speak. Wilkins accepted and was reported in the *New York Herald Tribune* the next day as assuring the mass audience at Abyssinian Baptist that Powell had "united support for Congress this fall in the new Harlem district."[20] This immediately incurred the wrath of some potential candidates, especially State Assemblyman William T. Andrews. Andrews wrote to Wilkins asking for clarification of the NAACP's position: "I am not any too certain that you, prior to Sunday, have been aware of my intention to seek election to Congress in November. Let me now assure you, however, that I intend to do so. With that, I would be very grateful to you for an expression of your preferences as far as the candidates so far declared are concerned."[21] In addition, an attorney in Harlem, Eardlie John, notified Wilkins of his intention to run, and wanted to know if Wilkins was speaking personally or if his remarks "irrevocably commit the National Office (of the NAACP)?"[22]

Wilkins, of course, had to correct the impression left by the *Herald Tribune*. He wrote the editor (with copies to Powell, John, and Andrews) that the NAACP did not endorse candidates and that the reporter took as an endorsement by Wilkins a statement made in jest. But perhaps Wilkins was a bit naïve. A mass meeting in Adam Powell's church at that time would be hard to characterize as anything but a political rally for Powell, notwithstanding his solemn vow to the speakers beforehand that no names of candidates should be mentioned. The very first speaker was Joseph Ford, who, according to Wilkins, proceeded to refer to Powell several times as the "next congressman." In this jocular atmosphere, Wilkins, surveying the scene, proceeded to call for unity in the overall civil rights and political struggle and jokingly stated that "I guess that all the people in this room appeared to be unified behind Adam."[23] Powell, of course, loved it all. There was no way he would lose an opportunity on his home turf to further his candidacy. In his response to Wilkins's letter of explanation to the *Herald Tribune* (which, incidentally, the newspaper excerpted in a later edition), Powell coyly wrote to Roy Wilkins: "As soon as you made that wisecrack at the Conference Saturday, I knew the press would grab it up. Your letter to the Herald Tribune was very good.

Incidentally, the Democratic Party gave me the nomination Thursday night. Will be picking you up soon."[24] Adam was off and running and enjoying every minute of it. His confidence was hard to subdue.

The "Soap Box" columns in *The People's Voice* became his regular campaign organ, setting forth his various views on a range of issues—labor unions, civil rights, the war overseas—but mainly elaborating on his antisegregation positions. The only Negro in Congress, William L. Dawson, Democrat from Chicago, attended a conference in New York on "Social Hygiene" and stated that he "would be happy to see Adam Clayton Powell, Jr. and as many other Negroes as we can get" in Congress.[25]

Powell stepped up his speaking engagements not only in Harlem but around the country, accepting invitations to preach and speak at NAACP meetings in places such as Anderson, Indiana, where he was introduced as the inevitable next Negro congressman. He lost no chance to appear with celebrities and entertainers, as well as with the Communist Party leader Earl Browder at mass rallies. At one Harlem wartime "victory rally" selling war bonds, he shared the platform with Browder and also Count Basie, Billie Holiday, Josh White, and Paul Robeson. And this exposure was combined with endorsements from local labor unions. *The People's Voice* printed almost weekly several letters from soldiers around the country and overseas praising Powell. Some sent financial contributions to his campaign.

The Powell wagon continued to roll. In June he picked up the endorsement of the American Labor Party in Manhattan, then under the chairmanship of Congressman Vito Marcantonio. (Marcantonio had previously been denied the endorsement of Tammany Hall in his own bid for reelection.) The leader of the black New York Elks, and a longtime Republican, J. Finley Wilson, agreed to chair a Republicans for Powell Committee. Local 65 of the Wholesale and Warehouse Workers (CIO) gave a check for three hundred dollars to M. Moran Weston of the Negro Labor Victory Committee to be delivered to Powell's campaign. Langston Hughes, the popular, folksy poet, playwright and author, wrote a campaign song for Powell: "Let My People Go—Now!"

Powell's candidacy was not destined, however, to go unchallenged. Over the years, he had angered too many activists in the community who now were in no mood to hand him the election without a fight. Some Democratic district leaders, led by Herbert

I. Bruce, were determined to resist their party's choice, and they frantically scoured the area for a viable candidate to run in the primary. The *New York Times* reported Bruce as saying that Harlem should not be represented by a "Communist-controlled rabble-rouser who may lead to bloodshed between Negroes and whites in this country."[26] But this in turn caused some of Bruce's constituents to rebel and rush to Powell's defense. The jockeying continued, with Powell's old nemesis, Frank R. Crosswaith of the Social Democrats, blasting him and saying "we do not want a dark edition of the Bilbo or Rankin [white Mississippi segregationist legislators in the Senate and House, respectively] ilk who thrive upon exploiting racial and creedal differences."[27] Another Harlem Republican district leader, Harold C. Burton, who had old political scores to settle with Powell, sought wisely to distinguish between Powell the preacher and Powell the politician. Recognizing the tremendous affection for the church in Harlem, Burton did not wish to alienate loyal churchgoing Harlemites by painting Powell with too broad a brush of attack. Therefore, it would be wise to commend Powell for his religious leadership, but condemn his ineptness as a political leader. "Whatever contribution Adam Powell, Jr. made to the community was as a minister, but as a politician he has been a dud."[28] These were two different Powells, Burton asserted. As a politician, he had "bungled" the case of discrimination at the city colleges. Discrimination in hiring Negro nurses at the city hospitals, likewise, Burton claimed, was never challenged successfully by Powell, notwithstanding the young preacher's claims. Powell, in other words, claimed more than he produced.

A columnist for the *Amsterdam News*, Earl Brown, took on Powell's political leadership as less than honorable, and concluded that in effect Powell was really no more than a "stooge" for downtown political bosses in Tammany Hall.[29]

Although Powell had received the Republican endorsement in his race for the City Council, the party was not interested in his candidacy for congress. Instead, the Republicans selected a Harlem lawyer and woman, Sara Pelham Speaks, as their candidate. A former social worker and teacher, Mrs. Speaks had strong credentials. A graduate of the University of Michigan, she received a law degree from New York University in 1936. She had been active in Republican Party circles for years as an executive in the women's division of the Republican National Committee in 1936 and 1940. She had also taught for a time at the college level in Orangeburg, South Carolina, and worked in government in the Office of the

Recorder of Deeds and the Census Bureau. Her father was prominent as the publisher of the Negro newspaper the *Washington Tribune*. Shortly after the party endorsed her, approximately two hundred Harlem women, one of whom was the wife of A. Philip Randolph, formed a committee to support Speaks. She immediately announced that she would take the fight against Powell into his own party, sensing the unrest among some Democratic district leaders, by filing for the Democratic primary. The well-spoken criminal lawyer felt confident that her style and record of quiet civic activism could be a tough match for the flamboyant preacher.

She indicated the difference between herself and Powell when she stated that her approach as a member of Congress would not be "emotional and inflammatory." "You get nowhere by rabble-rousing. A Congressman or woman has only one vote and you can't pass bills with one vote. A Representative must work through friendships and party associations."[30] In such a manner, she declared, she would work to end the poll tax, support legislation to make lynching a federal crime, and help to achieve effective enforcement of antidiscrimination laws. In substance, her stand on issues was little different from Powell's, but there was no ignoring the fact that Harlem was now voting strongly Democratic, and her opponent had the huge Abyssinian Church organization behind him. By any calculation, she would have an uphill fight.

As expected, the *Amsterdam News* liked her candidacy. In an editorial entitled "Women, Politics and Progress," the newspaper stated: "At long last the recognition rightly due Negro women from political leaders in the major parties has been given in the designation by the Republicans of Sara Speaks as a candidate for Congress. . . . She is able, experienced and politically-wise in her own right. . . . Sara Speaks has the foundation for the making of a good congressman."[31]

When she decided to challenge Powell in the Democratic primary, he countered by filing in the Republican primary. Thus, as the summer of 1944 wore on, Harlem was alive with a political contest for its first congressional seat. For the August 1 primaries, Harlemites of both major parties had the same two choices. While not too different on substantive issues, the candidates were worlds apart in their leadership styles. But style and substance sometime become fused. Powell had never been, to that point, hesitant about working with the Communists or with any group with which he was not entirely in agreement. This was not, to him, a permanent ideological commitment, but a political arrangement for convenience. To the masses in Harlem, he probably accurately calculated that they understood this relationship. Charges that he was an ally of Communists likely did not phase him. Therefore, in the heat of the race and the hot days of late July when Sara Speaks charged in a statement carried in the *New York Times* (in an obscure one-liner news item on a back page) that Powell was "bringing in Communists from sections as far removed as Gramercy Park and Flatbush to do his canvassing,"[32] Powell more than likely yawned—and smiled. True or not, it was hardly a charge with much political import in the congressional race taking place up in Harlem.

Early in the spring, however, Powell made one of his classic off-the-cuff remarks that he later felt obliged to modify. This would be a pattern throughout his congressional career, and for the most part he was able to rephrase a comment to minimize the damage and survive. Shortly after Tammany designated him its party's choice, he held a press conference in his home. Probably feeling some need to blunt the Tammany stamp of approval, he stated, "I will never be a machine man. I will represent the Negro people first. I will represent after that all the other American people."[33] He then proceeded to talk about his views on the war (peace abroad must also mean equal rights for all at home), Negro involvement in peace negotiations, abolition of segregation in the military, and making lynching a federal crime—rather standard positions for Negro leadership and pretty much what any candidate running in Harlem would be expected to say—except for the "Negro people first" statement. His enemies pounced on him, equating such a position with the white supremacist views of segregationists. "Any Negro, particularly any Negro leader, who comes out for 'Negroes First' today indicates clearly that he is irresponsible," Earl Brown wrote in the *Amsterdam News*.[34] "[The statement] is . . . filled with the irresponsible mouthings of a man bitten by the intense desire to get elected to Congress at the expense of sanity, decency, racial accord and progress. Let the Rev. Powell mend his statements and his ways."

Recognizing the controversial nature of his remark, Powell did amend his statement a few weeks later. Speaking before the Finnish Turva Lodge in Harlem, he said, "I promise to represent this district first—not only the Negroes but each and every citizen of this area, irrespective of race, creed or political affiliation."[35] How much this soothed the feelings of those who questioned him is not known but it is also the case that he probably did not spend much, if any, time worrying about it. He had a good notion, because he knew himself well, about the kind of congressman he would be and that made him comfortable in making the statement in the first place and subsequently revising it. His main policy agenda was civil rights for Negroes. He knew that issue best; it was an important issue, and he also believed that very much of what would be done for Negroes, especially the poor constituents, would rebound to the economic benefit of others. This had been the thrust of his many speeches and "Soap Box" articles over the years. To many who admired him and granted him leeway beyond the usual limits, he was already accepted as one whose mouthings at times might outdistance his meanings. So be it, they shrugged. Adam could clean it up later.

That was Powell's developing reputation. But there was another dimension to this ambitious, unpredictable personality that was not so easily accepted or explained away. More than a few people with whom he had worked over the years were concluding that there was a problem with Adam of personal integrity. The evidence continued to mount. In early June, 1944, Walter White of the NAACP invited several important Harlem leaders to an informal dinner at the Hotel Theresa on 125th and Seventh Avenue to discuss specific steps that might avert a repetition of the riot the previous summer. Powell agreed to attend, along with approximately twenty others representing various organizations in the community. It was a wide-ranging discussion covering youth gangs (which were presenting increasing problems of juvenile delinquency), police actions, adequate recreation facilities, curfew hours, loitering at bars, and measures to stifle rumors. It was agreed that a meeting would be sought with Mayor La Guardia.[36]

A few days later, the *New York Times* carried a prominent news story: "Powell's Church Wars on Hoodlums; Favors Stronger Measures by Civil and Military Police in Negro Communities; 5-Point Program Offered; Bigger City Patrol Corps, More Recreation Projects, Curfew for Children Are Urged."[37] Powell had gotten the deacon board of Abyssinian Baptist Church to issue a number of proposals which exactly duplicated the ideas discussed at the private NAACP meeting. The initiative, it appeared, came from Powell. In his "Soap Box" column, Powell did commend the NAACP for calling the meeting, but wrote that "this conference was called too late." He then proceeded to list recommendations, mostly as his own, that others had discussed. Walter White wrote to Powell, taking exception to the "too late" reference and reminded him of a similar conference over a year before to which he had been invited.[38]

White did not bother to mention the similarity in recommendations or the seeming credit Powell was taking for initiating them. But Powell's preemptive move did not escape the notice of an *Amsterdam News* columnist, who wrote:

> When Sara Speaks was designated Republican candidate for Congress from the 22nd Congressional District, she was on the short end of a 10 to 1 bet for election. Today she is even money, and is reported to be gaining. Adam C. Powell lost prestige mightily among leading Harlemites last week when he took credit for a program outlined at a meeting called by the NAACP and was off-the-record. The resolution adopted by the deacon board of Abyssinian Baptist Church and published in the daily press last week was the identical program considered at the meeting seven days previously. Nearly every important figure in Harlem was present at the meeting and they are burning up over what they term downright dishonesty.[39]

This analysis of Sara Speak's improved chances was wishful thinking but the article was doubtless accurate on the reaction to Powell's integrity. But, again, Powell's campaign was in high gear, and he would not be deterred by others who were piqued by his tactics.

This was a typical sound-truck, street-corner-rally, endorsement-gathering campaign. And Powell gave every indication of being a master at it. *The People's Voice* listed his weeklong nightly schedule of street-corner appearances, with the usual fanfare of local entertainers and speakers warming up the crowd. His stump speech demanded an end to discrimination, linking the war abroad to the civil rights crusade at home, taking, always, a swipe at the "Uncle Toms" who supported the opposition, and frequently reminding the listeners of his role in earlier Harlem protest struggles. He found time to join a picket line in support of striking sales clerks in front of a major store on 125th Street seeking higher wages and better working conditions. (*The People's Voice* headlined his involvement on the line, with a large picture of him carrying a picket sign. The *New York Times* duly noted that he joined the picket line "for ten minutes.") He joined celebrities at War Bond rallies in Times Square and at Madison Square Garden. His receipt of an award in June from the American Committee of Jewish Writers, Artists and Scientists, chaired by Albert Einstein, was obviously very important to him. Receiving the Dorie Miller and Meyer Levine Award for being the Negro who had done the most for better relations between Negroes and Jews in 1943, he responded with a speech that lashed out at anti-Semitism and said: "We cannot divorce anti-Semitism and jimcrowism. . . . I refuse to let people call Jews Christ killers, because I know that Jews were Christ creators."[40] At the same time, he advocated a form of quotas in hiring, warning 125th Street merchants, "You must hire Negroes along with whites at ratios that reflect the proportion of Negro trade."[41]

Both his own newspaper and the *New York Times* highlighted a summer program organized by Abyssinian Baptist Church (led by Isabel Powell) that sent seventy-nine Harlem youngsters to homes of white families for several weeks in Vermont.[42] This, of course, was good, nonpolitical publicity for the Powell campaign.

In the final analysis, the election of a representative from Harlem was not seen as a panacea by many people. Many surely were realistic in knowing that one more Negro in Congress could hardly produce the legislation called for by Powell or any of his staunchest, most radical supporters: a permanent Fair Employment Practices Commission; abolition of the poll tax; making lynching a federal crime; the end to racial segregation in the armed forces. And certainly not any items from the list of policies Powell endorsed in July: much higher taxes for incomes over $75,000; abolition of the Senate filibuster [filibustering Southern senators defeated civil rights bills passed by the House]; federal takeover of all public utilities; and "the establishment of a federal insurance system."[43] Even Powell must have seen these as rather visionary goals, hardly on the priority list of even his own Democratic Party and its Presidential standard-bearer, Franklin D. Roosevelt. This was understood. But the value and expectation of an Adam Powell in Congress at that time related more to "spokesmanship." Here was a person who would at least "speak out," who would provide a voice—very likely a loud and eloquent one—in the very visible corridors of Congress. *That* would be different. He could counter in words, at least, the frequent congressional speeches made—and as often unanswered—by Southern segregationists. Many Negroes were angry that no Northern liberals would get up on the floor of Congress and challenge the segregationists—even in words, not to mention with effective proposed legislation. Powell certainly promised to do that. To a certain extent he had done it in his single term on the City Council. Years later, the role of congressional spokesman would be much less needed, but in the United States of the 1940s, this was no sheer symbolic or salutary gesture. This is what was meant by an item in *The People's Voice* during the campaign:

> Militant Negro leaders throughout the country as well as liberals of other groups see in the election of Adam Clayton Powell to Congress the one effective antidote to the venom spewing of the race baiting polltaxers and their sympathizers in the nation's greatest legislative body. . . . For several years now the Bilbos, Rankins, Dies and the others of their ilk have used the august Congressional halls as forums in which to spout their anti-racial, anti-minority mouthings and smear campaigns. To date there have been none who would challenge these violations of the decency code in the name of democracy and respectability.[44]

This is the role Powell promised to play, and it was certainly one his constituents wanted of him. And this is what Sara Speaks (and even Congressman Dawson) misunderstood. Of course, they would support the correct legislative measures—even propose some. But what representative of Negroes (of *any* political party) would not—and expect to survive? That part was easy. But who would stand up in Congress and forcefully, rhetorically take exception when Southern racists used the word "nigger," as they often did? Who would give speeches in the nation's national forum—not only back home in pulpits and in friendly mass street corner rallies—to be recorded in the *Congressional Record* that championed civil rights unequivocally? *This* was missing, and *this* Powell would supply. Psychological? Cathartic? Yes. But for a people in such circumstances, political and economic and social, what might appear rather insubstantial to others could be extremely important. Simply calling to task a speech made by a segregationist and getting that challenge published across the country, including the South—this could have enormous positive consequences, to the soul, if not to the solution. The word "antidote" used by *The People's Voice* was aptly chosen. Sara Speaks was not temperamentally suited for that role. Clearly she was an intelligent, honest fighter for civil rights. But Harlem Negroes did not need a quiet bargainer in Congress. Others would do the trading and the compromising. Those times called for an outspoken, almost intransigent advocate out front, not behind closed doors, one who would not lose her job if she spoke out, or who could be punished in countless ways known to Negroes who were considered "uppity" or "militant" or "radical." *They* would protect such a leader with their votes and approval through reelection term after term.

Powell read this mood perfectly. And that mood also fit perfectly his own personal style.

On August 1, 1944, primary election day, he received the mandate he wanted.

The numbers told the story. Powell won both the Democratic and Republican primaries. He beat Sara Speaks on the Democratic ticket—3,358 to 734, and in her own party he triumphed 1,397 to 1,038. Thus he had the nomination of the three parties—including the uncontested American Labor Party designation—that virtually assured him victory in the November general election. So confident had he been that a few days before the primary vote he had taken off for his favorite annual vacation spot, Oak Bluffs on Martha's Vineyard. There was no need to interrupt his normal pleasurable summer routine in order to receive the results of a predictable conclusion.

Reporters gathered at Abyssinian the afternoon after the election, and Powell held a long-distance telephone press conference in between his leisurely fishing in the waters off the island. He would go to Congress as a Democrat, he told them. He would, of course, remain as pastor of the church, returning on weekends while Congress was in session to tend to his ministerial duties. What would he do when Southern racists insulted Negroes in Congress? He would immediately raise a point of order and "give them an old-fashioned lecture in real democracy," and if this were not enough, he would introduce a resolution calling for their impeachment.[45] This is what his constituents wanted to hear, and they were confident that the brash young legislator would do just that.

The disappointed *Amsterdam News* wished him well, but took one last die-hard swipe at him. Powell's record in the City Council was again characterized as unproductive; he had accomplished there "nothing noteworthy." He has "[u]nfortunately and needlessly . . . seen fit to claim credit for many things he did not do." Perhaps he would mend his ways and seize the "grand opportunity to perform invaluable service. . . . It is up to him."[46]

For the next few weeks, however, Adam Powell would be fishing in other waters.

Three months later, on November 7, he was elected, unopposed, to Congress. Given the favorable electoral circumstances Powell enjoyed in Harlem, it would be difficult to justify an assertion made more than four decades later by a historian commenting on Roosevelt's fourth-term reelection and its impact on Powell's election. Professor John Patrick Diggins wrote: "Roosevelt won the big industrial cities and the urban black vote. . . . The President also brought in on his coattails William Fulbright of Arkansas to the Senate and Helen Gahagan Douglas of California and Adam Clayton Powell, Jr., of New York's Harlem to the House."[47] Whatever political debts Powell owed, it would be hard to conclude that he was elected to Congress on President Roosevelt's coattails. He enjoyed the endorsement of three major parties—and ran unopposed. Powell would have had fun with such an academic assessment of his political fortunes.

In the interim between the primary and the general election, he spent most of the fall working on his first book, *Marching Blacks,* at Martha's Vineyard, and making a few speeches around the country for the Roosevelt-Truman ticket. Powell had made no secret of his preference for Henry Wallace as the Vice-Presidential nominee, but he accepted Truman as a border-state moderate, far preferable to the Southerners' wish for Governor Jimmy Byrnes. He concentrated his attack on the Southern "poll-taxers" and their alliance with the "Northern Republican reactionaries" who resisted the gains of the liberal New Deal. At a massive rally in Harlem's Golden Gate Ballroom on a Sunday afternoon in October, Powell praised both the President and Mrs. Eleanor Roosevelt. "We need both Roosevelts," he shouted into the microphone. "They have been our friends."[48]

Indeed, Eleanor Roosevelt, as much as if not more so than her husband, was widely viewed as a "friend" of the Negro, as a strong supporter of civil rights. She worked especially closely with Walter White of the NAACP and with Mary McLeod Bethune, president of the National Council of Negro Women, a former adviser to the Roosevelt administration's National Youth Administration, and president of a Negro college in Daytona Beach, Florida. (Mrs. Bethune's stature in the national Negro community was comparable to that of A. Philip Randolph's: she was viewed as having high integrity, and being forceful and persistent, although she was not a mass-movement organizer. Her telegram endorsing Powell's candidacy in July was prominently featured on the front page of *The People's Voice.* Powell knew it carried weight in Harlem, especially among the women church folk.)[49] Eleanor Roosevelt addressed NAACP meetings (later serving as a national board member), attended integrated meetings in the South at a time when such behavior was cause for public comment in the press, and urged fair treatment of Negroes in all New Deal projects. Everyone knew that she was a good contact to have in the White House, and she would do her best—not always successfully, of course—to intervene with her husband for a worthy civil rights cause. Southern segregationsits attacked her constantly for her racial views, and sought to ridicule and demean her every chance they got. Her public association and work with Negroes came to be labeled derisively as "Eleanor Clubs."

From time to time, Mrs. Roosevelt would receive mail from White Southerners objecting to her racial views and activities. And very often she took careful pains to respond. One Alabamian wrote to her:

> We, my family and most of my friends are so wholeheartedly for the President (we adore everyone by the name) we regret for there to be anything said against you that we *have* to agree with. You make yourself most unpopular in the South by parading your most absurd and obnoxious ideas as to how we should treat our most faithful and humble negroes. This in turn reflects on our President. I believe your ideas arise from a lack of complete knowledge of the negro situation in the south and particularly in the small towns in the south where you find almost as many negroes as whites.[50]

Mrs. Roosevelt answered the letter patiently: "I have never advocated any social equality whatsoever, and I do not know of any Negro leaders who advocate it. In this country we are completely free to choose our companions and no one has any right to interfere."[51] She stated that there were four "fundamental rights" Negroes should not be denied: an equal opportunity for employment according to ability and at equal pay; an equal opportunity for education; an equal opportunity for justice before the law; and an equal opportunity to participate in government through the ballot. She then wrote, recognizing the fears of some whites of black population dominance in some local communities:

> Perhaps one of the solutions will be to move the Negroes into places where there are only a few and thus prevent the unbalance. This has been suggested and even tried in the manpower shortage and has been bitterly opposed by some Southern states.
>
> We made a grievous mistake in bringing the Negroes here as slaves and we can not undo that.
>
> I hope you will understand my position.[52]

When this correspondence was released to the press (not by Mrs. Roosevelt), she was criticized by some, including the *Amsterdam*

News, for rejecting "social equality." But Adam Powell's *The People's Voice* came to her defense:

> It is clear, of course, that Mrs. Roosevelt's views are absolutely correct. . . . The White House has never seen a First Lady who has been so fearless as Mrs. Roosevelt in her own practice of "social equality," nor one so bold and consistent in going out of her way to fight for Negro "democratic rights." She is justly admired by the Negro people, who will go to the polls next November almost as much to vote for her as for her great husband. . . .
>
> We have no information about the views of Mrs. Frances Dewey, of Texas, wife of the Republican candidate for President, on the issue of the Negro's democratic rights. We do know, however, that the reelection of President Roosevelt will return to the White House a First Lady who is a genuine friend of the Negro people."[53]

Eleanor Roosevelt's correspondence is legendary, and one of her constant correspondents was Walter White, whom she respected and trusted. On July 7, 1944, White sent a handwritten letter to her on the eve of the Democratic convention:

> My dear Mrs. Roosevelt:
>
> Very considerable concern is being expressed among Negroes over the rumors that Mr. Wallace is to be replaced by a conservative Southerner as the President's running mate. They see clearly that the so-called "Southern revolt" allegedly over the Negro issue, is a calculated campaign to browbeat the Democrats into choosing a Southerner as vice president who would become president should Mr. Roosevelt resign after the war is ended.
>
> This fear is so genuine and widespread that the nomination of a Southerner would virtually drive the Negro vote into the Republican camp.
>
> Sincerely,
> Walter White[54]

A few weeks later, White sent her a copy of his speech before the NAACP convention wherein he strongly condemned the "Southern conspiracy to replace Mr. Wallace by a reactionary Southerner with an anti-Negro record." Mrs. Roosevelt frequently found herself in the middle between her husband's political constraints over civil rights on the one hand and the more ardent advocates for civil rights who were her friends on the other. (In this regard she was very much like Mayor Fiorello La Guardia.) Her response to

White's second letter expressed her feeling that it was unfortunately but understandably a "bitter" letter, but wondered whether such a tone was the best approach to "help us solve our extremely difficult questions." She indicated that she and her husband were "as disturbed as you" about the prospects of a Byrnes vice-presidential nomination, and she was glad that did not happen. She told White that while she did not know Truman, "from all I hear he is a good man. Of course, I would have preferred Mr. Wallace." And then she revealed a rather poignant feeling about her husband's pending bid for a fourth term: "To tell the truth, from a personal standpoint and not for publication, a defeat will not be an unmixed sorrow for me. The President has felt that it is his duty to continue and since it looks as though the alternative would not be helpful to us or to the world, I suppose we will have to work and hope for success in November."[55]

President Roosevelt would do little personal campaigning in the 1944 election. There was a war to tend to; his health had to be protected. And after eleven highly visible years in office, most voters likely knew what they did or did not like about the man seeking an unprecedented fourth term. Therefore, he ran little political risk by not stumping the country seeking votes.

This did not mean, however, that many would not want to get to him, civil rights leaders, among them. They had hoped to meet with the President before Congress adjourned, but that was not possible, much to A. Philip Randolph's chagrin. Finally, Walter White, Mary McLeod Bethune, and Channing H. Tobias were able to see the President on September 29. Randolph refused to attend since he felt a meeting *after* Congress adjourned was fruitless. The three had twenty-five minutes with Roosevelt during which time they listed several items of policy importance to them. They wanted Roosevelt to urge Congress to speed along proposed legislation for a permanent FEPC. Roosevelt agreed to make this a "must" item, saying, "I invented the FEPC." They wanted federal legislation to protect military personnel from civilian violence—Negro soldiers had been the targets of several assaults. The President agreed. He also promised to stop the proposed plan to provide racially segregated furlough-rest facilities for white and Negro military personnel. Would the President support the proposal that the reorganization of a peacetime military force be on a nonsegregated basis without racially separate units? The President answered: "Of course, of course." The delegation wanted to discuss the U.S. role in urging the Allies to end colonial rule in Africa, India, and the West

Indies—areas where white European powers ruled over nonwhite peoples. There was little time left to elaborate on this at the meeting, but apparently Roosevelt had time to give the group a sense of his conversations with Prime Minister Winston Churchill on British colonial policies. Walter White recorded in a memo that Churchill was not willing to consider any change in Britain's relationship to her colonies. In fact, the Prime Minister felt that only "bloodshed and revolution" would follow from Indian independence. White then recorded Roosevelt's own "theory of handling revolutions," namely, "to build a wall around the country, toss over it arms and ammunition and say that when the revolution is over, the people could ask for help if they wished it."[56] White shared his views of the meeting with Eleanor Roosevelt, calling the session "a most interesting talk" and concluding that he (White) felt "real progress was made." It was important to the civil rights leadership that Mrs. Roosevelt be kept informed.

As with Mayor La Guardia on the issue of civil rights, Eleanor Roosevelt was, in the environment of that time, a liberal. At the same time, she had to point out to persistent civil rights advocates that the President was in a difficult political situation. If he pushed too hard for civil rights in Congress, he would jeopardize the support he needed from Southern legislators for his other important measures. She could say and do things the President could not. When a Negro friend, Pauli Murray, criticized President Roosevelt and compared him unfavorably to Wendell Willkie on the civil rights issue, Eleanor Roosevelt expressed distinct annoyance in a letter to Murray:

> I wonder if it ever occurred to you that Mr. Willkie has no responsibility whatsoever. He can say whatever he likes and do whatever he likes without having to take into consideration the southerners who control the important committees in Congress. . . . Of course I can say just how I feel, but I cannot say it with much sense of security unless the President were willing for me to do so.[57]

She spotted the same article in the *Reader's Digest* that La Guardia's assistant had called to his attention. The article, written by a Negro, had taken Adam Powell and others to task for the strident nature of their newspaper accounts of race relations. Eleanor Roosevelt liked the piece. Although she had appeared with Powell several times at civil rights and war bond rallies, she nonetheless felt that his vehement attacks on segregationists were probably ill-advised and should be tempered. She commended the article to Walter White, who did not by any means share her favorable opinion of the writer. She responded to White: "It seemed to me temperate and fair and mature. . . . At a time when feelings were so tense, I thought he [the writer] wisely criticized such people as the Reverend (Adam Clayton) Powell who add to the tenseness."[58]

This would be a perennial disagreement between the Roosevelts and those who supported the leadership style and substance of Adam Powell. It was, indeed, a manifestation of the different responses to the American Dilemma.

8

President Truman and a Report: "To Secure These Rights"

In November 1944, Powell had a new job and a new romantic interest. Isabel Powell had had enough of her husband's obvious amorous attention to Hazel Scott, the jazz pianist and popular nightclub singer from Trinidad. She began a lawsuit for separate maintenance. Powell, of course, denied that he was affectionately involved, and accused his wife of being "over-suspicious."[1] Certainly, he admitted, his roles as preacher and public servant required him to see the "opposite sex," and at times they would get "demonstrative." But this was "merely indicative of their agreement with me concerning the religious or political issue under discussion." Harlemites who knew Powell must have chuckled over this rather disingenuous explanation of his extramarital affairs. A settlement was reached and Mrs. Powell agreed to start out-of-state divorce proceedings. Hazel Scott and Adam Powell would marry in August 1945.

The year 1945 was the beginning of Harry Truman's Presidency following Roosevelt's death in April. Truman and Powell were destined never to get along. Interestingly enough, their wives would be the source of their permanent split—each man defending the honor and integrity of his spouse. The precipitating incident occurred in October, one year after Powell, assured of his own election, had made strong speeches supporting the Roosevelt-Truman ticket.

Although Powell's *People's Voice* had preferred Henry Wallace for

Vice President in 1944, the newspaper came to Truman's defense in the course of the 1944 Presidential campaign. Charges were leveled that Truman, from the old Kansas City Pendergast machine in the border state of Missouri, had earlier Ku Klux Klan sympathies, if not actual membership. Truman denied this and wired the NAACP a strong affirmation of his civil rights record as a senator and of his support for Roosevelt's New Deal policies. "I supported FEPC, I voted for cloture on the anti-lynching Bill. I voted for cloture on the anti-poll tax bill."[2] *The People's Voice* editorialized: "Senator Truman is a friend of the Negro people. . . . he has been right on every major issue of especial concern to Negro citizens. . . . a true progressive."[3] In spite of this record, Southern delegates clearly preferred Truman over Henry Wallace as Roosevelt's running mate, and they gave him their support. Better to have a true Dixiecrat, but short of that, Truman would do. Thus the Northern liberals and the Southern segregationists in 1944 settled for Truman as a lesser of evils from their respective political positions. Truman was not in the camp of the anti-Negro-ranting Senator Bilbo of Mississippi. He had made a forceful, albeit general, speech in 1940 before a Negro audience at the Democratic convention calling for fair treatment to all citizens:

> Numberless antagonisms and indignities heaped upon any race will eventually try human patience to the limit and a crisis will develop. We all know the Negro is here to stay and in no way can be removed from our political and economic life, and we should recognize his inalienable rights as specified in our Constitution. Can any man claim protection of our laws if he denies that protection to others?[4]

Like Eleanor Roosevelt and Fiorello La Guardia, Truman always made it clear that he was not advocating "social equality." This was the phrase at the time that connoted a range of personal relations between the races—intermarriage, especially—that a majority of white Americans feared and found objectionable. Truman's views were very close to those of Eleanor Roosevelt's and in the context of those times, these could be accepted by most civil rights advocates.

Notwithstanding, it was still with some apprehension that Negroes viewed his succession to the Presidency in April 1945. In spite of his Senate voting record, he was a relatively unknown entity. And he certainly did not bring an Eleanor Roosevelt to the White House as the First Lady and inside contact for civil rights groups. It was, indeed, this contrast between Mrs. Roosevelt and Mrs. Truman that was part of the permanent personal antipathy between Congressman Powell and President Truman.

In the fall of 1945 the new Mrs. Adam Clayton Powell, Jr., was denied the use of Constitution Hall in Washington, D.C., to give a concert. The hall was owned by the Daughters of the American Revolution (DAR), whose rules prohibited the use of the building by any but white performers. Six years earlier, in 1939, the rule had been invoked against the Negro contralto Marian Anderson, whereupon Mrs. Roosevelt resigned from membership in the DAR. This resignation was a further symbolic statement by Eleanor Roosevelt of her abhorrence of racial discrimination, and it was received in black communities with considerable gratitude and respect. Shortly before the Hazel Scott rejection, the DAR invited Mrs. Truman to tea. Powell promptly sent her a telegram, telling her to refuse, reminding her of Mrs. Roosevelt's earlier actions. Mrs. Truman responded: "In my opinion my acceptance of the hospitality is not related to the merits of the issue which has since arisen."[5] President Truman likewise informed Powell: "I am sure that you will realize . . . the impossibility of any interference by me in the management or policy of a private enterprise such as the one in question.[6] Powell, however, was not interested in constitutional or legal arguments about Presidential powers. His wife had been insulted blatantly because of her race, and he wanted the President and his wife to take a personal stand against that sort of racial bigotry. The Trumans disagreed, and Mrs. Truman attended the tea.

Powell immediately called her the "last lady" of the land. Truman was furious. *His* wife had now been insulted, and he referred to Powell at a staff meeting shortly afterwards as "that damned nigger preacher."[7] The episode went no further, but for the rest of Truman's Presidency—Powell's first six years in Congress—he never invited the Harlem congressman to the White House, even for the ritualistic receptions held each year for members of Congress and their spouses. Each man was protecting the honor and integrity of his wife, with racial prejudice at the center of the antagonism. This personal relationship carried over into other realms. From that point on, the Truman White House channeled all patronage jobs for Harlem through the office of Chicago Negro congressman William L. Dawson. This ultimate political rebuke to Powell, of course, left no fond feelings between Powell and his Chicago colleague. The least Dawson could have done, Powell probably reasoned, was to refuse to cooperate in the personal political vendetta of the President.

Whatever the personal relationship between the new President and the new congressman, the increasingly explosive issue of civil rights in the United States had to be faced. America was returning home in 1945 from a successful world war. Conversion to a peacetime economy was the number-one priority. The "double V" slogan (victory abroad and at home) of many civil rights advocates would now be tested. And 1946 provided a devastating picture of racial strife and attacks by whites on Negro veterans recently returned from overseas. Racial tension, along with labor union strikes, mounted. To some people, the war against the Axis Powers only interrupted the unfinished internal struggle of America's Dilemma. Civil rights advocates wanted the new President to take a forceful lead in urging Congress to pass legislation against lynching and violence, in favor of establishing a permanent FEPC, and in guaranteeing protection to Negroes in the South who sought the right to register and to vote.

Like Roosevelt before him, Truman was mindful of the power of the Southern electorate. Southerners occupied strategic positions in Congress. The Southern states were important in terms of Electoral College votes to any Democrat in a Presidential election. In other words, the New Deal coalition put together over a decade earlier by Roosevelt included and required the support of Southern segregationists. But it also needed the growing power of the urban black vote in the North. This was the balancing act Roosevelt faced and Truman inherited.

Civil rights leaders were aware of Truman's position, and they were keen on keeping the pressure on him. A. Philip Randolph organized a small delegation in August 1945, two weeks after the victory over Japan, to meet with the President. He sent a telegram to each invited member of the group, which included Rabbi Stephen Wise, Walter White, Dr. Channing Tobias, Mary McLeod Bethune, Philip Murray, William Green, Monsignor Ryan, and Bishop Oxnam. The purpose was to urge Truman to put FEPC bills [S. 101 and H.R. 2232] on his "must list" of legislation to be passed. The postwar economic situation of black Americans urgently required this law, Randolph stated.[8]

This meeting with the President never took place. Truman was not willing at that time to receive the delegation.[9] Instead, the President continued to voice his support for a permanent FEPC, but he did nothing of a substantial nature in urging Congress in that direction. Neither did he advocate additional funds for the existing FEPC created by Roosevelt in 1941. (The wartime agency ultimately went out of business in June 1946.) Truman's language, without question, was what civil rights leaders welcomed, but his actions were less than forthcoming. In the meantime, during his first year in office into 1946, he put primary emphasis on the economic issues of peacetime conversion, and hoped to maneuver around the politically divisive issue of civil rights. He did appoint a Negro lawyer, Irvin C. Mollison of Chicago, as a federal judge on the United States Customs Court—a first to the federal bench, obviously responsive to the request of Congressman William L. Dawson. He also made a Philadelphia Negro lawyer and NAACP member, William Hastie, governor of the Virgin Islands. His record that year was seriously blemished, however, when he ordered the soon-to-be extinct FEPC not to issue "cease and desist" orders to a particular local transit company in Washington, D.C. This directive so disappointed the NAACP lawyer, Charles H. Houston, that he angrily resigned from the FEPC. Thus President Truman was walking a political tightrope in 1945–46 over the civil rights issue. He frequently asserted that there was just so much a President, acting through executive fiat, could do; the laws—requiring congressional action—needed to be strengthened. But he personally was not actively engaging himself in the effort to bring about those laws. He spoke noble, general words in support of the constitutional freedoms, but there was little else. One historian concluded:

> In spite of his many public commitments to FEPC, the president rarely exerted pressure on Congress to act on this legislation. . . . While avoiding a bruising fight, he could still make certain ritualistic gestures on behalf of a good cause. A speech here and a letter there would assure him of some liberal support and gratitude for his efforts.[10]

There is little question, however, that in 1945–46, Presidential rhetoric could be interpreted by some civil rights people as a rather major change from previous decades of Presidential leadership, despite few concrete results. Woodrow Wilson's Democratic administration was a disaster for Negroes: under Wilson, Washington, D.C., became a strongly entrenched legally segregated city. The three Republican Presidents of the 1920s were little better. Franklin Roosevelt had a surrogate, his wife who paid attention to the issue, but he personally was not noted for his especially strong positions on civil rights. Therefore, Harry S Truman from Missouri was the first President to even offer language that attempted to raise the consciousness of Americans on the gap between the democratic ideals of the constitution and the practices in everyday life. This was far more than any President (with the exception of Abraham Lincoln) had ever done, and for this many civil rights advocates were grateful.

But matters would not remain static in that highly charged postwar period. And the issue of civil rights certainly would not lie dormant while the country sorted out the priorities of a new day. The "double V" was by no means achieved. The country was poised—North and South—for a leap into the middle of the twentieth century with a major war and a great economic depression behind it. Veterans were returning home to start families and launch careers. Society's volatility was evident at every turn, and *the* American Dilemma was as much a part of that dynamism as any other issue. Ironically, what President Truman did in 1946–47, using his executive authority to create a study commission, in combination with his general pronouncements of support for the constitutional rights of all, contributed more to the civil rights cause than the action of any prior modern-day President.

The country was in racial turmoil. Obviously, there needed to be something more in the way of new laws to overcome intransigent state governments. But what exactly should be done remained the issue. In February 1946 a Negro war veteran, still in his uniform, was dragged from a bus in Batesburgh, South Carolina, beaten and blinded by the local police. A local jury acquitted the attacker, the police chief. The same month in Columbia, Tennessee, the Ku Klux Klan went on a rampage and twenty-eight Negroes were arrested. Two were killed while in custody. Other acts of violence continued. Meanwhile, a National Emergency Committee against Mob Violence was formed, including Walter White, Eleanor Roosevelt, Channing Tobias, and James Carey of the CIO. After several months, the group was able to obtain a meeting with Truman on September 19, 1946. Ticking off the atrocious incidents of racial violence, the group urged the President to act. "My God!" Truman stated. "I had no idea that it was as terrible as that! We've got to do something!"[11] He agreed to appoint a Presidential commission to study not just the violence but the entire matter of "civil rights" and "civil liberties" and to make recommendations to him. A fifteen-member group was formed.

The President's move was met with cautious optimism from civil rights leaders and the Negro press. At least there was, for the first time, recognition from the highest office in the country that the issue of civil rights should receive the nation's official attention.

This in itself was progress. Truman chose the members carefully: Charles E. Wilson, president of General Electric, chairman; Attorney Sadie T. Alexander of Philadelphia; James B. Carey of the CIO; John S. Dickey, president of Dartmouth College; Attorney Morris L. Ernst; Rabbi Roland B. Gittelson; Frank P. Graham, president of the University of North Carolina; Francis J. Haas, Catholic bishop; Charles Luckman, president of Lever Brothers; Attorney Franklin D. Roosevelt, Jr.; Henry Knox Sherrill, Episcopal bishop; Boris Shiskin, AFL; Dorothy Tilly of Atlanta; and Channing Tobias. It was a moderate-to-liberal-leaning group. No segregationists were selected. The two Negroes were Alexander and Tobias, both of whom had ties to the NAACP and the National Urban League, respectively. Professor Robert K. Carr of Dartmouth and a scholar on civil rights laws was appointed to head the committee's staff.

This was a prestigious, independent group, and the fact that Truman would take the political risk in appointing it "to inquire into and to determine whether and in what respect current law-enforcement measures and the authority and means possessed by federal, state, and local governments may be strengthened and improved to safeguard the civil rights of the people" was impressive. Precisely what the committee would say and recommend was not predictable, but it was likely to make a statement that could only facilitate the civil rights in the long run—or so many liberals felt. After all, it did not contain adamant foes of civil rights. While there were Southern sentiments represented, these were in the persons of two people—Graham and Tilly—generally recognized as willing to see reasonably paced change brought to that section of the country. And importantly, even the NAACP had not come to the point in its campaign where it was prepared to challenge the very existence of segregation per se.

The committee met with more than twenty organizations, held hearings, and relied heavily on data supplied by the Civil Rights Section of the Department of Justice.[12]

Truman had made it known that he would appreciate, to the extent possible, a unanimous report, recognizing that such unanimity would strengthen the influence of the recommendations as well as the hand of the President in supporting them. Such a preference in itself indicated that Truman was taking his committee seriously. He was prepared to risk the political fallout that might come from the careful deliberations of this thoughtful, prestigious group. One historian observed:

> The Truman civil rights committee was a collection of notables, a blue ribbon panel. All had admirable records of public service, nearly half had held government positions during the war, yet all Committee members had built their reputations outside the government and politics. Significantly, these were prominent, independent citizens, not likely to be easily controlled or silenced, whose stature would add respectability to their task.[13]

While the members clearly were oriented toward racial change—there were no die-hard resisters to civil rights—the leaders of the major civil rights organizations were not on the committee. This was an obvious and, to the NAACP and National Urban League, acceptable recognition that the group should be composed of persons with less than full-time involvement in the civil rights struggle. Again, this was an attempt to enhance the ultimate value of the committee's work. In the final analysis, in the environment of the postwar 1940s, such a committee was a major political development on the American scene. Whatever it reported would be scrutinized thoroughly by the President, Congress, and all segments of society. The issue of civil rights in the United States had been given its first prominent position on the national political agenda. To that point, the "civil rights movement" had consisted mainly of decades of court cases challenging the denial of the right to vote in the South, efforts to secure antilynching legislation, cases against unequal treatment in higher education, appeals against discrimination in New Deal programs and in war industries, discrimination in jury selections, and efforts to secure equal salaries for teachers. On the local level, there were periodic mass protest efforts. With Truman's Committee on Civil Rights, formally launched at a White House meeting with the President in January 1947, the issue would be joined, and specific recommendations made for policy action. Gunnar Myrdal's book, *An American Dilemma*, would surely be relied on, but the committee would go further and stipulate in quite concrete terms what needed to be done to alleviate racial problems in the country.

Also hovering in the atmosphere at the time was the growing realization of the impact of America's internal racial problems on its image and influence abroad. The Cold War had begun. Restless peoples in Asia and Africa were beginning to clamor for their independence from European nations. And the Soviet Union, anxious to engage the growing ideological contest between Communism and capitalism, lost no opportunity to exploit Western weaknesses in the human rights arena. Truman was sensitive to these developments.

In an unprecedented move in the middle of the committee's deliberations, Truman accepted an invitation to address the annual convention of the NAACP. No President had ever so honored a civil rights group before. Rejecting the advice of some of his closest counselors, he decided to make a lengthy, forceful statement on civil rights. His words were general—there was no call for specific legislation, which presumably would come from his committee—but the tone was decidedly up-beat and liberal: "We can no longer afford the luxury of a leisurely attack upon prejudice and discrimination . . . we cannot wait another decade for another generation to remedy these evils. We must work as never before to cure them now."[14]

Unknown to most at the time, major portions of the speech had been written by Professor Carr of the committee's staff. This, again, encouraged the committee to come forth with more than mild proposals, confident that the President's general sentiments were in favor of a more bold approach to the problems. Civil rights groups and the Negro press were ecstatic and expectant. Truman had, in their eyes, come out of the shadow of President Roosevelt on this subject at least. There was a new Presidential rhetoric which was not to be discounted. If nothing more, it would add legitimacy to the struggle being waged by civil rights forces.

The committee labored over the summer and into the fall and presented its report to the President on October 29, 1947.

The report was a noble statement of the "American heritage" of freedom and equality, and how the country had fallen short of those promises. Here, it picked up the Gunnar Myrdal theme of a distinction between creed and practice. Then it spelled out the need to have a forceful federal government presence on this issue, flying in the face of the advocates of "states' rights." In the final section, a "program for action" was presented. There should be a civil rights division (not just a section) in the Department of Justice; also a permanent commission on civil rights established by Congress. And Congress itself should have a joint standing committee on civil rights. An antilynching law should be passed, and poll taxes done away with. Washington, D.C., should have home rule and the right to vote in Presidential elections. In addition, segregation in the military services should be abolished. Action on claims of Japanese Americans—who had their property confiscated during the war—should get "further study." Admittedly, a weak proposal. A permanent FEPC with real enforcement powers should be phased in over a one-year period.

Two recommendations, however, received less than unanimous

support. A majority felt that states should enact fair educational practice laws, but a minority could not accept this. Unquestionably, the most forceful recommendation came over the issue of withholding federal grants from those educational institutions that persisted in maintaining segregation. Tilly and Graham, from the South, thought this would do more harm than good. In an interesting reversal, Franklin D. Roosevelt, Jr., sided with those advocating the proposal. It later developed that he had spoken to his mother, Eleanor Roosevelt, who persuaded him to take the side of the more liberal members.[15] (The ironic aspect of this episode, as we shall see in Chapter 10, is that only a few years later Eleanor Roosevelt was urging the NAACP to take a more pragmatic stand involving a similar proposal introduced in Congress by Adam Powell.)

In all, the report listed thirty-three specific recommendations. It was, for the times, a bold document in the cause of civil rights. *To Secure These Rights* had gone even beyond what the NAACP had been advocating up to that point, namely the complete dismantling of *de jure* segregation. And because of the report, the NAACP decided that it would put on its agenda the matter of denying federal funds to segregated facilities. Truman's committee, whether he wanted it or not, had abruptly changed the debate, and altered the terms of discussion and bargaining over civil rights in the United States. Southern segregationists from that point on were on the defensive in protecting their legally segregated systems. Some Southern politicians would attempt to punish Truman for this in the 1948 Presidential election, but for the moment, Truman was identified properly as the first modern-day president to be associated with forceful advocacy of civil rights. The political tightrope he was walking was still very much evident, but the direction he intended to go was unquestioned. Roy Wilkins of the NAACP characterized the report as "the greatest stimulant to our program." No new laws were enacted; segregation and discrimination continued. But there was now a new agenda, indeed, one might suggest, a new moral climate.

Truman and Powell would never have an amiable personal relationship. But each in his own way was elevated and moved along interestingly similar paths in attacking the American Dilemma. The border-state senator-President had launched a committee that had issued a report beyond the expectations of most citizens. The congressman from Harlem now had a peg to latch onto, enabling him to put his stamp of leadership on the historic struggle. Two thoroughly different politicians were caught in a political whirlwind over one of the most delicate and emotional issues facing the country. The President's career would be seriously jeopardized—but ultimately salvaged. The congressman's career would be secured for the next two decades.

Indeed, it took almost two decades to achieve the policy recommendations of the committee. Those were years of the gradual dissolution of legal racial segregation, filled with constitutional arguments, executive decrees, and congressional bickering and bargaining.

Adam Clayton Powell, Jr., assumed a new, prominent role in the struggle. He became the quintessential irritant within Congress, a role that suited him perfectly, and one he obviously relished.

9

The Communist Party, the FBI, and "Mr. Civil Rights"

As early as 1942, if not before, the Federal Bureau of Investigation (FBI) took notice of Adam Clayton Powell, Jr. Director J. Edgar Hoover sent a letter to the bureau's Special Agent in Charge (SAC) in New York City stating:

> In view of the strong indications of Communist affiliations on the part of Powell, you are requested to immediately institute a discreet investigation of this individual. Your investigation should be conducted with a view of ascertaining background information on Powell, his connections and affiliations, radical activities into which he has entered and his connection with the Communist Party.[1]

In some form or other, the FBI collected information on Powell over the next twenty-eight years. In July 1942, the Washington office sent a nine-page single-spaced memo to New York on the history and background of Powell, giving a brief biographical sketch of his early years and noting his activities in protest movements. The *Daily Worker*, the communist newspaper, was digested carefully and all references to Powell were cited.[2] Hoover advised his subordinates in the New York office to take care in pursuing the investigation in view of Powell's standing in the community: "It is pointed out that in view of Powell's reported ministerial capacity, his prominence in Harlem and his political activity, your investigation must necessarily be of a very discreet nature."[3]

A few months later, Hoover indicated an impatience with the New York office. Apparently, he had not received the report he requested. The office told him that there were "other urgent matters" to tend to, and the New York agents had not been able to get around to the Powell investigation. Hoover, on October 5, 1942, reminded the SAC that a lot of information had been given to Washington and this matter should proceed promptly. He ordered:

> Your attention is directed to the considerable amount of information furnished by you to the Bureau concerning Powell reflecting this subject's activities among the Negroes in your Field Division, as well as his connections and affiliations with the Communist Party and various Communist Party front organizations. As you are aware, the Bureau is vitally interest [*sic*] in the Negro situation as well as those forces responsible for unrest and dissatisfaction among the Negroes.
>
> You are accordingly instructed to immediately institute an investigation concerning Powell and submit a report to the Bureau within thirty days after receipt of this letter.[4]

The New York office got the message. Its preliminary report (not available under the Freedom of Information Act) outlined Powell's activities and scrutinized issues of *The People's Voice.* Noting that Powell was "co-publisher," the transmittal letter to Hoover stated:

> From a perusal of "People's Voice" over a period of a month it has been ascertained that it follows closely the Communist Party line. . . . In view of the favorable attitude of this paper toward the Communist Party program and the activities of Powell in connection with the Communist Party, the New York Office has taken a six-month subscription for two copies of the "People's Voice," and one copy will be furnished regularly to the Bureau.[5]

Hoover instructed that rather than send the entire paper, "you have the paper clipped in the New York Field Division for items of interest to the Bureau's work and forward the same currently. The newspaper should be scrutinized carefully, not only for Communist matters but for matters of interest to the negro situation."[6]

After several months, the FBI in New York submitted its full thirty-page report on Powell on February 26, 1943. It noted that his "nationalistic tendencies" were "communistic," that he "has also been active as a member of and speaker before many of the alleged Communist front organizations." Powell had a selective service classification of 4-D, and on the Selective Questionnaire relative to conscientious objection, Powell had written, "I haven't fully made up my mind." Noting that Powell received the endorsement of the Communist Party newspaper, the *Daily Worker*, in his City Council race, the FBI also reported several of that paper's favorable items on Powell. Powell's vehement attacks on racists and on Congressman Martin Dies were reported, as well as his endorsement of Communist Benjamin Davis, Jr., to succeed him on the City Council. The report cited Powell's praise for the Communist Party: "It is time that the Negroes participated in the political scene as members of the democracy, not just as Negroes. This is the one reason I have always given credit to the Communist Party, because they have had the courage to run Negro people in national, state and county elections." The New York FBI Field Division ended its report by saying: "Will keep in touch with Confidential Informants . . . and other sources of information, in order to obtain and report the future activities of Adam Clayton Powell, Jr."[7]

The FBI read *The People's Voice* with great care. And the results were enough to cause the agency to question whether criminal action should not be brought against Powell and his colleagues on the paper. Often the paper published letters from Negro soldiers complaining of racial discrimination on the battle front, and objecting to brutal treatment by their own white officers. One corporal in the North African combat zone wrote detailing physical abuse and racial insults, and said: "We had white American soldiers to spit in our faces since we have been overseas. What could we do? . . . One or two of our soldiers have been killed for nothing by white MPs." According to this soldier, white officers slapped Negro soldiers and dared them to report the incidents.[8] This letter was printed in *The People's Voice.* The FBI alerted Hoover that such a letter, "If read by some young selectees, may affect his [*sic*] willingness to be inducted into the Armed Services of this country." The New York office wanted a Department of Justice opinion as to whether publication of the letter might be a violation of the sedition statute. Hoover forwarded the letter to the assistant attorney general with this notation: "I shall appreciate your advice as to whether you believe the publication of this letter may be considered as violation of any Federal statute within the Bureau's investigative jurisdiction."[9]

The FBI files contained several instances of this sort of concern. The agency was interested in the impact the publications of these complaints would have on the war effort and citizen morale. And the FBI reports linked race issues and consequences with Communism. A typical phrase from the New York SAC to J. Edgar Hoover read: "It is reported that the publication of such instances in the People's Voice tends to cause considerable conversation among Negro elements and communistically dominated groups concerning discrimination in the South and in the armed forces which apparently results in the reluctance of Negro inductees toward entering the armed forces."[10] There is no evidence that Powell was aware of this FBI concern or surveillance, but he did editorialize about the FBI in one of his columns in *The People's Voice*:

> The FBI has done a good job in rounding up foreign saboteurs. It has distinctly failed its mission as regards domestic Fascists. It is high time that it busied itself—if it isn't already too late. If they had spent half the time they used on rounding up crackpot Negro nationalists in rounding up perverted Klu Kluxers, Christian Fronters, and Coughlinites, then there wouldn't be any riots in America today. Our government has been mysteriously soft-headed in dealing with the big-time Fifth Columnists of America. . . . The Attorney General of the United States and the head of the FBI, if they are really serious about this and are given a clear-cut go-ahead signal from the White House can clean up America's brand of Fascism in short order.[11]

For its part, the FBI wanted to know if such language constituted acts of sedition.

Clearly, Powell and the FBI were fighting different wars.

When Powell arrived in the nation's capital, he hit the ground running. A thoroughly segregated city and a discriminatory government, Washington, D.C., and Congress were immediate targets for the new congressman. Eating facilities and barbershops on Capitol Hill were segregated. Congressmen and their staffs accepted this, even the Negro congressman from Chicago, William L. Dawson. But not Powell. He ordered the black members of his staff to use all the facilities, and he conspicuously did so himself. His every move on this front was widely publicized. He delighted in responding to Mississippi congressman Rankin's refusal to sit next to him in the House chamber. Using language that would come to characterize his tenure, he said: "I am happy that Rankin will not sit by me because that makes it mutual. The only people with whom he is qualified to sit are Hitler and Mussolini."[12] This is what many wanted to hear—an outspoken legislator not kowtowing to the racial bigots. Powell blasted the decision to make the Dies Un-American Activities Committee a permanent body. This was the work, he asserted, of "domestic fascism."

Powell continued his weekly column in *The People's Voice*, now calling it "Soapbox—In Washington." He used it to address a range of issues as he had before, but now he spent more time reporting on pending legislation and maneuvers in Congress. He championed the full-employment bill, calling it a "revolutionary idea." And while he noted that the bill did not guarantee against racial discrimination, he nonetheless felt it was important, first, to establish the principle of "the guarantee of a job for all—by the Federal government." He wrote to his constituents:

> Not only does such a measure face a bitter struggle to get through Congress in any sort of decent shape at all, but it faces a more bitter fight to be made safe for Negroes and minority groups. This phase of the matter will need clear and hard thinking. But first, let us get behind this bill in whatever form. It is about the biggest legislative thing that has ever happened in this country—for all groups.[13]

Interestingly, a few years later Powell would not take the same position on similar social policy legislation before the Congress. The amendments (discussed in the next chapter) he proposed forbidding federal expenditures to various agencies that maintained discriminatory and segregated facilities and practices would create an intense debate within liberal circles. But in his first year in Congress, he was willing, as indeed was the NAACP, to subordinate the civil rights goal for the moment in favor of getting the legislation passed.

He told his readers that on the whole he was treated cordially and that "many such as Bender of Ohio and Madden of Indiana go out of their way to make me feel at home."[14] He assured his constitutents that he was working hard, introducing five bills and joining forces with those opposing the "work or jail" bill.[15] "All of this, of course, means that there is not time for playing in Washington. I am rarely in bed later than nine o'clock and am usually up in the morning between 6:30 and 7 o'clock."[16] This apparently was intended to allay the fears of some of his critics back home who doubted his ability to tend to the tedious duties of a congressman. He ended each column with a reminder to his constituents that he would be available for consultation without previous appointment at 9:30 A.M. every Saturday at the office of *The*

People's Voice, 210 W. 125th Street and during the week by mail or telephone at the U.S. House of Representatives. One of his first speeches on the House floor was a slap at Congressman Rankin and an attack against a quota system in New York dental schools relating to Jews. Rankin, in response to a speech by the Jewish congressman Emanuel Celler, from New York, had said: "Remember that white gentiles of the country have some rights." Powell rose to Celler's defense and, without mentioning Rankin by name, stated: "Racial bigotry has no place in this nation and least of all in the House of Representatives. I am not a member of that minority but I will always oppose any who tries to besmirch any group because of race, creed, or color."[17] Powell was losing no opportunity to engage the issue of segregation and discrimination. Here, at last, was a congressman who would use the congressional forum to constantly state the position of racial equality. His constituents and supporters appreciated this.

He also leveled his criticism at the institution of Congress itself. There were too many committees with overlapping responsibilities and with too few staff members to do a proper job. He cited an instance of veterans' affairs falling within the jurisdiction of at least three separate committees. Some bills were not given proper attention, he charged, citing the amendment of the Bankruptcy Act. This was a complicated measure, but few congressmen had adequate information on which to cast a sensible vote. One of the leaders stated that the bill was "loaded with dynamite." Well, for Powell, he wanted more information, but "it was passed without even a vote being recorded and with close to 100 members absent from the House." He complained "that there is not sufficient legislative counsel or reference service to advise the members on just what 'dynamite' there is in the bills that come before it."

One got the impression of a new, young congressman wanting to be responsible to his duties, but frustrated by the enormity of the task and hampered by lack of access to relevant information. The high absentee rate seemed to appall him also. He gave every indication of studying the details of those bills he was most interested in and could get information on. He dashed off a stream of letters to government agencies questioning discriminatory practices, especially in the armed forces and relating to recruitment of Negro nurses. He introduced a bill—H.R. 2708—prohibiting segregation in the army and navy six months after V-J Day. He strongly criticized discriminatory treatment of Japanese Americans as opposed to German Americans. He alluded to American silence on the

Adam Clayton Powell, Jr., at age five.
(Courtesy of Isabel Washington Powell)

The Reverend Adam Clayton Powell, Sr., about the time of his retirement in 1937. *(Courtesy of Adam Clayton Powell IV)*

Isabel Washington, first wife of Adam Jr., as a nightclub dancer in the early 1930s, before their marriage. *(Courtesy of Isabel Washington Powell)*

A meeting in Harlem in 1936 after the release of a Mayor's Commission report on the Harlem riots of 1935. Powell Jr. is at the lectern. Among the others are Powell Sr., smiling at his son; Mayor La Guardia *(left of Powell Sr.)*; attorney Hubert Delany *(left of La Guardia)*, member of the commission and tax commissioner of Manhattan. *(Austin Hansen)*

Pickets protesting employment discrimination at the 1939 New York World's Fair outside Fair headquarters in the Empire State Building. *(Courtesy of the Schomburg Center for Research in Black Culture, New York Public Library)*

A picketer in Harlem protests employment discrimination by the bus company, 1941. *(Austin Hansen)*

Powell at a rally in Harlem in 1946, campaigning for reelection to Congress. *(Austin Hansen)*

Adam and Hazel Scott Powell, his second wife, celebrate their first wedding anniversary in August 1946, at home with their two-week-old son, Adam III. *(Morgan Smith)*

Powell with Congressman Vito Marcantonio *(left)* and Franklin D. Roosevelt, Jr., 1950. *(AP/Wide World Photos)*

President Eisenhower receiving a gift from congressmen, including Powell *(last row, left)*. *(Courtesy of the Dwight D. Eisenhower Library)*

Powell and His Imperial Majesty Hailie Selassie, Emperor of Ethiopia, on the occasion of the Emperor's visit to Abyssinian Baptist Church, 1954.
(Morgan Smith)

Powell at the Bandung Conference, 1955, talking to Foreign Minister Sunarjo of Indonesia.
(AP/Wide World Photos)

Powell talking to reporters at the White House, October 11, 1956, explaining his endorsement of President Eisenhower for reelection. *(Courtesy of James L. Watson)*

Powell with political friends, 1962. *Left to right:* J. Raymond Jones; Edward Dudley, borough president of Manhattan; Minetta Anderson; State Senator James L. Watson; and Powell. *(Courtesy of James L. Watson)*

Campaign rally for Averill Harriman's reelection as gov of New York, 1958. *(Courtesy James L. Watson)*

Rally in Harlem for John F. Kennedy for President, 1960. *Left to right:* Averill Harriman; Mayor Robert Wagner; Jaqueline Kennedy; Powell; John F. Kennedy; Lillian Upshur; Eleanor Roosevelt. *(Courtesy of* Ebony *magazine)*

Holocaust. "Regardless of what atrocities have been committed by the Japs, none of them can in any way measure up to the recently publicized horrors of Nazi Germany. All during the years, however, outstanding spokesmen of the world kept telling America what the Germans were doing, but we refused to believe it. Yet we believed anything we heard concerning the Japs. . . . A fascist is a fascist whether he is black or white, brown or yellow. Any American, I don't care who he is, who tries to play up Jap atrocities over German atrocities is merely trying to fight a white man's war and win a white man's peace, and brother that's fascism!"[18] He wrote that he was horrified at the confidential newsreels—shown to the Congress only—of the Nazi slave-labor camps. These pictures were "too filthy and depraved to exhibit to the general public."

He took on the State Department's decision to keep Japanese government control over liberated Korea. His telegram to Secretary of State James Byrnes questioned this policy. "This is in direct opposition to everything for which we have fought this war," he declared, and he introduced a bill (H.R. 1901) to authorize the naturalization and admission of Koreans into the United States. His ire was also directed at Britain's policies toward Hong Kong, and the plans for England to resume imperial rule over that territory. Clement Attlee's Labor government, he concluded, was no better than Winston Churchill's Tories. American foreign policy toward the civil war in China also drew Powell's attention. He wanted American troops out of China and no American interference in that country's civil war. He introduced a bill to that effect, which was referred to the House Committee on Foreign Affairs.

It is not known, but Powell likely had a record for the most bills introduced and speeches made on the House floor for a freshman congressman. Legislatively, these bills were, to be sure, ignored, but he was building a very quick record of an active, attentive new member of Congress. In his eyes, and those of many of his constituents, that is why he was elected. He was not there to be a shrinking violet—to go along, and make no waves. He could be ignored, and—as far as results from the congressional leadership were concerned—he was. But there was now at least a voice, a presence. Adam Clayton Powell, Jr., from Harlem was fast becoming "Mr. Civil Rights" in the Congress and the country. Concrete results, given the times and institutions, were not his to achieve. But as he saw it, that was not his defeat. If he persisted in raising the issues, in being as much of an irritant as possible, he was performing a historic role.

In speeches around the country, he aimed his fire at both major parties for failure to pass an effective, permanent Fair Employment Practices Commission (FEPC) bill. "Any American," he told a New York audience in July 1945, "who continues to accept the campaign promises of the Democrats or the Republicans is a gullible fool."

By February 1945, FBI reports were labeling *The People's Voice* a "negro communist newspaper," and continually pointing out Powell's senior position with the paper.

In the midst of the frenzy of his first months in Congress, Powell and Hazel Scott were married on August 1, 1945, in Stamford, Connecticut. Powell's partner in *The People's Voice*, Charles Buchanan, was his best man. A hugh reception followed at Cafe Society in New York. After a month-long honeymoon, the new Mrs. Powell left for a national concert tour, and Powell returned to Congress and his preaching-politicking. It would be a marriage of two very busy, popular, professional black Americans, constantly in the public eye, and seemingly comfortable with the divergent demands their respective professional lives would make on the marriage.

Powell kept a hyperactive schedule—speaking around the country, engaging in local political party fights in Harlem, preaching at Abyssinian Baptist Church, helping run *The People's Voice*. There was no question that he enjoyed every one of his activities, and he molded them into one piece—projecting himself as the militant, uncompromising fighter for civil rights and liberal socioeconomic causes. One so involved inevitably would make enemies, personal and political. He never hesitated to label whites who disagreed with him as fascists or Dixiecratic racists, and those blacks who fought him as "Uncle Toms." His oratory was becoming even more renown, mixing biblical references with current events, always using the well-developed Baptist-preacher style he had been practicing for almost a decade and a half. After his first term, there was no doubt in anyone's mind that he would seek reelection.

An *Amsterdam News* columnist, Earl Brown (who would be Powell's opponent for the congressional seat twelve years later) realistically assessed the chances of those who thought of challenging Powell. "There is . . . one vast difference between Mr. Powell and the other three [challengers]: he is going to win and they are going to lose. . . . Congressman Powell is still Harlem's political champ."[19] This was patently true, although Brown noted the enigma associated with his conclusion. Powell, Brown said, was really not liked by any of the parties—Democrats, Republicans, American Labor Party, even the Communist Party. "The Democrats would dearly love to ditch him. From President Truman to Eddie Loughlin, Tammany Hall leader. But they can't because Congressman Powell would win even though neither party backed him. . . . He is one of the few politicians extant who is not wanted by any party, but is sought by practically all of them."[20]

Perhaps. But the Republicans, who had endorsed Powell in 1944, when he captured their primary, decided they would mount a serious campaign against him. Republican governor Thomas E. Dewey was reasonably popular in Harlem and was running for reelection. Perhaps a strong Powell opponent for the congressional seat in the Twenty-second District could be mutually productive—for Dewey, and to unseat Powell. They selected a well-spoken, militant black former army chaplain, with a record of employment with the NAACP in Washington and Cleveland, who was then a student at Columbia University Law School. His name was Grant Reynolds. He was also state commissioner of corrections. His base was not in Harlem politics, but the local black Republicans accepted him as their standard bearer nonetheless. He had come to the attention of the statewide Republicans after a speech he had made at Madison Square Garden on behalf of Governor Dewey in 1944. This was enough for the Harlem Republicans—a man who had access to Dewey. In addition, Reynolds was a very good speaker, tall, and as handsome as Powell. He made a good appearance. More than a few around Harlem began to call the impending contest "the battle of the giants."

Reynolds immediately threw himself into the campaign, confident that he could match Powell on civil rights as well as commitment to public service. He blasted Powell's congressional absentee record—missing fifteen of thirty-two roll-call votes. Reynolds labeled the incumbent "Part-time Powell," and called attention to the enormous speaking fees—five hundred dollars—Powell got through a lecture bureau. For his part, Reynolds was in favor of a seventy-five cent minimum wage (over the current forty cents), low-rent housing, and an end to segregation in the military forces. The latter was a major personal sore point with Reynolds. As an army chaplain, he had suffered innumerable racial indignities on army posts during the war, and he complained publicly and bitterly, finally receiving an honorable discharge after bitter complaints of personal mistreatment as a black officer.

Following his previous strategy, Powell sought the Republican nomination as well as the Democratic. Thus he faced Reynolds in the Republican primary. Reynold's strategy was to engage Powell in a face-to-face public debate, force him to defend and specify his supposedly productive first-term record. Years later, Reynolds reminisced: "I thought that if I could get him on the public platform, I could beat him. He was emotional, and I thought I could get him flustered."[21] But Powell was having none of that. He knew that he had a comfortable lead (in the Democratic primary, at least), and the political adage of not giving your underdog opponent exposure was good enough for him. At various planned forums in the district, Powell either sent a surrogate (one once was Congressman Vito Marcantonio) or simply declined. Reynolds and the *New York Age* tried to make capital with this dodging, but to no avail. Reynolds understood this, but the frustration was no less evident.

Reynolds was also comfortable with his role as a Republican in a predominantly black Democratic district. He was not as enamored with the Roosevelt New Deal as apparently many blacks were. His assessment of the New Deal for blacks was the following:

> We were the only components of the Democratic Party that got the shaft. Labor got rights to organize. The South got agreement that agriculture and domestic servants would not be covered by Social Security. Jews got access. Catholics got support for parochial schools. Blacks got an invitation to go on welfare. I got tremendous applause when I talked about this. The New Deal confined us to a period of dependency that has not been gotten over yet.[22]

The *New York Age* endorsed Reynolds, and the *Amsterdam News* covered his campaign in the same favorable way that *The People's Voice* lent positive space to Powell.

The primary was on August 20, 1946, and on that day Powell easily won the Democratic endorsement to go along with that of the American Labor Party. But he suffered his first electoral defeat in his career at the hands of Grant Reynolds for designation as the Republican nominee. Reynolds nosed him out by five hundred votes in the Republican primary, and this was occasion for blaring headlines in the *Amsterdam News*: "Reynolds Gives Powell 1st Defeat." Reynolds promptly stated: "I regard my nomination as an indication that the people of the 22nd district are sick and tired of buffoonery and showmanship in politics. Furthermore, I regard it as an endorsement of Gov. Thomas E. Dewey and his grand record of achievement which has meant so much to the Negroes of this State."[23]

Powell sent a note to Reynolds: "Congratulations on your primary victory. Your party machine stuck by you." It was a cryptic remark intended to negate the view some might have that Powell was losing his grip on the constituents in Harlem.

The fact is, and many knew it, he was never in serious political trouble. Although the *New York Age* optimistically editorialized several weeks later, during the general election contest, that a Grant Reynolds win was "extremely likely," it was not to be. Powell went on to beat Reynolds in November by a two-to-one vote.[24] He would not have to worry about a serious challenge to his seat in Congress for more than twenty years. His political career in Harlem was confirmed. Apparently, a substantial number of the voters approved of the way he had conducted himself the first term. He now turned his attention to that role and the consolidation of a reputation as Mr. Civil Rights that stuck with him for the next decade and a half.

First, Powell made a decision to sever his ties with *The People's Voice.* In December 1946, he issued a statement that his congressional duties and the pastorate of Abyssinian were more than enough to occupy his time. He was selling his stock in the newspaper and resigning his positions as editor and chairman of the Powell-Buchanan Publishing Corporation effective December 10, 1946. The *New York Times* reported that Powell was advised to leave the newspaper because it had developed a clear reputation as Communist-controlled. He was advised, the *Times* said, "to end his ties with all left-wing groups. Many of Mr. Powell's supporters expressed the view that any connection with organizations of Communist persuasion would handicap his activities in the next Congress, which will be under Republican control."[25] Powell made no reference to this in his resignation statement.

He returned to Congress in January, the father of a new baby boy, Adam Clayton Powell III.

Back in Congress, Powell could be expected to introduce civil rights bills—in favor of a permanent FEPC, antilynching proposals, against segregation in interstate travel—and he did. These moves, however, were not really what made his reputation. In fact, when he would introduce a measure, civil rights supporters either looked for cosponsors or assumed that the bills would likely not get out of committee or even go to hearings. This was not so much a result of the fact that Powell had little political influence as it had to do with the subject of the proposals. In those years, no civil rights bills introduced by anyone were going anywhere. The NAACP, however, had little hope that Congressman Dawson, who at least was liked by the Truman White House, would be of much help. One NAACP letter from its Washington lobbyist, Leslie Perry, to Roy Wilkins stated bluntly: "Dawson can hardly be expected to push any bill."[26] When Powell came to Congress, at least he offered a willing vehicle to have bills introduced. In a report from the Washington NAACP to the director summarizing the status of current bills, Perry wrote that Powell was the sponsor of a bill aimed at ending segregation in interstate travel. The NAACP had sought additional sponsors without success, but "even so," Perry assured the NAACP officials in New York, the organization would fight to have hearings on the bill.[27] Therefore, when another congressman was unavailable, the NAACP, which was the major civil rights interest group on Capitol Hill, could count on Powell to put a proposed bill into the legislative hopper. How hard he would fight for it, or, if he did, how much support he could muster was another matter. But to the legislative in-fighters, the ones who had to count votes, make deals, sway doubters, and craft compromises, in the immediate postwar years into the 1950s, Powell was not particularly useful. Indeed, that was hardly his role. Such tasks were usually performed by more senior people in any case, ones who chaired committees and had built up credit with their colleagues. Few, if any, freshmen legislators had those qualities. Thus Powell's value in those early formative years in Congress was as an outspoken advocate. It was in that capacity that he would make the headlines, command attention, and, in the process, begin to build the reputation as "Mr. Civil Rights."

An illustration of this occurred early in the eightieth congressional session, Powell's second term. Joseph Martin, Republican from Massachusetts, was presiding in the House as Speaker, and a staunch segregationist—Rankin from Mississippi, Powell's old nemesis—was making a speech. Powell knew he would eventually use the word "nigger" as he frequently did in his speeches on the House floor. Indeed, he did, and Powell was on his feet.

Powell: Mr. Speaker, a parliamentary inquiry.
The Speaker: Will the gentleman yield for a parliamentary inquiry?
Rankin: No. I will not yield for that purpose.
Powell: Mr. Speaker, a point of order.

The Speaker: The gentleman will state his point of order.

Powell: Is it within the rules of this Congress to refer to any group of our nation in disparaging terms?

Rankin: It is not disparaging to call them Negroes, as all respectable Negroes know.

Powell: I am addressing the Speaker.

The Speaker: The Chair is not aware of the disparaging term used.

Powell: He used the term "nigger" in referring to a group.

The Speaker: The Chair understood the gentleman to say "Negro."

Rankin: Mr. Speaker, I said what I always say and what I am always going to say when referring to these people.

The Speaker: The gentleman will proceed in order.

Powell: Mr. Speaker, a point of order.

The Speaker: The chair overrules the point of order.[28]

Powell publicized this exchange back in his home district and throughout the nation's Negro press. This was his role. He could speak out, protecting the integrity of people so long denigrated. And he seized every opportunity to do this. On Sunday mornings he would return to the Abyssinian pulpit and deliver his ringing sermons which became a mixture of biblical text, political commentary, and reports from Congress. His basic message was always the same: challenging the society to overcome the American Dilemma, to bring its practices into line with its Creed. This was his theme and his approach as he toured the nation on speaking engagements, projecting himself and being presented as "that dynamic, militant advocate of civil rights, racial justice, and economic advancement for the little people." He was always careful to include the latter point, making it clear that Negroes and whites should stand together in the struggle.

During his first fifteen years in Congress, his reputation as "Mr. Civil Rights" stemmed essentially from two sources: his constant, vigilant championing of the liberal, civil rights cause on platforms around the country as a highly visible speaker from Congress; and the very controversial "Powell Amendment." The reputation was deserved, but it should also be noted that he, of course, was not alone in the civil rights forefront. There were several organizations and individuals devoting their full time and energies to the country's racial problems. The NAACP was the largest group, with its companion legal arm, the NAACP Legal Defense and Educational Fund (LDF). This organization, led by Walter White, Roy Wilkins, and Thurgood Marshall, was probably as well known nationally as

Powell, if not as brash and outspoken. A. Philip Randolph continued the fight for a permanent FEPC, and maintained his position as an uncompromising, dignified leader in both the labor movement and in civil rights circles. In time, Clarence Mitchell would become the full-time NAACP lobbyist in Washington, D.C., and would become known as the "101st Senator" because of tireless efforts lobbying in the halls of Congress. And, of course, Mary McLeod Bethune was still active on the civil rights scene into the early fifties. There was Paul Robeson on the left, frequently aligned with the United States Communist Party, along with the aging but still highly regarded W. E. B. Du Bois. This was the period of the NAACP's successful challenge in the courts to overturn legal segregation in the schools and in other areas, notably against restrictive covenants in real estate contracts, and in voting discrimination cases coming out of the South. These people were joined by white liberal allies, and they persistently mounted a legal and political campaign at the national level that served as the backdrop to the more mass-based civil rights struggle that would burst on the scene in the late 1950s. In a few short years, new leaders, especially Dr. Martin Luther King, Jr., would emerge, engaging in mass boycotts, sit-ins, and other protest actions.

But in the first decade or so after World War II, from his highly visible base in Congress, it was Adam Clayton Powell, Jr., who gave flourishing voice to the burgeoning aspirations of millions who wanted to see the country finally and successfully come to grips with the Dilemma—to end racial segregation and discrimination.

Powell was given a seat on the House Committee on Education and Labor, serving there in the Eighty-first Congress along with two second-term congressmen—John F. Kennedy from Massachusetts, and Richard M. Nixon from California. He was also appointed chairman of the subcommittee on the FEPC. He readily cooperated with the NAACP in sponsoring an amendment to the Taft-Hartley Law that required that no union be certified as the bargaining agent if it segregated or discriminated on the basis of race, religion, or national origin.[29] Clearly, the NAACP was more pleased than not with Powell's ready availability. Walter White, Roy Wilkins, and Clarence Mitchell had no illusions about the young congressman; they knew he was prone to grab the spotlight, and his record as a reliable, loyal team player was questionable. But, on balance, he was at that time an asset. In addition, he did chair a congressional subcommittee on FEPC, and he was to be accorded respect in that role even if at times he could prove a bit difficult to reach. At one point, Clarence Mitchell wanted urgently to confer with Powell on legislative strategy but was put off. Mitchell wrote a memo for the NAACP files in which he noted that Powell refused to take his call on one occasion, even though he informed Powell's secretary that he was calling on the advice of congressmen who were referring him to Powell. Powell apparently would move on the business before his subcommittee in his own time, and in his own way.[30] This was something the NAACP simply had to live with. Powell was his own man, and friend and foe would have to accept him on his terms. Over the next several years, Powell and the NAACP had a relationship that was more cooperative than antagonistic. The organization needed him, even if he was not the easiest person to work with. This certainly was the reason the NAACP decided to include Powell in its major civil rights programs. The potential for disappointment in such a relationship was always present, but worth the risk. There would come a time years later when this would not be the case.

For this reason, the NAACP decided to include Powell in a prominent role in a major conference planned for early 1950: a mass national emergency civil rights conference in Washington, D.C. The NAACP board decided to invite a broad cross-section of liberal and civil rights groups to Washington in January 1950, to lobby Congress on FEPC and for comprehensive civil rights legislation. It would be a highly publicized three-day meeting of speeches, panels, and lobbying. Representatives from labor, religious, and civic groups were invited, along with selected legislators. This was a historic undertaking; it was the first such nationwide mobilization of political forces for civil rights in the history of the country. The letter from Roy Wilkins, who was to chair the National Emergency Civil Rights Mobilization, inviting Adam Powell to participate was to the point: Wilkins told Powell that because he [Powell] was "the number one man on FEPC," it was proper that he should be the one to address the conference on that subject. The FEPC bill before the House would be Powell's responsibility, and he knew as much as anyone what was required for its passage.[31]

The conference came at a time when civil rights forces were caught up, as the country was, in the explosive controversies of the Cold War and charges of Communist infiltration in the United States. Intense debates raged in liberal-left circles over the wisdom of making common cause with Marxist-oriented groups. The NAACP, which was the originator of the conference, had always protected its position on this issue. The organization was decidedly anti-Communist, and it had no intention of letting the "leftists" move in on the conference and dilute its emphasis on civil rights by introducing other issues—such as the U.S. role in foreign affairs. Roy Wilkins made it clear that neither was this intended to be a Truman-bashing meeting. The focus would be on mobilizing a national base of support for the Truman administration's civil rights program in Congress. The aim was to demonstrate to Congress sufficient nationwide political support for FEPC and other civil rights measures. In addition, the conference, consistent with NAACP style, would be one of orderliness and respect.

Over fifty organizations agreed to participate, including the Americans for Democratic Action, Jewish War Veterans, the Catholic Interracial Council, the CIO, AFL, National Council of Negro Women, the Negro Elks, and various Negro church groups. In all, there were approximately 4,037 officially registered delegates from thirty-three states. In his letter to Clark Clifford in the White House, Wilkins stated: "They are not of the extreme left wing. . . . The Communists would like very much to horn in on the proceedings, and they are doing their best to do so. We know that they will not be officially represented in the delegation, but a few of them may creep in as representatives of other organizations."[32] And he firmly informed Communist William L. Patterson that he rejected his offer of "cooperation" and "support." Patterson had suggested that Benjamin Davis, Paul Robeson, Henry Wallace, and Vito Marcantonio be invited to address the conference. They were not. "We are not here," Wilkins wrote, "for malicious heckling and embarrassment." And in an article prepared for the *New Leader*, Wilkins wrote: "It [the conference] is a non-partisan, non-left movement, rejecting the persistent proffers of 'cooperation' and 'assistance' made by individuals and organizations long identified as apologists for communist doctrine and Soviet foreign policies."[33]

The organizers of the conference tightly controlled credentials of delegates permitted to attend, drawing criticism from some quarters, especially from Louis Lautier of the Negro Newspaper Publishers Association, I. F. Stone, and others who felt the civil rights cause could benefit from a broadened support base on the left. NAACP spokesmen defended their actions. Thurgood Marshall, then special counsel of the NAACP and actively engaged in trying cases in the courts against segregation and discrimination, and later (in 1967) to become the first black Associate Justice of the U.S. Supreme Court, wrote to Lautier a long but most revealing letter.

He bluntly reminded Lautier that the American Communists had in the past used the civil rights cause for their own purposes, and at times, as with the Hitler-Stalin Pact in 1939, "the left-wing organizations sold Moses down the river." Marshall was wary of such relationships, having also experienced what he considered to be left-wing deviousness in the many court cases the NAACP was trying against segregation and discrimination. The civil rights movement should not be complicated with other issues, he felt, especially foreign policy, which was what the Communists would try to do. And he was intent on working with those "who consider the Negroes' problem the top problem." Therefore, it was entirely justifiable from his point of view to exclude the Communists from the Mobilization Conference and to thwart their infiltration attempt.[34]

The conference was a major event for civil rights advocates at that point in the struggle. The focus was simple and clear: to pressure Congress to move on civil rights legislation and to strengthen the hand of the President in this effort. This meant overcoming the House Rules Committee, which was blocking the bringing of measures to the floor, and beating the contemplated Senate filibuster. The conference wanted Truman to pressure congressional leadership in both congressional chambers in these fights. But there was decided preference in treating President Truman gingerly. This was not to be a meeting that laid blame at the doorstep of the Presidency. The problem, the organizers concluded, was the Congress, not the President. The point was to enlist President Truman in as courteous and polite a way as possible to use his position to persuade the congressional leadership to be supportive.

Congressman Adam Clayton Powell, Jr., understood this strategy. All the conferees did. The organizers had made the general line of attack known to all invited to speak. Powell decided not to involve himself in the Communist-delegate-exclusion issue that surfaced and created some dissension among some delegates. Already by then he was beginning to distance himself from the overt Marxists he had been allied with over the years. Whatever the earlier advantages of associating with the Communists, he now obviously concluded that that relationship was no longer viable. Instead, he would step up his attack on the political decision-makers, and reinforce and secure his militant niche in that way. Therefore, the January 1950 conference, with all the controversial trappings of Communism versus anti-Communism, offered him a good platform to reassert his militant civil rights credentials. He seized the opportunity. The previous speakers had pretty much followed the script outlined by the organizers, namely, to concentrate their attack on Congress. Powell would not be so contained. The other speakers might be soft on President Truman, but not Powell. The House Rules Committee had planned to offer to repeal the twenty-one-day rule whereby, after that period of time, a bill could come before the House if the Rules Committee failed to act. If repealed, the rule would offer a serious obstacle to civil rights legislation inasmuch as the Rules Committee was controlled by Southerners hostile to civil rights. This was Powell's handle.

Impeccably dressed in a bow tie, and a white handkerchief draped from his suit pocket, he was in his finest form as he mounted the platform and hovered over the four thousand delegates, many of whom held no brief for the Communists, but also wanted more than polite stroking from the administration, which they felt could, in fact, do more in pressuring Congress to act. One account, friendly to the radical left, reported Powell's "bombshell." Powell blasted into the microphone: "I demand that a delegation from this mobilization force an audience with the White House. . . . If the President doesn't call in House Speaker Rayburn, Majority Leader McCormack, Majority Whip Percy Priest, and John Lesinski, chairman of the Labor and Education Committee, to make them see to it that FEPC comes up under the 21-day rule and is passed—then Truman hasn't kept his promise to the American people."[35] Powell had thrown the ball into *Truman*'s court; the President should be forced to take more responsibility in leaning on Congress.

This was not the kind of demand or pressure the conference organizers had in mind. "The leadership was horrified. The delegates were overjoyed," one reporter wrote.[36] And several delegates began to press for more vigorous action: "What is going to be done about Congressman Powell's demands that we see the President, Rayburn, McCormack, Priest and Lesinski?" The organizers had, indeed, planned to see Truman, but not in such a strident manner, and certainly not with the intent of putting a kind of ultimatum to him to call in the congressional leadership. Powell had pushed the issue in a direction that would make the meeting with Truman more of a confrontation than one of friendly consultation on political strategy.

Wilkins and the other NAACP organizers of the conference surely were not surprised, although likely disappointed, by Powell's posture. They had known him as one inclined to speak with intent to ignite an audience. Dealing with Powell in such settings always carried that risk. Thus, at this important and historic first meeting of its kind, a mass coalitional gathering in the nation's capital for civil rights, Adam Clayton Powell had seized the opportunity to position himself as the most militant among the respected leaders. He was going as far as he could while remaining within the fold of acceptability. And in the process, he quietly skirted the anti-Communist issue as an ideological struggle he did not want to join openly, much as he had preferred to do in the 1930s and early 1940s on the picket lines in Harlem. Except that now, instead of attempting to reconcile and broker differences, he sensed—in the general national atmosphere of the early 1950s—a perceptible decline of the Marxist-left's appeal, and in his own way moved away from that group, always protecting his militant civil rights credentials.

This style of behavior was not always consistent with the calculated moves of the civil rights forces. The NAACP had wanted to work more methodically on the House leadership in getting legislation out of the Rules Committee. But Congressmen F. D. Roosevelt, Jr., and Adam Powell jumped the gun. Roosevelt initiated a discharge petition, and Powell took his own independent action. Roy Wilkins described his own frustration in a letter to Walter White, in which he pointed out that the strategy of the civil rights groups was to keep the pressure on Speaker Sam Rayburn to bring along as many votes as possible. This, he said, could best be done by the quiet buttonholing and persuading for which the Speaker was noted. But Congressman Roosevelt, without consulting anyone, introduced a discharge petition to get the FEPC bill out of the Rules Committee. To Wilkins, this was ill-advised, because it took the pressure off Rayburn to produce supporters. Powell erred, according to Wilkins, by "sending a threatening letter to all Republicans" promising to expose their positions against civil rights. Powell also blasted Congressman Roosevelt for the premature discharge petition. This was too confrontational for the NAACP forces and served to win no friends and to influence few if any supporters. Wilkins was indeed frustrated and concluded, "The stupid fight between Powell and Roosevelt made matters infinitely worse."[37]

Powell continued his independent line, blasting away at those in both parties dragging their feet on civil rights. Before a black college commencement audience at Wilberforce University in Ohio he lashed out at Democrats and Republicans for "selling the Negro down the drain." A "backlash of reaction," he charged, was sweeping over our country. A motion of his to end segregation in Washington, D.C., received only nineteen out of 433 votes, he stated. "The time has arrived for the major parties to either set up a bipartisan program of civil rights or give up and acknowledge that it is nothing more than the cheapest of political frauds."[38]

But Powell did not escape the harsh criticisms from some of his old allies on the left. In the midst of the Korean War, he announced on January 24, 1951, on the House floor, that for the duration of the war he would, in the interest of unity, suspend his attempts to get antisegregation amendments to military appropriations. He also noted that he disagreed with Paul Robeson earlier when Robeson asserted that Negroes would not fight a war against Russia. The *New York Times* took note of this announcement in a short news item.[39] But Powell's onetime ally, Benjamin Davis, who had succeeded him on the New York City Council, pounced on his decision as "a surrender to the powerful reactionary pressures exerted upon him by big business interests, with which he has strong financial, property and political ties, especially through the Democratic Party."[40] Now Powell was getting from the left what he had been leveling at segregationists and "Uncle Toms" for years. Although Powell still made "fiery speeches" and was one of "the most militant sounding of the Negro reformists," Davis wrote, Powell had "adopted a line of surrender to the warmongering oppressors of the Negro people." He accused Powell of being the perfect foil of "Wall Street masters," precisely because "Wall Street needs a radical-sounding orator who can dress up the 'white supremacy' war program so that it sounds like a militant struggle for Negro rights. That's Rep. Powell."[41]

A political marriage that had been tenuous at best for some time had now ended. In all likelihood, this was probably not too disappointing for Powell. He had for some time, probably since his break five years earlier with the now defunct *People's Voice*, been moving in that direction. He had likely concluded that there was little political advantage to a continued relationship with the Communists, especially in light of the growing Cold War antipathy to the American Communist Party. Powell no longer needed them, and he might well have concluded that they were, on balance, a greater liability than asset. He could protect his base without their support.

For its own part, the FBI had a rather confusing time over the years deciding how to deal with Powell's earlier flirtation with the Communists. On the one hand, Powell often shared platforms with Communists and lauded their civil rights advocacy. On the other, he clearly was not a card-carrying member, and the FBI files revealed a taped telephone conversation in 1945 wherein Powell specifically told a person to whom he was speaking that he, Powell, was not a Communist. Powell apparently was complaining about an article Benjamin Davis had written in the *Daily Worker.*[42] But time and again, the FBI field reports to J. Edgar Hoover noted his friendliness with the Communist Party. One report concluded: "Available information fails to indicate that Powell is a member of the Communist Party, however, he has participated in numerous Communist front groups."[43] This politically enigmatic young black activist from Harlem apparently did not fit the expected mold of what the Bureau understood to be the profile of one who conducted himself as Powell did. His actions and affiliations were not simplistically explained by those who saw such matters in cut-and-dried, loyalty-versus-disloyalty terms. While he was not an avowed party member as was Ben Davis, neither was he simply a strong advocate for civil rights who eschewed the Communists as did the NAACP leaders. The FBI in the 1940s at least had a difficult time with this type of civil rights figure. He would probably be characterized, though the FBI files did not use the term, in the popular jargon of the time as a "fellow-traveler," at most.

The FBI and the House Subcommittee on Un-American Activities (HUAC) also had their suspicions about Powell's second wife, jazz pianist Hazel Scott. She was called to testify before that committee on September 22, 1950. HUAC had released a list of suspected subversive organizations with which Mrs. Powell had been associated. Unlike some of her colleagues in the entertainment field, Hazel Scott agreed to appear and to deny that she was a Communist. Recognizing her special relationship as Powell's wife, the committee chairman, Congressman John W. Wood of Georgia, tended to be unusually solicitous of her, but nonetheless insistent in probing her associations. He permitted her to make an opening statement, adding: "I would like to point out, however, that we would not like this to be considered as a precedent for any other person who has been adversely mentioned in publications throughout the country to use this committee as a means of answering such charges. We are making an exception in your case in view of the fact you are the wife of one of our colleagues."[44]

Hazel Scott denied the "malicious charges" that she was a "communist sympathizer." She admitted that she had been associated as an entertainer with some groups that were considered disloyal, but when she discovered their purpose, she "discontinued [her] activity." She defended her membership in three entertainer unions and stated that ". . . the American entertainment industry has no place for Communists. The entertainment unions should oust any Communist member, but only through orderly procedures presenting opportunity for rebuttal and defense."[45] She maintained her strong support for civil rights, and insisted that this did not, notwithstanding her occasional associations, make her a Communist. At the conclusion of her testimony, Congressman Francis E. Walter (Pennsylvania) asked her the familiar question which some witnesses had refused to answer:

"Are you now or have you ever been a member of the Communist Party?"

Not choosing to take the Fifth Amendment right to refuse to answer the question, Mrs. Hazel Scott Powell responded: "I am not now, never have been, have never entertained the idea, and never will become a member, which is something nobody has ever asked me."

In her prepared statement, she was adamant: "I, for one, Mr. Chairman, am not ready to hand over America's entertainment industry to Moscow."

She insisted: "I will maintain my fight for the application of our liberties to all regardless of color and creed. Those of the far left and far right have no place in this fight. The latter have no respect for liberty; nor do the former, although they mouth the slogans. But the fact that Communists pretend to stand for the causes for which I stand will not make me abandon the battle. If they should infiltrate my organizations, I will try to rally my colleagues to oust them, so we can continue the fight most effectively. But I refuse to surrender the burning issues of our day to the enemies of democracy."[46]

This statement by his wife at that time very likely reflected Congressman Powell's general sentiments on the Communist issue and civil rights. More than a few civil rights fighters had always resented the effort of segregationists and conservatives to link the two causes, with the implication being that one who severely criticized the denial of civil rights in the United States somehow had to be influenced by subversive elements. Some civil rights workers were not able to escape the brush of guilt by association. But Powell's status as a popular congressman provided him added protection from HUAC and the FBI probing into his own activities in this area.

Powell's reputation as a civil rights fighter and astute politician also earned him the respect of the New York Democrats, who now recognized that he was, indeed, an entrenched political force to be reckoned with. In 1952 he became the state's first delegate-at-large to the Democratic National Convention. The *New York Times* bluntly declared that this was "to emphasize [the Democratic State Committee's] support of a strong civil rights program."[47] The 1952 Presidential campaign provided him another chance to assert his militant credentials. He went to the Democratic convention as a supporter of New York's W. Averell Harriman, but the convention chose Governor Adlai Stevenson, and Senator John Sparkman of Alabama as the Vice-Presidential running mate. Both the Democratic civil rights plank in the platform and Sparkman were immediately attacked by Powell. The platform was weak on FEPC and Sparkman had an anti–civil rights record. Following the convention, Powell returned to Harlem and launched his own intraparty political struggle. At a rally of three thousand at the Golden Gate Ballroom in Harlem he attacked the Democratic convention as a "sellout." He particularly singled out his Negro congressional colleague from Chicago, William L. Dawson, who was on the platform drafting committee and reportedly argued for a mild, compromised civil rights plank. Dawson, said Powell, was an "Uncle Tom." "I am not saying that any money had to pass to Dawson, for there always have been men who for a slap on the back are willing to sell their people down the river."[48] He also blasted House Speaker Sam Rayburn for trying to win over the Southern delegates at the convention. "I charge now openly that Speaker Sam Rayburn used every trick at his command to bring back into the convention the Dixiecrats who had been overwhelmingly put out. He disregarded all principles of fair play and rules of parliamentary procedure. . . . It was an absolute disgrace."[49] Blasting Dawson was one thing, but to take on the most powerful leader in the House of Representatives was another. Some questioned Powell's wisdom, even if he had cause to be, as many liberal Democrats were, unhappy with the candidates' stands and the platform on civil rights. But Powell also knew that some people would see his blasts as acts of political courage and praise him even more for speaking out. Pending satisfactory responses from Stevenson and Sparkman in meetings he would have with them, Powell suggested the possibility that Negroes should boycott the 1952 Presidential election. Vote only for county, city, and state candidates, he urged, unless there would be firm assurances "from Governor Stevenson and Senator Sparkman that they will campaign on a more forthright civil rights program than the ambiguous one adopted in the party platform."[50]

At the Harlem rally, where he was introduced to an admiring

crowd as "Mr. Civil Rights," he rose to his best oratorical heights when he stated that he was advised against bucking the national party leadership. It was, he was counseled, "political suicide." He told the receptive audience that he rejected such caution: "They failed to realize that before I was a politician I was a Negro and that before I was a Negro I was a man. . . . We are the new Negro and we will continue to walk together. Nobody can stop it. If this is Armageddon, let it be Armageddon. You can't sell out Harlem." And his Harlem constituents ate it up. Adam Powell, indeed, was their man . . . and he knew it.

There were also cooler heads in Harlem who knew that there would be no organized boycott of the Presidential election by Negroes. It was, on balance, not in their interests. Powell would have his time on the platform (and possibly up the ante for his support for the ticket), but he would come around. Perhaps it was simply his way of keeping the pressure on, but many other Negro leaders felt a Stevenson-Sparkman ticket was still preferable to an Eisenhower-Nixon slate. Walter White was one, as were several Harlem district leaders, including Joseph Pinckney and Herbert Bruce. The latter two wired Sparkman that Truman's and Senator Herbert Lehman's support of the platform was "good enough for us." Powell was being "irresponsible," said several Negro organization spokesmen, including A. Philip Randolph of the Brotherhood of Sleeping Car Porters. But Powell had reinforced once again his position as an outspoken advocate of no compromise on civil rights. Of course, he *would* compromise and come around to supporting the ticket. Very few who had come to know the voluble congressman from Harlem really ever doubted that he would. In their view, he was simply pursuing his traditional practice of having his cake and eating it, too. There were some, also, who believed that Powell was simply putting a high price tag on himself before the national party for his ultimate support and active campaigning. This latter assessment of Powell's criteria for political endorsement of candidates followed him throughout his political career.

10

The Eisenhower Administration, the "Powell Amendment," and the Liberals' Lament

With the Republican victory in 1952, Powell was faced for the first time with a different party in the White House. This would not necessarily mean too much, since he had never benefited from a Truman Democratic White House. In fact, there was the distinct possibility that Democrat Powell would enjoy *more* access to the Republican Presidency than he had to the Democratic one. This turned out to be the case, although Powell continued to push for strong civil rights measures. But his political posture toward Eisenhower was far different from that toward Truman. He decided to attack Eisenhower's "official family"—his cabinet officers—and to publicly assume that they were *not* doing the bidding of the President in moving faster on civil rights. In all likelihood, this strategy was pursued in recognition of the high personal popularity of the President. At any rate, it gained him access to and recognition from the new White House team that was in stark contrast to the treatment he received from the Truman White House. (Of course, he would not make the political mistake of insulting Mamie Eisenhower as he had Bess Truman.)

But the new man in the White House was diametrically opposed to Powell on several crucial issues regarding civil rights. Eisenhower had testified before Congress in 1948 that he opposed integration in the army below the platoon level,[1] where soldiers were housed together in army barracks. It was not wise, he felt, to try, through laws, to force one to accept another. He clearly did not believe that the federal government should step into the racial arena, where, to his mind, the state and local authorities were the more preferable actors, if at all. Above all, relying on the age-old argument of the defenders of segregation, he was against "social mingling" and rejected the thought that "a Negro should court my daughter."[2] FEPC at the national level was abhorrent to him; if anything, states should deal with such problems. But time and again, Eisenhower went on record as one who believed that it was not proper to rely on legislation. America's racial problems—and he often indicated that he hated to use the words "racial" and "discrimination"—could best be overcome through patient devotion to education and the development of goodwill. Such views, therefore, would obviously lead him to eschew any approaches except the quiet, least-publicized efforts. This stance certainly made him out of step with the developing attacks against legal segregation and discrimination then being made by the NAACP in the courts.

Perhaps one of the most insightful analyses of the new President's views on the subject came, painfully, from Arthur Larson, who served for a time as his special assistant, and as Under Secretary of Labor. After revealing that Eisenhower once flatly stated that the Supreme Court's school desegregation decision in 1954 "was wrong," Larson concluded: "There emerges the inescapable conclusion that President Eisenhower, during his presidential tenure, was neither emotionally nor intellectually in favor of combating segregation in general."[3]

When Eisenhower talked about not wanting a Negro to "court" his daughter, Larson was convinced that this was a President out of step, on this issue, with the dynamic developments beginning to unfold. Larson concluded:

> There it was. The oldest cliche in the race relations dialogue, a cliche that was threadbare even at the time of the Lincoln-Douglas debates. From that time on, I realized that this man, whose views on so many other subjects were easy for me to identify myself with, had views on race relations that to me were distinctly old-fashioned or of another generation, and not a little Southern. Indeed, he himself made a practice, particularly when trying to conciliate some of the more intractable Southern Senators, of stressing the fact that he was born in the South and had lived in the South a considerable part of his life.[4]

Eisenhower's personal secretary, Ann Whitman, likewise recorded her experience with the President on the civil rights issue. She, like Larson, was far more a proponent of civil rights than her boss. She knew, to her consternation, of his disagreement with the Supreme Court's 1954 ruling against school segregation, and at times she gently tried to nudge him in the direction of a more progressive view.[5]

This was the man who would occupy the White House for the eight years that Adam Powell was building his reputation as a vigorous congressional civil rights defender. It would not be easy to attack Eisenhower directly. He was so popular—a war hero, kindly and dignified in many ways, obviously seen by many in the country as a welcomed change from twenty years of the Democrats in the White House, especially, the last seven under Truman.

Powell had to develop a political strategy that would not openly antagonize and alienate Eisenhower personally, but yet maintain his role as a strong advocate for civil rights. He chose to go after the President's appointees, and to charge that *they* were not carrying out the *President's* policies of "equal justice." This would be no easy task, especially since those appointees were familiar with Eisenhower's deep-seated convictions on the subject. And at the same time, Powell wanted to be able to keep open his own lines of communication with the new Republican regime. There were always favors a congressman could get from the Executive Branch. Powell had never experienced that. Party aside, he would attempt the delicate balancing act.

His first major salvo came on June 3, 1953, when he released a telegram he had sent to the President, who had been in office six months. In it, Powell charged that the Secretary of Health, Education and Welfare Oveta Culp Hobby, Secretary of the Navy Robert Anderson, and an official of the Veterans Administration were definitely defying the President's policies of ending racial segregation in federal government facilities. The *Washington Evening Star* ran a large headline: "Hobby Flouts Seg Order, Powell Charges." Powell softly stroked Eisenhower and proceeded to blast the others:

> The hour has arrived for you to decisively assert your integrity. You cannot continue to stand between two opposite moral poles. You stated publicly to the White House press and the news rang around the world in the hearts of freedom-loving people everywhere: "I find no moral or legal justification for the use of Federal funds in the support of segregation." . . .

> Your official family in the past 5 days has completely undermined your stated position on segregation.[6]

Powell proceeded to cite instances where the three appointees specifically indicated that they would continue to implement past practices of segregation—in Southern VA hospitals out of respect for "local customs"; in naval shipyards in Charleston, South Carolina, and Norfolk, Virginia; and in segregated schools on army posts. Seeking, apparently, to play on Eisenhower's long, illustrious career as a top-ranking general in the military, Powell labeled the acts of the three as "insubordination"—a term any military officer would understand and reject. Powell wrote to Eisenhower: "This is insubordination. This is not support of you as the Commander in Chief and the President of the United States. This detracts from the dignity, integrity, and power of your office." Powell was using all the references and symbols he suspected might get General cum President Eisenhower's attention. And he continued the soft stroking. He referred to the President as "a man of good insights, decent instincts, and strong moral character." He wanted these traits to be used, and he asked of the President "the courtesy of a personal reply."[7]

The White House was alarmed and furious. But Eisenhower and his aides seemed less perturbed at the conditions Powell described than at the manner in which he raised them. The congressman had gone public first, before informing the White House of his intentions. *That,* to the President's aides, apparently was not courteous—if one wanted to talk about "courtesy." The chief aide in the White House at the time who dealt with delicate racial matters was Maxwell Rabb, who later said that although most people certainly knew that what Powell described was correct, the issue of civil rights was so "lacking in visibility" that to so expose conditions "came as a great surprise." But apparently the issue at the White House was one of "protocol." Powell, Rabb said, should have sent the letter to the President first.[8] Rabb was immediately dispatched to Capitol Hill to see Powell.

"Well, Max. You're a little late," Powell reportedly greeted Rabb. "I expected you a bit sooner than this."

Rabb was aware that he had to handle Powell carefully. Rabb and Powell proceeded to discuss how they could work things out. There should be a "bridge built between" the two, in Rabb's words. Rabb suggested that Powell write the President "and tell him how sorry you are that you went to the press without giving him the courtesy of seeing the letter first. I can assure you he will remedy all this because it deserves to be remedied. And we'll go to work on it immediately."[9]

Thus began a relationship between Powell and Maxwell Rabb—not really Eisenhower. Rabb was to be Powell's main contact in the administration, and eventually a respectful relationship developed.

Three days later, Eisenhower sent Powell a reply to his telegram. (If Powell sent a letter of apology it was not made public.) The President continued the mild mutual-respect approach. He thanked Powell for his "kind expression of confidence," and he assured him that his Administration would pursue "the purpose of eliminating segregation in federally supported institutions." He then made a pledge to move forward on these issues.[10]

For the moment, this was good enough for Powell. He immediately answered and his encomiums became even more effusive, bordering, characteristically, on hyperbole. He told the President that his letter "justified my confidence in you." Powell was pleased that Eisenhower would assert his leadership as President. Powell went on:

> The most significant statement in your letter, and the one which makes it a Magna Carta for minorities and a second Emancipation Proclamation is: "We have not taken and we shall not take a single backward step. There must be no second class citizenship in this country."

Two such sentences in a Presidential letter to a Negro congressman, even in 1953, could hardly compare with the Magna Carta or the Emancipation Proclamation, but then, too, Powell was known to engage at times in excess. He proceeded to list five specific things he hoped the President, acting solely through the Executive Branch, would see to: the continuance of FEPC by Executive Order; continuance of the Committee on Government Contract Compliance; elimination of the naval policy of segregation in on-shore establishments; a change in the policy of the Federal Housing and Home Finance Administration to give aid to segregated housing; and ending discrimination in the Foreign Service of the Department of State that then, according to Powell, had "only 50 Negroes in Foreign Service out of 6,000 employed." Concluding his response to the President, Powell obviously signaled that he would maintain a ready access to the White House, obviously through Maxwell Rabb. "'Whenever and wherever I find any instance which seems to indicate that any of your official family is not cooperating with your program, I shall communicate immediately with the proper persons on your White House staff."[11] In other words, the teacher would send a note home to the parent.

This was the bridge, then, that Rabb and Powell built. To be sure, it would wobble at times, but each clearly judged that this sort of relationship at the start of this new administration was preferable to one of open criticism and no communication. Why not give it a try? Powell clearly had something to gain politically, even if the "official family" did not perform as the fatherly figure in the Presidency generally and often vaguely stated. Powell now had access, something the Truman people denied him. He might as well make a soft peace with this Republican regime that was now in office and, quite frankly, could be there for some time. And neither was Powell naïve about his potential value as a civil rights spokesman to the administration. In fact, he and Rabb likely understood that as a friendly but militant civil rights advocate, Powell would be more helpful to the administration than someone without Powell's outspoken ways and credentials.

This was by no means a partnership. That would imply too much conscious, deliberate mutual calculation. It was more likely the result of distinct political assessments based on each one's needs and understandings of differential roles and styles. Certainly, the Eisenhower administration preferred to work on the racial issues quietly, privately, without fanfare, and at times even through indirection. For example, one account of the way Robert Anderson handled "quiet desegregation" in naval facilities was as follows:

> Desegregation without public controversy was Anderson's aim, and commanders were advised to promote local cooperation by explaining the changes privately to civic leaders, local businessmen, and veterans' organizations. . . . In addition, Anderson conceded the insensitivity of his initial reply to Powell, attributing it to his lack of information on base conditions.
>
> Following Anderson's urgings for secrecy in the transition process, local commanders devised ingenious methods to achieve quiet desegregation. Buses with signs designating racial seating areas were removed for "maintenance" reasons and not replaced. Bathrooms were closed for "modernization," which actually consisted only of painting over racial designations above doorways. Lunchrooms were similarly adapted for integrated use.[12]

This was the way Eisenhower preferred to deal with these sticky racial issues. In fact, he was "decidedly impressed by the secretary's skill in achieving the desegregation goals without incident or political embarrassment."[13]

The results were fine with Powell, but his own experience and background made him less sanguine that these things would have been achieved at all without the more public denunciation of the blatant conditions in the first place. He had built a potential career on "going public," raising civil rights issues loudly and sharply. He was not likely, even in deference to a President with whom he wanted to maintain a "bridge," to detour too much from tactics and a lifelong strategy that, up to then, had been reasonably successful—at least for his reputation, if not always in terms of final concrete results.

This was the accommodation the Powell-Rabb "détente" would have to accept. On balance, it would be easier to reconcile conflicting styles than to smooth over differences of basic views. Powell clearly believed in the high efficacy of strong federal laws to enforce desegregation; Eisenhower did not. Powell certainly supported the Supreme Court's 1954 school desegregation case; Eisenhower did not. And as we shall see, Powell was prepared to withhold federal funds from those facilities and programs that practiced segregation; Eisenhower clearly was not. The two men, then, were very different in their worldviews on the issue of civil rights—probably more so than Powell was with La Guardia, Eleanor Roosevelt, and perhaps even Truman—but they would try under the circumstances of their respective political roles and the steadily evolving events of the 1950s to effect a reasonable working relationship. Or at least Powell and Rabb, acting on behalf of the President, would.

After the initial June 1953 meeting of understanding, relations between Powell and Rabb did indeed seem to develop rather nicely. Rabb sent the congressman a "Dear Adam" letter "in the nature of a progress report in order to keep [Powell] advised of activities here in the field of equality of opportunity."[14] (This was sent to Powell in Paris, where the congressman was on a trip with his son, inspecting American military bases in Europe. This trip, incidentally, coincided with a European concert tour by Hazel Scott.) He informed Powell of progress in desegregating naval installations. ("Secretary Anderson deserves real credit for what he has done. . . ." Rabb was making sure to credit the "official family.")

Rabb, however, was not able to accommodate his new friend in one instance—to meet him at the dock when he and his son arrived from their European trip. A cable was received at the State Department and passed on to Rabb.

> COG. POWELL AND SEVEN-YEAR-OLD SON DEPARTING SS QUEEN ELIZABETH ETA NEW YORK A.M. SEPTEMBER 29. CONGRESSMAN REQUESTS

MAXWELL RABB AT WHITE HOUSE AND NEW YORK OFFICE BE INFORMED OF TIME OF ARRIVAL.[15]

Rabb wrote dutifully that unfortunately he could not rearrange his schedule, and added somewhat cryptically that he was sure Powell had a "stimulating experience." The "détente" did not go that far.

> I was delighted to learn that you and your son will be returning to the United States next week and I very much wish that I were able to meet you at the dock. Unfortunately, I must be here in Washington to keep a speaking engagement of long standing; otherwise, I would be in New York to welcome you home. I would like to get at first hand your impressions of the trip.
>
> I am sure that your trip to Europe has been a stimulating experience and that, on your return, you will renew, with your accustomed energy, your distinguished efforts on behalf of your constituents and of the country as a whole.[16]

Powell kept Rabb informed of his speeches complimenting President Eisenhower, sending him copies and news items. Rabb, in turn, sent some of these along to colleagues in the administration and in the Republican Party. To the Assistant Secretary of State, Rabb sent a copy of one of Powell's sermons praising Eisenhower. In one instance, the *New York Herald Tribune* reported "Rep. Powell Lauds Eisenhower." The news item read:

> "Many criticisms have been aimed at President Eisenhower," Mr. Powell said, "but I can bear witness to the fact that there has not been a single problem of a moral or ethical nature which I have presented to the White House that he has not done his best to solve, and when he has given his word he has kept it."[17]

The Negro newspaper the *Atlanta Daily World* of October 17, 1953, carried the same story.

This obviously delighted Rabb, and he wanted the Republicans to take note. To the State Department, he appended the comment: "I think you can see that such a ringing endorsement at this time from a Democrat who holds the highest position in the minds of the Negroes certainly is a wonderful tribute—and very helpful to the Administration."[18] Powell had asked that he be designated as official representative to an upcoming celebration in Haiti. Rabb passed the request on to the State Department saying: "My suggestion—and I feel very strongly that it should be done—is to designate Congressman Adam Clayton Powell, Jr. as the person to go over. I think it will pay great dividends." (The State Department, as it turned out, did not have to act on this particular request, because the Haitians decided "in the interest of economy" not to invite delegations. The State Department noted to Rabb: ". . . suggests that you relay this information to Cong. Powell—that it should make him feel better.") Thus continued the care and feeding of Adam Clayton Powell by the Eisenhower Administration—some members of it, at any rate.

Rabb sent the news clippings of Powell's praise of the President to Leonard Hall, chairman of the Republican National Committee, with the following attached memo regarding Powell:

> . . . I wanted you to at least know that he has been talking in all his official pronouncements in a way that has been of inestimable help to us to develop a strong pro-Eisenhower sentiment among Negroes.
>
> . . . I wanted you to see the basis for my friendly feelings toward him.[19]

And to Sherman Adams, the President's chief assistant, Rabb sent the same material with this note: "You might be interested in seeing how a difficult Democrat, who originally blasted the Eisenhower Administration, has reacted to a little friendly treatment."

Powell clearly felt the arrangement was mutually beneficial. He could now make personal requests with high expectation of a sympathetic hearing. These were, to be sure, in the easy realm—they by no means extended to the passage of civil rights legislation, which was another matter of substance altogether. On several occasions, Powell contacted Rabb to intervene for a friend—one in trouble with his post office job in Boston, to solicit letters of praise for individuals back in his home district, to help a white soldier whom Powell had met overseas who was seeking to have his enlistment extended. In the latter instance, Powell sent the soldier's letter on to Rabb with the notation "Dear Max—This is a white officer who did tremendous work in morale. He needs to be saved." Sometimes Rabb was able to accommodate his congressman-friend.

The White House was able to deliver on one Powell request of enormous personal importance to him. In April 1954, Powell wrote to Rabb:

> In May of this year, His Imperial Majesty, the Emperor of Ethiopia is visiting our country. In the course of his visit, I would like the State Department to arrange for him to either visit the Abyssinian Baptist Church or to arrange a motorcade through Harlem, which I

> will be glad to organize, and in the motorcade, have them briefly pause at the Abyssinian Baptist Church.[20]

This one Rabb wanted to deliver on. He knew of the extreme symbolic value of a visit by Haile Selassie to Powell's church in the middle of Harlem. He immediately transmitted Powell's request to the State Department: "I would definitely recommend the request that Congressman Powell makes in the attached copy of the letter. He has been most friendly and has made speeches in favor of the President of the United States. We should encourage friendly Democrats."[21] The State Department was cooperative, agreeing to pass the request on to the Ethiopian embassy in Washington for ultimate approval in Addis Ababa. But the department cautioned Powell: ". . . I hope that no mention will be made of your invitation until we have confirmed plans with the Embassy." Powell had no intention of blowing this most significant event with a premature announcement. As matters developed, the visit was approved. Emperor Haile Selassie visited Abyssinian Baptist Church and presented Powell with a gold medallion which he constantly wore and displayed the rest of his life. The emperor's visit was an ornament on the Harlem scene, and Powell basked in the glory, further enhancing his role as a most important public figure, even on the international stage. His friends at the White House had come through for him. On one level at least, Powell had to conclude that the quid pro quo with the Eisenhower White House was paying off.

To the obvious pleasure of Rabb and the administration, Powell directed some of his strongest barbs away from the Eisenhower people and toward the Congress. In early February, 1955, Rabb circulated to various high Republican officials and to Ann Whitman a speech Powell made on the House floor. On February 2, 1955, Powell took the House podium and praised the Executive Branch and the Supreme Court, but blasted Congress for its lethargy on civil rights. He made one of his most fiery, impassioned speeches for congressional civil rights action:

> Tremendous changes are taking place in our country eradicating the concept of second class citizenship. Yet the United States Congress has done absolutely nothing in this sphere. . . . So many changes . . . have taken place under the leadership of President Eisenhower that many of the civil rights bills which I used to introduce are no longer of any value. This year, for instance, I did not introduce the bill to abolish segregation in the Armed Forces—it was not needed. . . . Two

> years ago, this Capital was a cesspool of democracy where not only I, as a Negro congressman, was banned from all public places but also visiting chiefs of state and their representatives, if their skin happened to be dark. But under the vigorous leadership of H.V. Higley, Administrator of Veterans' Affairs, there is no longer any segregation in any veterans' hospital. . . . For 10 years, my colleagues and I have introduced civil rights amendment after amendment, civil rights bill after bill, pleading, praying that you good ladies and gentlemen, would give to this body the glory of dynamic leadership that it should have. But you failed and history has recorded it. . . . This is an hour when a world waits breathlessly, expectantly, almost hungrily, for this Congress, the 84th Congress, through legislation to give some semblance of democracy in action. Our President and our Supreme Court cannot do all this by themselves and, furthermore, we should not expect it. . . . The opponents of a fair employment opportunities bill state that they do not believe that the Federal Government should intrude in States' rights. I do not agree with them, but until such time as we do pass a national FEPC, I am introducing today an FEPC bill for the District of Columbia.[22]

Of course, Powell did not mention that the President he had praised so highly also did not believe in a *national* FEPC. But his speech was satisfying to Rabb and the White House. Powell had linked Eisenhower with the Supreme Court, which had only nine months earlier struck down legal segregation in public schools. Some of Eisenhower's aides, at least, must have appreciated the company. Powell was continuing his practice of not directly, publicly attacking the President.

At one point—in 1954—the relationship between Eisenhower and Powell seemed to reach its zenith. Quite elated with the way Powell had spared the President his sharpest public attacks, and, indeed, often praised him, Rabb went so far as to suggest to friends at the *Reader's Digest* that that magazine publish an article by Powell lauding Eisenhower. Rabb, apparently, had been encouraged in this by a speech Powell had given in February 1954 in Chicago praising Eisenhower no less than eight times. The magazine liked the idea. A short article was written for Powell's signature entitled "The President and the Negro: A New Era!" It was an extraordinarily laudatory statement, listing progress under the President in military desegregation, minor appointments in the administration, and desegregation in Washington, D.C. "I was wrong," the article confessed, when talking about Powell's doubts in 1952 about

Eisenhower's candidacy. And it concluded: "As a Democrat, I nonetheless believe that Dwight Eisenhower is proving to be President of all the people and that, not Negroes only, but all the people will be better and America stronger because of it."[23] Quite a statement. A press agent could not have done better, especially in view of the opinion of some of Eisenhower's closest aides of the President's *real* positions on civil rights.

The senior editor of the *Reader's Digest* sent Rabb a draft of the article, even before it was shown to Powell, noting in the accompanying letter that Rabb's idea for the article "was a grand suggestion, both editorially and politically." The magazine was going to reach Powell in Paris (where he was on vacation) to get him to approve it.[24] Of course, Rabb enthusiastically sent the letter and article to Ann Whitman to show the President. The stroking of Adam Powell had returned dividends again. The article was published in the October 1954 issue under the shortened title, "The President and the Negro"—five months after the 1954 Supreme Court school desegregation decision, which President Eisenhower thought, according to Ann Whitman and others, was a terrible mistake and would "set back" the cause of civil rights. This seeming contradiction between the President's views and Powell's public statements about him apparently did not bother Powell. And the congressman's White House friends were happy that he felt the way he did about the President—whatever his reasons.

At the same time, Powell knew he had to keep up the pressure on the Executive Branch on the civil rights front. In spite of optimistic but general pronouncements coming from officials, government military and civilian facilities were still segregated in many places, notwithstanding Powell's comments on the floor of the House in February 1954. Some progress was being made, but not nearly enough nor at the pace most civil rights advocates desired. Powell could take comfort in his personally congenial relations with the White House, but he could not be perceived as relaxing his fight against segregation and discrimination. Therefore, in addition to notes on personal-political matters, he also kept up a steady stream of correspondence to and pressure on Rabb and other high administration officials. There were some instances where it was not possible to avoid leaning heavily on the Executive Branch. But equally important, to the Eisenhower people, at least, Powell was not *as* prone to condemn the administration *publicly* as he was to attack his own body, Congress.

Just five months after Powell had made his speech about the end of segregation in the armed forces, the American Civil Liberties Union issued a detailed press release charging "pockets of discrimination and segregation" still existing in the navy. A five-point program was proposed to overcome this situation. Powell immediately sent a letter to the Secretary of the Navy requesting a "reply to this, point by point!" The navy duly responded, outlining steps to be taken. Powell noted in the margins of the letter that in order to more fully publicize to Negroes opportunities in the navy, "Recruiting posters should show *all* Americans, not just *white*."[25] The navy responded as follows:

> We appreciate your recommendation as to the recruiting posters. The Navy is constantly revising its recruiting literature and posters in an effort to make a maximum nation-wide appeal, especially under present conditions of critical manpower shortages. I have referred your suggestion to the Chief of Naval Personnel for consideration and possible adoption.[26]

As was his practice in such matters, Powell sent the letter to Clarence Mitchell of the NAACP Washington bureau "to read and comment." Powell and Mitchell were continually in touch, copying letters to each other, and generally coordinating their efforts. It was a relationship Powell found quite useful. Mitchell worked full-time as the NAACP lobbyist on the Hill, and was considered one of the most effective, knowledgeable, and respected civil rights activists in Washington. He was a good ally for Powell to have. With its numerous local branches around the country, the NAACP had contacts with local, grass-roots interests that fed directly into Clarence Mitchell and ultimately, if necessary, to Powell. And, of course, the information flow was reciprocal. It was a perfect example of interest-group action hooking up with sympathetic forces in Congress. Powell frequently sought Mitchell's advice on appointments, proposed legislation, witnesses to invite to give congressional testimony, and, of course, voting tendencies of some members of Congress.

Mitchell, likewise, respected the Powell connection. Years later, he recalled that he and Powell had a comfortable, mutually respectful working relationship. Mitchell appreciated that Powell was usually available and willing to introduce antisegregation amendments to bills. Not only would Powell introduce the proposal, but he "would work for it."[27]

The military continued to be a source of frustration for Powell and a sore point between him and the White House. Attempting to balance his insistence on ending segregation and discrimination in the armed forces with patient treatment of the President, Powell exhibited more patience in some instances than he was usually prone to practice. In one case—a notice posted on a bulletin board at Fort Bliss, Texas, called for "Caucasians only" for the military police—the matter dragged out for nine months while letters of protest and response circulated between Powell and the White House.

September 28, 1954—Telegram from Powell to the President: "I have just discovered segregation and discrimination at Fort Bliss Texas 591st Military Policemen. Order was posted September 21 Quote For Caucasians Only Unquote. In the event that this is denied I have just procured the original order personally signed by the Company Commander and will be happy to turn this over to you."

December 6, 1954—Telegram from Powell to Maxwell Rabb: "I have received no reply to my wire to President Eisenhower on September 28th and to Honorable Charles E. Wilson on October 7th concerning situation at Fort Bliss, Texas. Kindly reply immediately."

December 9, 1954—Letter from Rabb to Powell: "Dear Adam: I was very disturbed to receive your wire of December sixth. The file on that particular problem was inadvertently misplaced and I had assumed that it was under consideration in another department.

As soon as I received your wire, I instituted a search for the material and I have already started work on it. I hope that we will have a reply for you very shortly, and I want you to know that I am indeed sorry about the delay. With warm regards."

January 31, 1955—Letter from Rabb to Powell: "Dear Congressman: In response to the inquiries from your office, this is to advise you that I have requested the Department of Defense to look into the problem which you raised relative to Fort Bliss. As soon as a report is received, I will get in touch with you. . . . With kind personal regards."

February 4, 1955—(two days *after* Powell made his speech on the House Floor stating that he had not introduced a bill this year "to abolish segregation in the Armed Forces—it was not needed.")—Letter from Powell to Rabb: "Dear Max: . . . As regards Fort Bliss, I cannot understand why this is taking so long. . . . You must realize that over four months have now gone past since I first made representations concerning this to the Department of Defense. . . . Best personal wishes."

March 3, 1955—Letter from Powell to Rabb: "My dear Max: I have discovered that a report was made to the Pentagon on the Fort Bliss M.P. situation within a month and a half after I made my first protest, which was September 21st. That report is buried at the Pentagon and I am now entering the sixth month since the incident and have received no reply.

"I do not want to do anything drastic but I am sure you will agree that half a year is long enough for a Member of Congress to wait for an answer to an inquiry to any government department.

"Much as I am loath to place a deadline on the matter, I am forced to and I must say that I will have to take the Floor of Congress and introduce a resolution of inquiry within the next few days if the Defense does not reply to my telegram concerning the aforementioned incident.

"Kindly do what you can so that I will not be forced to take this kind of action. Best personal wishes."

March 17, 1955—Letter from Robert Tripp Ross, Assistant Secretary of Defense, to Congressman Powell: "Dear Mr. Powell: This is in response to your telegram to the Secretary of Defense regarding certain conditions at Fort Bliss, Texas.

"The circumstances surrounding the conditions mentioned in your correspondence on the subject have been investigated by an Inspector General, and it was determined that racial discrimination was not involved. In this regard, Inspectors General are confidential agents of the Secretary of the Army and Chief of Staff of the Army or commanders whom they serve. Their reports may constitute not only factual data but advice and recommendations of a privileged nature. It is therefore not considered desirable to release such reports of investigation outside the Department of Defense.

"I understand that representatives of the Department of Defense have discussed the above with you on several occasions. [At this place in the margins of the letter, Powell wrote in bold letters: NO! NEVER!] I believe the salient points of those discussions gave clear indication of the absence of racial discrimination intent in connection with the display of an item on a Fort Bliss bulletin board. [Powell underlined this sentence and wrote in the margins: A LIE!] The Department of the Army is vigorously implementing its policy of complete integration, including the elimination of known instances of discriminatory treatment. In view of the complete exploration of this subject and the information subsequently provided you, I hope this clarifies the issue to your satisfaction. Sincerely yours."

Powell wrote across the top of the letter: "Max Rabb. This is a stupid letter!" At the bottom, he wrote: "I must blast this *openly!*"

At this point a White House memo signed March 19, 1955, by "nsc" was sent to Rabb reading: ". . . when I spoke with Mr. Evans [Department of Defense] he told me the reasons which the Dept. gave—and which they refuse to give Cong. Powell—I just do not understand their refusal unless they are covering up a blunder (which they obviously are doing)—

"I have not shown this [an attached letter] to Mr. [Bryce] Harlow [of the White House Staff] per usual instructions, because I think there is going to be trouble and that you might want to handle personally!!

"A few searing phone calls from you to people higher up than Evans would take care of it??????????????????????????????

"This makes me absolutely furious!!!!!!!!!!!!"

March 25, 1955—Letter from Powell to Rabb: "My dear Mr. Rabb: After six months of repeated requests, I have just received the enclosed letter signed by Robert Tripp Ross from the Department of the Army in relation to the Military Police matter at Fort Bliss, Texas. I am sure that I received this reply only because of the insistence of the White House. . . . In my six terms as a member of the U.S. Congress, I have never had any agency treat me as shabbily, and, virtually to ignore me. I want to thank you for your cooperation in this matter. . . . The enclosed reply [Ross's letter to Powell] is incredibly stupid. As you know, I gave the White House photostatic copies of the original order which was taken off the bulletin board at Fort Bliss, Texas, specifically stating that volunteers were needed for Military Police and that they *"must be Caucasians only."* For this letter to say that there is no instance of race discrimination is unbelievable. I am insisting that there be a complete investigation. I completely reject this letter as a reply. I further suggest that the time has arrived for a high level conference between representatives, if not the secretaries themselves, of the various branches of the Armed Services and myself with preferably you present. . . .

"We cannot allow this great crusade for democratic Armed Forces to bog down now because somewhere along the line there are some underlings who may not be sold on the proposition. President Eisenhower has covered himself with too much glory to allow the luster of it to be dimmed by someone cutting the ground from underneath him. Before this continues any further, let us see what we can do cooperatively. Yours truly."

June 21, 1955—Letter from Rabb to Powell: "Dear Adam: After receiving the message from your office with reference to your continued interest in the Fort Bliss matter, I checked with the Department of the Army to inquire if any further report was available to you. I am advised that the whole problem is still under study there and that, if any report can be made, they will get in touch with you.

"I am sorry that I can not give you a more responsive reply. However, I know that the Army is giving some real thought to your protest. With warm regard."

June 20, 1955—Memorandum for the Record, from James E. Evans, Assistant Secretary of Defense for Manpower and Personnel: ". . . the responses on the Fort Bliss item having not been found acceptable to the Congressman, we are in the position of attempting to get from the Army further modification in line with the expressions which the Congressman has made further to various officials with whom he has dealt on this matter."[28]

The entire matter lingered and faded, as the army ultimately ended the practice of recruiting M.P. volunteers on a racial basis. Powell's patience in this affair demonstrated his willingness to restrain himself in some instances. He continued to keep Eisenhower above the fray, insisting that subordinates and "underlings" were not doing the President's bidding. He also knew that his threat to go public was precisely what the administration did not want him to do. But this kind of experience probably exacted its toll on him. Instead of nine months of evasion and bureaucratic defiance and hypocrisy, he probably would have settled for an early honest admission of discrimination, ending the practice, and perhaps a simple apology. In return, he likely would have agreed to keep the episode quiet if asked to do so by Rabb. But the way the Defense Department handled the matter contributed to his cynicism and contempt. To be sure, he was willing to play along with the White House, but in light of such treatment, he could hardly respect the officials who were giving him the run around. And all over such petty incidents as an ill-advised notice on a bulletin board. To him the government was simply a bastion of deceit and humiliation. Any assessment of Powell's seemingly cavalier, unpredictable style would have to take these experiences into account. He very likely took his role as a congressman to mean that he was entitled to the respect he had seen given to others. That did not happen, and it obviously fed his own defiance and bitterness. This in turn made him that much more an enigmatic, difficult, and politically unreliable person to understand and deal with. He was willing to cooperate with Rabb and Eisenhower, praising the latter beyond what some less generous civil rights figures were prepared to do, but he wanted the respect of reciprocity, and certainly in the realm of overt evidence of racial discrimination on a military base. Inevitably, he was a product of America's dilemma—sensitive enough to be righteously indignant, cunning enough to match the system's hypocrisy. In the long run, neither he nor the system was well served by the elusive responses.

The armed forces overseas and at home continued for several years throughout the 1950s to be a target for Powell's proddings. He was known to most black servicemen as the one to contact if there was an incident of racial discrimination or any lingering practice of segregation. On more than a few occasions, some veterans and servicemen recalled that only the mention of the *intent* to write to Powell was sufficient to change some discriminatory policy or practice. In his annual trips overseas, Powell would visit military bases in an official capacity as a member of Congress, thus guaranteeing VIP treatment. He would meet with commanding officers and enlisted men, and get several personal accounts of racial conditions on the particular posts. Frequently, he sent item-by-item reports back to Maxwell Rabb. He was known to take up the cases of individual military and civilian personnel who charged discrimination against them. Occasionally these efforts were released to the press, requiring the military authorities or the Department of Defense to respond.[29]

At times, his prodding concerned subtle practices of individual discrimination by white officers, even extending to the use of latrines on military bases. Powell required detailed explanations, often writing long, point-by-point letters outlining transgressions. Neither was he beyond sending off biting responses to the Department of the Army. In one such letter, he told a colonel: "I totally reject your reply . . . to my inquiry." After taking meticulous issue with the army's effusive and evasive explanation regarding segregated latrines, he concluded: "Again, I categorically reject your reply and I demand a prompt response directly from the Secretary of the Army concerning this matter. My patience is running out on this continued double-talk, double-dealing, shilly-shallying on this whole question."[30] He sent copies of his two-page single-spaced castigation to Vice President Nixon, the Secretary of Defense, the Secretary of the Army, Maxwell Rabb, and Sherman Adams in the White House. He was also likely, at times, to send copies of correspondence to Clarence Mitchell. In one case, involving a denial from the Department of the Army regarding charges that only white personnel were being given choice assignments, Powell wrote in the margins a note to Mitchell: "Clarence—what junk?"

While he did not issue a press release every time he engaged in a confrontation with government officials, his insistent attention did not go unnoticed in the Negro press and in civil rights circles. Neither were there criticisms that such attention to seemingly minor transgressions—segregated bathrooms, notices on bulletin boards, subtle racist statements by white officers—was trivial and not worth the effort. Many understood, in the context of the United States in the 1950s, that it was important to challenge such activities if only to signal the uncompromising intent to end any racial discrimination. That context included decades of assuming that such practices were normal, indeed healthy and respectable. The only way to fight that national mentality was to be persistent against even the slightest evidences of its existence. The psychological impact of Powell's protests was enormous in black communities. In addition, the military was a relatively easy target. It was wholly within federal jurisdiction, and there were existing Executive Orders against segregation and discrimination. Neither were civil rights advocates unmindful of the ideological advantage offered by the Cold War environment. Segregation in America's military certainly did not sit well with those attempting to respond to the Communist challenge from abroad. Thus a Powell crusade against the armed forces was a good substantive issue to take on, even if it did not address major problems of FEPC, segregation in housing, education, and other areas of American life. These issues he would deal with in another way, through legislative action, but he could take on the Defense Department more directly and personally.

It was clear that the military authorities were aware that they were caught between contending forces. On the one hand, they took care to assure Powell that *they* were not sanctioning segregation; on the other, they felt they had to abide by local (meaning Southern) customs in conditions existing off military bases. When Powell complained about transportation at Barksdale Air Force Base in Louisiana and in the nearby town, he received a carefully worded letter from the Office of the Secretary, Department of the Air Force:

> There is no segregation on buses operated by the Air Force on the base. In furnishing commercial bus transportation, which is available to military and civilian personnel, the local transportation company practices segregation off the base in compliance with state law. Segregation on commercial bus transportation on the base is not sanctioned by the Air Force. However, to avoid the awkward and embarrassing position of having to change seats in transit, passengers may voluntarily sit in spaces where they would be required to sit when off the base. There is no intent on the part of Air Force commanders to enforce any particular seating arrangement for any personnel on a commercial bus. It is left to the individual's own preference where he will sit while the commercial bus is on the base. Of course, the Air Force has no jurisdiction concerning commercial bus transportation off the base.[31]

Powell made sure that Clarence Mitchell got a copy of this letter.

Not all the mail Powell received from Negro GIs complained of discrimination, however. Infrequently, he was told that his constant harping on the military was uncalled for and likely doing more harm than good:

> Dear Mr. Powell:
>
> I appreciate your motives in attempting to eliminate discrimination wherever it exists in order that we may enjoy our constitutional rights on an equal basis with our fellow citizens. There are certainly many instances where bigotry and intolerance have resulted in shameful and disgusting unfairness to us Negroes. . . . There is no government environment in existence in the world today through which our hope for stamping out segregation and discrimination can become a reality than our own democracy—and I am proud to be a citizen of this country.
>
> There are *con*structive and *de*structive methods of dealing with this problem. . . . I refer to your repeated attacks on the Armed Forces. Based on a few isolated instances in which it appears to me you have left out most of the facts you manage to imply that the Armed Forces foster, encourage, and operate on a policy of enforced segregation. This is a slap in the face of the tremendously influencial [*sic*] organization which has made more progress in the last five years and done more for our cause, both directly and indirectly, than any other single factor. It would seem to me that it would serve us better to praise them and to point to them as examples of how integration can and does work.

I am a Negro WAF 1st Lieutenant. I have been commissioned in the United States Air Force for five years. I have yet to experience one single instance of discrimination as far as my own personal career is concerned nor have I been aware of any instances concerning others. On the contrary, I have seen numerous situations in which a Negro member has created a problem for himself that the service has "bent over backwards" to solve for him so that there could be no charge of discrimination. . . .

I am an average Air Force Officer. To compare my standing, with regard to equality and privilege, as an Air Force Officer, with my standing as a civilian school teacher in Virginia gives the very best case for the Armed Forces. So long as I perform my duties satisfactorily and conduct my personal life in the high standard required of all officers I AM EQUAL.

I'm as concerned as you are, but I'm not going to hurt the cause by blindly insisting that progress is not being made.[32]

There was no need for Powell to send *this* one to Rabb. He did, however, send a copy to Clarence Mitchell. It did not make an argument with which he was unfamiliar, and on the political stump he likely would have dismissed such a person as an "Uncle Tom." (There were times, however, as we shall see in the next chapter when Powell could come pretty close to expressing the same sentiments, albeit in a quite different setting.) He had enough correspondence and personal experience to the contrary to justify in his own mind his persistent pressure on the military.

At the same time, in his own way, he was capable of soft-pedaling criticism of the President personally. In a letter to Rabb dealing with two other matters where he wanted favors from the White House, he concluded on a congenial note, albeit one that indicated his displeasure with Eisenhower's less-than-wholehearted support for the Supreme Court's 1954 school desegregation decision:

. . . Of course, I will say my usual good thing about Eisenhower although I think that a definite slip-up occurred on the aftermath of the Supreme Court Decision. It would have been so much better if Eisenhower had just said the matter was now in the hands of the courts and leave it at that. Of course we both know that the President will speak his own mind and tell the truth even if it hurts him.[33]

Likewise, Powell was clearly prepared in the mid-1950s to identify himself, in the eyes of the White House at least, as a reliable anti-Communist. In early 1955, Powell's old Harlem political buddy and successor in the New York City Council, Benjamin J. Davis, was serving a five-year prison sentence. He had been convicted under the Smith Act along with ten others as a member of the Communist Party advocating the violent overthrow of the government. A Communist-front organization, the Civil Rights Congress, published a four-page article charging racial discrimination in federal prisons. The article noted that Ben Davis had filed a petition in the federal court to end segregation in the U.S. penitentiary at Terre Haute, Indiana, where he was confined, and at other federal prisons. The lawsuit also charged that white prisoners were given better treatment and more benefits and privileges. The Civil Rights Congress called for a nationwide campaign to get Attorney General Herbert Brownell to act to "eliminate jimcrow in Federal prisons."

Obviously wanting to end segregation in the prisons no less than in the military and other segments of American life, Powell sent the article to Rabb with the attached note:

> Dear Max:
>
> What can we do about this so that the Communists will not take the play away from us?[34]
>
> Adam

The congressman did not restrict his probing to the Defense Department and federal agencies dealing with federal programs. He also turned his attention to the FBI. Throughout the 1950s, there were numerous instances of denial of the right to vote to Negroes in the South. Very often such denials took the form of violence against civil rights workers attempting to register to vote. And in 1955 there was the highly publicized case of the lynching of a young Chicago Negro boy, Emmett Till, in Mississippi. Till had allegedly insulted a white woman by whistling at her. All these cases, especially Till's murder, received national attention. But local law-enforcement authorities were not prone to be vigorous in investigating them. Powell, along with other civil rights leaders, wanted Washington FBI intervention, believing that even FBI agents based in Mississippi could not be trusted to pursue justice diligently and impartially.

Powell's office called the FBI in Washington in an attempt to get the names of the FBI agents in Mississippi who were investigating both the Till murder and the voting denial charges. In fact, the Till murder was considered a matter for local law enforcement, no evidence of a federal crime having been committed; thus there was no FBI investigation of that matter. As for the voting denials, Powell was informed that the FBI conducted investigations at the request of the Department of Justice, and that he should go to that agency for any information. And in any case, the FBI said, its practice was to use locally based agents in its investigations. Obviously, this official response would not satisfy Powell. He had addressed a mass rally in New York City's garment district on October 11, 1955, clearly condemning FBI actions. The FBI in New York duly monitored the meeting, and the agency filed a report of the rally, citing an article in *The National Guardian*, a socialist journal. Powell told the "20,000 unionists" at the rally that "no crisis facing America is more serious than the crisis of racism." He then proposed "(1) A delegation to the White House to demand that a special session of Congress investigate violence in Mississippi and (2) A delegation to J. Edgar Hoover 'on the problems of the FBI in Mississippi,' because its 'native' agents are mistrusted by Negroes."[35] An FBI office memo noted that the FBI "files do reflect he [Powell] has been affiliated with numerous front organizations some of which have been cited by the Attorney General. . . . Correspondence with him has been on a 'black letterhead basis.' "[36]

Powell continued his personal requests to his contact, Rabb, in the White House, at times leaving Rabb at a loss as to how to deal with them. On one occasion, Powell forwarded a request from a doctor seeking a job with the American embassy in Paris. In a somewhat exasperated tone, Rabb responded:

> Dear Adam:
>
> I have been pondering over your letter of June fifteenth. You know, we all too often tend to say that there is "nothing new under the sun"—but I think that I have really met up with something new in this request from Dr. Cordice for appointment as embassy physician in Paris. I have no idea at all on how to go about it! I am therefore sending your letter and Dr. Cordice's request on to the State Department with the request that they put it in the right office there.
>
> I hope that this will do the trick.[37]

Obviously, Powell viewed Rabb as the main White House contact for sundry matters, assuming, perhaps, that Rabb could start an inquiry or get action even when the issue was remote from White House responsibility. For instance, Powell wired Rabb complaining of the promotion of an employee in the Washington, D.C. fire department. That employee allegedly had opposed the "program of integration of your Administration. I earnestly request that he not be promoted because if he is, the public and many of us will regard this as a retreat on your part. May I have an immediate reply." Rabb patiently, but in a mildly rebuking tone, explained his position:

> Dear Adam:
>
> I have your wire regarding promotion in the Fire Department of the District of Columbia. Frankly, I don't understand it and I wonder if there is not some misunderstanding about the work which I am doing here.
>
> I don't believe that anyone would ask that this office try to supervise the hiring, firing and promoting of every Federal and District employee in the Government—but that is, essentially, what your wire suggests. This Administration is concerned with general policy and we are proud of the progress we have made. . . .[38]

He proceeded to scold Powell on the charge of "retreat," and gave every indication that this request and implication were not within the realm of their agreement of bridge-building and cooperation.

At times, however, Powell was able to get better results. He complained to Rabb about conditions in the federally sponsored New York City slum clearance program, specifically in Harlem. The relocation of families was a sore point, with conditions for tenants violating several rules of safety and habitability. The city official in charge of slum clearance was Robert Moses, Powell's old nemesis from the Stuyvesant Town project debate in the 1940s. The federal authorities admitted "that there are several respects in which the site management and relocation operation can and should be improved."[39] The Housing and Home Finance Agency promised to pursue "steps to require the redeveloper to improve the handling of family relocation at this project site."

So the politically peripatetic congressman from Harlem was all over the civil rights terrain, taking Rabb and the Eisenhower White House with him—using, in his mind probably, the offer to "build bridges" between himself as *the* preeminent representative of his people (not just in Harlem, but throughout the country) and the Eisenhower administration. Sometimes quietly, other times not, he kept the pressure on. That was his role as he saw it at that time: the Congressional Irritant. There is sufficient evidence to suggest that he took it seriously, even if, at times, he seemed to exasperate his White House contacts. And neither was the White House naïve about the importance and volatility of this man. They respected his political influence, even though they knew they had to be constantly wary of him. In October 1955, during the FBI–Emmett Till affair and in the midst of intensifying racial problems in the South, Powell requested a meeting with Rabb. A handwritten White House memo to Bryce Harlow read: "Cong. Powell wants to come in and see Mr. Rabb tomorrow. Mr. Rabb doesn't know what about—and would like to be sure it is OK with you."[40]

Harlow indicated it was "OK," but scribbled at the bottom: ". . . with fingers X'd!" Indeed. With Adam Clayton Powell, Jr., who could tell?

Throughout the history of the civil rights struggle in the United States, going back as far as the immediate post–Civil War years, if not before, there have been perennial debates among civil rights advocates about the best strategies and tactics to pursue. Invariably, these discussions have focused on how hard to push for particular goals, if and when compromises should be accepted, and, above all, the extent to which agreements should be reached that seemingly moved the struggle along, even though maintaining an overall system of segregation and discrimination. In one form or other, the disagreements evoked language such as "half-loaf or whole loaf," "principle versus pragmatic politics," "morality versus sell-out." Harold Cruse provided an important historical context in his presentation of the defeat of a congressional bill in the 1880s—introduced by Senator Henry W. Blair, Republican of New Hampshire—to provide federal funds for education, albeit on a segregated (but equal) basis.[41] Many blacks accepted the bill, believing that education, even segregated, was sorely needed by the recently freed blacks. One Southern black leader of the Afro-American League pleaded in 1890: "Our people are hungering and thirsting for education. . . . If we can't get the whole loaf don't in heaven's name withhold the half loaf that is offered us."[42] But the bill never passed, thanks, according to Cruse, in large measure to the Northern (white) liberals who deserted the cause of federal aid to education in favor of the South working out its own problems without federal intervention. Cruse concluded: "The northern liberal retreat from support of Blair was one of the last actions in the northern ritual of washing its hands of the Southern Negro."[42]

The compromise issue came up again in World I. The NAACP worked diligently in favor of more Negro army officers. But it was clear that the Woodrow Wilson administration was only willing to consider this if officer training camps were segregated. Many blacks protested such a policy, calling it, understandably, an affront to Negroes and contradictory to the principle of fighting "a war to make the world safe for democracy." W. E. B. Du Bois of the NAACP was no shrinking violet in such matters. He had long established a scholarly reputation as a staunch opponent of the more accommodating policies of the popular Negro leader, Booker T. Washington of Tuskegee Institute in Alabama. If anyone's civil rights credentials were intact, surely Du Bois's were. But he weighed the arguments in 1917 and came down on the side of accepting a segregated officers' training camp, a decision that angered and bewildered some Negroes who were disappointed that he would submit to such a compromise. Du Bois, who was also the editor of the NAACP's widely read journal, *Crisis*, wrote in his defense: "We face a condition, not a theory. There is not the slightest chance of our being admitted to white camps, therefore, it is either a case of a 'jim-crow' officers training camp or no colored officers. Of the two things, no colored officers would be the greatest calamity."[44]

There was hardly a year or an issue that did not present this dilemma in one way or another—the Stuyvesant Town project in New York in the 1940s; whether to attach an FEPC provision to a proposed full-employment bill in 1945; A. Philip Randolph's and Grant Reynold's 1948 vow to encourage young men not to serve in a segregated army. Always the basic questions were the same: How far should one go in insisting that segregation and discrimination be totally eliminated? Should the benefits projected under less than full elimination of segregation be accepted as the best that could be obtained? When was the latter a "sellout" of one's principles? How does one balance pragmatic politics based on objective reality with a clear, pure stand on moral grounds? By the late 1940s and 1950s, this was an old dilemma in civil rights circles. Up to that point, however, there was little real chance of playing out this debate in a meaningful way in serious political circles. That is, the political cards were so stacked against civil rights that the issue was usually little more than an academic debate. However adamant the no-compromise forces were, there was little they could do, little impact they could have. The political lineup and the social climate simply were not conducive to an extended hearing of the arguments.

But the years beginning with the late 1940s presented a new era. The war against fascism and Nazism was successfully over. There was a growing anticolonial spirit in Asia and Africa. Black voters were growing in numbers in Northern urban areas. More Northern white Americans were becoming less tolerant of the blatant signs of racial segregation and discrimination in the South. The United States Supreme Court was beginning to render decisions challenging the *de jure* segregation system. President Truman's independent-minded Committee on Civil Rights had written a report that called for the first time for much more aggressive action in favor of civil rights on the part of the national government, putting Southern states clearly on the political and, likely, moral defensive. More organized liberal, labor, and religious groups were beginning to be involved in civil rights issues at the national and local levels. Blacks in the South, led frequently by returning war veterans, were organizing local civic-political voter leagues pushing for the end to racial barriers in voting and other forms of discrimination. The NAACP had given notice that it would step up its fight on the legal front through the courts, as well as in the legislative and executive arenas. Racial insults and discriminatory practices previously accepted as inevitable and unchangeable were now optimistically challenged.

There was clearly the birth of a new ethos in the country concerning America's dilemma.

At its 1949 annual convention, the NAACP, taking its cue from the Civil Rights Committee report, decided to adopt a policy of opposition to any federal financial support for any racially segregated facilities.

To be sure, as always, there was not unanimity of agreement in the Negro community on this issue. In April 1949, the National Council of Negro Women issued a nationwide appeal to its members urging that an antisegregation amendment *not* be attached to the pending public housing legislation in Congress.[45] Feeling that segregated housing could best be fought through the courts, with the Supreme Court ruling against restrictive covenants in *Shelley* v. *Kramer* having been rendered in 1948, the council argued: "Do We Put Our Eggs in One Basket? We have every reason to believe we can have *housing* and *non*-segregation if we fight for enactment of S. 1070 and H.R. 4009. For we can still fight for non-segregation through executive and judicial action. Didn't we win in the U.S. Supreme Court decisions against racial restrictive covenants?" The NAACP did not accept this reasoning, but maintained that "in a few communities it has already become apparent that Urban Redevelopment and public housing will be used to perpetuate segregated residential areas. In other communities, organizations other than the NAACP are taking a lead to see that redeveloping will be along unsegregated lines."[46]

The liberal bind was a familiar one. Some groups such as the National Council knew that if an antisegregation amendment were attached to proposed public housing legislation, this would lose the political support of Southerners who wanted the money but not the desegregation, as well as conservatives who hated any federal support for social programs. At the same time, some liberals did not want to be caught arguing against provisions to end segregation. Again, what was politically realistic had to be played out against what was the constitutionally right, and some would even say moral, thing to do. In addition, no one denied that a liberal social policy agenda stood for more federal government support for social programs—housing, education, health, extended social security benefits. But to insist on obtaining *both* the social programs and civil rights could mean, in the cold calculating world of vote counting in Congress, ending up getting neither.

Congressman Adam Clayton Powell, Jr., lost no time getting into this thicket. In early 1950 he introduced an amendment to a federal aid to education bill before the House Education and Labor Committee, on which he sat, stipulating that federal funds should be distributed without discrimination on account of race or color. The committee adopted it. But this did not satisfy the NAACP at all, probably much to Powell's surprise. The fact was that Powell's amendment language could be entirely compatible *with segregated* facilities. His amendment could simply mean a continuation of the "separate but equal" doctrine endorsed over fifty years before in *Plessy* v. *Ferguson* (1896). In other words, funds could go "equally," that is on a nondiscriminatory basis, to whites and Negroes, but the races could and would remain separated. Powell had not been careful in his drafting. Probably sensing this and not concluding that Powell was deserting the civil rights ship, Leslie Perry of the NAACP dashed off a "Dear Adam" letter to him; stating that the NAACP's Board had adopted a resolution calling for the end of any federal funds going to "states, schools or countries" that maintained *segregated* facilities. Perry noted that Powell's amendment did not cover "racial segregation," and he offered to provide the proper language for Powell's use.[47]

Clearly, Powell was caught short in his attentiveness to the distinction between segregation and discrimination. At that time, just two months after his dynamic militant appearance before the

Emergency Civil Rights Mobilization meeting in Washington, he was not about to be upstaged by the NAACP. His reply went not to Perry, but to Roy Wilkins (then the Acting Director of the NAACP during Walter White's leave; Powell would hardly deal with lesser staff if he could go higher), and exhibited a bit of pique, not daring to admit his own error, or failure to check with his allies. He noted that Perry's letter came too late for his consideration: "It would have been absolutely impossible to have made any amendments whatsoever after Leslie Perry's letter was written. . . . The Committee is to consider the Burke Bill, H.R. 5939 [another education bill] after April 17. I will be glad to bring up your amendment at that time if it is prepared and in my hands before the Committee concludes action."[48]

From that point on, the NAACP and Powell worked hand in hand on such amendments. While the legislative label bore Powell's name—they were "Powell Amendments," and, indeed, Roy Wilkins years later referred to him as "the Great Amender"—this civil rights strategy was really the brainchild of the President's Civil Rights Committee in conjunction with the subsequent tedious political work for over a decade by the NAACP. That organization was the quarterback that threw the ball to Powell, who, to his credit, was more than happy to catch and run with it. They had distinct, important collaborative roles to play, and they played them. As early as April 1950, the minutes of the NAACP board of directors reflected that that body had settled in to a strategy that would apply to an array of proposed bills dealing with the liberal social issues. "Upon motion, duly seconded, it was voted that we follow our previous position and ask Rep. Powell to introduce *our customary amendment.*" (Italics added.)[49]

An old issue, albeit in a new mid-twentieth-century legislative context, was resurrected.

By 1955 the NAACP was strongly committed to its new approach. The antisegregation amendment focused its major attention on a proposed piece of legislation to provide federal funds to build badly needed new schools in the country. The Eisenhower administration was willing to support a proposal making such funds available on a rather complicated but more liberal basis than ever existed before to those districts that clearly needed them. Certainly, everyone except conservatives agreed this move was a progressive step. Federal resources should be channeled to areas suffering from a shortage of schools. But the NAACP was adamant that such funds not be used by those districts that maintained segregated school systems. In addition, in May 1954, and a year later in May 1955, the United States Supreme Court had declared that racially segregated schools violated the Fourteenth Amendment's provision for "equal protection of the laws." Surely, the NAACP felt, a "Powell Amendment" was now more defensible than ever. After all, it sought to support the declaration of the Supreme Court. The civil rights organization mounted an extensive lobbying campaign behind Powell's amendment. In a definitive, unambiguous letter to Clarence Mitchell in Washington, Roy Wilkins emphatically noted that he had informed the Leadership Conference on Civil Rights of the NAACP's no-compromise position. The NAACP would remain adamant, even if this meant that the total bill was defeated.[50]

President Eisenhower, of course, rejected the amendment, calling it "extraneous."[51] Roy Wilkins dashed off a long letter to Powell attacking Eisenhower's position as "shocking," and evidence of the President's ability "to close one's eyes to realities, political and moral." Clearly, the letter was intended to bolster Powell's resolve. The NAACP did not want him backing down in the face of Eisenhower's charge, a response they were not entirely sure he would not make. Thus Wilkins closed his letter as follows: "We know that this development will not deter you from your intention to introduce an appropriate anti-segregation amendment to the school construction bill in the House. This Association, I need not say, will support you to the fullest."[52] The NAACP, indeed, went all out, taking out a full-page advertisement in the *New York Times* ("Who Is Blocking Federal Aid to School Construction?"[53]); writing local NAACP branches around the country, as well as numerous liberal, religious, and labor groups; and buttonholing Democrats and Republicans in both chambers of Congress.

Powell, of course, was flooded with mail—pro and con, and oftentimes simply seeking advice—and he frequently sent these on to Clarence Mitchell. One handwritten letter came from Hallettsville, Texas, seeking advice on how to vote on a local school bond. The writer noted that $315,000 of the $800,000 would be used for a "colored school." What should the voters do? The writer added: "I am in the *South* and you know the conditions down here." And he concluded: "We want to know just what the Federal Government wants us to do."[54]

It was the Blair school aid bill all over again, seventy years later. Except this time, the blacks in the South at least had a black congressman to write to for advice. In fact, the letter seemed to equate Powell with "the Federal Government." In the writer's frame of reference, this was probably appropriate enough. Powell at first wrote across the top "vote against bond issue," then scratched this out, and sent the letter instead to Clarence Mitchell with the notation at the top: "What should I say?"

The NAACP was true to its word in backing up Powell and defending him from editorial attacks, sending letters to critics at the *New York Times*, the *Washington Post*, and other prominent journals and columnists.

For his own part, Powell rose to eloquent heights in several speeches he gave on the House floor in favor of the antisegregation amendment. In well-prepared texts, in all likelihood worked out in consultation with Mitchell, he answered all the arguments of the adversaries, point by point. He outlined the evidence of continued school segregation even in the face of the 1954 and 1955 Supreme Court decisions, reciting testimony of Southern politicians and school officials who vowed never to yield to desegregation. He cited letters to Clarence Mitchell, and responses from HEW and the Comptroller General, who stated that either the Court should act or the Congress should do so. He inveighed against these officials and pleaded with his colleagues: "How shocking that we Americans, who are supposedly religious, have so lost our sense of values that we are willing to support illegal and immoral un-American actions and attitudes!"[55] And: "The issues before us are legal, but more than that, moral and ethical. . . . You cannot teach respect for law and order in schools built in defiance of law and order. . . . From where do we get this new concept that the protection of basic liberties should be left solely to the courts? In reality, are not the courts the last and not the first resort for the protection of basic rights?"[56] Sensitive to the Cold War environment of the time, he argued:

> The fight between the free world and the slave world will be won on the basis of moral stamina only. We acknowledge that the Soviet is basically immoral and atheistic, but all reports indicate that religion is growing. Shall we let an immoral Soviet grow in grace while we supposedly Christian Americans through default, expediency and compromise become unmoral? . . . Here and now we must make the choice: shall it be Marx or Christ; Lenin or Lincoln; Stalin or Roosevelt; Kruschev or Eisenhower? . . . This is our Challenge. Have we the moral courage?[57]

With the concurrence of the NAACP, Powell sought to mitigate the charge that his amendment was "extremist." He proposed that the provision be applied only to those school *districts* (not to the entire state) that refused to desegregate, and he offered to give them four years to *begin* the process. In addition, the appropriated funds would be held in escrow for potential use by resisting districts that subsequently decided to comply within the four-year period.

Ever diligent in rounding up and holding committed votes, Clarence Mitchell kept Powell informed of rumors about possible defections and efforts "to torpedo our amendment." In one instance, Mitchell wrote to Powell about an item in a Drew Pearson column that Representative James Roosevelt (son of FDR) "was trying to defeat the amendment." Mitchell was not sure of this, inasmuch as the liberal Roosevelt had supported the amendment in committee. (This could well have been the position of Congressman Roosevelt in view of the position his active and prominent mother had taken against introducing the amendment at the committee stage.) Mitchell wrote to Powell, "I would like to urge that you and Mr. Roosevelt issue a joint statement making it clear that this vital amendment must be part of any bill passed and that you urge all of its supporters to stand fast."[58]

There were other outspoken supporters in the House. Congressman T. Millet Hand of New Jersey, noting that Powell allowed four years to start desegregation, stated, "That does not seem to be proceeding with unreasonable speed."[59] Walter Reuther, president of the United Auto Workers, who, several months earlier, had joined with Eleanor Roosevelt to try to persuade the NAACP to forgo introducing the amendment at the committee stage in preference to presenting it on the floor, released a statement to the press putting the burden on Eisenhower. He wanted the President and the Attorney General to "state clearly and emphatically" that if there were no amendment they would deny funds to segregated districts. "In the absence of such a clarifying statement the UAW will urge the enactment of legislation providing for specific safeguards against federal funds for education being used in violation of the Supreme Court decision."[60]

The Powell Amendment, however, always had its liberal opponents, and the issue, in their estimation, was not an easy one to resolve. They fully understood, and in some cases leaned in the direction of, the moral and constitutional arguments of the NAACP and Powell. Some had rather impeccable records on civil rights in the context, certainly, of the 1940s and 1950s. They truly resented any linking of their rejection of the amendment to the objectionable views of segregationists; and they wanted no partnership with conservatives who opposed most federal support for social programs dating from the New Deal. Indeed, these liberals would style themselves New Dealers in the social policy sense—even perhaps the liberal Republicans, such as Jacob Javits of New York and Wayne Morse of Oregon. Their dilemma was pure and simple: they desperately felt the need for such measures as federal aid for school construction, but they did not feel that they could garner enough votes in Congress—especially to break a Southern filibuster in the Senate—if the Powell Amendment were part of the bill. It was a matter of political reality.

Some liberals such as Eleanor Roosevelt and Walter Reuther tried heartily in 1955 to get the NAACP to shift its tactics. Do not, they pleaded, offer the amendment in the Senate committee, but wait until the bill reaches the Senate floor. At that point, it would be difficult to raise the filibuster. Their letter to Roy Wilkins put the case: The bill should go before the entire Senate without the amendment. That would get it out of the committee safely. Once on the floor, the amendment could then be introduced. What this would accomplish, they reasoned, would be to cut the ground from under any attempt to filibuster a motion to even consider the whole bill.[61] To be sure, there would be a filibuster attempt after the bill was on the floor, but, they reasoned, the debate would center on the entire bill rather than simply over the narrower issue of whether to bring it forward in the first place. This strategy, they believed, would more likely yield more votes for cloture (to end the filibuster), plus it would give the liberal supporters an opportunity to debate the substantive merits of the bill, rather than be hemmed in by a procedural debate. If this advice were followed, the proponents of civil rights would be strengthened in the moral arguments they could make and in mobilizing "the broadest possible support behind our efforts."[62]

The liberals were caught in another bind. The fact that it was the NAACP that was behind the rigid, no-compromise position made liberal opposition more difficult. The NAACP was by no means, even in the 1950s, perceived as an unreasonable, "irresponsible" group. Certainly not "radical." If anything, Wilkins and Mitchell had established their reputations as Cold War liberals, men willing to speak out against those wanting to embarrass the country over the civil rights issue. Perhaps Powell, personally, could not be fully trusted, but not the NAACP. Powell, perhaps, could be tarred with the brush of irresponsibility and, indeed, as an "extremist" (in spite of his publicly kind words for Eisenhower) but hardly the

NAACP. Thus the NAACP/Powell alliance put an additional political burden on liberals who knew that it was more difficult to question the veracity of the oldest civil rights organization than it was to dismiss the Harlem Congressman. The NAACP's record lent legitimacy to the argument that liberals had to respect. This was certainly the view of Joseph Rauh of the Americans for Democratic Action (ADA). He had the highest respect for Clarence Mitchell and he stated that, as vexing and "divisive" as the issue was among liberals, he simply had to go along with his trusted friend Clarence Mitchell.[63]

In a letter to a liberal critic, Roy Wilkins's words hit with a particularly telling blow. He restated the NAACP's commitment to federal aid, but by no means on a segregated basis. He wanted the liberal critics to redirect their efforts. He did not question their commitment to civil rights, but: "It would seem that the friends of federal aid might well expend some of their persuasive powers on those who want to have their cake (segregation) and eat it too (federal aid)."[64]

Likewise, Clarence Mitchell's strong rebuke to a liberal friend must have strained relations in a painful way. Charles Abrams had questioned the use of antisegregation amendments in a "reckless" way, that is, by attaching them to any and every valuable piece of social legislation. They should be used more selectively, he said in a speech at Fisk University and in correspondence with Clarence Mitchell. Mitchell shot back: "We may as well face the fact that when reactionary elements try to kill legislation with civil rights measures they are stepping into a breach created because some *liberals simply do not have the guts to make a good fight for this just principle.*"[65]

A liberal friend of the NAACP, Senator Paul H. Douglas of Illinois, urged the group to pursue a strategy similar to that suggested by Mrs. Roosevelt and Reuther. He was particularly confident that the Supreme Court's 1954 desegregation ruling was a major plus in their fight, and this might make the amendment less politically necessary. But Wilkins wired the Chicago NAACP branch: ". . . Current propaganda in Washington to which we believe Douglas lending ear is to omit our legislation [the amendment] from committee version and offer it as amendment later on the floor. . . . Keep protest in good taste but make it strong."

This was the organization's posture: polite but persistent. The liberal critics, after all, were friends, but they had to be held to the fire. The NAACP could do this much more effectively than Powell.

The congressman's motives could be questioned. He had demonstrated his unreliability too many times over the years by blasting critics summarily, especially linking liberals with racists. But the NAACP had no such suspect political liabilities, and liberals knew this. When that organization took a rigid stand, it had to be noticed.

The dilemma was poignantly illustrated by an exchange between Congressman Stewart L. Udall, whom the NAACP highly respected, and Clarence Mitchell. Udall wrote Mitchell:

> Dear Clarence:
>
> . . . Of course, there is room for honest disagreement on this whole question. Perhaps our main differences arise from the fact that by habit we are schooled in the art of the possible, while principle is the central thing in your work—and rightly so. Sometimes in our desire to get half-a-loaf our principles hang on the brink (and sometimes go over) but generally speaking we have found that a modest program is better than none.
>
> One hardly needs to invoke tolerance on your part. Although most of us work closely with various groups which concern themselves with legislation, not infrequently we reject their opinions and follow our own convictions. Invariably they are broadminded and judge us on our record after the final decision is in. Surely you will approach this matter in an equally liberal spirit.
>
> After all, we may be right.
>
> Sincerely,[66]

Udall had suggested dropping the Powell Amendment in favor of a substitute that would provide extra funds for those school districts that were "impacted" by the serious court-ordered process of dismantling the dual school system. He reasoned that such an approach would offer an incentive to Southerners to desegregate. The measure would operate in a manner similar to laws aiding areas "impacted" by the pressure of federal military establishments.

> . . . Few will dispute that the [1954 Supreme Court] decision of the judicial arm of our government produced a "federal impact" equal to, or greater than, the war and defense activities recognized by Congress when Public Law 815 (our existing school aid legislation) was passed. . . . My bill would authorize an annual appropriation . . . as direct aid to school districts faced with reorganization. . . . It should be apparent that only through such a program as this can many of the affected districts make any start toward integration. . . . Instead of self-righteous criticism, the rest of the country would hold out a

helping hand. Instead of threats, we would use understanding. In place of compulsion, we could offer cooperation.[67]

Udall's approach was offering a carrot rather than using a stick. Firmly committed to desegregation, he not only believed that his approach was best in principle as a means of achieving the goal, he did not believe the Powell Amendment had a chance, politically.

The NAACP understood the sentiments behind his move, and likely would not oppose extra money to assist the desegregation process. But the Udall proposal would not guarantee that districts would take the bait; in fact, more than a few Southern officials were on record as forever maintaining segregation, the Supreme Court decisions notwithstanding.

Therefore, Mitchell in responding to his friend, recognized the difficult position he was in. But Mitchell, as Wilkins had done earlier, urged the liberals to "devote their energies to supporting rather than opposing our amendment." Perhaps what should happen is to have a public record (through a vote) of those who were prepared to stand up for civil rights. If the amendment was withdrawn, such a "list" would not be known. Mitchell sympathized with Udall and appreciated his efforts to find a solution, but "nevertheless, I believe it is a terrible mistake for you to oppose our amendment."[68]

In the end, the school construction aid bill was defeated. Blame was spread around by all members in the liberal and civil rights camp. "Intransigence" was leveled at the Powell/NAACP forces. The tension within the NAACP itself surfaced even more. One NAACP board member who had earlier written a letter to the editor supporting the Powell Amendment as "wise and necessary statesmanship,"[69] subsequently circulated a caustic memorandum to his colleagues on the NAACP board. He was not at all pleased with the no-compromise stance of his NAACP colleagues. By maintaining such a position, they got neither education funds nor integrated education. And because they had insisted on the latter, they lost the former. In addition, "we have been made to look like political suckers and amateurs because passing the Amendment was exactly what the enemies of the Federal aid for schools wanted." He reminded his colleagues that they needed "friends and allies" and the way they were proceeding would make this difficult. They needed liberals in religious and union circles, and these forces should not be alienated by intransigent tactics. To compromise on this issue, he argued, did not mean that they had to give up the fight to end segregation.[70]

It was indeed an old problem in the civil rights struggle. Half loaf versus whole loaf. When to compromise? Principle versus pragmatic politics.

When the bill was finally defeated in 1956, Powell received a telegram from the president of a black college in Mississippi: "I guess you are happy today you have burned the bridge for every Negro child and white to get the education they need. You would do anything to reach a political end."[71] Powell sent the telegram to Clarence, who he knew would make an appropriate response. Mitchell wrote to the college president that the Powell Amendment was aimed at protecting the rights of "colored people." And he reminded him that the Mississippi congressional delegation was against the bill even without the Powell Amendment. He asked pointedly, "What kind of telegram have you sent to your own representatives?"[72]

The Negro congressman from Chicago, Democrat William L. Dawson, did not, however, agree with the NAACP and Powell. He voted against the amendment, stating, "I can never do anything that I conscientiously believe will deprive any child of an education."[73]

This particular issue raised by the Powell Amendment would not finally be resolved in legislative form until a decade later with the passage of the Civil Rights Act of 1964. It would be, some would say later, a crowning achievement, a major legacy, of Powell's congressional career. The ultimate victory was no less a tribute to the relentless efforts of Clarence Mitchell and the NAACP.

For his own part, Powell could also claim to have carried the fight—literally—with honor. In July 1955, during heated committee discussions, one segregationist committee member from West Virginia, sixty-nine-year-old Cleveland M. Bailey, became enraged and accused Powell of trying to wreck the public school system. Tempers flared. Powell called Bailey a "liar," whereupon the older man landed a surprise punch on Powell's jaw, sending him sprawling. Colleagues quickly stepped in, calmed feelings, and persuaded the two to shake hands. Later to the press, Powell sported his widest grin and simply dismissed the affair with: "Cleve Bailey and I smoke cigars together and are old friends."[74]

One more blow taken for democracy.

11

The Bandung Conference and a (Surprising) Voice for America

The year 1955 was a characteristically frenetic time for Congressman Powell. In addition to his persistent prodding of military and civilian government authorities, as well as engaging in the intense congressional debates over the antisegregation amendment, he became involved in international affairs in Asia at a time when the Eisenhower administration was dreadfully fearful that an atomic war could conceivably break out with the People's Republic of China. There were two dramas developing in Southeast Asia and in the Formosa Straits, both of which involved delicate foreign negotiations and potentially dangerous consequences. Powell thrust himself prominently into the first, while the Eisenhower administration carefully navigated through the latter.

In early January, 1955, the prime ministers of India, Ceylon (later Sri Lanka), Burma, Pakistan, and Indonesia decided to convene a Pan-Asian/Pan-African conference of twenty-nine independent nations. The purpose was to discuss issues of colonialism and the growing desire for self-determination on the part of the peoples of what years later came to be called the Third World. This would be the first such meeting of its kind, and obviously in the heated environment of post–World War II international politics, it would be one watched with much interest by the superpowers of the East and West. These were nations often referred to as the ones ardently pursued in the ideological struggle between Communism and capitalism. They were a crucial element of the Cold War confrontation. Which way would they turn? Who would gain their favor?

The conference was called for April 18–24, 1955, in Bandung, Indonesia.

The People's Republic of China (popularly called Red China in the United States) and India together represented almost half the population of the world. One was Communist, the other fiercely attempting to chart a course of neutrality, or nonalignment. There were conspicuous omissions from the list of invitees: Israel, because the Arab nations objected to her presence; South Africa, because of its official policy of racial apartheid; the Republic of China (Chiang Kai-shek's exiled government on Formosa), because of the objection of "Red" China; and both North and South Korea, because of the ideological differences between them.

Such a forum clearly offered an opportunity to score ideological and political points, and few persons in the United States expected otherwise. Certainly the United States would have its supporters there, the Philippines and Pakistan being the most likely. But since the Western capitalist countries were the ones with colonies remaining in Asia and Africa, these were expected to receive the brunt of condemnation at Bandung. And it was expected that Chou En-lai of China would lead that attack.

At the same time, political affairs were heating up between the United States and Chou En-lai over Formosa and two islands just off the coast of China—Quemoy and Matsu—under the control of Formosa. There was serious speculation that China would attempt to take the two islands, which she claimed belonged to the mainland, as a preparatory step to attacking Chiang Kai-shek on Formosa. Chiang, in the meantime relying on American defense promises, had never given up the hope of using the two islands as an eventual launching pad for a strike against mainland China. Such a war surely would involve the United States and the probable use of atomic weapons. In March 1955, Eisenhower, Stephen E. Ambrose reported, was speculating that the situation would possibly lead to a war.[1] The American President was prepared to defend Formosa, but not Quemoy and Matsu if a Communist attack on the latter two did not presage a move against Formosa. Eisenhower did not believe world public opinion would sanction a United States atomic fight in the Formosa Straits.

These delicate calculations were taking place at the same time plans were moving forward to convene the Bandung Conference.

Enter Adam Clayton Powell.

On January 26, 1955, Powell took the floor of the House of Representatives and made a speech. Mistakenly noting the date to be the fifth anniversary of India's independence, he called attention to the upcoming Bandung Conference. Granted, the United States was not invited, properly so since the conference was for Asian and African nations, he urged the U.S. nonetheless to send an interracial delegation of observers, "not an all-white Department of State team, but an all-American Department of State team, a team composed of Negroes and whites, of Jews and Gentiles, and of Protestants and Catholics."[2] In this way, he argued, the U.S. could demonstrate its identity with the colored peoples of Asia and Africa. He also took the opportunity, once again, to praise Eisenhower and the Supreme Court for leadership in "showing the world that we are beginning to practice at home the democracy that we preach abroad." The problem, he asserted, was with U.S. foreign policy, not its progress in civil rights on the domestic front.

He followed this speech with a letter to Rabb, making the same points, and even suggested some Negro names: "the Assistant Secretary of Labor, Mr. [J. Ernest] Wilkins, and one of the three Negro members of the House of Representatives—Congressman Dawson, Diggs or myself."[3] So that his own name be understood as especially appropriate, he immodestly added: "I know personally many of the Chiefs of State and members of the foreign offices of these countries, both in Africa and in Asia, and I can assure you that the appearance in Indonisia [*sic*] at that time of American officials, both Negro and white, will be of tremendous value."

Rabb sent the letter on to the State Department "for such action you deem appropriate."

Two weeks later, Rabb informed Powell of State's decision, enclosing a memo from the department. The Department of State "was currently working on the problems posed by the conference," the memo read, but noted that there were "no present plans to send observers" and that "Congressman Powell should not be encouraged in his apparent hope to attend the Conference as an observer."[4] The memo duly noted that neither the Republic of China (Chiang Kai-shek's Formosa) nor the Republic of Korea was invited.

Powell's secretary acknowledged Rabb's correspondence and added: "Mr. Powell states that he will attend the Conference and will pay his own way."[5]

This was not pleasant news for the State Department. A volatile gathering at that delicate time in that part of the world was not what American foreign policy interests needed. It would be politically safer if Powell and all others connected in any way with the

U.S. government simply stayed away. On March 2, a handwritten note was put on Rabb's desk: "Thruston Morton called. State people don't want Powell going to Asian Conf.—would like to talk to him—get him other assignments. Talked to him 2 March—He will talk to Morton & probably will go along."[6]

Whatever "probably will go along" meant, Powell had already decided and announced publicly that he was going "with or without the approval of the State Department." In the meantime, the State Department, already in the middle of the Formosa Straits crisis, was attempting to strike the proper stance toward Bandung. As a member of the South East Asia Treaty Organization (SEATO), the U.S. supported a short statement of "cordial greetings," to be given to the conferees by Pakistan, Philippines, and Thailand. It reaffirmed SEATO's commitment to "the principle of equal rights and self-determination" and "independence of all countries whose peoples desire it and are able to undertake its responsibilities."[7]

Secretary of State John Foster Dulles issued a statement to his colleagues in SEATO saying there was no conflict between the SEATO nations and others attending the conference. Everyone wanted peace, justice, freedom.

> Therefore it seems to me that a message of fraternal greeting to those who will be gathering presumably, and we hope actually, to promote the same goals that we seek, is extremely desirable and will tend to dissipate any feeling that there is a conflict between us, or that there is a strain between us, or any fear of apprehension on the part of one gathering as to the purposes and intentions of the other gathering.[8]

That would take care of the U.S. position coming out of SEATO and the State Department. But that might not be sufficient. The President might still be pressed to say something. In late March, Nelson A. Rockefeller, then a special assistant at the White House, tried his hand at a short four-page speech Eisenhower might make, outlining the various U.S. economic programs for Southeast Asia. On the morning of March 31, there was a lengthy State Department staff meeting on the proposed speech and it was rejected. Dulles sent a memorandum to Sherman Adams explaining:

> Our view is that a major Presidential speech along the line proposed is neither desirable nor feasible at this time, but that a less formal statement from the President, either at a press conference or during the course of some informal address, might be very helpful. . . . We

> feel that any such speech would have to be delivered by at least April 10 in order to avoid being regarded as a purely propaganda effort and having the appearance of interference from an outside party. . . . One possibility would be next week's Press Conference, at which *prepared questions would have to be planted.*[9]

Rockefeller readily agreed and helped draft a short potential press conference answer for the President which essentially reiterated Dulles's earlier statement at SEATO. Rockefeller's proposed statement did add, however, a swipe at the Communists, specifically naming the "Soviet Union" and "Communist China" as "the only powers in the world today that are seeking to extend a dominating control over other peoples in the time-worn pattern of colonialism."

Powell was not giving up yet on trying to get Eisenhower to make a statement. On April 6 he wired the President urging him to "send greetings of good will." He reminded Eisenhower:

> . . . I think my presence there as an American Negro will do much to counteract any propaganda of Red China concerning the United States and its minority problem. A message of good will from you will be of tremendous strategic importance. It will not cost this country anything and I am sure we will gain much for it. . . . I will be extremely happy if while in Bandung to note that you have sent at least greetings of good will and cooperation for peace for our world and for Asia and Africa.[10]

Powell could not budge Eisenhower on this one. Instead, Assistant Secretary Morton wired Powell, restating portions of the earlier U.S. position. At the same time, Powell had wired Morton, noting that a *New York Times* article had indicated that the State Department had issued directives to various U.S. embassies to have a "friendly and cooperative" attitude toward the conference. If this was the best Powell could get, he would take it. In his wire to Morton, he stated: "May I place myself entirely at your disposal and any special instructions which you may want to convey. I will look forward to receiving them at various embassies along the way and at Djakarta. I can be reached tonight at Lincoln 4–7770 if there are any last minute instructions."[11] Morton simply thanked him and suggested he "consult Ambassador Cumming at Djakarta."

Apparently Powell wanted desperately to have some kind of official U.S. blessing or recognition of his appearance in Bandung. Although he was paying his own expenses and was certified as a correspondent for the *New York Age–Defender*, a black weekly newspaper, he obviously felt his stature at the conference could be enhanced by a friendly word or gesture from his government. As events developed, his independent, nonofficial status very likely served him better than if he *had* received State Department instructions. He was free to chart his own course at the conference, and to make the most of whatever benefits might ensue.

Thus, while the administration was tiptoeing through the potentially explosive Formosa Straits crisis, trying to deal with Chou En-lai, Chiang Kai-shek, and a host of other problems in that part of the world, Adam Powell arrived in Bandung—his own man, with his own portfolio. He could be what he had official credentials to be—namely, an unofficial observer and reporter. Or he could make news, something he had always done when the scene was right and the audience was available.

Of course, he chose the latter.

There were five hundred reporters and journalists from around the world interviewing officials, recording arrivals, checking rumors, filing stories. Each delegation had several stories it wanted told to the world. There were three South Africans, two blacks and an Indian, who had come invited but not as officials because their country, obviously, was not invited. They were there to plead their cause against apartheid in South Africa. They held a news conference the day before Powell arrived, and in the course of the session they indicated that they hoped the United States, among other major powers, would aid their fight. A young Ceylonese woman reporter asked them how they could expect the U.S. to be sympathetic to their plight in South Africa when racial segregation and discrimination existed in the States. Their answer is not known, but news of the press conference reached Powell on his arrival. That was his opening.

He immediately called his own press conference and at least one hundred reporters showed up at his hotel. This surely would be news. His arrival at the conference was not at all comparable to the pomp and ceremony accorded heads of state, but he was a known figure, a black congressman from the United States who had a wide reputation as a fighter for civil rights in his country. The mood of the press conference was expectant, the atmosphere one of high excitement. Powell indicated that he was sorry the Ceylonese reporter was not present, because he wanted to correct the record. And he was off and running.

Without question there were racial problems in his country, but "racism in the United States is on the way out.

> Second class citizenship is on the way out.
>
> A few years ago Washington was an open cesspool of United States democracy. Today it is a place of complete equality. Every hotel, restaurant, amusement place, school and golf course is completely integrated.
>
> It is a mark of distinction in the United States to be a Negro. To be a Negro is no longer a stigma.
>
> A Negro has been elected to a city-wide office in Atlanta.
>
> Negroes are in office in Richmond and Norfolk.
>
> Virginia has decided not to resist the Supreme Court decision in favor of ending segregation in schools."

Reporters from Communist countries were astounded and disappointed, some noticeably putting away their notebooks when they saw where Powell was going.[12] He might have lost their attention, but he certainly had grabbed the Bandung spotlight back home. He was deluged for the next several days by reporters from the States asking him to elaborate, to give his opinions on the conference, on Chou En-lai, Nehru. The first gathering of twenty-nine Asian and African countries in a conference aimed at ending colonialism might have limited news value back in the States in 1955, but what one of the most prominent civil rights leaders, a black congressman, on the scene had to say about U.S. domestic racial problems was definitely worth the time and space, especially after that opening salvo that caused some Communist journalists to turn away in derision. Powell hardly cared about them. He knew who his audience was. And now, having gotten the appropriate attention of the U.S. media in this mountain resort city in Indonesia, he would use the platform to expound on U.S. foreign policy. *U.S. News & World Report* got him for a lengthy interview which was cabled back to New York for immediate publication. It was his most authentic statement following the first press conference. But now, to his satisfaction, the subjects dealt more with U.S. foreign policy toward colonialism. To a series of leading questions, Powell waxed eloquently against Communists, Chou En-lai in particular; for a progressive policy toward anticolonialism; and for a bright future for pro-Americanism if the United States took certain steps. He emphasized that the delegates were not anti-American, but they were decidedly against American foreign policy. Red China should not be seen as the dominant power among these countries, but simply as another force; the delegates were concerned with being under *no* domination from East or West. Powell took care to stress that military force should not be used in the Formosa Straits, even though Chiang Kai-shek had "very little" support among the delegates. And, of course, he carefully noted how, simply by "holding a press conference," he was able to "stop Communist propaganda concerning the American Negro." How, precisely?—"simply by telling the truth about the race problem in the United States."[13]

Powell had had his say in Bandung. His strong defense of America's race relations did not consume the conference. Delegates had their own agendas to push. There was even a minimum of discussion over the Formosa Straits issue. Even Powell admitted in the *U.S. News* interview: "Non-Communist countries didn't want to raise this question . . . because they didn't want to antagonize anyone, including the United States. But behind the scene, many delegates told me Quemoy and Matsu should go to Red China."

Throughout the week Powell circulated among the delegates, meeting many anticolonial advocates he had never heard of and learning a lot. He even attempted to intervene with the Chinese to get some American flyers released who were being held prisoners by the Chou En-lai government. When he did say unfavorable things about the U.S., he stuck to the subject of America's need to be more aggressive in its anticolonial policy. After a week, it was time to go home, and he embarked with the self-assured feeling that he had acquitted himself well. He was prepared to return and launch into this latest role of world statesman. He knew there would be criticism in some quarters about his lavish defense of racial affairs, but he also knew he would take up where he left off—dashing off letters of protest against discrimination and segregation, fighting for the Powell Amendment.

In all honesty, he might not have been prepared for the standing ovation he received from his congressional colleagues when he appeared on the House floor the first time back. Speeches were made lauding his courage and patriotism. A congressional resolution applauded his defense of American democracy against evil Communism. Congressman Ray J. Madden (D.-Ind.) went so far as to announce that, thanks to Powell, this was the "first world-wide moral defeat for Communist aggression."[14] It was, indeed, the one and only time he would be so hailed by so many of his colleagues. They were demonstrating their appreciation, for surely many if not most had not the slightest inkling that this maverick among them would be *so* vociferous in his defense of his country in what was assumed would be hostile foreign territory. For a brief time, Powell soaked up the glory. The Veterans of Foreign Wars gave him a citation.

Shortly after his return, he sought an appointment with President Eisenhower. In a telegram, he wrote: "Imperative that I see you as soon as possible preferably before your Tuesday conference with the Republican and Democratic leaders concerning inside report of Asian African Bandung Conference."[15]

What he soon found out, however, was that the welcome-home reception went just so far. Eisenhower was still unwilling to see him personally. What followed over the next ten days after the telegram was a series of telephone calls, memos, press speculation of an administration "snub," and growing Powell anger.

Powell's secretary called twice on May 2, seeking an appointment. Bryce Harlow returned one call, telling Powell the President's schedule would not permit an appointment the next day. A White House memo to Bernard Shanley, special counsel to the President, read: "He [Harlow] feels it better that you tell him [Powell] not possible—and that is his advice—that no appt. be arranged for Powell."

Another Powell call pushed for "definitely this week." Harlow and Rabb advised Shanley to consult first "with State, and if they think it is OK, . . . we should try to accommodate him with an appt."

Two days later, Powell's secretary was put off again. Then Shanley called Powell to suggest that the congressman talk to Mr. Herbert Hoover (son of the ex-president) at the State Department "and then decide whether he still felt he had to see the President." (It was not lost on the administration that while Powell had some strong words of support for his country's progress in race relations, he had also strongly attacked America's foreign policy in the Far East and on colonial issues.) Of course, Powell wanted to talk to Eisenhower personally, but he would also see the people over at the State Department.[16] Meanwhile, a news item appeared in the *New York Daily News* menacingly titled: "No One Will Hear His Report, Administration Snub Rouses Powell's Ire."[17] Powell was quoted as saying that if he could not see the President or John Foster Dulles, he would make his report public and "that will not be pleasant." An appointment finally was set up with the President for May 11. Maxwell Rabb sat in and took notes.

Basically, Powell made the same points to Eisenhower that he had been making in Bandung and afterwards. He said he "went to Bandung in order to give living proof to the fact that there is no truth in the Communist charge that the Negro is oppressed in America." He felt the next big Communist propaganda attack would concentrate in Africa, and that he heard from "reliable sources" that twenty million dollars' worth of ammunition was being "smuggled into Tunis and Algeria from Communist-inspired sources." The prime mover of this group, according to Powell, was someone known as the "Grand Mufti of Jerusalem," an Arab leader who was in Bandung urging delegates to support Chou En-lai and not America. Powell's proof of the Grand Mufti's activities and plans apparently came from newspaper clippings which the American press had not picked up. Powell described Nehru and Krishna Menon of India as "bitter men." He urged, nonetheless, that aid to India be continued, with which the President agreed. Powell also suggested that more Negroes be assigned to U.S. embassies in Asia and Africa. Eisenhower appeared skeptical when Powell informed him of low morale in the Foreign Service, but he promised to look into the matter. Powell informed the President that Chou En-lai would have lost any attempt to obtain an anti-West vote at the conference. He concluded by repeating his suggestion of a summit meeting between SEATO and the "Colombo Powers."[18] Such a meeting might be held in Manila, and Powell urged that it be held "in order to annihilate the propaganda drive of Red China."

So Powell had his meeting with the President. It lasted thirty-five minutes. Bandung was behind him, but the fallout continued.

More than a few commentators—friend and foe—were dumbfounded by Powell's actions at Bandung. In hindsight, perhaps, they should not have been, because Powell was clearly on record back home as praising Eisenhower and the Supreme Court, even if from time to time he loudly denounced Congress and other governmental bodies. But the surprising thing to many was that he would choose an international forum to be such a patriotic defender of race relations in the States. If he wanted to make an impressive mark in anticolonial circles abroad, one might have expected him to deliver a speech more similar to one he might give on the corner of 125th Street and Seventh Avenue in Harlem. Then, again, why should he do that? His hometown constituents of twenty years knew where he stood. He was not seeking votes in Bandung. And he certainly came down on the right side on the colonial issue and against American *foreign* policy. These were the two issues of highest concern to the audience in Bandung. Apparently, it was not necessarily planned as a U.S.-bashing conference. *Most* delegates in all likelihood wanted to steer a nonaligned course. Thus Powell's defense of America's civil rights record would do him little damage that week in Indonesia. And he probably correctly calculated that reaction back home would be mixed, leaning toward favorable. He had not, after all, embraced the Southern segregationists. His basic message was one of progress, not final victory. Ultimately, the plaudits he would gain from rather stunned and grateful sources would far outweigh the reaction of temporary dismay and disappointment from those who wanted a more accusatory voice at Bandung.

At any rate, aside from general approbation from his congressional colleagues, reaction in the media was predictably mixed. One columnist, P. L. Prattis, in the prominent Negro weekly newspaper the *Pittsburgh Courier*, was amusingly cautious in his open letter to Powell. Prattis admitted there were certain parts of Powell's Bandung remarks he did not quite grasp—such as "it was a distinction to be a Negro" in America, given the racial slights he experienced in everyday travels around the country. He also subtly called Powell's attention to a kind of racial breakdown in responses: these were "raves" from the white press, while Negro papers were "somewhat non-committal, or downright critical." And he concluded: "Maybe the colored writers aren't quite so sure—they're not certain you have meant all you said. Some of them may feel that you are pulling Uncle Sam's leg."[19]

Predictably, the Communist *Daily Worker* weighed in with all guns blasting: "He [Powell] insulted the intelligence of his conference hosts by statements exaggerating the victories against racism."[20]

The president of the Washington, D.C., local branch of the NAACP said: "All Congressman Powell had to do was tell the truth, not go overboard."[21] Still another critic took him to task for politically tactical reasons: "Why . . . did Negroes resent what Mr. Powell is reported to have said at Bandung? Because they know that outside pressure, chiefly from the Communists, is probably the strongest factor in forcing a betterment of their status here; that an attack on colonialism (which is nothing else but racialism) anywhere, is an attack on it here, too."[22]

Dr. Marguerite Cartwright, a Negro correspondent who had covered the conference and rode back on the plane with Powell, thought his portrayal of Chou En-lai was "not true." In fact, she concluded that Chou gained prestige by just "being invited to the conference. He was in top form and was followed by adoring mobs wherever he went."[23]

But Powell, the experienced politician that he was, knew that all the precincts weren't in. Indeed, the usually critical *New York Mirror* was so pleased with him that it editorialized: "On the basis of what he has accomplished so far, we'd suggest that Congress pass a special bill to reimburse him."[24] The Republican-oriented *Pittsburgh Courier* wondered: "Is the Harlem Congressman seeking to get into the good graces of the powers-that-be, and if so, why? Whatever the reason, we are glad to see this *new* Congressman Powell in the role of defender of God's country."[25] The liberal *New Republic* noted with irony that Powell "did more than anyone else at the Bandung Conference . . . to persuade delegates of America's decency in racial relations," but he would still have "to ride in the back of buses in the South, can't stay at certain hotels, or eat in many restaurants."[26] The widely read, influential Ralph McGill of the *Atlanta Constitution* expressed an appreciative view when he concluded: "Rep. Powell did a great service to his country."[27] He pointed out that Powell's voice carried even greater weight because he paid his own way and, therefore, no one "could charge him with being a paid voice."

The affair finally simmered down, of course, but once again the unpredictable Powell had left his mark. He moved on to other issues, always commanding center stage, and virtually always leaving admirers and adversaries wondering how and where—never if—he would strike next.

12

Alleged Kickbacks and an Income Tax Investigation

On July 3, 1953, an interoffice memorandum was sent to the FBI director. The subject of the memo was "Congressman Adam Clayton Powell, Jr., New York."[1]

The Department of Justice had received information that suggested that the congressman might be involved in a salary kickback arrangement with an employee on his staff and he might be vulnerable to income tax fraud charges. The writer of the memo, D. M. Ladd, conveyed the opinion of the Justice Department official, Warren Olney:

> Mr. Olney stated he could initiate an investigation with reference to the so-called kickback, which he felt would be very difficult to prove, in view of the fact that [name censored] was allegedly not cooperative; further, he indicated that Congressman Powell has recently made several attacks against the Attorney General and an investigation by the Department would be attacked by him as being political in nature. He, therefore, thought it would be much easier to make an income tax case and to refer the matter to the Internal Revenue as an income tax matter. He wanted, however, to mention this to the Bureau.[2]

The FBI was agreeable to any decision the Justice Department made, that the FBI "would not object" to proceeding "on the income tax angle."

For the next eight years, Powell was involved in an income tax investigation and an eventual trial for tax evasion and fraud.

The catalyst, as it later developed, was a tip from an old Powell former political ally, Joseph Ford, who had served as Powell's campaign manager in his earlier Harlem elections. He was also an accountant who prepared the income tax returns for Powell and several members of the staff and congregation of Abyssinian Baptist Church. Ford was also a member of the church. Ford and Powell had a bitter political parting of the ways in 1951, and now Ford, who had taken many of Powell's personal financial records with him, had no intention any longer of maintaining loyalty to his one-time political protégé. According to inquiries made by the journalist Jack Anderson (then on the staff of columnist Drew Pearson) in 1954, Ford went to a Herbert Bruce who was opposing Powell in the Democratic primary for Congress that year. Ford and Bruce wrote a "John Doe" letter to the Department of Justice.[3] This account, however, places these events several months after the FBI memo of July 1953. In any case, there is no dispute that Ford and the records in his possession were the principal sources for the subsequent investigations. It seems that a Mrs. Hattie Freeman Dodson was drawing two salaries from 1945, one as congressional secretary to Powell and the other as business secretary for Abyssinian Baptist Church. In addition, her husband, Howard T. Dodson, drew a salary of $3,000 as Abyssinian's choirmaster. Ford reported that Mrs. Dodson filed two income tax returns, one as a joint return with her husband including only their church salaries. The other return she filed under her maiden name of "Hattie Freeman." Mrs. Dodson had gone to Washington when Powell entered Congress, but she married Mr. Dodson at the end of the year and returned to New York still remaining on the government payroll as Powell's Washington-based secretary. She did not return to Washington. According to Ford, Mrs. Dodson told him that "the money she received was not kept by her but that she gave it back to the Congressman." Ford also testified that Mrs. Dodson told him: ". . . The Congressman told her that she could keep any refund of taxes she got on her withholding tax." In addition, both the joint return and Mrs. Dodson's individual return listed seven fictitious dependents: three nonexistent children, a brother, aunt, and grandparents, none of whom lived with the Dodsons. The Dodsons denied any wrongdoing, but insisted that they had relied on Ford, the "so-called tax expert to prepare their taxes properly."

Thus the government was faced with two possibilities: salary kickback charges against Powell with income tax implications, and tax fraud against the Dodsons. For the moment, the decision was made to move on the second, and to continue the investigation of Powell.

At nine o'clock one morning in May 1954, Mrs. Dodson answered a knock on her door. According to an affidavit she later filed in the United States District Court, the following events took place.[4] She received four persons into her home that morning—Assistant United States Attorney Samuel R. Pierce, Jr., two U.S. Treasury agents, and a woman "who appeared from the case she was carrying to be a stenotype operator." Pierce informed her that she was subpoenaed to appear before a grand jury at ten-thirty that same morning. When she stated she would appear on her own, Pierce wrote "forthwith" on the subpoena and suggested they wait until she dressed and take her downtown with them. When they arrived at Pierce's office, she was questioned for two hours. Her account reads:

> On my arrival at the Court House Messrs. Pierce and Bolson took me to Mr. Pierce's office and proceeded to question me vigorously about certain tax returns which they alleged I had filed jointly with my husband under the name of Dodson, and individually under my maiden name of Freeman. Mr. Pierce was not satisfied with my answers to his questions. On a number of occasions during the questioning, he told me that he was going to lock me up. He seemed to be seeking additional information about something unrelated to my case. He kept saying to me throughout the questioning "You know what I want to know. Now tell me what I want to know," or words to that effect.[5]

After a half-hour lunch break, during which time Mrs. Dodson was unsuccessful in reaching her lawyer, she was taken before the grand jury and proceeded to answer incriminating questions. Her affidavit continued:

> Subsequent to this occasion, I found out what Mr. Pierce had been driving at in our interview. In the course of later interviews with him, Mr. Pierce said that he wanted me to testify against my employer, Congressman Adam Clayton Powell, about various alleged irregularities in the conduct of his office. I then realized that Mr. Pierce's behavior in my home and during the first interview in his office was designed to intimidate me into testifying against Congressman Powell

> on matters that I knew nothing about, as well as into incriminating my husband and myself.[6]

Notwithstanding her hurried appearance before the grand jury with neither a warning nor legal counsel, an indictment was not handed down until seven months later, on December 16, 1954. All of this, Mrs. Dodson pleaded, constituted self-incrimination under duress and intimidation. She moved to dismiss the indictment, but to no avail. She and her husband were brought to trial for income tax evasion and fraud in May 1956.

The main witness against them was their former tax accountant, Joseph Ford. He testified that Mrs. Dodson had specifically told him that Congressman Powell was receiving the money from her government salary and that Powell therefore wanted her to file two tax returns. She agreed, Ford asserted, because she said "the money belonged to the congressman and she didn't want to mix it with her income."[7] At one point in his testimony, he admitted that he could not explain why one of the returns signed "Hattie Freeman" was, in fact, his handwriting. For three years, 1948 to 1951, Ford insisted that he advised Mrs. Dodson that what she was doing was wrong, but each time she insisted, saying she had checked with Powell.

Mrs. Dodson's lawyer pressed Ford on the reasons for his now disclosing this information. Was it because of enmity toward Powell, his former political colleague? Ford replied: "I have nothing at all against Congressman Powell. I voted for him at the last election." Had Ford told Samuel R. Pierce about the kickbacks? At first Ford said no, but when asked again, he replied, "I told him the truth." What did that mean, the lawyer asked. Ford responded, "I did."

The prosecution read into the record a statement made by Mrs. Dodson to the grand jury in May 1954, wherein she told Ford to list fraudulent dependents.

Mrs. Dodson did not take the witness stand at her trial. Her lawyer explained that he did not want the prosecution to "mock and sneer" at her, and that she had been treated "miserably" in her 1954 grand jury appearance.[8]

Further, in her grand jury statement, Mrs. Dodson told a story that sought to explain the fate of the money from the congressional salary. She stated that she never gave the money to Powell. She got every cent. And she kept it in a safe deposit box, never telling her husband about it, because she wanted to "surprise" him someday when they were ready to buy "a little house." The approximate amount was $9,000, but she said she had spent much of it. Indeed, her husband had testified that he knew nothing of his wife's income from the reputed congressional job. The checks were often cashed by a Sunday school teacher and secretary at the Abyssinian Church.

Adam Powell appeared to testify on behalf of the Dodsons. This was a surprise move, and the courtroom was packed with sympathetic supporters, many from Abyssinian. Earlier in the day, just prior to Powell's appearance, the judge, with the prosecution's consent, had dropped the charges against Mr. Dodson.

Mrs. Dodson's lawyer put the straightforward question to Powell: "Did Hattie Freeman Dodson ever kick back any of her congressional salary to you?"

"Unqualifiedly no," Powell answered. "Never. Not a penny."

All news accounts reported Powell's appearance, and noted that his voice was so subdued that it sometimes was inaudible in the courtroom. Powell denied that there was ever an agreement between himself and Mrs. Dodson regarding her check or any aspect of her tax return. Probed about his relation to Joseph Ford, Powell had nothing kind to say about his old political buddy. Ford ran a "tax mill" at the church; he was not a man to be trusted. How had Powell come to be associated with him over a decade ago in such a close relationship that he had Ford serve as his campaign manager several times?

"I didn't know anything about practical politics," Powell responded. "He was a practical politician, and I needed someone like him."

The one light moment in his testimony came when Powell was asked by the prosecution if he would change his mind about Mrs. Dodson if she admitted lying before the grand jury.

No, Powell said. He would not base his opinion of a person on just one wrongdoing.

Prosecutor Thomas A. Bolan: On how many occasions do you have to be informed that Mrs. Dodson lied before you would change your opinion as to whether she was capable of lying?

Powell: I don't know. The Bible tells me seventy times seven.

Bolan: Seventy times seven?

Powell: That is what the Bible says . . .

Bolan: That is 490 times, is that right?

Powell: That is what Jesus said, yes sir.

Bolan: . . . until Mrs. Dodson admits that she has lied on 490 occasions you will stick to your opinion that she is not capable of telling a lie, is that right?

Powell: Yes it is, yes it is.

Bolan: . . . did that passage refer to forgiveness, or did it refer to the capacity to do sin?

Powell: Forgiveness.

Bolan: . . . I didn't ask you whether you would forgive Mrs. Dodson if she lied 490 times. I asked you if your opinion would change as to her capacity for lying.

Powell: Her capacity to sin?

Bolan: Yes.

Powell: Okay, yes. I believe we all have it, a capacity to sin. Yes sir.

Following Powell on the witness stand was Samuel Pierce, who had first approached Mrs. Dodson at her home two years earlier. Pierce had since left his post as Assistant U.S. Attorney and was then serving as an assistant to the Under Secretary of Labor, one of the few Negroes in the Eisenhower administration. (Twenty-five years later, Pierce would be appointed Secretary of Housing and Urban Development and serve eight years in the Reagan administration.) He denied that he acted improperly in bringing Mrs. Dodson before the grand jury in 1954. And he denied that he or his associates were really attempting to get Adam Powell, rather than his secretary. Finally, under questioning, he termed "ridiculous" a suggestion by Mrs. Dodson's attorney that he possibly had personal designs on winning Powell's congressional seat.[9]

That might be Pierce's version, but Mrs. Dodson's attorney, Frederick H. Bloc, was having none of it. He summed up: "The Government is prosecuting my client because they don't have the guts to indict Congressman Powell. They want to send her to jail so they can brainwash her every day and beat her down to get her to give them information against Mr. Powell."[10] He accused the main government witness, Joseph Ford, of "a dastardly character assassination committed . . . for political revenge." And he challenged: "If Powell has done anything wrong, the government would have brought it out."

The jury of ten men and two women, however, returned a guilty verdict, and the judge sentenced Mrs. Dodson to seven months in prison and a one-thousand dollar fine.

Powell sent a letter to the judge asking for leniency, but Judge Irving H. Kaufman took his own counsel on the matter. He was, in fact, influenced by her "impeccable record" in the past, and therefore did not impose a harsher sentence, which could have been a maximum of forty-five years in prison and $90,000 in fines. The kickback charges did not enter into his consideration, Judge Kaufman said: "If you believe her assertion that she received and retained her congressional salary, the seriousness and brazenness of the tax evasion becomes more masked. . . . It is hardly likely that a woman of her executive ability could be as slovenly in her personal affairs as she pretends."[11]

Powell blamed the entire affair on opponents of his who were part of an effort "to stop [Powell's] congressional fight against White Citizens Councils. There is someone, or group, trying to stop the fight I am making. I'm accumulating evidence in both parties, and the number is beginning to narrow. I think definitely that I will be able soon to put my finger on who it is."[12]

For her part, Mrs. Dodson went to prison insisting on her innocence, and criticizing the "completely erroneous" impression that she and Powell were involved in a salary kickback arrangement. As she surrendered to be taken to prison, she defended her congressman: "I regret very much that there should have been any such unfounded reflection upon Congressman Powell."[13]

In an interview over thirty years later, Mrs. Dodson still remembered Adam Powell fondly. "I think that he was a great man. I don't think he gets the credit for what he tried to do. . . . He did a lot for our people. . . . As far as I know, Adam has never actually hurt anybody, but himself."[14]

There were others, however, just as fond of Powell as Hattie Dodson, and equally respectful and admiring of the former secretary, who believed, privately and anonymously, that she, indeed, was hurt by her association with Powell. There was always a suspicion lurking in the shadows that this woman, whatever her own faults in terms of the false listing of dependents, was making a great sacrifice in protecting Powell. To be sure, she was vulnerable with the fictitious dependents. Therefore, it was not necessary to prove a kickback in order to convict her. But her story of the congressional salary stashed away in a safe deposit box did not ring true to some who knew her and Powell. They believed *she* saved Powell, and was due *his* loyalty and gratitude.

Powell told a *New York Post* reporter in early 1956 an interesting story involving steady private contributions to him from his mother over a period of at least fifteen years. These mounted to $100,000, according to Powell, "from the time I was at Colgate until she died." It seems that the money, unknown to the senior Powell, came from a wealthy white man, Powell's maternal grandfather. Obviously, the reporter hinted that Powell was laying the foundation to explain his own access to funds that could explain his rather exceptional lavish life-style.[15]

The federal government was not finished with its investigation of Powell's tax returns. The authorities continued probing. And in the process, three other aides to Powell were indicted and convicted, two on charges of income tax evasion and one for embezzlement of church funds. None of these cases involved hints of salary kickbacks, but Powell was, in the minds of government officials, suspiciously linked to the tax evasion defendants. Each person had served on Powell's congressional staff as well as been members of the church. Acy Lennon and William L. Hampton were involved with Powell in a real estate and apartment sales deal. A real estate developer, David Kent, had approached Powell to help sell cooperative apartments in an interracial housing project in Queens. Powell agreed and dispatched Lennon and Hampton to Kent. Kent subsequently wrote a check for $3,000 to Powell as a "loan," payable on demand after six months at 1 percent interest. In July 1952, Kent wrote another check for $3,000 payable to the Tenants Protective Association (TPA), an organization formed by Powell in 1948 to combat slum conditions in Harlem. Ostensibly, this $3,000 was for commissions earned by Lennon and Hampton for selling apartments in the co-op. But the money was deposited in the TPA bank account and withdrawn three days later by a check paid to a Paul Klein, a close friend of Powell's. The authorization for this check remained a mystery since neither the TPA treasurer nor cotreasurer recalled signing for the withdrawal. And Klein surprisingly admitted that he did not recall receiving the money. At that point, Powell refreshed everyone's memory by stating that the $3,000 was paid to Klein "for services rendered . . . because Klein had worked so very hard for many years in many capacities and had never been paid by me." In court, when Powell was ordered to produce the records of the TPA, he informed the court that, unfortunately, some of the records had been stolen through vandalism connected with a political election against him a few years before—apparently his opponent was attempting to get at his papers. And the remainder of the TPA records were lost in a church fire, the debris being carted away by a junkman. Again, unfortunately.

Neither the first $3,000 to Powell from Kent nor the second payment was ever pinned down—no parties apparently reported the transaction in their respective income tax returns. It was becoming reasonably clear to the federal authorities that they were on the trail of questionable monetary dealings of the congressman from Harlem. In the meantime, however, they were not yet able to trace any specific money to Powell. Thus the aides, Lennon and Hampton, were indicted and convicted for filing false tax returns—the same charges that were made against Dodson—by listing nonexistent dependents. Powell announced that they got a "raw deal."

A fourth Powell associate and church member, John H. Harmon, was indicted and convicted of embezzlement of church funds in January 1957. Harmon, an accountant, handled the books of the Federal Credit Union of the Abyssinian Baptist Church. Powell, who helped organize the credit union in 1940, served as its president until he resigned in 1955. Harmon was found guilty of embezzling $2,619.

Thus, within a one-year period, four church employees and Powell aides had run afoul of the law and gone to jail. So far, Powell had not been charged with any wrongdoing. There were only hints, implications, raised eyebrows, and a growing sense that as the tax probes continued, one more shoe—Adam Powell's—would drop. All this was happening during the 1956 Presidential campaign, and Powell was making noises that he just might not be willing to support his own party's nominee, Adlai Stevenson.

Meanwhile, as the government was returning indictments against and winning convictions of Powell's aides, the income tax investigation against him personally would become embroiled in a tangled web of Presidential politics, conservative journalistic pressure, and local Harlem–New York City politics. The political Powell and the personal, legal affairs of the congressman would, from that point on, be continuously linked in one form or another. His career, always controversial, was now headed toward one drama after another. For the next fourteen years, he and his supporters would characterize his personal and legal problems as vendettas against him for his outspoken, independent political behavior—especially behavior against segregation and discrimination.

He was becoming the *cause.* Defending Powell was equated with defending civil rights.

Without question, he lived on the cusp of suspicious wrongdoing. Persons around him were going to jail, sometimes because of questionable but unproven financial dealings with him. And it was equally clear that virtually any political decision he took from then on would be subject, by friend and foe, to scrutiny for its relation to his personal problems.

This certainly was the case in the fall of 1956 when Congressman Adam Clayton Powell, Jr., six-time elected Democrat from Harlem, bolted his party and endorsed Republican President Dwight D. Eisenhower for reelection. Powell, of course, defended his action on the basis of his comparative assessment of the civil rights potential of an Eisenhower administration versus a Stevenson administration. With others, however, rumors ran rampant—thus the ongoing income tax investigation.

13

Switch to President Eisenhower, 1956

If, over the years, Adam Clayton Powell, Jr., was an enigma to many people, surely President Dwight D. Eisenhower for eight years presented a special challenge to the political dexterity of the Harlem congressman. Given Eisenhower's deep-seated views on race, he did not make Powell's periodic praise of him an especially easy task. But Powell saluted the President more often than he denounced or criticized him.

Racial tension was growing rapidly, particularly in the South. Civil rights activists were being intimidated and killed; the Montgomery, Alabama, bus boycott led by the then little known Reverend Dr. Martin Luther King, Jr., was beginning to attract the world's attention. In 1955 a Negro student, Autherine Lucy, was denied admission to the University of Alabama because of her race; White Citizens Councils opposed to integration were multiplying in the South. In a twenty-four-page report to the President's cabinet on March 9, 1956, J. Edgar Hoover detailed the growing explosive situation. White and Negro leaders were coming close to calling for open, organized violence. And if not, they were certainly predicting mass "bloodshed" on both sides. Negroes who advocated the right to vote were being subjected to economic harassment: loss of jobs, loss of credit and supplies. Hoover cited a speech by Senator James Eastland the previous month in Montgomery wherein he stated: "The Anglo-Saxon people have held steadfast to the belief that resistance to tyranny [meaning, resistance to federal insistence on integration] is obedience to God." The FBI director blamed "extremists on both sides" for creating a volatile situation. He referred to the FBI's "certain knowledge, 127 organizations have come into being since May 17, 1954, all designed to maintain segregation." He also described the efforts of the Communists to take advantage of the racial tension.[1]

It was, indeed, a pretty grim picture being sketched before the President and his cabinet that morning. Among other items on the agenda, the general outline of a proposed civil rights bill was discussed. The Attorney General, Herbert Brownell, briefly discussed four points: the creation of a bipartisan commission to study the problems; further protection of the right to vote; further protection for civil rights; and creation of an Office of Assistant Attorney General for a new Civil Rights Division in the Department of Justice. This was as far as the President was willing to go, and he wanted Brownell to stress "that what is needed is calmness and sanity." Maxwell Rabb later passed on to Brownell the thoughts of the President. "Make your statement [that is, the message to Congress that would accompany the proposed legislation] like your brief to the Supreme Court—don't take the attitude that you are another Sumner [the "radical Republican" during Reconstruction after the Civil War]." And the President once again admonished his aides on his true feelings on this subject:

> I believe that Herb Brownell should put forward what he has got here, but with a statement that many Americans understandably are separated by deep emotions on this subject. One of the prime reasons for this is that, after all, another system was upheld by the Supreme Court for 60 years. These people in the South were not breaking the law for the past 60 years, but, ever since the "separate but equal decision," they have been *obeying* the Constitution of the United States. Now, we cannot erase the emotions of three generations just overnight. . . . People have a right to disagree with the Supreme Court decision—since the Supreme Court has disagreed with its own decision of 60 years standing—but, of course, the new decision should now be carried out.[2]

In addition, the Cabinet discussion made clear that the legislative proposal would be from the Justice Department, not from the President directly.

Powell certainly was not privy to these cabinet deliberations at the time, but he was not happy with what he had been hearing—

or not hearing—from the President. In one of his rare public blasts at Eisenhower personally, he told a Howard University audience just one week prior to that cabinet meeting that he was becoming frustrated with and disappointed in the President. He accused Eisenhower of "dodging the issue, passing the buck, trying to wash his hands like Pilate of the blood of innocent men and women in the Southland."[3] He had no kind words for the Democratic leader Adlai Stevenson, either, but his public rebuke of the President was quite uncharacteristic.

A few days later, Powell continued his attack. He was critical of both parties, he said, and suggested that he and other Negro leaders might well start a third party if neither of the two major parties improved their stands on civil rights. He offered an option, however, noting that Eisenhower was much better earlier in his administration. "If President Eisenhower goes back to where he left off two years ago on civil rights—and Stevenson or other Democratic candidates continue to stand in the middle of the road [on civil rights]—I'd probably vote Republican [in the upcoming presidential election]." If both parties were to "stand still" on the issue, a third party was a possibility.[4] But if Eisenhower "resume[d] his leadership," this could present a different result.

In the midst of these observations, Powell was getting press coverage for other comments and plans. He was organizing a National Day of Prayer to give moral support to besieged Negroes in the South, especially in Montgomery where King's home had been bombed. At first he called for a day-long work stoppage, but then backed away from the idea as too disruptive. Then he made the startling announcement to his church that he might resign from the pulpit and Congress to devote himself full-time to the civil rights struggle.[5] He did neither, of course, and few political observers expected him to. Powell, they figured was simply grabbing news space.

Meanwhile, officials inside the White House and the Republican Party were trying to devise an effective stance—aside from the proposed legislation—toward the escalating racial tension. Sherman Adams had circulated the results of a Gallup poll showing Negroes still preferring the Democratic Party. E. Frederick Morrow the negro staff member in the White House, and Val J. Washington, the Negro official on the staff of the Republican National Committee, responded with almost pleading memos to Adams. Of course, Morrow wrote, the present administration had done more "to raise the Negro to the status of a first-class citizen than any other admintion in history." If this is the case, Morrow asked rhetorically, why aren't Negroes more appreciative—meaning more inclined to reward the Republicans?

> Any non-Negro would expect evidence of extreme gratitude on the part of the Negro race, but the average Negro feels that he has merely come into something that should have been his at the dawn of the Republic, and while he rejoices in his new status, he feels no extreme obligation to anyone for giving him what he believes to be his inalienable rights.[6]

Morrow proceeded to indicate that masses of Negroes felt the administration "has completely abandoned the Negro in the South and left him to the mercy of state governments that have manifested their intention to violate all laws, human and divine, as long as it results in 'keeping the Negro in his place.' " He noted that not enough publicity had been given to the quiet things the administration had done. What he recommended, however, was largely salutary: a "responsible member of the Administration" to make a statement "deploring" violence in Mississippi; more Negro speakers at the "Salute to Eisenhower Dinners" around the country; an administration-sponsored conference "of a dozen or more leading ministers, white and Negro" to talk about conditions and suggest what could be done. Undoubtedly, Morrow's recommendations were tailored to fit the mood of the people in the White House he had come to know. He later wrote that his suggestion of a conference "was vetoed by higher authority in the White House."[7] Later, when he consulted Rabb, he revealed that Rabb gave him a "tongue-lashing." Negroes were ungrateful, surly, too aggressive. "He felt that the [Negro] leaders' demands were intemperate ones and had driven most of the liberals to cover. . . . In effect, he was telling me that I should walk softly from then on and ask fewer questions of the members of the Administration on this matter."[8]

Val J. Washington was equally blunt in his response to Adams on the Gallup poll. The poll told him nothing he did not already know. To be sure, Eisenhower was more popular than his party. He candidly noted that most Negroes believed that the administration was "catering" to the white voters in the South in hopes of gaining their political support.[9] There had not been "one word" from the administration on the Emmett Till murder the previous summer. He concluded: "Negroes have accepted Eisenhower, but not the Republican Party, and some of his advisors."[10]

Morrow kept trying. In February of 1956 he pleaded to Sherman Adams to permit him to take a trip South to speak privately with some Negro leaders in Alabama. He noted that he had spent much of the previous weekend "trying to reason with Congressman Adam Powell's cohorts who are sponsoring the 'National Day of Prayer.' "[11] He thought he was successful in keeping it from becoming an antiadministration demonstration. But "One of the tragedies in the present situation is the fact that Adam Powell is a flamboyant opportunist who, while in the process of trying to assist his race in this hour, will also use what success is obtained as political ammunition."[12] Morrow continued:

> I should like official permission to go to Birmingham, Alabama this week, to have conferences with the Negro leaders (they trust me and my judgment) in the Montgomery situation, and to apprise them of what the Administration has done and is doing in the field of civil and human rights. I should like to counsel them to use wisdom and forbearance in their present actions, and that under no circumstances should they be led along the wrong path by politicians who intimate that they can get better assistance and more consideration from some other party.

By all estimates, this would be a difficult sell under the circumstances. Surely Morrow understood this, but he also had personal reasons, which he candidly disclosed, for making the request.

> All these conferences would be unofficial, and off the record, and I would not promise anything, but my presence would give these leaders the assurance of our interest and the feeling that we are not completely indifferent to the plight that besets them. It would also get me off a tremendous "spot" and erase the belief that I am too comfortable in my own position to be concerned about the plight of my brothers.[13]

The day after he wrote this memo to Sherman Adams, he got his "tongue-lashing" from Rabb. A few days later, Adams called him in and told him that he appreciated the request "but . . . it would be politically and personally dangerous . . . to be sent into the situation."[14] Adams promised to keep him informed of what the administration was planning, including briefing him on the upcoming cabinet meeting with J. Edgar Hoover. And then, solicitously, he told Morrow that he (Adams) "could appreciate [Morrow's] position as a Negro and as a member of the President's staff, but that [Morrow] must not become deeply involved in the problem because [Morrow] would be a target for recriminations that could be bad."[15]

Apparently, the "spot" that Morrow was in with some of the Negro critics was less important than the possible "recriminations" he might face from other sources. His White House employers would protect him from the latter.

There is little evidence that Powell or most other Negro leaders—politicians or civil rights activists—viewed Morrow as an influential insider. And therefore his role was seldom if ever part of serious political calculations in dealing with the White House. In the spring and summer of 1956, with the approaching Presidential election, that certainly was the case.

Adam Powell was continuing to make headlines with his various digs at both parties. He would wait and see whom he would support, if anyone. He'd have to confer with the various candidates, take their measure on civil rights. And with each salvo, media interest in him increased. He was, after all, always good copy. The *New York Post*, beginning in late March, 1956, ran five consecutive lengthy biographical articles on him, going back to his college days, with pictures. The major highlights, largely already known, of his career were retold, coming up to his current income tax investigation and threat to sit out the 1956 election. The articles also duly noted his many positive activities over the years in Harlem and for civil rights in Congress. Whether Powell particularly liked the concluding three sentences after a weeklong dissection is not known: "His proposals may be flamboyant and impractical, but he has made himself a vehicle of genuine protest. The more responsible leaders of the Negro community are left to pick up the pieces, but it is Powell that the voter remembers. On that simple truth he has built a career."[16]

Whether he liked the evaluation or not (and he probably did), Powell knew that it was just such thinking about him on the part of national and local politicians that gave his 1956 Presidential ploy credibility.

In the meantime, Powell's colleagues on the New York State Democratic Committee cast wary eyes at him and decided not to select him as a delegate to the upcoming national nominating convention. One report indicated that his 1954 *Reader's Digest* article praising Eisenhower was the cause.[17] This exclusion was in all likelihood quite comfortable for Powell. The independent path he was charting would only be complicated by a commitment at that early stage to any candidate (Governor Harriman was the New York delegation's choice for nominee) or party selection. The real action for him would not be at the convention, but afterwards when both parties had made their choices. If he had gone to the Democratic convention, this would have uncomfortably bound him, as a participating delegate, to the convention's choice. He wanted more time to do his own negotiating. Thus, skipping the Democratic National Convention, he took off on July 19 on a European tour that included attendance in London at the World Conference of Parliamentarians (he was a vice president), and several military bases. The trip lasted three months.

The Democrats nominated Adlai Stevenson again for President and Senator Estes Kefauver of Tennessee as his running mate. The Republicans' only decision was the Vice-Presidential slot, ultimately going to Richard M. Nixon for reelection. But Eisenhower had definite opinions about what the party platform should say about civil rights. During the convention, he telephoned Herbert Brownell and was emphatic that the platform not misstate his views on the Supreme Court's 1954 school desegregation ruling. Ann Whitman monitored that call, and her notes recorded the following directions from Eisenhower:

> The President called the Attorney General in San Francisco. His quarrel was with efforts to insert the words "The Eisenhower Administration . . . and the Republican Party" have supported the Supreme Court in the desegregation business. He wanted the words "Eisenhower Administration" deleted. He reminded the Attorney General that the Attorney General was, in his brief before Supreme Court, appearing as a lawyer, not as a member of the Eisenhower Administration. He said it had never come before Cabinet, for instance (and could the Attorney General imagine what a storm Mrs. Hobby would raise, had it?). The Attorney General agreed that was true. The President asked him to talk to [Prescott] Bush and [Senator] Dirksen and if they did not come around, he would refuse to "go to San Francisco."
>
> The President said that in this business he was between the compulsion of duty on one side, and his firm conviction, on the other, that because of the Supreme Court's ruling, the whole issue had been set back badly.
>
> General Persons (of the White House Staff) told me [Ann Whitman] later, he also refused to accept the word "concur." He will let go the "Republican Party accepts."[18]

So Eisenhower was holding true to his very moderate views on civil rights, apparently even to the point of being willing to embarrass his party by not showing up to accept the nomination.

If this was the candidate Powell had to use in his bluff with the Democrats, he'd play the hand dealt him.

"Despite his veiled threats, don't expect Harlem Rep. Adam Clayton Powell to bolt the Democratic Party this fall. As a Democrat, the veteran Negro congressman enjoys seniority which he'd have to give up if he left the party. But he won't stump for the national ticket."[19] This was the opinion of *Newsweek* magazine on October 1, 1956. The editors were right—and wrong.

Powell did not "bolt" the Democratic Party. He ran for reelection on the Democratic ticket in Harlem and won handily. But he did publicly announce his support for Republican President Dwight D. Eisenhower, formed an organization—Independent Democrats for Eisenhower (IDE)—with headquarters at 270 Park Avenue in New York City, and *did* stump for the national ticket—the Republican ticket.

How did this come about? Characteristically, there were several "inside" versions, speculative views, and Powell's own public explanation of his decision. Given their conflicting nature, the actual truth will likely not be known. But there were so many dimensions to the saga that there could well be kernels of accuracy in most of the accounts, as well as distortions and outright fabrications. Lurking in the background always was the speculation that Powell made a "deal" with the "Eisenhower people" involving his current income tax investigation. He would support the President in exchange for a quashing of the investigation and other personal favors, including leniency for his aides, and money.

The source of one scenario was a former political associate of Powell's who worked with him throughout the campaign as executive director of the IDE, Frederick S. Weaver.[20] When Weaver told his version in 1959 to the columnist Drew Pearson, he had broken with Powell and was furnishing a steady stream of reports to Pearson about Powell's personal and political affairs. According to Weaver, he and two others met with Powell in the summer of 1956 and interested the congressman in switching support to local Republicans as a way of gaining political leverage for Negroes in Harlem. The original idea was to concentrate on state and city races. Powell was receptive, and even suggested "the national election as well." Weaver says that meetings were arranged between Powell and Rabb, Republican Party leaders, Sherman Adams, and White House staff aide Charles Willis. The Negro bandleader and longtime Republican Lionel Hampton attended one of the exploratory meetings. Powell indicated he needed $50,000, paid in advance, and other personal housing accommodations—a room at the Waldorf-Astoria and an apartment in the Middletown Hotel. Weaver then wrote that Powell suggested that the Republican leaders should consider the detrimental effect on the campaign if he were indicted on income tax charges. This "would embarrass the President," and Weaver noted that Adams "agreed to discuss the matter with the Attorney General." Hopefully, the grand jury investigation could be called off.

Powell, Weaver said, also tried to put in a word for his friend, Acy Lennon, then under indictment, but to no avail. Powell's own legal fees were to be paid, and a tax lawyer obtained for him.

The overall strategy was for Powell to seek appointments with Stevenson and Eisenhower to ascertain their views on civil rights with the hope that Stevenson would be hesitant and Eisenhower cooperative in granting an interview. Powell could then publicly announce for Eisenhower. As Weaver recorded, "That was the way it went down." Weaver quit his job as a clerk of the municipal court, joined Powell at the IDE, and became Powell's "advance man" as the congressman went around the country campaigning for Eisenhower. Charles Willis was assigned to raise a budget of $100,000.

According to Weaver, Powell had another personal problem he needed help with. He and his wife, Hazel Scott, were having marital problems. Weaver disclosed that a possible suit by Powell's wife could be embarrassing. If she named names of women associated with Powell, this could only complicate Powell's role in the campaign. Weaver wrote that a tax attorney was engaged who worked out an agreement with Mrs. Powell whereby she would leave the country for the duration of the campaign. In his memo to Pearson, Weaver spared few details of Powell's sexual exploits on the campaign trail over the next several weeks. In fact, he revealed, "one of the requirements of the advance man was to have dates waiting for him on arrival."

This Weaver account came to Drew Pearson in 1959. But in the middle of the 1956 campaign, Pearson received a memo from his assistant, Jack Anderson, describing another version of the circumstances of Powell's switch.[21] According to Anderson, Vice President Richard Nixon was the one who worked out the agreement with Powell to support the President in exchange for "help on his income tax troubles." Then Powell informed Nixon that he was "ready and willing" to campaign for Eisenhower.

Anderson stated that Powell, while in Europe, dictated by long-distance telephone another letter to Nixon and one to Rabb, restating his willingness. When the letter was mentioned in a Jack Anderson column in September 1956,[22] Powell denied it. Anderson admitted to Pearson that the only evidence he had was the word of two sources, one who had seen the letter, and another who allegedly was told about it by Powell himself. Both of these sources, independently, used the words "ready and willing." Neither could Anderson prove, he said, that Powell discussed his tax problems with Nixon.

In a denial, Powell wrote to Pearson: "I have never written Vice President Nixon or anyone else at any time offering to campaign for the Republicans."[23] Anderson's source told him that Nixon turned the Powell letter over to Charles Willis, "who worked out the details for Powell's switch to Eisenhower."[24] The deal included quietly dropping the tax investigation of Powell. Anderson added: "I don't know how we could document this, except that Powell boasted of it to my source." Hattie Dodson was to be released from prison. "Another Powell crony, Fred Weaver, will be given a federal job."[25] Powell reportedly told Anderson in Weaver's presence at the ceremonial opening of the IDE headquarters that he (Powell) was going to see that Weaver got a job, and he would speak to Rabb about it right away.

Anderson also heard from his source, "who got it from Powell," that Charles Willis's father-in-law, Harvey Firestone of the rubber company, was putting "up $150,000 to bankroll Powell's campaign."

Thus the various versions existed over the years of the circumstances surrounding Powell's switch. But money and the tax investigation were central in each unsubstantiated account.

Of course, Powell's own version was straightforward enough: He decided to back Eisenhower over Stevenson because Eisenhower would be better for the civil rights movement—period.

Thirteen years later, in an oral history interview concerning his time as Eisenhower's press secretary, James Hagerty was asked if he knew of any reports or rumors that a campaign allowance for Powell was involved in the Powell switch. Hagerty, who attended the meeting between Eisenhower and Powell that preceded Powell's announcement, replied that he knew of no such deal, but neither would he be surprised if campaign funds were supplied to Powell. That was not an unusual practice in such circumstances. And, of course, this was "Adam's stock in trade."[26]

However he got there, the fact is that on October 11, 1956, at

3:02 P.M. Democratic Congressman Adam Clayton Powell, Jr. from Harlem walked into Republican President Eisenhower's Oval Office and came out twenty-five minutes later at 3:27 P.M. Three other persons were present: Bernard Shanley of the White House Staff, James Hagerty, and Val Washington. Shanley took notes.

(Interestingly and inexplicably, Ann Whitman's normally copious diary of the President's daily activities does not include any entry indicating the Powell meeting on that date. She began the diary with: "A bad day, which the President bore with wonderful grace."[27] She then listed each appointment, including the Prince and Princess of Monaco, and added, as she frequently did, brief comments from the President to her or her own observation. For instance: the President told her "Grace Kelly was aloof but . . . the Prince was nice." And "the President got a letter . . . that disturbed him." She recorded that the "President hit golf balls for about thirty-five minutes, then went to House to dress for the visit of the members of the Supreme Court, scheduled for five o'clock." In any case, the diary notes of the usually meticulous personal secretary notwithstanding, there is no historical dispute that Eisenhower did meet Powell that afternoon—apparently sometime before or after golf.)

Shanley's one-page, single-spaced notes of the meeting indicate that Powell "started the discussion" with an account of his trip to Yugoslavia and of that country's interest in selling its copper to the United States. The President wondered about Chilean copper, and told Shanley to check this out.[28]

Powell then told the President that he was going to support him, "that he was forced to do so" because of the "vacillating" position his own party had been taking. He mentioned this twice, "and also pointed out that he recognized what the results of this would be vis-à-vis his relationship with the Democratic Party." Eisenhower replied by saying he was "greatly honored" to have the support of a member of the Congress "who is elected by the people." Powell "then raised the question, as agreed" of the Powell Amendment, saying he was willing to accept instead an amendment by Congressman Javits. Shanley had already briefed Eisenhower on this subject. Congressman Jacob Javits (R.-N.Y.) had proposed that federal funds be withheld only from school districts that defied a specific federal court desegregation order.

The President told Powell his staff would study the Javits proposal. Powell indicated his wish that the school construction bill would be submitted promptly in the new congressional session.

Eisenhower agreed. Powell stated that "he was prepared to lead an independent movement for the President on a nationwide basis and take an active part in the balance of the campaign."

Shanley's notes concluded: "During the course of the conference, the President explained again his position on the integration problem as he has done so often in press conferences."

That was it. Powell and Eisenhower shook hands, and Powell adjourned to Hagerty's office. A short time later, Hagerty assembled reporters on the White House steps where Powell made his announcement. The reason for the switch? Quite simple: civil rights would be better served under an Eisenhower Presidency than a Stevenson administration.

Back in New York over the next several days, reporters pressed Powell to elaborate on his meeting. At the same time, he appeared to testify in the tax evasion trial of his friend Acy Lennon. Powell indicated that Eisenhower had made three specific commitments to him: First, he supported a voting rights bill giving the Justice Department added powers, and permitting civil suits against anyone who denied a person's civil rights. Second, the President favored the arrest of school officials on contempt-of-court charges when they refused to obey court orders to desegregate; if more federal marshals were needed, then those should be hired. Third, he supported a school-aid bill that Powell would draft, including a cutoff of funds to districts that refused to obey court orders, and providing funds to states on the basis of need rather than on a per-capita basis.[29] These commitments plus Eisenhower's record in hiring 316 Negroes in top jobs "as compared to 25 under the Democrats" were the main factors in Powell's decision, he explained. He also made it clear that he did not like being "snubbed" by Stevenson, after seven unsuccessful attempts to see the Democratic candidate.

The Republicans might have been pleased to receive Powell's endorsement, but they were also finding out that they had best stay on guard. Southerners and conservatives immediately wanted to know about the "arrest for contempt" policy Eisenhower, according to Powell, was supposedly advocating. This bore no resemblance to what they had been hearing the President say over the years. Hagerty had to spring into action. Obviously Powell was misstating the conference discussion. The President *had* made a statement in his press conference on September 11, 1956, in response to a question regarding federal responsibility in segregation disputes. What if officials refused to admit Negro students after being ordered to do so by a court? Did the federal government have a responsibility to intervene? The President's verbatim response, which Hagerty restudied, was, in part, as follows:

> . . . Now, that Court must decide whether it believes it—someone is in contempt of that Court. And at that point I think it is customary for the Court to call in the Justice Department to assist in bringing the evidence and thrashing the case out. And, then, that having been done, if anyone is in contempt, I assume that it is the job of the U.S. Marshall to serve the warrants and to take the men, the offenders, to jail or to pay their fines or whatever happens. . . .[30]

That was as close as Eisenhower came to the Powell claim. And, anyway, as Hagerty well knew, this particular topic had not come up at the Powell meeting. He immediately drafted a statement for Powell to issue. Reached in New York, Powell agreed to the following retraction which Hagerty released from the White House in Powell's name:

> I want to correct a mistake made by me a week ago last Saturday when I delivered an extemporaneous speech at an open air rally in New York, quoting the President at our meeting on October 11. I want to set the record straight by stating that he did not make the remarks on enforcement of school integration which I attributed to him.
>
> I inadvertently confused this interview with my recollections of what the President said at his public press conference on September 11 when he did mention the subject of enforcement of school integration.[31]

Now, at least on this point, the public could focus on Eisenhower's words, not on what Powell said the President told him. Such was the nature of the rear-guard action necessary when one aligned oneself with Powell—or so the administration was learning. The *New York Herald Tribune* ran the retraction under the headline "Rep. Powell Admits: He Misquoted Eisenhower on Jailing Segregationists."[32] The *New York Times* also informed its readers: "Powell Retracts Report on Talks. Now Says President Did Not Advocate Jail for Defying Courts on Integration."[33]

The Republican-leaning *New York Daily News* focused its editorial—"Rep. Powell Now Likes Ike"—on the virtues, from its point of view, of Powell's decision:

> The New-Fair Deal and Liberal Party smear apparatus has already gone to work on Rep. Powell—for which we want to offer him our congratulations. When that mob tries to ruin your reputation, it

> means you're okay. We also want to congratulate Mr. Powell on his vision and realism in coming out for the Republican national ticket of Eisenhower and Nixon.
>
> The Republicans consistently down the years have done most of the real work on behalf of civil rights for Negroes and other minority groups, while the Democrats have done most of the talking on the subject.[34]

But as expected, the loudest reaction to Powell's switch came from those most disappointed with his decision—Democrats, Negro and white.

In a way, it was the Bandung fallout all over again. Powell had created another, if not indefensible, highly controversial event. His single, individual act had caused a situation requiring response. Only this time there was more at stake than merely beneficial effects for Powell. This latest move *could* challenge the political base of his Democratic colleagues in Negro communities. It was one thing to praise the United States in a far-off land, with possible personal advantage for himself back home with his congressional colleagues and the administration—praise, incidentally, that might be a bit excessive on the race issue. It was an entirely different matter to tamper with and attempt to divert the loyalties of an otherwise Democratic Party–based Negro vote. His opponents now were not easily dismissed Communist reporters in Bandung who were no match for his expertise on America's race relations, or Chou En-lai bent on embarrassing the United States. Now he would be challenged by his own kind, politicians who had come through the civil rights political struggles the same as he, even if they did not have his national prominence and image. And even more to the point, this contest would have specific measurable results. At the end, there would be votes to be counted—winners and losers.

Among the first groups to renounce Powell's switch were Negro Democratic politicians in Harlem. Led by the Manhattan Borough President, Hulan Jack, six elected leaders issued a statement saying they were saddened that Powell had allowed himself to be "pressured" by the White House to change his convictions. The "pressure," of course, related, they intimidated, to Powell's current income tax problems.

"That is a complete lie," Powell shot back in a radio interview. "I didn't have any convictions to change." And then, as if recognizing that did not sound just right, he quickly added, "I had no convictions about Adlai Stevenson to change in this campaign."[35]

Powell's Negro congressional colleague, Representative Charles C. Diggs from Detroit, said he was not surprised by the switch to Eisenhower. After all, Powell had praised the President before.

But Democratic congressman Emanuel Celler of Brooklyn was most emphatic in his outrage. He called Powell a "backslider," "a turncoat," and then he voiced a serious suggestion that sanctions should be imposed against Powell by the party, namely, by denying him his seniority rights as a member of the Committee on Education and Labor.[36] (Exactly ten years later, as described in Chapter 1, Celler would chair a congressional committee charged with dealing with that exact issue involving Powell's later activities.) Paul M. Butler, chairman of the Democratic National Committee, also suggested that Powell's congressional seniority be taken away. To this Powell responded that "the Negro people—for that matter, all decent Americans—will rise up against the Democratic candidate for communist-type suppression of freedom of speech."

The Negro press was divided on the issue. In Powell's own Harlem, the *Amsterdam News* sided with him over the six elected officials, suggesting that "more Harlemites support Mr. Powell than stand against him."

The front-page editorial in the *Chicago Defender* endorsed the Stevenson-Kefauver ticket, concluding, "The Republicans have failed under Eisenhower to realize its greatest opportunity . . . to emerge as a liberal party."

The *Pittsburgh Courier*, long a Republican Party supporter, liked very much what Powell had done.

A Negro labor leader, vice president of the AFL-CIO and president of the United Transport Service Employees, Willard Townsend, labeled Powell's switch "a shocking betrayal of his race and his party."[37]

In the meantime, Powell hit the campaign trail, speaking before large audiences in Cleveland, Chicago, Gary, Toledo, Los Angeles, and San Francisco. In Los Angeles a picket line by local Democrats heckled his appearance. Local Republicans were enthusiastic. In Gary, Indiana, the chairman of Citizens for Eisenhower reported back to the IDE that he had received overwhelming favorable reaction to Powell's speech, which was tape-recorded and "distributed throughout Indiana." He also informed headquarters that of all the speakers he had heard, Powell "is absolutely the tops."[38]

The Illinois Citizens for Eisenhower wrote Powell: "Your appearances in Chicago last Saturday were among the highlights of our campaign to date."[39]

At each stop, pictures of Powell and Eisenhower (not together) appeared on posters announcing his appearance.

The Republicans also were aware that Powell's stomping for Eisenhower could have a spin-off effect for local candidates. Senator Everett Dirksen was faced with a tough challenge in Illinois. Maxwell Rabb sent a letter to the senator outlining White House efforts on his behalf: "Congressman Powell is going to Chicago and his appearance will be strongly supported by many of Chicago's leading ministers who are joining forces to give him a good send-off."[40]

Powell was cautious, however, in not seeming to be endorsing *all* Republicans everywhere he went. His was a switch explicitly to Eisenhower, but he was aware, of course, of the coattail effect. He did not appear on platforms with any and every Republican who wanted to reap the spillover benefits. But in New York he did decide "reluctantly" to support Republican Jacob Javits for senator against Mayor Robert Wagner. Wagner, he explained, had aligned himself with the Negro Harlem leaders (Powell called them "smear artists") who had attacked him. Wagner, Powell argued, had done nothing to end *de facto* school segregation in New York City "comparable to the Dixiecrat areas in the South."[41]

Liberal columnist Max Lerner took Powell to task by questioning the congressman's off-again, on-again support for Eisenhower. Lerner wondered how Powell could explain his earlier attack in March on the President (the "Pilate" speech) as well as Eisenhower's dilution of the Republican platform. And the columnist rejected Powell's insinuations that Negroes should not listen to whites on these matters. Powell had told his Abyssinian congregation that what Democrats Eleanor Roosevelt and Senator Herbert Lehman wanted was not relevant, that they could hardly decide what was good for Negroes. Lerner wrote: "No doubt Powell will scorn what I have written as an outsider's talk. . . . He talks as if he were the only person who has a right to ask American Negroes to listen to him. He talks as if there were no white person who is worth listening to. This is arrogant talk, and dangerously close to racism."[42]

Assured of his own reelection, Powell stayed on the election circuit for Eisenhower. In his own Sixteenth Congressional District, he was opposed by candidates on the Republican and Liberal party lines, which was fine with him, because that would only split the opposition against him. But neither of the other two candidates put much faith or effort into their hopeless quests to unseat Powell.

* * *

Election day came. Eisenhower won by a landslide, carrying forty-one out of forty-eight states. He beat Stevenson with 35,585,316 votes to the governor's 26,031,322, and took New York State by a margin of nearly 1.6 million votes.

Powell's own congressional district, of course, was important to watch. In 1952, Eisenhower got 17 percent of the vote in that district. This was almost doubled in 1956, to 32.8 percent. Stevenson ran on both Democratic and Liberal tickets in 1956. The Harlem results were as follows:

Eisenhower (R)	Stevenson (D)	Stevenson (L)
30,689	55,099	7,677

Running for the Senate with Powell's endorsement, Javits received 27,485 votes in Harlem to Wagner's combined Democrat-Liberal vote of 61,875.

Powell's own vote in his district declined from 72 percent in 1952 to 62 percent in 1956, though he still won by a comfortable margin.

Powell (D)	Bailey (R)	Taylor (L)
58,631	16,762	8,930

In 1952, Eisenhower received only 1,860 more votes in Harlem than the Republican congressional candidate. In 1956 this figure was 13,927. Eisenhower got almost twice as many votes for President in Harlem than the Republican candidate for Congress. Of course, this led the IDE to claim the significant influence of Powell's endorsement. Marty Snyder sent the election data to Sherman Adams, saying, "This . . . indicates the effect of the Powell switch to Eisenhower, wherein the voters are still Democrats but voted for Ike on the Presidential line."[43]

Apparently, the President was upset that he was not able to bring along more Republicans into Congress. While his own victory was enormous and comforting, the Democrats were able to maintain control of both houses of Congress. It was the first time, Javits later observed, "that a triumphant President had been unable to carry at least one house of Congress for his party."[44]

In his own frame of analysis, this was probably just fine with Powell. He had switched to Eisenhower, not the Republican Party, and, as added comfort, his endorsed candidate for the Senate, Javits, had won. It would not be in Powell's interest for the Democrats to lose the majority in the House of Representatives. After all, there he was gaining important years toward seniority, and was soon in line for a chairmanship if the Democrats maintained control of the House. In a sense, 1956 represented a year when Adam Powell could have his cake and eat it, too. Normally, that was a pretty good spot for a politician to be in.

But was it? Already, before the election, there had been talk that he should be punished for his switch. Of course, he was not the first member of his party to jump ship for a particular election and remain as an official party member. The columnist Murray Kempton, by no means a fan of Powell's, nonetheless saw fit to point this out. Several Southern Dixiecrats had bolted the Democratic Party in 1948 without being punished. Senator Price Daniel was elected to the Senate in 1952 from Texas on the Democratic ticket while supporting Eisenhower for President. Senator J. Strom Thurmond (then a Democrat) bolted in 1948, supported Eisenhower in 1952, and again deserted the Democratic ticket in 1956—without punishment. So, according to Kempton, Powell was in good company. "He [Powell] is self-seeking, a nuisance, and a ham practiced to the point of insufferability, in this case, if no other, sharing the attributes of the average Southern Congressman."[45]

The first disciplinary move against Powell came when the House Democratic Patronage Committee fired two employees sponsored by Powell. One worked in the House post office, the other as a member of the Capitol police. Both were from Harlem, attending Howard University in Washington.

"Let's put it this way," said California congressman Harry E. Sheppard, a member of the patronage committee. "The patronage committee is charged with taking care of Democrats, period."[46]

What about Representative John Bell Williams, Democrat of Mississippi, who had bolted in 1956 and supported a segregationist States' Rights Party candidate?

Sheppard simply replied that the committee had not as yet "gone through the entire employment category and classified Democrats versus Republicans."

And, of course, it never did.

The NAACP leaped to Powell's defense with strong letters to House Speaker Sam Rayburn, and Congressman Emanuel Celler, who was expected to lead the New York delegation in punishing Powell. Noting that no action had been taken against Williams or other Southern segregationists in the past, Roy Wilkins wrote to Rayburn that if Powell was punished, there could only be one conclusion: it was "because of Powell's race," and because of his strong advocacy of civil rights.[47]

Rayburn replied that the appointments were "entirely in the

hands of the Patronage Committee" but he would discuss the matter with them. "And if anybody is punished, which I doubt, it will not be on account of race, as far as I am concerned."[48]

Meanwhile, as word got out that there were plans afoot to punish Powell by denying him his patronage and seniority, forces began to mobilize in his behalf. The Americans for Democratic Action (ADA) released a press statement carried widely in the Sunday papers asserting that denial of patronage to Powell but not to Williams "would indicate that the Democratic Congressional majority views desertion of the Party by a pro–civil rights northerner as a much more grievous sin than desertion of it by an anti–civil rights southerner."[49]

A group of Negro Republicans, led by a Philadelphia attorney, Cecil Moore, planned to organize a "March on Washington," if necessary, if Powell was punished.

The Reverend Gardner C. Taylor of New York joined a group from that city in telegrams to the New York political leaders, saying: "The Negro community may not agree with Congressman Powell but will look upon this as an anti-Negro move." They threatened retaliation at the polls in future elections.

Powell's defenders were growing. A two-day Ministers' National Civil Rights Conference was organized by the Baptist Ministers Conference of Greater New York. It would be held in Washington at the opening of the new Congress in January to lobby on his behalf. They planned to collect trainloads of supporters along the Eastern Seaboard to journey to the nation's Capital.

The *Amsterdam News* featured an editorial, "Chastise Powell," vowing this was "a bigoted anti-Negro fight" and "We don't intend to let Mr. Powell fight alone."[50]

Even Communist Benjamin J. Davis put aside his enmity toward Powell and came to his defense. "Rep. Powell is an outstanding leader of the Negro people, whose record in Congress is one of exceptional service to the cause of civil rights, labor and social legislation."[51]

Obviously beginning to feel the pressure, Celler and others decided against any attempt to deny Powell his seniority status. Celler wrote to Roy Wilkins: "I will not make any move against Adam Clayton Powell unless every one of the members of the House, guilty of the same political omission, is treated exactly as he is."[52] But Celler wanted to make it clear to the NAACP leadership that he was disappointed with Powell's activities regarding civil rights legislation. Celler, apparently, was not as impressed with Powell's record as some others were. He felt obliged to remind Wilkins:

> Frankly, I was disheartened at the attitude of Adam Clayton Powell. The day the Civil Rights bill came up on the floor of the House, I found, to my amazement, that he had left for Europe. Here was a bill that meant a great deal to all of us. A few days before that bill was scheduled for a vote, I alerted him to the fact that its consideration was imminent and that I would like him to speak on it as I was in charge of such arrangements. He said, "Of course I will be present." He defaulted on his promise to me and betrayed his own people.[53]

Celler was not telling the NAACP something the civil rights leaders did not know, and they surely were equally frustrated with Powell. But such was the bind his behavior put them in. Without question, he should have kept his promise and been present to support the civil rights bill. He was wrong for not doing so. But his "punishment" could not be for transgressions similarly engaged in by others and overlooked. Celler was rightfully complaining about the unreliable habits of a most difficult civil rights ally. To punish him for political party reasons without applying the same rules to civil rights opponents simply would not be acceptable.

Powell's everlasting confidence was that he knew this assessment was his strength.

What subsequently happened was a successful move on the part of the Committee on Education and Labor to deny him a subcommittee chairmanship. Graham Barden as chairman of the full committee had moved to reorganize it into five permanent subcommittees, which had previously been temporary. Barden sought and received permission to appoint the subchairmen without regard to seniority. Powell was the third-ranking member of the full committee, which meant he had seniority and normally would be entitled to a subchair. But Barden bluntly told him he stood no chance. Another fight ensued. Powell even sought the aid of his White House friends, without success. Rabb sent a memo to Sherman Adams:

> ... I spent an hour and a half with Powell in his office last night and he is well aware of our general sympathy and friendly feeling.... He is still distressed that this move was taken because he feels it may deprive him of a Chairmanship but he fully understands the situation and appreciates our position.[54]

Once again the NAACP came to Powell's defense. And this time it was even more difficult, because basically the NAACP did not favor the seniority rule in principle. Because of that rule, Southern chairmen were able to gain positions of power and block civil rights and liberal legislation. Now, however, they were supporting the use of the rule for Powell. Clarence Mitchell explained the situation to Roy Wilkins: He believed that as long as the seniority rule existed it should not be used discriminatorily or arbitrarily. Thus, since Powell had seniority, he should be given recognition.[55] In other words, if seniority would apply to places on the full committees, including the chairmanship, it should apply to subcommittee chairmanships. Nobody was being fooled by this change of the rules just as Powell was moving up in seniority, Mitchell declared. A press release from the NAACP sought to state the political punishment or racial motivation as clearly as possible:

> No matter what technicalities any of us in Washington may use to explain what happened [in the vote to support Barden], in the eyes of most people around the country this will be regarded as either a penalty because he [Powell] supported President Eisenhower in 1956 or committee discrimination because Mr. Powell is colored.[56]

Thus, while Powell's seniority on the full committee was not effected as such, he was still denied the interim privilege that came with his already senior status. He would have to wait longer. The irony in this is that he was gaining seniority the same way his Southern adversaries had done for decades—by being continuously reelected from a very safe, virtually one-party district—and in each instance the issue of race was paramount. Therefore, it was in his interest not to leave the Democratic Party. That party in the majority in the House, along with his growing seniority, would inevitably lead to the chairmanship. Everyone knew that.

His switching to Eisenhower was not really a great risk. He still won his own district handily. His constituents did, in fact, show a reasonable increase for Eisenhower, enough at least for Powell to claim an impact there and around the country. And his own party kept control of Congress.

The speculations continued on the reasons for his switch. Apparently, not too many people were convinced that Powell's reason was the *only* motivation. To be sure, Stevenson was rather moderate on civil rights, but Eisenhower was quite his equal if not better—or worse—on that score. And, of course, the matter of a "deal" over the income tax investigation always crept into more than a few speculations. This aspect of the event would remain in the "highly speculative" category, however, since those in a position to know were either denying a deal or not saying. But cynicism being so prevalent, especially where Powell was concerned, many simply shrugged and assumed it was true. To be sure, a few commentators, even Powell's most severe critics, were willing to exclude the President personally. The *National Review*, the ardently conservative magazine that stayed on Powell's income tax investigation trail, summed up what many suspected: it was highly unlikely that Powell confronted Eisenhower personally on a deal—this would not have been proper or necessary—but it was quite possible that Powell did have an unspoken understanding with party officials regarding a Powell endorsement in exchange for ending the income tax investigation.[57]

Naïveté notwithstanding, it *is* conceivable that Powell had additional motives for the endorsement that need not have included a tax investigation deal. The fact is that Powell did have a history of not being too respectful of either party. From his earliest days he had let it be known that firm loyalty to one or the other major party was not the wisest strategy. In addition, he had been locked out of the Truman White House, and at least during the first Eisenhower term he got his memos answered and telephone calls returned. Interestingly, a *New York Post* reporter doing a profile on Powell in October 1956 interviewed several "people on the street" in Harlem, getting reactions to his switch. The reporter approached "an elderly grey-haired worker, currently unemployed" who was "disdainful" of Powell. The reporter thought his reason for Powell's switch was "eccentric." Namely: "The Congressman had gone for Eisenhower . . . because Powell didn't have the pull when Truman was President. . . . Eisenhower gave him pull in the cabinet."[58]

Why "eccentric?" This explanation could well have as much legitimacy as many of the other speculations around at the time. On a personal level, Powell felt comfortable with Rabb and some of the others in the White House—but especially Rabb. A Stevenson White House need not be as accessible. And given Powell's limited expectations for Democrats *or* Republicans at that time on civil rights, an endorsement of Eisenhower need not have been such a bad tradeoff. But as with many complicated issues, this one likely had several motivations behind it.

At any rate, the deed was done. The numbers were in; he had survived.

Or had he?

* * *

The next several months would tell just how much "help" Powell could expect from his friends now reelected to a second term. One month after Congress convened, he sought a meeting with Sherman Adams to discuss four matters: (1) the Gold Coast (Powell wanted to be a member of the official United States delegation to the upcoming independence celebration of that country, later renamed Ghana); (2) federal aid to education; (3) public relations between the White House and the "Negro people" and (4) "Powell's problem re the ignoring of his seniority on the Labor Committee." Adams wanted the advice of Rabb, who replied, "I recommend that you see Congressman Powell tomorrow *IF* you are prepared to discuss item 2—the school construction bill."[59] As to the other items, Rabb informed Adams: "We are in good shape on this. We have gone to bat at State for Powell and he knows it." Apparently, Speaker Sam Rayburn did not want Powell included on the African trip, preferring Charles Diggs of Michigan. (Rabb's memo mistakenly listed Diggs as from Illinois, unless Rabb meant Congressman Dawson from Chicago.) Regarding "public relations with Negroes," "There is nothing we can do except listen on this. It is the same story which I get daily from Negro leaders all over the country." And with the Labor Committee, "there is nothing we can do. . . . the White House cannot, after all, tell a Congressional Committee what to do on something like this."

Powell's White House friends could not help him on the first item, the delegation to Ghana. Knowing of Powell's love for travel and the pomp and ceremony of international events, Rabb was particularly upset about Powell's exclusion from the Ghana trip. Rabb lobbied congressional minority leader Joseph Martin, who had no objection as long as Powell was not "an official member of the delegation." Perhaps, Martin suggested, he could go as "special assistant to the Vice President." Rabb then talked to contacts at the State Department who informed him that they hoped Powell would *not* be included "in any capacity at all." The reason was that "Rayburn is very upset at the Powell defection and does not want him there in any form." Therefore, Rabb wrote in a memo to Adams, "In view of this, I recommend that we forget the whole thing; there appears to be no way to help Powell." He then added ruefully: "However, this does upset me very much. What it means is that anyone who goes to bat for us in the future will know that he will be heavily penalized and that we will not be able to help him. In my mind, this is a major reason why we will remain a minority party."[60]

In fact, Rabb was so upset that he mildly rebuked E. Frederick Morrow for putting his own name forward as an official member of the delegation. Perhaps this was "overdoing it," Rabb told Morrow. After all, he had been a marshal in the inaugural parade. Of course, Morrow was dismayed, but he did not know, apparently, that Rabb had his own Negro candidate, namely, Powell.

As it turned out, Powell did go to the Ghanaian independence celebration—as a member of the party of Dr. Martin Luther King, Jr. King had received an official invitation from the new prime minister, Kwame Nkrumah.[61] But it was clear that this was not Powell's show. Martin Luther King was the main attraction, lunching privately with Nkrumah and having a highly publicized impromptu meeting with Nixon at a reception. So uneventful from a publicity point of view was this for Powell that in his autobiography, *Adam by Adam*, he only mentioned that in March 1957 in Ghana he introduced King to Nixon.[62] He did not mention the nation's independence, and there is no confirmation that he, in fact, made the introduction.

The spring of 1957 saw more acts of violence—bombings, beatings, harassments—in the South against Negroes. And still there was no word or action from the President. Racial tension was growing. More threats of an all-out race war came from all sides. Civil rights leaders repeatedly called for the President to go South and make a speech, or, at the least, meet with a representative group of Negro and white leaders. Eisenhower refused.

In February, before he went off to Ghana, Martin Luther King, through his newly formed Southern Christian Leadership Conference, announced plans to hold a "Prayer Pilgrimage" in Washington that spring. The purpose was to have as many as 50,000 people from across the country assemble to protest in favor of progressive civil rights legislation. Wilkins was reluctant, but agreed to go, along with A. Philip Randolph. In late March, they sent a telegram to about fifty people inviting them to meet in Washington on April 5 to make final plans for the mass "pilgrimage."

Powell was invited. He immediately called Sherman Adams in the White House to tell him. Speaking to Adams's secretary, he apparently indicated that the purpose of the pilgrimage "is to protest refusal of the President to see these [King, Wilkins, Randolph] leaders."[63] Powell conferred instead with Rabb, who wrote to Adams: "Powell is very much opposed to such a march and will do what he can to stop it. He did suggest that I talk to Clarence Mitchell, Legislative Director of NAACP."[64]

Mitchell informed Rabb that May 17, the third anniversary of the Supreme Court *Brown* decision, was the chosen date. And Mitchell did not think that Eisenhower would be the main target of the mass gathering. Sherman Adams was, indeed, very interested in these developments and urged Rabb to follow up "very closely"—when, where, who, etc. Rabb agreed and told Adams that the planning meeting was to take place at 11:00 A.M. Friday, April 5, 1957, at the Metropolitan Baptist Church in Washington. And he advised that the White House had its friends looking out for them:

> Congressman Powell will attend the meeting and will report to me what takes place. He is still a little fearful that, despite Clarence Mitchell's representations, Martin Luther King may still try to make a march on Washington. Powell and Mitchell will do their best to try to keep the meeting under control.
>
> When I get another report, I will let you know.[65]

Indeed, Rabb got a report on the meeting from Powell and Mitchell. They seemingly reported that King wanted an anti-President march, but "fortunately, this did not develop"—according to Rabb, thanks to Powell and Mitchell.

> Congressman Powell, Clarence Mitchell of the NAACP and Reverend Jernigan successfully changed the entire character of this meeting into an occasion where there will be an observance of the anniversary of the school decision through prayer. The President, I am assured, will not be adversely affected.
>
> At the present time this matter is well in hand and I will continue to watch it carefully. I do, however, feel we must keep a constant vigil relative to this matter. There is always the possibility that a prayer pilgrimage cannot be kept under control, and I am in constant communication with the leaders to ensure keeping it in hand.[66]

Powell especially seemed bent on depicting King to the White House as the villain, the one intent on embarrassing the President. And Powell wanted it known in the administration that he (Powell) was the one keeping the lid on. According to other sources, this was not necessary, inasmuch as King never really intended such a confrontation.[67] But Powell clearly was beginning to perceive King as a viable challenge, albeit not a hostile one, to his role as the most charismatic, popular spokesman on the civil rights scene. And Powell wanted the advantage of access. He had switched and supported Eisenhower. He now wanted dividends. In his correspondence with the President and Sherman Adams, nudging them to speak out more in favor of civil rights, he gently but pointedly observed that he was coming under criticism, allegedly for his defense of the President. To Adams, he wrote that there had been much criticism from Negroes and whites, Republicans and Democrats, Northerners and Southerners aimed at the President for not speaking out, and that he (Powell) "personally to a lesser degree received quite a little. . . . I personally am being subject to bitter criticism in my district among Negroes and in Mrs. Roosevelt's column of Friday, March 22nd."[68] The point was that he wanted his friends in the White House to know what burden he was bearing—for them.

Burdened or not, Powell did not let the many political and civil rights problems erupting in the summer of 1957 interfere with his annual trip to Europe. And in doing so, he left his Democratic colleagues, who sorely needed his vote on an important bill involving the building of a dam in Hells Canyon, Idaho, in the lurch. As a member of a public works subcommittee, Powell had promised Congresswoman Edith Green of Oregon he would vote for the dam. The Republicans did not want it, and had asked Powell to absent himself on the day of the vote as a favor to them. Powell flew to New York. Green pursued him by telephone. He refused to take her calls. She flew to New York. He refused to see her. She sought help from Tammany Hall leader Carmine De Sapio. No luck. From Mayor Robert Wagner she got the same result. Finally, Negro congressman Charles Diggs got through to Powell and asked if he would return and vote with the Northern/Western liberals for the Hells Canyon dam. "No," Powell replied.

Then A. Philip Randolph and Clarence Mitchell were asked to help. Mitchell reported that Powell would vote for the dam if the liberals would make certain concessions for a stronger civil rights bill then being debated in Congress. No deal. The Hells Canyon vote was lost in committee, mainly because of Powell's absence. His liberal colleagues once again interpreted his motives as catering to the Eisenhower people for personal gain, not as bargaining for civil rights.

It was this summer of 1957 that saw the passage by Congress of the first civil rights bill in eighty-two years—since 1875. The House had passed its version in 1956 (with Powell absent, as Celler had noted), and the action centered now on the Senate and the filibuster. The main forces outside Congress pushing for action were the NAACP and the ADA, not Powell. In itself, this was not too unexpected. As a member of the House, Powell carried no influence in the other chamber, and his major House committee, Education and Labor, was not the central focus of the bill in the House. In his legislative capacity, he would not become a major player until the 1960s, and then not on civil rights legislation but on social welfare issues that came within the jurisdiction of his committee. But he maintained the civil rights leadership mantle in Congress, nonetheless, in the late 1950s. His speeches and bureaucratic pressures had become legendary.

In the maneuvering and negotiating of interest-group politics in America, it is always useful for interest groups and leaders to have a meeting with the President. Whether such sessions have any substantive value or not, they signal "access," "influence," "clout," the point being that a group is thought highly enough by the White House to receive some portion of the President's time and ear. This is valuable political leverage. The media are informed; issues are raised in public. The President can be expected to "go on record" in a way that is usually more or less favorable to the group's wishes, inasmuch as such sessions normally do not take place unless there is a reasonable assurance—especially when the issue involved is controversial or volatile—that the President's and the group's views can be acceptably reconciled.

In the annals of the civil rights struggle, this event was especially important. In the Negro political community up to the late 1950s, there was a long history of exclusion from such circles of influence—thus the critical importance of having Eleanor Roosevelt pleading the cause within the White House during FDR's Presidency. This was the reason for some civil rights leaders courting Truman. The ability to "get in to see the President" was a sign, however slight, of sympathetic feeling from the most powerful seat in government. And in the early days of the civil rights movement, symbol came very close to substance in many instances, given the lowly condition of black Americans. That Eisenhower had not met with a civil rights group during his first term was a point of severe irritation to many Negro leaders, and one of growing embarrassment to sympathetic supporters within the administration. E. Frederick Morrow, for one, was keenly sensitive to the problem, as one would expect. In spite of his earlier "tongue-lashing" from Rabb not to push too hard, he decided to take up the cause one more time, responding to an inquiry from Sherman Adams on the "repeated requests from Negro leaders that the President confer with them on the many domestic problems plaguing the race at this time."

There was no denying that racial tension was growing, with increasing violence in the South, local protest demonstrations, and the escalating rhetoric of confrontation from whites and Negroes. Many Southern school districts, especially Little Rock, Arkansas, remained adamantly opposed to desegregation, and vowed never to concede. Segregated public facilities—buses, beaches, libraries, restaurants, hotels—were targets of sporadic attack and racial violence. Negroes continued to be blatantly denied the right to register and vote. Southern white vigilante groups on more than a few occasions bombed Negro homes and churches and harassed civil rights activists, physically and economically. Instances of the peaceful desegregation of schools, as in Louisville, Kentucky, were the exception, and the cause for relieved announcement by Eisenhower and his aides. But the rule was otherwise. Morrow decided to be as blunt as possible in his reply to Adams:

> I can state categorically that the rank and file of Negroes in the country feel that the President has deserted them in their current fight to achieve first-class citizenship via Civil Rights legislation, etc.
>
> . . . There is tremendous unrest in the country among the Negro population. Tensions are great, emotions are at a high pitch, and the time is approaching when peaceful resistance and oratory may give way to efforts not conducive to the welfare of our country. I feel the time is ripe for the President to see two or three outstanding Negro leaders, and to let them get off their chests the things that seem to be giving them great concern. I feel the psychology of the President seeing these men will have a great effect upon the morale, sentiments and attitudes of Negro citizens. Their present feeling is that their acknowledged leadership is being ignored, snubbed, and belittled by the President and his staff. Even though we may be aware of what these men will say when they meet the President, it is important that they be able to meet him and say it face to face.[69]

In other words, for goodness' sake, grant the meeting.

Adams sought the opinion of Rabb, who, apparently persuaded that this much could now go forward, agreed with Morrow's memo. But Rabb did not want to be hasty. He informed Adams that "our plans call for such an appointment being set up [with King, Randolph, and Wilkins] after Congress leaves or after the civil rights bill has been acted upon."[70] He also said that he had talked to Martin Luther King who "has agreed to be patient."

Two weeks later, Rabb sent another memorandum to Adams. Apparently, Rabb was beginning to warm up to King as a reasonable leader to deal with. He was taking his own measure of the newly emerged civil rights leader. King had met with Nixon in Washington after their Ghana session. Rabb wrote:

> Incidentally, the Vice President was very much impressed with Reverend King and thinks the President would enjoy talking to him. He is not, he says, a man who believes in violent and retaliatory pro-Negro actions, but sponsors an evolutionary but progressive march forward.[71]

Meanwhile, the summer came and went, and the civil rights bill was passed.

But September meant the beginning of a new school year and new desegregation problems in the South. It was, indeed, the autumn of Eisenhower's most serious confrontation with the issue of civil rights. Governor Orval Faubus of Arkansas was stubbornly resisting desegregation efforts in the face of a federal court order to admit nine Negro students to Little Rock's Central High School. A personal meeting between the governor and Eisenhower in Newport, Rhode Island, was nonproductive. Mob violence had broken out, and federal court orders were being flouted. Eisenhower ordered federal troops from the 101st Airborne Division into Little Rock to restore order and to escort the Negro students to the school. Reluctantly returning from Newport where he had been working and relaxing, the President delivered a nationally televised address explaining the reasons for his troubling decision. "Mob rule cannot be allowed to override the decisions of the courts," he said.

In the midst of these dynamic events, and before the troops were sent in, Powell, noting that the President had met with Faubus and other white leaders, renewed his request for a meeting between the President and "any Negroes you desire." Eisenhower, on September 17—one week before he spoke to the nation—wired Powell that he would meet with him and that he had "directed [my] staff in Washington to confer with you for this purpose."

Powell's telegram to James Hagerty, the press secretary, in Newport was almost ecstatic. In this frantic time, when the nation's attention was focused daily on the unfolding traumatic events over race, he could now resume center stage and, he hoped, gain significant civil rights—and personal—concessions. He could reassert his leadership roles. He wired Hagerty:

> Am very gratified for prompt reply of President Eisenhower. His statement is in keeping with those things that I have always

> applauded him for. Am I to deal personally as regards to the appointment or am I to make my arrangements through Max Rabb or Sherman Adams? Telegrams are already being received from individuals such as Martin Luther King praising the President's action and wishing the very best for my conference with President. I would personally like to talk to you before the conference so that you can help me to make it as successful as possible.[72]

Perhaps what Powell was not aware of initially was that Rabb was taking his own counsel about a forthcoming meeting. In addition to Powell, he was consulting with Roy Wilkins and Jackie Robinson, the former baseball player and prominent Republican. And, as events developed, the order to send troops to Little Rock intervened, along with the President's national speech. In addition, other sources were communicating directly with the White House recommending other persons who should be included in the meeting. For example, Louis Lautier of the National Negro Press Association had written to Rabb suggesting "that some top flight Negroes be brought in—and not political hacks."[73] He had in mind such people as the Reverend Joseph H. Jackson, president of the National Baptist Convention; Dr. Channing Tobias, chairman of the NAACP board; Lester Granger of the National Urban League; A. Philip Randolph; Carl Murphy of the *Afro-American* newspapers, Baltimore; Dr. Rufus E. Clement, president of Atlanta University and member of the Atlanta Board of Education; Dr. Mordecai W. Johnson, president of Howard University; and a bishop from the African Methodist Episcopal Church, as well as a bishop of the A.M.E. Zion Church. He also suggested Ralph Bunche of the United Nations. Rabb thanked him and told him his suggestion "will be given very favorable and sympathetic consideration here."

Another source suggested to Rabb the inclusion of the president of the National Council of Negro Women, and then cautioned: "You would probably want to avoid Martin Luther King, who has become a symbol, as well as anyone from the NAACP."[74]

Thus the politics of this important "meeting with the President" was taking shape. Rabb was sensitive to all these crosscurrents. In his memorandum to Sherman Adams, he sized up the situation. The list was getting too large, and yet the White House did not want to offend friends, or create problems for itself with contending religious and political factions within the Negro community. Care had to be taken not to have overrepresentation from the NAACP. Inclusion from one segment of the Negro community—for instance, Negro college presidents—would generate requests from others. Rabb advised that Wilkins felt "very strongly that the meeting should be completely divorced from the Little Rock situation and that the farther away the meeting is held from that incident the better it will be for all concerned. He understands that circumstances may call for the meeting to be put off until sometime in November."[75]

As matters developed, the meeting was not held. Events rushed in, and Powell's earlier euphoria proved premature. As the weeks went by, Little Rock stabilized; the troops remained but overt violence subsided substantially. A mild civil rights bill was on the books, and attention was turned to appointing the members of the newly created United States Commission on Civil Rights, established by the law. If serious civil rights problems remained, and they did, the public's attention had waned, and turned to other front-page news.

On October 4, 1957, the Russians launched Sputnik. In addition, the country was in the throes of a serious economic recession. From the administration's point of view, this was no time to be meeting with a selective group of America's Negro leaders on a problem that was so vexing and highly charged. The best strategy for the moment was to ignore it—or at least not encourage public attention, which is precisely what a meeting would have produced.

Obviously disappointed, Powell nonetheless had a personal matter to take up with the Eisenhower people—a matter left over from the 1956 Presidential campaign. Namely money.

On September 27, 1957, he wrote a detailed letter to Sherman Adams, reminding him that it would soon be a year since his announced support of Eisenhower and stipulating that several of his aides were still owed back pay for their services in the campaign. He listed amounts and names, and indicated that the promise of future employment for one person had not been met. Adam Powell was on the warpath again—at least for the moment. When he endorsed Eisenhower, he curtly told Adams, he asked for nothing for himself.

> However, the following facts [names and amounts owed], which I have not yet made public, leave me wondering what has happened to the word of Republican leaders. I have waited patiently, held many conferences, telephone conversations and the like. I can wait

> no longer. I am not complaining about my loss of seniority and related benefits in the House Education and Labor Committee, or anything else that has happened to me. That was a calculated risk. But I am most definitely complaining to you for the last time concerning your broken word to me—your, in this case meaning the leadership of the Republican Party.[76]

Powell was clearly perturbed over the treatment he had received from the President's party. His income tax returns were still being investigated. His patronage agreements were not being honored. In his reflective moments years later, he concluded that his Eisenhower switch had angered Democrats *and* Republicans in New York and in the South. They resented his independence. And he wrote, in uncharacteristic admission of vulnerability and naïveté: "The simple fact was that they had used me and now wanted nothing more than perhaps to destroy me. . . . I felt like giving up."[77]

But, of course, he would not. Even as the likelihood of an Eisenhower meeting was receding, he resurrected a proposal he had made shortly after his return from Europe in September 1957. He would ask the administration, through the United States Information Agency (USIA), to send him (and he included possibly the two other Negro congressmen, Diggs and Dawson) on a worldwide speaking tour, discussing and defending America's progress in race relations—"holding press conferences and taking on all comers."[78] Undoubtedly, Powell had in mind something similar to his Bandung performance, and he remembered how much that episode raised his stock in important circles back home. With things not going particularly well for him personally and politically, this might be the propitious time to have an encore performance.

Bryce Harlow wanted to know what Rabb thought, after telling him "I vote no." Rabb wrote back: "You are quite right. If we could be sure of what he would say I might vote the other way."[79]

Likewise, Morrow was not about to support such a trip. He wrote to Harlow: "It would be fatal for this Administration to sponsor this trip of three Democrat congressmen who love neither the Administration nor most of its policies. Powell is noted for his impulsive 'headline-making' statements."[80] And then, without wanting to appear to be making a "pitch" for himself, he reminded Harlow that he (Morrow) had made a similar request involving himself. At any rate, if consideration were given to such an assignment, "we should send our own team."

Harlow, in turn, advised Sherman Adams to tell the USIA "to find suitable reasons to disapprove the suggested trip abroad."[81]

A few months later the matter was finally disposed of by the USIA and the White House. And they were quite candid with Powell: "They agreed to take the position with Mr. Powell that Little Rock had fortunately faded as a burning issue abroad and that it was in the interest of the United States to avoid stirring this up."[82]

Powell was quickly getting the message. There appeared to be little policy benefit coming from his switch to Eisenhower. And, failing that, it seemed that he was not even able to realize the courtesy of favorable action on more personal requests.

The political marriage between Powell and Eisenhower was clearly on shaky grounds. It would not be long before the congressman would, in effect, announce a separation.

That time came in January 1958, with one of the strongest criticisms Powell had made against the President in their years of tenuous relationship. In all likelihood, Powell was beginning to conclude that the bridge he and Rabb had constructed five years before was on the verge of tumbling down. He could not have been particularly happy about these developments, but neither his pride nor his politics would permit any other conclusion. The USIA's blunt representation to him that "Little Rock fortunately had faded as a burning issue" must have been especially galling. A younger Adam Powell never would have accepted such a characterization of America's dilemma. That would have been precisely the time for him to apply more, not less, pressure. He must have been wondering what his evolved "insider" status was getting him. Had he come so far that he was now prepared to give up on the one sure tactic—open, public defiance and criticism—that had catapulted him to leadership? Was he now being co-opted and taken for granted in the way that he had so often effectively accused others of being used, thus nullifying their challenge to his leadership? He well knew the consequences if this happened to him. The administration always preferred quiet discussions. Powell's stock in trade essentially had always been the opposite—noise. As things were developing in his personal and political life, both in Washington and back in New York, he was realistic enough to know that he was in another critical stage of his political career that would require some serious recalculations on his part.

On January 28, 1958, he sent an 810-word telegram to the President and released a copy to the press—shades of 1953. The

President and "your administration," he asserted, were being branded as indifferent to and procrastinating on the civil rights issue. He cited Nixon's failure to follow up on a promise to Martin Luther King to hold hearings in the South of the Government Contract Compliance Committee. He outlined his disappointment over the aborted conference with the President. And, obviously smarting from the USIA's conclusion about a fading interest in Little Rock, Powell told Eisenhower, "Little Rock has not quieted down." Bombings continued, along with murders. Indeed, there could be more Little Rocks. Russia could reap benefits in Asia and Africa "on the basis of the dilatory tactics of our government in the field of equality and time is not on our side." He assured the President that if "you think that a conference is no longer necessary, then you are the recipient of some very bad briefing and advice by your aides."[83]

For all practical political purposes, this was the coup de grace between Powell and the administration. From that point on, correspondence between Rabb and Powell became more guarded and stilted. Rabb answered the telegram with a sort of the-President-asked-me-to-acknowledge-but-these-are-involved-issues letter.[84] Powell now would take off all the other self-imposed constraints. He always knew that the administration eschewed public discussion on civil rights. He flatly stated that he wanted a better reply "within the next couple of weeks" which he could release "to the Negro press, and for that matter, the dailies as well."[85]

From the White House end, the matter was finished. Rabb wrote a "Note to File" that Jack Watson, a presidential aide, had suggested not responding to Powell and concluded "we cannot always agree with the kind of approach desired by someone who seeks publicity."[86]

That was it. The bridge was down.

"Powell says Ike Reneges on Civil Rights," read the headline on a *New York Mirror* news story on the telegram.

If Powell was finished as the fair-haired boy of the administration, the White House was still willing—quietly—to pursue the possibility of a meeting with civil rights leaders. That spring, Rabb retired and was succeeded by Rocco C. Siciliano as the one to deal with touchy racial issues. In June, Siciliano met with King to get the minister's views on a possible meeting with the President: who should attend, and what did they want to talk about?[87] King made it clear that Roy Wilkins should be part of the group. (Four weeks prior to this meeting, on May 8, 1958, a federal grand jury in New York returned an indictment against Adam Powell for income tax fraud.)

Powell's name came up in the King-Siciliano meeting. Should Powell be invited? Siciliano recorded King's reaction:

> With regard to Congressman Powell, he [King] appeared to agree with us [Deputy Attorney General Lawrence E. Walsh and E. Frederick Morrow] that Powell's present indictment and forthcoming trial would make it impossible to include him in the group. He made no effort to press for Powell's attendance.[88]

Powell clearly was hurt by the exclusion. This was, after all, he claimed publicly, a meeting *he* had arranged as far back as the previous September. Of course, the White House denied this. Powell attempted to keep his hand in by writing to King and other leaders advising them on matters to discuss with the President. But he was politically astute enough to know by then that as far as *his* access to the White House was concerned, he was out. In his autobiography years later, he wrote: "And so, the meeting I had fought to arrange was held without my presence. I could only conclude that the Administration feared that I would take too militant a stand. If so, the fear was justified."[89]

Perhaps. But it was more likely that by 1958, events were moving beyond the type of insider-outsider leadership Powell had been offering. He had probably reached the peak of this style's effectiveness with the "informant" role he played over the Prayer Pilgrimage episode in the spring of 1957. But there seemed to be little reciprocity; he was getting *very* little in return. To his many supporters, he was still "Mr. Civil Rights" and would remain so for a little time longer. But there was a growing Southern-based mass civil rights movement with Dr. Martin Luther King, Jr., becoming increasingly prominent. And the White House was forming its own independent judgment—increasingly favorable—of King as one it could deal with. There was the established Negro leadership—NAACP, National Urban League, Randolph—with reasonably well-staffed organizations around the country. Adam Clayton Powell would have to adjust to these fast-developing changes. He still had what no others possessed among the Negro leadership cadre, namely, an important base in Congress. And he was on the verge of gaining senior status in that body. He would not need to be number one on everybody's guest-speaker list at civil rights gatherings. He would have to share the mantle now, and with a King who was being recognized in his own right as an eloquent, spellbinding speaker. King was, after all, also a Negro Baptist preacher. And it must be said, there was enough work to do for the civil rights movement nationally to have more than one or even a few outspoken leaders.

All this was true, of course, but Powell nonetheless had to take stock, reassess his role. His marital problems and his tax problems, notwithstanding, he had to get his political life straightened out. In addition, his detractors back in Harlem and Tammany Hall were already sharpening their attacks on him in preparation for a serious challenge to his congressional seat.

Therefore, he had little time to spend feeling sorry for himself for being slighted by his former buddies at the White House. It was time to move on, time to put the open flirtation with the Eisenhower administration behind him. And anyway, *that* administration had only two short years to go.

Powell was savvy enough about Congress to know that political influence in that body came from seniority. Throughout the 1950s, he was slowly accumulating this status, but he had not yet achieved what he desired. He was not given a subcommittee chairmanship, which was the normal incremental progression up the power ladder. His influence was less with his congressional colleagues and more with the public, aided by media exposure. Thus essentially he had to capitalize on his role as an irritant, one who could draw attention to himself and the issues he espoused. His annoying amendments and his constant harping on segregation and discrimination in the military and other government agencies were examples of this role. In this capacity, he was perceived by many as a member of the liberal forces, but not as a formidable *institutional* power. His exceptionally high absentee record on roll-call votes and committee attendance was well-known. But this behavior could be excused, some supporters argued, because he *was* being denied the congressional courtesy—from his chairman—of a rightfully earned subchairmanship. Why should he attend such committee sessions and be subjected to continued humiliation?

In spite of this, he continued to define himself as a major player on the liberal front. And he was certainly so identified by civil rights groups around the country. In 1958 and 1959, there was a general recognition by such groups that Congress would be asked to strengthen the 1957 Civil Rights Law, especially in regard to voting rights. In many parts of the South, the denial of such rights had continued to be blatantly ignored. Tuskegee (Macon County), Alabama, was a good example. Home of the famous Negro college, Tuskegee Institute, many of its black professors were denied the right to vote. The local civil rights group, the Tuskegee Civic Association (TCA), wrote thirty-five congressmen and senators, including Powell, to urge consideration of a proposal, prepared by the TCA, to set up a federal voter registration committee. The idea was to provide federal registrars in those areas where, as in Tuskegee, local authorities were using all means at their disposal to deny access to registration and voting. (In Tuskegee, the local registrars simply refused to open their offices to take applications for months at a time.) The strategy was to build broad-based liberal support in Congress for such a plan.[90] But this meant extensive consultation with liberal legislators, and careful plotting of legislative strategy. When the proposal was made to the thirty-five congressmen, the TCA indicated a hope that there would be formal and informal discussions before a final bill was drafted. The NAACP's Clarence Mitchell was contacted. The TCA began to hold meetings with other local Southern civic action groups to gain support. A regional conference was held in Atlanta in January 1959. This was expected to be a tedious, educative political process, involving building national media support. The basic idea was to implant the concept of a federal voter registration process in those places where local and state processes had broken down. The idea was based to some extent on the theory of the President's sending federal troops into Little Rock: enforcement of law and order was a local responsibility, but failing that, the federal government would step in and enforce constitutional rights. But the TCA wanted to talk up the idea first, consult in Washington, get sympathetic Northern press editorials, and build a political coalition. In other words, the groundwork would be laid carefully before there was a formal proposal introduced in Congress.

But Powell jumped the gun. He took the initial TCA draft, shaped it into a bill, and introduced it into the House hopper in June 1959. It became H.R. 7957, and was referred to the Committee on House Administration, not the House Judiciary Committee, which handled civil rights measures. TCA officials were somewhat perplexed at this premature action on Powell's part. Some even thought his sponsorship was a "political kiss of death." Not enough political work to build support had been done. Several attempts were made to contact Powell. Finally, a TCA official was able to reach him by phone and explain the possible harmful effects of such a premature move.

"You want the bill passed, don't you?" Powell impatiently argued. "Then you've got the right man. I'll take care of it."[91]

He did not speak out for it, and H.R. 7957 got lost in the shuffle of other proposals being introduced. A 1960 bill was passed that, unlike the TCA proposal which envisioned a federal *administrative* apparatus, provided mechanisms for the federal courts to deal with vote-denial issues. On the whole, the judicial process promised to be much slower in registering large numbers of people. But the bill was a vast improvement over the 1957 law.

Some local Tuskegee activists were never convinced that Powell gave serious attention to the proposal, but they had to live with his characteristically independent style. With Powell, you took the good with the bad, and hoped the former would outweigh the latter.

Powell's relative ineffectiveness and lack of influence inside the corridors of Congress in the late 1950s stemmed from a mixture of the racism of many of his colleagues who refused to accord him positions of responsibility and respect, the controversial nature of the civil rights issues he espoused, and certainly, the unpredictable character of his own political behavior. This made him, at best, during that time a congressional irritant. This would change drastically and abruptly in just a couple of years when he assumed chairmanship of the full committee. But in the last few years of the 1950s, he was in a political holding pattern—clearly not part of the inner leadership circle of Congress, in spite of his almost fifteen years there, and not entirely fitted yet into the newly emerging civil rights leadership being launched in the South.

He continued to speak out against discrimination, and met with Justice Department officials in 1958 and 1959 on a civil rights legislative agenda. He was received courteously by the new Attorney General, William P. Rogers, and the Deputy Attorney General, Lawrence Walsh. But there is no evidence that these meetings were particularly productive.

In 1959 Powell sought to have Eisenhower officially invite the new prime minister of Cuba, Fidel Castro, for a visit. After a trip to Cuba in February of that year, Powell indicated in a telegram to Eisenhower that Castro would look favorably on such an invitation.[92] Castro was scheduled to address the American Society of Newspaper Editors in Washington in April 1959. Powell urged Eisenhower: "Will you as quickly as possible invite Dr. Castro so that what little is left of the mishandling of Cuban relationships can be saved. This wire is confidential pending a reply."[93] Powell, however, was no more successful in getting a meeting with the President for Castro than he was in 1957 for himself. The White House politely acknowledged Powell's efforts, but equally as politely advised him: "Any questions of appropriate official courtesies would, of course, be handled by the two governments."[94] In other words, the President and his State Department would conduct American foreign policy with Cuba without the assistance of the congressman from Harlem.

In the meantime, ever since Powell's switch to Eisenhower in 1956, the speculation had not ceased that somehow or other his tax problems were a factor in his decision. This was enhanced when the Justice Department's investigation of his tax records lagged and was even thought by some members of the conservative press to have been called off. Obviously, these rumors had to be denied by the government. On May 23, 1957, Deputy Attorney General William P. Rogers had felt it necessary to write to the U.S. Attorney in New York, Paul W. Williams, explicitly assuring him that no favors should be shown the congressman. He should be treated "like every other case in your office."[95] It seems that Mississippi senator James Eastland had heard some rumors to the contrary, and had "disinterestedly" spoken to the Justice Department about them. Rogers wanted the U.S. Attorney to know: "If in your opinion the facts justify action, we want you to take it. If the facts do not justify action, do not act. . . . We want and expect you to make the decision in collaboration with the Tax Division in accordance with our standard procedures for all cases."

So much for an endorsement deal.

After that, the investigation proceeded. A grand jury was recalled, and issued subpoenas for the tax records of Adam Powell and Hazel Scott. On May 8, 1958, he was indicted.

But it would be two years before the case came to trial. In the interim, he had to face—for the first time in over a decade—a concerted attempt on the part of Harlem and New York Democrats to defeat him at the polls. Tammany Hall's leader, Carmine De Sapio, was sufficiently fed up with the maverick Powell to actively attempt to deny him the party nomination for reelection in 1958. And De Sapio proceeded to mastermind the attempted purge. Even then, local Harlem politicians, who had no love for Powell, knew this would be an uphill battle for Tammany Hall.

"I told them that Powell could have been elected if he ran on a laundry ticket," Edward Dudley, a prominent Harlem lawyer and politician, said.[96]

Perhaps true. But Powell knew the value, in terms of his seniority in Congress, of being nominated on the Democratic Party ticket. And it was *that* party's nomination he needed. Otherwise, thirteen years of tenure would go down the drain. If defeated in the primary, he would have to run as an independent and/or Republican, since the *local* Republicans were anxious to endorse him. To be sure, he stood a good chance, even then, of winning in the general election. But to return to Congress a freshman? Hardly.

Those were the stakes in the spring and summer of 1958. Everyone knew this.

14

Victory over Tammany Hall, 1958

On a hot August Sunday morning in 1988, a member of Abyssinian Baptist Church stood in front of the Gothic structure on West 138th Street in Harlem reminiscing. It was 9:30 A.M. and parishioners, some in cars, were already arriving for the 11:00 A.M. service. Several of the six-story buildings directly across the street stood abandoned, with boarded windows. The member greeted the early arrivals, some of whom were white visitors from France, Germany, and Italy. They would be introduced and welcomed along with other visitors later during the service by the new young minister, the Reverend Calvin Butts.

"He's sort of like Adam was," the member said. "You know. Young, smart, full of energy."

Gradually, the street became lined, double-parked on one side with cars.

"Be sure to see the Adam Powell Memorial Room before you leave," the greeter told a visitor.

A bulletin board in front announced the order of service, the sermon, and the preacher for the day. Dr. Calvin O. Butts was to preach on "The Ministry of Truth." It was Sunday, August 7, 1988, and in a short time the church would be 90 percent filled.

The greeter continued. "I came here from North Carolina in '44, and I just decided to join here because I'd heard of Powell. And I thought it'd be a good place to worship. I liked what I'd heard about him and his father and what they were doing with the church and all."

He moved away for a moment to help an elderly lady up the two steps into the vestibule. Another parishioner came out, swept the front sidewalk, and placed "No Parking" signs immediately in front of the main entrance. The two chatted a few minutes about the summer heat. Then the first turned to the visitor and said: "The politicians didn't like Adam much, I guess. Lot of reasons. He got into a lot of scraps and things." He paused and softly laughed and squinted his eyes in reflection. "I remember one time back in the fifties, I think, they tried to run somebody against him. But it didn't work. The only people who supported Adam was the people."

Exactly to the month and week thirty years earlier in August 1958, Powell would need "the people" in one of his many "scraps" with "the politicians."

On the heels of his 1956 switch to Eisenhower, his continuing income tax problems, and his lack of support in Congress for his seniority recognition, local Democratic politicians decided to make their move against him. Never considered a loyal clubhouse player, Powell had off-again on-again relations with the local district leaders in Harlem and with Carmine De Sapio. If he was an irritant legislatively in Congress with his constant criticisms of civil rights denials, he was no less a thorn in the side of New York politicos who would have preferred more predictable support from one of their party when it came to local and state politics. After all, Powell had also endorsed Republican Jacob Javits over Democrat Robert Wagner in the 1956 senatorial race.

Now was the time, his New York detractors concluded, to go after him, to rid themselves of this irritant. Their motives were many and varied. De Sapio certainly wanted to solidify his own power as county leader, and help national congressional Democrats, who would be grateful, in the process. Local Harlem district leaders, obviously concerned about their hold on local political power, would rest more easily without the volatile Powell in their midst, even though his civil rights stands were laudatory. To them, he was just too undependable—which meant, at times, independent. Therefore, early in 1958, talk began that Tammany Hall would not select Powell as its nominee for reelection to the Sixteenth District congressional seat that year. Ostensibly, the choice was to be made by the party district leaders—eight in all—whose assembly districts were wholly or in part in the congressional district. Their choice would then be ratified by the large New York County (Manhattan) committee, that is, Tammany Hall. But no one doubted the involved hand of De Sapio. He was, after all, the county leader. And he needed half of sixteen votes—four coming from Harlem—on the committee to retain that position. His mark as a strong leader was being tested. Effective leaders had one sure way of proving their political mettle—slating winning candidates and maintaining their loyalty. Having happy district leaders was one way to ensure this goal. District leaders had their own small but disciplined party followers who were experienced vote-getters, petition gatherers, and all-around party workers—keeping in touch with neighbors, doing favors for those in need. To be sure, Tammany Hall was seeing a steady decline in its political machine power: patronage jobs were eroding to civil service; fewer and fewer working-class people, in fact, needed the public sector jobs in the first place; "reform" elements, mostly professional and middle class, were making their way into local New York City politics focusing more on issues than on party machine loyalty.

But in 1958, Tammany's Harlem problem was not so much changing socioeconomic demographics—some of that to be sure—as it was the personal magnetism of Adam Clayton Powell, Jr.

The "drop Powell" talk continued, picked up by the daily and weekly press.

"I dare them," Powell taunted from the pulpit of Abyssinian. "If they buck me for reelection then there will not be a Democratic Governor in Albany next year. I promise them that."[1] He knew that incumbent Governor Averell Harriman would be facing stiff competition possibly from liberal Republican Nelson Rockefeller for the governorship in November. This meant the Democrats needed their loyal black voters in Harlem. Antagonizing Powell could eat into that base.

"If I don't get the support of the Democratic leaders of Harlem," Powell elaborated a few weeks later, "then I don't think I am bound to support the Democratic nominee for Governor this year."[2]

Throughout March and April, 1958, rumors, speculations, charges and countercharges filled the Harlem political air. Some heard that Tammany would not be "so stupid" as to drop Powell. Others reported that Ralph Bunche, then Thurgood Marshall, then the Reverend James Robinson had been approached, the latter by Harriman, to run, but all declined for various reasons. It soon became clear that Hulan E. Jack, the first Negro Manhattan Borough president (elected in 1953), was not going to support Powell. "Mr. Powell's behavior has not been in the best interests of the Democratic Party," Jack told a newsman in early May.[3] Jack was also one of the eight Harlem district leaders who would vote on the party's nominee. More names hit the political pundit columns: former congressman Franklin D. Roosevelt, Jr.; State Assembly member Bessie Buchanan; State Senator James L. Watson; city councilman and journalist Earl Brown; mayoral assistant Anna Hedgeman. All but Roosevelt were Negroes.[4]

Then on May 8, Powell was indicted for income tax fraud.

De Sapio and the eight Harlem district leaders convened and voted, six to one, with one abstention, not to nominate Powell. Lloyd Dickens was the lone dissenter. William Fitts Ryan did not vote. The official reason for rejecting Powell was his switch to Eisenhower two years earlier. The other startling news was that the party did not yet have a candidate of its own. The only thing the Tammany forces were sure of at the moment was that Powell could be beaten. For the first time, he would have the organization's resources against him, and if properly mobilized in a low-turnout primary, this could spell trouble for the congressman in spite of his immense popularity. After all, it was hoped, many of "Powell's People" really did not vote. They simply packed rallies and applauded him loudly.

Over the next weeks, the scramble was on to find someone willing to take on Powell. While it was true that Powell would have to rely on "amateurs" to get his primary petitions properly filed, no one was honestly complacent about how easy it would be to defeat him. They all knew the kind of campaign Powell would wage—us against them, "them" meaning the white bosses downtown—and it was hard to dodge the brush of "Uncle Tom" when Powell was wielding the charge. It definitely would be, as the editor of the *New York Age* said, "a nasty war."[5]

Just how nasty began to be seen at an NAACP rally on Saturday, May 17, in Harlem. The New York branch of the NAACP was commemorating the fourth anniversary of the Supreme Court decision against school segregation. Several speakers, including Powell and Hulan Jack, were invited to address the outdoor meeting. When Jack began, he was loudly and continuously booed until Powell stepped forward and quieted everyone down, graciously urging them to hear the borough president. Jack was visibly shaken and hurriedly finished his remarks. Powell then rose to speak to thunderous applause, and he turned the civil rights rally into a political rally for his candidacy. Denouncing De Sapio, he blasted those Negro politicians (clearly intending to include Hulan Jack) who supported the Tammany leader as Uncle Toms. The crowd in front of the Hotel Theresa loved it. The gloves were off. The next day from his pulpit, Powell continued swinging. He warned De Sapio and Jack "to stay off the streets of Harlem or we'll make it mighty uncomfortable."[6]

This was a bit too much for the NAACP. The organization criticized Powell for using the rally for political purposes, and it rejected his veiled references to violence. "The NAACP is not in partisan politics. The trouble between Mr. Powell and the New York County Democratic organization will have to be settled by contests between party members and party factions. That is not our business and we repudiate any effort by Mr. Powell or anyone else to drag our name into it."[7] Even here Powell had his defenders. A group called the Jersey City Progressive Civic and Social League Inc. wrote to Roy Wilkins of the NAACP and complained about the NAACP statement. The group admonished: "We feel that in these days of 'strife and strove,' for our first-class security, we should not display feelings of discord toward any of our prominent racial leaders at any time. . . . It is an established fact that our honorable U.S. Representation [*sic*] Adam Clayton Powell has done far more 'Good' than 'Wrong' as an elected official and public servant."[8]

For his part, Hulan Jack swung back, charging Powell with "spewing hate" and acting irresponsibly. Lurking beneath the surface of some of the anger was a feeling, Jack insinuated, of anti-Catholicism and resentment against West Indians. Jack was both Catholic and West Indian, coming to New York in 1932 from Barbados. The religious issue stemmed from a proposed Harlem public housing project backed by the local Catholic church. There was a dispute over relocation practices of current residents, and Jack sided with the church and the Catholic leaders in Tammany Hall.

Charges, denials, and countercharges flew back and forth.

Seeing an opportunity to take advantage of the internecine Democratic Party battles, the Harlem Republicans decided to capitalize on the situation. They knew they could hardly capture the congressional seat with one of their loyal own. So why not endorse Adam Clayton Powell, Jr.? The City Republican Chairman, Thomas Curran, was opposed, but Harold Burton, who had challenged Powell in 1948 and 1954, Cary Blue, Charles S. Hill, and William A. Cornelius insisted. They prevailed.

Powell, hedging his bets, saw no reason to turn them down. He issued a statement of acceptance that took a swipe at the Tammany selection process by contrast:

> These men [Harlem Republicans] were not summoned downtown by the county chairman, Thomas J. Curran, and told what to do. These Harlem leaders expressed the will of their people by setting up their own conferences and asking Mr. Curran to respect their rights. Mr. Curran, disregarding what he personally may think of me, is to be

> highly respected by obeying the rightful demand of his Harlem leaders and agreeing to my nomination.[9]

In other words, the Negro Republicans of Harlem were calling the tune, unlike the Harlem Democrats. In fact, Curran remained personally opposed to Powell, calling him an "opportunist" and asserting, "He [Powell] considers only the future of Mr. Powell."[10]

Indeed, Powell, by accepting the Republican nomination, was guaranteeing he would be on the ballot in the 1958 general election *in case* things went awry in the Democratic primary in August. He also had received the party line designation of the Communist Party, but this was, by his calculation, hardly useful. He had his campaign manager issue a polite thank-you statement.

But even with the Republican designation, which he valued almost as much as that of his own party, Powell was keenly aware that the *big* stake was not so much his seat but his seniority. If he had to go back to Congress as a Republican, he would lose the thirteen years of accrued seniority, and that was hardly what he relished. No. The main prize was the Democratic nomination, and he made no mistake about that. Thus he was pleased with the endorsement of prominent Negroes such as A. Philip Randolph and Dr. Martin Luther King, Jr. King sent him a letter in June that said, in part, "For many years you have been a militant champion of justice, not only as a Congressman from Harlem, but necessarily as a spokesman for disenfranchised millions in the South."[11]

Armed with such support, Powell felt comfortably situated to go forth and do battle. He also knew, however, that he needed the sage counsel of someone who knew the nuts and bolts of party politics in New York City. And for this he was shrewd enough to turn to one of the best, J. Raymond Jones. Jones had retired from politics in 1953 and was working in a lucrative ($12,000) patronage job as secretary to Judge Gerald Culkin. Never completely rid of the political bug since his days in the 1930s and 1940s when he pioneered the establishment of active Democratic clubs, Jones leaped at the chance to return to the political arena. He became Powell's campaign manager. Jones recalled: "I outlined a plan of action, suggested the themes of 'plantation' and 'bossism,' and he [Powell] concurred. I remarked that it would be best if he did the talking and I handled everything else."[12]

"Everything else" first and foremost meant getting 750 signatures on petitions that could not be successfully challenged as invalid. This could be a most tricky business, because the technicalities of proper filing were enough to dazzle the most astute lawyer. There were innumerable ways entire bundles of petitions could be disqualified because of the slightest deviation from precise requirements. Years later, sitting in his scenic hillside home in his second retirement in the Caribbean, he jovially recalled his experiences in the 1958 Tammany/Powell fight:

> Soon after I joined Powell in 1958, 15 people came to me to work. I knew that they were sent by De Sapio. But I let them work anyway, getting signatures on petitions. But I kept those petitions in my files and never used them. If I did use them, I know we would have been successfully challenged, and Powell never would have gotten on the ballot. Those petitions were defective, deliberately so. Thus, Tammany knew that I knew.[13]

Jones was not called the "Harlem Fox" for nothing, and Powell was lucky to have him.

In the meantime, Tammany Hall had to go through the rather embarrassing process of finding a candidate to run against Powell. There were many who would have loved to be Harlem's congressional representative, but the prospects were simply too onerous. Finally, De Sapio, after surveying a bevy of nationally prominent names—none of whom gave the faintest hint that they would be interested—settled on a city councilman from Harlem, Earl Brown. A Harvard graduate, Brown was an associate editor of *Life* magazine, and wrote a column in the *Amsterdam News*. He was, therefore, not an unknown. And he was not considered a "political hack." He spoke softly and carefully, phrasing his thoughts in the cultivated manner expected of one with his training and profession. He was also a most reluctant candidate.

One evening Edward Dudley was asked to confer with De Sapio about possible choices. Dudley met him and Brown at De Sapio's apartment in Greenwich Village. After reviewing several names together, Dudley told De Sapio: 'You've got the man right here. Earl Brown."

Brown, seated behind De Sapio, was frantically—and quietly—waving his hands and shaking his head no.[14]

But the county leader had decided. The delay was becoming politically devastating. The longer they procrastinated, the more certain it appeared that Powell would be unbeatable. Brown relented after extracting two promises: that the party would pick up the tab, and Hulan Jack, whom Brown had criticized often enough in the past, would not be a part of the campaign.[15] Both conditions were easily met. The party's treasury would hardly feel it, and Hulan Jack probably appreciated the reprieve. He had had enough of Powell's attacks.

The campaign provided delightful entertainment throughout the Harlem community during the hot summer days of June and July. Not having campaigned so actively in over a decade, Powell was enjoying the nightly forays on a sound truck, drawing crowds that were happy to have diversion from the stuffy tenements. Powell's entourage frequently included live music—once led by Dizzy Gillespie—preceding his talks. He poked fun at Brown and blasted the "plantation boss," Carmine De Sapio. Brown's style of speaking was more academic than rally-rousing, with thoughtfully phrased points, at times delivered meditatively while he cast his eyes at his feet. This was perfect for Adam Powell, who labeled his opponent "Look Down Brown." The crowd roared. And at another time, Powell mockingly shouted: "White doesn't have to be right. Black doesn't have to be right always either. But, in this present case, Brown—if it is named Earl—can't possibly be right." More laughter. Powell recounted his record of attempts to pass the Powell Amendment, the pressure to end military discrimination, his challenge to Southern Dixiecrats, and, of course, his defiance of "Downtown (Tammany) bosses." He accused the Tammany leaders of collusion with the Dixiecrats to deprive him of his seniority and eventual chairmanship. They were out to get him, he yelled, because they feared his independence and leadership of the civil rights movement. He reeled off a long list of prominent supporters who knew he "couldn't be bought." All the names—Randolph, King, Jackie Robinson, Joe Louis—were instantly recognizable to his Harlem street-corner audiences. And they yelled back in responsive approval. It was political church—vintage Powell.

He sent letters around the country soliciting funds both for his legal defense against the income tax indictment and for his reelection fight. Campaign finance laws then not being very strict, he could write: "Will you . . . rush to me . . . a contribution for either or both of my funds. If you desire to do so anonymously, let me know or you can place cash in an envelope marked PERSONAL—CONFIDENTIAL." Checks were to be made out to "People for Powell" at the Hotel Theresa, or "For Legal Defense." In a mass mailing to "Fellow-Democrat," he encouraged voters, to "make your summer plans now so that you will be in New York ready to vote on August 12th."

Earl Brown was an intelligent man. He knew the odds against him, and he knew his style of campaigning was no match for Powell. Therefore, unlike Grant Reynolds back in 1946, Brown did not seek to debate Powell in an open forum. In fact, one evening Powell parked his sound truck outside the Brown headquarters and taunted the city councilman to come out and debate him. Brown confined his appearances more to small coffee-klatches and professorial lectures before orderly, behaved groups indoors. He concentrated on Powell's absentee record in Congress and on his opponent's flamboyant style. He reeled off data showing the few times Powell attended committee meetings. Brown had received a warm, supportive, detailed letter from Congressman Stewart L. Udall who served with Powell on both the Education and Labor Committee and on the House Committee on Interior and Insular Affairs. Udall wrote to Brown:

> Perhaps it is a slight overstatement, but in my opinion the plain truth is that Rev. Powell has not won the genuine respect of a single colleague during his many years of casual service in the House. One of his most serious shortcomings is that he carries none of the workload of his committees. . . . Believe me, you will render a real service to the country—and to your people—if you defeat Mr. Powell.[16]

Udall had a list compiled of Powell's eighty-fifth Congress committee attendance record for the full committee on Interior and Insular Affairs: forty-seven absences, two presents. For the Subcommittee on Safety and Compensation in 1958, eleven absences, zero present. Udall informed Brown: "From what I have heard of Powell's campaign methods, I suppose such devastating facts will not compel any votes against him, but nevertheless I thought you should have these summaries at your disposal."

Udall was right. The attendance records meant virtually nothing to the Harlem voters.

In addition, Brown received the endorsement of the Liberal Party, which had never supported Powell. The Liberal designation meant that come what may in the August 12 Democratic primary, both Powell and Brown would be on the ballot in November, inasmuch as Powell had the Republican Party designation. But everyone knew that the Democratic Party designation was the main prize. For Powell it meant, if he won it, continuation of his party seniority; for Brown, a much stronger chance to unseat Powell in the general election.

As lively and entertaining as the summer campaign was, it was hardly a cliff-hanger in the minds of most voters and political pundits. As early as May, and into July, Powell seemed to enjoy upwards of three- and four-to-one support over his opponent.

Voters in Harlem told *New York Post* reporters:

"I don't know if he [Powell] did wrong or not. But I know he did all right for us Negroes. I'm going all down the line for him."

"I always voted for him and I'm voting for him again. He's done a lot for my folks. He was the first to get us jobs."

One anti-Powell voter admitted: "I'm not going to vote for him, but that won't make any difference. When he stands up 6-foot-3, shakes that hair of his down in his face, and shouts just once, he'll get the support of every woman in the sound of his voice. And you can't outvote the women."

Of course, Powell had more than a few men supporters too, as everyone knew. His physical attraction was always a plus, but this was hardly his only or main asset—either in the pulpit or on the political stump. The *Post* survey left little doubt about the outcome. Of 145 persons who said they would vote, 130 chose Powell.[17]

Brown pointed with pride to his own record of success as a city councilman in getting legislation passed against housing discrimination. In his campaign, he described three types of Negro leaders: the Uncle Tom, cryptically referring to Hulan Jack; the "Loud Mouth," meaning Powell; and the quietly effective leader, meaning, obviously, himself. Eleanor Roosevelt, calling Powell a "demagogue," came out for Brown. So did the first Negro Wimbledon tennis champion, Althea Gibson. The athletic contrasts in support must have been quietly amusing to Powell's people—tennis against baseball (Jackie Robinson) and boxing (Joe Louis). Neither did the white metropolitan press help Brown. Editorials attacking Powell in the *New York Times* and the *Herald Tribune* were read derisively by Powell to the Harlem audiences gathered around his sound truck. The more they attacked Powell, the more ammunition they gave him to use against his opponent. The Harlem-based *Amsterdam News* endorsed Brown, and although the weekly had been criticizing Jack and De Sapio, Powell lumped them all together. Without question, many of Brown's supporters were simply albatrosses around his neck.

Ten days before the primary, Powell held a news conference at Abyssinian Baptist Church. He was relaxed and confident of victory, he assured the press. But he was still going to start ten days of intensive street campaigning. Unspoken, but probably understood, was that Powell hardly needed to close out the campaign with such last-minute activity, but he actually enjoyed it. He had not had to campaign in this manner since 1946 against Grant Reynolds. It was fun getting back on the stump for himself for a change, and especially in Harlem, with the press giving good coverage, and crowds shouting love and approval. He could use this to revive the political juices, and—certainly not articulated, but just as surely felt—to buoy his spirits for the impending income tax trial hanging over his head. This was a good way to charge the political support batteries, and also to take his mind off the sorry turn of events between himself and the Eisenhower administration.

Puffing on his ever-present cigar, and surrounded by doting campaign aides, he blew an occasional smoke ring and confidently predicted he would defeat Brown and Tammany Hall by a two-to-one margin.[18]

He was wrong.

Powell won by a three-to-one margin—14,837 to 4,935.

In spite of a highly publicized campaign, turnout was about 40 percent of the registered 50,000 Democrats. Some observers had predicted a higher rate of participation. Low turnout usually redounds to the benefit of the organized party, but in this case, Powell's essentially volunteer forces were superior. There was also speculation that several Tammany workers subtly and privately worked for Powell on election day, whispering to voters that they would not be disappointed in a vote for Powell.

The *New York Times* declared him "the political equivalent of the one-man band."[19] In an editorial strongly reminiscent of an *Amsterdam News* editorial fourteen years earlier when Powell was first elected to Congress, the *New York Post* wrote:

> . . . The man now has a tremendous opportunity to influence events on a national scale. . . . We hope Powell truly appreciates the responsibility that goes with his victory. . . . If Powell . . . attends to his business in Congress, perhaps the doubts many people have about him will eventually be dissipated.[20]

There were more immediate matters on Powell's plate, however. The statewide Democratic Party was locked in a tough fight to reelect Averell Harriman as governor. Nelson A. Rockefeller was the Republican opponent. Whom would Powell support? After all, he *was* endorsed early by the Republicans. And it was clear that the Republicans could use his blessing for the November election.

Powell took off for a brief vacation in Puerto Rico—where he was beginning to spend more time—and decided to let the offers and counteroffers come his way. He was in the driver's seat.

Before he left, however, he let it be known that there would be some Tammany Hall business that would be taken care of the following year. He served notice that he and J. Raymond Jones fully intended to challenge Tammany in 1959 for total control of the district leadership in Harlem—Hulan Jack and all. There was good reason to believe that they could pull this off. After all, Powell had not only beaten Jack in the latter's own assembly district, he had carried Jack's own apartment building. That would be the ultimate political victory—to beat an opponent in that person's own bailiwick. And to top it off, Jones declared that his return from retirement was now official. He and Powell would maintain their political alliance—a most formidable Harlem political force indeed.

Although faced with a nominal challenge from Brown on the Liberal Party ticket, Powell's problem now was to decide how—not if—he would come out for Harriman and the Democratic ticket in the general election. For a few weeks, Harold Burton of the Harlem Republicans harbored notions that Powell would campaign as and for the Republicans, Rockefeller on down. Burton insisted he had an earlier such commitment from Powell in exchange for the GOP's primary endorsement. He tried vainly to reach Powell in Puerto Rico. Powell, of course, was not interested. He would be foolish now to risk his seniority chances in Congress. He certainly did not want a repeat of the January 1957 denial of a subcommittee chairmanship. At the same time he wanted the New York Democrats to sweat a little and possibly to pay.

Word was sent to Powell in Puerto Rico that the Republicans were willing to be reasonable financially—that is, help pay off his primary campaign expenses, as well as provide money for any expenses he needed for the general election and any incurred in his help for Rockefeller. This was another way of saying they would listen to his ideas about money. Such matters are not the stuff of formal, explicit letters and memos; thus, no verifiable paper trail is available on these discussions. One source, however, indicated that Charles Willis, formerly of the Eisenhower staff, was designated to deal with Powell.[21] Burton wanted Powell as a step toward making Republican inroads into Harlem. Powell's support could help Republican Negro candidates running for the state legislature. According to Frederick Weaver, the Republicans were willing to talk in terms of $50,000 in cash. Powell supposedly was not interested in such a small sum. Weaver, writing later to Drew Pearson, said that Powell recognized that his move to the Republicans would jeopardize his political future, probably finishing it. Therefore, he had to have options in the form of greater "financial security." The least he could consider, Weaver advised, was a handsome position in a private company "as a vice president in charge of public relations at $50,000 a year for ten years," along with an advance of $50,000. Nonsense, Willis allegedly responded. And when Powell made the fifty-thousand-dollar offer public weeks later, Willis strongly denied it.

Meanwhile, the Democrats knew they had to reach Powell. A silent, neutral, inactive Powell would hardly be beneficial for the Harriman candidacy against Rockefeller. An emissary was dispatched to Puerto Rico. Weaver then claimed that the Democrats offered Powell $100,000 if he would agree to support the entire Democratic slate, top to bottom. Half of this would be paid up front, and the rest over a ten-year period at $100 per week. In addition, he would be reimbursed for his campaign expenses.

Again, none of the supposed deals could be verified. Powell, however, felt he could use the Democrats' help with his seniority tiff back in Congress. Support for the ticket in exchange would certainly be worth it.

After further discussions with the Democrats, and meetings with Harriman and Rockefeller—shades of the 1956 meeting with Eisenhower and the "nonmeeting" with Stevenson—Powell called for "party unity" and endorsed the Democrats.

Howls went up from the Republicans. Powell was back on the De Sapio "plantation." Powell had "sold out" to Tammany Hall.

Powell countered by saying the Republicans tried to "buy him." He revealed the discussions with Willis, but added, "I wouldn't say it was an attempt to bribe me because no specific amount was mentioned to me by Willis—only that he had a bundle for me."[22] Willis categorically denied this: "Adam Powell was never offered any money by me at any time in behalf of the Republican Party or for any other reason."[23] The most Willis offered, the *New York Times* reported, was that "as a candidate on the Republican ticket, he could expect the Republican Party to raise funds for him."

Frankly, this Powell-Republican tiff was less newsworthy than Powell's reconciliation with Tammany Hall. His endorsement of Harriman, he asserted, was conditioned on three main requirements, which were met: Harriman and De Sapio would agree to appoint "Negroes and all minorities" to positions of high authority in state and local government; De Sapio would use his influence in Congress to support Powell in obtaining his entitled seniority rights; there would be a major campaign role for Powell statewide, not only in Harlem. The agreement was reached, and Powell became associate campaign manager for Harriman's reelection. Of course, Harriman's statement said: "I welcome also Congressman Powell's support of my program of appointing and advancing qualified Negroes and members of other minority groups in the state government. I intend to continue and advance this expression of real democracy in New York State."[24] De Sapio, likewise, had no difficulty in agreeing to urge that Powell be accorded his rightful seniority privileges in Congress.

At a press conference announcing his endorsement, a smiling Powell said, "I am no longer purged."

He had protected his political base at home. He would deal with his Democratic primary adversaries later—the following year. For now, he would level some charges against Rockefeller, namely, the Rockefeller family's meager support, according to Powell, of the NAACP; Rockefeller's poor hiring record of Negro professionals; and the Rockefeller interest in South African diamond mines, exploiting "slave labor." All these were promptly denied by the Republican camp, but Powell was not deterred.

Neither was he likely surprised nor distracted by the *New York Times* editorial a few days before the November election endorsing Earl Brown. The *Times* recognized the futility of Brown's candidacy on the Liberal ticket, but Powell was more than the newspaper could take. His attendance record in Congress was "disgraceful." His Powell Amendment "helped kill the Federal school construction bill." The editors equated his "racist positions" to those "of the Rankins and the Bilbos [of Mississippi]." "His outrageous statements in the present campaign and his party flip-flopping are a disgrace to both the Democratic and the Republican parties that have accepted him because of the power he holds in his Harlem fiefdom."[25] The *Times* suggested a protest vote against Powell for Brown.

Powell, of course, won easily.

The editorial correctly decided to "pass over" Powell's income tax indictment, inasmuch as he had yet to be tried. But Powell knew that with all the political victories he was chalking up, he was still faced with a date in court. He might not have been worried—his style was such that it would be hard to tell on the surface—but he was astute enough to know that he should not take this next impending challenge lightly.

15

Surviving an Income Tax Trial

In December 1956, a federal grand jury was empaneled to take testimony regarding Congressman Powell's tax returns for six years, 1950 through 1955. Assistant U.S. Attorney Thomas A. Bolan began presenting evidence for the next three months purporting to show that for those years Powell falsified his tax returns. According to an article in the *National Review*, Powell, irked by these developments, called the White House "twice since the election to straighten out his tax troubles."[1] The implication was that the investigation violated an understanding between Powell and the Eisenhower administration arising from his endorsement of the President.

Meanwhile, James V. Johnson, an attorney who had prepared Powell's 1951 and 1952 tax returns, refused to turn over certain records. He claimed a lawyer-client privilege. Bolan insisted, however, that Johnson was acting as Powell's accountant, not his lawyer. Other records from the House of Representatives payroll and Abyssinian Baptist Church were ordered to be produced for the grand jury.

Clearly, the probe was moving forward, and Powell formally complained to the Attorney General that he was being unnecessarily harassed. In early 1957, Bolan was temporarily reassigned to other business, and the Powell tax probe was put on hold. Then, when he turned his attention again to the Powell case, he was told to cease Department of Justice involvement and turn the matter over to the Treasury Department. Bolan was disappointed, because he believed the grand jury phase could be wrapped up in rather short order with an indictment. This did not matter. "That's the way we want it handled," he was allegedly told by his superiors. "It's just too hot to handle." This occurred on March 18, 1957.

Two months later, Deputy Attorney General William P. Rogers wrote his letter to U.S. Attorney Paul Williams denying any rumors that Powell was being given special treatment.

But for the remainder of the year the grand jury did not sit on the Powell probe.

Following an earlier decision to return to private practice, Thomas Bolan resigned from the Justice Department in September 1957. He had not worked on the Powell case since March of that year.

More than a few who had been following the case speculated that notwithstanding the Rogers letter, Powell was being protected as a quid pro quo for his switch to Eisenhower. While never substantiated, suspicions persisted.

After March nothing happened for the rest of the year until the *National Review* printed an article in December 1957 outlining the various twists and turns, starts and stops in the Powell case. The foreman of the grand jury, seeing the article, asked the U.S. Attorney for an explanation. He received no satisfactory response and then approached the magazine's editors. They agreed that copies of the article should be sent to each member of the grand jury. And then, on the possible heels of a "runaway" grand jury, the investigative process started up again.

One witness, Acy Lennon, formerly Powell's aide and now serving a sentence for tax fraud, argued that he should not be required to appear before the grand jury. The fact that the *National Review* had sent the article to the grand jurors amounted to "contamination" of the process. The judge disagreed.

For its part, the magazine was openly indignant at any intimation that it had acted improperly. In an open letter to U.S. Attorney Paul Williams, editor William F. Buckley, Jr., defended contact with the grand jurors. Buckley understood that the attorney was examining whether a law had been violated by the magazine's acts—namely, that "whoever attempts to influence the action or decision of any grand or petty juror of any court of the U.S., upon any issue or matter pending before the jury of which he is a member, or pertaining to his duties, by writing or sending to him any written communication in relation to such issue, shall be fined not more than $1,000 or imprisoned not more than six months or both."

Buckley was defiant. The "*National Review* pleads guilty," he wrote.

But to what?

"*National Review* never urged the jury to indict Adam Clayton Powell, Jr.: we merely asked that it investigate the abrupt suspension of the investigation you launched, and Washington arbitrarily froze." The editor insisted that the jury was simply being asked to do its duty, come what may. And if the law prohibited such action by the press, then the law should be changed.

This issue was not joined. The probe of Powell's tax returns moved forward. Bolan, by then a law partner of Roy M. Cohn, offered to appear and present evidence. (Meanwhile, the statute of limitations had run out on Powell's 1950 tax return. Attention then focused on 1951–52.)

The controversy escalated. The investigation resumed at the time Powell was gearing up to fight Tammany's decision to dump him. A close Powell friend, Dunbar S. McLaurin, drew a connection: "Without passing on the merits of the investigation, it certainly seems odd to many members of the Harlem community that these charges are being reopened against New York's only Negro Congressman just before the primary campaign. . . . It may well be that this is another link in what appears to be a pattern of discrediting any type of independent Negro leadership."[2]

Powell was adamant before his Abyssinian congregation that he was being persecuted, and many agreed with him. He compared himself to the nineteenth-century antislavery preacher, Henry Ward Beecher, and vowed that if he were not a similarly outspoken, independent champion of human rights, he would not be such a target of attack. His parishioners responded with overwhelming agreement and support.[3]

After marathon sessions over a three-week period, the grand jury returned a three-count indictment against Powell on May 8, 1958. He was charged with knowingly advising the fraudulent preparation of Mrs. Powell's (Hazel Scott's) 1951 tax return. Instead of a claimed net income of $3,815.31, she actually had taxable income of $9,181.08, the indictment charged. The second count charged Powell with aiding and abetting in the preparation of a fraudulent return for another person, his wife. The third count charged tax evasion in a joint return for 1952. Mrs. Powell, performing in Europe at the time of the indictment, was not named as a defendant. If convicted on all three counts, Powell could be sentenced to fifteen years (five years per count) in prison and fined $30,000.

The daily press covered the grand jury action widely and each story gave a history of the saga, reminding readers of the rumored link to the 1956 switch, as well as the record of convictions against Powell's former aides. Powell was not called before the grand jury, and he was obviously worried by the action when he got word of the indictment in his office on Capitol Hill. For the moment, he had no comment.

His first move, and a clear indication that he understood the seriousness of the situation, was to hire the renowned criminal lawyer Edward Bennett Williams to represent him. Williams's legal skills were already well established in defense of such clients as Frank Costello, James Hoffa, the late senator Joseph McCarthy, and Dave Beck, the union leader. The thirty-seven-year-old Washington lawyer had never met Powell before then, and his only knowledge of the case to that point came from newspaper accounts.

Powell appeared the following week in court and pleaded not guilty to all three counts.

The legal case was now in the hands of his attorneys, and his public statements wisely steered clear of any reference to the specific charges in the indictment. But Powell would handle the political side, where, of course, he was the expert. He lost no opportunity to link his tax trial with the Tammany Hall challenge, and he noted the outpouring of civil and religious support for his political contest—and by implication, his innocence of the tax charges. Rallies were held for him. The officers of his church issued a statement: "We call on the religious community to stand with us and to offer constant prayers to Almighty God that his [Powell's] enemies may be confounded so that he can continue to fight wherever God gives him an opportunity for the rights of common men."[4]

Powell was particularly pleased with the statement made by Roy Wilkins of the NAACP. At a civil rights leadership meeting in Washington, Wilkins stated that "many Negroes and some whites as well are asking themselves whether Adam is being singled out because he does not bite his tongue on civil rights." He then wondered "if certain political sources are trying to close Adam's mouth and put down his influence. The goverment got itself in an awful mess picking on Powell."[5] (That same week, Wilkins had to scold Powell for his threatening remarks against Hulan Jack and Carmine De Sapio at the NAACP rally in Harlem.) Powell loved this kind of public respect paid him by such a highly regarded civil rights leader. He repeated the "awful mess" statement at a Brooklyn fund-raising rally in his behalf. That was the sort of public-political image he could nurture to make the legal case against him seem even more of a political vendetta. Ministers around the country preached sermons on his behalf, and sent contributions. One minister in Miami, Florida, wrote to him that Negroes would not forget how Powell had stood up over the years for "freedom and human rights. Your great father Rev. Adam Clayton Powell, Senior, has trained you and prepared you for leadership, and the battle of life. You will therefore face these trying moments with that degree of fortitude and determination which has brought the Negro race from the depths of slavery to the threshold of the Promised Land."[6]

This minister also wrote to Wilkins to urge "that the NAACP and its legal staff will stand by him."[7] Wilkins responded, reminding him that Powell had obtained "a very distinguished attorney" and "It will not be necessary, therefore, for other lawyers to take part." But Wilkins did add that he hoped Powell would be accorded justice and "that an outspoken champion" would not suffer because of his adamant stand for civil rights.[8]

Therefore, in the minds of many, Powell's civil rights record was more important than any particular income tax transgressions he might be guilty of. Even assuming the latter, it would be difficult to convince many that the underlying motivation for the tax trial was *not* to punish Powell for his civil rights advocacy. And this was precisely the way Powell wanted to be portrayed—as a man on trial for his crusade for civil rights, not because he allegedly falsified income tax returns.

The trial, under Edward Bennett Williams's deft hand, would turn on legal evidence. For his part, Powell was handling the extra-legal political terrain. This was a pattern to be replayed several times in the next decade of his controversial career.

Always more critical than complimentary of Powell, the *New York Times*, following the indictment, published an article depicting the frustrating dimensions of the man. Clearly one who had "won a reputation as the nation's most militant Negro leader," the *Times* wrote, Powell at the same time was accused by many "of being obsessed with fancy living, of having an alarming capacity for alienating close friends, of being vain, childish, insincere, undependable, disloyal and ungrateful." Many saw him as an opportunist who "exploited the race issue in pulpit and legislative hall to gain the prestige, adulation and money he needs for the purpose of pleasure." But the article felt obliged to inform its readers of another aspect of the man:

> . . . even his most severe critics admit that he has done more to dramatize the civil rights issue than any other man in modern times.
>
> His critics also concede that he probably has done as much as any

> man to stimulate the Negro's race consciousness and to sharpen his awareness of the value of the ballot, the boycott, the mass meeting and the picket line in the race's drive toward full equality.[9]

The *Times* got one of its facts wrong: "The Rev. Adam Clayton Powell, Sr. established the Abyssinian Baptist Church when young Adam . . . was graduated from Colgate University in 1930." Hardly so, and Abyssinian parishioners must have shaken their heads in tolerant bemusement at this bit of historical revisionism—off by 122 years. And they might have wondered what else the newspaper got wrong about their pastor. But they would hardly deny the many sides of their volatile leader. He could indeed be, as the old folk saying went, "a puzzlement."

The trial was postponed several times due to conflicting attorney schedules, motions to amend the original indictment, and in 1959 a major operation Powell had to undergo to remove a tumor near his esophagus. From all outward appearances, he stood up well during the various developments and delays. His congressional office continued to function as normally as possible; he attempted a liaison with Castro; and he kept a reasonably active speaking schedule.

Finally, in early 1960, the trial was set, and jury selection began. His lawyer made a point of the means used to empanel jurors. The court clerk admitted that prospective jurors were taken from rent-lease lists in well-to-do communities in order to insure a "better" class of jurors. Relying, as earlier, on voter-registration lists yielded oftentimes less than highly qualified jurors. Edward Bennett Williams protested that this new method smacked of geographical and economic, and even possibly racial, discrimination, noting that lower-income people were hardly likely to appear on the rent-lease lists.

The final jury consisted of nine women and three men—all white. One negro woman, who would later replace one juror who became ill, was chosen as the first alternate.

The trial began March 7, 1960. Government witnesses would consist of Internal Revenue agents, U.S. government officials stationed overseas, foreign citizens flown from Europe—agents and others involved in promoting Hazel Scott's tours—and a reluctant Hattie Dodson. Hazel Scott returned from Paris for a brief stopover on her way to performances around the country and in Canada. She was not asked to be a witness, and she was blatantly coy when reporters tried to get her opinion on the trial.

"What trial?" she toyed with one reporter. "I go to Chicago Monday for a three-week engagement, then to Minneapolis and finally to Canada for some work over the Canadian Broadcasting System. That's the only trial I know of."[10] Although she attended church services at Abyssinian during her brief stopover, she stayed at a hotel in midtown instead of at the family home in suburban Mt. Vernon, New York. Those close to Powell and his wife knew that their marriage was virtually over. But they also knew that during the course of the trial, she would do nothing to jeopardize her husband's chances of being acquitted.

During the opening days of the trial, the small courtroom was packed with news reporters, leaving little room for the hundreds of Powell supporters and curiosity seekers who had to mill around outside waiting for a chance to get in or even to catch a glimpse of Powell and Williams. These were clearly the two stars of the legal drama.

The government's case hinged on its ability to prove that Powell falsely claimed deductions on his wife's 1951 tax returns, that he also did so on their joint 1952 return, and that he understated his own income for 1952. Much of the testimony consisted of item-by-item analyses of the various documents: presents in Europe for his son, restaurant and liquor bills, rail fare tickets between Washington, D.C., and New York, costs of clerical attire, etc. Questions were raised whether, in fact, he was on official business during the time he traveled with Mrs. Hazel Scott Powell to various foreign cities.

The trial droned on, monotonous at times to those who wanted less tedious accounts of deductible or allowable expenditures. But Williams was patient, and Powell had no choice. Entertainment bills at famous nightclubs, Sardi's and "21" and other well-known night spots, which were claimed as expense deductions were scrutinized. (At one point, Powell whispered to his counsel that he wished these food and liquor bills would not be brought up before lunch. They made him hungry.) But for the most part, Powell was a study in seriousness in the courtroom. Before the twelve-person jury that could send him to jail, this was not the time for pomposity. There was inconclusive testimony from a U.S. Embassy official in London about exactly what Powell did while he was in that city, and whether the official did or did not understand Powell's visit to be an official one. Hattie Dodson was quizzed about her role in preparing worksheets on Powell's income and expenses, and how she obtained the information—from Powell or not—to pass on to the lawyer-accountant Johnson. She stated she really could not remember some details, but overall, although called as a government witness, she was more protective of Powell than harmful.

Clearly pressing to have Powell explain how he had large sums of cash—in one instance at least $7,500—to carry with him on an overseas trip, the government was suggesting that such monies likely came from the salary kickback of his former secretary. In addition, the government wanted Mrs. Dodson to explain how she handled payments of Powell's alimony to his first wife during his absence abroad.

Powell's possession of large sums of ready cash was always a source of interest to investigators and reporters, even though four years earlier, he had told a *New York Post* reporter that his mother periodically gave him sizable sums.

When Powell took the stand, he explained that beginning in 1945 his father gave him $3,000 each year for vacation expenses. This money, when not used, Powell explained, would be kept in a safe at the church. In 1951, apparently realizing that his son was going on an extended European trip, the father had offered to give him $7,500. Powell testified that to avoid a gift tax, he asked his father to give him the usual $3,000 and to make the rest in the form of a loan of $4,500. In return, Powell executed a note dated August 24, 1951, that read "Received from my father, A. Clayton Powell, Sr., $4,500, payable to him on or before January 15, 1952 without interest." It was not signed. This money, he testified, was deposited in the Manufacturers Trust Bank by Hattie Dodson before he left the country. He also testified that the loan was repaid in 1952 from the father's annual $3,000 gift plus his own $1,500.

On cross-examination, Powell testified that he did not get the note back from his father, who died in 1953. But mysteriously, the note was mailed to him in 1960 from an unknown source three weeks before the start of his trial.

The safe in the church, he stated, always contained large sums of cash—contributions for birthdays, anniversaries, trips. The government's attorney, Morton Robson, obviously was skeptical of this explanation. And he wondered aloud how the father could be so generous when he died leaving an estate of less than $4,000. But Powell was less interested in convincing Robson; his target was the jury.

A church official gave testimony about $17,075 Powell failed to report as income from the church in 1951 and 1952. Before the trial began, the official had told Robson a different story about the money. Under oath, however, he explained that the money was really not income for those years, but $12,000 in two years' back salary due Powell, plus parsonage allowance, repayment of a loan from Powell, postage expenses, and a sum for customary vacation expenses. This testimony did not help the government's case, although again, it was coming from one of its own witnesses. Robson told the court that he was completely surprised by the church official's testimony.

Some of the most damaging testimony against the government's case came when Hattie Dodson and James Johnson admitted that they had made mistakes in compiling Powell's returns. Namely, they had duplicated income items, listing some income for Hazel Scott *and* Powell. In addition, a $2,500 tax-free congressional allowance was listed as taxable income. The government hurriedly tried to explain that it was unaware of this duplication when the original indictment was filed. But, Williams countered, the full extent of the duplication *was* known in April 1959, and these would have completely wiped out the understatement of income. The government's tax witness had to admit that that was true. In addition, the government had sent letters to 350 Negro colleges and Negro newspapers in an attempt to find out if Powell had spoken at any of them without reporting fees. The results were not a part of the court record. In fact, Powell had *overstated* his income. Williams argued that once the government found it could not prevail on the charges of understatement—due to the duplications and errors—it tried to build its case on charges of phony expense deductions.

Federal judge Frederick Van Pelt Bryan dismissed two counts of the three-count indictment. The 1952 charge of tax evasion was thrown out, with the government conceding that it had not offered enough evidence to support the charge. And the 1951 understatement charge was dropped, because of the "overstatement" evidence. That left only the charge that Powell, in 1951, willfully intended to defraud the government.

Williams admitted that mistakes were made in the 1951 tax return, but they were not mistakes made by his client. Rather, according to testimony of both Dodson and Johnson, these errors were caused by them, not by Powell. He hammered away that these were witnesses called by the government, not by defendant Powell. He also wanted the jury to remember that the errors were made "by persons who made errors against the taxpayer more than for the taxpayer."

The trial was drawing to a close, and the government's case was slowly unraveling. Summations followed.

Edward Bennett Williams lost no time in reminding the jury of the various mistakes made by the government in preparing the case. "They [the Government] had these records for 18 months. If after 18 months these experts made these mistakes, how can they ask you to convict this man and find him guilty beyond a reasonable doubt?" Was this not a trial of "political intimidation"? He questioned why hundreds of letters were sent to Negro colleges and newspapers stating that Powell's tax affairs "were under grand jury investigation." "I say that if the intent was to help a tax investigation, the letters would have been sent to other than Negro papers and Negro schools. I say it was wrong. I say it was indecent to conduct this investigation this way."[11] Why wasn't Powell called in to explain his returns, which was the normal procedure in such matters, Williams wanted the jurors to wonder. There was no doubt in the defense attorney's mind, and he wanted those twelve jurors to share his confidence, that this case was a political vendetta against Powell. "I ask you to consider whether you believe, really and truly, that there is behind this trial simply the charge, recklessly and carelessly put together in this indictment, or whether he is on trial for political liquidation." He paused, looked at the jury for a long moment, and walked slowly back to his seat next to Powell. His summation had taken three and a half hours.

Robson followed the next day. He urged the jury to really question whether Powell would be so casual as to *not* check the tax work of his aides. Of course not, he contended, and stated: "He lied to you. He lied to the government." He derided Powell's explanation of the cash and loan from his father, calling it a "fabricated" story.[12] Powell perjured himself, Robson argued, and that was what he wanted the jury to ponder, not the charges of political motivation raised the previous day. He should be convicted "not because Mr. Powell is a congressman, a minister, a Negro, but because he has willfully cheated millions of Americans who each year do pay their taxes." Robson took one hour less than his opposing counsel to sum up the case.

The trial had lasted just over six weeks. In his two-and-a-half hour instruction to the jury, Judge Bryan made some telling points that seemed to favor Powell: Powell's 1951 trip to Europe was official and not for pleasure; Powell and his wife were professionals who would be expected to have rather "substantial" deductible business expenses; Powell's tax lawyer was, in fact, careless in preparing the returns.[13]

Sensing the pro-Powell impact of these observations, Robson, when asked by the judge if he wished to say anything else, simply—

one reporter said "wearily"—responded: "I have no wish to be heard."

The jury deliberated for about twenty-six hours and took a total of twenty votes. At first, there was a vote of eight to four for acquittal. Then the jury sent a note to the judge informing him they were hopelessly deadlocked. He enjoined them to keep trying. More deliberations and votes followed: two switched; now ten to two for acquittal. Another weary note was sent to the judge: "Your Honor, the jury has reached a deadlock. Cannot possibly be changed by any further deliberation. Further consideration this morning has actually created additional difficulties in arriving at a verdict." The judge was equally insistent, as could be expected. Such matters, everyone knew, were always difficult, but the legal system depended so much on the jury process. The jury obeyed, but a third note finally revealed the abject truth—still at ten to two, this was a hung jury. The judge threw in the towel and reluctantly dismissed them.

One juror felt most of her colleagues had made up their minds even before the deliberations began. Another felt that the judge's instructions "left us with an empty bag. When he was through, there was nothing left of the government's case."[14]

Thus, for the moment, Powell was not convicted. The jury's indecision left some options: the judge could have rendered a verdict, anyway, in favor of Powell by acquitting him altogether or dismissing the case; failing that, the government could retry the case on the remaining count.

Meanwhile, temporarily relieved from the pressures of daily courtroom attendance, Powell announced he would return to his pulpit and to Congress. In a revealing omen of his political life to come, he commented on the current activities in Congress that led to the passage of a second civil rights bill, the Civil Rights Law of 1960. Powell had been preoccupied in a federal courtroom in Foley Square in New York City. "I'm sorry," he said, "I missed the civil rights fight."[15] He and others were keenly aware that civil rights issues were becoming increasingly manifest. Black college students in the South had launched a series of dramatic, highly publicized sit-ins against discrimination in places of public accommodation. New voices were on the horizon as the decade of 1960 began. Martin Luther King, Jr., himself had just successfully won a tax fraud case brought against him by the state of Alabama. There were mass, grass-roots stirrings around the country. In just one short year, CORE (the Congress of Racial Equality) would initiate Freedom Rides in the South on interstate buses, protesting segregation. King's SCLC (Southern Christian Leadership Conference) would take its nonviolent campaign into Albany, Georgia. And observers knew that the battle in Congress would heat up over the next few years, with pressure from liberal forces to strengthen the civil rights laws.

Anyone in Powell's position who was preoccupied with his own personal fights would not be available for leadership in this escalating social movement. There could not be many more such distractions if his credibility was to remain intact.

Several weeks after the hung jury, Edward Bennett Williams went to court to ask the judge to dismiss the remaining count. He forcefully argued that the action of the *National Review* editors in contacting the grand jury was highly improper. He stated: "Their action was no different than that of people leading a lynch mob. It just happened in New York instead of Mississippi."[16]

Robson conceded that "the grand jury may have been improperly contacted."

Judge Bryan suggested, "The contacts were pretty unsavory."

But he would not dismiss the case, believing that the government should still have its chance to retry Powell and prove its case.

This chance was declined one year later when the Department of Justice announced that it was dropping the tax case against Powell.

In the interim, the country had elected a new President, John F. Kennedy. And Powell had finally achieved the vaunted role of chairman of a major congressional committee. The two men needed each other if they were to succeed in their respective leadership roles. His criminal tax problems now behind him (the government would still press him for taxes it claimed he owed), Powell could turn his attention to what would amount to yet another major plateau in his political career, and at precisely the time when America's dilemma, which he had for so long made his number-one priority, was fast becoming more central to the society's concerns. Powell and these issues arrived on the front pages at a propitious moment in the nation's history. The next ten years would be the most important decade in the nation's political struggle over civil rights since the Civil War—indeed, in exactly one hundred years. Because of his new position in Congress, Powell would be well situated to play a leading role. How he would proceed remained to be seen. But one thing was certain: he was no longer a mere legislative irritant, a "spokesman," one tacking on annoying amendments, a senior member without proper recognition from his colleagues. He was now in possession of something never before possessed by a black man in America's complex political system. As chairman of a major congressional committee, which he achieved in January 1961, he now had *institutional power*. And he got there the system's way—through seniority.

The big question for many was this: how would he use this new power?

Power and Paradox, 1960s

16

The New Frontier, a New Chairman, and President Kennedy

One of the happiest days in Adam Powell's political life undoubtedly was January 22, 1960. On that day, he received some news which startled most Congress watchers and apparently was not even expected by the venerable House Speaker, Sam Rayburn. When Powell heard the news in New York in his office at Abyssinian, he later told a hastily called news conference: "The first thing I did was to thank God on my knees."[1]

Representative Graham A. Barden, chairman of the House Committee on Education and Labor, had just announced he was retiring from Congress after the current session. Powell was the highest-ranking Democrat next in line to succeed him in the committee chairmanship. All those years of waiting and enduring insults would soon be over. In the next term, if Congress acted as it always had, Powell would become the chairman. Of course, the Democrats still had to maintain a House majority after the coming November election—very likely to happen. And Powell, himself, would have to be reelected from Harlem—very certain to happen. Finally, Powell had to survive the upcoming tax trial—its outcome impossible to predict. For the moment, however, all these contingencies were in the near future, and Powell proceeded to exude confidence. He predicted no difficulty whatsoever in being chosen as chairman. After all, his seniority entitled him to it. He also bluntly asserted that the committee, under his leadership, would be more active and decidedly more liberal. In addition, he had received assurance, he alleged, from

Speaker Rayburn that led him to anticipate no problems in getting the appointment when the time arrived for such consideration.

Barden's surprise announcement was indeed a shock, especially to the Southern and conservative forces who had approved of the way he had effectively blocked progressive legislation coming before his committee, and certainly approved of his successful efforts to curtail Powell's committee service. His arbitrary, disdainful treatment of Powell over the years, including denying him a subcommittee chairmanship, was well-known. But now the sixty-three-year-old North Carolinian, after twenty-six years in the House of Representatives, was going home to spend more time with his family. Powell surely welcomed his trip.

But the conservatives and Southerners were not the only ones chagrined at the prospect of a Powell chairmanship. The *New York Times* editorialized against both Powell and the "anachronistic seniority system" that made his likely ascension possible. Powell's "racist attitudes," his "miserable record" as a legislator, and "his extreme absenteeism" were deplorable. "Mr. Powell is not the kind of legislator who ought to be chairman of a committee of the Congress."[2] The seniority system should be modified. And now that system, the editorial stated, was coming to haunt the conservatives and liberals who had failed to do anything about it over the years. Powell's Harlem supporters immediately leaped to his defense. "The *Times* is employing a specious argument," one letter writer charged.[3] Powell was hardly a racist; that label belonged to one who believed in racial superiority, which meant, if applied, that "no Southerner and few Northerners could qualify as a committee chairman."

In addition, Powell was a prodigious worker for far more than the Negroes in Harlem; his workload far exceeded that of most of his colleagues, precisely because many Negroes in the country looked to him for help. And the writer added a reminder that was obviously felt by many critics and supporters alike:

> In his sixteen years in Congress Mr. Powell has done exactly as his constituents in Harlem have wanted him to do: continue to introduce all forms of civil rights legislation whether the Congress passed it or not. It would be far more accurate to say of Mr. Powell that a good legislator has been operating in a poor Congress.[4]

One of the earliest and most prominent critics of a likely Powell chairmanship was George Meany, president of the AFL-CIO. Powell would make a "terrible" chairman, he stated. His history of stirring up racial hatred "at the least provocation" was divisive.[5] And, as could be expected, this blast triggered pro-Powell responses, especially from A. Philip Randolph, who had been having his own arguments with Meany over segregation in some labor unions. Not denying that Powell's attendance record could stand improvement, Randolph was quick to point out that Powell's voting record on labor and civil rights issues was very good. The retired president of the United Mine Workers, John L. Lewis, accused Meany of "sheer stupidity" in blasting Powell. "Representative Powell has a fine voting record on matters of interest to working people."[6] And Lewis added that Powell had thus far been denied a subcommittee chairmanship "simply because he is a Negro."

But while Powell needed the support of his party in Congress to gain the chair, which he would more than likely get, there were, as always over the years, almost hand-wringing sessions among his friends across the country who worried about him and his leadership capacity. At many informal gatherings of Negroes the talk frequently turned to the state of the race, leadership, and general prospects in the upcoming decade. There was no question that sensitive, concerned Negroes recognized the power and influence Powell wielded, especially among his constituents, and now probably even, at last, in Congress. Some had been making a career of imploring the Harlem congressman to rise up and realize his full "potential for great effectiveness." But always they remained in suspended anticipation. So often, Powell seemed to fall just short. But now, perhaps not until now, he had a golden opportunity to prove his mettle, to seize the reigns of leadership. Jackie Robinson voiced such a heartfelt plea in his syndicated column shortly after the Barden announcement. Robinson wrote that he had recently been a part of an informal social gathering where everyone agreed that Adam Powell had it within his grasp to do great things, and *really* be a leader. But there was a lingering undercurrent of doubt. Robinson recognized that Powell was enormously popular, and because of this, there was understandable reluctance to criticize him where he fell short of expectations. But, hopefully, Powell would "show more of an aggressive follow-up." Fiery speeches were not enough. Now he should use his new role as the chairman of a vital committee to "affect the course of Negro progress" in labor and education. Robinson remained hopeful that his congressman-friend would rise to the challenge.[7]

These were the pleadings of Powell's friends, not his enemies. They wanted him to be their leader. They wanted to continue to support and protect him, but they wanted him to reciprocate. Powell might have asked exactly what they expected. His voting record was quite correct. His insistent pressure to end segregation and discrimination was clearly known. True, his attendance record was low, but hardly the lowest, and, anyway, who could blame him based on the treatment in Congress from the racists he despised. Still, there *was* something to the Robinson pleading. And everyone knew it. Was it Powell's haughty, arrogant style? Probably not—in itself. Everyone recognized he was prone to showmanship and strutting. There was a lot of the ham actor in him. Some even chalked it up to his role as a Baptist preacher.

But style was not the central issue. Was it the matter of his party switch for Eisenhower? No; Robinson and some others who supported him were Republicans. And at that time, with many Negro leaders and concerned activists, civil rights really crossed party lines. Was it his tax problems? These were court matters and would be handled in the proper judicial forum. But this did suggest that he might be more careful in the future about his personal finances. Were his friends worried that Powell would somehow flagrantly betray the civil rights movement? Quite unlikely. Ideologically, Powell had established his credentials long ago. He was an unquestioned advocate of civil rights and liberal, progressive policies. But still there was some intangible, gnawing uneasiness with the congressman that left his staunchest supporters less than certain that Powell could ultimately be depended upon to devote his full time and energies to the struggle. Robinson used the term "follow-up." Whatever it was, this was the man many Negroes had in Congress who was on the verge of becoming a powerful figure in his own right. Many hoped it would not be a precipice. Powell was about to obtain power based on the established structures of the system itself. He could now be more than a "spokesman," more than an "irritant." He would head a major congressional committee, with a large staff overseeing legislation vital not only to Negroes but to all Americans. And he got there the old-fashioned way: through seniority. He earned it.

Indeed, the turn of the decade and Barden's "gift" had the makings of a new political life for Adam Clayton Powell, Jr.

And whatever else was certain, 1960 would also present the country with a new President.

Eight years of the Eisenhower administration were drawing to a close. Democrats had fielded an array of aspiring candidates, and the Republicans, with some favoring Nelson Rockefeller of New York, were getting used to the idea that Richard Nixon would be their standard bearer in the 1960 Presidential contest. Powell always loved the role of publicly assessing the field for his constituents and the media. He could always be counted on to give caustic, headline-catching comments evaluating the relative strengths and weaknesses of the various candidates. He was always good copy. He seized this opportunity at an outdoor rally in Harlem. The occasion was a Saturday afternoon annual achievement award ceremony in June 1960. The recipient that year was none other than Powell's tax case lawyer, Edward Bennett Williams. As far as Powell was concerned, with the hung jury episode recently behind him, there was no one else who had, indeed, distinguished himself so thoroughly. Powell took the occasion to evaluate the list of the then surviving crop of Presidential contenders.[8]

If he were a Republican, he told his audience, he would favor Rockefeller "because he is boss-free, has never subscribed to the reactionary school of the Republican Party and has spoken out incisively on foreign policy and civil rights." (He overlooked or forgot his criticism of Rockefeller on these issues two years earlier when he had campaigned against him for Harriman in the New York gubernatorial race.) Nixon, on the other hand, clearly had no commendable record on civil rights—voting against FEPC, against antilynching amendments to the Draft Act. Powell did not bother to reconcile these views with his rather friendly relations with Nixon four years earlier in the 1956 Presidential campaign. That was then, this was now. And for Powell, politics was what the present moment required.

As for the Democrats—it was clear that this year Powell was not going to desert his party—he ticked off three top runners: Senators Lyndon Johnson of Texas and Stuart Symington of Missouri, and former governor Adlai Stevenson. Senator Hubert Humphrey had by then been eliminated in the primaries by another strong contender, Senator John F. Kennedy. Powell began with Kennedy: "I do not like his softness on McCarthyism." And Kennedy's civil rights record left a lot to be desired. The Massachusetts senator had voted to recommit the 1957 civil rights bill to Senator Eastland's judiciary committee. But more important and more recently, Kennedy had been currying favor with the segregationist Alabama governor, John Patterson, a known supporter of the Ku Klux Klan, Powell concluded. As for Stevenson, his 1956 civil rights stand was woefully deficient in comparison with his 1952 views. He could possibly redeem himself if he "would admit he was wrong in '56 and reaffirm his position of 1952." Powell also recounted Stevenson's refusal to see him in 1956. Clearly, as far as Powell was concerned, Senator Johnson was "the most able man in the United States Congress, the best leader that Congress has had in many a decade." And if the choice came down to one between Nixon and Johnson, surely "there could be no choice." Powell was willing, however, to suggest that either Senator Eugene McCarthy of Minnesota or Senator Kennedy would make very good Vice-Presidential candidates. He was careful to mention the Catholic identities of both of these men because he did not want to be accused of rejecting either for President because of their religion.

This was the political life Powell loved. Making big, bold, simple statements to his constituents, teaching them the intricacies of politics, giving them the "inside dope" on personalities and deals. He was their astute, monitoring leader, couching each assessment in terms that appeared to be the thoughtful process of agonizing scrutiny. And he knew the media would pick up his words. They would be reported widely, and he would again be center stage. This was his milieu. And on that afternoon in Harlem he was performing well.

At that moment, those were his public pronouncements. There would then ensue a rather familiar Powellian game of having the various candidates vie for his favor. And in this process he was not always as forthright and candid with his friends and colleagues as the public assessments would lead one to believe. In the spring before the Democratic convention, he was still allied with Ray Jones, who was willing, as a shrewd politician, to go along with the congressman to extract the best political deal possible. Both knew that their endorsements had value, and they were prepared to extract maximum return for their nod. But apparently Jones was not entirely prepared for all the maneuverings Powell engaged in. They both decided to sit back and watch the bidding proceed. Powell informed Jones that Speaker Sam Rayburn wanted to see him in Washington. Jones obliged, and Powell introduced them. When Powell left the room, Rayburn made his pitch for support of Senator Johnson by Jones and Powell. In return, Rayburn would guarantee that Powell got his chairmanship. Fair enough, Jones thought, and told Johnson so in a subsequent meeting later that day. Powell, obviously, was happy and agreed. Jones, Rayburn, and Johnson felt they had a deal.

As Jones saw it, he and Powell had little to lose. Johnson had only an outside chance of grabbing the nomination away from Kennedy, who was by then far ahead in delegate support and gaining momentum. A victory on the first ballot at the convention for Kennedy was not out of the question. Kennedy hardly needed them at that point, but he *would* need them in the general election race against Nixon. It would be nice to have the Harlem politicians beforehand, but if that were not possible, it would hardly sink his nomination bid. Therefore, if Jones and Powell stuck with Johnson until after the convention, they would have fulfilled their end of the bargain, and Powell would get his chairmanship. If they worked for Kennedy as the nominee, they would be able to reap the benefits of that support if Kennedy became President. As far as Jones was concerned, it was a no-lose deal.[9]

The fragmented nature of the American political system made such political calculations possible. Politicians could calculate when and how to give their support to maximize their political leverage, and remain legitimate in the process. Senator Johnson needed them before the convention much more so than Kennedy did in order to get delegates. Besides, Johnson (and Rayburn) had more to give Powell at that stage. If, as seemed likely, Kennedy won the nomination, he would certainly need Powell—and, to a lesser extent, Jones—to help turn out the large Negro vote he would need against Nixon. They could then easily oblige, and thus reap those benefits if Kennedy won. Surely, this was a no-lose situation. So Jones, Johnson, and Rayburn assumed they had a deal, and they had every reason to believe Powell was on board. After all, Powell was the reason Jones got involved with Johnson in the first place. Jones took the train back to New York that night prepared to work to round up preconvention delegates for Johnson.

But Powell was not finished.

Without Jones's knowledge, Powell a few days later told Mayor Robert Wagner that Jones was not yet committed, and, therefore, he (Jones) might be interested in a meeting with Kennedy. Unaware of this when Wagner approached him, Jones nonetheless agreed to meet with Kennedy off the record, and he knew he would have to inform Kennedy that he could not then support him. But Jones made the mistake of telling his friend Powell of the planned meeting, which, of course, was not to be made public. (At the same time, Jones had a meeting with a Kennedy supporter who offered a six-figure check if Jones endorsed Kennedy. Jones declined the offer.) But the next day, the *Herald Tribune* ran a story essentially saying "Kennedy Coming to See Jones." Jones, knowing of his deal with

Rayburn and Johnson, was furious with the leak. Immediately, he accused Wagner, who had arranged the meeting. But Wagner thought Jones was the source of the leak.

Several weeks after the convention, the journalist Theodore White visited Jones in St. Thomas and told him that Kennedy was angry with him for the double cross and the leak. Apparently, Powell had told Kennedy's people that Jones was the source of the leaked story on the meeting. Jones, again, was upset and he told White to "tell JFK I think he's a stupid bastard if he believes what Powell said." White delivered the message. John Kennedy was inclined to accept Jones's version over Powell's, but Robert Kennedy was in no mood for peace with Jones. White gave Jones Robert Kennedy's response: "Why that black bastard. I'll never forgive him."[10] Jones traced his later political troubles with Robert Kennedy in New York politics to that Presidential campaign incident.

This was the beginning of the breakup of the short-lived Powell-Jones alliance. Jones felt he simply could not trust Powell, who was always willing to trade—not only with the highest bidder, but apparently also with the latest bidder. To strike a deal with the highest bidder, even if the stakes were for personal gain, was acceptable. But once made, the deal had to be kept. Jones was not convinced that Powell felt particularly obliged to honor that rule.

Meanwhile, Powell became involved in another preconvention hassle with Martin Luther King and A. Philip Randolph. King and Randolph were planning to stage civil rights marches at both the Democratic and Republican conventions. The purpose was to pressure the parties to take strong pro–civil rights positions in their platforms and to commit the respective candidates to those positions. For reasons unknown to them, Powell was opposed to such action. He threatened to embarrass King if King did not withdraw and break off his association with Bayard Rustin, who was to help organize the demonstrations. Apparently, Powell was prepared to accuse King and Rustin of a homosexual relationship. Knowing this to be blatantly false, King nevertheless was upset and worried about the impact of such a charge. (Rustin was homosexual, though at the time this was not public knowledge. King was not, but he knew of Rustin's sexual orientation.) He wanted Randolph to accede to Powell's wishes to cancel the demonstration. Randolph refused. Aware of King's intense discomfort over Powell's threats, Rustin regretfully agreed to disassociate himself from the SCLC and King. His anger, however, was as much toward King for buckling under to Powell's unfounded threats as it was toward Powell. Rustin never held Powell in the highest regard in any case. Powell was not able to stop the march, but he did force Rustin to resign as King's aide.

Shortly before the convention, Powell preached a sermon extolling the virtues of Lyndon Johnson, but bluntly stated, "I am not endorsing Lyndon Johnson for the nomination. . . . My candidates were Hubert Humphrey and G. Mennen Williams and Stuart Symington, and only Symington is left."[11] Nonetheless, he wanted his audience to know that Johnson should not be rejected simply because he came from the South, "'and that if Lyndon Johnson does get the nomination he will be acceptable." Some pundits speculated that Powell was using Symington as a stalking horse for Johnson. As late as two weeks before the convention, Powell was drawing loud cheers from a Harlem audience when he sharply criticized Senator Kennedy on civil rights.

But Kennedy captured the Democratic nomination on the first ballot, and Powell lost no time in telling a news conference at Sardi's restaurant in midtown Manhattan that he would campaign vigorously for the nominee. He planned to go to thirty-three cities in nineteen states in support of the Democratic ticket. And he indeed hit the campaign trail once again.

His personal life was also taking another turn. Hazel Scott confirmed reports that she had filed for a divorce, which was granted in early December in Juarez, Mexico. She sought no alimony, only support for their fourteen-year-old son and costs for the divorce suit.

Kennedy squeaked out a narrow win for the Presidency over Richard Nixon, with Lyndon Johnson from Texas as his running mate. In a sermon at Abyssinian Baptist, Powell hailed the election as "'the first national poll taken on the issues of religious and regional prejudice. . . . A new frontier of faith was opened." He was cautious in assigning credit to the Negro vote, but he said that "if some of us had not worked as we did, the razor-edge margin of victory would have been a razor-edge margin of defeat."[12] And he offered the opinion that now that a Catholic candidate had broken the Presidential barrier, he saw no reason why the way should not now be opened for a Jew, and "once we get that out of the way, we can proceed to the Negro." He might have been serious, but his congregation merely laughed in skeptical amusement.

In the interim between the election and opening of the new congressional session, Powell, now divorced, went off to Puerto Rico, where he married his twenty-nine-year-old Puerto Rican secretary, Yvette Diago. The new Mrs. Powell was from a Puerto Rican family prominent in business and island politics. Powell said that he planned to take a much-needed rest and work on his autobiography at the new fifty-thousand-dollar house he was building on the beach at Cerro Gordo, just outside San Juan. But he also dropped another small bombshell about his future plans. He revealed that he planned to retire from politics in 1964 as well as from the pastorship of Abyssinian. He hoped to live in Puerto Rico and become an overseas executive in a Miami-based insurance company. He had first announced his retirement plans six months earlier, but now he was being a bit more specific. Still, however, his colleagues—and enemies—were not sure he meant it or if this was simply another Powell ploy to keep the pundits guessing—and talking about him.

With the election behind him, and before he took off for Puerto Rico, Powell lost no time in establishing a relationship with the new President-Elect and in asserting his impending leadership of the Education and Labor Committee. On November 30 he met for an hour with Kennedy at the latter's Georgetown home to discuss legislative plans for the next congressional session. Aid to education and a minimum-wage increase would receive top committee priority, they agreed. Even a few weeks before then, Powell started with a flurry of assignments to the members of the committee. By then everyone was confident that there would be no successful effort to block his chairmanship. He asked Kentucky congressman Carl D. Perkins to develop a "crash" program aimed at closing the gap between American and Soviet scientific education. Congresswoman Edith Green was assigned to study juvenile delinquency problems; Representative James Roosevelt got the task of drafting a measure to provide scholarship aid to students from Africa, Asia, and Latin America. Powell said he hoped this would rival Russian efforts in that field. In addition, Kennedy and Powell agreed on a move to establish a domestic peace corps and hoped James Roosevelt would explore this possibility. Another committee member, Frank Thompson, Jr., was asked to develop proposals for cultural activities in the United States and abroad. Herbert Zelenko of New York was designated to deal with labor-management relations. Elmer J. Holland would study unemployment issues and the impact of automation on unemployment.

All this came several weeks before the opening of the new Congress. Powell was off and running, giving every indication that he would be an active chairman of a major aggressive legislative committee. His supporters were pleased and impressed. Powell was at last coming into his own.

One matter caught the NAACP's attention, however, and was cause for some concern about their longtime civil rights ally. An item in the *New York Times* indicated that Powell had stated that he would not present to his committee the customary Powell Amendment to deny federal funds to school districts that remained segregated. He did reserve the option, however, of offering the amendment on the floor of Congress, after committee action.[13] This did not sit well with the NAACP. Clarence Mitchell, who had been hearing other disturbing comments around Washington regarding the new administration's lack of intent to push civil rights legislation, met with Powell on December 7, 1960. They discussed three issues: the school aid amendment, FEPC, and segregated facilities on Capitol Hill. Mitchell's memo to Roy Wilkins describing the meeting was a harbinger of things to come for the NAACP. Mitchell wrote that Powell informed him that he (Powell) would exact a commitment from the Secretary of HEW, Abraham Ribicoff, to forbid segregation by "executive action" in education-aid programs. Mitchell was not pleased with this strategy, because it did not cover areas such as housing, health, or airports. It was too narrow. But Mitchell reported that at least Powell did not *refuse* to introduce the customary amendment. The matter was left at that, but there was a feeling that Powell was not as willing as he had been in previous years to serve as the vehicle for the controversial Powell Amendment.[14] Powell told Mitchell that Representative James Roosevelt would handle FEPC issues, and, at Powell's request, Mitchell promised him a memorandum on the matter of segregated congressional facilities.[15]

It was becoming clear to the NAACP that the very cooperative (though self-serving) Powell they had known and worked with over the previous decade on civil rights issues might not be the same Powell in his new role. This could only be a disturbing development for the civil rights organization that had supported and looked forward to Powell's assumption of the chairmanship.

But Powell was sworn in as the new chairman, and a gala testimonial banquet was held in his honor on January 29, 1961, at the Hotel Commodore in New York. Roy Wilkins sent his regrets ("NAACP business trip to Omaha") and congratulations. The new administration, however, turned out in force. Speakers for the occasion included Secretary of Labor Arthur J. Goldberg and HEW Secretary Abraham A. Ribicoff. President Kennedy wired "warm regards," and words of high admiration and respect. The *Christian Science Monitor* described the affair at length and drew political conclusions sure to delight Powell:

> Coming at a time of strongly spotlighted reluctance by President Kennedy to be associated with New York Democratic leaders because of a bitter intraparty fight here, these words [Kennedy's telegram] as well as the presence of two key Cabinet members made it clear that the new administration regards Mr. Powell as a major power in Washington.[16]

The *Monitor* duly noted the importance of Powell's role as chairman of the Education and Labor Committee. What he did or did not do "could seriously affect the fate of the Kennedy legislative program." If Powell pushed for his traditional amendment, this could seriously jeopardize Kennedy's other bills. By its conspicuous presence at the testimonial dinner, the administration clearly was telling Powell that they wanted his friendship and cooperation. Characteristically, in his speech that evening, Powell challenged the President to move by legislative *or* executive action to withhold federal aid to segregated agencies. He knew that Kennedy did not want to deal with the Powell Amendment in Congress. Thus he had something quite concrete to bargain with. But specifically what did the Kennedy people have that Powell wanted? Aside from the passage of progressive legislation unimpeded by a Powell Amendment, what could Kennedy offer Powell in return? To be sure, it was nice to get official recognition of his power and importance. But that was reasonably self-evident, and this derived from Congress, not from the White House. If Powell was to incur the disappointment of his NAACP friends and others for not introducing his amendment, he would have to set a price, a price only the administration could pay.

On April 14, 1961, Powell gave Kennedy what the President wanted. He announced that he would withhold his antisegregation amendment from school aid legislation then under consideration. And if anyone else offered the amendment, he would lead the opposition to it. Powell told a news conference: "The Russian challenge to the United States in space is now so great that no one can afford to do anything that would slow up Federal aid to education at all levels."[17]

On the same day, U.S. Attorney Morton Robson told a federal judge in New York that the Department of Justice was not pursuing its tax case against Powell on the one remaining count left undecided a year earlier by the hung jury. Any further investigation, Robson told the court, would prove "fruitless." Powell was now free of the legal cloud that had been hanging over him for years.

Powell jokingly wearing a "Faubus for President" button, 1960. *(Courtesy of Adam Clayton Powell IV)*

Powell in his Jaguar at the Capitol in Washington, D.C., 1961. *(AP/Wide World Photos)*

Clarence Mitchell of the NAACP, known as "the 101st senator," in 1963.
(AP/Wide World Photos)

Powell with Malcolm X *(center)* and Dick Gregory, 1962. *(Courtesy of the Schomburg Center for Research in Black Culture, New York Public Library)*

Powell meeting with President Lyndon B. Johnson, 1965. *(Courtesy of the Lyndon B. Johnson Library)*

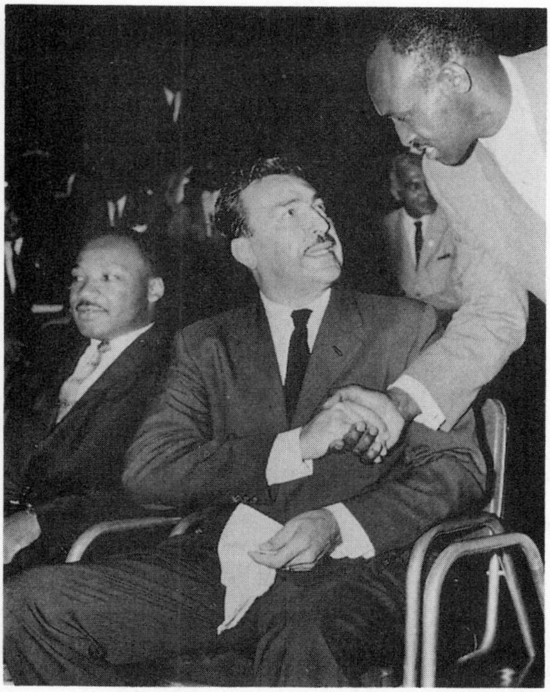

Powell with Martin Luther King, Jr. *(at left)*, shaking hands with an unidentified man at a 1964 civil rights meeting in New York. *(Courtesy of* Ebony *magazine)*

Yvette Powell (his third wife), Adam IV, and Powell at home in Puerto Rico, 1963. *(Courtesy of Adam Clayton Powell IV)*

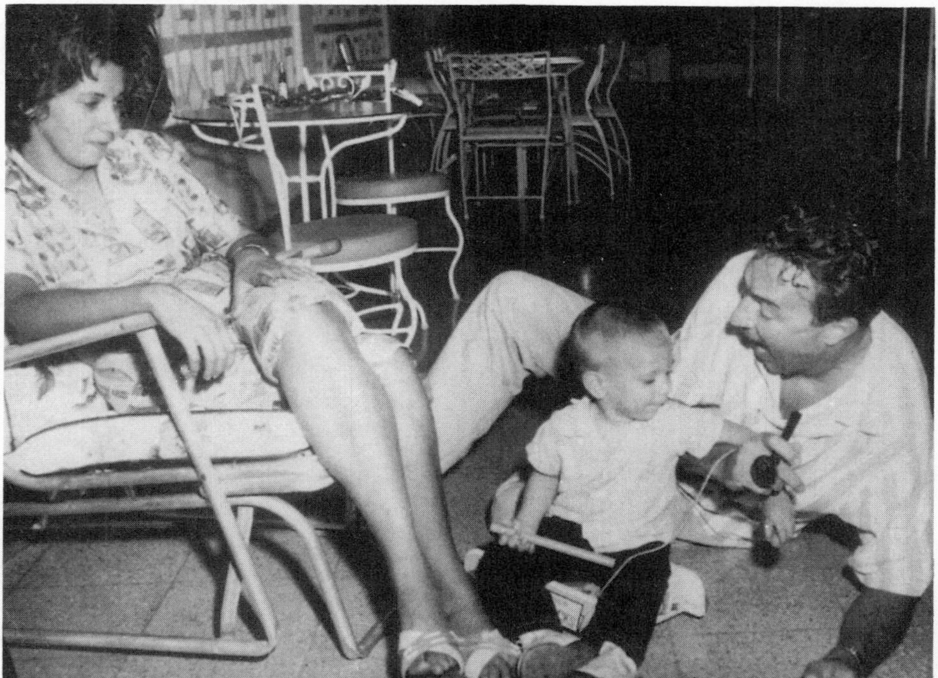

Powell with A. Philip Randolph (at Powell's right, shaking hands with an unidentified man) at a civil rights rally in Harlem in the early 1960s. Jackie Robinson is on the far left. *(Austin Hansen)*

Powell at lunch with his lawyers, Edward Bennet Williams *(center)* and Harrison S. Jackson *(left)*, during a recess in his income tax trial in 1960. *(Courtesy of the Schomburg Center for Research in Black Culture, New York Public Library)*

Yvette Powell appearing before the Celler select committee with her lawyer, Joseph Rauh, in February 1967. *(Courtesy of Joseph Rauh)*

Powell with his aide Chuck Stone in 1965. *(AP/Wide World Photos)*

Powell strolling in Bimini in 1967. Floyd McKissick of CORE is on Powell's right; the Reverend A. Kendall Smith is on McKissick's right; others in the photo are unidentified. *(AP/Wide World Photos)*

Powell with Darlene Expose Hine *(far left)* outside Abyssinian Baptist Church, 1970.
(AP/Wide World Photos)

Powell in Bimini with the lawyers representing him before the Celler select committee, 1967.
(AP/Wide World Photos)

HARLEM CAN NO LONGER AFFORD ADAM CLAYTON POWELL

HR No.	DATE	BILL TOPIC	
HR 514	April 23, 1969	Extending the Elementary and Secondary Education Act programs.	POWELL ABSENT
HR 5554	May 6, 1969	Expand and make permanent special milk program for children.	POWELL ABSENT
HR 11651	July 21, 1969	To make available $1,000,000 in additional funds for meals for needy children.	POWELL ABSENT
HR 13111	July 31, 1969	Adding $894,547,000 to the appropriation for Office of Education programs.	POWELL ABSENT
HR 13194	Sept. 15, 1969	STUDENT LOANS — Bill amending the Higher Education Act of 1965 to provide emergency student loan guarantees.	POWELL ABSENT
HR 13310	Oct. 6, 1969	Educational Assistance for programs for aid to children with learning difficulties.	POWELL ABSENT
HR 14705	Nov. 13, 1969	UNEMPLOYMENT COMPENSATION—Extend and improve the Federal, State unemployment compensation system to cover an additional 4.5 million workers.	POWELL ABSENT
HR 4249	Dec. 11, 1969	To extend Voting Rights Act of 1965.	POWELL ABSENT
S 740	Dec. 16, 1969	Establishing opportunities for Spanish speaking people.	POWELL ABSENT
S 3016	Dec. 20, 1969	Extending the anti-poverty program $6 billion.	POWELL ABSENT
HR 8644	June 27, 1969	Aid to dependent children.	POWELL ABSENT
HR 11102	June 4, 1969	Medical facilities for hospital construction and modernization.	POWELL ABSENT
HR 13827	Oct. 23, 1969	Extending Housing and Urban Development Program, authorizing $4.9 billion.	POWELL ABSENT
HR 15095	Dec. 15, 1969	Bill increasing Social Security benefit payments by 15%.	POWELL ABSENT

Elect

CHARLES RANGEL

TO

Congress

18th C.D.

Vote Democratic Primary ★ June 23, 1970

Campaign leaflet for Charles B. Rangel in his race to defeat Powell, 1970.

Powell in Tallahassee, Florida, on a speaking tour during his exclusion from Congress, 1968. *(UPI/Bettmann)*

Powell's funeral at Abyssinian Baptist Church, 1972. *(AP/Wide World Photos)*

Abyssinian Baptist Church.

The Adam Clayton Powell State Office Building, 125t
Street and Seventh Avenue in New York.

No one was openly charging a deal between Powell and the new Attorney General, Robert F. Kennedy, the President's brother. But more than a few drew a possible connection between the two announcements.

"We certainly weren't claiming and could not prove a deal," one NAACP official stated privately. "But, knowing Powell as we did, well—it was not a good day for civil rights."

President Kennedy's narrow victory over Nixon and the slim Democratic control of Congress left him with little political leverage on Capitol Hill. Any successful legislative proposals would require the most intense process of bargaining, trading, and negotiating. The administration was keenly aware that any plans it had for a "New Frontier" of progressive-liberal legislation would have to run the formidable gauntlet of resistance from conservative forces in Congress, led by the Southern Democrats and Republicans. This combination, buttressed by a conservative-dominated House Rules Committee, and the constitutionally permissible Senate filibuster, could frustrate virtually any attempt to move in a liberal direction. None of this, in itself, was new. But what was different was a new administration that was perceived, at least, as having the will, if not the way, to conduct an active government. This objective political situation would cause more than a few headaches for Kennedy's people and civil rights advocates. It soon became clear that Kennedy would not pursue a *legislative* strategy for civil rights "early in 1961" as he had intimated during the campaign. He would rely more on what could be done exclusively by the Executive Branch, acting through executive decrees, and relying on the persuasive force of moral arguments. He would forgo for the time being asking Congress to enact new civil rights laws. Presidential assistant Theodore Sorensen put it simply: "The reason was arithmetic."[18] The votes were not there for civil rights legislation; and if such a fruitless effort *were* made, this could alienate people who might otherwise support other measures, such as an increase in minimum wage, aid to education, a health bill, and housing aid.

In the early 1960s, while there was certainly growing activity on the civil rights front, especially in the South, with mass demonstrations and sit-in protests, and increased efforts to desegregate colleges and universities, this escalating situation had not yet reached the halls of Congress. Sorensen summarized the judgment of many in the White House at the time: "In view of solid Southern Democratic intransigence, greater Republican and Western Democratic support was required, and with no broad public interest in such legislation outside of the various civil rights organizations, that support was not obtainable."[19] Therefore, a pragmatic decision had to be made: hold off on any new major civil rights proposals for the moment in hopes that other laws could be passed. This was the classic American Dilemma all over again. Civil rights advocates had been grappling with it politically since the New Deal. Except that now there *was* a difference. For the first time, at least in the minds of some blacks, there was a man in the White House who was genuinely interested in doing something. Kennedy was perceived as one who would use his office, if not to pressure Congress, to exert influence on the bureaucracy and the private sector to loosen the binds of segregation and discrimination. This perception came not only from his rhetoric, but from specific acts, acts that were small and incremental in themselves, but when viewed against the backdrop of relative silence over the previous eight years loomed large and significant. And so dire were the straits of civil rights victims at the time that little things meant a lot.

Two episodes occurred that indicated a welcomed Kennedy approach—and bought him time with some civil rights proponents. The first happened toward the end of the Presidential campaign. Martin Luther King, Jr., had been jailed in Georgia, and many feared for his life. Senator Kennedy called King's wife to comfort her. Robert Kennedy called the Georgia judge to persuade him to release King. King was released shortly afterwards. Both calls were widely reported, especially in the Northern black communities. There are no reliable measures of the impact on black voters, but few analysts doubted the likely effect. This was precisely the kind of show of personal interest and involvement blacks had been seeking from the Eisenhower administration over the years. (Nixon had also been urged to call Mrs. King, but his campaign staff advised against it.) King's father publicly announced he was voting for Kennedy—even though the senator was a Catholic. Kennedy's telephone call, in the context of American race relations in 1960, was an enormous boost to black American morale—in a sense, it helped legitimize King and the civil rights struggle at the highest levels of government; it was *action*, not just rhetoric—and many took it as a signal of the kind of leadership that would come from a Kennedy White House.

The other incident also involved a telephone call from then newly inaugurated President Kennedy. On the day of his swearing-in, viewing the inaugural parade, he noticed there were no blacks in the Coast Guard marching band. The next day he called the Treasury Department inquiring about this. Black recruits to the Coast Guard began showing up in the next year's class. Again, black people were impressed and elated. On such a great celebratory day, here was a man who would be sensitive enough—in 1961 when such matters were not necessarily uppermost in the minds of many in high places—to notice such a thing. He would not deny, ignore, or excuse it. There was indeed a new President.

These decisions bought Kennedy time with some of his civil rights critics who were also impressed that now, at least, they had little trouble meeting with the President. To a person, they labeled him charming and sympathetic, albeit harshly realistic in his political calculations. And on civil rights *legislation*—not telephone calls—Kennedy concluded that the time was not ripe. He would move, he and his associates kept saying, when there was a reasonable prospect that civil rights proposals to Congress had a chance of passage.

As pleasant and charismatic as Kennedy was, he was also insistent that his no-legislation-now approach was best. After one of several meetings with White House officials, Roy Wilkins recorded his frustration: "As I left the White House that day, I thought to myself, It's nice to be able to get through the door again. But I began to wonder how much good it was going to do."[20] The NAACP understood the Kennedy reasons, but argued that there was no guarantee that even if he held off on civil rights legislation he would get his other measures. Then the NAACP pressed the President to issue a broad, all-inclusive Executive Order—if that was the route to choose to take—barring segregation and discrimination, including withholding funds, in all arenas of American public life. This could be in the form of a Second Emancipation Proclamation. Kennedy was wary of this, and simply asked for a memo on it.

In his favor, the NAACP had to concede that Kennedy made some significant appointments of blacks to judgeships and high-level administrative posts, and was seriously prepared to appoint Robert Weaver to head a proposed new Department of Housing and Urban Development, making him the first black cabinet member. All these appointments were good, substantively and symbolically, but they were limited in impact if there were no new, stronger laws for them to implement and enforce. Civil rights advocates gently kept the pressure on, but the Kennedy people were equally adamant. The administration did not like its choices; it agreed with the *principles* of the civil rights forces, but the time was not right. The costs were too high. So much else was at stake. Wilkins concluded: "It was the same rationale we had been hearing for twenty-five years."[21]

And, indeed, Wilkins was correct, because the American Dilemma in its classic form was still very much a part of American life. Very much had changed, but very much remained the same. It was the argument put forth by the New Deal; Fiorello La Guardia had agonized over the Stuyvesant Town project in similar terms. Truman was faced with the same issues when his Civil Rights Commission raised them; some liberals had fought the Powell Amendment in the 1950s with identical arguments. And now for the first two years of the New Frontier, here were the same obstacles. Everyone understood each other's political arguments and philosophical premises, but after months of badgering, Wilkins summed up his frustration: "I think 1962 was perhaps the lowest moment for the civil rights movement during the Kennedy years."[22]

And no one misunderstood the basic source of this frustration. It was not so much that conditions had worsened; in fact, there were some positive advances. It was not the inaccessibility of the new administration; it was light years ahead of its immediate predecessor in this respect. Rather, it was that expectations were much higher now than before, and this would inevitably raise the criteria for judging performance. There were, after all, new people in positions of power, people who were more liberal, more openly sympathetic. And these were people not on the fringes of power, but in the very seats of power. Still, however, the frustration persisted. There was the realization that even with all the new positive developments, there remained a complex, cross-checking political system that civil rights opponents could take advantage of. And Kennedy was at the vortex of this seemingly intractable situation, requiring every bit of political skill he could muster.

An additional factor in the political equation now was the new chairman of the thirty-one-member House Committee on Education and Labor, Congressman Adam Clayton Powell, Jr., from Harlem, still recognized by many in the country as "Mr. Civil Rights."

Having established that he would not rock the Kennedy legislative boat by introducing the controversial Powell Amendment, it remained to be seen how Powell would proceed to function. He was keenly aware that more than a few critics had predicted that he would not be a good chairman. George Meany and the *New York Times* were not the only ones who had expressed doubts about him. Columnist Murray Kempton confidently predicted that Powell will "do a terrible job, because he is a lazy, careless, and selfish man."[23] Others simply did not imagine that the Harlem congressman could give up a lifetime record of disruptive independence and inattention to detail. He had seldom demonstrated the capacity to be a loyal party man, able to operate as a team player and prepared to maneuver as required in the complex political role of a major congressional committee chairman. It was important to Powell, one of his professional staff members, Dr. Deborah Partridge Wolfe, recalled, to establish first and foremost that these critics were wrong. He set out to prove that he would be a "fair" chairman—fair with his fellow members of both parties, and especially in assigning subcommittee chairman slots.[24] And above all, he wanted his committee members to respect him as the chairman.

It was clear that he was the ideological opposite of his predecessor, Graham Barden. And the committee had its share of those who were liberal and inclined to agree with him legislatively. Therefore, if he gave them coveted subcommittee slots with budgets and staffs, something denied him by Barden over the years, this could be the first test. In addition, Wolfe stated, he knew that if he introduced his divisive Powell Amendment at the outset of the congressional session, this would only irritate the liberals on his committee and complicate their lives much as before. Thus, by "sharing the wealth"—that is, giving subcommittees adequate budgets to operate—and withholding the amendment, he would be demonstrating a sensitivity to his colleagues they surely had to appreciate. That was the way "good" chairmen acted, and Powell clearly wanted that reputation. He was also aware that committee members would appreciate the opportunity to manage bills on the floor of the House that came out of their subcommittees. Powell had no objection to this. Under Barden's reign, the chairman of the full committee almost always reserved this highly prized role for himself. But Powell would, in this regard, share the spotlight.

Dr. Wolfe likewise was quick to point out that one of the major feats of a successful chairman was to delegate responsibility to good people—staff and fellow members—and then let them pursue their talents. Their success could only redound to the chairman's credit. A young member of Congress at the time, John Brademas from Indiana, was one of the new (elected in 1958) liberals on the committee. A Rhodes Scholar, Brademas had a strong interest in education issues. Powell was quite willing to treat him as Barden never would have. Brademas later became president of New York University. Years later, he recalled:

> [Powell] took a great deal of pride in the fact that on his committee were several very well-educated, intelligent, articulate young Democratic members. And he liked that. . . . He was perfectly willing to delegate authority and opportunity and responsibility to them. . . . I remember very early on . . . shortly after he had become the chairman. He called me in. I was a second-term congressman . . . and he said, "John, I want you to be chairman of a task force to take a look at what the federal government should be doing in the way of higher education." Well, for a fresh second-term congressman to be given that kind of opportunity was a marvelous thing. And he said, "Here is some staff money. You pick out the other members of your task force." . . . And we worked hard and we produced a report that had thirteen recommendations, twelve of which have since been enacted into law.[25]

On another occasion, Brademas went to Powell regarding support for colleges in international studies and research. He asked Powell to "let me run with it." Brademas's letter to Powell was unapologetically candid in the political effect such an assignment could have for a young congressman, the request coming during an election. Powell, understanding the politics of such matters, readily agreed. "So Adam," Brademas stated, "was perfectly willing to delegate responsibility and to give credit. He, of course, was very pleased to assume credit. And he would say, 'Why, most of these pieces of legislation were written in my committee, and I have a great record, and I'm very proud of it.' "

Powell gained the favor of his committee colleagues because he respected their talents and interests. He knew that members served best by representing their constituents and getting their names before the public—and all the better if this was associated with concrete legislation. There is every indication that he acceded to their wishes when he could. And, indeed, it was mutual, as Brademas stated:

> . . . a lot of us, in all candor, did the hard work, did the nitty-gritty, conducted the hearings. Adam supported us. He gave us an opportunity to lead. So Adam, quite properly, as politicians are in the credit-taking business, took credit for the legislation that came out of his committee. And that's perfectly all right. . . . So it all blended together. And Adam was in the right place at the right time.

Of course, the important thing is that Powell was willing to facilitate matters for his members in a way that was a refreshing contrast to Barden's chairmanship. One could only imagine what might have been Powell's career record if he had been given serious committee assignments back in the late 1940s when he first joined Congress. Now, in the first years of his chairmanship, he was cooperative, not obstructive, and he recognized the political needs of his committee members back home. For this style and attitude, his members, or at least certainly those in the majority party, were more than grateful.

One of the first important things Powell did was to request and receive a major increase in budget allocation for his committee. If he was to be generous in rewarding his members with substantive assignments, he had to have the resources to facilitate their work. Under Barden, the Education and Labor Committee received $175,000 for its annual operations. Powell requested an enormous increase to $600,000, and he got it. One former New York congressman, Ludwig Teller, who later worked for a year as consultant to Powell on the committee, described how Powell restructured the subcommittees.[26] Barden had set up permanent subcommittees. Powell, instead, designated subcommittees on the basis of particular topics or subjects being dealt with. This permitted subcommittees to come and go as legislative needs required. Under the old system, some subcommittees continued to exist even if they had no business to conduct. Under Powell's system, the subcommittees would always have something to do, and, of course, Powell, with his increased budget, would be able to support the work with much greater control over the allocation of funds. For the chairman, it was a more efficient way to allocate resources and maximize subcommittee productivity. For the members, it meant they were always serving on a working, active subcommittee. In this way, also, Powell, as chairman, would have more control over the overall flow of committee business.

Adopting this approach, he needed highly qualified staff people serving him on the full committee. He did not rely on political cronies to fill such important posts. As his education chief, Dr. Wolfe had not known Powell personally before he appointed her. He only knew of her professional reputation. She had been a Dean of the School of Education at Tuskegee Institute in Alabama, later a professor of education at Queens College in New York City, from which she took a leave to join Powell's committee for three years. She had been a member of Educators for Kennedy in the 1960 campaign, and was initially offered a position as Assistant Secretary of HEW under Abraham Ribicoff. She turned this down and subsequently accepted the post as education chief on Powell's committee.

Her task was to coordinate all educational matters coming before the full committee, to keep the members informed, and, as she put it, "to teach them" about the complexities of the bills.

Wolfe remembers Powell being completely supportive in her work. "He read what I gave him. He definitely did his homework. I could tell from the way he asked questions of witnesses on technical matters relating to a bill." At one point, she took the entire committee to a nearby Montgomery County, Maryland, school to see new teaching techniques and equipment being used. Powell encouraged her in all such activities, recognizing the substantive value—and positive public image—of such committee work. "He did not get in my way," Dr. Wolfe added. "He let me plan hearings, and work with others." Powell was particularly impressed at the way she carefully organized committee hearings, preparing a brief summary for each section of the bill to be considered, and presenting the witnesses in a consecutive, orderly manner that would facilitate the committee members following the testimony. Clearly, Powell was proud of the work of this black woman educator with a Ph.D.

In fact, she stated, he made a point of insisting that she be addressed as "Dr. Wolfe." This, she concluded, signaled his respect for her talents and pride in her race.

But she conceded that Powell could be a most difficult person to work with at times. The problem was his extreme egocentrism, which had to be massaged at all times. He insisted on being accorded the highest respect as chairman. On one especially discomforting morning for Dr. Wolfe, Powell entered the office and an administrative assistant did not rise immediately and greet him. Powell fired her on the spot because she had not shown the proper deference. Dr. Wolfe recognized that such a self-centered person could be brutal in personal relations. And she vowed never to let herself be put in a position of being totally reliant on him for a job. She had tenure as a professor at Queens College, and she always let others—including Powell—know this. She recalled: "I always introduced myself as Dr. Deborah Wolfe, Education Chief of the House Education and Labor Committee, *on leave from Queens College*." One day, Powell mischievously asked her why she always added that last bit of biographical identification. She smiled, and did not answer. But he knew why; and she knew he knew.

But Powell recognized and respected such professionals around him. They gave him the substance he needed. In the same way that he relied on the legal skills of Edward Bennett Williams, he relied on and rewarded the professional talents of his committee staff.

For one with such a vulnerable, volatile political life, having his substantive flanks covered was a necessity.

There were times, however, when Powell would, indeed, be a source of frustration for the staff. He did not attend committee hearings as often as Dr. Wolfe wanted. In this sense, Brademas's characterization of him as "being bored" with the tedious committee work was correct. Dr. Wolfe said that she was usually able to get him to come when big political figures were to testify, such as a cabinet secretary, or a big-city mayor. She admitted amusingly that he could get "a little wiggly at hearings." But in the early years of his chairmanship, there was no question of his interest and attention to the political requirements of his job. Wolfe admired the way he was able to "work both sides of the aisle"—Republicans as well as Democrats. He understood the necessity for coalitions and compromise. He knew when to call for a vote when the supporters were lined up. He saw his chairmanship in that light: getting the best possible proposed bill out of his committee into the House Rules Committee and onto the House floor. In this process, according to Dr. Wolfe, he was a "master politician."

Powell disagreed with President Kennedy on the minimum wage increase and made it known publicly, but he went along with his committee's decision on its final vote. Early in 1961, Kennedy asked Congress to increase the minimum wage from one dollar to $1.25 an hour in three steps over a three-year period. In addition, workers for hotels, motels, restaurants, laundries, and motion picture theaters were not to be covered. Powell quickly made it known that this proposal "does not measure up to what I had expected." He objected to the three-step increases, and he wanted the excluded workers brought under coverage. His committee rejected his attempted amendment by a vote of eighteen to thirteen. A White House memo noted Powell's position: "Powell feels very strongly about hotel, motel and restaurant people. As you know, they've [the committee] removed the exemption and in the Committee vote Powell took two or three Democrats with him, and almost solid Republican support." [27] Powell lobbied vigorously for his views, but he accepted the final result. He was also mindful that his old civil rights allies were watching developments in his committee. It was important that he keep his own liberal record intact even in the face of necessary pragmatic politics of the New Frontier. This new political era would be touchy indeed. John A. Davis, of the New York State Commission Against Discrimination, wrote to his old friend Clarence Mitchell and sent a copy to Powell. In the letter he sadly noted the exclusion of laundry workers and cotton gin workers from the minimum wage bill, and wondered about the liberal policies of the new administration. "It seems to me more and more like an old deal," he concluded. What would happen to Negroes in education, he wondered. And he asked, "Are we not in danger of losing everything we have been fighting for since 1954?"[28]

Powell was keenly aware of such views. If the new politics would concentrate on legislative action in the economic realm, he had to be sure that Negroes were not left out of the benefits. After all, his committee would be the vehicle for such advances, if they were to be made. He had agreed with the administration to ease up on his overt civil rights demands, but he did not want to be caught with no benefits to show the constituents who had relied on him—and who expected his chairmanship to have concrete meaning. He was astute enough to know that the New Frontier would not push for civil rights laws. But if, at the same time, Negroes—who were employed overwhelmingly in the low-paid jobs—were not to be helped, then doubt and cynicism could set in, and his credibility would be in jeopardy. This would be a difficult row to plow, and he knew it. It was a new ballgame for him. Over the years, he had used his seat in Congress as an outspoken champion of civil rights, being perceived as a symbol as much as anything else. But now, after all the excitement and enthusiasm surrounding his chairmanship, surely the symbolism had to be joined by substantive gains. Otherwise, what was—in the minds of many who held high expectations—the point?

Powell was sensitive to these concerns. But he also knew that he was still a relatively small—albeit much larger than before—part of a vastly complex, fragmented political system. He definitely had power in Congress now. As chairman of a major committee he had control over resources and, to an extent, could seriously help the political careers of some members. But he was also aware that such leverage went just so far. The minimum-wage-increase proposal was a good example of the new political process he was engaged in. He was still not able to produce completely for those who needed him the most. This would be a vexing situation for any liberal representative, but it was especially so for a black congressman with a large low-income constituency. In some ways, it was another dimension of the American Dilemma—this time with a socioeconomic face. Sorensen records that Kennedy, likewise, "Deeply disliked dropping laundry workers—whose plight he had often cited in the campaign—from the extended coverage provisions of the minimum wage bill. But the alternative was no bill at all and thus no protection for millions of others."[29] Powell understood this, but his political problem was somewhat different from Kennedy's. Kennedy could at least point to an increased wage bill that covered many workers. But Powell had to answer to those left out—continuously. In a way, his political burden was just as great as, if not greater than, those politicians who represented more affluent and resourceful constituents.

Given these political realities, Powell continued to work with the administration. The fact is that he had no viable alternative. He kept up a steady correspondence with the President, advising him of conditions in his committee on education proposals and other matters. It was clear that Powell intended to be a strong administration advocate, and the White House knew this. Powell would ask for meetings with President Kennedy to discuss legislative strategy. A typical letter read:

> April 27, 1961
>
> My dear Mr. President:
>
> The relationship of the Committee on Education and Labor with the Administration has reached a very serious point. The Speaker is aware of this and to some extent agrees with the almost solid Democratic caucus. It is imperative, therefore, that a meeting be held immediately since as matters now stand, not only is there increasing resentment but the entire education program is grinding to a halt.
>
> With every good wish.[30]

And Powell would not fail to point up the political-partisan consequences, if necessary, knowing how sensitive the Kennedy White House was to such matters:

> July 21, 1961
>
> My dear Mr. President:
>
> The impasse concerning the education bills reported out from the Committee of which I am the Chairman can be surmounted. During this week I have had extensive conferences with the Democratic Members of my committee, the authors of the legislation and the chairmen of the subcommittees on education.
>
> I am requesting an opportunity to meet with you briefly as soon as possible to discuss with you the plans at which we have arrived

and by which we believe that these bills can be brought before the House and passed during this present session.

The Republican Members of my Committee and the Republican leadership of the House are now united around a project for which they can claim victory and will result in the loss in this coming election of at least thirty Democratic seats in the House, or enough to give the Republicans control, if their plans are not stopped.

Time is of the essence.

With every good wish.

Sincerely your friend and supporter,[31]

On another occasion he wrote:

January 17, 1962

Dear Mr. President:

The gentlewoman from Oregon, Mrs. Edith Green, and I would like to confer with you concerning a very important item facing our Committee. The educational program of our Government is now fragmented into 46 different agencies, with a total amount of $1,500,000,000 a year being spent for educational purposes. This, of course, leads to not only a shocking cost but to a loss of impact of our educational thrust.

This probe could be a dramatic and meaningful maneuver on your part and we are prepared with documents, etc., to go into action.

With every good wish.[32]

In this effort, Powell was assisting Congresswoman Green, who had indicated a concern about waste in educational spending three years earlier to Chairman Barden. Barden was not supportive; Powell now was. They met at the White House with Theodore Sorensen. The new chairman indeed was a refreshing change for those on the committee who had suffered for ten years under Barden's reign of do-nothingism. Powell supported his subcommittee chairmen, and moved their bills through the full committee into the Rules Committee with dispatch. He consulted, and compromised when he had to, and overall performed in a manner pleasing to most of his members.

He did have his little tiffs with some Republicans on his committee, especially the senior minority member, Carroll D. Kearns. With Kearns, Powell was convinced that the Pennsylvanian resented his chairmanship—and him. Powell wanted Kearns to relinquish some of his office space to make room for an expanded committee staff.

Kearns refused, saying he would do so only upon orders from the Speaker himself. Powell resented this, and proceeded to build extra office space behind a partition in the hall. "Due to his ridiculous obstinacy," Powell told the press, "it is costing the Government $2,000 to build this partition in the hall. As chairman, I could move his things right out of the office and lock him out. But I wouldn't do that, and that's why we're building the partition."[33] But the chairman also knew that he had other ways of reminding the resistant that he was in charge. A few months earlier, Kearns had requested Powell to approve the assignment of a military aide to accompany him on a six-week world tour. Powell refused, stating that he did not even have such an aide on his own travels as chairman. His letter to Kearns must have given him some delight to write. He wrote:

> I do not believe that in times of National crisis such as these, that any Member of the Congress, including Committee chairmen, should have as aides men who are now needed so desperately. While we are calling up tens of thousands of American boys, it just doesn't make sense to me that we of the Congress take scores of the commissioned officers to travel with us. I have so communicated my views to the Defense establishment. I am sure you agree with me.
>
> With every good wish for a good trip.[34]

Powell was willing to be cooperative and supportive, but he expected reciprocity. It would be difficult to see how his detractors on the committee could miss that. And if they did, he knew how to remind them.

At the same time, he continued to play the civil rights watchdog role he had pursued during the Eisenhower administration. From time to time he would contact the White House complaining of or inquiring into a reported practice of segregation or discrimination in the bureaucracy. Why should the racial identity of the spouse of an applicant to a military school be noted on the application? (The Department of Defense, respecting state laws against interracial marriage, responded: "This was done not to permit preference in school selections but rather to prevent embarrassment when service personnel report to a new situation. . . . In any event the requirement that a married service school applicant state his wife's race if different from his own will be dropped."[35]) Was there any substance to the suspicion that a public stadium being built in Texas with federal funds could have segregated air-raid fallout shelters?

(Adam Yarmolinsky, in a "Dear Adam" letter, replied that the government assumed that the facility "would be operated on an integrated basis" and then added a P.S.: "My assumption has just been confirmed by definite assurance."[36])

And so the Powell monitoring continued, and in the early 1960s the results appeared to be increasingly favorable.

He also served notice on organized labor that he would use his position as chairman to fight discrimination in apprenticeship training programs. At a labor banquet at the NAACP's national convention in 1961, Powell promised to introduce measures withholding federal aid to any apprenticeship program that practiced racial discrimination.[37] He would not support labor's request for a common-situs picketing bill until the craft unions "get in step with Democracy." Repeatedly, he referred to the "new day" evidenced by the black college student sit-in movement in the South and the recent Freedom Rides conducted by CORE. And he admonished the NAACP to begin thinking beyond "legalisms" toward a new time of mass, nonviolent protests. Phase One, he said, of the civil rights struggle was, understandably, preoccupied with legal, courtroom battles. But "Tonight I call for the immediate acceleration of Phase Two; namely, economic freedom." Through direct action, the Negro masses, he predicted, would be demanding more and better jobs and entry into nondiscriminatory training programs. And he advised his NAACP hosts to "radically change its thrust or be by-passed by the new Negro and the new white man in this new world of rising expectations." Another interesting aspect of this speech was that several times (at least five in the prepared four-page text) he used the term "Afro-American."

Clearly, however, he was beginning in 1961 to emphasize the economic dimension and the possible utility of mass, direct action, including boycotts. He was also aware of the "selective buying" campaign then being conducted by several black ministers in Philadelphia, led by the Reverend Leon Sullivan. In a sense, he likely recalled his earlier years in Harlem, and he undoubtedly was responding to the increased mass protest led by King, the Student Nonviolent Coordinating Committee, and CORE. Through it all, there was the impression that Powell was taking his measure of new circumstances—in his own political life as a major congressional committee chairman; of the new rising young black protesters; and, from his vantage point in Harlem, as early as 1961, the obvious appeals that a fiery young black speaker, Malcolm X, was having on the street-corner crowds of his community. His advice to the

NAACP to "change its thrust" was very likely another way of suggesting that he personally was rethinking the requirements of his own unique leadership role. This role required him to be a party leader—Mr. Chairman—in Congress, and at the same time maintain his title of "Mr. Civil Rights."

Powell signed his letters to Kennedy as "friend and supporter." As chairman of his committee, this meant that he would do whatever he could, along with the other congressional party leadership, to push the President's program. This was the normal expectation when the same party controlled the White House and the Congress. Lesser congressmen might stray, but party loyalty was expected from the more senior members. This, of course, did not apply when some very divisive issue—for example, civil rights—pitted national party against hometown interests, as with the die-hard Southern segregationists. Always, the constituents' interests had first call on the legislator's votes. Powell had an advantage here. He was a liberal; his committee was largely liberal, and there was a liberal-leaning administration in the White House. Unlike his experience with the Eisenhower administration, he was now a frequent visitor to the White House—for social occasions as well as political meetings. Powell now had access. He was invited to bill-signing ceremonies, and his recommendations, or veto of proposed nominations, were frequently respected when patronage appointments were involved. One such successful recommendation involved the wife of J. Raymond Jones as comptroller of the Virgin Islands.[38] On another, Attorney General Robert F. Kennedy felt obliged to clear some federal judgeship nominations in New York City with him. When one such potential nomination involving NAACP attorney Robert L. Carter unfortunately and indefensibly did not receive Powell's blessing, the appointment was not made.[39] (Ironically, Carter would serve five years later as one of Powell's lawyers in his fight against exclusion from Congress. Carter was later appointed to the Federal District court in 1972 by President Richard Nixon.)

The Kennedy White House had good reason to appreciate the work of Powell's committee. In the first congressional session of 1961, Kennedy got 48.4 percent of what he asked for from Congress. He had great success overall with Powell's committee, winning favorable action there on nineteen of twenty-six requests. He was able to get his minimum wage increase, but not the aid-to-education bill he had made one of his priority items. Clearly, the roadblock was not the Education and Labor Committee, but the

House Rules Committee or the conservative coalition in Congress. When the subcommittees under Powell reported their bills to the full committee, Powell was diligent in bringing them to a vote of the full committee and moving them along. On education matters, the committee's record was not too good once on the floor: seven bills approved in committee lost later in House action; five won. The committee was not more successful on labor issues. It approved all four of the administration's proposals, but was able to gain House approval of only one—to raise the minimum wage to $1.15 per hour immediately.[40] Clearly, however, Powell's committee was, indeed, supportive of the President, but there was little the chairman or his liberal colleagues could do to overcome the full House conservative opposition.

Powell recognized this, and he made it clear that failure to pass the aid-to-education bill should not be laid at his committee's doorstep. In June 1961, when he returned from a ten-day trip to Europe during which he attended the International Labor Organization meeting in Geneva, he announced that the education bill was beyond his committee's salvation. There were too many obstacles—mainly divided over aid to parochial schools, and fought by aid opponents to *any* federal support—and he warned: "Someone's got to blow the whistle. Someone beyond the Committee and Congress."[41] Notwithstanding the fact that Powell had not supported an antisegregation amendment, the Southerners still resisted the measure as one aimed at forcing the end to racial segregation in the South.

For his own part, Powell kept his liberal voting record intact. He received a 100 percent rating from the liberal Americans for Democratic Action for 1962. And on those roll call votes calling for a large federal role in various programs—meaning increased federal dollars—he voted 89 percent in favor. In 1961, he had a 0 percent voting record *in agreement* with the conservative coalition in Congress, and 57 percent *in disagreement*. The following year, these percentages were 0 and 69. Not only did the ADA like Powell's voting record in 1962, he also received a 100 percent rating from the important COPE (Committee on Political Education, AFL-CIO), and 90 percent from the liberal National Farmers Union (NFU). In contrast, the three conservative interest groups rating congressmen had him down at the bottom: American Farm Bureau Federation, 9 percent; Civic Affairs Associates, 0 percent; Americans for Constitutional Action, 0 percent.

Actually the question about Powell was not *how* he would vote, but, on important roll call votes on the floor, *if* he would be around to cast a vote. His absentee record, though improved, was still not at the level his friends preferred it to be. To be sure, he had adopted a much different attitude toward his congressional responsibilities since assuming the chairmanship, but he was still afflicted by the travel bug and a short attention span in, to him, boring congressional sessions answering roll call. In 1961, the average Democratic member of the House voted 88 percent of the time on roll calls; Powell's record was 54 percent. In 1962, the Democratic House average was 83 percent; Powell's again was 54 percent. He was by no means the lowest, but some people felt these numbers were too low for the chairman of a major committee.[42]

Most colleagues and staff who worked with Powell in Congress appear generally to agree that he always preferred off-the-floor political work to the time-consuming task of appearing to cast a vote on a measure, the outcome of which was frequently known beforehand. His interests were in the small strategy meetings, the bargaining and lining up of support, and striking a compromise deal. When he put his talents to these tasks, he was recognized, as Dr. Wolfe concluded, as "a master politician." And this same style led John Brademas to assess him in those early years as a "very effective chairman." His committee's legislative defeats were the result of the ideological lineup in Congress and the political environment in the country, by no means the result of leadership faults on his part. With more allies on Capitol Hill like himself the New Frontier programs would have enjoyed far greater success. The Kennedy White House and other liberals knew this. Powell was not the problem. If anything, his expeditious movement of bills through his committee facilitated the liberal social policy agenda. And, in addition, many observers were clearly aware of the contrast with the previous chairman.

At the same time, he kept the White House on notice that he was not giving up entirely his old fight against use of federal funds for segregated facilities. His support of the New Frontier's political strategy had limits. In May 1963 he sent a letter to the President complaining of segregation in hospitals built in the South with funds supplied by the Hill-Burton Act. A year earlier, he had called attention to a situation in Augusta, Georgia, where $400,000 was used to operate a hospital that set aside twelve beds for Negroes in the basement. This "separate but equal" approach was unacceptable, and he would introduce legislation to end such practices. He was no longer able to wait until the country's "climate" had changed. "It is time to call a halt to this type of subsidization in defiance of the Constitution. Although I believe this can be done without the enactment of additional legislation, it is not being done."[43] By 1963, Powell was no longer going to play the Kennedy restraining game. A letter from the White House was still not comforting: "I think you are aware of the very strong position that the Administration has taken in opposition to the [separate but equal] provision. . . . You may be assured that we will continue our efforts to correct the situation so far as it relates to segregated use of hospitals constructed with Federal assistance."[44]

The fact is that Powell was beginning to feel political pressure from the civil rights movement. Impatience was growing. Demonstrations in the South were capturing worldwide headlines. More than a few critics were becoming disenchanted with the cautious civil rights strategy of the New Frontier. Appointments to "breakthrough" positions had been made, but continued civil rights denials were being exposed in dramatic form.

The climate in Congress might not have changed, but there clearly was a mood of growing militancy in black communities, South and North. This was the pressure Powell was feeling. It was good to be chairman of a powerful committee, but congressional politics was, at the moment, not where the civil rights action was. He had always been the militant, the recognized outspoken critic of America's abominable racial problems. Now there were other voices capturing headlines, and risking danger on picket lines and in mass boycott protests. Powell remembered his days in Harlem. Where was he now? Was there a new movement for racial justice that was passing him by? Was his important role in Congress less than what these new times and the growing civil rights issue required? Was he to be quietly relegated to the ranks of the steady but cautious NAACP? Would his voice continue to be the one that drew the greatest applause at Harlem rallies? How could he compete with the obviously growing appeal of a Martin Luther King braving police dogs in Birmingham, Alabama, and the strident crowd-pleasing speeches of a Malcolm X in his own Harlem community and other black communities across the North?

Coming with the fiery speeches was the growing language of black nationalism. The Black Muslims were now deriding the "so-called Negro," and asking Negroes to think of themselves as blacks, as descendants from a proud heritage in Africa, and as Muslims. This was language Powell had heard before in the 1930s in Harlem, but he had always been able to chart a middle course and survive as a prominent, relevant leader. But in the early 1960s the challenge was there again. Powell's own status had changed considerably, but he still saw himself as *the* mass black leader—"Mr. Chairman," to be sure, a black man in a position of institutional power in Congress, without question. But he was always more comfortable as the unpredictable irritant, the maverick, the one who led the charge, who always closed the rally.

Perhaps more than his particular leadership, his ego was on the line as he contemplated his moves in the spring of 1963. He had to show that he had not become a comfortable insider, prepared to make congressional compromises from the safe haven of Congress. And in another sense, how could he tell that his Harlem base, in this turbulent time, just might be slowly eroding beneath him? Could there be the possibility of a Malcolm X looming on the horizon to challenge him for his congressional seat? In spite of the fact that the Nation of Islam eschewed electoral politics at that time, there were rumors that this could change. And in the dynamic, fast-developing times with dramatic protest events unfolding almost weekly in some part of the country, who could tell? No political career was untouchable—even, some speculated, Powell's. And precisely because he had been the recognized leader for so long of a people now beginning to surge forward, it was not unknown in history for a leader to be overtaken by his followers.

Powell had options. He could hit out at the Southern segregationists in the Ku Klux Klan–ridden towns oppressing blacks. But this was already effectively being done by the new wave of youthful sit-inners and mass protesters led by King, SNCC, and CORE. They were challenging that old order not only with words but with their bodies. Powell's speeches would be welcome and supportive, but also supplementary, secondary. He could goad his conservative colleagues in the Congress for blocking effective, progressive legislation. But this was striking too close to home in the arena where he had to live every day and bargain and negotiate ultimately for votes. Such an overt attack, at that particular time, would make an already politically bad situation infinitely worse. He likely never considered as a viable option *openly* prodding the Kennedy administration to be more aggressive in its legislative thrust. His position as chairman with ready access to the White House was too valuable to jeopardize by possibly chilling relationships there. He certainly was not going to take on Malcolm X and the Black Muslims, although they espoused religious beliefs at variance with his own Christian faith.

He was not prepared temperamentally or substantively to attempt to give well-reasoned lectures about the necessity for political astuteness and the need to compromise—as much as this might well have reflected his own deeper inclinations. He was always the irritant, the one who believed that stirring up matters and creating tension were preferable to moderate, balanced, calm appeals to patience and reason.

He read the evolving social and racial scene and made his move. He decided to attack his old friends in the NAACP. He would position himself on the side of the racial "radicals." He would hit out at the one target, at that time, that was most vulnerable and, for him, safe to attack—namely, the civil rights "moderates," and their white liberal allies. In the midst of the dramatic protest demonstrations in Birmingham, Alabama, with the fire hoses and police dogs being used against the protesters by the local officials, Powell chose a platform at a Baptist church rally in Washington, D.C., to launch his new thrust for first-rank leadership. To a cheering audience of 1,200 he said: "The white man has given the Negro just about all he intends to give him. From now on we will win only what we fight for. There is no future for the Negro man except what he fights for. Now this may sound like black nationalism—and maybe it is."[45] He followed this a few days later at a massive outdoor rally in Harlem. Joined on the platform now by Malcolm X and some local politicians, he launched his strongest attack on the NAACP and the National Urban League. "I don't agree with some of the things Malcolm X preaches and he doesn't agree with some of the things I preach. But one of the things I am very close to agreeing almost completely with is Malcolm X's analysis of our present national Negro organizations."

He then criticized these organizations for having whites in many positions of leadership, and noted that the reverse was not true of such groups as the B'nai B'rith, the Italian or Irish or Polish ethnic organizations. Black organizations should be led by blacks. Whites could, of course, be members, but not leaders. He accused the white NAACP board members of voting to reject the Powell Amendment in the 1950s. He called for more consciously black collective efforts in education, economic enterprises, and political bloc voting. And, again, if this sounded like black nationalism, "then what is wrong with it? Why is it that racism and nationalism are only dirty words when applied to Negro people?"

These views created a storm of pro and con reaction in the media. As Powell's words came across the airwaves and in the headlines, he was interpreted as saying that blacks should boycott the

NAACP until that organization reorganized its leadership structure, got rid of the white officers, and put more grass-roots blacks on the board of directors. Powell later denied calling explicitly for a boycott of the NAACP, but he stuck to his criticism regarding whites in leadership roles.

He sketched the main outlines of his new position in a four-page handwritten outline, labeled "Re-Cap," dated May 17, 1963.

1. So called Negro org. must be *black* led.
2. Black masses must finance their orgs.
3. Whites *follow* black leadership
4. Black Rev. (Political Sophistication and economic development)
5. Civil Rights Act
   Meaningless for 2/3 outside of the South
   Aimed at Black Middle Class
6. Most important for the 2/3 is ECO Development
   Here is where [word unclear] have moved
   1. Manpower
   2. Voc. Ed.
   3. Juvenile Del.
   4. Equal Pay
   5. SBA
   6. War on Pov.
7. Rev. of Black Mod. vs. Black Radicals (respectable rebels)
8. Parity Concept of power and production
   White man cannot own the black man
9. Harlem should not tolerate outside leadership
   To do so is to abdicate that community's responsibility to itself and to its children—*develop indigenous pride*
10. Power would be non-violent
    —More important dimension, grounded in Christian principles
    —well led org., disciplined, clearly defined goals.
11. The principle of *desegregation* as a tenet—distinguish between desegre & integration—
12. No demonstrators who are not voters (over 21—wear voting reg. card on lapel when you protest)
13. Defy law of man when in conflict with law of God
14. Unashamed preference of black man in politics
15. Political sophistication of black masses
16. Negroes must follow only those leaders who can sit at the bargaining table and bargain as equals.
17. A new massive involvement with ourselves.

18. Black clergy must take the lead in getting black people off their knees. In Chicago, where is your Rev. Martin Luther King, Jr., Shuttlesworth, Leon Sullivan, and, yes, your Adam Clayton Powell.[46]

Across the top of these four pages of notes and down the margins, Powell wrote: "New dimension—what was merely the Black Revolt must now mature into the Black Revolution. What was merely protests must now [words missing] into products. Black people must now seek audacious *power.*"

These talking points would become the basis of Powell's public pronouncements as he moved into the summer of 1963, with the civil rights movement reaching a peak of protest and public attention. (Years later in his book *Adam by Adam,* he called the points, with elaboration, his "black position paper.") There was a little bit of the old 1930s Powell there with its emphasis on the economic, as well as the recognition of the power of the ballot. He was recognizing the mass appeals of black nationalism, but he was not a "separatist" in the sense of advocating a separate political nation, as the Black Muslims were demanding at that time. He wanted to talk about "desegregation" not "integration," the former being more legal, the latter more social. And he certainly was intent on pushing for black leadership of organizations in black communities, even prepared to use himself as a good example. Again, mindful of the kinds of problems that afflicted many in the urban ghettos, he wanted to stress economic issues. Such issues, of course, came through his committee, and, therefore, his sixteenth point of following those black leaders who could sit at the bargaining table was not lost on those who understood his message. *He* was chairman of one of those most important bargaining tables. (He spelled this out later in his book, specifically, the fact that his committee would handle virtually all the economic issues that concerned black urban citizens.)

This was a document crafted by Powell to reflect his sharpest personal, political, and intellectual sense of where his lifelong struggle was headed. Clearly, there were several points in it that his NAACP friends could accept, and those were the points Powell proceeded to emphasize in his speeches and media interviews—economic issues, voting, nonviolence, need for political sophistication. But it was also clear that he *had* taken a very strong slap at the NAACP in his earlier rally speeches. And that organization and its supporters were not going to give him a free shot. A veteran of the civil rights wars and once a newspaper man sensitive to the role of publicity and the media, Roy Wilkins lost no time in reporting the incident to the NAACP board and sending out press releases rejecting Powell's attacks on the organization. Powell's call for a boycott of the NAACP, Wilkins said, was "more than silly. It is vicious."[47] It would "fall on deaf ears," because the NAACP's record was well-known and highly respected by Negro Americans. Wilkins defended the organization's stand as an "interracial and interfaith" group who had prided itself on having long-standing white citizens associated with it from its beginning. The NAACP stood for integration and could hardly endorse a call to kick whites out of its leadership ranks. Whites certainly did not "control" the NAACP, whose funds came overwhelmingly from its grass-roots membership—80 percent. Therefore, Powell was "talking through his hat." And in an explanation that he had used before and would reiterate subsequently (especially during the later years of the Black Power movement), Wilkins said that white people helped create the racial problems in the country and thus had a responsibility and role in helping to eradicate those problems. Powell should know better, Wilkins chided. And apparently referring to Powell's recent troubles stemming from exposure of his European junkets (discussed in Chapter 18), Wilkins suggested that Powell was chafing over such attacks against him. If there was to be a "reappraisal," it was Powell's task, not the NAACP's.

The NAACP really decided to go on the offensive. Sensitive not only to Powell's attacks, the organization was aware that others—less publicly—were beginning to hint that the new mass militancy was eclipsing the NAACP's cautious but steady style of struggle. And some were suggesting that perhaps the NAACP was "too moderate" and, indeed, outdated. The organization issued a twelve-page pamphlet entitled *Adam . . . Where Art Thou?*"[48] It opened with a July 21, 1955, letter from Powell to Wilkins thanking the NAACP for its support, and, after citing Powell's 1963 criticisms, proceeded to list four pages of NAACP positions and achievements over the years. All these were aimed at refuting Powell's charges and at reaffirming the organization's long-standing commitment to the civil rights cause. Then the pamphlet presented four pages of Negro editorial and individual reaction to Powell's attack. The *Philadelphia Tribune* bluntly stated that Powell "is confused. How in the name of heaven can he logically advocate segregation within the ranks of the NAACP which has as its basic purpose the ending of segregation in America?" The *Atlanta Daily World* concluded:

"His [Powell's] position is extreme, irrational and vindictive." The *California Eagle* said that "Powell opened the spring silly season . . . with advice to Negroes to boycott the NAACP." Lumping Powell with racists Talmadge, Eastland, Hitler, and Malcolm X, the *St. Louis Argus* simply ended, "We wished he hadn't said it." "Every Negro in the United States, with an ounce of sense, should be against practically everything Powell is for," the *Carolina Times* wrote. The (Baltimore) *Afro-American* noted: "We have come to Mr. Powell's defense on numerous occasions. We have not hesitated to speak out when we felt he was right and his attackers wrong. But this time Mr. Powell errs."

The NAACP was pleased to reprint and circulate Jackie Robinson's syndicated column, an open letter to Powell. Robinson called Powell's attack "vicious" and told the congressman that he had "grievously set back the cause of the Negro, let your race down and failed miserably in the role which our people justly expect you to play as an important national leader of the Negro in this nation."

J. Raymond Jones, Powell's on-again, off-again political ally in Harlem, announced that he was purchasing a life membership in the NAACP for his grandson.

In the middle of this flare-up, the Oakland, California, NAACP branch wrote the national office seeking some advice. The branch had planned to invite Powell to speak at its area-wide conference in June. What advice would Wilkins offer about this? Wilkins wired an immediate response. He did not recommend that Powell be given "a platform in view of his attacks upon the Association." Powell was wrong in these attacks, and the NAACP, including all its branches, stood fast against the "racism" he was espousing.[49]

So Powell was in the middle of yet another "family" feud, a familiar spot for him. But in a WNEW Radio interview the first week in April, he shrugged it off. The interviewer asked, "Why do you think the fire against you is increasing these days?"

"Because, probably, I'm saying the truth more," Powell responded. "You see, I have gotten to this period in life where I don't give a hoot about anything, and I might as well say the truth. But it isn't anything new. Go back and read a book I wrote twenty years ago. It's the same thing that I have been saying the past few weeks. It's called *Marching Blacks*."[50] (In that book, Powell did emphasize economic issues, but his treatment of the role of whites was quite different than in 1963. Then he had lauded the position of "outstanding whites such as Pearl Buck, Wendell Willkie, Homer P. Rainey, Frank Graham, Lillian Smith, and the greatest of all, Eleanor Roosevelt.")[51]

Others joined the chorus of critics of Powell's 1963 blast. The president of City College of New York, Buell G. Gallagher, defended the role of some whites on the NAACP board, including himself, and reminded Powell in a "Dear Adam" letter that they had supported the Powell Amendment. And Gallagher had to admonish Powell that "the NAACP continued to support its established position when, later you reversed yourself and did not offer the 'Powell Amendment.' "[52] Mike Masaoka, Washington representative of the Japanese-American Citizens League, likewise expressed "resentment" at Powell's position, asserting that it represented "racism in civil rights," and, recalling the undemocratic treatment of Japanese Americans in this country during World War II, "that only with the help and cooperation of others may civil rights be secured for any group of frustrated Americans."[53] In a speech at a black school, Tougaloo Southern Christian College, in Mississippi, Ralph Bunche told the students, "I regard Powell's attacks not only as stupid and irresponsible, but as revoltingly racist."[54]

Not all reactions were negative, however, as Powell knew would be the case. He knew the enthusiastic applause he received when he made his statements tapped some depths of feelings among some blacks. And the *Washington Afro-American* cautioned Roy Wilkins in an editorial that perhaps the congressman had more of a valid point than some were willing to admit. (The editor, C. Sumner Stone, would later serve as an assistant to Powell on his committee.) The newspaper reminded its readers: "With all of Mr. Powell's failings and weaknesses, the people have continued to place their deepest confidence in him by electing him."[55]

This episode passed, but it left a bitter feeling toward Powell in the minds of some civil rights advocates. It was additional evidence for them that he was not a trustworthy ally and would say virtually anything to draw attention to himself, even at the expense of hurting his friends. This was the unfortunate side of Powell one had to learn to live with. He probably did not mean everything he said, Clarence Mitchell charitably intimated years later. He liked to appeal to street-corner crowds, to get their applause and approval for the moment.[56] It was not an appealing side of his personality, and it could be disruptive at times. But many, such as Mitchell, had come not only to expect such behavior from the volatile Harlem congressman but to adjust to it.

This might be true, but to others such behavior was politically irresponsible and downright unethical. Powell seemed at times to be thoroughly insensitive to the blatant falsity of some of his remarks. For the record, he would make statements easily refuted, but the explanation, if necessary, could come later. This was the case, for example, with his mischaracterization of his meeting with President Eisenhower in October 1956. He claimed the President had made statements to him which were clearly not the case. James Hagerty had to rush a correction over Powell's signature. President Kennedy's White House was faced with a similar situation in June 1963. This came in the wake of Kennedy's important speech on June 11 on civil rights, wherein he called the issue a moral one the nation had to face, and revised his legislative agenda, introducing a more comprehensive set of proposals to Congress. Dynamic events in the South had created a crisis and changed the political climate drastically. Kennedy would now shed much of his cautious civil rights approach. Civil rights activists were elated.

On the West Coast at the time, Powell praised the speech and told reporters that he personally had stayed up half the night helping the administration draft the historic speech. Indeed, he stated to reporters, he was responsible for most of the thoughts in the speech. This, of course, was absolutely untrue. Powell had nothing to do with the drafting of that talk. He knew it; the White House knew it. When a Kennedy aide contacted Powell to clear up his statement, one account recorded the exchange as follows:

> Aide: About that statement . . .
> Powell: What statement?
> Aide: (Explains the wire-service report read by the President)
> Powell: Oh no, I said over half the President's legislation would go through my committee.
> Aide: But newsmen have a tape recording of what you actually said, and it corresponds to what was published.
> Powell: Well, you know those tape recorders. They have all those knobs that you turn on and off . . . they put other things in other places . . . that's what happened.[57]

Very likely no one in the White House actually believed "that's what happened." But when the inquiries and complaints began to flow in, they had to play it straight. Senator Strom Thurmond of South Carolina—long a Powell foe and a segregationist—wanted the President to declare whether, in fact, Powell's claim of major authorship of the historic speech was true. Lawrence O'Brien, special assistant to the President, responded:

> . . . I assume you have seen Congressman Powell's statement that the report of his address was inaccurate. According to the Congressman, as we understand it, the confusion arose from the statement that a great deal of the legislation proposed by the President would be within the jurisdiction of the House Committee on Education and Labor of which he is Chairman.[58]

A few months later, at the historic March on Washington on August 28, 1963, Powell was given the ceremonial role of leading a special congressional delegation to its reserved seats among the 200,000 gathered at the Lincoln Memorial. He would have preferred a speaker's role, but only nongovernmental civil rights leaders were selected to address the audience. This decision—some suggested it was a direct effort to exclude Powell—meant that there was now a duly recognized civil rights leadership that did not include Adam Powell. There was now a "Big Six" among that leadership, King being the most prominent. (The others were Roy Wilkins, NAACP; Whitney Young, the Urban League; James Farmer, CORE; Dorothy Height, National Council of Negro Women; and John Lewis, SNCC. A. Philip Randolph was then the revered dean of the movement and was not expected to play a day-to-day leadership role.) King's "I Have a Dream" speech that closed out the day-long rally was now the new clarion call of the civil rights movement. The informal crown of "Mr. Civil Rights" had now passed to another dynamic preacher, younger than Powell by twenty years, who was prepared to assume that role. But it was also clear that King and many others would recognize that after that point, it would be impossible for any *one* person to lay exclusive claim to *the* top leadership role. The struggle was proliferating. New groups, especially in the North, were beginning to flex their muscles. Mass, direct action was capturing the attention of editors, reporters, and news cameras, vying for print space and air time. The United States Commission on Civil Rights was gathering facts, monitoring changes, and issuing reports with quite liberal policy recommendations. On the black nationalist front in 1963–64, it would be difficult to challenge the Muslim minister, Malcolm X, as the leading spokesman. Thus, while Powell might adopt some of their current sentiments, he knew he could hardly preempt the leadership of the Muslims—and he likely would not have wanted to in any case, given the substantive nature of the positions they were taking. In April he had told the WNEW Radio interviewer that he and King were "getting ready to organize a national organization next month—that might be the end of the NAACP—did you know that?" This group would be called "the National Christian Leadership Action Conference." This was not true, of course. But Powell was casting about for a viable, visible role for himself. During this period, he invited Malcolm X to speak at Abyssinian Baptist Church as part of a series of weekly sessions on "the Black Revolution."

Through it all, he knew he had one important base—in Congress. He would continue to function there as the chairman of an exceedingly important committee. His friends knew he was capable of doing an excellent job in that role for the cause of civil rights and social justice. What they did not know was whether that role—with much of it involving less glamorous, tedious work—would satisfy his ego and varied interests in a fast-changing political environment.

Certainly the most traumatic specific change was the assassination of President Kennedy on November 22, 1963. A shocked, saddened nation was numbed by this tragic event, but it also provided the occasion for a concerted attempt to achieve some of the liberal goals envisioned by the fallen young President. That challenge devolved on now President Lyndon B. Johnson, who knew the American political system as well as anyone, and who understood the political necessity to seize the moment.

17

The Great Society, "Mr. Chairman," and President Johnson

The new leadership in the White House would soon—very soon, within two weeks of taking office—find out just how sensitive Adam Powell also was to the political nuances in town and to his insistence that he be accorded proper recognition in his chairmanship. Early in December, 1963, the House and Senate reached an agreement on $1.2 billion in aid to higher education. The two chambers also agreed on vocational education grants. Johnson was elated to sign the higher-education bill, and he issued a statement, reported in a lead article in the *New York Times*, complimenting the legislators, specifically singling out Senator Wayne Morse and Congresswoman Edith Green. The latter, of course, served on Powell's committee. The President's statement read: "The Senate is to be commended on its passage today of the conference report on higher education. This Congress is well on its way to doing more for education than any since the Land-Grant College Act that was passed 100 years ago. Members of the House and Senate Education Committees, Republicans and Democrats alike, are to be congratulated on this major step forward. I extend my special congratulations to Senator Morse and Congressman [*sic*] Green, who have a long record of interest and leadership in this field."[1] The news story proceeded to name Morse and Green as "the chief sponsors and managers of the college-aid bill." But it also discussed aid to vocational education, and the account made it seem that Green was instrumental there also.

This interpretation and public understanding of what happened did not please Powell in the least. He had not yet reached the point of resentment of Green (which became mutual) that developed later, but neither was he prepared to let it appear that she was the one on his committee mainly responsible for the legislative achievements. Powell shot off an indignant telegram to the new President:

> Shocked to read your statement concerning the Education Bill in the N.Y. Times. I trust that they misquoted you. At no time was Mrs. Green the manager for the House. I was the manager and according to Senator Morse, I played the major role in getting agreement.
>
> Also the author of the bill and ranking subcommittee chairman, Mr. Perkins of Kentucky, was not mentioned.
>
> Mrs. Green does have a fine history in the field of education but it so happens that vocational education was not under her subcommittee nor was she the author.
>
> May I suggest that this be changed by another statement since not only I but many members of the Committee on Education and Labor, are deeply perturbed by this quotation in the press.[2]

Of course, no subsequent clarifying statement was issued, but the White House and other political players in Washington were on notice that Powell would brook no slights, especially regarding his committee. This was a constant concern with him. Being "Mr. Chairman" was too important to him and his constituents—he spoke effusively of his role wherever he went around the country, in small black church pulpits or in mass rallies. He could not afford the image that could, he well knew, be fostered by persistent press reports of him as a titular leader, one who was not really in command of his committee. He was prepared to share some of the limelight, but never to give it up completely. Therefore, he read the media reports concerning his committee's work with a careful eye. Those reports had to coincide with his repeated public pronouncements of his central role. He was keenly aware of the cynicism among some blacks in any case about the political system, and it was important for him to be a living refutation of those negative feelings.

In this regard, it was especially important that his committee and he as chairman be accorded a crucial role in the impending antipoverty legislation that was being prepared in the Johnson administration. At that early stage, it was not at all clear how the proposed bill to deal with poverty would be handled in Congress. Thus he sought a January 1964 meeting with President Johnson. Lawrence O'Brien informed the President that Powell wanted to talk about three things: (1) the President's priority list on major bills in his committee; (2) how the President wanted him to handle the Juvenile Delinquency bill in relation to the Poverty bill; and (3) the 1964 campaign—"what to do now in order to avoid snags later." O'Brien bluntly advised the President: "Powell likely will presume that the Poverty bill will go to his committee. This fact certainly is not settled."[3] Granted, the Education and Labor Committee would seem to be the natural choice, "but the standing of Powell and of the Committee generally would not be a plus for the bill on the floor of the House." Powell had created a furor a year before over his highly publicized personal junket overseas in the company of two women staffers. This had caused scrutiny of his use of government funds. He had become the target of widespread national newspaper criticism as well as sharp attacks from some of his colleagues in Congress. He had flaunted the matter then, angering some of his colleagues who resented his arrogance and what they perceived as his total lack of contrition. (This episode is discussed in the next chapter.) It certainly would not be good if some members opposed the antipoverty bill simply in retaliation against Powell. Therefore, O'Brien urged President Johnson to be cautious and noncommittal with Powell if his committee's role came up, advising:

> At any rate, for your immediate purposes, I strongly advise that you not say anything concerning jurisdiction which Powell could interpret as a commitment or stretch into a quote for the press. And, of course, it would be highly unfortunate if he got wind of the fact we are considering the select committee approach.[4]

Indeed it would. The Democratic leadership was clearly aware that Powell had to be treated gingerly. To smooth the way for convincing him that no embarrassing slight was intended or in the offing, notwithstanding how the antipoverty bill was assigned, Speaker John W. McCormack went on record praising Powell and his committee. With the previous December episode in mind, and mindful of the delicate committee jurisdictional decisions over pending antipoverty legislation yet to be made, McCormack decided to send Powell a "Dear Adam" letter in late January, 1964:

> I am very proud of the outstanding record that you have made as Chairman. . . . If it were not for the fact that you were Chairman . . . we would never have had the Minimum Wage Bill [and] . . . the

> Vocational Education Act. These two measures came out of your Committee and passed through Congress under your brilliant and courageous leadership. . . . I am always happy when there is a Bill on the Floor of the House that has come out of your Committee because I know that, under your leadership, its chances of passage are excellent, even when it receives the "blind opposition" of the opposite Party.[5]

That, for the moment, should help soothe the feelings of the highly sensitive chairman, in case a decision was made not to assign the antipoverty bill to his committee. At least he could show his public and constituents such fulsome compliments.

And the White House deliberations went forward. While virtually all authoritative accounts of the initial formulation of the antipoverty bill indicate that the substantive issues were drafted in the Executive Branch,[6] there was still the necessity to get the bill through Congress. Should there be a special select committee in Congress to handle this omnibus proposal? If it were assigned to the Education and Labor Committee, would there be a way to deal with Powell? Normally, these kinds of matters are determined by the Speaker and the congressional leadership, but it was clear that this was President Johnson's show. And the Democratic leaders in Congress, especially McCormack, were willing to let the White House pretty much call the shots. The various sections of the bill conceivably could fall within the jurisdiction of several House committees: job training and employment to Education and Labor; public health to Interstate and Foreign Commerce; public assistance and welfare services to Ways and Means; urban renewal and community facilities to Banking and Currency; local community action to Government Operations. A special joint committee or even a special select committee could be set up, but these presented problems. They were usually used when protracted study and deliberations were called for. And the administration wanted none of that. Time was of the essence. The thinking and drafting were already being done in the Executive Branch. Assistant Budget Director Charles L. Schultze sent a detailed memo to the White House outlining the various legislative options. On balance, he concluded: "The major portion of funds . . . will be devoted to programs falling in the Education and Labor Committee's bailiwick. If the bill is to go to a single standing committee, it would almost have to go to Education and Labor."[7] In addition, "we may get more committee chairmen in our hair if we go the select committee route than if we go the Education and Labor route." Neither was it wise to contemplate splitting up the bill, inasmuch as "central coordination" of the antipoverty efforts was the desired goal. Thus this called for one omnibus bill going to one congressional committee.

These arguments were persuasive enough to convince the White House that Powell's committee should handle the proposals in the House. Henry Wilson so advised Lawrence O'Brien: "I'm about to come to the conclusion that the difficulties inherent in setting up a select committee are so broad that it would be wiser and possibly as helpful to arrange instead for a special subcommittee with Education and Labor chaired by Landrum."[8] This was fine so far, but Phil Landrum of Georgia was not Adam Clayton Powell, Mr. Chairman. And Powell would have to agree. In addition, Landrum had incurred the wrath of organized labor a few years before with his cosponsorship of the antiunion Landrum-Griffin bill. George Meany of the AFL-CIO would have to be pacified.

Landrum was the White House choice to head the subcommittee because it was perceived that he could bring along much needed Southern congressional votes. Landrum was also shrewd enough to know that his chairman, Powell, would have to agree to this assignment. Wilson was straightforward in his memo to O'Brien:

> . . . I took it upon myself to ask Landrum if he would take the chairmanship of a special subcommittee on Poverty if we asked it.
>
> He responded very enthusiastically that he would. He said the only thing that needs be done would be to get Powell's concurrence, and that he anticipated no trouble with that. He said his relations with Powell these days are excellent and that within the last week or two Powell has urged him again to accept a subcommittee chairmanship.
>
> However, he feels that we rather than he, will have to approach Powell first on the subject.

Indeed, Powell, for his own personal reasons, would have to be asked directly by the White House. If he was to give up such a major role, he wanted to be owed by the President, not a member of his committee. The arrangement was agreed to. When the bill was sent up to Capitol Hill and assigned to Powell's committee, the chairman opened hearings on it on March 17, 1964, and subsequently turned the management of the bill over to Landrum. Powell fully understood the politics of all this, and he also knew that the Johnson administration would be grateful for his cooperation. In this way, he could build credits with the new administration and still maintain face. After all, the Landrum group was a subcommittee, and Powell was still the duly recognized chairman of the full committee that would have to report out the bill to the floor of the House.

That was the scenario, and it worked. Powell could and did afterwards assert that the antipoverty bill was a product of *his* committee, and, indeed, largely *his* work. In a television interview during the opening week of subcommittee hearings, Powell confidently told the interviewer that he was sure the bill would get through the House. His strategy ensured that. He stated:

> . . . The way I have outlined my strategy, it will [pass the House]. I have given the authorship of the bill to the gentleman from Georgia, Mr. Landrum, and am moving the hearings right along. I will conclude them the last week of April. I will write the bill up the week of April 26th and send it over to the Rules Committee May 1st, and I think we will have it on the Floor May 15th for passage.[9]

In the course of the interview, Powell had some complimentary things to say about President Johnson. ("I think that under our present President Johnson we will continue [to cross new frontiers begun by President Kennedy]," and "he's got everything that Jack Kennedy had in terms of vision and legislation. Then, he's the greatest living pro in the field of politics.") These were kind remarks and the White House was appreciative. In preparation for a meeting several days later that Powell was to have with Johnson, the President's staff sent a copy of the television transcript to the President with a note: "Thank him for comments on TV show."[10] In the world of Washington politics, little things meant a lot.

After the March on Washington on August 28, 1963, and other dynamic developments on the civil rights front, it was clear that Adam Powell would not be, as he had been for over a decade, the main spokesman in the country on civil rights. His was still an important voice, but not at all the preemptive authority. Events were simply moving too fast; new leaders and organizations had moved on stage and to the front. Also his role as chairman of the Education and Labor Committee required his attention to specific legislation coming before that body. Nonetheless, he continued his monitoring of developments from his congressional seat, especially as they related to issues over which his committee had some authority. He knew it was necessary and possible to conduct his own "legislative oversight" functions. There would still be a role to play in seeing that policies were carried out in a nondiscriminatory manner. In early December, 1963, he sent a letter to the Secretary of HEW, Anthony J. Celebrezze, complaining about fellowship awards to colleges. Such a matter surely fell within his committee's domain. He wrote:

> Upon examination of the November 15 announcement regarding the awarding of National Defense Educational Act Title IV graduate fellowships, I was disturbed to find that, out of 694 fellowships approved for programs at 156 colleges and universities for 1964–65 academic year, only one Negro institution (Howard University) was included, and only for six graduate fellowships.
>
> This is inexcusable when there are 127 Negro colleges, nearly 20 of which offer graduate education. I should like an explanation regarding this matter.
>
> Simultaneously, would you also provide a breakdown in the 1,500 graduate fellowships which will be available during the Spring of 1964.
>
> Thank you for giving this matter your immediate attention.[11]

He knew he could get action when others outside government could not. A letter from the chairman, before whom agencies would have to come for future appropriations, could hardly be ignored. This was not an insignificant role.

He also knew that his inquiries into administrative hiring and promotion practices in the civil service and, for example, the Peace Corps, as well as other top policy-making positions would require attention and response.[12] And he did not let up. Very often detailed explanations followed, offering clarifications, numbers, promises to do better, and always recognizing the authority and influence of the chairman. He spoke to the President personally about his concerns, and followed up with a detailed listing of Negro appointees. On December 18, 1964, he sent Johnson a memorandum, "Lack of Status of Negroes in Top Jobs in Poverty Corps, Peace Corps, HEW, HHFA, as Ambassadors and in Federal Regulatory Agencies." An attached letter complained that there were "fewer Negro ambassadors today than during the Kennedy Administration"; "Only one Negro as one of the 95 Commissioners and members of 17 Federal regulatory agencies"; "The absence of Negroes in policy-making positions in the Poverty Corps in Washington in contrast to local and state programs"; "The failure of Negroes to advance significantly in higher positions in both HEW and HHFA, particularly the latter." His attached memo specified that "in the top 151 positions in the Department of Health, Education, and Welfare, there are no Negroes." Out of ninety-five members or commissioners of federal regulatory agencies (for example, the Interstate Commerce Commission, Civil Service Commission, Federal Reserve System) in seventeen agencies, there was only one Negro—that one being on the five-member National Labor Relations Board. And "While there have been several white women ambassadors, there has never been a Negro woman ambassador." He pointed out that although six Negroes headed *local* poverty programs around the country, of the seven top divisions and key jobs *in Washington*, "None of the seven are headed by a Negro."[13]

The White House did not take such Powell prodding lightly. Lawrence O'Brien gathered all the correspondence from the congressman and sent it over to John Macy, chairman of the U.S. Civil Service Commission. His attached memo to Macy was clear and candid:

> You will find the attached self-explanatory. As you know, Powell is key to many of the most important measures on the President's program. Also you probably know he is not above withholding action on bills if the information he seeks is not made available to him. I believe he should get some kind of response on his request. I will leave to your good judgment as to where the response comes from. Possibly the information could be furnished verbally by someone you deem appropriate.[14]

Then followed a scenario like the one Powell had been engaged in early in the Eisenhower administration—polite, respectful responses from the Executive Branch, followed by more prodding from the congressman and his staff, followed by still more promises to "do better." It was a very familiar script with Powell. Except now in the mid-1960s, there, in fact, were more positive changes taking place. And, indeed, as the changes occurred, Powell kept the pressure on, always probing for more and better results in various agencies and categories of employment. For example, John Macy answered Powell's letters and memo to Johnson with the following to Powell:

> . . . As you know, the President has asked several members of his White House Staff to investigate and to analyze the minority employment situation in the various Federal agencies. While we feel that, as based on the results of our inquiries, we might have determined that a more

> favorable pattern exists than you suggest, we do not feel that there is anything to be gained by a comparison of statistics. . . .
>
> This Administration is dedicated to removing all traces of discrimination. . . . The past injustices are rapidly disappearing. We are aware, of course, that much remains to be done in this vital area. Your constructive criticisms have assisted us in reviewing the effectiveness of our program. We want you to know that serious consideration will be given your suggestions and proposals.[15]

By now, the former editor of the *Washington Afro-American*, C. Sumner Stone, had joined Powell's staff as special assistant to the chairman. "Chuck" Stone took up the duties of pursuing many of these crucial "oversight" roles. Acting with Powell's authority, Stone patiently but persistently pursued the point with Macy. It was Stone who had prepared the statistics relating to employment, and he responded to Macy "to clarify with hopefully greater precision the exact nature of the chairman's criticism, i.e. that Negroes in the higher echelons or better jobs in government are not making significant progress."[16] He then noted:

> That there has been solid progress in the middle and lower grades, there can be no denial. But virtually no activity has occurred in the sub-cabinet, Federal regulatory and ambassadorial positions. . . .
>
> In the grades, GS 12–15, naturally there has been a greater increase of Negroes. But a refinement of that group breakdown to GS 16–18 reveals a barely perceptible change in numbers. . . .
>
> Progress is an inevitable byproduct of human existence and I think we have made progress in Negro employment, but I doubt if any Negro in America would concur with your statement that "the past injustices are rapidly disappearing."

And the administration knew that while Stone was writing over his own signature, he was representing the thinking and intentions of the chairman. Thus this congressional aide could not be dismissed or ignored. In a few months, high-level appointments were made—Patricia Roberts Harris as the first Negro woman ambassador (to Luxembourg); Aileen Hernandez to the Equal Employment Opportunity Commission, created in 1964. A short time afterwards, there would be several more appointments: ambassadorships; a seat on the Federal Reserve Board; Robert Weaver to the cabinet as HUD Secretary; and several high-level posts in other agencies.

These developments were perhaps not as dramatic and visible as the important March on Selma in February–March 1965, which led to the Voting Rights Act of 1965. Nor were they as significant as growing tensions and issues raised by the various mass protests in local areas around the country calling attention to serious social and economic problems in the urban ghettos—Watts in Los Angeles would explode in rage in August 1965. But this persistent pressure Powell and his staff were exerting was something only he could do. When he had been in the streets earlier in his career, leading protest demonstrations, there was no comparable force on the "inside" in Congress. And in this new work, he very likely was achieving—given the nature of the system and the issues—about as much as one so inclined to act could achieve.

This kind of action did not capture headlines, but those who knew of his efforts did not minimize its importance. Powell was astute enough to realize that the highly dramatic and publicity-reliant nature of the burgeoning civil rights struggle would lead the media to the more visible, mass-action leaders. This was a fact he would have to accept. To be sure, he could still call a press conference and get an audience. But he was hardly the first source for reporters to call when a major event—a demonstration, a shooting in the South, announcements of further protests—occurred.

A group of young activists in the South, the Student Nonviolent Coordinating Committee, was bringing college students south to work in Mississippi on civil rights in the summer of 1964. This was an action story the media wanted to know about. Powell could not help them. Black and white civil rights forces formed the Mississippi Freedom Democratic Party and challenged the all-white state Mississippi delegation to the Democratic national convention in Atlantic City, New Jersey. This was a front-line, front-page story. Powell was not a primary source for information on that dynamic development. There were other leaders now engaged in work in various parts of the country who were sharing the civil rights leadership spotlight.

In many ways this unfolding reality was an inevitable consequence of a social movement that had grown enormously and was broadening its base of participation. It was not so much that Powell was becoming less relevant or losing his stature or growing out of touch. Rather, the struggle was taking on vastly new dimensions, and there would be much more division of labor and sharing of leadership roles.

This was not to suggest that Powell, beyond prodding the administration from the inside, ceased an interest in national civil rights events. Quite the contrary. In early March, 1964, he wrote a letter to President Johnson suggesting that the President consider establishing a bipartisan, interracial, crisis-preventing, fact-finding committee to deal with potentially explosive civil rights issues.[17] "When it is anticipated that a given area will become the center of tension and where the problems involved have National significance," he wrote, "I believe an interracial, bipartisan fact-finding committee composed of citizens with unblemished reputations sent into the area by the President to ascertain the facts, would have a very favorable effect on public sentiment and could act to bring all sides together." A report from such a group, he felt, issued by the President would carry great weight and make it "extremely difficult for an irresponsible group to operate effectively." Such a process "could be a successful deterrent to further hostilities and possible violence." He told the President that he did not believe the current Civil Rights Commission was composed to function on such an immediate, crisis-prevention basis. That body was useful for longer-term studies leading toward future policy and legislative action.

The White House circulated his letter for comment from appropriate administration sources. Assistant Attorney General Burke Marshall was not sanguine that such a fact-finding body as Powell proposed

> could anticipate potential trouble areas sufficiently in advance of an outbreak of hostilities, immediately go into that area, make investigations, sift fact from rumor in a tense and complicated atmosphere such as surrounds such disturbances, and come up with a solution that would prevent or avoid hostilities.[18]

But more important, in Marshall's view, there was a provision—Title 10—in the pending civil rights bill in Congress that would establish the Community Relations Service, which would be able to come close to doing what Powell had in mind. Why not wait and see how this developed? And this was the position the White House took, informing Powell that the upcoming civil rights bill was being looked to as a major vehicle for achieving many of the goals he sought.

The Civil Rights Act of 1964 was signed by President Johnson on July 2, 1964, a vast improvement over the 1957 and 1960 laws. It did, indeed, set up the Community Relations Service, as well as the Equal Employment Opportunity Commission. Title 6 of the new law contained the culmination of years of struggle to adopt the "Powell Amendment." The provision authorized federal agencies to terminate financial support to any agencies that practiced racial segregation or discrimination. Thus, after fifteen years of struggle, Powell and his closest allies in that struggle over the years—Clarence Mitchell of the

NAACP and Joseph Rauh of the ADA and Leadership Conference on Civil Rights—had won. It was a clear victory.

Ironically, while it likely was, as Roger Wilkins said years later,[19] Powell's greatest legacy, he was not a major participant in the year-long, day-to-day struggle preceding passage of the bill. Powell's contribution, especially to Title 6, would be missed, however, if one did not understand the decade-plus battle that he had led in the Congress throughout the 1950s. During the 1963–64 congressional debates, the main lobbyists were organized by the Leadership Conference on Civil Rights, led by Mitchell and Rauh.[20] Joe Rauh recalled that Powell was not a part of the central core of the lobbying efforts. He certainly supported the bill, and even suggested that when the equal-employment provision seemed to hit a snag it should be brought to the floor under the congressional procedural rule known as "Calendar Wednesday." This meant that the provision would have to be dealt with and voted up or down on that day. The Leadership Conference did not back this tactic, and Powell did not push it. Rauh stated later that other congressional offices, especially those of Congressman Frank Thompson of New Jersey, were used as command posts, not Powell's, during the last hectic weeks and days of the legislative struggle.[21]

After years of a most prominent, visible position in the forefront of the national civil rights struggle, it was perhaps a bit strange to some not to see him intimately involved at this mid-1960s historic stage. But such was the nature of the developments of that important social movement. In addition, Powell was increasingly attracting headlines for his personal foibles—extravagant European junkets, a New York libel suit against him—that tended to leave an image that made some of the other civil rights leaders uncomfortable. The civil rights movement had always relied heavily on moral arguments to state its cause, and Powell's personal life-style left something to be desired. He was by no means persona non grata with the civil rights leadership, but neither were his name and cooperation considered absolutely essential for the success of a particular campaign.

Powell knew this, although no one would state it so candidly. He also knew that he was still a congressional chairman, and, as such, could command recognition. Indeed, he continued to function with deft political skills from time to time in that role, although such activity was not nearly as public or visible as the dramatic civil rights protests. In a sense, Powell had to accept the inevitable consequences that his entrenched congressional role would not be so dynamically visible, even as he performed otherwise very important political tasks. Many politicians who seek power could easily accept this. But Powell wanted both power and publicity, and it was becoming increasingly difficult to have these simultaneously. Most of the publicity—of a front-page variety—he was getting was not the kind that particularly contributed to enhancing his power. And the effective congressional power-wielding he was pursuing did not necessarily lead to the positive headline publicity he coveted. A good example was his role in extending the National Defense Education Act in 1964.

The NDEA was passed in 1958 in response to the Soviet Sputnik launched in 1957. This scientific feat signaled Russia's clear achievements in higher education, and was the catalyst for Americans to give serious attention to the quality of their own educational systems, especially in science, mathematics, and foreign languages. The feeling quickly spread that "the Russians were ahead of us." The 1958 NDEA provided grants and loans, college fellowships for Ph.D. study, and hundreds of thousands of high school, undergraduate, and graduate students benefited. About 15,000 elementary and secondary school language teachers attended language institutes. Instruction in science, mathematics, and modern languages was strengthened. In 1964 the NDEA was up for renewal, and President Johnson and the Democrats wanted to broaden its coverage to include civics, English, geography, and history.

Senator Wayne Morse handled hearings in the Senate. Congresswoman Edith Green, chairman of a subcommittee in Powell's full committee, had charge of hearings in the House. But Green was prepared to be more cooperative with the Republicans who were not intent on expanding the program. She accepted virtually all the Republican proposals that would limit the bill. This infuriated her Democratic colleagues, who now knew that Chairman Powell would have to come to the rescue if this important measure was to receive any substantial boost.[22] The draft bill Green had agreed to was miles apart from what Morse's Senate colleagues had reported. A conference committee between the House and Senate was necessary to iron out the differences. Powell and Speaker McCormack quickly developed a strategy to counter the Republicans and Green. Powell, feeling that Democrat Green might well vote with the Republicans, arranged the House conferees so there would be eight Democrats and five Republicans. If he had followed the normal route and appointed seven Democrats and five Republicans, and if Green voted with the Republicans, thus creating a 6–

6 tie, there could be no action on NDEA. This was an important move, because, indeed, when the provision came up to add the other subjects, Green voted with the Republicans, but Powell's vote, as chairman, broke the tie. He had saved the day, and the NDEA was significantly expanded. It is generally recognized as a major piece of Great Society legislation.

Equally as important, politically, was President Johnson's public acknowledgment of Powell's role when he signed the bill at a formal White House ceremony. Initially, the legislation had been referred to as the "Green-Morse" bill. Johnson was not to repeat his earlier gaffe. This time he heaped praise on the Congress and referred to the measure as the "Powell-Morse" bill, quietly but obviously indicating his appreciation for the role Powell had played in saving the education bill and making it much better. This was Johnson's not-so-subtle way, one observer concluded, of making it clear that he appreciated the work of those two legislators "with the remarkable accomplishments in the field of education."[23]

Senator Morse, likewise, was grateful to Powell for the way he handled the episode. Of course, congressmen frequently sent each other little notes of praise and admiration, but Morse's "Dear Adam" letter to Powell shortly after the NDEA skirmish was more than a mere pro forma salute:

> Although I know you know how much I appreciate your wonderful leadership in handling the NDEA bill through conference, nevertheless I want to put it down in print. In all my 20 years in the Senate I have never seen a chairman of a conference committee do as effective a job as you did in handling the NDEA bill through conference. I am well aware of the problems that existed for you among the House conferees and the way you handled the problems made me only that much more an admirer of your generalship.[24]

This was Powell at his political best, maneuvering on his committee, supporting liberal legislation, putting together coalitions, marshaling and counting votes, and serving as a loyal party man and White House supporter. It was not front-page civil rights material, but very important in its own way. This was the Powell his staunch defenders would portray a few years later when his career was waning and he was in trouble. This was the master politician, the "Mr. Chairman" they wanted people to remember and respect.

President Johnson, in 1964, was also enjoying more than a modicum of success. He won 88 percent of the roll call votes on his bills then—131 out of 149. Powell was one of his main supporters. The *Congressional Quarterly* reported him at that time as supporting Johnson 50 percent of the time. But this figure, relatively low, reflected Powell's frequent failure to vote on House roll call votes. He was often out of town or simply did not go to the chamber to answer the roll call—an old habit he had not given up. If Powell had been present most of the time, his recorded vote support would have been much higher. He was recorded in opposition to Johnson 4 percent of the time.[25] Powell's floor absentee record continued to plague him. On 113 roll calls in 1964, his percentage voting participation was 49; on 232 roll calls in 1963 *and* 1964, his percentage was 55. Again, he was not the lowest in the New York delegation (Congressman Charles A. Buckley from the Bronx was 24 and 28, respectively), but Powell *was* an important committee chairman. And his supporters wished, ever so much, that somehow he could match his political skills and issue support with an improved attendance record. But that simply was not—never had been—Powell's way of doing his congressional business. This could be explained to and accepted by those who were his staunch supporters. But it *was* a perennial point of vulnerability, and it would not help him when he needed added support to save his political life a short time later.

The year 1964 was not a time for Powell to play his Presidential-preference guessing game with the media and public. As early as March in the television interview where he praised Johnson, he also unhesitatingly predicted that in the November Presidential election "he [Johnson] will sweep the country." And Powell promised to campaign for him, adding, "it is much more important for a white man from Texas to demand a civil rights bill than for a Negro congressman from Harlem. It makes him of greater importance."

Indeed, Lyndon B. Johnson did sweep to victory, winning the greatest popular vote plurality in the country's history. He surpassed Franklin D. Roosevelt's plurality of 11,072,014 over Alfred Landon in 1936, by gaining 15,949,707 more votes than his opponent, Republican Senator Barry Goldwater of Arizona. He won 486 electoral votes to Goldwater's fifty-two, carrying all but six states.[26]

What was equally impressive was that President Johnson outpolled Powell—who easily won reelection to his eleventh term—in the congressman's own Harlem. Johnson was endorsed by both the Democratic and Liberal parties, and Powell by only the Democrats. But looking only at the Democratic line, and checking those assembly districts (A.D.s) that wholly encompassed Powell's Eighteenth Congressional District—five in all—Powell ran behind Johnson in each district. In a couple of districts, the margins were quite impressive:

11th A.D.—Johnson, 24,934; Powell, 21,016
12th A.D.—Johnson, 43,275; Powell, 26,401
13th A.D.—Johnson, 28,179; Powell, 6,556
14th A.D.—Johnson, 20,344; Powell, 17,722
16th A.D.—Johnson, 16,332; Powell, 14,293

Some analysts attempted to explain these figures by suggesting that the vote for the Presidency at the top of the ticket always exceeds that for those positions less salient, the usual "trail-off" vote. Another explanation suggested that Harlem voters were certain that Powell would win, but definitely wanted to make sure they voted against Goldwater, who was widely perceived as anti–civil rights, and for Johnson, the political heir to the Kennedy legacy.

Others were less sure of these explanations. They saw in these figures a lingering discontent with Powell. To be sure, the congressman was virtually unbeatable in a general election; his total vote was 93,681 to his Republican opponent's 11,656—84 percent to 10 percent. But in an off-year (1962) election, Powell got 59,125 (70 percent) to his Republican opponent's 18,313 (22 percent), and the Liberal candidate's 7,457 (8 percent). He had no serious opposition in the primary election, which made him a shoo-in in a heavily Democratic congressional district. But perhaps there *was* a soft spot there. Perhaps a strong primary challenge at a propitious moment by an exceptionally appealing candidate *could* pierce the wall of seeming Powell invincibility. Seventy percent of the primary vote in 1962 surely was substantial. But it was not absolutely impenetrable—under the right circumstances. All politicians knew this. And in 1964, even with the "trail-off" factor, this argument suggested, Powell should not have trailed Johnson *in his own home base* by 47,076 votes!

But for the moment—1964—things were fine. Powell would have preferred to match or exceed the top of the ticket. All congressional candidates would want this. Although the margin of difference between him and Johnson in Harlem might have been privately embarrassing, he could live with it. And he was quite comfortable enough. While there might have been lusting eyes cast in his direction for his seat, no one seriously suspected that he was in trouble.

He was confident enough, in fact, that he prepared to return to Washington and see what could be done about reestablishing himself as the preeminent "civil rights" leader on the political scene. In this he knew that his major challengers were the often-referred-to "Big Six" of the major civil rights organizations. These leaders were prominent and effective, but they were not party politicians in the partisan, organization sense of the term. What the Democratic Party should do was to recruit more blacks into the party ranks at the state and local levels, to serve on party committees and run for office. What was needed, Powell felt, was more traditional *party* workers who understood grass-roots voter mobilization and party management. Apparently, Powell had discussions with Hobart Taylor, Jr., associate counsel to the President, on the matter. A few weeks after the election, Taylor sent a memo to President Johnson outlining his and Powell's thinking. Johnson had had several meetings with civil rights leaders, especially during the legislative struggle over the civil rights bill, and it was clear that Johnson felt close to "Big Six" member Whitney Young, Jr., of the National Urban League, as well as to Clarence Mitchell. He sought their counsel, especially Young's, constantly. In his memo, Taylor recognized that such meetings were "helpful,"

> but as Adam Powell has recently warned, they are no substitute in the long run for the development of effective political leadership in the traditional sense. . . . If the Republican Party moves toward the center, as most observers now predict, the political struggle for minority votes will become more organizational and less ideological and the usefulness of civil rights leaders will decline in a corresponding degree. . . . I think that we would do well to . . . urge that there be more appointments to state Democratic committees and that more persons be selected to hold offices in the local Democratic hierarchy. . . . You may wish to de-emphasize to some extent the closeness of your coordination with the so-called Big Six civil rights leaders because this tends to downgrade regular political leadership.[27]

Such an analysis certainly had elements of legitimacy although it probably overstated the competing roles of the two types of leadership. The rise in black electoral political leaders would come—especially after the passage of the Voting Rights Act of 1965—in a few years, but even that phenomenon owed a great deal to the civil rights protests in the Selma, Alabama, demonstrations in the spring of 1965. Powell and Taylor surely must have known of the interconnection between protest and subsequent political gains. This had, in fact, been a hallmark of Powell's earlier career. But at the moment, there were more immediate political concerns, such as access to and influence with the White House. Their particular interests might have been to undercut the civil rights leaders, but this could hardly be a trade-off for the President. Johnson could have both—a continuing relationship with friendly civil rights leaders *and* a buildup of the state and local parties with increased participation of black (and these *would* be mostly Democratic) voters, especially in the South. Powell's leadership challenge came from the national civil rights leaders. A savvy President Johnson well knew that he did not have a dog in that fight.

In addition, Johnson was well aware that Powell was not always on the best of terms with the very local black party leaders he and Taylor urged him to woo. In his own Harlem, in 1964, Powell was feuding again with the powerful J. Raymond Jones who would soon be chosen to head Tammany Hall. The Powell-Jones relationship had been one of the most volatile in local politics dating back to their short-lived alliance in the 1958 defeat of Tammany Hall and Carmine De Sapio. How could Johnson steer a consensual course in that quagmire? His wisest bet was to stay out of it. He had already been alerted by Powell that there was no love lost between the congressman and the astute local practitioner of Harlem and New York politics. In early 1964 Larry O'Brien received a memo from a White House aide, Chuck Daly:

> Powell understands that during a visit Saturday, Ray Jones told the President he was getting along well with Powell in New York.
>
> Powell says: "Please tell the President there has been no marriage with that guy and me, and there never will be."[28]

Without question, Johnson would not touch this one, any more than he would favor the party politicians over the civil rights leaders. As far as Johnson was concerned, these various leaders in their respective roles could be courted by the White House on their own distinctive terms and merits.

By all accounts the Eighty-ninth Congress of 1965 was one of the most productive in modern times. "In the course of the year," the *Congressional Quarterly Almanac* reported, "Congress approved major programs which had long been on the agenda of the Democratic party."[29] Three factors were mainly responsible:

> The decisive Democratic majorities elected in 1964, the personal leadership of President Johnson, and the shaping of legislation to obtain maximum political support in Congress. On a number of occasions (most notably in connection with the Elementary and Secondary Education Act) the word was passed to approve the bill and worry about perfecting details later.[30]

Of course, some Republicans labeled the swift, cooperative legislative action as a "rubber-stamp" Congress. But this hardly fazed the Democrats. More than a few Congress-watchers compared the legislative output with the early years of Franklin Roosevelt's New Deal. Especially commendable were laws on medical care for the aged, voting rights, and elementary and secondary education. These were heady, hectic times, and Chairman Powell was in the middle of the political thicket—bargaining, negotiating, politicking. For the first time in his twenty years in Congress, the national political scene provided him and his liberal colleagues the opportunity to move forward on both civil rights and social programs—both agendas he had championed throughout his combative political career. Finally, there were major breakthroughs. And even in the midst of all this activity, Powell miffed a few of his allies, including President Johnson, by his personal political tactics.

Powell's committee was the key to quick action on the elementary-secondary education bill. Everyone—in Congress and at the White House—knew this. But they also knew that there was strong sentiment in the House of Representatives to curtail the budget of Powell's committee. Thanks to his widely publicized spending habits, Powell was the target of some who wanted to decrease his appropriations. This angered the chairman, and he fought back: no full committee allocation of funds, no quick committee action on pending education legislation.

President Johnson noted this temporary stalemate when he wrote in his memoirs:

> One unforeseen obstacle was Chairman Adam Clayton Powell. . . . Powell usually voted with the progressive forces in Congress, but he could be unpredictable. Because we hoped to get the bill through quickly, before lobbyists in the special groups could congeal the opposition Powell made a firm commitment to take it up in full committee. . . .
>
> Instead Powell held the bill hostage to force the funds he had requested for his staff expenses. . . . Because delay was dangerous to the education bill, the leadership now had to consider ways of

> freeing the committee from Powell's control, if that became necessary.[31]

But such action turned out to be unnecessary. Powell simply wanted Congress to play ball with him in return for his cooperation. White House assistant Jack Valenti sent a memo to the President: "Adam Clayton Powell called—asked to pass along his apologies to the President for delaying the full committee meeting, but he had to turn the screws on the House leadership to get his full appropriation. He has that now."[32]

Thus Powell returned to the fold and became once again a good member of the Democratic team. As such, he had to contend with Congresswoman Edith Green, who was now his nemesis on the committee. Green wanted further delays, and she proceeded to try to work a deal with the Republicans. A lengthy White House memo detailed her concerns and efforts.[33] Larry O'Brien reported: "She began agitations to stir up the religious issue which culminated Friday in her calling Protestant leaders into her office to tell them this bill will put Catholic priests in the public schools." She promised to support another bill if her wishes on still other matters were granted. Then she apparently reneged. All this angered Powell, who felt she was not being a cooperative committee member. He had to act, lest his own authority over his committee be undermined. The White House was kept fully informed and was prepared to support the chairman. Adviser Douglass Cater told President Johnson:

> Adam Clayton Powell is burning mad over Edith Green's behavior on the Education Bill. He has threatened three reprisals:
>
> 1. Remove vocational rehabilitation from her subcommittee jurisdiction.
>
> 2. Fire her sister from the Committee Staff.
>
> 3. Entrust John Brademas with sponsorship of the Higher Education Bill.
>
> Brademas is uncertain about no. 3, but is willing to undertake the job if it will serve the good of the bill.[34]

Johnson scribbled at the bottom of the memo "OK all 3."

Powell knew how the game was played, and he was prepared to reward his friends and punish his enemies. He also had a pretty good read on when he could expect support from the powerful White House.

Finally, on April 11, 1965, the President signed the major piece of education legislation in a one-room schoolhouse near Stonewall, Texas—where he had first started school. A short reminder memo was sent to him by Larry O'Brien: "In my judgment, I think it would be well if in your remarks at the 5:00 Education Ceremony this evening, mention was made by name of the contribution of Senator Wayne Morse and Congressman Carl Perkins to the enactment of the bill. Also Chairman Powell—(Lister Hill, too?)"[35] Johnson obliged, and at a reception on April 13, 1965, in honor of those who contributed to the legislative struggle, he stated: "I was never prouder than I am right now. I was never prouder of the Congress, of men like Carl Perkins, and Wayne Morse and Adam Clayton Powell, and Lister Hill who expedited the hearings in his Committee."

No mistaken mention of Mrs. Green this time, or oversight of Powell.

The following year, 1966, Powell continued his close attention to education issues, meeting with officials of the Department of Health, Education, and Welfare. HEW characterized the chairman as "cordial and cooperative." There would be four bills brought forward: international education, elementary and secondary education, higher education, and library construction. Powell outlined his plans to assign responsibilities to various subcommittees and discussed the political problems with various provisions as he saw them. "He anticipates trouble with big city Democrats over the repeal of incentive grants," an HEW memo of one strategy session reported.[36] "He believes NDEA loan conversion probably is a mistake at this time." "He thinks the impacted areas program should be phased out, but not in an election year." "He wants the land-grant college funds restored." Clearly, he was on top of the substantive business before his committee, giving political assessments, and detailing his own preferences. Powell also alerted the administration that he would introduce a bill on de facto school segregation and handle it in an ad hoc subcommittee chaired by himself.

One week after this session, Powell made his promised move against segregation in Northern public schools. He introduced a bill (H.R. 13079) and convened the Ad Hoc Subcommittee on De Facto School Segregation under his chairmanship. The committee would take testimony in several cities, including New York, Boston, Philadelphia, Detroit, Cleveland, St. Louis, Los Angeles, and San Francisco. Powell's bill was a forerunner of an issue that would plague Northern urban school systems over the next two decades. He was concerned that school desegregation, especially in the

North, was not proceeding with the "deliberate speed" the Supreme Court in 1954 envisioned. Of course, that court decision spoke directly to school systems that had previously legally segregated schools. In the North, the problem was one of *de facto* segregation, leaving a serious "racial imbalance" in many schools. Powell wanted Congress to legislate on this situation. At that point, only the federal courts were dealing with the problem in a slow, tedious, case-by-case manner.

Powell's proposed bill defined racial imbalance "as a condition that exists in any school if the percentage of non-white pupils in the school is over 20 percent greater or less than the percentage of non-white pupils in comparable schools in the same school district." For example, if 50 percent of a city's high school enrollment were "Negro,"[37] any high school in that city which had less than 30 percent or more than 70 percent Negroes in attendance would be racially imbalanced. Similarly, in a school system whose junior high population was 90 percent Negro, an all-white junior high would be imbalanced. In a school system in which 10 percent of the public elementary school children were Negro, an all-Negro elementary school as well as any elementary school which was more than 30 percent Negro would be labeled "imbalanced." Powell's bill indicated that "nonwhite" applied not only to Negroes but to "American Indians, Chinese, or any population viewed as 'non-white' under applicable state law."

What did he propose? He wanted $600 million to be made available over a three-year period as grants to local areas to initiate projects to eliminate the racial imbalance. This would be the "incentive" grants. Such projects could include the construction of "educational parks" or any such projects designed to attract a racially and economically diverse student body. This could also include "cooperative ventures" between contiguous urban and suburban school systems which would otherwise have homogeneous school populations, and the preparation of new forms of testing that would not separate out the "culturally deprived."

All this should be accomplished, he urged, by June 30, 1970. If a school system was not in compliance after that date, then no federal financial assistance in any form would go to that system—the Powell Amendment sanction again. When he introduced his bill, he released a press statement that harkened back to his old days on the civil rights stomp. "The time has come to thrust away the false slogans and the blinders of hypocrisy and see the public schools in many large northern urban centers as they really are."[38]

He was also critical of the Democratically controlled Executive agencies:

> We cannot wait for the Departments of Justice or Health, Education, and Welfare to develop any courageous consistency and make up their minds that Negro children in New York, Chicago, Los Angeles, Washington, D.C. and most northern cities are the innocent victims of a hand-me-down school system. In fact, had HEW attempted to enforce the Civil Rights Act regardless of "race, creed or *region*," we might have made some headway against northern de facto school segregation, in itself a social cancer as destructive of the human spirit and intellect as southern de jure segregation.[39]

This was the Powell his many admirers knew and supported. He was on the cutting edge of a racially explosive issue, challenging old practices, taking on his own party in the administration, introducing into Congress an issue that body likely would prefer to avoid, using the language of the American Dilemma.

The year was 1966, what was to be Powell's last effective year in Congress. After then, he would become embroiled in congressional and legal battles to save his seat, and his energies would be diverted to protecting his political life. Years after he left Congress, the courts would be entangled in a web of various plans and proposals dealing with the knotty issue of racial imbalance in the urban schools. He did not propose busing as one possible solution, but soon that remedy along with others would be splitting Northern communities apart in vehement debates, protests, boycotts, and generally heated disagreements, often violent, over what to do about segregated schools. Powell's bill did not get very far—clearly the administration and most of his liberal colleagues did not want to engage the matter. The White House proceeded to apply pressure on him to go along with a more moderate bill. Douglass Cater sent President Johnson a memo urging him to lean on Powell:

> Adam Clayton Powell has accepted the invitation to be present at the Teacher Corps signing at 11 o'clock today. Congressman Perkins is hopeful that you can apply a little pressure to Powell to help get the Elementary and Secondary Act out of committee. . . . Powell is going off to his Geneva Conference at the end of the month and we want to avoid a log jam-up on education legislation. . . . The subcommittee knocked out the incentive grants provision and Powell should keep it out. . . .
>
> You might warn Powell that you don't want any more expensive

amendments tied on to the bill in full committee. It has gone as far as you can stand.[40]

Powell understood the politics of all this activity, and he certainly wanted to be considered as still a cooperative, loyal team player. At the same time, he wanted to exact the maximum from the White House in return. If he was being asked to compromise, he wanted administration respect and support for his own particular political and personal needs. His committee was beginning, in 1966, to act against his wishes; he sensed he was losing their respect, and he needed White House backup. There had to be a quid pro quo. One internal administration memorandum in the heat of negotiations read:

> Chuck Stone called Thursday, July 7, appealing for strong White House support in promoting a quorum for Powell committee meeting on Monday, July 18, at 10 a.m. This is the day when the committee is expected to report out a clean bill for the Elementary and Secondary Education Act. But Mrs. Green is giving trouble.
>
> The Committee met recently without a quorum and ruled that there could be no amendments to the bill without unanimous committee support. Stone believes that Mrs. Green is unaware of this move to thwart her amendments—but he warns that if she learns about it before July 18, she may boycott the meeting, taking several Republicans and a couple of Democrats with her and making it impossible to report out a clean bill.
>
> At this point, Stone foresees only 14 Democrats attending the July 18 meeting—2 short of the 16 needed, he says. He urges that we pressure Sam Gibbons to attend the meeting and support the bill. He also feels that strong White House support will be needed to pull this one out of the fire.
>
> I assured Chuck of our deep interest in this one, and promised him you would call early Monday.[41]

It was becoming clear that Powell did not have the control over his committee that a powerful, respected chairman should have. His position was becoming increasingly weakened. Any time a chairman had to appeal for outside help in this manner, he gave up some of his bargaining power and leverage. Everyone knew this. Certainly Powell's committee members knew it. The White House was willing to help him, but obviously on its own terms. And the administration, given the opportunity to go directly to the committee—in effect circumventing the chairman *by invitation of the chair-*

man himself—would feel quite free to cut its own deals with each member. This was hardly the best position for a chairman to be in. And surely Powell must have known this. Such contacts and maneuvering are hardly kept secret in a town as totally political as the nation's capital. White House aide Henry Wilson candidly outlined his activity with Powell's committee to the President:

> I secured agreement this morning from John Brademas, Jim O'Hara and Hugh Carey that they will help in cutting back the House Elementary and Secondary Education bill by deleting $170 million of the 1967 authorization and all of the 1968 authorization. . . .
>
> I have talked with Perkins also, and he is reluctantly agreeable.
>
> I intend to talk with each member of the Committee beginning now.
>
> The final hurdle will be Powell who is out of town this week.
>
> I am sure we can expect blackmail here, but we'll cross that bridge when we get to it.[42]

Thus as far as the White House was concerned, on important education legislation, Powell was not the first to check with by mid-1966 but likely the last. His political clout was dwindling rapidly. The White House and his committee members were shaping the content of legislation themselves, going around him, and they simply would have to deal with his objections later. To be sure, there would continue to be pro forma, symbolic gestures of respect toward the chairman, but any reasonably sophisticated observer of the Washington scene could see the handwriting on the wall—indeed, even if, at the time, they were not privy to the written memos.

Powell was equally puzzling to the White House because, while he clearly was a liberal who supported the progressive measures, he was also a constant—albeit friendly—critic of the antipoverty programs. From the beginning, he endorsed the legislation. But his complaint was with the way many of the local programs were being administered. His criticisms were widely reported: salaries of local antipoverty officials were too high, intended to enrich the rich; too often jobs went to political cronies in the form of patronage and favors; blacks in the South were excluded from the planning boards and staffs. "There has been an over-emphasis on planning and dismal de-emphasis on action programs."[43]

The various antipoverty programs around the country were, indeed, vulnerable to these and other criticisms. The swiftly enacted legislation was heralded with much fanfare and high expectations.

The money flowed. There were so many opportunities for diverse handling of the funds, leaving open the attractive possibility for opportunism and fraud. It is not surprising that many of the programs came under sharp scrutiny from friend and foe alike. Powell was in the middle of this fray, attempting to use his position as chairman of the congressional committee charged with overseeing the programs to exert his maximum influence on the shape of the programs. He held committee hearings, inviting witnesses sympathetic to his criticisms. He urged the comptroller general to hold up funds for certain cities until his complaints were addressed. One White House memo bluntly concluded, "There is no way of predicting Mr. Powell's course of action in this regard."[44]

Overall, however, the White House had confidence that in the end it could rely on Powell to be a friend, not a foe. Powell did not ultimately want to kill the program, only to put his own imprimatur on it, and possibly to have a greater voice in how certain local programs were funded and administered. He also knew that in the long run it was better to play ball with the White House. His enemies were not the people in the administration but those in Congress who either wanted no such programs at all or wanted to exclude blacks from leadership roles. In this struggle, he and the Johnson administration were allies. Thus, while he criticized certain aspects of the program, he also sought White House help. In addition, he kept up his active travel schedule—to his home and rest haven in Puerto Rico, to the island of Bimini in the Bahamas, and to international meetings. He was not always around to tend to the personal day-to-day prodding necessary to move his committee's legislation through the congressional labyrinth. On more than one occasion his office would call the White House for help. Presidential assistant Claude Desautels sent a note to O'Brien:

> I just took a call for you from Mrs. Dargan[s]. Adam Clayton Powell called her from Puerto Rico, asking her to get in touch with you immediately. He needs help in getting a rule on poverty. He has asked Howard Smith twice without success. He wants it this week because he is going to Geneva probably next week on the ILO Conference. She said that she expected him back from Puerto Rico tomorrow but no later than Wednesday. I advised him we would be back in touch.[45]

And Powell was aware that it was in his best interest to stay in favor with the White House. The powerful, popular Executive Branch could exert various kinds of influence on Congress, and Powell could use that intervention from time to time. He knew that he was not personally liked by many of his colleagues, and they might well use any reasonable means to diminish the influence and power of his committee. There were times when the White House, if it wanted, could be helpful. For example, Powell was anxious that certain bills be assigned to his committee. Depending on how a bill was drafted, it could be given to any number of committees, and, of course, committee jurisdiction carried with it influence over the bill. He felt no hesitancy in seeking administration support. He was also aware that every such instance involved reciprocity. As Desautels wrote to O'Brien:

> I took a call for you from Maxine Dargan[s]. The Chairman [Powell] had asked her to relay to you the understanding that there is a draft of a bill at the White House presently regarding employment of Older Americans.
>
> He wants the language of the bill drafted in such a way that the bill will be referred to his Committee rather than to Ways and Means. Do you wish me to check here?[46]

Check it, O'Brien replied.

"I have checked this out with everyone," Desautels later informed O'Brien. "There is no foundation to it at this time and I have so advised Mrs. Dargan[s]."

All these political contacts and favors were part of the process of policy-making. Powell understood that as long as he did not stray too far from the cooperative circle, he could expect a positive quid pro quo relationship with the Johnson White House. At the same time, sensitive to his reputation and image beyond Congress with his Harlem and national supporters, he had no intention of relinquishing his outspoken role. He constantly took aim at the relatively low amount of money appropriated to fight poverty. Instead of a requested $1.75 billion, there should be $4.5 billion, he asserted. "If we can spend billions of dollars to save a quasi-democracy in Vietnam, we must spend more to preserve democracy at home," he told a crowded news conference in December 1965.[47] Invariably, his press conferences were well attended. Frequently held in the large, impressive committee hearing room, he would hold forth for the television cameras and reporters who knew they would get caustic, newsworthy quotes from the acerbic congressman. Always, at this time, his subject was the state of the antipoverty programs around the country—this was now his special domain of expertise. On occasion, he spoke of racial segregation and discrimination, but both he and the reporters knew that the civil rights leaders were better sources for those stories. There were instances when he tied civil rights to antipoverty, especially in criticizing some local programs for excluding blacks or for taking federal antipoverty money and still not doing much to end de facto segregation, especially in the North. And he often reminded the press that he was a friendly critic of the antipoverty program, one who was "wholeheartedly committed" to the legislation. He reminded everyone: "It is better for a supporter of the program to make these charges."[48] He was also aware that when he criticized the programs in some Northern cities, as he did when he attacked Mayor Richard Daley of Chicago, he was attacking local leaders of his own party, because most of those mayors and city leaders were Democrats.

In doing this, surely he knew that he was not making President Johnson's leadership role any easier. As the national party leader, Johnson had to get along with those big-city mayors. But Powell's attacks, as much as anything else, were likely calculated to remind the President that he, Johnson, could not ignore Powell either. And he insisted on extracting from the White House the maximum in this regard. Whatever else this meant, it certainly involved access to Johnson. Others in and out of government might have difficulty getting in to see a busy President, but Powell clearly wanted preferred status. And he knew his bargaining chips. In December 1965, Johnson was informed by an aide:

> Mr. President:
>
> Chuck Stone called and I asked him to write, which he has done. He states that Chairman Powell and Congressman Gibbons would like to see you the week of January 10. Purpose is to discuss the War on Poverty legislation for 1966.
>
> The Chairman says he does not plan to hold any hearings on the War on Poverty until he has had an opportunity to have this discussion with you.
>
> Do you want to see Powell and Gibbons?
>
> Yes ______ No ______[49]

This was the busy opening week of the new congressional session, but Johnson checked "yes" and then scribbled at the bottom of the memo: "OK if absolutely off record so I don't have this precedent for 535 members I can't see 1st week."

Fair enough. But Adam Clayton Powell ought to be accommodated. He got his appointment with the President.

All the while, the antipoverty program remained mired in bitter political squabbles. Republicans continually pointed out various administrative failures and waste, as well as political favoritism in the programs. Various congressmen sought funds for their own pet projects and districts. Powell sent committee staffers around the country investigating projects and reporting back to him. He stressed jobs for the unemployed and teenagers, and he instructed his staff to seek out the "common folk," not the elite who ran the programs, to find out what was needed. "Get down to the nitty-gritty. Talk only with the masses."[50] Of course, some saw this as a Powell move to undercut the local elite black and white leadership over which he had no control. He was noted by then as having a low regard for some of the established black organizations which he felt were out of touch with the large number of young people in the ghettos who were participating in the summer riots beginning to plague the inner cities. He pointed especially to the Watts area in Los Angeles. He called for the dismissal of OEO officials who felt the programs could be phased into other agencies of government over a period of time.[51]

One of his most dramatic—and final—statements on the antipoverty program came in August 1966, when he testified, at his request, at a Senate hearing held by Senator Abraham Ribicoff.[52] What was needed, he urged, was $35 billion more in federal funds over the next decade. He called for a national multipurpose council to administer a self-directed, self-help program for the involvement of residents of urban slums in the redevelopment of these areas through nonprofit organizations.[53] He took his swipe at Sargent Shriver, suggesting he resign; at the Department of Housing and Urban Development, under the leadership of the black Secretary, Robert C. Weaver; and he renewed his attack on the National Urban League. The League, led by Whitney M. Young, Jr., one of the Big Six civil rights leaders, was "fattening its operational budget at the unknowing expense of the Federal Government," Powell asserted.[54]

Clearly there was no love lost between Powell and the major civil rights leaders. He seemed intent on denying them a major role in running antipoverty programs. One of his successful efforts was scuttling a potential grant to James Farmer, head of CORE. But this episode was not fully explained, at least not to Farmer's satisfaction. Powell reportedly was not the only actor in that play, and the various political motivations and maneuverings remained unclear. In any event, it was not one of Powell's most honorable moments—whether, as he maintained, he was doing the bidding of others, or pursuing his own purposes.

Farmer had developed his own ideas for a major program to stamp out adult illiteracy in the country. He discussed these with the President, who was enthusiastic but advised him to get the endorsement of other civil rights organizations; Johnson did not want to be perceived as favoring only CORE. This was fine with Farmer, and he also "touched base with" Harold Howe, the commissioner of education; Vice President Hubert Humphrey; and Adam Powell. All "enthusiastically endorsed" Farmer's proposal against adult illiteracy.[55] He had established a nonprofit organization, the Center for Community Action Education, to run the program once it was funded by the Office of Economic Opportunity (OEO). As far as Farmer was concerned, the center's application for a grant was moving along nicely and would be approved any day by Sargent Shriver. But that was not to happen. Time passed; no grant was approved: Farmer sought answers—from the White House; from OEO—but received no responses. Finally, A. Philip Randolph was able to get through to the President, who told him to check with "the Chairman"—Adam Powell. But calls to Powell were not returned until Martin Luther King, Jr., finally was able to talk to the chairman about Farmer's proposal. In the interim, Powell had told a press conference that he planned to ask HEW to run a major adult literacy program. He saw no need for a new, separate organization to be set up to do this.

According to Farmer, King was told by Powell that President Johnson "told me to axe it." Why? "Oh well, they're going to give me something I need very much; in fact, something I've got to have." Powell did not elaborate, and this left Farmer hanging. A few days later, Farmer was told by a black reporter that Powell had made a deal with the White House: in return for his scuttling the literacy program, Powell would be given White House assistance in having a libel judgment against him in New York (discussed in Chapter 19) reduced. Farmer remained skeptical, but his application was never approved and the judgment was later substantially reduced. Farmer was never able to authenticate this account, but he knew enough about the congressman to remain wary of his credibility in such matters.[56] Even if the White House did help Powell, it was not clear why the administration, which apparently had earlier expressed such enthusiasm, would subsequently turn against the literacy project. In fact, Vice President Humphrey had even sent Farmer a premature congratulatory note, assuming the project had been approved and launched.

In July 1966, the *New York Times* reported:

> Political pressure crushed James Farmer's proposed project to combat illiteracy with an $860,000 antipoverty grant. Sargent Shriver, director of the Office of Economic Opportunity, was on the verge of signing the grant more than six months ago, but outside forces deterred him. Subordinates in the agency pointed to Representative Adam Clayton Powell, Democrat of Manhattan, as the pressure point.[57]

Chuck Stone of Powell's staff stated that "the chairman received a number of telephone calls from congressmen saying that they were opposed to it [the literacy project]." One White House memo seemed to indicate that Powell was the main culprit. Henry Wilson wrote to Bill Moyers (both were Presidential assistants):

> You should be aware that Chuck Stone called me today with the news that Powell is back in town and that he has ruled that he will not schedule hearings on the OEO authorization until the administration has publicly announced that it is discontinuing the operation headed by James Farmer. Stone said he has given this message to Sargent Shriver and that he is quite unhappy about it. My reaction is to let Sarge wrestle with Powell a few days on this before we get into the act or push the Speaker into it.[58]

But Farmer still could not pin down the exact nature of the objections or the specific sources of political opposition. Virtually all accounts, however, pointed to Powell as the hatchet man, and this left a bitter taste in Farmer's mouth, toward both Powell and Shriver.

Years later, in an interview, Farmer recounted the incident and spoke about Powell's subsequent friendliness toward him. As for the literacy program and Powell's role, as Farmer saw it, Powell was simply doing what he had to do to get help on his New York legal problems. Farmer stated:

> . . . I don't think it was anything personal between Adam and me, because very shortly after the program was killed—effectively killed, with Adam taking the posture that killed it, I saw Adam and he behaved toward me as though nothing at all had happened between us.
>
> Hi Jim. How's it going? How are you man? It's good to see you!

> Frankly, I do not think Adam was an immoral man or a moral man, even. I think he was amoral. I think he was almost completely political . . . [and] would do whatever served his purposes, politically.[59]

Powell's influence over antipoverty programs was indeed considerable, but he was by no means omnipotent. He won some battles and lost some. He was not able, for instance, to get a favorable reconsideration of an OEO rejection of a business training grant to a group he supported, in spite of lengthy correspondence with and pressure on Shriver. On the other hand, he kept OEO on its toes with his detailed inquiries about the conduct of certain projects and procedures for awarding or rejecting grants. In each instance, OEO felt obliged to respond with respectful attention. In a sense, Powell was carrying over his earlier civil rights monitoring into the antipoverty area. On August 24, 1966, he sent a letter to Shriver informing the director: "I plan to call a press conference and issue a major statement on the War on Poverty and the Office of Economic Opportunity this weekend. I would deeply appreciate your reaction and response within 48 hours of receipt of this letter to the following *8* issues and questions."[60] He wanted to know such things as the following: Had OEO funds for a child-development program in Mississippi been terminated? If so, why? (Powell knew that segregationists in that state were opposed to the racially integrated program.) Why had OEO turned down "Project Spin-Off" after officially encouraging a proposal? (Powell had sought to intervene on behalf of the applicants.) What was OEO's precise administrative position on funding self-help housing proposals? Why had OEO not concentrated on recruiting teenage Negro females for its Job Corps Centers? What *specifically* was OEO doing to develop a consistent policy on representation of the poor on Community Action Agency policy or advisory boards? What were OEO's minimum requirements for suspending funds for an OEO-subsidized project?

Two days later he received a response: a detailed six-page, single-spaced reply. It might not have completely satisfied him, but few people could command such quick bureaucratic response around Washington, and Powell knew it. Apparently, he still had clout.

Powell realized that his most unique, direct contribution to the civil rights cause at this point lay in his persistent prodding of the Johnson administration to hire blacks in top policy-making positions. In this constant monitoring he was performing the way he had in the previous decade when he had lit the fires under the

Eisenhower White House to eliminate segregation and discrimination. It was his own individual campaign that he, as a congressman, could pursue with reasonable likelihood of favorable results. His unique position as a prominent congressman gave him the opportunity to push and probe in ways not always available to the civil rights leaders. And in this role he was persistent. He fired off inquiries concerning employment in the Peace Corps, and at the higher GS ranks in the various departments. In each instance, the responsible administration officials felt obliged to respond, sometimes confirming Powell's figures, other times pointing out that he had missed an appointment or two. And they kept the President informed so he would be able to report developments to Powell when the two got together. Powell had put them on notice, and they were sensitive to his interest. In early 1966, Douglass Cater sent a note to Johnson:

> If Chairman Powell comes to call in the next day or two, you may wish to tell him of the appointment of Lisle Carter to be Assistant Secretary (for Individual and Family Services) of HEW. This puts a Negro into one of the Department's top positions. In addition, here is a current status report on Negro employment in the Office of Education. . . . You may also wish to point out that four leading Negroes have declined the post of Associate Commissioner for Adult and Vocational Education.
>
> I am hoping that the new Commissioner, Harold Howe, will give increased impetus to this recruitment.[61]

At times, Powell could be somewhat mirthful in his communications with officials on the subject. He chided the chairman of the U.S. Civil Service Commission in a letter that took the commission to task on its emphasis on "quality" appointments. Of course, Powell agreed, but "too often the factor of race is still a determinant in the concept of 'quality.' " He added:

> There is an abundance of quality in the Negro professional communities all over America. I believe it can be channeled into valuable contributions of public service to our government if continuing vigorous efforts are made to find these highly qualified Negroes. I think the Biblical injunction still obtains here. . . . "Seek, and ye shall find."[62]

Playful, perhaps, but the commissioner got the congressman's point.

At the same time, the White House wanted to accommodate

Powell, where possible, for strictly political reasons. As with most politicians, Powell made recommendations for certain political appointments. Often enough, these were understood as part of the political bargaining process—quid pro quo. A memo from the White House to the Civil Service Commission illustrates this point involving a Powell recommendation:

> To: John Macy
>
> From: Henry H. Wilson, Jr.
>
> You will recall our conversations regarding the reappointment of Howard Gamser to the Federal Mediation Board. It is my recollection that last June you told me that Gamser was not a bad appointment, but that there was hope someone better could be found, and it is my impression that his term expired June 30. You will recall that while we sat at the Mess Table, I called Adam Powell and told him that Gamser would not be named and that Powell thereupon threatened blackmail with respect to legislation then pending. It was my advice to you to forget blackmail and to proceed to get someone else. As I understand it, you to date have no better thoughts for the appointment. Three months have gone by. Powell yesterday performed well on the Minimum Wage bill, and it occurs to me that unless there is some reason now not to appoint Gamser, it would be an appropriate time, with relation to our dealings with Powell, to name Gamser.
>
> At this time, it could come almost as a reward to Powell and we still have to work with him on the OEO authorization, the Elementary and Secondary Education bill, and various conference reports, in which we will be asking that he stand up against Senate bills with vastly inflated sums.
>
> You should know also that many members of the Democratic side of the Education and Labor Committee are interested in Gamser.[63]

Likewise, administration officials were ever alert to comments in the black press that praised black-American appointments. Such praise was always useful to have to show to Powell. The administration had made several significant "breakthrough" appointments by mid-1966, notably Andrew Brimmer to the Board of Governors of the Federal Reserve Board, and Robert C. Weaver as the first black cabinet secretary over the newly established Department of Housing and Urban Development. A black newspaper in California editorialized at length in laudatory terms. The President was worthy of "the highest accolade," and "all of these show that the President not only recognizes superior ability but he continuously does so at the exclusion of race and color."[64]

Powell's favorite target, John Macy at the Civil Service Commission, could not let such commentary go unnoticed. Macy sent a copy of the editorial to the President with a covering note: "In view of Congressman Adam Clayton Powell's recent carping at your record of Negro appointments, I thought you would be interested in the attached editorial from *The Voice*, a San Diego Negro newspaper."[65]

Powell likely would have smiled and simply admonished the administration to keep seeking—and finding.

But he was not always in agreement with the White House choices, even at times offering a white candidate over a black. It was generally known that Powell had no particular affection for Robert Weaver, the highly regarded housing expert who was widely expected—as far back as the Kennedy administration—to assume the HUD post. Powell was never able to establish the kind of preferred position with Weaver that he wanted, especially in dealing with certain housing development contracts. Weaver was fiercely independent and a stickler for merit in every respect of his work. And he had been in and around Washington politics and government since the New Deal days in positions that brought him close to FDR's Interior Secretary, Harold Ickes, and others. He was not easily intimidated. At times Powell simply found this quality in Weaver annoying and vexing, and he made his views known to the White House. Several months before Weaver's appointment, Powell went so far as to offer himself as a lead player to derail Weaver's selection.

To: Larry O'Brien July 29, 1965

From: Claude Desautels

I took a call for you from Adam Clayton Powell.

He says that Bob Weaver has got to go, and wants you to get this to the President.

Also he wants you to know that if you and the President deem it advisable he will issue a public statement in support of someone like Albert Rains for the new Cabinet post, and it will be issued whenever you deem it most advisable—

a- prior to Senate debate of the Departmental Bill

b- During debate

c- After passage.

He wants you to know he will be out of the city about 10 days. He can be reached in this period through the Miami Marina.

He said, "I'm going to be on a ship called The Little Seas, Claude-Baby."[66]

O'Brien sent the memo on to President Johnson. It had no effect, because six months later, Weaver was appointed. This was not an instance when Powell felt obliged to congratulate the administration, although virtually everyone else in the civil rights and liberal activist community saw it as an excellent appointment. On the other hand, Powell let the White House know that he hoped Thurgood Marshall would eventually be considered for appointment to the United States Supreme Court.[67]

On balance, Powell's relationship with the Johnson White House through mid-1966 was one of mutual political respect. They were all professional politicians who understood the game of politics and knew how to push levers of power and trade and bargain. Powell was not above seeking White House help when he needed personal political support—to get a bill passed, to protect his committee's jurisdiction and powers—and the White House was willing to reciprocate with the volatile congressman under many circumstances. At one time in 1966, Powell got wind of a possible move to split his committee into two parts. He immediately called the White House for help in heading this off. Jack Valenti advised that he check with Larry O'Brien, but nothing came of it. The White House was keenly aware that Powell carried negative political baggage, but it also knew that he had considerable support in some national circles. When he pushed hard on civil rights issues, especially for more appointments of blacks, he was on solid, acceptable ground, and most people recognized this. When he lobbied for or against certain political appointments and favors, he could be treated on the political merits of the case. President Johnson and his aides fully understood that Powell had enemies who were not at all disposed to comfort him. But this simply meant that in dealing with him, one had to be careful not to be drawn into his political battles unnecessarily. This was perhaps more true with Powell than with others, since the chairman had a reputation for not always honoring his commitments, and even misstating the facts in a particular situation. With Powell involved, you always checked.

He could be a persistent advocate, and if he felt he was getting less than respectful treatment, he could be especially bothersome. Everyone knew this. When Joseph Califano joined the White House staff, he sent a coyly worded note to John Macy inquiring about a Powell recommendation, noting to Macy that "I inherited Adam Clayton Powell from Jack Valenti."[68] It was likely an inheritance he could just as well have done without. Invitations from Powell to attend certain functions had to be handled very carefully, even to the extent of checking at times with the President. On one occasion, Jack Valenti sought the President's counsel:

MEMO for The President March 29, 1965

I have been invited to a buffet dinner honoring Adam Clayton Powell on Friday, April 2.

Before I decline I thought I should check with you since he becomes quite sensitive about these things.

accept ______ decline ______

Jack Valenti[69]

Johnson checked "decline."

The problem the administration had with Powell was not whether he would ultimately support the Great Society legislation. He would; he wanted it. But he was not dependable in two very important ways. In the heat of some legislative battles he was prone not to be around. He would be out of town, and his promise to show up for a crucial session or vote could not be relied on. Henry Wilson outlined such a frustration to the President involving negotiations on the minimum-wage bill in 1966. He concluded his memo with: "Powell swears he will be back in town on Monday. I doubt it."[70] And on another occasion, even when Powell had clearly given his word to appear and support a measure, there was lingering doubt. "It would be my guess," Wilson informed the President, regarding OEO legislation, "that if things are allowed to sit, the odds are that Powell will come in Wednesday, make the motion to adopt the rule, and then proceed to speak for the bill. But he is, of course, massively unpredictable."[71]

The frustration was compounded by the number of instances when Powell simply could not be trusted to speak the truth. The *Washington Post* had quoted Powell once as saying that White House sources had asked him to add more funds to a particular bill. No one in the White House owned up to this request, and Wilson sought out Powell for clarification. "I finally caught up with Adam Clayton Powell. . . . I . . . asked him whether he had been accurately quoted. He said, 'Well . . . you know.' " Wilson then reminded the President of the incident in 1963 when Powell had been tape-recorded as claiming—falsely—to have stayed up half the night writing Kennedy's civil rights speech. Wilson concluded his memo to President Johnson by saying, "That's about the kind of story this is."[72]

Thus his political allies always had to be especially on guard against some unforeseen—and inexcusable—act. He was a power, but also an unreasonable pain. His personal life and problems were becoming flagrant. What was once perceived as simply a lavish, fun-loving life-style was becoming one bordering on excess and even hints of misuse of congressional funds. His associations with numerous women were now quite open, and he made little effort to conceal them. Without question, he could be a good, effective chairman, a loyal party member, a liberal. The President and his party appreciated this part of his life. And even though he often criticized the established civil rights leaders, he could always be found on the side of those championing stronger civil rights measures and the end to racial segregation and discrimination. And at the same time, he was never at a loss for words in pushing for more federal support for those of all races at the lowest end of the economic ladder. His liberal credentials in this respect were in order.

Yet, in spite of this powerful presence, there was a problem. There was always an aspect of Adam Clayton Powell, Jr., that left even many of his supporters with a lingering doubt, a skepticism, a hesitancy. And it is equally likely that he was aware of—and unfazed by—this paradox.

18

"I will always do just what every other Congressman . . . has done."

On February 5, 1963, Senator John J. Williams, Republican of Delaware, took the floor of the Senate and did a most unusual thing; he sharply criticized a member of the other chamber of Congress for that member's alleged questionable personal and political behavior. His target was Adam Clayton Powell, Jr.

Williams was irate at what he considered the unconscionable political favoritism shown Powell by government agencies in awarding grants and loans to him. The senator recalled the wide publicity a few months earlier of Powell traveling to Europe in lavish style on government expense in the company of two female congressional staffers. Ostensibly on a fact-finding trip to investigate the conditions of working women in the NATO countries, Powell and his companions were reported and photographed in popular nightclubs, attending theaters, and dining in opulent restaurants. In addition, Williams charged, there was no sign that the Internal Revenue Service was seriously trying to collect back taxes it claimed Powell owed. Without question, Senator Williams concluded, this member of the House was a disgrace to Congress and something ought to be done about it.

The charges were so severe that Senator Wayne Morse, Democrat of Oregon, introduced a resolution the next day to strike from the record Williams's speech, because it "reflected on the character and reputation" of another member of Congress. Williams was not deterred. In fact, he ingeniously defended his remarks and indicated that he was rather restrained in his attack.

> I made the remarks and I stand behind them. I checked carefully and was advised it was not a violation of the rules. I did not discuss this person's conduct in the House of Representatives. I never said one word yesterday, nor will I today, about this person having relatives on the public payroll who are not working. . . . Neither will I say that he is not fulfilling his duties and is guilty of a great deal of absenteeism.[1]

Indeed, and by so cryptically raising these other "unmentioned" matters, everyone knew the senator was putting his finger on issues often discussed privately about Powell's behavior. The congressman's flamboyant life-style was now front-page news, and he did little to conceal it. If anything, he seemed to revel in it, almost taunting his critics—in and out of Congress—and daring them to make an issue of the way he acted.

Powell had left Washington for Puerto Rico on February 5, the day Williams leveled his blast, and returned two weeks later ready to do battle. He held a press conference on February 20, 1963.

It was vintage Powell.

Puffing on his cigarillo, surrounded by staff, he reclined in the chairman's seat in the crowded committee room amidst reporters and cameras. The questions came from all sides, but the reporters knew they were sparring with a veteran political professional. He would answer their questions, he promised them, but he insisted first on revealing the anti–civil rights record of his critic, Senator Williams. Here was a senator, Powell asserted, who purchased property with a racial restrictive covenant on it—not only against Negroes, but Jews and Orientals. Here was a senator who voted against an amendment to desegregate airport facilities; against extension of the Civil Rights Commission; against federal assistance to school desegregation—and "on and on we go."

But the reporters wanted to get at Powell, not Williams. What about his travels abroad "with two young ladies?" Powell quickly corrected: "Two staff members."

He then explained the report that was prepared by his traveling companions, dealing with equal opportunity for women in Europe, leading to the equal-pay-for-equal-work legislation passed by the House and then pending in the Senate.

He denied that he had misused "counterpart funds" on his trip. This was money set aside in foreign currency in U.S. embassies to be used only in those countries for congressional expenses and other purposes. The money was not convertible into dollars and did not go into the U.S. Treasury. It was money accrued to the United States from governmental transactions in the various countries, but was held in those respective countries. Therefore, as far as Powell was concerned, this was not money taken away from the American taxpayers. These funds were always used by traveling congressmen, made available to them through the State Department in the country visited. He was not acting improperly, therefore, in drawing on these funds. He mentioned several other congress members who, as it turned out, were traveling in Europe at the same time he was (during the particular trip under question—August–September, 1962)—Senator Estes Kefauver, Congressman Otto Passman, and others—and even seen in the same nightclubs.

He strongly made his point that he saw nothing wrong with this. It was within the law. If the law was wrong, then it should be changed.

But—and he eyed the gathered reporters defiantly and sternly—"I wish to state very emphatically that I will always do just what every other Congressman and committee chairman has done and is doing and will do."[2]

As for relatives on the payroll, he had acknowledged before that his wife worked for him out of Puerto Rico where she was busy translating and answering his mail from his Spanish-speaking constituents in Harlem. And anyway, when a reporter asked if he thought having relatives on the payroll was "a good thing," he responded: "Yes. Very good, very good. . . . Over 100 members of the House of Representatives have their relatives on payrolls that we know about. . . . As long as 100 plus members of the House and 'X' number of senators, then I am going to do it." For him there would be no double standard, no second-class status. He was especially annoyed when he was asked if he felt he had a special obligation as a civil rights leader to "lean over backward to avoid criticism." Powell quickly replied "No, that's the view, you see, that a lot of people say, the minorities have got to be twice this as compared to others. I take the view that equality is equality and I take the view that I am a Member of Congress as good as anybody else."[3]

But the reporters persisted. Wasn't the use of "counterpart funds" for attending nightclubs or going to luxurious resorts an abuse of congressional privileges?

"No," Powell shot back, "because it's done by all of them."

But did that make it right?

"Well, there is no right or wrong in it. It's nonprohibitive. It was set up that way," Powell insisted.

"Was it set up to go to nightclubs?" a reporter asked, sensing he had the Harlem congressman on the ropes.

Powell leaned back, blew a smoke ring, half turned in the direction of the reporter with a smirk on his face, and lowered his voice as he spoke slowly in a contrived air of impatience: "Well, I am sure that you don't go to Paris and stay all the time in Notre Dame."

The frustrated reporter was not finished. He was determined: "But is that part of committee business?"

Assuming the same posture of slight incredulity, Powell looked at his inquisitor, smiled, gave a slight but discernible wink, and answered quietly and slowly: "Of course it's part of it. You're going abroad. Travel is a very broadening kind of education and I wish to assure you that it is practiced by every member of the House and the Senate."

He was enjoying himself now. His staff knew it. The press knew it. There had been rumors that he would retire after this term. Would he run again in 1964?

"Most assuredly now," Powell replied. "You of the press have just put me in an untenable position. I've got to run whether I want to or not. . . . If I didn't run again, it would look like I am running out."

For the moment, Powell had, in his own mind, met his antagonists and won. He had set the framework for responding to any criticisms of his personal behavior. And try as they may, his critics could not shake him, or faze him. He was certainly not going to change, at age fifty-five, the habits of a lifetime, and he seemed determined to put his congressional colleagues who criticized him on the defensive. His counterattack would be the charge of racism combined with the charge of hypocrisy. He refused to let them accuse him of doing any more than they were "guilty" of.

Many Powell supporters firmly believed he was correct in his assessment of the motivations and vulnerabilities of his attackers. It was precisely this element of truth that provided his own actions a certain cloak of tolerability—if not outright approval. If he was, as one reporter indicated, being referred to as an "adult delinquent," he and his defenders knew that he was in good company.

But the Powell Problem always seemed to be a bit more blatant than that presented by his colleagues. Many of them might engage in similar behavior, but he was *too* public, too flamboyant, too reckless. And in acting this way, he was inevitably calling attention to similar practices of his more discreet colleagues. On the other hand, Powell would likely have concluded that it was his race, not his overt acts, that drew the attacks, and he was not going to be constrained by *that* criteria of selective criticism.

Several months earlier, in 1962, columnist Drew Pearson had obtained and published a copy of the State Department cable to the U.S. embassies outlining Powell's trip abroad with the two female staffers, Corinne Huff and Tamara J. Wall. The cable read:

> August 8 sailing SS Queen Mary arriving South Hampton 8/13; Paris 8/16; Venice 8/20; Rome 8/23; Athens 8/27; Delphi 8/30; sailing Leonardo da Vinci 9/15 from Gibraltar. . . .
>
> . . . Codel [Congressional Delegation] and party authorized use local currencies 19FT561 funds [counterpart funds]. Meet assist control officers.
>
> Request one single and one double with bath as follows: London 8/13, 14, 15 Cumberland Marble Arch Hotel; Paris 8/16–19 Hotel San Regis; Venice 8/20–22 Royal Denieli; Rome 8/23–26 (1) Excelsior (2) Flora (3) Victoria—whichever has special Embassy rate; Athens 8/27–29 Beachhouse at Astir Hotel in Glyphada; Delphi 8/30 new governmental hotel name unknown.
>
> Confirm Department soonest.
>
> London—Request three tickets 8/14, 15 best shows playing except Broadway plays.
>
> Paris—Codel desires use U.S. army car and chauffeur. Reserve three for first show and dinner best table Lido 8/16.
>
> Venice—If film festival going on request three tickets 8/20 or 21.
>
> Codel also requests use Consulate's motorboat.
>
> Athens—Arrange use rental car trip to Delphi payable 19FT561 funds 8/30.
>
> Delphi—Codel inquires whether boat trip about 6 days around islands possibility?
>
> Possible visit Rhodes.
>
> South Hampton—Codel requests be met at Queen Mary Cherbourg with $100 U.S. equivalent in local currencies for each member party.[4]

Pearson's account of the three-week trip was meticulously detailed. Powell had left his back brace in Washington; it had to be flown to him immediately in London.

The three travelers went to nightclubs, "quaint restaurants," and did a fair amount of sightseeing. In Paris, Rome, and Athens, Powell met with the American labor attaché. The itinerary, however, left little doubt that much, if not most, of the time was taken up with relaxed enjoyment, including cruising the Grand Canal in Venice. Powell was well known to the headwaiters in the best restaurants throughout the continent, and thus was able to get the best tables. From Rome he and Huff flew to Athens, while Wall stayed on a little longer with friends. In Athens, an American embassy–chauffeured car was at their disposal for sight-seeing trips. At one point, in the hotel lobby, Powell bumped into Lady Bird Johnson, who was there with Vice President Lyndon B. Johnson on an official mission in Greece. Pearson reported: "Adam looked a bit embarrassed, excused himself, and walked on across the lobby." The six-day cruise through the Greek islands was canceled, and Powell and Huff flew to Madrid, while Wall went to Vienna and Copenhagen.

Then the famous State Department cable was made public and the American press picked up the story. "After that," Pearson wrote, "the trip became an overpublicized bore. The Congressman cut short his trip and flew back to New York and Puerto Rico."[5]

By this time, Powell's trip was front-page news and the subject of widespread editorials and media comment. Pictures of Powell and Corinne Huff in nightclubs appeared. Meanwhile, his wife and new young son, Adam Clayton Powell IV, were back in Puerto Rico. She had heard about the trip from reporters who constantly called for her reaction. In an article a few years later, Mrs. Yvette Diago Powell picked up the story and gave her account of the obviously tension-filled return of her husband.[6] Earlier that summer, he had suggested that she not make the trip with him, because caring for their young baby on the trip would be too expensive. When the stories of his trip and traveling companions hit, she became concerned. To reporters, she had "no comment." But certainly there were things to discuss with her husband. She wrote: "I had a wire from Adam; he was cutting his trip short; I should meet him at the airport. He came off the airplane all smiles, swept me into his arms and kissed me. The newspaper people were waiting for him too; a picture of our embrace was in the next edition."

Later, he explained to her:

> Yes . . . there had been two women from his office. He needed them along; they were helping him. No, he had never been out with either of them—not alone. That evening in the nightclub was a big party,

> attended by most of the United States delegation. A lot of people were there. It was just another case of the newspapers singling out Adam Powell and trying to brand him as a playboy. "How could I greet you so affectionately at the airport," he asked, "if I had been with another woman?" I believed him. The rest of his stay in Puerto Rico was like another honeymoon. *Poor* Adam, I thought. *Always being hounded by the papers.*

But Mrs. Powell's trust began to wear thin over the next few years. She accidentally discovered a picture of another woman in her husband's wallet. Powell ardently claimed it had been put there by someone out to frame him. She did not bother to point out to him that the picture was taken in their Washington home. Her calls to their home in Washington at times were answered by a woman. Powell claimed it surely was a man who used the house. Perhaps she should have her ears examined. Powell tried to explain to her how important he was, with "tremendous responsibilities," and how much the White House relied on him. He often longed to be able to put the hectic political life behind him, he assured her, and remain with his family in Puerto Rico.

In time, it was clear that Powell's affections for his third wife had waned. Although she wanted to join him in Washington, she remained in Puerto Rico, at his insistence. His trips to visit his family became fewer and fewer, and, eventually, in the summer of 1964, he was not returning her calls. Finally, Powell admitted that "he had got himself a little involved." Mrs. Powell wrote that her husband assured her that he still loved her and their son and not anyone else. He was constantly being chased by women, and he admitted that, being human, he had "done wrong." He asked her forgiveness. He promised to clean up this affair and bring his family to Washington. That was 1964. It was never to be.

Mrs. Powell's article was one of sadness, disappointment, and more than a bit of anger. She told of her son's longing for his father—especially at Christmastime, when what he wanted most was for Santa to bring his daddy. Over the years, as she tried to contact Powell, he was never available, even to see his son. She asked a staff member if the congressman would see their son, if only for five minutes. She was advised that "the Chairman" was too busy to see his son. Mrs. Powell concluded: "Try to explain that to a young man. I tried—but I probably failed."[7]

The other women in Powell's life certainly would attract attention. Corinne Huff was a former Miss Ohio, the first black woman to win that recognition, and a contestant in the Miss Universe pageant. In a book he wrote shortly before he died, Powell simply described her as the "first soul sister to be in the Miss Universe contest." He called her Huffi. "She stood by me for many years and carried her burden in the heat of the day. And I will never forget what she did to help me when everyone had turned their backs upon me."[8]

The New York *Amsterdam News* managed to get an exclusive interview with Tamara Wall shortly after the publicized European trip. A lawyer, she served as assistant counsel on Powell's committee. She was divorced, with a young daughter. She denied that the trip was a high-living junket. "We had very little leisure time. Our itinerary was arranged by the embassy and Congressman Powell, in typical fashion, saw to it that we kept the schedule."[9] They had a busy schedule of meetings, with little time for pleasure. Whatever "courtesies" were extended to them, such as theater tickets, were no more than was the norm for traveling congressional parties. As for the trip being ended abruptly because of the sensational news stories back in the States, she emphatically insisted that Powell simply decided that "work . . . still remained to be done at home and . . . we had been rather successful in gathering the data that we were seeking."

Notwithstanding this explanation, her name was continually linked to the trip, much to her consternation, by columnists and others. Four years later, in 1966, when Powell's past was being spotlighted again in the midst of his committee's fight to curtail his powers, Drew Pearson once again cited her as one of the two women on the 1962 trip. The article, "Negroes Found Ashamed of Powell," stated: "Fishing and women . . . became Adam's number one concern. They still are. At least they rate ahead of his duties in Congress."[10] The columnist again named Tamara Wall and Corinne Huff as the two female staffers on the 1962 trip. This new reference to her hurt Wall deeply. A friend of hers wrote Pearson pleading that the columnist have "compassion" for her and "refrain from spreading her name in the press the next time you recount Congressman Powell's exploits."[11] Wall, indeed, was upset. The next day she wrote to the columnist complaining that he had used her name in his story. She doubted that this served any useful purpose or made him "a better, or more thorough, reporter."[12] Drew Pearson responded in a one-sentence letter: "Dear Tamara: I was needlessly thoughtless and I am sorry. Sincerely."[13]

* * *

But Adam Powell's travels were not the only matters of concern to his critics. His wife was on his staff payroll at $12,974 per year while living in Puerto Rico, and more than a few wondered how she earned her pay. "I have more than 100,000 Spanish-speaking people in my district," Powell explained, "and I get a lot of mail. It's all sent to her and she answers it for me. But I maintain no office there." Indeed, no office, the *New York Times* had editorialized, but the newspaper noted that the congressman was building a fifty-thousand-dollar home outside San Juan "against the time—the sooner the better—when he retires from political life."[14] Powell then explained that his wife had been staying in Puerto Rico where she could be cared for by her personal physician, while awaiting the birth of their baby. She would return to Washington later, he promised. And her salary continued, with Powell receiving and depositing the checks long after any constituents' correspondence was sent to her to answer. Before a congressional committee in February 1967, she testified that for six years she had received only four salary checks, that presumably the other checks went directly to her husband. And she had not done any work to earn the money for the last year and a half.

In addition, Senator Williams had charged that HHFA loans had been made to "Powell and his associates" totaling nearly $11 million. Robert C. Weaver, then administrator of HHFA, had to deny in detail that any special treatment or favors were accorded to Powell.

There were other real estate dealings and a grant to a youth training program in Harlem that caught congressional and media attention. In each instance, Powell denied any wrongdoing or undue influence. Of course, he admitted, he had endorsed the Harlem project, but this was no more or less than what any responsible congressman would do for his district. Besides, the project had been praised by a Washington newspaper as a good example of a worthwhile domestic peace corps effort to lift youth out of poverty. Powell insisted that while he initiated the idea and was on the board of the organization for a time, he did not control the grant of $250,000. His friend and former staff member, Livingston L. Wingate, became director of the project. Wingate told the press: "It's a fact that Adam Clayton Powell negotiated this grant. His influence was used to get it. How in the hell does a community get a grant if not through its Congressman? If he didn't negotiate it, he should be run out."[15]

In the meantime, Powell had his own suspicions and complaints regarding invasion of his privacy. In March 1963, in the midst of the furor over his personal behavior, he complained to Attorney General Robert F. Kennedy that his telephone had been tapped. Apparently, the private line in his office had been hooked up with another line—it appeared to be crossed with a telephone line to a local Washington bar—and there were suspicious interruptions when his secretary was on the line. Kennedy had the FBI contact Powell for further information. The congressman, however, was not very forthcoming, referring the agents to his secretary. After several discussions and checks, the phone company concluded it had made a mistake, but Powell clearly was not willing to settle for such a bureaucratic explanation. Immediately following his brief interview with the FBI in Harlem he took the platform at an outdoor rally and announced a wire tap on his telephone. The press naturally reported this, and the FBI noted in its files: "Powell has been interviewed by NYO, afterwards he went on with speech and mentioned wire tap—knowing full well it seems only a telephone snafu."[16] For Powell's purposes, this could serve as further evidence of harassment and surveillance, thus confirming in the minds of his supporters that he was being unduly hounded. But to the FBI, this could hardly convince the agency that he was sincere in his complaint.

The spring of 1963, following Senator Williams's attack, was a period of fast-developing, dramatic events in the civil rights movement. Martin Luther King, Jr., led protest marches in Birmingham, Alabama. The White House attempted negotiations with white business leaders in the South to avoid further violence, and in the meantime got ready to introduce major new civil rights legislation. All this activity was the prelude to the mass March on Washington in August.

Throughout these frantic weeks and months, Powell was drawing press criticism for his questionable behavior as well as his political flirtation with Malcolm X and the Black Muslims. The most direct consequence for him would be Congress's refusal to appropriate the full amount he requested to run his committee. "Clip His Money Wings," the lead editorial in a Tampa, Florida, newspaper, said the $700,000 he was requesting should be reduced. The chairman sought $200,000 for an "investigative task force." As far as the editorial was concerned, this was "little more than a personal political agency for Powell," and it should be denied.[17] The *New York World-Telegram* ridiculed him on its editorial page with a reprint of a poetic ditty, "The Powell and the Glory":

Anything whites can do he can be better:
Junketer, demagogue, loafer, go-getter.

Anything whites can do, he can do louder—
Preach and not practice and then take a powder.

Anything charged him, he labels a figment
Leveled by white men because of his pigment.
—SEC[18]

And the press dutifully reported his flouting of efforts to curtail his travels. He told an enthusiastic civil rights rally in Englewood, New Jersey: "They tried to stop me, but I'm going again . . . this Sunday . . . the luxury flight to Paris . . . with lots of relatives . . . at the government's expense . . . as the delegate to the World Labor Congress in Geneva."

Someone in the crowd shouted approvingly, "First class!"

Powell flashed a broad grin, acknowledged the comment, and shouted back, "That's right, First Class. All the way."[19]

The news story was headlined "Unreconstructed Adam—Another Junket, First Class."

The crowd loved it. Adam Powell loved it. He was in his element. This was the support he sought and knew he had. He could also count on editorial support from some of the Negro press. He was aware that some Negro newspapers would come to his defense as, indeed, the *Amsterdam News* had done months earlier in a front-page editorial. That editorial asserted that Powell was to be treated as all other members of Congress. Those members took trips abroad, received government funds and courtesies in doing so, and hired many consultants and staff, and by the same token, Powell should not be singled out for criticism in doing these things. As the "duly elected" representative of his district, Powell should be respected as all other elected officials were respected.[20]

But, of course, some of Powell's colleagues in the House clearly resented the assertion that he was no worse than the rest of them. The Republicans led the charge, of course, with Congressman John M. Ashbrook of Ohio admitting that the "rules of the House" were "not conducive to a public airing of our own dirty linen." In February 1963, he urged that Powell not be given the large amount he had requested to run his committee. Ashbrook was, in fact, a member of Powell's committee. But he felt that Powell had wasted funds, built too large a staff, and been inequitable in his treatment of

Republicans on the committee. Powell, he charged, was too lavish with consultants' contracts—for his friends, while reducing the staff of the Republican members. He put into the *Congressional Record* itemized expenditures over a two-year period, some of highly questionable nature, such as over thirty trips to Puerto Rico for members and staff. He wanted the *Record* to make clear that he resented Powell's statement that "every other Congressman" was vulnerable to charges of excessive, questionable travel at government expense. He stated, "I object to the reference that we all practice this type of activity. I certainly would not nor would many Members of the House and yet the impression is given, accidentally or otherwise, that this is the standard routine for all of us."[21]

Several other Republicans rose to commend Ashbrook for his "courage" and "forthrightness" in bringing the matter out in the open.

"I want to commend him [Ashbrook]," stated Congressman Thomas B. Curtis of Missouri, "for doing something that many Members have felt needed to be done on the floor of the House." The "entire reputation of the Congress is at stake," others agreed. Several others spoke in righteous indignation at being tarred with Powell's broad brush of accusation, and they reported that their constituents back home were becoming impatient with their unwillingness to reprimand the errant Harlem congressman.

Adam Powell was surely not endearing himself to his congressional colleagues.

For the moment, the protests had an effect. The House severely cut Powell's requested allocation for the 1963 session—by $148,500—and approved $200,000 for only the first term. Of this amount, $150,000 was made available directly to the six subcommittees. This was, as the *Congressional Quarterly* reported, "an unusual step that meant Powell would have no direct control of the funds."[22]

Some Democrats attempted to defend the chairman, pointing out the "notable achievement" of the committee in the previous congressional session. But their defense was hedged against the consideration that it might provoke even more attacks on the chairman and the committee. Everyone recognized that Powell had put his supporters in a most uncomfortable position. Perhaps if they could escape with only a reduced committee budget, the overall damage could be contained, and Powell just *might* get the message and mend his ways.

Get the message—perhaps; mend his ways—hardly.

In such circumstances, Powell invariably raised the race issue—

either asserting that the criticisms were made because he was black or calling attention to the critics' records on civil rights. Either charge made the attacks suspect in his own mind and in the assessment of his supporters. He knew that his willingness to expose the racism in others always made his opponents uncomfortable and gun-shy. And at times he did not go only after those who had attacked him publicly. It was sufficient if he revealed bits of previously unknown information that would best be kept unmentioned—even if the information was later denied or went unverified. The mere audacity to say certain things was testimony to his brashness and irritating style. For example, at the 1963 rally in Englewood, New Jersey, he singled out the UN ambassador, Adlai Stevenson, his former "foe" in the 1956 Presidential campaign.

"I'm going to tell you something that has never before been told," he said to the audience in an air of let's-really-tell-the-truth-about-our-so-called-white-liberal-friends. "Last week when Stevenson was told he had to hire some Negroes for his staff, he asked for three secretaries. But Stevenson said they must be light-skinned."[23]

True or not (Stevenson's office later denied it), the point was that no other liberal congressman would dare make such a public statement about a high official of his own party. This was part of Powell's protection—his willingness to say what others deemed wise to keep secret. And when he was attacked on other grounds, he could easily charge an attempt to silence him as the main motivation. He was too dangerous, he intimated, not because he was too flamboyant, but because he was too honest—too honest not only about his own behavior, but that of others, who were really hypocrites. This sort of defense resonated well with many who were already suspicious of America's true commitment to racial progress—the American Dilemma. In other words, the defense was plausible if only because it cast doubts on the motives of those who were quick to condemn Powell, but reluctant to attack the issue of American racism. The conservative columnist David Lawrence recognized this fact when he wrote that "Powell's Claim of Racial Bias Keeps His Colleagues from Moving Against Him."[24] Citing a *New York Times* editorial, Lawrence concluded that Powell's congressional colleagues "are afraid to remove him [from the committee chairmanship] because they, too, might be branded as having racial prejudices." As virtually everyone admitted, the only legitimate rebuke to Powell had to come from those who elected him, and Lawrence wrote: "But leadership of such a movement would have to come from the highly respected Negro leaders in the country. They could not be charged with racial antagonisms."

True—to an extent. Indeed, they would be in a stronger position to resist charges of racism, but they still would have to contend with charges of "Uncle Tomism." Powell had vanquished more than a handful of Negro critics with that label. But the "respected Negro leadership" was no less concerned about the problems Powell raised, and that leadership had to have its own doubts about the seeming "double standard" being applied to Powell. The NAACP received more than a few letters protesting Powell's behavior, and imploring the civil rights organization "to influence him to do right." This was an understandable concern, John Morsell of the NAACP wrote to one person in Illinois. But the NAACP also recognized the other, broader, problem that Powell presented. Of course, Morsell reminded, the NAACP had no influence over Powell, who "plans his own course of action without reference to others." At the same time, it was important to note that Powell was by no means the major offender in spending on foreign trips, as news stories pointed out. To be sure, Congress needed reforming, but until that happened, we could expect individual congressmen to "take advantage" of the system "in ways which we might not approve."[25]

This was probably not an answer that would satisfy those frustrated with Powell, but it was one some of the most respected black leaders felt necessary to give. Powell was perhaps not the best example of an exemplary congressman, but neither was he alone in his seeming transgressions. In order to get at him, it was necessary to come to grips with the larger problems he both exposed and reflected. This was a tall order. It was likely his strongest defense. Society's vulnerability was his greatest protection, as paradoxical and vexing as that was to those who resented this maverick politician from Harlem.

"If it's not illegal, immoral, or fattening, I'll do it," Adam Powell was fond of saying jocularly to taunting reporters—and admiring black audiences. He never attempted to hide his love for the comfortable, indeed, opulent life. There was about him a sense of entitlement, that he *should* take advantage of the finer things of life offered to him. The pity was, as he rationalized, that such opportunities were not open to others less fortunate than himself—white and black. Therefore, he was not an apologist for his behavior; he saw no reason to be contrite, to apologize, to offer to mend his ways. Such an attitude, to him, was hypocritical, and he was contemptuous enough of many of his colleagues who enjoyed the same privileges and perks, but constantly sought to conceal their relatively luxurious life-style from public view.

After years in politics and obtaining such a lofty status, he was in a position to observe the doings of others. It was part of the game, the process, the system. They might be more circumspect, but not himself. It was a system *they* created, and he had no intention of denying himself the fruits of *their* creation. He knew the political deals for personal gain others entered into. He was aware of the benefits—trips, payoffs, patronage, padded payrolls, contracts for friends—available to those in power. He would be foolish, in his estimation, not to avail himself of those same opportunities.

"If it's wrong," he often chided, "then change the law."

And he was aware no less of what was possible on the fringes of the law. There were things congressmen could do that were not particularly honorable, but neither was there an avalanche of moral outrage at such activities. Consequently, Powell saw no reason to challenge those unwritten conventions and limit his own behavior.

The FBI, however, was not as willing to concede this realm of permissibility, at least as far as Powell was concerned. Perhaps it was because he was *so* flagrant, or because he was *so* racially troublesome, not a team player. At any rate, in 1959, the FBI files indicated an investigation into possible bribery charges against Powell. The agency had received a tip from the Immigration and Naturalization Service in Hartford, Connecticut, that an alien had reportedly paid $500 to have Powell introduce a bill that would grant the particular immigrant permanent residence in the United States.[26] The money allegedly was paid to a third party and passed on to Powell. The record showed that Powell had, in fact, introduced such a bill, but the FBI could not determine if Powell received any money for doing so. The most the FBI could say was that "one can only guess that the money possibly was eventually passed on to Congressman Powell." Powell's name, the FBI noted, was "brought into the picture . . . on the basis of conjecture." If Powell was guilty of bribery, the government could not prove it, and the matter never surfaced. But there were more than a few Washington observers who were aware that fees were paid from time to time to lawyers to make a case before congressmen in such matters. This was, as such, quite legal, but certainly not if any of the fees found their way into congressional pockets. It would take a very naïve person to conclude that the latter did not occasionally happen, however. But this was the system in which Powell lived.

He was certainly not the only legislator who introduced such "private bills."

The real problem with Powell was not the possibility—slim or likely—that he engaged in questionable legal behavior. Instead, it was that one always had to be on special guard against his *open* moves. No one who operated on the Harlem political scene was naïve about Powell, or at least no one should have been. It was frequently the case that a political deal with Powell, seemingly signed and sealed, might really not be the final word after all. J. Raymond Jones knew this, as the account of the 1960 Presidential primary illustrated. But there were several other such instances, some of which simply left his "partners" shaking their heads in frustration and amazement.

A prominent New York State Democratic Party lawyer, Justin Feldman, had his share of dealings with Powell. In 1962, the Republican-controlled state legislature reapportioned the congressional districts, providing a reasonably safe district for Powell of black and Latino voters. At the same time, a safe district on the East Side of Manhattan was carved out for then Republican congressman John Lindsay. The word was out that the Republicans, led by Governor Nelson Rockefeller, had cut a deal with Powell, with Thurgood Marshall as the go-between: a safe seat for Powell in exchange for the same for Lindsay. The New York Democrats, not sure of this, but also not liking the redrawn lines, decided to bring a lawsuit charging malapportionment. Powell moved to join the suit on the side of the Republicans. The Democrats, with Justin Feldman as the lawyer, welcomed this, hoping to get a deposition from Powell on exactly what had happened. Under oath, he would have to tell the truth.

Meanwhile, at the same time in 1962, Robert Morgenthau was running for governor against Rockefeller. Feldman became Morgenthau's campaign manager, and he sought Powell's support. Powell was receptive, but he made it known that he would need $50,000 for "campaign expenses" to travel around the state for Morgenthau. Believing that this was a bit steep, Feldman hoped to negotiate a smaller figure; $15,000 to $20,000 would be more reasonable. He and his wife were invited to one of Powell's political club affairs at Smalls Restaurant in Harlem. After this they were to go to dinner at another favorite Powell spot in upper Harlem, the Flash Inn. Powell was his usual gracious, effusive self. He knew that the state Democrats had suspected him of working out a congressional reapportionment deal with the Republicans, and he knew the Democrats wanted to gain his political support in the upcoming gubernatorial race.

He was the happy, charming host with the Feldmans and several political club friends at the dinner table. He announced to Feldman: "You want to know about those districts and how they got drawn up. You thought it was Thurgood. You're wrong. A 60 percent black district would be bad for me in a three-way primary with two blacks and a white. So Nelson [Rockefeller] sent Sam Pierce down to see me, and at this very table we redrew those lines. And I end up with a protected district." Powell beamed, knowing he had his audience, especially Feldman, in his grasp. "Now," he continued, "Justin, you know the truth. If you want to put me on the stand and ask me about this, and you're that kind of S.O.B., then I'm the kind of S.O.B. who would deny it." Everyone—except Feldman—roared with laughter.

The dinner that evening cost $160, but in his generous manner, Powell waved off Feldman's offer to contribute to the bill, and he picked up the tab.

The next morning, Feldman received a call from an irritated Morgenthau, his candidate. "What are you doing with Adam Clayton Powell in Harlem?" Morgenthau wanted to know. He had already received a call from Powell. "He said you also stuck him with the check. Why did you do that?" Clearly, Morgenthau was disappointed with his campaign manager. Feldman patiently explained the evening dinner meeting and promised to clear up matters. He called Powell at Abyssinian Baptist Church to reprimand him for what was obviously a big bag of misunderstandings, if not misstatements, especially about the dinner check. Surely, Powell remembered Feldman's offer to pay for his and his wife's share? Powell, according to Feldman, simply laughed into the phone, and proceeded to explain to the astute lawyer how an astute politician—this one, at least—saw things: "I was making a point. Morgenthau won't dare let it be known that he is a cheapskate. Now, I'll get my full $50,000 for campaign expenses."[27]

That Powell played hard-ball politics on his home turf everyone knew. And no one understood this better than J. Raymond Jones. "I often wondered," Jones wrote years later in his memoirs, "why I had to be burdened by this very brilliant but oh so mercurial colleague."[28] Jones told of a joint venture he entered into with Powell to build cooperative housing for middle- and low-income residents in Harlem. The relationship fell apart, although the housing was subsequently built, over Powell's "surrogates" demanding what Jones felt were unreasonable subcontract fees. Powell and his associates sued Jones and his partners, claiming the latter had not been entirely honest in their dealings and had created a "dummy front" corporation to squeeze out the Powell group. The suit sought to keep the city from paying certain fees to the Jones group. "In the background of the controversy," the *New York Times* reported, "is a cleavage between two groups polarizing around either Councilman Jones or Representative Powell as primary elections approach."[29]

The entire episode left the impression in the minds of many that here were two giants of Harlem politics squaring off against each other for the financial and political rewards that go with political power. There was enough suspicion and criticism to be shared by everyone involved, and the reputations of all undoubtedly were tarnished. Powell and Jones had been known to be shrewd businessmen as well as astute politicians, and the credibility of both suffered in the aftermath of this open, vicious legal battle between two who once were allies. Their alliance, prominently displayed in Powell's successful 1958 fight with Tammany Hall, never lasted long. In 1961 Powell and Jones were on opposite sides in the hotly contested Democratic mayoralty contest between Mayor Robert Wagner, supported by Jones and the "reformers," and Arthur Levitt, supported, by Powell. Wagner and Jones won that one, but the two Harlem politicians made up long enough to enter into the housing deal.

No one knowledgeable, however, about the dynamic ways of Harlem politics assumed that the two could get along for too long. They were too different in style, and neither ever felt comfortable with the other. In the spring of 1964, when Jones paid a visit to President Johnson, Powell had sent that message to the White House: "Please tell the President there has been no marriage with that guy and me, and there never will be."[30]

But, of course, this was in the spring. A few months later, when Jones became the first black leader of Tammany Hall, he and Powell held a public kiss-and-make-up meeting in Powell's Washington office. Jones later wrote that he knew he had to have harmony in the New York party if he were to be a successful leader: "I first had to take care of schisms in my own bailiwick, and that meant I would have to show all New York that I could pacify, if not tame, that temperamental leopard in my backyard—Congressman Adam Clayton Powell."[31] This time Powell was cooperative. The co-op housing legal battle was behind them, and Powell received Jones with open arms and generous words of praise and support. "We've never been opponents," Powell told the press waiting outside his office. "We merely differed once on a candidate. Ray and I have been close together all our lives." Jones merely smiled and decided to enjoy the hyperbole.

No one would have more experience with Powell on the local Harlem New York scene during the turbulent 1960s than Jones. Whether in business deals turned sour, or in political alliances that proved problematic, Jones and Powell were, indeed, two old pros in a protracted love-hate relationship. No other city, at no other time in black political history, offered such a saga of two protagonists of such skills and power locked in combat on the same turf. They shared the same constituents; they dealt with the same political leaders at the city, state, and national levels. They both had strong reputations for political brilliance, and they both had respective hard-core loyal supporters who would never desert them. In their own ways, they represented the positive aspirations of their people, and each clearly understood the complex requirements of being a "race leader" and trying to use that leadership to the maximum advantage of their followers. Equally important, both were aware of the pressures imposed on one who chose the roles they carved out for themselves. In December 1964, when Jones became the first black leader of Tammany Hall—albeit only a shadow of its earlier powerful self—his assumption of that position was comparable in the minds of some to a Jackie Robinson breaking into major-league baseball in 1946. It was an important political "first" in the largest and perhaps most vibrant ethnically political city in the country.

If their respective positions represented the power and the promise of black New York politics, they also represented the stresses and strains of political ambition and survival. And this situation came at a time—the flowering of the Great Society programs—when money from Washington would be flowing into local communities throughout the country.

Chairman Powell never lost an opportunity to remind everyone that his committee was the central vehicle for the passage of the antipoverty legislation. He exaggerated at times, of course, but there was enough truth in the claim to let it stand. What was also certain was that such bursts of appropriations would ignite intense interest throughout the country over how various local programs would be controlled and run. Obviously, Powell's Harlem was no exception, and Powell would take more than a casual interest in this in his own congressional front yard.

The issue there focused on control of the major antipoverty

agency in the community, HARYOU-ACT (Harlem Youth Opportunities Unlimited–Associated Community Teams). The two agencies merged in the summer of 1964. HARYOU was mainly the result of the intellectual work of Dr. Kenneth B. Clark, a prominent social psychologist and college professor who became its director. But if Clark was anything, he was, by his own admission, not a politician, and certainly not one in Powell's league. Neither was he ever on Powell's team. Clark envisioned an antipoverty program that would be free of political pressure—in staffing, devising programs, etc.—and would rely heavily on professional social service people and indigenous residents. The managers of such an important task would have control over millions of dollars.

Within a month after the merger of HARYOU and ACT, Clark resigned as director, charging that Powell "had seized control of the organization to use for his own purposes."[32] Columnist Murray Kempton wrote that Washington, D.C., saw Harlem as "simply a geographical expression for Adam Powell's private property." And Powell's old nemesis William Buckley concluded that HARYOU-ACT was merely "another of Mr. Powell's expensive hobbies." Powell denied these charges, of course, but the leadership fight over the agency continued. Powell countercharged that Clark and his wife, Dr. Mamie Clark, an accomplished psychologist like her husband, would "come out of this making a tremendous sum of money" if they were given control of the agency. This infuriated the Clarks even more. Jones attempted to mediate the dispute, but without success. It was becoming clear that Clark's battle with Powell was a losing one, and his respect for the congressman had virtually disappeared. He had quite the opposite view of Jones, whom he regarded as a shrewd politician but a man of integrity. Several years later, Clark recalled those hectic fights with Powell: Powell, according to Clark, clearly saw HARYOU as a political base, a mechanism for exerting powerful political control. It was a potential source for patronage jobs, and Clark indicated that Powell bluntly told him so. Therefore, Powell could not give Clark a free hand in developing the program. Clark felt that Powell "did a pork barrel job," and he had the support of Senator Robert Kennedy. As far as Clark was concerned, this "was an omen as to what was going to happen to the war on poverty in general."[33] And more than a few times later, Clark told of a conversation with Powell wherein the congressman bluntly stated: "Kenneth, with your brains and my power, we could split millions or split the loot." Clark always believed that Powell saw the antipoverty program as a means of enriching himself and his friends.

Clark stepped aside from HARYOU-ACT, and a Powell supporter, Livingston L. Wingate, became the director. A lawyer and former member of Powell's congressional staff, Wingate strongly disclaimed any political pressure: "HARYOU-ACT by its very nature, must be scrupulously guarded from politicians and other interests who might seek to divert its program to their own interests."[34] The only order he received from Powell concerning the antipoverty agency, he said, was to "keep it clean." This did not mean, of course, as Wingate stated at another time, that having Powell as one's congressman could not be a good thing. Powell was a powerful committee chairman; it would be expected of him to look after the interests of his constituents, especially in getting grants. They all do it . . . and they should. But this was not the same as using the program as a patronage funnel and employment service for one's political cronies.

But suspicion of political favoritism and documented inefficient accounting procedures were precisely the problems that plagued this important and vulnerable agency virtually from its inception. Audit report after audit report revealed no fraudulent use of funds or involved Powell in any illegal way regarding money. But few ever doubted that Powell's friends—efficient or inefficient—were the ones running the program. Powell himself for a time took an open interest in seeing that the agency's books were put in order, and insisted that Wingate do whatever was necessary to weed out the "leeches" on the agency's staff.

But no one suspected that Powell would let such an important project exist in his district without his political input. The major source of funds was Congress. The people involved at the grassroots level were potential and actual civic activists, if not outright political operatives. The social and economic issues being addressed were too vital to the entire community. Mayors around the country soon realized the potential political threats that could come from such embryonic activity. For Powell *not* to take an active interest in HARYOU-ACT would have been unthinkable. The battle in Harlem was repeated in various forms in many urban areas around the country as established political figures sought to control the programs.

The volatile Harlem scene was especially tense. And everyone understood, sometimes cynically, that with so much money flowing and so many opportunities, personal and political, the power brokers in Harlem would clash. Powell was in the middle of this dynamic development.

At the same time, it was clear that Powell's reputation for cunning and connivance would follow him. He could not be ignored, but even the White House had to be wary of its relationship with him where matters of New York politics were concerned. One always had to be cautious of questionable requests from the chairman and his friends. One White House memo clearly illustrated the problem. In response to a Powell request in 1964, Lee White, a member of Johnson's staff, wrote to Jack Valenti that the White House should be careful about committing the President to attend a housing dedication ceremony in New York. One of the developers, a friend of Powell's, was "under investigation for some sort of hanky-panky in the housing field." The President's appearance could be sticky and embarrassing, therefore, "it looks like a good one to avoid."[35]

Such an attitude very likely compromised Powell's role as chairman, but on balance he maintained his status as a political power to be reckoned with into the mid-1960s. His flamboyant life-style, cavalier response to his critics, and questionable activities on the Harlem home front all made him, in the minds of some, a difficult, if not dubious politician to deal with. He could not be rejected out of hand, but at the same time it was foolish to place complete faith in dealings with him. Such an assessment, ultimately, could not serve him well.

But through all this, there was an unfolding drama in the New York courts that would prove to be one of the major factors in his political undoing.

19

Exposing Crime and Corruption, and the "Bag Woman" Case

Throughout his career Powell was frequently involved in several controversial battles simultaneously. In early 1960, his plate was overflowing.

—He was bedeviled by the income tax indictment and trial.
—He had to fight off critics, especially George Meany of the AFL-CIO, who did not want to see him accede to the chairmanship of his committee.
—He became involved in questionable maneuvers over endorsement of candidates for the Democratic Presidential nomination, which was not unrelated to his quest for the chairmanship.
—He challenged Carmine De Sapio and Tammany Hall for a greater share of political power—through control of district leaderships and patronage jobs—in Manhattan and New York City.
—He launched a crusade from the floor of Congress against crime and police corruption in Harlem.

All these things were taking place—any one of which would have been more than enough to occupy the full attention of the most active politician—while his second marriage was coming to an end, and he was spending more time in Puerto Rico where he would build a home and take on a new bride. This latter move even fueled speculation that he was preparing to concentrate his long-term political interests on Puerto Rico, even with the view of that island's eventual statehood and his own role as its future senator or governor.

Powell *always* had many political irons in the fire.

Surely one of the hottest was the charge he made in a sermon from Abyssinian's pulpit on January 10, 1960: "I am stating one unchallengeable fact, that the Mafia and the syndicate are in complete control of Harlem." There is strong speculation that Powell made this move in an effort to divert the attacks on him involving his income taxes. If he chose to go public with startling accusations of crime and corruption, perhaps this would scare off his detractors or at least make his charges of attempts to silence him more plausible.

A week earlier, from the House floor, he had launched a series of ten weekly speeches accusing the New York police of being involved in protecting organized crime, especially the "numbers racket" in Harlem. "Numbers" (also referred to as "policy") was a form of gambling whereby bettors placed bets with local contacts on a combination of three numbers each day. The bettor won if the three numbers corresponded to three numbers appearing in the same order in a previously designated portion of the day's pari-mutuel betting total at a selected racetrack. Reliable estimates were that about 1.5 million people in New York "played the numbers" each day, betting as little as a nickel or dime up to hundreds of dollars, wagering about $100 million per year. Payoff odds were usually six hundred to one. Bettors could place bets at candy stores, bars, newsstands, barbershops, cafés, with individual "runners," and various other places known as "drops." All this was illegal, of course, and it could only survive on such a large scale with the protective cover of the police. Powell charged, and most Harlemites believed, that the police were "on the pad," that is, were being bribed by the operators of the racket who thus avoided arrest. That this major criminal industry operated fairly openly throughout the city, and in countless other communities throughout the country, was an open secret.

Powell launched his crusade, charging that the police were corrupted, and that this illegal activity, known as the "poor man's hobby," was taking millions of dollars out of poor communities. He also charged that organized crime, under the control of Italians and Jews, was squeezing out the local Negro operators. "If this low-income community," he stated, "has drained from it between $3 million and $4 million a month, then the first fact I wish to point out is that the numbers is pauperizing Harlem." When arrests were made, invariably, he accused, it was the lowly Negro "runners," not the big-time white operators, who were hit. He promised that he would take the floor of the House once a week and expose the gamblers involved, giving names and addresses of "drops," the operators, and those protected by the police.

As soon as he leveled his blast, New York police officials denied any wrongdoing and immediately swooped into Harlem and arrested many low-level bookies, all black. This hardly satisfied Powell, who then charged racial discrimination in law enforcement, and he raised the issue in a way that disappointed some of his defenders. Specifically, he wanted it known that as long as the illegal racket operated, then Negroes should have their share of the profits! He told a rally at his church: "I am against numbers in any form. But until the day when numbers is wiped out in Harlem—I hate to say this from the pulpit—I am going to fight for the Negro having the same chance as an Italian."[1]

In his speeches on the House floor, Powell got very specific. He listed names of operators, addresses where bets could be placed, and in some instances the amount of money paid to the police. He pointed out that most of the legal defense of the few arrested from time to time was handled by a few known lawyers, as well as the bail bond business. Who paid these people? The Mafia, Powell charged. He promised more, and he called on the governor and the mayor to appoint investigative committees with subpoena powers to dig into the charges he was making.

Adam Powell was asking probing, embarrassing questions. He had turned up the heat. The *New York Post*, spurred on by his charges, picked up the story, and sent its own investigative reporting team into Harlem. The newspaper confirmed virtually every charge the congressman made, and proceeded to run a series of detailed articles outlining the operation of the numbers racket, police corruption and all. Powell, feeling vindicated, was elated. He introduced the *Post* articles into the *Congressional Record*.

It was also clear that he sensed he was onto a worthy cause, and he would not let pass the opportunity to drive home his points with biting sarcasm. He knew he had the issue of gambling and police corruption as a good one to stand on; too many people were involved as bettors, low-level employees, big-time operators (they were called "bankers" in the gambling business), and police on the take. He also knew that the issue of civil rights in the country was beginning to get more attention. That spring of 1960 would see renewed efforts to pass a civil rights bill. It was also the beginning, on February 1, of the Southern black college student sit-in protests at segregated lunch counters. Both of these issues, crime and civil rights, were grist for Adam Powell's mill. In one of his weekly exposés to Congress, he amusingly told his colleagues: "If I was preaching, with my Scripture background, I would take the Book of Numbers on gambling, and the one on Civil Rights would be the Book on Revelations."[2]

But as always, he caused some who otherwise supported him in his efforts to admonish him in some respects. Roy Wilkins of the NAACP did not care for his comment on support for more Negro numbers operators, if whites were to be protected. Wilkins had to answer a letter from a woman who objected to Wilkins's criticism of Powell on this point. She had written to Wilkins telling him that everyone who lived in Harlem knew that Powell was correct in his description of the racial employment patterns in the numbers racket. The lower level jobs were held by Negroes; the "bankers with few exceptions are white." To pretend otherwise was hypocritical, and Powell should be supported, not criticized, for being "willing to give his life for the long-overdue exposure of this racket."[3]

Wilkins could not agree with her or Powell on the racial inference. He certainly agreed that gambling and police corruption should be exposed, but he was not prepared to support any movement or campaign that called for "equal rights in gambling." There should be no toleration of any effort to suggest that there should be a serious "discussion of gambling rights on a racial basis." He found this incredible. As far as Wilkins was concerned, this was not his understanding of the purpose of his lifelong struggle for civil rights.[4]

But for his part, Powell knew what he was doing in raising the issue of racial discrimination in the allocation of gambling profits and law enforcement. He knew that many of his constituents and church members would, indeed, continue to gamble illegally, and he knew that no amount of moralizing on *that* issue from him would change that practice. But he also knew that many of those same people were resentful that whites controlled the operation to the exclusion of blacks. And when the authorities denied police complicity, this only fed the cynicism and resentment. Therefore, when he raised the race issue, he was, in his mind, only once again speaking to the true feelings of many residents in the Harlem ghetto. Not all, but certainly many who would identify with and admire his courage in even opening up the subject. It was Powell again being the honest purveyor of the true feelings of many. "Equal rights in gambling"? As saddening as that might be, it very likely reflected the reality on the minds of many Harlemites. Therefore, Powell was not only revealing a legally corrupt system; he was exposing a morally vulnerable situation, even if the remedy he offered at the moment was less than morally or legally satisfying. In fact, that remedy was full of the contradictions characteristic of ghetto life in general—revulsion against immorality, injustice, and illegality on the one hand, yet insisting on a piece of the immoral, illegal action on the other. And some people simply concluded that Powell was pursuing that old hustler's game: "Cut us in or cut it out." At the same time he was building a protective wall around himself: they were going after him on the tax case to silence him—to intimidate him.

Neither were matters helped by the denials and evasive responses from the police. Powell called for the resignation of the police commissioner, for periodic reassignment of vice squad officers, and for more Negro police, as well as a Negro deputy commissioner. When the official response was that he was asking for racial preference, this simply aggravated the Harlem cynicism. When the district attorney and police commissioner prodded him to meet with them and to bring any other evidence he had, this simply increased the Harlem anger. It was as if the police did not know everything he knew—and then some. The police commissioner scolded Powell that it was not necessary to stir up "anti-Semitic or anti-Italian feeling to demonstrate that policy is evil." And on a local television program, Congressman Emanuel Celler raised the same point. Powell gave a somewhat contemptuous apology: "Maybe I should have said that all bankers in Harlem are whites then."[5]

He was equally incensed when the police commissioner rejected his suggestion that a Negro be appointed as deputy commissioner. Such appointments, the commissioner responded, were made on the basis of merit and qualifications, not on the basis of race. This was more than Powell could take. Such an answer was "a new dodge," a "pious attitude," and a "counterfeit position."[6] Powell accused the commissioner of "posing as some kind of righteous American." He said:

> Since the Negro people were freed as slaves, the whole of this country has been working to correct a terrible wrong and balance the sheet of democracy. One of the means of balancing the sheet has been the appointment of qualified Negro citizens to high office. It is part of our record that whenever these precedent-making appoint-

> ments occurred, all of us have been proud of the fact that we were accomplishing the American dream of full democracy for everyone.[7]

This was an argument that would burst full force on the civil rights policy agenda a few years later in the form of "affirmative action." Powell was engaging the issue in his way, insisting that his suggestion did not deny attention to qualification:

> When I asked the Commissioner to appoint a Negro, I laid emphasis on qualification and representation. To appoint a Negro on the basis of race would mean making such an appointment regardless of qualifications. I did not, as the Commissioner well knows, ask for such an appointment. It is foolish on the Commissioner's part to pretend in public that I did. On the contrary, I called for adequate representation of our vast Negro population in the higher councils of the Police Department. I feel . . . that a qualified Negro commissioner could not only make a fine contribution to the solution of minority problems, but lift the prestige of the department in the eyes of our minority citizens and give a higher morale to minority rank-and-file members of the department.

Years later, the argument, and its counter views, would become a major issue in deciding how to remedy the effects of past discrimination. At that moment, Powell was having none of the commissioner's "arrogant" and "lofty" rationalizations. He well knew how many political appointments were made to various high and low positions, and he certainly well knew that race and ethnic identities were some criteria frequently used. The commissioner's response not only infuriated him; it insulted him. And in this reaction, he likely was joined by many of his constituents who were weary of such blatant evasions and hypocrisies.

In this same speech on February 25, 1960, Powell, pursuing his tactic of being specific, mentioned the name of a woman, Mrs. Esther James, as a person "extorting" money from gamblers and "transmitting this money to police officers." This was known to the police authorities, he charged, because a letter, which he introduced into the *Congressional Record*, had been sent from one of the gamblers to the police complaining of Mrs. James's extortion.[8] Nothing had been done about the complaint, and Powell wanted to know why. The complainant was ready to testify under oath against her, but there had been no official action. Powell stated that "no investigation has been made, and Esther James continues to be the payoff woman for the police department higher ups."

A few weeks later, on March 6, 1960, Powell was a last-minute fill-in guest for Senator Hubert Humphrey on a New York television talk show. Of course he would be asked about his charges of crime and police corruption. He repeated his several charges and proceeded to name Mrs. Esther James as a "bag woman" carrying money from gamblers to the police. As long as he confined such remarks to the floor of Congress, he was immune from any suit on the basis of libel or slander. But now he was on television.

Mrs. James filed suit for defamation of character against Powell, the television station, and the program's sponsor. From the beginning it was clear that Powell did not take this action seriously. Mrs. James was seeking $1 million from him, but in comparison to the other battles he had fought and was fighting, this surely was only a slight annoyance. The television station and the sponsor, however, shortly settled for $1,500. Powell certainly was not in a conciliatory mood for even such a relatively minor sum, and he was more than convinced that his allegations about her were substantial and accurate. However questionable some of his other pronouncements on politics and persons had been over the years, this one, in his mind, was beyond any taint of falsehood. The runners and payoff people in the neighborhoods were matters of common knowledge. The operations were just that extensive and open. In addition, he was now an exceedingly busy congressional committee chairman, and this minor irritation was far down on his list of priorities. This turned out to be a major miscalculation on his part. In his last book, he candidly admitted that he had made a "grave mistake." At first, he did not take the lawsuit seriously, considering it "just another of the smear tactics." Then it became clear, later, that it would be hard to persuade witnesses to testify in his favor, complicating the process of gathering the evidence necessary to justify his public statements. He also asserted that he was then so busy in Washington that he could not concentrate on the lawsuit.[9]

This admission only matched the frustration felt by Charles McKinney, the lawyer Powell engaged to handle the case. At first, McKinney had to get several continuances because the demands of Washington business made his client unavailable. But this was vexing because the lawyer never knew when the judge would simply order the case to be heard. "It was hard to get Powell's time and attention," McKinney recalled.[10] "He would agree to be in court on a certain date to start the trial, but then send word at the last minute that he couldn't make it." This meant McKinney had to plead for still another continuance.

Finally, no more delays were possible, and a definite trial date set. McKinney informed Powell, who assured him he would be present. McKinney insisted he wanted Powell in the courtroom throughout the trial, but the congressman apparently felt he need only be there to give his own testimony. This hardly suited the lawyer's planned strategy, which called for Powell being at the trial and having the jurors see him. McKinney stated that he had studied Powell's income tax trial, and he wanted Powell's charisma in the courtroom as well as on the stand. But Powell never appeared, and he sent a note at the last minute when he was scheduled to take the stand instructing his attorney to proceed without him. He also told his frustrated lawyer that he would not hold him responsible for the outcome. This could be small comfort for the attorney. His task was to defend his client, but there had to be cooperation. McKinney noted that for the most part throughout the period of preparing the case, he had to deal with Powell through intermediaries. Powell simply was too busy or too uninterested.

On April 3, 1963, the jury returned a verdict against Powell for a total of $211,500: $11,500 for compensatory damages, and $200,000 for punitive damages.

One juror told the press later: "We felt that nobody has a right to shoot off his mouth that way, especially a member of Congress who should know better. He did not offer any concrete evidence that she was a 'bag woman' as he had stated."[11]

McKinney was convinced that Powell's constant nonappearances were taken by the jury as acts of defiance and disrespect. After the trial, one juror revealed that Powell's failure to appear did not sit well with many of her juror colleagues. "We had to be there. So why couldn't he come?" In addition, there was no problem in establishing that Mrs. James actually took money from gamblers; there were two witnesses who testified to this. But the defense could not establish that she actually paid over the money to the police. McKinney's hope was that with Powell on the stand, the congressman could be so persuasive that the jurors would have to believe him. But this was not to be, and, McKinney lamented years later, that in fact the case could readily have been settled for $5,000 to $7,500 at the most.

Mrs. James was jubilant. "The King is dead," she announced. "Adam Clayton Powell is dead. Now he will just have to keep his big mouth shut."

What followed for the next three and a half years was a series of legal maneuvers that included countless appeals, motions, arguments, delays, and even another lawsuit by the relentless Mrs. James and her lawyer, Raymond Rubin. Powell had replaced his original lawyer with a team headed by Henry Williams. The libel suit was appealed through the state and federal courts to the U.S. Supreme Court, which refused to hear the case. In the process, James and Rubin accused Powell of transferring his property in New York and Puerto Rico to his wife's Puerto Rican relatives in an attempt to avoid having his assets attached. Powell had received $900 for an *Esquire* article he had written, and he gave this money to his wife. James stated this was another ruse to avoid paying the judgment against him.

Along the way, a state court reduced the original judgment from $211,500 to $46,500. But time after time, Powell refused to respond to court orders to appear and answer various charges and to submit to an examination of his financial records. Ultimately two civil citations were issued against him. He still refused to appear. The state laws did not permit a civil contempt warrant to be served on Sunday; thus for over a year Powell came to New York only on Sundays to preach at Abyssinian and leave before the end of the day. The press followed these various legal maneuvers every step, detailing the growing frustration of the plaintiff and highlighting the deft ability of the congressman to prolong the final judgments. At one point when he insisted, unsuccessfully, that a contempt warrant was illegally served against him, Powell's air of confidence persisted. One press account read that he showed no interest in the various judicial decrees. He was relaxing at his home in Puerto Rico when a reporter reached him by telephone. His attitude was one of indifference and defiance. He bantered with the reporter, commenting on the weather and his concern for what the lack of rain was doing to his lawn. "The weather here has been very beautiful," he said. "I am getting fat and suntanned. When I get back to Washington they are going to think I am a Negro." This was the old self-confident Adam Powell, teasing his questioners, having fun.[12] When a criminal warrant was issued, permitting him to be served on Sunday, the judge agreed to hold off enforcing it until another appeal was heard.

Newspaper headlines recorded the long-running legal saga:

"Powell Fails to Show for Libel Case Probe"
"Powell Loses In Bid to Stay Arrest Order"

"Powell Rebuffed in Court Fight Here"
"Sees Powell 'Feeling the Heat' "
"Powell Account is Frozen by Writ"

The Johnson White House was obviously interested in and following the drama. One internal memo, written at the time hearings were being held on the important new antipoverty bill, read: "As you know, we have been helpful to Chairman Powell on several occasions. . . . I mentioned to him that Jack Valenti and you might be willing to work with him on the following items: 1. Helping with his libel problems. . . ."[13]

During the 1964 Presidential campaign, when Powell was stomping the country for the Johnson-Humphrey ticket, another White House memo was sent:

To: Larry O'Brien October 26, 1964

From: Henry Wilson

Adam Powell called me last week about an AID loan for a textile firm in the Dominican Republic.

Totally impossible, of course.

I had AID give him the bad news.

I later talked with him—he expressed appreciation for effort—especially since I had AID point out another route.

Yesterday he called with a new one—wants the Justice Department to defend him against the effort to invoke civil arrest in the matter of the libel judgment against him.

I attach carbons of an exchange of letters with Katzenbach.

You can't say he doesn't make things interesting.[14]

Powell had asked Acting Attorney General Nicholas Katzenbach to explore the possibility of the Justice Department defending him against the second suit involving transfer of his property. Katzenbach informed Powell that this was not possible. Although the Justice Department had represented Powell when an attempt was made to enjoin the payment of his congressional salary, this other matter, specifically the suit charging property transfer, was not proper for consideration by the department. Katzenbach wrote:

. . . The various orders entered by the courts . . . are incidental to the defamation action (*James* v. *Powell*) which has already gone to judgment and received appellate review. Also, Judge Chimera's order of June 1, 1964 (which recites that it is based upon an asserted failure to obey a subpoena issued September 5, 1963) was issued after pre-

> sentation of affidavits on your behalf and after hearing arguments of counsel and provided that execution would be stayed while the House of Representatives is in session. Throughout the course of this litigation you appear to have been represented by private counsel, both in connection with the underlying litigation which resulted in the judgment, and during the period subsequent to the issuance of the subpoena in September 1963.
>
> The material which you have furnished us indicated that this litigation, from its inception, has involved acts which were not done in the discharge of your official functions and has not involved government property or activities. . . . the dispute in question arose from statements made by you over television.[15]

This was not a satisfactory response for Powell, who wrote back that he clearly disagreed with Justice's interpretations. He sought to show how all the proceedings, in fact, stemmed from the judgment in the defamation suit. And he raised the point that he would make a few months later in a speech in Congress:

> . . . You contend in your letter that the litigation involved acts which were not done in the discharge of official functions nor government activities. In fact, the statements made on the television program had been previously made on the floor of the United States House of Representatives. They related to matters of vital public interests. I feel I would have been derelict in my duty as a United States Congressman had I not brought these matters to the attention of the public. On such an important question, neither the Supreme Court of New York nor the Court of Appeals of New York have rendered a legal opinion.
>
> Because the rights, duties, and privileges of the United States Congressmen were involved, I am certain that the United States has an interest and, for this reason, I again request representation by the Department of Justice.[16]

The Department of Justice did not change its mind, and Powell had to proceed on his own.

Meanwhile, his friends had formed an organization to help pay off the first judgment. He indicated he would pay the amount of the defamation judgment—now $51,000 with interest—but he would continue to fight the second suit alleging illegal transfer of property. Apparently money would come from a group called "Harlem Justice for Powell," which had, by early 1965, raised "about $30,000 from friends," according to Powell.[17]

At the same time, Powell advised the FBI that his office had been approached by an "unknown individual" who was willing to offer Powell a deal involving the libel suit. In essence, it was a bribe. Apparently, this person would "come up with $51,000 to settle the libel suit and in turn Congressman Powell would appoint this individual's son to West Point." When the FBI sought to confirm this information, it could find no substance to the charge. The agency had long been wary of Powell, and a notation in the FBI files on this recent matter indicated less than full confidence in the congressman's veracity. In advising its agent how to proceed, the FBI noted: "It is entirely possible that Powell is attempting some sort of a maneuver which would be to his benefit in connection with the libel suit pending against him in New York and interviews of——— should be handled most thoroughly and most circumspectly."[18] Nothing resulted from the complaint.

This was not the only time during that period that the FBI heard from Powell's office concerning mysterious doings. And the FBI was beginning to suspect that perhaps Powell might be nervous about his safety. Powell's secretary obviously shared his concerns, given the nature of the charges he was leveling against the underworld and the police in New York. In a couple of instances in early 1964, Mrs. Maxine Dargans called the FBI to report unusual things at Powell's Washington home. Powell had noticed something wrong with the electricity, causing the lights to flicker. He called the power company, and the trouble was traced to a manhole in the courtyard. Mrs. Dargans told the FBI: "The Congressman felt this was suspicious and wondered what might cause such a condition." To allay his fears, she wanted to assure Powell that it could be defective wiring or a current overload.

A few weeks later, Mrs. Dargans called the FBI to report that Powell had noticed a suspicious car "hanging around the house." He noted the license number—a Virginia tag—and wanted the FBI to investigate. The 1962 Buick station wagon had two white men in it. The FBI files noted: "She [Mrs. Dargans] was most anxious to determine if there was anything about this man [the one in whose name the car was registered] that might require special attention, and if there was anything at all that could be done to ease the Congressman's mind regarding this situation." The FBI advised that its information, thus far, did not warrant a federal investigation, and that Powell should rely on local authorities. The agency then noted in its files: "It will be recalled that last week Mrs. Dargans called and advised that Congressman Powell was worried about flickering lights at his home. It seems that the current action pending in New York against Powell has him jumpy."[19]

Under the circumstances, this was understandable.

In the meantime, Powell made one last effort at convincing his congressional colleagues that his New York legal problems were more than personal, but also raised issues about the constitutional rights of congressmen to speak off the floor. If he could not persuade the Department of Justice of this, he would, in February 1965, at least make one more stab on the floor of the House, where this business had all started in the first place back in 1960.

It was clear that he felt he had a constitutional point that had not been fully appreciated. To him, he told the fifty-odd members in the chamber, the principal issue was: "Can any Member of the U.S. Congress repeat, off the floor of Congress, that which he has said on the floor?"[20] This was the overriding constitutional question that his case presented, and, he emphasized several times, it had never been adjudicated, not by the state or federal courts. What more important issue could be presented, especially when the purpose of the repetition was to inform the public and one's constituents of transactions that had taken place within the elected body. Under such circumstances, he pleaded, the constitutional immunity that protected congressmen's speeches *on* the floor ought logically to be extended beyond the chamber. In addition, he argued, this was such a vital matter of freedom of speech that he felt the media likewise ought to be concerned. Otherwise, what if the press printed a speech made on the floor that someone felt was libelous? Would not the fate engulfing him in New York be precedent for suing the media? His issue, in other words, not only involved congressional immunity but serious questions relating to the First Amendment and freedom of the press.

It had been five years, he told his colleagues, since he first took the floor and launched his crusade against crime and corruption in New York. Inasmuch as some were new members, they might not know the background of his case, but he wanted them to know. He introduced the series of articles published by the *New York Post*, as well as the sermon he preached on the subject. And then he mentioned Mrs. James and how the case against him developed. But this time, he also disclosed that she had a criminal record, convicted, he asserted, in Buffalo "4 times for assault and battery, but this was not reported in the press." (Two years later, columnist Drew Pearson published the record of Mrs. James and concluded that Powell might well have reason to believe he "suffered a miscarriage of justice." Pearson questioned whether such a person as Mrs. James, who had had "six brushes with the law," really justified the kind of support she received in her suit against Powell.[21])

But in 1965, before Congress, Powell wanted his colleagues to know this. And he also reminded them that he had been tried and convicted in Manhattan, a borough with 50 percent Negroes and Puerto Ricans, by an all-white jury.

"What I am bucking here is the entire underworld," he charged. And he cited a recent *Newsweek* article that linked narcotics and the numbers racket. Powell said, "The narcotics pushers have all the protection they want from the police department." He was not holding back now, pulling no punches. The courts, police, the press "mobilized against me in my fight against vice and corruption. But I will continue to fight. I will not be deterred by these irrelevant suits or other devices that have been brought against me."

He tried to convince his fellow members that there were unlawful aspects of his case: the fact that he was served with an arrest warrant on one occasion when Congress was in session, thus violating congressional immunity; that one subpoena was delivered to his church office, not to his New York home. But these technical procedural points were likely less impressive than the constitutional point of protected speech to which he referred several times. He again asserted, hoping obviously that his colleagues would agree and see the relevance to them, "There is no relevant difference between communication of congressional speeches by the printed pages of the *Congressional Record* and communication through the facilities of television and radio and by the words that come from a human being's mouth."

He noted that Mrs. James offered to settle for $8,000, but on the advice of counsel, he refused. "Whether this advice was good or bad," he said, "is not important, but the point is that it has ballooned out of all proportions—from $8,000 to a quarter of a million dollars." And he emphasized: "The sole object is to keep Adam Powell out of New York."

Neither would he let up on the campaign against police corruption, he promised. As to the matter of transferring $900 to his wife, his position was: "Why is it a crime to give $900 to your wife and not a crime to give $3,000 to a cop who operates a numbers drop?"

And: "Why is it that my Harlem, Spanish Harlem, Italian Harlem, Black Harlem, is the dumping ground for dope in the United States?"

He promised to renew his charges against crime and corruption each week on the House floor. And he ended his speech with the flourishing oratory usually reserved for the pulpit and mass rallies:

> I do not know how long I will be able to do it, but as long as I have breath I will not allow the criminalization of my people or any people, the pauperization of my people or any people, the degradation of any people.
>
> I am only one, but I am one. I cannot do everything but I can do something. What I can do, that I ought to do; and what I ought to do by the grace of God I will do.[22]

By all accounts, it was one of his most stirring speeches on the House floor.

But this was an impassioned speech delivered to an unresponsive body. It was perhaps the only place left to him, but Congress clearly was going to let the New York judicial system run its course against him.

The next year, 1966, the legal limits for Powell would be reached. The various contempt citations were being prosecuted. He was ordered to appear in court on penalty of arrest.

On November 28, 1966, the day before Powell's fifty-eighth birthday, a court order was issued to the city's fifty-three deputy sheriff's: "Without further process, take the body of Adam Clayton Powell, the defendant judgment debtor and commit him to the Civil Jail—on any day of the week including Sunday."[23] Of course, Powell's lawyers appealed, but the end was nearing.

Now it was time for serious private negotiations aimed at a settlement of the remaining judgment of $165,000 against him. A state court indicated the intent to order him to pay sixty dollars per week, and Powell's lawyer said he would recommend this to his client. But Mrs. James's lawyer was unsatisfied, and the judge allowed that he would not order the settlement without Mrs. James's agreement.

The *New York Times* noted that at the rate of sixty dollars per week—$3,120 a year—"it would take the 57-year-old Mr. Powell almost 53 years to pay the judgment to Mrs. James. . . . Now 68 years old, she would thus be 121 by the time the judgment was paid."[24] And this did not take into account the 6 percent interest charge on the unpaid balance of the judgment.

The *Times*, never a friend of Powell's, editorialized: "Mr. Powell's annual payment would have been less than a third of the interest, with no allowance at all for liquidating the principal. No wonder he was ready to jump at the bargain."[25]

But by all calculations, the "Bag Woman" case was coming to an end. Powell would have to pay. It only remained to determine how much and on what terms. This was something Harlem political pundits would never have predicted; Powell had established an image of invincibility in such matters, the income tax indictment being the most prominent. He had been in and out of so many legal and political scrapes and never really seemed to have suffered a definitive defeat, even when candidates he had strongly endorsed lost. Such defeats never seemed to rub off on him. He always had a way of turning loss into victory. But now he was brought down by the sixty-eight-year-old widow. Six years earlier, not many people would have bet on *that* outcome.

By December 1966, if this much was certain, it was also certain that these personal judicial developments would have to compete for Powell's attention with another major problem beginning to descend on his head. A House subcommittee, appointed in the fall, was looking into his handling of committee funds and was preparing to make its report the first week in January 1967. The findings did not look encouraging for Powell. There was open talk now that not only would there be a move to strip him of his chairmanship, but there might be a motion to deny him his seat when Congress convened on January 10, 1967. The next phase of the political drama of Adam Clayton Powell, Jr., would shift for the next several weeks to the Congress, the place that had been his anchor for twenty-one years.

By any definition, he was an embattled man.

20

Congressional Rebuke, Supreme Court Victory, and Electoral Defeat

By the spring and summer of 1966, few Congress watchers doubted that Chairman Powell was losing control of his committee. Several members were sensing that they could do business with the party leadership and the White House by going around him. His prior stamp of approval was becoming less necessary. On May 5, Powell sent a "My dear Colleague" letter to his committee, with a copy to the President:

> I am shocked to learn that you do not have enough interest in the War on Poverty legislation to attend a meeting on Friday, May 6, at 10 a.m., for the purpose of writing up the bill, especially in view of the fact that the appropriation for this bill cannot be enacted until we have passed it on the Floor and the fiscal year closes June 30.[1]

A few months later, he had to appeal to the White House for support in rounding up his committee for a quorum to deal with the Elementary and Secondary Education bill.

But his members and the White House were making their own assessments and charting ways to circumvent him. This was partly because he was becoming increasingly difficult to deal with. He announced that he would not move the "common-site picketing" bill that organized labor wanted until the unions met certain conditions relating to racial discrimination in local unions. This decision stalled matters. He took off for a three-week trip to Europe to attend the

International Labor Organization meetings, thus holding up further consideration of the antipoverty bill. House leaders had to plot to send the bill to the House Rules Committee from his committee without his cooperation, if necessary. Normally, the chairman or his designee would handle the debate on the floor, but now the Speaker was authorized to designate any majority member of Powell's committee to manage the bill. This was a clear signal of what was developing.

More than a few congressmen were feeling that in addition to Powell's differences on certain bills, he was simply too distracted with all his other problems. He was too often unavailable to work out disagreements over pending legislation. And when he did convene his committee, it was frequently at the inconvenience of many who had already readjusted their schedules several times to accommodate him. The *Congressional Quarterly* observed: "It was within that context that the members of the Education and Labor Committee quietly organized to change the rules to limit much of Powell's power as chairman."[2]

In addition, by this time the White House had concluded that the chairman was not to be relied on for sustained future leadership, and the administration was also taking its readings of the top leaders in Congress. In mid-July, 1966, a memo to President Johnson from Presidential aide Henry Wilson read:

> Adam Powell has requested an appointment with you for this week.
>
> I do not urge that you see him, though of course you cannot treat lightly such a request from the chairman of a major committee.
>
> . . . Powell's attitude about the OEO bill has been peculiar, to say the least. Two or three weeks ago, while Powell was out of town, he had Chuck Stone call Shriver and me to ask whether we would be agreeable to postponing consideration of this bill until after the election. I don't want to read too much into this, but the Speaker is understandably jumpy after his experience with Powell recently on the Situs Picketing bill.[3]

Wilson also noted in his memo: "Powell is scheduled to be in New York in court tomorrow."

In September 1966, Powell's committee decided to move to restrict his powers as chairman. (See Chapter 1.) While Sam Gibbons of Florida was the point man in this move, the major participants were the senior subcommittee chairmen, led by Representative Frank Thompson of New Jersey. In the course of this developing sentiment, Powell's handling of committee funds for travel and hiring surfaced. For some time there had been rumblings that travel authorizations were being abused and some persons, especially Powell's wife, were on the payroll illegally. Now, with dissatisfaction against him growing, this would be a good time to have the House delve into those various rumors and unconfirmed allegations. The House passed a resolution directing a subcommittee, to be chaired by Wayne Hays of Ohio, to investigate the matters. The subcommittee began its work on September 26, 1966, reviewing all the audits of expenses of the committee as well as the payroll records. It was also certain that Powell, his wife, and several staff members would be called to testify.

The major case against Powell revolved around two matters: the use of airline tickets issued in the names of some staff members but actually used by others, especially Powell and Corinne Huff, and the employment of Mrs. Powell as a staff member and another person as a maid. Subpoenaed records indicated that scores of tickets were purchased—all authorized by Powell—through the use of committee credit cards of some staffers, but those particular persons never took the trips. In some instances, the persons supposed to have been on a particular trip were actually in other cities on committee business. At the same time, the trips coincided with the travel of Powell and Huff. Virtually all the questionable tickets were for travel between Washington and Miami, or Washington–New York–Miami. Investigators made the assumption that the Miami trips were for travel to Bimini. Committee investigators charted dates meticulously. In one instance, the evidence strongly suggested that tickets were issued in one staff member's name but actually used by Powell's son Adam Clayton Powell III, and friends as they left a social gathering in Washington to return to New York. Since tickets on the air shuttle between Washington and New York could only be purchased and signed for on the plane, the credit card had to be given to the alleged unauthorized user. The point was, of course, that any issued tickets could only be used by persons employed by the committee and on official committee business. The evidence was mounting that in very many instances this simply was not the case.

In addition, Powell had hired a young woman as a clerk but, according to her testimony, she served mainly as a domestic servant for Powell and Huff on a three-week trip to Bimini. She was fired upon return to Washington after being on the payroll for only one month.

Mrs. Powell's status as a committee employee was of great concern to the investigators. Payroll records showed that monthly salary checks continued to be issued in her name, but they were sent to Powell's congressional office, endorsed in his name, and deposited in his bank account. The investigators, of course, were quite interested in ascertaining the nature of Mrs. Powell's work, since it was known that she had not worked in Washington or New York for her husband in several years.

Throughout the fall of 1966, the evidence of travel and payroll abuses mounted. The Hays subcommittee prepared to hear witnesses to explain the seeming irregularities they were discovering. They issued subpoenas to several staff members, Powell, and his wife.

Powell, however, would not cooperate. On December 17, 1966, he sent an indignant letter to Wayne Hays laying down the conditions under which he would appear before the subcommittee:

> . . . Unfortunately, several well-documented reports have already reached me indicating specific improprieties by the Subcommittee's investigators. These reports reveal that staff members have been pilloried, asked personally embarrassing questions concerning matters which have no relation to the investigation and that the Subcommittee investigators have operated from the presumption that all of the Committee staff members have no integrity.
>
> . . . Several staff members have even been asked intimate questions and details concerning my personal life. This represents an unconscionable abuse of my right to be free from an invasion of privacy, a right which I am confident you value as tenderly as I do.
>
> That the Education and Labor Committee has been singled out, that only certain staff employees have been subpoenaed and that I personally am the obvious target of the investigation is a sorry commentary on the sense of fair play the Congress is supposed to extend to all of its colleagues.[4]

Powell insisted that "the investigation include a comparative analysis of the travel vouchers of staff members of other full Committees and Subcommittees, including your own." He also insisted that "the investigation include a comparable analysis of the travel undertaken by all other Committee and Subcommittee Chairmen."

Of course the Hays subcommittee would have none of this. Although the House Resolution establishing the subcommittee did not specify that only Education and Labor would be investigated, it was clear to everyone that Powell's committee would be the focus of its work.

At the same time, the investigators had no success in getting Mrs. Powell to come to Washington from Puerto Rico to testify. They notified her, setting a December date, but she replied that she needed time to make arrangements for the care of her young son, Adam Clayton Powell IV. In her correspondence she continually indicated: "I am willing to attend on a future date should you so desire." Once, her attorney informed Hays by telegram: "Mrs. Powell willing to cooperate." And then the investigators were advised that it was "impossible to appear at hearing before January 5." In the meantime, on November 22, 1966, she wrote to the Finance Office of the House of Representatives requesting that her future payroll checks be sent to her in Puerto Rico.

The Hays subcommittee had already received a Secret Service report of an interview with Mrs. Powell back on October 5, 1966, in Puerto Rico. At that time, when questioned about past payroll checks, she stated that the checks did not bear her genuine endorsement, that she had not authorized the endorsements, and she had not authorized her husband or anyone else to endorse the checks. She also stated that she had not seen or heard from her husband in more than a year. If the Hays subcommittee was in no mood to entertain Powell's conditions for his appearance, neither was it prepared to delay its report beyond the first of the year to accommodate Mrs. Powell. Everyone knew that it was desirable to wrap up the investigation and have a report issued before the new session of Congress convened in early January.

By all accounts, the evidence was damaging to the chairman from Harlem. On January 3, 1967, the Hays subcommittee issued its report. Its conclusions were predictable:

> . . . The deceptive practice of using the names of staff employees on airline tickets which were not used by the named employees appears to be a scheme devised to conceal the actual travel of Representative Powell, Miss Huff, and others, in some instances at least, so as to prevent questions being raised by the Committee on House Administration as to the official character of travel performed. . . .
>
> Persons having no official connection with the Congress have been provided with transportation by Representative Powell and the travel purchased by air travel credit cards of the Committee on Education and Labor. Said transportation costs have been charged to and paid from the contingent funds allocated to the Committee on Education and Labor.
>
> . . . All vouchers for payment of travel costs of the Committee on Education and Labor bore the signature "Adam C. Powell," certifying

> said vouchers to the Committee on House Administration for payment from the contingent fund. . . . The record of hearings raises a strong presumption that Y. Marjorie Flores (Mrs. Adam C. Powell) is receiving compensation, as a clerk for Representative Powell, in the sum of $20,578 per year in violation of Public Law 89–90, 89th Congress, in that she is not performing the services for which she is compensated in the offices of Representative Powell in the District of Columbia or in the State or the district which he represents, as required by said statute.

In all the testimony taken, each witness testified that the authorization for use of various credit cards came from Powell. Even when they knew they personally were not taking the particular trip, the staff members could assume that the ticket would be used by a legitimate staff member on official committee business.

The Hays subcommittee, however, recommended that "accounting controls" be strengthened for *all* committees, that monthly reports from *all* committees be filed, and that prior approval for a trip be obtained from the Committee on House Administration. Couched in these terms, these recommendations did not single out Powell's committee. But it did recommend that Mrs. Powell's employment be terminated. And it recommended "that the report and record of these hearings be made available to each Member of the Congress and that the Committee on House Administration forward the report and record to such agencies and departments of the Federal Government as it shall deem appropriate"—namely, the Department of Justice for a follow-up investigation to see if there were civil or criminal charges that should be brought.

Now the die was cast. The damaging evidence against Powell was out in the open as Congress got ready to begin a new term in January 1967. Powell continued to exude confidence and, many concluded, arrogance. He remained in Bimini over the Christmas holidays, bantering with reporters who reached him by telephone about how delightful the fishing was and that he had not a care in the world. Photos showed him languishing on his yacht or casually visiting with his friends in the streets of the quaint little island town.

Those close to the scene on Capitol Hill certainly were aware that Powell was in trouble, even if his own actions in Bimini did not show it. Speaker McCormack was trying to head off moves to discipline him. The Democratic Party Caucus in the House was ready to receive a motion that he be stripped of his chairmanship, and there was now more than small sentiment for going so far as to exclude him from Congress. It was crucial, McCormack thought, that Powell return immediately and help head off a disaster, but he was unable to reach the congressman. Finally, in desperation, he asked the venerable A. Philip Randolph to persuade Powell to come back and work out a compromise. Bayard Rustin put through a call for Randolph, but Powell was the epitome of defiance. He would not talk to the Speaker; he would not return immediately. He would come back in time for the Caucus meeting, and present his certificate of election and be sworn in like everyone else. Rustin had to communicate this disappointing news to Speaker McCormack.[5]

Powell's attitude proved fatal.

When the Democratic Caucus met on January 9, it voted to give the chairmanship of Education and Labor to Carl Perkins of Kentucky. The motion was put by Representative Morris K. Udall.

A few days earlier, Powell issued a lengthy statement entitled "15 Facts" which attempted to defend himself and head off the rising tide against him. He expressed gratitude for the "unexpected outpouring of support from thousands of Negroes and Negro organizations all over the country," mentioning Randolph, church groups, the Puerto Rican "community leadership of New York City," the California president of the Mexican American Political Association, "and that always loyal and important source of support, the Negro press." He charged that the fight to retain his chairmanship ("and this is the only issue in this struggle") "must be militantly pressed." He reviewed the circumstances of the complex legal case in New York. The case was "still in litigation." Therefore, "I am not a fugitive from justice which has been so loosely and irresponsibly bandied about in editorials." He accused the House of Representatives of "racial bigotry" in employment in its own chamber. And he constantly raised the "double standard" issue: why him, and not many others who were also guilty of holding up legislation, especially civil rights bills? Apparently, he asserted, there would appear to be "two standards of conduct—one for white congressmen and one for Negro Congressmen." He implied the misdeeds of others in Congress when he said:

> I have committed no crime. I have not tarnished the name of the House through any violation of Federal laws, particularly the U.S. Civil Code governing conflicts of interest for Congressmen. Nor have I misused my position to obtain Federal contracts for corporations represented by me or by my law firm. Nor have I derived any income

> from such contracts. Nor have I bilked the United States government out of $1,000,000 by selling it inferior merchandise which affects the conduct of the war in Vietnam.

He blasted the Hays subcommittee report for leaks to the press which led to wild speculation about his guilt. Were not five white Mississippi congressmen charged by Negro candidates with electoral fraud in 1965? The charges were well documented, he stated, but the group was seated anyway. "Nor was there a spate of hysterical editorials angrily demanding the Mississippi delegation's unseating."[6] For the moment, this would be Powell's argumentative brief in his defense.

But it was too late. The Caucus voted to remove him as chairman.

In the long saga of Adam Clayton Powell, this particular action probably was the one blow—short of exclusion or expulsion from Congress—that effectively ended his career as an important political figure. He would no longer have what no other black politician had ever had before, namely a substantial share of *real* control over substantive policy-making. All those years of waiting were down the drain; twenty-two years of seniority now meant virtually nothing. This was surely the most crushing blow in his long, stormy ordeal as a controversial politician. And this act by the Caucus could not be challenged in court or anywhere else. It was clearly within the purview of the majority party to choose the chairmen of committees. He was not finished, but no one would deny that he was severely diminished in his potential for political effectiveness, even if he retained his seat in the House.

And as matters were shaping up, even that was no longer guaranteed. But for the moment, his outward appearance remained unruffled. Reporters questioned him about his feelings. "Are you worried?" one asked.

Powell leaned back and slowly blew smoke from his cigar and asked: "Do I look it?"

"Wouldn't you rather be in the Bahamas?" another reporter seemed to taunt him.

Remaining unflappable, Powell laughed and parried: "Wouldn't you?"[7]

But it was also clear that Powell now was, in fact, becoming worried, if not desperate, about his political fate. Later in the evening after the Caucus took away his chairmanship, he was in his office with some staff members trying to get President Johnson on the telephone. After several attempts, he got through to Henry Wilson. An hour later, Wilson wrote a memo to the President:

January 9, 1967
8:10 p.m.

Memorandum For the President
From: Henry H. Wilson, Jr.

. . . At about 7:15, when the meeting in the Cabinet Room was breaking up, Powell again called and I took the call.

He talked for 10 or 15 minutes. The entire burden of his conversation was to say that this was a black day for the Democratic Party and probably meant loss in 1968. He said he was cut to death by the northern liberals, such as Frank Thompson and Jim O'Hara.

He then ranged west and implied that there was a dark plot among Romney, Stewart Udall, and Mo Udall, and referred to the creed of the Mormon Church. I asked him whether he had any reason to suppose that Stewart Udall had participated in today's activities.

He ducked that by saying that Stewart at one point had been a missionary of the Mormon Church.

He then said that someone should be sent up to the Hill to talk with him, preferably in the company of Louis Martin [a black staffer with the Democratic National Committee]. At this point, I realized that throughout the conversation he had the impression that he had been talking with the President rather than with me, and I had to make the judgment whether to disabuse him and to leave him screaming for a conversation with the President and telling the press the President would not talk with him, or to close the conversation with the hope that in his present circumstances he would think twice about fabricating any stories about what he told the President for purposes of press statements.

I think it is of interest that he was not insisting that he come down here nor demanding action from here concerning the meeting tomorrow.

I chose the latter course and got him off the phone.[8]

The next day the new session of Congress opened and all elected candidates except Powell were sworn in. Powell had been directed, on a motion from Congressman Lionel Van Deerling, "to stand aside." A debate ensued, and the House voted to exclude him, pending an investigation and report of a special nine-member, bipartisan committee to be appointed by the Speaker. The committee was to make recommendations to the House in five weeks from its selection. Once again, Powell was the center of a nationwide political controversy.

Prominent black leaders, including Martin Luther King, Jr., Roy Wilkins, A. Philip Randolph, and Bayard Rustin, issued strongly worded statements condemning the exclusion of Powell. Randolph planned to call a "summit" meeting of Negro leaders to deal with the situation, looking also at the civil rights voting record of those who had voted against Powell. The action against Powell, Randolph told the press, had caused a "crisis" in "Negro-white relations."[9] Bayard Rustin issued a statement:

> In no sense can I condone Congressman Powell's exceedingly mixed record. But I must ask why the activities of other Congressmen are not also the object of scrutiny. . . . to single out Congressman Powell while blithely ignoring the misdeeds of his colleagues can only arouse in the Negro community the unfortunate and demoralizing suspicion that Congress is governed by a double standard—that actions against Mr. Powell are motivated not by lofty idealism, but by subtle racism.

And this was a statement from one, Rustin, who had been attacked more than once by Powell for his homosexuality. In addition, Rustin, as a Social Democrat, had long been one who preferred to minimize racism as a cause for the Negroes' problems, but rather stressed basic economic causes.

Other voices were heard. The major civil rights leaders issued a joint statement which also raised the "double standard" issue: "We do not close our eyes to the shortcomings of Mr. Powell or of any other congressman. . . . We ask only that Mr. Powell be judged by standards equally applied to all Congressmen."[10] Dick Gregory called for a national strike for one day to protest the action against Powell.[11] Sammy Davis, Jr., wired Powell's office that he was "appalled to hear about what has happened" and would do "anything I can possibly do to help."[12] The *Pittsburgh Courier*, also not noted for blind adulation of Powell over the years, came to his defense now in an editorial that concluded that the punishment was "overly severe and unnecessarily excessive."[13] The editorial proceeded to remind the readers of the many concrete accomplishments of Powell's over the years. Floyd McKissick of CORE stated that very many black people had complained to him of the "political castration" of the congressman.[14] The American Civil Liberties Union and the New York Civil Liberties Union prepared a legal brief challenging the constitutionality of the exclusion and sent it to the Special Committee appointed by the Speaker. The brief argued that only the criteria of age, citizenship, and inhabitance were to be considered, and Powell met these.

The congregation of Abyssinian Baptist adopted a resolution supporting its pastor and proceeded to set up some mechanism to coordinate protest on his behalf. The associate minister, the Reverend David N. Licorish, admitted that there were some in the church who did not agree, but the support, he said, was overwhelming.[15] Powell sent Licorish a letter asking the minister not to preach a sermon on the issue, but expressing his appreciation for support and vowing to continue the fight. Licorish called for continuous prayer meetings. New York City councilman Edward Koch introduced a resolution to present to the Special Committee asking it to review the "bag woman" case as part of its investigation.[16] J. Raymond Jones noted that the case grew out of complaints of crime and corruption made to Powell by his constituents. "The fundamental question," Jones concluded, "is the right of a Congressman to express the feelings of his constituents."[17] Apparently Koch and Jones hoped that if Congress really looked into the circumstances leading to the case—the charges of crime and corruption—this would help Powell retain his seat.

In the nature of things, there were several handles people grabbed onto to defend Powell. Some stressed the "double standard" issue; others emphasized the unresolved complications of the protracted libel suit, and that Powell was entitled to play out the legal options open to him. Still others focused on his years of civil rights activism. Congress, however, seemed prepared to concentrate on his handling of committee funds and his chairmanship. Here, many legislators felt, relying on the Hays subcommittee report, they were on firmer ground. But it was also certain that Congressman Van Deerling was as impressed by the several civil and criminal warrants back in New York as anything else. What to some might be an attempt on Powell's part to get his full day in court was to Van Deerling an abuse of the judicial system.

It was becoming clear that the sudden outburst of support for Powell was likely too little, too late, and, above all, not very organized. For the most part, there were only outcries of anger and resentment, calling for various forms of protests, most of which never materialized. There were more than a few observations that perhaps those who would have been expected to organize an effective move to protect him really did not do so. "Where Were New York's Congressmen When Their Colleague Was Ousted?" the headline in the *Daily Worker* news story asked.[18] "Where there was a 'defense' of Powell it was at most apologetic and half-hearted. . . . And even these were actions which appeared strictly for the record. . . . There were no public protests from the Reform Democratic city body." Perhaps the sharpest observation focused on the civil rights movement. The *New York Times* ran a story that raised this point, commenting on "a notable absence of organized, effective support of Mr. Powell by distinguished civil rights leaders." It stated:

> Ordinarily, when the Leadership Conference on Civil Rights is interested in a cause, it organizes a formidable lobbying operation led by its chairman, Roy Wilkins. The Conference . . . never swung into action for Mr. Powell until after he had been disciplined by the House.[19]

This was true but there was an explanation, and Wilkins was not going to let this reference go unanswered—as the press probably knew. In a candid interview, Wilkins explained that, true, there was no organized effort from the civil rights leaders, but it was hardly an oversight. Powell, Wilkins bluntly stated, never came to them (the major civil rights groups) for help. Powell was his own man, and he never confided in Wilkins or other leaders "how serious" the situation was either with the New York case or the move against him in Congress. "It is hardly to be wondered," Wilkins concluded, "that the civil rights organizations did not spend sleepless nights in defense of Powell." Those groups were unaware of the large amount of mail building up against Powell. "If we had known this we could have done something."[20]

Perhaps so, but given Powell's nature and his long problematic relationship with the civil rights leaders, especially since the early 1960s and the March on Washington in 1963, it is difficult to imagine that he would have initiated such a move. It was probably the price he had to pay for the independent style he so cherished. Powell was not even prepared to accept the help of the Speaker of the House. And he very likely calculated, rightly or wrongly, that he had more influence *within* the House on such organizational matters than did any of the civil rights groups. It was a calculation born of his style and ego. His fierce independence would not permit him to turn to the very civil rights leaders he was prone to attack at a moment's notice if he felt so moved. He could hardly be contrite before his fellow congressmen—his peers. He certainly was not going to go, now, at this stage in his volatile career to those whose leadership he had so often criticized. In addition, Powell probably felt that he could rely on a ground swell of mass support nationwide. This, beginning with his own Harlem community, had always been his bedrock political support and protection. Working with other established civil rights leaders and organizations (except with Clarence Mitchell in the 1950s) had never been his strong suit. At the proper time he could rely on the masses to support him. This strategy suited him better, and indeed it had sustained him over the years. Aside from his large church, and tightly knit, but relatively small Alfred Isaacs Political Club in Harlem, he really did not have anything approaching a structured, ongoing organizational base. As those who knew his career well over the years so often would say, "Powell only has the people with him."

In 1967, as the House of Representatives prepared to decide his fate, "Powell's People" had to contend with representatives who were listening to "their own people" as well. The mail *was* running heavily against him. Some congressmen *were* beginning to feel more than slight pressure "to do something about that Powell." It was clear that as the evidence of abuse of funds grew and the New York trial dragged on, press reports on Powell only focused on those negative aspects of his life. This would make a vote against him that much easier. To be sure, there would be charges of a "double standard" and of racism. But it was becoming easier even to deal with those attacks. The *New York Times* undoubtedly reflected the view of many Americans in an editorial following the vote to exclude him. Rather than being a victim of race, Powell was really the "beneficiary" of a reluctance on the part of his opponents to attack him for fear of being accused of being racists. The *Times* believed Powell should be required to take care of his legal problems in New York before being permitted to take his seat in Congress.[21] "What to Do About Adam Powell?" an editorial in *Life* magazine asked.[22] Was it really the case, the editors pondered, that his only crime was "being black," as one Harlem rally was told? "Maybe that used to be true," the editorial concluded. "It isn't now. Adam's crime now is contempt—both civil and criminal—of the courts of New York." The problem was, the editorial continued, that if Powell were punished beyond being censured, "Negroes generally are likely to get the message wrong." Why was this? Because Powell represented race achievement, "clout," "more than any Negro before him." Therefore, the best thing in a difficult, delicate situation was "to investigate Powell's conduct fully and fairly, and decide whether it brings Congress into public contempt."

Perhaps this would ease *some* of the tension, but probably not.

In any case, the Powell matter was causing political problems in many corners for those who had to grapple with it. Henry Wilson told the President that "[Congressman Wilbur] Mills [of Arkansas] has been worked over by the Negro leadership in Little Rock about the Adam Powell situation and he is very hopeful that the outcome of the scuffling around on this subject next week will be to suspend Powell in mid air, until he straightens out his problems with the courts in New York."[23]

A few weeks later, after the exclusion vote and while the Special Committee was preparing to go to work, Wilson gave President Johnson his own assessment of the Powell situation and its impact on the President. Fully aware that many blacks had written the President urging him to act on Powell's behalf, and some had even suggested that the White House was heavily implicated in the ouster move, Wilson informed the President:

> On balance, I think you came out of this very mean situation about as well as possible.
>
> Emotions were so high that someone had to get hurt, and it turned out to be the Speaker.
>
> It is not over yet of course. There remain:
> a. the report of the special committee;
> b. action in the House concerning it;
> c. in the event Powell is seated, the
> determination as to which rank he will occupy
> on the Education and Labor Committee.
> If he is seated, he could cause us a great deal of trouble in the #2 spot as head of one of the major Subcommittees.[24]

Meanwhile, Speaker McCormack named a nine-member special committee to investigate the Powell matter and make recommendations to the full House in five weeks. Emanuel Celler, the Brooklyn Democrat, was asked to serve as chairman. The other members were James C. Corman (D.-Calif.); Claude D. Pepper (D.-Fl.); John Conyers, Jr. (D.-Mich.); Andrew Jacobs (D.-Ind.); Arch A. Moore, Jr. (R.-W. Va.); Charles M. Teague (R.-Calif.); Clark MacGregor (R-Minn.); and Vernon W. Thompson (R.-Wisc.)[25] This looked reasonably good for Powell, inasmuch as the group was evaluated by the press as "liberal." They were all lawyers, and they all would have preferred to have been given other assignments from the Speaker. Celler told the press he was likely entitled "to commiserations, not congratulations." But "as a good soldier," he was willing to serve.[26]

Andy Jacobs later noted in his account of the committee's work that earlier a colleague had told him that "only someone passionately interested in political suicide will get mixed up with that Adam

Clayton Powell Select Committee."[27] As a second-term congressman, Jacobs had not been expected to be asked, but he was—telling the Speaker that it sounded like jury duty—and he concluded: "It was not an enviable appointment."

In the meantime, Powell lined up his legal team. He asked eight lawyers to represent him: Jean Camper Cahn, Washington, D.C.; Robert L. Carter, New York; Hubert T. Delaney, New York; Arthur Kinoy, New York; William M. Kunstler, New York; Frank Reeves, Washington, D.C.; Herbert O. Reid, Washington, D.C.; and Henry R. Williams, New York. From Powell's point of view, the case was uncomplicated: the United States Constitution sets three qualifications for serving in the House if elected—a minimum age of twenty-five, citizenship, and state residency. He met all three and thus was constitutionally entitled to be seated. No other issues were pertinent. That was it. He came and testified to that effect and, on the advice of his lawyers, refused to answer any questions beyond those boundaries.

But the committee was not so sure, and neither was it of one mind on exactly how much it could probe and even what it *could* recommend in the way of punishment. It only knew that in five weeks it had to make a report, and the media were watching its every move and noting the witnesses being called. The Hays subcommittee report figured prominently in its deliberations, which meant that it would not be bound by the three constitutional qualifications. Mrs. Powell was also to be called to testify. On recommendation of the Hays subcommittee report the House had terminated her employment, but she agreed to come. She contacted Washington attorney Joseph Rauh, who had a strong reputation in civil rights, civil liberties, and as counsel to prominent witnesses before congressional committees. (In the latter role, he had represented playwrights Arthur Miller and Lillian Hellman.) A very close associate of Clarence Mitchell over the years as a civil rights lobbyist, Rauh recalled Mrs. Powell calling him to ask if he would serve as her counsel. She asked if "people were scared of Adam." Rauh chuckled and said he wasn't, and this was exactly the kind of assignment he liked to accept.[28] If the committee was going to probe into Powell's committee activities, then his wife's salary checks would be important evidence. The committee also decided to take testimony on the "bag woman" case, as well as "matters of Mr. Powell's alleged official misconduct since January 3, 1961." (This was the date on which he had become chairman of his committee.)

Chuck Stone testified that Powell directed him several times to purchase airline tickets in the names of other staff members, but the actual travel was for Powell and Corinne Huff. Surely the most dramatic testimony would come from Mrs. Powell. She appeared on February 16, 1967. Impressing the committee members with her quiet demeanor and candor, she testified, after declining to request a closed hearing, that she did virtually no work for the chairman after 1965. Although asking her husband many times to let her return to Washington or remove her from the payroll, he refused. She had last seen Powell in September 1965, and he refused to see her in August 1966 when she came to Washington to discuss "our personal life." Neither had she authorized the endorsement of her salary checks. Jacobs wrote: "I scanned the audience and noticed frowns of sympathy on the faces of women. Without much question, Mrs. Powell's decision to testify openly had won her this public's affection."[29] However, aware of the trouble her statements could cause, Mrs. Powell closed her testimony with a plea for her husband: "Although we have not been together for some time, Adam is my husband and the father of my child." She hoped the committee would rule in his favor and permit him to "continue his career in the service of our country."[30]

In a few weeks, the Special Committee would make its report, but in the meantime the new chairman of Education and Labor, Carl Perkins, announced the firing of twelve staffers employed by Powell, one of whom was Chuck Stone.[31]

The Celler committee proceeded to debate the options available. From the beginning, none of the members appeared to be inclined simply to recommend seating Powell with no further action. Sentiments ran from no seating, to seating with a move to then expel, to seating with censure, to seating with censure *and* a fine to recoup the funds inappropriately used. It was also generally agreed that if Powell were expelled and ran in a special election, he would probably win hands down. Representative Teague was fearful of making a martyr of Powell by expelling him. There was strong interest in levying some sort of fine or forfeiture of salary if Powell were seated. The committee should try to provide a means of financial restitution. After several days of debate in closed sessions, the committee agreed to recommend that Powell should be seated, that he should be publicly censured, that he should pay $40,000 to Congress, and that he should be stripped of his seniority. It was a grueling, tiring five weeks of work, but the members felt they had done the best they could. Throughout, Congressman Jacobs was perplexed by the lack of adequate rules or standards to guide their work. They were, in a sense, making up the rules as they went along. In one week they would submit their work to the full House for its consideration.

When the House convened on March 1, 1967, to consider the Celler committee report, Powell was not present. (His appearance was not expected, although, technically, he could have attended inasmuch as the original resolution excluding him permitted him access to his office and presumably to the floor.) The debate ranged far and wide, covering historical issues at the 1787 Constitutional Convention, concepts of separation of powers and the right of Congress to judge its elections, the *Federalist Papers*, all the way to the practical concerns of what to do if Powell *were* excluded, ran again in a special election, won, and again presented his certificate of election. How long could this go on? No one had an answer for this or any of the other sticky legal, constitutional and political issues raised. Passionate pleas were made to support the Celler committee's report as the best, fairest solution. Congressman Arch Moore assured his colleagues that if seated, "the only thing the Member [Powell] . . . will have in this House is a key to . . . a suite in some one of the several office buildings." Congressman Albert Watson (R.-S.C.) was less charitable: "The public knows that Powell is guilty." Even now, he charged, while the House was tying itself in knots over this affair, Powell was lounging in Bimini "with a glass in one hand and a woman in the other."

John Conyers undoubtedly made the most agonizing speech of the debate. He had already registered his objection to the unusually severe nature of the recommendations, which he had reluctantly agreed to. He had preferred seating with censure, not a fine nor the denial of seniority. As a young black congressman from Detroit, he was sensitive to the vexing problems caused by Powell and this case. Earlier in the committee deliberations, Conyers had told the committee: "When I was a little boy in Michigan, Adam Clayton Powell was the first and only black hero I ever heard of. He used to come to Detroit, and we'd have big celebrations. Adam became a personal hero to me. But now, no hero placed so high on a pedestal ever showed such feet of clay before." But now Conyers wanted to assure the full body that he supported the recommendations in order to help save Powell's seat. He spoke of Powell's "special role," reminding his colleagues of Powell's years of struggle against segregation; and he was sure that black Americans remembered this record. Those same blacks also knew that "many white Americans" disliked Powell because of that record and now it was likely one of the reasons, in addition to his "personal conduct," he was under attack.[32] All these things were on the minds of black Americans and Conyers wanted his congressional colleagues to know that.

It was Representative Holland (D.-Pa.) who laid down the racism gauntlet. It was clear to him that race was a factor here. He had read his mail, and racism was pervasive in most of the letters against Powell. Neither was Holland impressed, he said, by the argument that if Powell were white, he would have been punished long since. "Like who, Mr. Speaker?" Holland wanted to know. "Is Adam Clayton Powell the only sinner in this House? Does the House have such a long and complex list of precedents of censuring and demoting and fining Members who do not meet its high moral standards?" And then Holland reminded his colleagues that Powell was having to answer for the fiery speeches of Black Power advocates that created dissension and hatred in the country. Powell was experiencing what many other blacks knew all too well: although they themselves were law-abiding, they were discriminated against and accused of criminality because they were lumped together with some Negroes who "break the law."[33]

All this might be true, but the House was in no conciliatory mood. Powell did not have enough supporters in that body that day. Too many people remembered the defiant, arrogant Powell. Too many resented his handling of committee funds in an obviously unlawful manner; too many were angered by the New York court business that made him appear as if he were flaunting his disregard for the judicial process. Would censure be sufficient humiliation?

"Who are we kidding?" argued Congressman Samuel L. Devine (R.-Ohio). "Humility does not appear to be one of his virtues."

Representative Durward G. Hall (R.-Mo.) argued that "this man [Powell] is uncensurable, unembarrassable, and irresponsible."

Referring to the recent scandals involving Walter Jenkins, a former Johnson White House aide, and Bobby Baker, another protégé of Johnson's, and commenting on the need to raise ethical standards in government, Congressman H. R. Gross (R.-Iowa) urged: "The House of Representatives today can either help this moral climate or it can further destroy it. Mr. Speaker, I have a reasonably strong stomach, but it will revolt at the aroma that will arise if today Adam Clayton Powell is offered a seat in this chamber."

Gross did not have to worry. After four and a half hours of debate, the House voted to reject the Celler committee's recommendations, and then voted to support a resolution by Congressman Thomas B. Curtis (R.-Mo.) that Powell "is excluded from membership in the 90th Congress."

The roll-call vote was not even close: 307–116.

Whatever else the vote that day decided, it certainly set the stage for something Congressman Arch Moore predicted. If the Celler committee's recommendation was rejected, Moore warned, "we would be on a collision course with the courts of this land."

He was so right.

One week later, March 8, Powell established another "first" in American political history. He filed suit in the federal district court challenging his exclusion from Congress.

Meanwhile, a special election to fill the vacancy was set for April 11. Powell announced his candidacy. Then James Meredith, the first black to attend the University of Mississippi back in 1962, and now a law student at Columbia University, announced his candidacy on the Republican ticket. Then, a few days later, Meredith withdrew and was replaced by Lucille Pickett Williams. The Conservative Party also fielded a candidate.

The only bets around Harlem were not *if* Powell would win, but by how much. He did not return from Bimini to campaign, of course, because of the outstanding court orders, but very few doubted that this would hurt him. The feelings in Harlem were so intensely aimed at supporting him in the face of the House action that his physical appearance would only have been symbolic. The voters would rally around him as they had done before, especially when he was challenged nine years earlier by Tammany Hall. The House had rejected Harlem's choice, so in a sense it was questioning the community's judgment.

The special election result, therefore, was never in doubt:

Powell (D.)	27,900 (86.1%)
Williams (R.)	4,091 (12.6%)
Erwin F. Yearling (C.)	427 (1.3%)

Then Powell added a new wrinkle to the drama; he decided not to present his certificate of election to the House, thus forestalling for the moment what the House would do. The resolution of exclusion had stipulated that he was not to be seated in the Ninetieth Congress. Powell decided he would press his case before the courts first. This was important to him, because a favorable court decision could mean he was not only entitled to his seat but also to his seniority. If he were sworn in as a result of the special election, presumably he would have to start over as a freshman. For the moment, then, the constitutional challenge was more important. It was nice to have the voters' confidence; that could only help. And it was wise to run in the special election, unless complications developed that might suggest his case was either moot or not subject to court review. Thus he had it both ways. He was the only duly elected person from New York's Eighteenth Congressional District, and he had a lawsuit pending that argued he should have been there in the first place.

For the next year and a half, Powell pursued his case through the courts, went on the college lecture circuit, and became increasingly militant in his speeches. His main targets were the war in Vietnam and racial injustice. The Department of Justice, receiving the Hays subcommittee and Celler committee reports, began an investigation into the charges. The FBI files indicated investigations into possible bribery charges as well. He was a man without an institutional base, but he still represented defiance and protest to many, black and white, who were becoming increasingly militant. Protests against the war in Vietnam were gaining steam. Powell clearly was identified with that sentiment. Urban riots in the summer of 1967 heated up tension in the Northern urban ghettos. Powell's speeches were received by many as sharp criticisms of the social, economic, and racial problems facing the nation. Some of his comments came just short of calling for a revolution. The FBI began filing reports of him under the heading of "Agitator Index."

A bill was introduced in Congress, cosponsored by, among others, Conyers, Charles Diggs of Detroit, Jacobs, and Frank Thompson, to provide normal congressional services for the constituents of his congressional district. Powell criticized this effort as "white colonialism" and a "return to slavery."[34] He particularly blasted John Conyers, saying he had "played into the hands of white racists." Conyers had taken his lumps from Powell, probably because of his vote on the Celler committee. The fact of Conyers's wrenching agony over the affair and effort to mitigate the penalty obviously gained him no respite from Powell's anger.

The FBI kept close tabs on his travels and speeches. At one gathering of six thousand students at UCLA, he urged white students to "join the black revolution." He told the throng: "I know you white boys and girls are frustrated. You need something to move you. One day you are going to say this man Powell is our man and he doesn't belong with those senile people in Washington." To this he received a standing ovation. And the FBI report carefully noted that he described America as a "sick society."[35] Throughout 1967 and the early part of 1968, this was his itinerary and his stock speech. When asked, he carefully explained that he would not return to Congress until the federal courts "had the guts" to decide finally on his case. The case was moving slowly. The district court had ruled against him, and he appealed. He had hoped to have the Supreme Court make an exception and take his case immediately from the district court. The Supreme Court refused. When the Court of Appeals finally ruled, on February 28, 1968—almost one year after he was excluded—the three-judge panel held that he was not entitled to his seat. Now Powell could take his case to the highest court of the land. On November 18, 1968, the Supreme Court would agree to hear his case.

The judicial wheels were turning slowly, but 1968 was also another election year, and Powell had to decide what he would do. It was not a difficult decision. Obviously he had to run again, if only to keep his case alive and, by winning, keep the seat from falling into someone else's hands. There was no telling what the Supreme Court would do if the seat became occupied by another elected representative. The issues were already complicated. If the Court wanted a reason to avoid the issue—perhaps on the basis of separation of powers—another incumbent might give added strength to that inclination. So it was best to run—and win. The running part was easy, but it was becoming known that there were more than a few dissatisfied forces in Harlem who were growing tired of the Powell business. Some had not liked his decision not to present himself for swearing in after the special election. It seemed somehow to be disrespectful of the electoral process, and some even felt that he was putting his personal needs above those of the constituents. People began to talk more openly and confidently about seeking a challenger to him. Respected leaders in Harlem, some with political ambitions of their own, others clearly nonpolitical, began to call for him to clear up his libel suit problems, return to Harlem, become a full-time congressman—or step aside. Harlem needed a representative in Congress, they argued. It was becoming easier to say these things openly as the weeks and months went by.

There were others on the national scene who were beginning to back away. Powell's fiery speeches were clearly on the edge of revolutionary calls, and these were more than some of the national civil rights leaders could countenance. An FBI tape recorded a telephone conversation of one of Martin Luther King's close advisers, Stanley Levison. Levison told his caller in early 1968: "Just between us, Martin considers Powell finished by his own errors. He would never say this publicly, but he's been double-crossed so many times by Powell pleading with him for support and then getting it from

Martin. Like when he ran for election against De Sapio's opposition and all that and Martin came to his support. And then Powell denounced him from the pulpit."[36]

A 1968 election bid meant that Powell in all likelihood would have to find a way to return to New York, if only for brief campaign appearances. But the matter of the outstanding arrest warrants had to be negotiated. His lawyer, Henry Williams, began the process. An agreement was reached in March 1968 whereby Powell would turn himself in to a New York judge, receive "parole," and then let the judicial maneuvers proceed again. On March 22, 1968, Powell flew to Newark, New Jersey, and was driven to Justice Arthur Markewich's New York apartment at 11:30 P.M. Technically he was arrested, but parole was immediately granted, and for the moment, Powell was free to walk the streets of New York again. Word spread of his return, and he went to a "Welcome Home" rally in Harlem. He told a wildly cheering throng the next day, "They've never seen a scene like they're gonna have if they try to touch Big Daddy." A driving rain did not dampen his followers' spirits. "I am no longer Martin Luther King saying 'We Shall Overcome.' I don't call for any violence and I don't call for any riots, but the nonviolent days are over, and if we must die let us not die like hogs in some inglorious spot," he said. That Sunday, he preached at Abyssinian Baptist. His sermon: "If a Man Falls, He Shall Rise Again." He was surrounded on the pulpit by young bodyguards dressed in military attire; one carried a machete with a Bible impaled on it.

The primary election was held on June 18. Powell had one opponent, a former aide of his, John H. Young. The people wanted "a new Harlem of dignity and self-respect, a young Harlem of courage and foresight, and most of all, a new Congressman," Young told those who would listen to him in his campaign.

But this was not the most exciting campaign Harlem had witnessed. In spite of the dramatic, triumphant return of Powell, Harlemites seemed distracted, less interested in the rhetoric and histrionics of electoral politics. In some ways, it was a sideshow to other, more dynamic, and indeed much more traumatic events taking place. On April 4, 1968, Dr. Martin Luther King, Jr., was assassinated. This cast a pall over the nation that signaled much deeper problems and feelings than were manifested in the ongoing Powell affair. Somehow King's death made everything else less relevant, even more frivolous. Frustration, anger, and racial tensions were increasing. And two weeks before the primary, Senator Robert Kennedy was killed. Political violence seemed to be the order of the day. All else seemed tame by comparison.

Powell's speeches grew more strident, although he returned only a few times from Bimini to campaign. On one occasion, he hinted that he would accept censure and even loss of his seniority if the 1967 exclusion resolution were rescinded. "I'd sooner be low man on the totem pole, and in Congress," he said, "because the nation needs me." The weeks passed, and primary day came. There were close to 80,000 registered Democrats in the Eighteenth Congressional District. Only 11,174 bothered to vote. Powell won: 6,723 to Young's 4,451. He had his victory, but by only a 3–2 margin. Professional politicians looked at those figures—the low turnout, the relatively small margin by which a not-too-popular challenger lost—and they saw something that interested them. *Powell could be beaten.* Something was taking place. Whatever it was, and there were many different speculations, there surely were ominous signs for Powell in those numbers.

But for the moment, he had the Democratic nomination to sustain him in the November general election. He did not campaign vigorously for himself, assuming quite correctly that his Republican and Conservative party opponents stood little chance in heavily Democratic Harlem. Neither did he do much of anything for the Humphrey-Muskie Presidential ticket, which needed support much more in New York against the Nixon-Agnew Republican slate. Powell made it known that he did not like Humphrey's defense of Johnson's Vietnam policies, that he preferred the views expressed by Senators Eugene McCarthy and George McGovern, who were much less "hawkish" on the war.

At any rate, Powell easily swept his district, taking 80.6 percent of the vote—36,973 to 7,290 (15.9 percent) for the Republican, and 1,616 (3.5 percent) for the Conservative.

Once again his Harlem constituents sent him back to Congress.

It would be the last election he would win.

Two weeks later, the Supreme Court agreed to hear his case. He now had to figure out a way to go to Congress as he waited out his chance to go to Court. He knew he had to do both. If the Court ruled in his favor, perhaps he could retain his seniority. If the Court ruled against him, at least he would still be in Congress, albeit low man on the totem pole. Negotiations proceeded to ease his reentry into the legislative body. It was also clear that very much depended on his ability to settle the libel case still hanging over his head in New York. His congressional colleagues seemed much less vindictive now than they had been two years earlier, but the Esther James case still lingered.

After the election things began to break in his favor. First there was the Supreme Court news, and then, on December 9, the Department of Justice decided not to seek an indictment against him. The department had investigated the various allegations and concluded "that available evidence did not warrant prosecution." As it turned out, the four Justice lawyers on the case could not agree among themselves. This was certainly good news for Powell. Another indictment, and by the federal government at that, could really complicate his life.

Meanwhile, in Congress, there was growing sentiment in favor of seating him, if he presented himself with a certificate of election. John Conyers and Charles Diggs were leading a quiet effort to remove any obstacles. They met with the party leadership and with the Republicans, putting together various acceptable terms that most could live with. Van Deerling was now satisfied that Powell was making serious efforts to pay off the libel judgment; he had surrendered to the New York judge and was no longer "a fugitive from justice." In addition, this time, there was no avalanche of mail from constituents around the country calling for Powell's exclusion. Moreover, some members likely felt that this exclusion-reelection business could go on and on only to the embarrassment of Congress and contribute to heightened racial tensions. This was hardly constructive in a society already being torn asunder over the Vietnam war and racial violence. Why bother?

Congressman Gross of Iowa remained adamant, however, and insisted that he would challenge Powell's seating again.

When the time came on January 3, Gross moved that Powell stand aside. After a one-hour debate, Gross's motion was defeated. After more debate, Congressman Celler introduced a motion, worked out by Conyers, Diggs, Ford, and a few others, that Powell be seated, fined $25,000 for the money wrongly paid out in his wife's salary and inappropriately used committee air travel funds, and that his seniority begin as of 1969. The motion also stipulated that $1,150 be deducted each month from his congressional salary until the fine was paid.

This motion carried 252 to 160.

Powell, after two years out of Congress, was sworn in as a freshman. He was assigned to his old committee, Education and Labor, but as the junior member on the Democratic side.

It was the best that could be worked out, and Powell accepted it. He told a press conference, "Well, maybe I'm an emancipated slave. . . . It wouldn't be a bad idea if everyone had to pay $25,000 to get in here." Clearly, he was stung, but probably relieved that, at least, he was back in Congress. He indicated he was consulting his lawyers about whether to challenge the fine, but one thing was certain: he would concentrate his energies on his two remaining concerns. He wanted to clear up the remaining judgment debts hanging over him from the libel suits, and he wanted to await the Supreme Court's ruling on his ouster.

On the former, his lawyers had been working on a deal whereby the last money owed Mrs. James would be paid. This was finally done in April 1969, and the Esther James case was behind him—nine years, the entire decade of the sixties, after he first made his "bag woman" charge.

In the meantime, he became, by his own description, a "part-time" congressman ("part-time work for part-time pay," as he put it), spending much of his time that spring on the lecture circuit. He could use the money. His roll-call attendance record was a dreadfully low 5 percent. He introduced a few resolutions to establish a special antipoverty investigating committee which he would chair, and to investigate combat deaths of blacks in Vietnam. Neither was acted upon. He was, without a doubt, one of the least effective, and some would say least important, members of the Congress of the United States. The fall had been tremendous. He once had power. He now had an office with, as Congressman Moore had predicted, only a key.

He resumed regular preaching at Abyssinian Baptist Church.

Those who knew him certainly concluded that in no way was he his old fiery, energetic self. He was back in Congress, but with absolutely none of the power and influence he had enjoyed a few years earlier. And now word was beginning to circulate in Harlem that Adam Powell was ill—possibly with cancer.

The years of embattlement were beginning to take their toll. On the platform, he could still deliver a rousing speech or sermon, but the contrast in demeanor and appearance from an earlier time was becoming evident. Clearly ill, looking older than his sixty-one years, moving slower, no longer the haughty strut, he was beginning to show signs of a serious health problem.

His spirits would be lifted temporarily by one more victory—from the United States Supreme Court.

On June 16, 1969, in a 7–1 decision, the Supreme Court ruled that Powell had been unconstitutionally excluded from Congress. Chief Justice Earl Warren, who would retire later that month, wrote the majority opinion. The Court held that the only issue was the interpretation of the constitutional provision stipulating three qualifications for membership in the House: age, citizenship, and inhabitancy. It was the duty of the Court to be the final arbiter of the meaning of that provision, and this duty did not violate the principle of separation of powers. The Court was not, the opinion held, intruding into the internal affairs or the exclusive domain of another coequal branch of the federal government. Likewise, the Court took pains to distinguish this case of exclusion from one of "expulsion." It was not saying anything about the latter situation, which was not an issue before the Court. Justice Potter Stewart was the one dissenter, basing his opinion on the grounds that the case had become moot. That is, Powell was, in fact, back in Congress, so there was nothing to decide. He had been excluded from the *Ninetieth* Congress. That congressional session was ended; Powell had now been properly elected to and indeed seated in the Ninety-first Congress. If Stewart's colleagues wanted to avoid this sticky political issue, they could have taken the Stewart route. They did not. But in deciding to address the constitutional issue of qualifications, the Court's opinion avoided the other main issue Powell was interested in, namely, his seniority. It sent the case back to the lower court for proper disposition in line with the Supreme Court's decision. In other words, the lower court should grapple with issues of the fine, seniority, and lost salary.

The Supreme Court decision, then, was only part of the battle for Powell, an absolutely crucial part, to be sure, but he still had no ruling on whether he could claim the salary lost from the two years of exclusion. But more important, he had no ruling on his seniority. The Supreme Court presumably had given him a peg on which to hang such claims. And Powell's lawyers did start proceedings in federal district court. These maneuvers would be as much political as strictly legal. Many of Powell's colleagues in the House were incensed at the Supreme Court's decision, and they were in no mood to give him any more than he already had. Powell hinted that he would be willing to trade: if the House would revoke the $25,000 fine, he would forgo efforts to get the back salary. He received no takers on this. The issue of seniority was even trickier. Seniority "rights" were more properly understood as matters falling within the exclusive purview of the legislative body, especially a chairmanship gained through seniority. It was abundantly clear that there was no positive mood in the House to give Powell these two claims.

In effect, the Supreme Court decision established a major constitutional principle at no cost to anyone but the Congress. The Court issued a ruling that required the Congress to do nothing it had not already done—seat Powell. In so ruling, the Court had said this could be a precedent for the interpretation of the "qualifications" provision. This was important as a significant constitutional point, more important to the electorate and aspiring congressional candidates than to Powell. But it was certainly a psychological and political boost for Powell, who had maintained all along that his exclusion was unconstitutional. On the matters of seniority and back salary, everyone was left hanging. Emanuel Celler noted that all the Supreme Court did was satisfy the issue of qualifications. That was the "essence" of the decision. All the other issues were "housekeeping" matters.

When news of the decision reached him in Bimini, Powell understandably was pleased, but uncharacteristically moderate in his response: ". . . the fact that we have fought before the Supreme Court to establish the principle of three branches of government is more important than Adam Clayton Powell," he said. He told reporters that the seniority and chairmanship issues were "secondary." He was also likely aware that if he were to press his claim for back salary, this would involve more legal wrangling and create still more tension between himself and his colleagues. He did have his lawyers file motions in the district court, but anyone seeing Powell at that time knew that he was a man distracted. His health was now an open topic of discussion. He admitted that he was suffering from "proliferating lymph glands" which could be cancerous, and he was beginning to hear real noises back in Harlem that his political days were numbered. He must have wondered privately whether he had the physical stamina and political fire to take on these growing problems.

In late 1969 and early 1970, more than a few Harlem politicians were concluding that Powell, sadly, did not "have it" anymore. He had served well during his long political career, but he should now retire. He was clearly ill; he was seldom in Congress, and certainly no longer an influential, energetic force to be reckoned with. For his own sake, and Harlem's, he should not seek reelection. Rumors of his failing health had now become confirmed by Powell himself and his doctors when he canceled several speaking engagements and went into the hospital for extensive tests. The newspapers began regularly referring to the "ailing" representative. Private meetings were held by Harlem politicians seeking to sort out the possible successors. Certainly, the hope among most of them was that Powell would graciously retire and not seek reelection. They did not relish an open fight in a primary with him which could only be divisive and demeaning to him. But the talk, news leaks, and plans continued. In most instances, the public comments on Powell were deferential, but obliquely dismissive.

"Adam has done one hell of a job, but . . ."

"He was hell on wheels as chairman of the House Education and Labor Committee, but . . ."

"Adam was a giant we can all be proud of, but . . ."[37]

His health and long absences from Congress made the talk that much more legitimate and acceptable. Perhaps, some felt, it would be a favor to *him* if he were not reelected.

What was also clear to these various politicos was that this had to be a Harlem affair. Whatever was decided, whoever would possibly challenge Powell could not be seen as associated with or the hand-picked candidate of "downtown" white leaders. That could be a kiss of death and exactly what Powell needed. In this sense, everyone knew that Harlemites always came to his defense when he was attacked from outside. Some aspirants immediately announced their intention to run. A local community activist, Jesse Gray, who had led several rent strikes declared his candidacy. John Young, who had made an impressive showing in the 1968 primary, honestly stated: "I would be crazy not to run." Others were less forthright, but equally as willing. The Manhattan borough president, Percy Sutton, a black considered by many as the next most popular Harlem politician to Powell, if not fast overtaking him, disclaimed any interest, but he was not shy in indicating that he had a candidate for the job—the young state assemblyman from Harlem, Charles B. Rangel. The Puerto Ricans were thinking of a candidate of their own from East Harlem, attorney Ramon Martinez.

In December, Rangel was quoted as saying: "The real question is where do we go from here. Whether or not Adam resigns, it is clear from his conduct that he has resigned from that office—a de facto resignation."[38] Years later, Rangel said that if he had been a part of the Powell "team," he never would have challenged him. He never worked with Powell personally, never sat on the same boards or belonged to the same political club. Rangel was a member of Sutton's Martin Luther King Democratic Club, and had succeeded to Sutton's seat in the State Assembly when Sutton became borough president. "We'd known for years," he said, "that a good man could really beat Adam."[39]

More meetings were held, one of which Powell attended at the home of Floyd McKissick of CORE. Several sensed that the CORE leader wanted to run, but would not openly champion his own cause. At that meeting Powell announced flatly that he intended to seek reelection. His health problems were under control, and he looked forward to returning to Congress in fighting form. In late January, he made the public announcement and confidently stated that he had "already raised $78,000 in campaign funds."[40] A few weeks later a large testimonial luncheon for him was held at Manhattan's midtown Americana Hotel. Again, he announced his candidacy, read a message of congratulations from former President Johnson, cited his own accomplishments over the years, especially as chairman, and blasted the Nixon administration. It was the opening round in his bid to retain his seat. Among those attending were Congresswoman Shirley Chisholm from Brooklyn; Congressman Charles Diggs; Congressman William F. Ryan of Manhattan, and his old Harlem adversary back in 1958, now political ally, Assemblyman Hulan Jack.[41]

Something else, however, had happened that month that would spell serious political trouble for Powell. He had always been sensitive to the need to keep the geographical boundaries of his congressional district in line with his Harlem-based political supporters. After all, it was a redrawing of those lines twenty-six years earlier that had given him the chance to be elected. He had paid close attention in the early 1960s to the redistricting, but now the Eighteenth Congressional District was redrawn to add a sixteen-block area outside Harlem on Manhattan's West Side. Here the population was substantially middle-class whites, decidedly not Powell's people. Earlier, the *Amsterdam News* had warned: "It is almost a fact that the Republican-controlled State Legislature is about to redistrict Harlem's 18th Congressional District. . . . Harlem's solid black vote will be diluted as to not only rout the strength of Adam Clayton Powell, but any other black congressional candidate. . . . Let us wake up. Now."[42] Bad news for Powell, but not necessarily for a black candidate.

Meanwhile, the field ended up with five candidates: Powell, Rangel, Gray, Young, and Martinez. Ordinarily, even with the redistricting, this would auger well for Powell, the incumbent and the most well-known: the more opponents, the greater the opportunity to split the opposition votes. The other candidates hit the campaign trail throughout the district. Powell continued preaching on Sundays at Abyssinian, made a few appearances in other churches in the community, but for the most part he hit the lecture circuit again around the country. His speeches were becoming more fiery and incendiary. He told college audiences that a sinister "power structure" conspiracy was responsible for the deaths of the Kennedys and King. He continued to condemn the war in Vietnam, and he predicted an "Armageddon" in American cities that coming summer if racial justice was not achieved. The days of nonviolence were over, he stated, and the politicians in Washington had best prepare for worse days of violence. In a speech at a Cleveland college, he stated that he saw no future for the country as long as it continued its exploitative policies at home and its "imperialist" policies abroad. What had happened to him in Congress was only a small taste of what would happen to anyone who took a stand against the "status quo."*

His speeches on college campuses were drawing increasing attention from the FBI. One report of his appearance at Chicago State College on February 26, 1970, was particularly biting. The agent was furious at what Powell was saying and wrote in the report:

> This so-called legislator, far more insolent and obnoxious than usual, approached the edge of treason as he sanctioned the use of weapons by Panthers and other black extremists, lamenting only the lack of marksmanship and ability to construct effective bombs. Sans logic and sans reason, he ranted, raved, and railed against the United States Government and its officials. . . . His career has been marked consistently by his chronic inability to open his mind and shut his mouth. As a legislator, he is a disgrace to the Congress of the United States. As a national figure, he is a disgrace to his race. . . . In the twaddle-tongue of black extremism, this congressional legislator lauded the infamous Black Panthers. . . . The shame here is that Powell is an American![44]

Back in Harlem, his opponents were campaigning vigorously against him. They knew he was the target, and they now felt no restraint in attacking him. Charles Rangel clearly was the strongest of the four challengers, and the gloves were off. Powell would receive his due respect, but 1970 was a new day. Powell saw no need to engage his opponents in debates—"The people know where I stand"—and this was fine with his challengers. A rousing series

*As a speaker at the forum with Powell, I talked to him later in his hotel room. This was the only time I had met him in person. I asked about the reelection campaign back in New York. He seemed genuinely unconcerned, even impatient with the question. "No way I can lose. After all I've done for the people of Harlem," he confidently stated. "They know it. Of course, I'll win. Won't even be close." He seemed honestly surprised that I would even think it was a question worth raising.[43]

of debates might elicit a sympathy vote for Powell. Rangel's campaign was relentless, gathering momentum with each passing week. He spoke in churches, on street corners, and in the newly carved out section of the district on the West Side. His confidence grew. He knew his initial weakness. Because he was not too well known outside his own assembly district, he decided that one of his first pieces of campaign material should focus on "Who is Charles Rangel?" True, he had cut his political teeth in the trenches of Harlem political clubs, doing things such as servicing constituents and building credits that a rising young, politically ambitious lawyer typically did. This was not dramatic, high visibility activity, but it was precisely the way one established a local political base. In addition, and most important, he was identified as one who had defended Adam Powell in the past against "outsiders" who tried to tell Harlemites to dump Powell. This meant that his challenge now could be understood as a legitimate, home-based move to change the old guard.

Rangel's campaign materials hammered away at the theme of Powell as a part-time congressman. He circulated leaflets showing Powell's absentee voting record on bills throughout 1969: fourteen bills (for example, extending the education programs, special milk programs for children, student loans, aid to dependent children, increasing Social Security benefits)—fourteen absences. The leaflet read: "Harlem can no longer afford Adam Clayton Powell." Another pointedly asked: "Are *YOU* the voter that Adam Powell takes for granted?? Harlem needs a Congressman. Write and ask the absent Powell to retire!" He reminded voters that Powell had stated on television, "My people would elect me . . . even if I had to be propped up in my casket."

Early in the campaign Rangel picked up endorsements from Percy Sutton, Jackie Robinson, Roy Campanella, David Dinkins (elected in 1989 the first African-American mayor of New York City), attorney Robert Carter (one of Powell's lawyers in the exclusion hearings before the Celler committee three years before), Jimmy Breslin, Paul O'Dwyer, Lionel Hampton (a Republican), the Reverend Wyatt T. Walker (a former associate of Martin Luther King, Jr.), and Assemblyman Frantz Leichter of the West Side. Harlem must rid itself "of tired, old public officials," Rangel urged the voters. He also talked about issues: drug addiction ("Congress has the power to stop the importation of drugs into this country overnight"); the Vietnam war (". . . promise not to vote one penny to continue the immoral war in Vietnam or elsewhere until our country fulfills its commitment to the burning domestic and social programs facing the people in New York City"); education (more federal funds); housing (for the aged and larger families). But above all he offered energy, youth, and "full-time" service. On the issues, Powell could match him. They were both liberals. But on the matter of physical energy, there was no contest; Rangel had him.

Operating out of campaign headquarters at the centrally located Theresa Hotel in Harlem, Rangel issued press releases almost weekly. In one, he and several West Side political leaders called for the impeachment of President Richard Nixon for the invasion of Cambodia. In another, he blasted Powell for planning a trip to Vietnam. Powell, the press release said,

> sank to a new low in political opportunism in his plans to visit Black G.I.'s in Vietnam during his election-year campaign. . . . If Congressman Powell truly wants to be of assistance to Black G.I.'s, he would make certain that he is present on the floor of Congress to vote on measures seeking to limit the powers of the President, eliminate defense funds for Cambodia and other bills to end the war. He would also be there to press for legislation on housing, employment, welfare and education to make life more bearable for the families of the Black troops in the Harlems across the nation.[45]

Rangel picked up more endorsements from Congresswoman Shirley Chisholm, Mayor John Lindsay, and Floyd McKissick.[46] Rangel led a picket line in front of the French consulate to protest the continued importation of heroin from that country. "Drug addiction has become the leading cause of death for people between the ages of 15 and 35 in New York. These are our young people," Rangel announced. Hearing him, Powell probably would have had a sense of déjà vu.[47]

But Powell probably did not hear him. He stayed on the nationwide lecture circuit, receiving rounds of applause from receptive college audiences, calling J. Edgar Hoover "that senile old bastard." He praised the Black Panthers and called for Black Power. "We're proud of our Black Panthers. Proud. Proud. But if I say this in Harlem I lose votes because I got a bunch of bourgeois Negroes."[48] He did not bother to open a campaign headquarters in Harlem until three weeks before the election. By then, it was clear that he was in a fight. He could not, or chose not to, match the flood of activity coming from Rangel and his three other opponents. He was engaged in one of the sharpest attacks he had experienced in his reelection bids. He issued few pieces of campaign material on his own, receiving one-line endorsements in the mailings sent out by a few other candidates (Hulan Jack was running for the State Assembly, Anthony Mendez for the State Senate) who supported him. But this would not be enough. Rangel was endorsed by the *New York Times* and the *New York Post.* The *Amsterdam News*, however, stuck with Powell:

> It would seem to us that he would relish, at this time in his life, the opportunity to return to the Congress as the "Adam of old," where in the past he has distinguished himself, and by virtue of his experience, give his constituents and blacks elsewhere his needed leadership of old.[49]

But this was not the "Adam of old." He had never really had to campaign vigorously for himself, even in his fight against Tammany Hall in 1958, and therefore he probably did not actually know how. He was not experienced at facing a serious challenge on his own territory. Signs of this began to show in the 1968 primary, but he was then still riding the crest of support from indignant Harlemites who were not going to be told by Congress who they should select. But now, in 1970, this was an intracommunity "family" argument. The challengers kept it that way by focusing on Powell's absentee record and cryptically noting his lack of physical energy, his declining health. They could not be easily labeled "Uncle Toms." They were locally based, home-grown products who were no longer willing to put their political careers on hold out of deference to Adam Powell. And they had just enough grass-roots support to make their challenges credible. Finally, there was that very important new dimension—a new section added to the congressional district, one that promised not to add to Powell's strength. Powell never campaigned in that West Side area, but Rangel and his forces saturated it.

With all this, the feeling was still there that Powell would pull it out. After all, Harlem had not chosen anyone else since 1944—twenty-six years. The mystique, some figured, would last this one more time. And in the minds of some, there *was* the feeling that that was what Powell wanted, one more victory. Now that he had declared his candidacy, he wanted to go out a winner. And, in the minds of some, perhaps in acknowledgment of all the fights in which he had engaged, he was entitled to one more win.

It was not to be.

On primary day, June 23, 1970, Adam Clayton Powell, Jr., lost. This was only the second defeat he had suffered in an election in

Harlem. (The first was to Grant Reynolds back in 1946 in the Republican primary. That one didn't really count since he had already won the Democratic nomination and went on to be re-elected in the general election.) But now in 1970, *this* one counted. It was a cliff-hanger. The tally:

Rangel	7,804	(32.6%)
Powell	7,599	(31.8%)
Martinez	4,327	(18.1%)
Gray	2,562	(10.7%)
Young	1,627	(6.8%)

Rangel's 205-vote margin was reduced to 150 after a recount demanded by Powell. Powell claimed election fraud and went to court. Then he and his supporters tried to circulate petitions to get him on the November ballot as an independent candidate. They were unable to get the sufficient number of valid signatures. His court challenge fell apart when, in December 1970, the federal court ruled that he was late in filing an appeal. Meanwhile, Rangel had won the general election in November and was preparing to go to Congress as Powell's successor.

The June primary defeat was Powell's end. The *Amsterdam News* editorialized:

> About the only true explanation one can make about the defeat of Mr. Powell is that had the congressman waged as vigorous a campaign before the election as he has been doing afterwards, in demanding a recount and declaring election machines missing and challenging votes, it is quite possible he would have received over 200 votes and emerged a winner.[50]

The FBI noted his defeat in an entry into its files. A handwritten comment on the page read: "Good riddance of bad rubbish!"[51]

Powell returned to Bimini, announced to his church in April 1971 that he was retiring from its pastorate, and decided to write a book about his life. His health was declining rapidly now. The cancer was taking its toll. On April 4, 1972, in Bimini, he was stricken with complications from prostate surgery, and flown immediately to Jackson Memorial Hospital in Miami, Florida. He died that night.[52]

A funeral was held several days later at Abyssinian Baptist Church. His body was taken to the Bahamas, cremated, and his ashes scattered over the waters off South Bimini.

21

Legacy

It is not surprising that controversy immediately erupted after Powell's death. As his entire adult life had evoked intense disagreement among his supporters and opponents, it continued even before his ashes were scattered across the Caribbean waters. Noting that he died coincidentally on the fourth anniversary of Martin Luther King's assassination, the *New York Times* compared the influence of the two men in a short two-paragraph editorial. Both men "played their roles in the emergence of blacks from the abuses of a white-dominated society. Both brought enormous personal gifts to the struggle for racial equality, and both attracted devoted followings."[1] Nonetheless, the *Times* was moved to distinguish the two leaders: " . . . one was an aspiring leader whose name adds luster to the American tradition; the other, lost in a sea of cynicism and self-indulgence, leaves no lasting heritage."

As far as the editorial writer was concerned, King "sought to appeal to the best in the American spirit . . . Mr. Powell . . . took as the measuring rod for application of his talents the grossest of white standards for personal and political success."

Such an assessment from that source was certain to provoke a reaction. Even before the funeral, two news conferences were held by Harlem political leaders and Powell supporters at Abyssinian Baptist Church. David Dinkins, who would become New York City's first African-American mayor seventeen years later, running on a pledge to bridge the city's racial divisions, stated: "Mr. Powell taught us pride in ourselves. There was a time when we would only read the *Amsterdam News* in public when it was hidden inside the *New York Times*." Basil A. Paterson, who would serve as the state's first black secretary of state three years later and who had run a respectable but unsuccessful race for lieutenant governor two years before, saw no need to compare King and Powell; blacks, he asserted, understood and appreciated both leaders, notwithstanding their different styles and appeals. The fiery black nationalist community activist from Brooklyn, Robert (Sonny) Carson, told the news conference: "I am his heritage. We are all his heritage."[2] (Seventeen years later, Carson, in campaigning for mayoral candidate Dinkins, stated that he did not wish to be considered anti-Jewish; he defiantly stated he was antiwhite.)

At the funeral before an overflowing audience, Dr. Samuel Proctor, who would succeed Powell as Abyssinian's senior pastor, gave the eulogy. "He gave us our first evidence that American institutions were capable of any change at all. He gave us a new basis for hope when our churches, colleges, unions, hotels—all were segregated. When my country, America, screamed at me, telling me I'm a nobody, he gave us all hope."[3] Mayor John V. Lindsay remembered Powell as a "man of style, brilliance and compassion—a skilled politician." The black congressman from Detroit, Charles C. Diggs, received shouts of approval when he told the audience that Powell was denied his seat in Congress by "envious and mediocre men" and by doing so had "made the Congress a smaller place."

Hazel Scott and her son were there; Yvette Diago Powell attended with her son. The woman with whom Powell lived at his death, Darlene Expose Hine, occupied a front-row seat. Powell's first wife, Isabel, did not attend the funeral.

It was inevitable that Powell's career would elicit comparison with that of other political leaders. The conduct of his office over the years was often compared with that of Congressman William L. Dawson of Chicago. Completely opposite men, both black and representing inner-city, low-income black districts, they were a study in contrasts. Dawson, the product of the powerful Cook County Democratic organization, was a loyal party man who eschewed publicity and preferred to identify himself as a "team" player. He held his seat and power through the party-patronage-based machine on the South Side of Chicago. He delivered services rather than speeches to his constituents and for these he was strongly supported. Powell, on the other hand, was from New York City, where machine politics began crumbling as far back as La Guardia's time.

Individualized politics was the order of the day at that time, and Powell was the epitome of independent politics. He neither belonged to nor built a coherent "machine," and patronage was not the incentive—there being relatively little of it to hand out—for his sustained support. Political scientist James Q. Wilson once noted that Dawson's Chicago circumstances pretty much determined the kind of congressman he would be—old-style, favor-dispensing, ward-boss politician. With Powell, there was a difference. In the absence of a strong citywide party structure thriving on patronage, politicians in New York City tended to build their own independent bases. Powell started in his church, linked it to his political association, the Alfred E. Isaacs Democratic Club, and was master of both simultaneously. Intangible benefits in the form of appeals to race pride and egalitarian goals largely attracted and held Powell supporters.[4] Individual services where possible, to be sure, were delivered, but if Powell never got one club member or constituent a job he likely would have continued to be elected. That would have been very unlikely for Dawson.

Clarence Mitchell also noticed this difference between Dawson and Powell. Dawson, a product of the "Chicago school of politics," believed in going along with the party, as did his other congressional colleagues from that city. But Powell was more like his New York City colleagues, who were more prone to be "pretty free wheeling." Thus, in some ways, the difference between Dawson and Powell reflected the difference between the respective political environments from which they came.[5]

At the same time, some black leaders were willing to go a long way toward explaining and even accepting Powell's maverick style. They recognized his appeal to many of his black constituents, again, as Wilson had described it. Bayard Rustin concluded that a large part of Powell's appeal to blacks was his willingness to dare to do what other leaders were not prepared to do. His constituents admired the "magnificent way he would thumb his nose at the white establishment." Why could not other civil rights leaders be like that, they asked. "He's not afraid to give the white folks hell."[6]

In this sense, Powell received the same response Malcolm X got from many in the most fiery days of his leadership. Gordon Parks once wrote that Malcolm was "fearless." He spoke defiantly and said "what most of us black folk were afraid to say publicly." Therefore, when Malcolm X condemned police brutality or Harlem slumlords, he was appreciated and loudly applauded.[7]

This, too, was Powell's value, not exclusively, but substantially.

And any black leader who played that role would always find more than a modicum of support, and his heritage would be viewed by those supporters as lasting and positive. Such reactions are intimately linked to one's view of the American Dilemma and how that issue should be faced.

Powell's career spanned almost forty years, and his contributions can be assessed over time in roughly the three periods outlined in this book.

In the first period, before going to Congress, he was perceived by many as an outspoken, tail-twisting, tongue-lashing protester. As a young minister, he spoke out and joined picket lines when many of his station in life kept silent and played it safe. Much of what he gained for his followers was psychological release, but in those times that was very much, indeed, for them. He would deliver a rousing speech when everyone knew there was no likelihood of getting effective bills through the City Council whether one spoke softly and tried to persuade gently or blasted the evils of racial segregation and tried to shame those who countenanced it. In that case, simply to shout the words of defiance and anger was something, and should not be discounted in assessing the worth of a leader otherwise so severely constrained by objective political reality. Surely, this took courage, and political scientist John A. Davis has noted that Powell's willingness to defy authority began long before he challenged racial segregation and discrimination. Davis noted that Powell went against the strong and clear wishes of his father and married Isabel Washington. This could not have been an easy thing to do, especially in a middle-class, prominent black family in those days. Even then Powell Jr. was demonstrating an individual, independent streak that could have tipped off any observer that the Bilbos and Rankins and other segregationists would be easy to defy by comparison.[8]

When he went to Congress, he had no intention of keeping quiet and solely playing by the rules. He once told a television interviewer that it was as an irritant that he wanted to be remembered and characterized. "All my life, an irritant. My father before me. It's my heritage. Whenever a person keeps prodding, keeps them squirming . . . it serves a purpose. It may not in contemporary history look so good. But as the times roll on, future historians will say, they served a purpose."[9] Even while he defended his country's record on race relations in an international forum, the Bandung Conference, he kept the pressure on to desegregate government facilities, and he achieved some results. Prior to his protests, black journalists were excluded from the press gallery of the House of Representatives. Powell immediately interceded and that policy was dropped. He gladly made himself the vehicle for introducing the controversial Powell Amendment, supported by the NAACP. He became the symbol for a staunch, no-compromise position on that issue, and in the process gained the national reputation of "Mr. Civil Rights." In prodding federal officials, he could, at times, shame them into concrete, albeit at times only small, results. At the same time, he curried favor with the reluctant Eisenhower administration, and more than a few times angered and confused his civil rights allies by going overboard in praising a President who was decidedly mild in support of the civil rights goals Powell himself advocated. Such seeming contradictory behavior always exposed Powell to charges of being self-serving and unpredictable. He could not be trusted, his friends and adversaries lamented, but he was always able to bring his constituents along with him at least to the point of rising to his defense in his reelection bids.

As chairman of an important congressional committee at a time when vital new social legislation was being passed, Powell played a crucial role. He was a liberal who, more often than not, used his position to expedite an ordinarily slow legislative process.

Interestingly, he probably achieved more as a leader acting on his own, given the constraints of each period, in the earlier two periods than in the last. There were clear victories as chairman, to be sure, but *that* liberal role could conceivably have been played in the 1960s by any number of other liberals on his committee. The times had changed, and there was a new, different ethos in the country and in Congress. He was at the center of power in this era, but he was not alone. And during the Johnson Presidency, he had a powerful, active White House to work with. But earlier, in the 1940s and 1950s, he was, indeed, virtually alone, or at least a lonely voice. And precisely because of that, he was exceptionally crucial. In many instances during those earlier times, if *he* did not speak out, the issue would not have been raised. If he had not persisted in some of the earlier protest marches in Harlem, bringing his massive church base with him, as with the protest against the local bus companies, the protest might not have succeeded. Many different ideological groups in Harlem at the time—black nationalists, integrationists, Communists—recognized this and appreciated the delicate, if at times bedeviling, balancing role he played in holding such contentious groups together for the duration of the particular movement. His skills as a preacher/protester were rare and singularly important. For example, only *he* could (or would dare to) challenge Congressman Rankin of Mississippi on the House floor in the 1940s for using the word "nigger." He certainly did not change Rankin's mind or behavior, but he gave solace to millions who longed for a little retaliatory defiance. There was a point beyond which the country should not "wink" at the insults of racists, pretending they were never uttered, or even perhaps should not be taken seriously. Powell knew the mood of his people, and on some matters, he was not willing to wink. This was of incalculable value to those who could look forward to little more at the moment. Powell had a unique platform, and he used it with the intense agreement of his followers.

In the 1950s, before mass civil rights marches were popular, he offered a focal point for the kind of outspoken protest that would characterize newer leaders soon to come on the scene. In a sense, he, along with only a small number of others, kept the protest fires smoldering until they would burst into flames a few years later in the 1960s. Without question, he cut deals, stroked adversaries, made compromises. He also extracted, where he could, more than personal benefits. Often, it was enough for a soldier on a military post simply to mention his name and a *de facto* segregated practice would end. Powell clearly was the point man, the weapon to be used in many different ways to strike at a racially segregated society that was, in the forties and fifties, not nearly as vulnerable to attack as it would become in the 1960s.

These were the things those old enough to know very likely objected to in the *Times* editorial. A lasting heritage? Surely, to them, the answer was clear and affirmative. And some of those who organized to defeat him in his last election bid did not confuse this point. Percy Sutton, Manhattan Borough president at the time of Powell's death and a strong supporter of the victorious Charles Rangel in the 1970 contest for the Harlem seat, noted that Powell was a "giant at a time when giants were few."

At the same time, he had his sincere detractors, not all of whom were by any means opponents of the civil rights cause he championed. He fought with them over patronage and power. He failed to keep some promises, and in this he could not be defended. There *were* times when he put his personal fortune ahead of everything else, and he frustrated and angered those who wanted more honest dealings from him. He very likely did scuttle the James Farmer literacy proposal, and never explained that apparently inexcusable behavior. Without question, he compromised his political power by his callous handling (by his own admission) of the "bag woman" case. There he certainly miscalculated. And he should not have abused his committee funds. He was clearly at fault, and could not be defended, whether he was one among many or not. He should have been more forthright; he owed it to his integrity, his cause, his constituents, even if he knew that his transgressions were no worse than those of some of his colleagues. For a man in such a powerful, controversial role, he should have been much more careful about keeping his record clean. He and his supporters might have seen this as requiring a double standard, but it was already long since established that he was not dealing with an absolutely honorable system. Powell had it mixed up. He often would say that if certain things could happen to him, then look what could happen to the poor and powerless. It really was just the opposite. If the political system could for so long oppress and permit the subjugation of a whole people, then why would he expect, as a spokesman for that people, to be accorded any better treatment? Surely he knew this. But he was never able to subordinate his personal desires to an obvious obligation for probity that his self-chosen role of public leader would require. In this he was his own worst enemy. And, it must be said, the people who needed him most were deprived of the greater leadership he could have provided.

Surely reaction to Adam Clayton Powell, Jr., invariably would be determined by reaction to the American Dilemma. His supporters who were inclined to rage against the gap between American ideals and practices were prone to overlook his personal faults. Criticizing him where and when he was most vulnerable—and there were many such opportunities—could be seen by his supporters as giving aid and comfort to the enemies of the civil rights cause. Powell knew this, and, therefore, he could raise the "double standard" issue with great effectiveness. Why him? The NAACP, Martin Luther King, Jr., and many white and black civil rights advocates were constantly in this bind. They had to bite their tongue, hold their peace, and try (mostly unsuccessfully) to get private word to Powell to mend his ways and be less personally obnoxious.

Others, more willing to take a more conciliatory, tolerant approach to the Dilemma, were less lenient toward and less forgiving of him. They were no less committed to the ultimate ends—perfecting the American Creed—but they differed with him and his supporters on the means to achieving those ends. Thus, while his supporters saw him as an admirable irritant, others saw him as an unreasonable demagogue, an opportunist. Why raise the "double standard" issue? Is this not, as the *Times* editorial suggested, choosing the lowest standards to judge leadership? These detractors wanted more patience and understanding from Powell (and his supporters) than he was willing (or able) to give. And when he refused and questioned *their* sincerity, this infuriated them even more. He was, menacingly, questioning *their* veracity on this most delicate and divisive of America's social issues.

Above all, these contending forces demonstrated fundamentally different responses to the Dilemma gap. Powell was in a constant state of creedal passion. Others were more prone to tolerate that gap and accept less than full compliance at the moment, as vexing as that would be.

Certainly, Powell seized the opportunity to portray this tolerating response as hypocritical and dishonest. In a sense, the *Times* editorial describing him as in "a sea of cynicism" was not too far off the mark. But it is important to explore the source of that cynicism. He had known and experienced the begrudging societal response to racial injustices over the years. He had seen the society ignore the issue for so long, and he had seen how Southern segregationists were coddled and catered to by many in his own party. *They* bolted the party time and again, and were not punished. *They* scuttled civil rights bills in committee or on the Senate floor for years, and were treated gingerly. Powell saw all this, and he had an additional peak into white American society from his personal peculiar vantage point.

As a white-looking black man, a marginal person, he was able to experience two quite separate worlds. Being accepted for a time as white by unsuspecting white racists early in his life, he could see the folly of racism. He could see the privileges a mere white skin brought without any obvious basis of merit—beyond skin color. Thus he could sneer at racists who gave, for him, contorted explanations for segregation. And he could hold such people in utter contempt. It is quite conceivable that this "privileged perspective" infuriated him and made him even more cynical in his own personal and political life. This was facilitated by his proclivity anyway for a carefree, cavalier life-style. In a sense, he likely concluded that if he had to accept America's toleration of the Dilemma, America would have to tolerate him also. He was entitled. If he "kept the faith" with his country (defending it at times, prepared to compromise on some legislation), then why could not Congress, likewise, be willing to reciprocate and allow him some latitude? He ultimately hoped—and privately expected—that his congressional colleagues would look at his transgressions and tolerate them with a wink. They were not willing to do so. And his cynicism deepened.

Without question, after Powell was stripped of his chairmanship in January 1967, he was finished as a power in Congress, even if he would regain his seat. He had wanted his political colleagues to provide him the same leeway he knew they were capable of providing others and he apparently hoped they would tolerate his actions in the same sense many of them had tolerated the inconsistencies between America's creed and its practice. They were in no mood for such a deal.

But perhaps more important, finally, neither were the voters of his Harlem. They were always furious (or at least more so than their fellow Americans) with the slow pace of dealing with the Dilemma, and they were growing increasingly uncomfortable with the seeming necessity to tolerate either their country or their congressman. It was time to move on to other strategies with new leaders, away from Powell as the Issue.

But an overflow crowd turned out for Powell's funeral, and in his death as in his life they were moved to support him. Surely they understood his value over time, and they, by their presence, would attempt to protect and define the meaning of *their* enigmatic leader *to them.* Other tangible evidence would appear over the succeeding years: a large government building was built on the corner of 125th Street and Seventh Avenue and named the Adam Clayton Powell Jr. State Office Building; Seventh Avenue in Harlem was renamed Adam Clayton Powell Jr. Boulevard. There would likely be no national holiday commemorating his birth and career, and very few in future generations would likely know precisely the circumstances of his decline and fall. But he was also likely to be accorded more historical attention than the vast majority of the people he served with in Congress—and remembered for the good as well as the bad.

Nineteen years after his defeat in 1970, a crossword puzzle appeared in the *New York Times.*[10] One entry clue read: "A memorable Powell."

The correct four-letter answer was ADAM.

Notes

Prologue

1. Gunnar Myrdal, *An American Dilemma* (New York: Harper & Bros., 1944), p. 4.
2. *Ibid.*, p. xlv.
3. *Ibid.*, p. 863n.
4. Adam Clayton Powell, Jr., *Adam by Adam, The Autobiography of Adam Clayton Powell, Jr.* (New York: The Dial Press, 1971), p. 71.
5. *Ibid.*, pp. 41–42.
6. Myrdal, p. 37.
7. Myrdal, p. 37.
8. Samuel P. Huntington, *American Politics, The Promise of Disharmony* (Cambridge, Mass.: Harvard University Press, 1981), p. 16.
9. *Ibid.*, p. 39.
10. *Ibid.*, p. 69. (Italics added.)
11. *Ibid.*, p. 70. (Italics added.)
12. *Newsweek*, January 16, 1967, p. 26.
13. See David Garrow, *Bearing the Cross* (New York: William Morrow and Company, Inc., 1986) p. 364.

Chapter 1

1. Two memos from Henry Wilson, administrative assistant to President Lyndon B. Johnson, January 10, 1967, in Adam Clayton Powell File, White House Central Files (WHCF), LBJ Library. University of Texas, Austin, Texas.
2. Actually, the official vote was 363–65, and not as the secretary's second memo reported: 354–64.
3. Congressional Record. 90th Congress. H4. January 10, 1967.
4. See news story by Jimmy Breslin in the *New York Post*, January 11, 1967, for this account of Powell's afternoon activities.
5. *New York Times*, March 30, 1966.

6. Memo in WHCF, Adam Clayton Powell, Jr., LBJ Library, July 16, 1966. Notation on memo from LBJ agreeing to reschedule the meeting.
7. *New York Times*, March 30, 1966.
8. Letter in Collection of Powell Memorial Room, Abyssinian Baptist Church, New York, New York.
9. *Adam by Adam*, p. 213.
10. Letter from Powell to President Johnson, September 9, 1966. President—Confidential File, Box 63, LBJL, University of Texas.
11. Memo to President Johnson from Henry Wilson, September 10, 1966. White House Central Files, LBJL, Box 280. (The White House Diary entries did show a call from President Johnson to Powell on September 6, 1966, returning a call from Powell.)
12. Clayborn Carson, *In the Struggle: SNCC and the Black Awakening of the 1960s* (Cambridge, Mass.: Harvard University Press, 1981), p. 224.
13. Correspondence from Roy Wilkins to Adam Clayton Powell, August 30, 1966; August 31, 1966. NAACP Washington Bureau Papers, Box 136, Library of Congress.
14. Roy Wilkins, "Powell on Very Solid Ground," *Amsterdam News*, November 12, 1966.
15. *Adam by Adam*, p. 203.
16. *Adam by Adam*, p. 208.
17. *New York Times*, September 25, 1966.
18. *New York Times*, September 23, 1966.
19. *New York Times*, September 3, 1966.
20. Press release, Whitney M. Young, Jr., Papers, Columbia University, New York.
21. *New York Times*, September 23, 1966.
22. Arthur Spingarn interview, Columbia University Oral History Collection, New York, July 1966.
23. *New York Times*, August 4, 1966.
24. Interview with J. Raymond Jones, December 2, 1972, St. Thomas, Virgin Islands.
25. *New York Times*, August 21, 1966.
26. *New York Times*, September 19, 1966.
27. Report of Select Committee Pursuant to H. Res. 1, 90th Congress, 1st Session. House Report No. 27, February 23, 1967. "In Re Adam Clayton Powell."

Chapter 2

1. See Lenworth A. Gunther III's unpublished Ph.D. dissertation, *Flamin' Tongue: The Rise of Adam Clayton Powell, Jr. 1908–1941,"* Columbia University, Department of History 1985, for the best account of the early years and family background of Powell.
2. See *Adam by Adam*, pp. 4–5.
3. Adam Clayton Powell, Sr., *Against the Tide* (New York: Richard R. Smith, 1938), p. 13.
4. *Adam by Adam*, p. 24.
5. *Ibid.*, p. 28.
6. In the high school, one for high-achieving students in the city, he was one of very few Negro students at the time.
7. *Adam by Adam*, p. 29.
8. *Ibid.*, p. 30.
9. *Ibid.*
10. See interview with Ray Vaughn in David Balch, "God, Caesar and Powell—Adam Clayton Saves 'em All," April 3, 1963, pp. 49, 62, one in a series of articles on Powell in the *New York World Telegram*. Other articles in the series appeared on April 1, 2, 4, 5, and 8.
11. *Adam by Adam*, p. 33.
12. Interview with Isabel Washington Powell, November 18, 1988, New York City.
13. *Adam by Adam*, p. 35.

Chapter 3

1. The members of the commission were Charles H. Roberts, chairman; Oswald Garrison Villard, vice-chairman; Eunice Hunton Carter, secretary; Countee Cullen; Hubert T. Delany; John G. Grimley; Arthur Garfield Hays; Morris Ernst; William R. McCann; A. Philip Randolph; John W. Robinson; William Jay Schieffelin; and Charles E. Teney. It was known officially as the Mayor's Commission on Conditions in Harlem.
2. *New York Post*, March 21, 1935.
3. *New York Sun*, March 21, 1935, p. 24.
4. *New York Herald Tribune*, March 22, 1935, p. 18.
5. *New York Post*, March 27, 1935, p. 1.
6. The Mayor's Commission on Conditions in Harlem, *The Negro in Harlem, A Report on Social and Economic Conditions Responsible for the Outbreak of March 19, 1935* (New York, 1936), p. 15.
7. *Ibid.*

8. *Ibid.*, p. 18.
9. *Ibid.*, p. 33.
10. Mayor's report, p. 47.
11. *Ibid.*, p. 56.
12. *Ibid.*, p. 4.
13. *Ibid.*, p. 73.
14. *New York Times*, June 30, 1936.
15. *New York Times*, July 1, 1936, p. 2.
16. *New York Times*, July 1, 1936, p. 2.
17. *Amsterdam News*, July 18, 1936.
18. *New York Times*, July 23, 1936, p. 12.
19. *New York Times*, August 25, 1936, p. 20.
20. *New York Times*, July 23, 1936, p. 12.
21. *Amsterdam News*, February 29, 1936.
22. *Amsterdam News*, June 6, 1936, p. 12.
23. *Amsterdam News*, July 11, 1936.
24. *Amsterdam News*, March 2, 1936, p. 12.
25. *Amsterdam News*, August 1, 1936.
26. *Amsterdam News*, May 30, 1936, p. 12.
27. *Amsterdam News*, May 5, 1936, p. 12.
28. *Amsterdam News*, April 4, 1936, p. 12.
29. *Amsterdam News*, September 5, 1936, p. 12.

Chapter 4

1. A rather substantial body of literature has developed on this subject. See Carter G. Woodson, *The History of the Negro Church* (Washington, D.C.: The Associated Publishers, 1921); Benjamin E. Mays, *The Negro's God* (New York: Atheneum Publishers, 1968); E. Franklin Frazier, *The Negro Church in America* (New York: Schocken Books, 1963); Charles V. Hamilton, *The Black Preacher in America* (New York: William R. Morrow, 1972).
2. This was Powell Sr.'s alma mater, renamed and moved from Washington, D.C., to Richmond.
3. 732 St. Nicholas Avenue, purchased from a couple who were members of the church.
4. Adam Clayton Powell, Sr., *Against the Tide* (New York: Richard R. Smith, 1938), p. 229.
5. See *Baltimore Afro-American*, December 27, 1930, p. 1; *Pittsburgh Courier*, January 17, 1931, p. 1; *New York Age*, January 10, 1931, p. 10.
6. Myrdal, *American Dilemma*, pp. 873, 875, 877.
7. Note his charge against the recently deceased and popular Reverend

L. K. Williams of Chicago. Powell Jr. even intimated that the late clergyman, who died in an airplane crash, had ordered a fellow minister killed over a battle for church power. This created quite a stir for a while in the Negro press, and Powell generally gave as good as he got in the exchanges.

8. See Gunther, *Flamin' Tongue;* and John William Kinney, *Adam Clayton Powell, Sr. and Adam Clayton Powell, Jr.: A Historical Exposition and Theological Analysis* (unpublished Ph.D. dissertation), Columbia University, 1979.
9. *Against the Tide*, p. 87.
10. *Ibid.*, p. 259.
11. See *Amsterdam News*, September 25, 1937, pp. 1, 4, for reference to this point.
12. See *Against the Tide*, pp. 283–87.

Chapter 5

1. William E. Leuchtenburg, *Franklin D. Roosevelt and the New Deal* (New York: Harper Torchbooks, 1963), xii.
2. *Adam by Adam*, p. 37.
3. *Ibid.*
4. Interview with Isabel Powell, November 16, 1988, New York City.
5. The wedding was originally planned for June, but was moved up apparently to avoid a large, drawn-out, elaborate gala. Nonetheless, the ceremony attracted thousands.
6. *Adam by Adam*, p. 39.
7. *Ibid.*, p. 43.
8. *Ibid.*, pp. 39–40.
9. *Ibid.*, pp. 37–38.
10. See *Amsterdam News*; *New York Age*.
11. Estimates of the eventual number ranged from several hundred to 6,000. Powell later recorded in his autobiography that there were 6,000. But he also misstated the event as occurring in the spring of 1930—when he was still at Colgate.
12. See Lenworth Gunther dissertation, p. 215, and Minutes of the Board of Estimate, Municipal Archives and Research Center, New York, New York.
13. In a 1958 document prepared by Powell's congressional staff, he claimed "The Negro doctors were reinstated" after his speech before the Board of Estimate. This is not accurate.
14. Gunther, p. 221.

15. Arthur M. Schlesinger, Jr., *The Coming of the New Deal* (Boston: Houghton Mifflin Company, 1959), pp. 401–4.
16. *Ibid.*, p. 403.
17. See Charles V. Hamilton and Dona Cooper Hamilton, "Social Policies, Civil Rights, and Poverty," in *Fighting Poverty, What Works and What Doesn't,* edited by Sheldon H. Danziger and Daniel H. Weinberg (Cambridge, Mass.: Harvard University Press, 1986), pp. 287–311.
18. Claude McKay, *Harlem: Negro Metropolis* (New York: E. P. Dutton & Company, 1940), p. 194.
19. Claude McKay, *Harlem: Negro Metropolis* (New York: E. P. Dutton & Company, 1940); and Roi Ottley, *New World A-Coming: Inside Black America* (New York: Arno Press and the *New York Times*, 1969).
20. See Gunther dissertation.
21. Beck shoe company case.
22. *Adam by Adam*, p. 63.
23. Gunther dissertation, p. 363.
24. Neil Hickey and Ed Edwin, *Adam Clayton Powell and the Politics of Race* (New York: Fleet Publishing Corporation, 1965), p. 56.
25. Gunther, p. 347.
26. *Ibid.*, pp. 314–15.
27. *Amsterdam News*, January 7, 1939.
28. Gunther, pp. 389–90. See also *New York Age*, May 20, 1939; *Amsterdam News*, May 27, 1939; June 10, 1939.
29. Memo from Roy Wilkins to Walter White re Standard Brands, Inc., May 23, 1939. NAACP Papers, Library of Congress, Group I, C-418.
30. *Ibid.*, p. 388.
31. *Amsterdam News*, March 23, 1940; April 20, 1940; *New York Age*, March 23, 1940; April 27, 1940.
32. Ralph Ellison, Introduction, *Invisible Man* (New York: Vintage Books, 1981), xiv.
33. "Soap Box" article in *Amsterdam News*, September 16, 1939.
34. Letter from Adam Clayton Powell to NAACP, August 3, 1939. NAACP Papers, Library of Congress, Group I, C-305.
35. Letter from James E. Allen to Roy Wilkins, April 26, 1935. NAACP Papers, Library of Congress, Group I, G-144.
36. *Adam by Adam*, p. 224.
37. *Ibid.*

Chapter 6

1. See "Soap Box," *Amsterdam News*, November 13, 1937, p. 13.
2. See "Powell Joins F.D.R. Backers," *Amsterdam News*, August 15, 1936, p. 1; "Church's Aid Asked for F.D.R.," *Amsterdam News*, September 5, 1936, p. 1.
3. *New York Age*, October 24, 1936; *Amsterdam News*, October 24, 1936.
4. Lenworth Gunther dissertation, p. 424.
5. *Amsterdam News*, October 18, 1933; November 1, 1933; *Harlem Heights Daily Citizen*, October 23, 1933.
6. *Amsterdam News*, January 12, 19, 26 1935; February 28, 1935; August 8, 1936.
7. John A. Morsell, "The Political Behavior of Negroes in New York City" (unpublished Ph.D. dissertation), Columbia University, 1951; Ira Katznelson, *Black Men, White Cities* (New York: Oxford University Press, 1973) pp. 66–71; Gilbert Osofsky, *Harlem: The Making of a Ghetto* (New York: Harper & Row Publishers, 1966).
8. Morsell, p. 33.
9. Morsell, pp. 39–40.
10. Morsell, p. 44.
11. Mark Naison, *Communists in Harlem During the Depression* (New York: Grove Press, 1983).
12. Interview with Isabel Powell, November 16, 1988, New York City.
13. *New York Times*, November 13, 1941.
14. Letter from Powell to La Guardia, January 21, 1942. Box 2614, FHLP. Cited in Dominic J. Capeci, *The Harlem Riot of 1943* (Philadelphia: Temple University Press, 1977), p. 23.
15. *Ibid.*, p. 24.
16. *Amsterdam News*, January 17, 1942, p. 1.
17. *New York Times*, February 4, 1942, p. 21.
18. *Amsterdam News*, reprinted in *The People's Voice*, February 14, 1942.
19. *The People's Voice*, February 14, 1942, p. 20.
20. *The People's Voice*, March 28, 1942.
21. *The People's Voice*, "Soap Box," Adam Clayton Powell, Jr., March 28, 1942, p. 5.
22. *New York Times*, April 14, 1943, p. 25.
23. Capeci, *The Harlem Riot of 1943*, p. 8.
24. Letter from Walter White to Negro ministers, club presidents, labor organizations, women's clubs, and other organizations in Harlem and Brooklyn, June 28, 1943. Files of NAACP, Group II, A-506, Library of Congress, Washington, D.C.
25. Dominic J. Capeci, "From Different Liberal Perspectives: Fiorello H. La Guardia, Adam Clayton Powell, Jr., and Civil Rights in New York City, 1941–1943." *Journal of Negro History*, Vol. LXII, No. 2, April 1977, p. 168.

26. *New York Times*, June 25, 1943.
27. FHLP, Box 3531, Folder 10.
28. *Ibid.*
29. Report, May 17, 1942, from Acting Lt. Schillersky, Criminal Alien Squad, to Commanding Officer, Criminal Alien Squad. FHLP, Box 3531, Folder 10, MARC.
30. *New York Times*, March 12, 1942.
31. *The People's Voice*, "Soap Box," April 25, 1942, p. 5.
32. *The People's Voice*, May 23, 1942, p. 20.
33. Letter from George Gove to Hon. William T. Andrews, April 22, 1943. FHLP, Box 3561, Folder 2, MARC.
34. Letter from William T. Andrews to Mr. George Gove, April 26, 1943. FHLP, Box 3561, Folder 2, MARC.
35. Letter from George Gove to William T. Andrews, May 6, 1943. FHLP, Box 3561, Folder 2, MARC.
36. The Board of Estimate was a body distinct from the City Council. It had jurisdiction over such matters as the budget and authority to approve or reject capital budget items such as this proposed housing development. The voting members were the mayor (three votes); the president of the City Council, Newbold Morris (three votes); and the five borough presidents (two votes each), for a total of sixteen votes.
37. Letters to Fiorello La Guardia in FHLP, Boxes 3560, 3561, Folders 14, 16, MARC. The letter from the New York City League of Women Voters took its stand on nonracial grounds: "We note the absence of provision for schools or recreation facilities."
38. Letter from Adam Clayton Powell, Jr., to Commissioner Robert Moses, August 16, 1943. FHLP, Box 3561, Folder 8, MARC.
39. Arthur Simon, *Stuyvesant Town, U.S.A., Pattern for Two Americas* (New York: New York University Press, 1970), p. 34.
40. *New York Times*, June 5, 1943.
41. *New York Herald Tribune*, June 5, 1943.
42. Letter from Walter White to Mayor La Guardia, June 16, 1943. FHLP, Box 3561, Folder 8, MARC.
43. Interview with Newbold Morris, June 30, 1954, reported in: Charles Garret, *The La Guardia Years, Machine and Reform Politics in New York City* (New Brunswick, New Jersey: Rutgers University Press, 1961), p. 386n.
44. Capeci, p. 14.
45. Letter from Mayor La Guardia to Frederick H. Ecker, July 31, 1943. FHLP, Box 3560, Folder 13, MARC.
46. Whether La Guardia's letter was ever transmitted to Ecker is not known. A copy remained in the mayor's files for future reference.

47. Letter of June 21, 1943, in FHLP, Box 3491, Folder 2, MARC. La Guardia, appreciatively acknowledged the letter. Other correspondence, one a detailed five-page critique of *The People's Voice*, was sent to the mayor and the City Council (July 3, 1943, FHLP, Box 3316, Folder IA). This was, however, signed: "A Former Associate of Powell." Its basic conclusion was "Powell is a notorious demagogue. . . . Only an ingrate and a professional troublemaker would attempt to turn New York's Negroes against Mayor La Guardia after all the Mayor has done for our people."
48. Warren Brown, "A Negro Warns the Negro Press," *The Reader's Digest*, January 1943, pp. 32–34.

Chapter 7

1. The "one-man, one vote" ruling would not be issued by the U.S. Supreme Court until 1962 in *Baker* v. *Carr*. 369 U.S. 186 (1962).
2. *New York Times*, January 16, 1941, pp. 1, 13.
3. Statement by Assembly Majority Leader Irving M. Ives, *ibid.*
4. *New York Times*, "Reapportionment When?," January 17, 1941, p. 16.
5. The committee was chaired by Republican assemblyman Harry A. Reoux. It was composed of five assemblymen and five senators.
6. *New York Times*, March 30, 1942, p. 19.
7. The two at-large congressional seats, existing since 1932, resulted from the 1930 census when New York State became eligible for two more congressional seats, but the state legislature failed to reapportion.
8. *New York Times*, March 31, 1942, pp. 1, 24.
9. The state constitution permitted an increase in Senate seats for counties having three or more senators. The issue was, did this mean three or more *before* the reapportionment was made, as the Democrats argued, or *after* the ratio was established for a new apportionment, as the Republicans maintained?
10. *New York Times*, April 15, 1942, p. 18.
11. *New York Times*, April 18, 1942, p. 1. The congressional reapportionment bill had slightly more support than the legislative bill, but both were rejected.
12. Congressman Arthur Mitchell, Republican from Chicago, who would be defeated and replaced by William L. Dawson, Democrat, in 1942.
13. *The People's Voice*, April 18, 1942, p. 5.
14. *Ibid.*

15. *Ibid.*
16. Presumably, this could be done on the basis of Article 1, Section 4 of the United States Constitution, which gives Congress the right to fix the time, place, and manner of holding congressional elections.
17. A. Philip Randolph, Columbia University Oral History Interview, July 25, 1972.
18. *Ibid.*
19. *Ibid.*
20. *New York Herald Tribune*, March 19, 1944, p. 12.
21. Letter from Assemblyman William T. Andrews to Roy Wilkins, March 23, 1944. NAACP Papers, Library of Congress, Group II, A-481.
22. Letter from Eardlie John to Roy Wilkins, March 21, 1944. NAACP Papers, Library of Congress, Group II, A-481.
23. Letter from Roy Wilkins to Eardlie John, March 24, 1944. NAACP Papers, Library of Congress, Group II, A-481.
24. Letter from Adam Clayton Powell, Jr., to Roy Wilkins, March 25, 1944. NAACP Papers, Library of Congress, Group II, A-481.
25. *The People's Voice*, April 22, 1944, p. 5. Dawson's style would later be in sharp contrast to that of his fellow congressman from Harlem. Dawson was not outspoken or flamboyant, and was seen by some as not vigorous enough in his attacks on segregationists. Even in 1944, Dawson (elected from Chicago's all-black South Side district) stated at the Harlem conference: "I am a Negro first, last and always. I will speak at any time I think I will get results." He and others would find that Powell in years to come would speak on the presumption that his mere speaking would elicit some sort of results. The two were very different, Dawson from the Cook County Democratic machine, Powell bent on being his own one-man machine.
26. *New York Times*, April 13, 1944.
27. *Daily Worker*, April 31, 1944.
28. *Amsterdam News*, July 22, 1944.
29. *Amsterdam News*, June 17, 1944. Ironically, fourteen years later in 1958, this same Earl Brown would be the candidate of Tammany Hall against Powell. The charges of "bossism" and "stooge" would be reversed.
30. *New York Times*, May 13, 1944.
31. *Amsterdam News*, May 20, 1944.
32. *New York Times*, July 29, 1944.
33. *New York Times*, April 9, 1944.
34. *Amsterdam News*, May 20, 1944.

35. *New York Times*, April 30, 1944.
36. Notes of Walter White, June 26, 1944. NAACP Papers, Library of Congress, Group II, A-496.
37. *New York Times*, June 16, 1944.
38. Letter from Walter White to the Rev. Adam Clayton Powell, Jr., June 16, 1944. NAACP Papers, Library of Congress, Group II, A-496.
39. Roland Stokes, "Political Stuff," *Amsterdam News*, June 24, 1944.
40. *The People's Voice*, "Soap Box," June 24, 1944, p. 5.
41. *The People's Voice*, "Soap Box," May 27, 1944, p. 5.
42. *New York Times*, July 30, 1944; *The People's Voice*, July 29, 1944, p. 6. This program was a collaboration between the Junior League of Abyssinian and the Reverend A. Ritchie Low of Johnson, Vermont. Isabel Powell helped raise the transportation costs.
43. *The People's Voice*, July 8, 1944, p. 19.
44. *The People's Voice*, May 27, 1944, p. 5.
45. *The People's Voice*, August 12, 1944, p. 7.
46. Julius J. Adams, "Adam C. Powell to Face Grand Opportunity as Harlem's First Negro U.S. Congressman," *Amsterdam News*, August 12, 1944.
47. John Patrick Diggins, *The Proud Decades, America in War and Peace, 1941–1960* (New York: W.W. Norton & Company, 1988), p. 22.
48. *The People's Voice*, October 7, 1944, p. 3.
49. The Bethune telegram read: "Three years ago I stood on the platform of your church and predicted a seat for you in Congress. My vision is not lessened today. You now have my unqualified endorsement. My prayers mean something. They follow you. This endorsement comes in my own personal right." *The People's Voice*, July 29, 1944, p. 1.
50. Letter from Mrs. Catherine D. Stallworth to Eleanor Roosevelt, August 18, 1944, NAACP Papers, Library of Congress, Group II, A-511.
51. Letter from Eleanor Roosevelt to Mrs. Catherine D. Stallworth, NAACP Papers, Library of Congress, Group II, A-511.
52. *Ibid.*
53. *The People's Voice*, September 16, 1944, p. 16.
54. Letter from Walter White to Eleanor Roosevelt, July 7, 1944. NAACP Papers, Library of Congress, Group II, A-511.
55. Letter from Eleanor Roosevelt to Walter White, August 3, 1944. NAACP Papers, Library of Congress, Group II, A-512. The rest of her letter inquired about other civil rights matters concerning the War Department, and ended "I have been glad to notice the recognition given the work of the colored Supply Corps in Normandy." In

her own account a few years later of the fourth-term quest, Eleanor Roosevelt wrote: "Another election lay ahead in the fall of 1944. I knew without asking that as long as the war was on it was a foregone conclusion that Franklin, if he was well enough, would run again." *This I Remember* (New York: Harper & Brothers Publishers, 1949), p. 328.

56. Memo prepared by Walter White on conference with the President, September 29, 1944, dated October 3, 1944. NAACP Papers, Library of Congress, Group II, A-511.
57. Quoted in Joseph P. Lash, *Eleanor and Franklin* (New York: W.W. Norton & Company, Inc., 1971), p. 672.
58. *Ibid.*, pp. 673–74.

Chapter 8

1. *New York Daily News*, November 25, 1944. Adam Clayton Powell Scrapbook, Vol. 2. p. 17, Schomburg Library, New York City.
2. Telegram from Vice-Presidential candidate Harry S Truman to Walter White, NAACP, October 31, 1944. NAACP Papers, Library of Congress, Group II, A-512.
3. *The People's Voice*, November 4, 1944, p. 20.
4. Quoted in Jonathan Daniels, *The Man of Independence* (Philadelphia: J.B. Lippincott Company, 1950), p. 338.
5. Quoted in Robert J. Donovan, *Conflict and Crisis, The Presidency of Harry S Truman, 1945–1948* (New York: W. W. Norton & Company, 1977), pp. 147–48.
6. *Ibid.*
7. *Ibid.*, p. 148.
8. Telegram from A. Philip Randolph to Walter White, August 24, 1945. NAACP Papers, Library of Congress, Group II, A-481.
9. William C. Berman, *The Politics of Civil Rights in the Truman Administration* (Columbus, Ohio: Ohio State University Press, 1970), p. 28.
10. *Ibid.*, p. 33.
11. *Ibid.*, p. 51. See also Donald R. McCory and Richard T. Ruetten, *Quest and Response, Minority Rights and the Truman Administration* (Lawrence, Kansas: The University Press of Kansas, 1973), p. 48.
12. William E. Juhnke, "President Truman's Committee on Civil Rights: The Interaction of Politics, Protest, and Presidential Advisory Commission." *Presidential Studies Quarterly*, Vol. XIX, No. 3 (Summer 1989), 593–610.

13. *Ibid.*, p. 597.
14. Quoted in *ibid.*, p. 602.
15. *Ibid.*, p. 604.

Chapter 9

1. FBI Files. No. HQ 100-51230. Letter, June 29, 1942, from J. Edgar Hoover to Special Agent in Charge, New York, New York.
2. FBI Memo. No. HQ 100-51230. July 10, 1942.
3. FBI Files. No. HQ 100-51230. June 29, 1942.
4. FBI Files. No. HQ 100-51230 7X2. October 5, 1942.
5. FBI Files. No. HQ 100-51230-15. Letter, October 14, 1942, from P. E. Foxworth, assistant director, to Director J. Edgar Hoover. The SAC noted: "A subscription has been entered under a fictitious name by this office."
6. Memo from J. Edgar Hoover to "SAC, New York." FBI Files. No. HQ100-51230. October 22, 1942.
7. Report FBI Files. No. HQ 100-51230-25. February 26, 1943.
8. FBI Files. No. HQ 100-51230. Vol 4. Letter in *The People's Voice*, May 29, 1943, from Cpl. John Marshall, 28th Quartermaster Regiment.
9. FBI Files. Memo for Assistant Attorney General from J. Edgar Hoover, July 1, 1943.
10. FBI Memo. *from E. E. Conroy to J. Edgar Hoover, June 19, 1943.*
11. *The People's Voice*, June 26, 1943.
12. *The People's Voice*, January 13, 1945, p. 5.
13. *The People's Voice*, January 27, 1945, p. 5.
14. *The People's Voice*, February 3, 1945, p. 5.
15. This was a measure that provided penalties or jail fines for those who engaged in strikes against war plants or other facilities involved in the war effort. It was strongly opposed by labor unions, and had been passed over President Roosevelt's veto.
16. *The People's Voice*, February 3, 1945, p. 5.
17. *The People's Voice*, February 17, 1945, p. 32.
18. *The People's Voice*, May 12, 1945, p. 4.
19. *Amsterdam News*, Earl Brown, "Timely Topics," June 22, 1946, p. 10.
20. *Ibid.*
21. Interview with Grant Reynolds, July 31, 1989, White Plains, New York.
22. *Ibid.*
23. *Amsterdam News*, August 24, 1946, p. 1.

24. Powell received a total of 32,573 votes (22,641 on the Democratic line, and 9,932 on the ALP line) to Reynolds's 19,514 on the Republican line.
25. *New York Times*, December 25, 1946. The FBI duly clipped the *Times* article and one in the *Daily Worker*, but made no comment on the resignation.
26. Letter from Leslie Perry to Roy Wilkins, January 21, 1944. NAACP Papers, Library of Congress, Group II, A-663.
27. Letter from Leslie Perry to Walter White, March 15, 1945. NAACP Papers, Library of Congress, Group II, A-663.
28. *The People's Voice*, March 1, 1947, p. 17. The "Soapbox" column of Powell's in which this appeared was clipped and put in his FBI files. FBI Files. No. HQ 100-51230-A, March 20, 1947.
29. Press release, NAACP, March 17, 1949. NAACP Washington Bureau Papers, Library of Congress, Box 103.
30. Memo. NAACP Washington Bureau Papers, Library of Congress, Box 103.
31. Letter from Roy Wilkins to Adam Powell, January 10, 1950. NAACP Papers, Library of Congress, Group II, A-193.
32. Letter from Roy Wilkins to Clark Clifford, December 20, 1949. NAACP Papers, Library of Congress, Group II, A-193.
33. Article (manuscript) by Roy Wilkins for publication in the *New Leader*, January 1950. NAACP Papers, Library of Congress, Group II, A-193.
34. Letter from Thurgood Marshall to Louis Lautier, January 25, 1950. NAACP Papers, Library of Congress, Group II, A-193.
35. Hessell Hartmen, "FEPC Crusaders in Washington," *Jewish Life*, Vol. IV, No. 5, March 1950, pp. 5–8.
36. *Ibid.*
37. Letter from Roy Wilkins to Walter White, February 3, 1950. NAACP Papers, Library of Congress, Group II, A-193.
38. *New York Times*, June 2, 1950.
39. *New York Times*, January 25, 1951. See Martin Duberman, *Paul Robeson* (New York: Alfred A. Knopf, 1988), p. 344, for reference to Powell's reaction to Robeson's speech.
40. Benjamin J. Davis, "Rep. Powell's New Line," *Daily Worker*, March 15, 1951.
41. *Ibid.*
42. FBI Files. No. HQ 100-51230-161. August 30, 1945.
43. FBI Files. No. HQ 100-51230-99. February 5, 1944.
44. *Testimony of Hazel Scott*. Hearing before the Committee for Un-American Activities. 81st Congress, 2nd Session. September 22, 1950.
45. *Ibid.*, p. 3613.

46. *Ibid.*
47. *New York Times*, May 2, 1952.
48. *New York Times*, August 4, 1952.
49. *Ibid.*
50. *Ibid.*

Chapter 10

1. Robert Frederick Burk, *The Eisenhower Administration and Black Civil Rights* (Knoxville: The University of Tennessee Press, 1984), p. 28.
2. *Ibid.*, p. 16.
3. Arthur Larson, *Eisenhower, The President Nobody Knew* (New York: Charles Scribner's Sons, 1968), p. 128.
4. *Ibid.*, p. 127.
5. Robert J. Donovan, *Confidential Secretary, Ann Whitman's 20 Years with Eisenhower and Rockefeller* (New York: E. P. Dutton, 1988), pp. 112–15.
6. *Congressional Record*, 1953. Appendix A3555.
7. *Ibid.*
8. Maxwell Rabb, Columbia University Oral History Archives (CUOHA).
9. *Ibid.*
10. *Congressional Record*, 1953. Appendix A3555.
11. *Ibid.*
12. Burk, p. 36.
13. *Ibid.*
14. Letter from Maxwell Rabb to Honorable Adam C. Powell, Jr., September 18, 1953. Dwight D. Eisenhower Library, Abilene, Kansas.
15. Memo dated September 9, 1953, from State Department to Maxwell Rabb. DDE Library.
16. Letter dated September 28, 1953, to Congressman Powell from Maxwell Rabb. DDE Library.
17. *New York Herald Tribune*, October 12, 1953.
18. Memo from Rabb to the Honorable Roderic O'Connor, Assistant to the Secretary of State.
19. Memo from Maxwell Rabb to Honorable Leonard Hall, November 2, 1953. DDE Library.
20. Letter dated April 2, 1954, from Powell to Rabb. DDE Library.
21. Memo from Rabb to Roderic O'Connor, Department of State, April 5, 1954. DDE Library.
22. *Congressional Record*, February 2, 1955. House of Representatives.
23. Draft of article in DDE Library.

24. Letter from Stanley High to Maxwell Rabb, July 16, 1954. DDE Library.
25. Letter from Albert Pratt, Assistant Secretary of the Navy, to Honorable A. C. Powell, Jr., July 20, 1955. NAACP Washington Bureau Papers, Box 157, Library of Congress.
26. Letter from Albert Pratt to Honorable Adam Clayton Powell, Jr., September 7, 1955. NAACP Washington Bureau Papers, Box 112, Library of Congress.
27. Clarence Mitchell, interview, Columbia University Oral History, pp. 1–68. Mitchell's recollection of their relationship is at variance somewhat with one account by Chuck Stone, *Black Political Power in America* (New York: Bobbs-Merrill Company, 1968). Stone recounts an incident in 1966 involving "Clarence Mitchell, Jr. (whom Powell despised and called 'Uncle Tom,' to his face)," p. 197. The nature of Powell's volatile relations with colleagues was such that both assessments of the Powell-Mitchell relationship might have credibility.
28. DDE Library.
29. *New York Times*, August 25, 1956. "Powell Sees Bias by the Army Abroad, Asks President and Brucker for Inquiry."
30. Letter from Adam Clayton Powell, Jr., to Colonel Dale E. Buchanan, Chief of Legislative Liaison, Department of the Army, June 12, 1956. DDE Library.
31. Letter from James P. Goode, Deputy for Manpower, Personnel and Organizations, Department of the Air Force, to Honorable Adam C. Powell, Jr., October 19, 1955. NAACP Washington Bureau Papers, Box 112, Library of Congress.
32. Letter from Brooksie L. Goins, 1st Lt., USAF, to The Honorable Adam Clayton Powell, 30 August 1956. NAACP Washington Bureau Papers, Box 112, Library of Congress. (Powell's secretary acknowledged the letter while Powell was traveling overseas.)
33. Letter from Adam Powell to Maxwell Rabb, December 10, 1954. DDE Library.
34. Letter from Powell to Rabb, February 15, 1955 (with attached article: "The Charge is . . . Jimcrow, the Official Government Policy in Federal Prisons," *Civil Rights Congress*, n.d.).
35. FBI Files. No. HQ 100-51230-197. November 8, 1955.
36. *Ibid.*
37. Letter from Rabb to Powell, June 22, 1955. DDE Library.
38. Draft of letter from Rabb to Powell, n.d. DDE Library.
39. Memo from Albert M. Cole, Administrator, Housing and Home Finance Agency, to Maxwell Rabb, March 16, 1955. DDE Library.
40. White House Memo to Bryce Harlow, October 5, 1955, 3:20 P.M. DDE Library.

41. Harold Cruse, *Plural But Equal, Blacks and Minorities in America's Plural Society* (New York: William Morrow and Company, Inc., 1987).
42. Quoted in *ibid.*, pp. 15–16.
43. *Ibid.*
44. W. E. B. Du Bois, *The Autobiography of W. E. B. Du Bois* (New York: International Publishers, 1968), p. 266.
45. Memo. "Negroes' Stake in Housing Legislation." National Council of Negro Women, April 12, 1949. NAACP Papers, Group II, A-114, Library of Congress.
46. Memorandum from Marian Wynn Perry (NAACP) to Roy Wilkins, April 19, 1949. NAACP Papers, Group II, A-114, Library of Congress.
47. Letter from Leslie S. Perry (NAACP) to Congressman Adam C. Powell, March 10, 1950. NAACP Papers, Group II, A-267, Library of Congress.
48. Letter from Adam Clayton Powell, Jr. to Roy Wilkins, March 15, 1950 (Special Delivery). NAACP Papers, Group II, A-267, Library of Congress.
49. Minutes. NAACP Board of Directors, April 10, 1950. NAACP Papers, Group II, A-112, Library of Congress.
50. Letter to Clarence Mitchell from Roy Wilkins, March 4, 1955. NAACP Washington Bureau Papers, Box 70, Library of Congress. Wilkins attached a memo he had sent to the NAACP branches in Illinois urging them to lobby Senator Paul Douglas. Apparently Douglas had received "less than five letters from Illinois on this matter," the memo said. In fact, Wilkins told Mitchell, "that *one* letter only had been received by Douglas, so I softened it by saying less than five."
51. Press conference. President Dwight D. Eisenhower, July 6, 1955.
52. Letter from Roy Wilkins to Adam Clayton Powell, Jr., July 7, 1955. NAACP Papers, Group II, A-481, Library of Congress. A few weeks later, Powell wrote to Wilkins: "My dear Roy: Just a brief note of thanks for the magnificent support of the NAACP given me, both in New York and Washington, with the hope that it will continue to preserve [*sic*]. With every good wish." NAACP Papers, Group II, A-481, Library of Congress (July 21, 1955).
53. *New York Times*, July 18, 1955.
54. Letter from A. H. Clay to Adam Powell, March 7, 1956. NAACP Washington Bureau Papers, Box 112, Library of Congress.
55. Speech by Congressman Powell before the House of Representatives, January 24, 1956. NAACP Washington Bureau Papers, Box 71, Library of Congress.
56. Speech by Congressman Powell before the House of Representa-

tives, June 29, 1956. NAACP Washington Bureau Papers, Box 71, Library of Congress.

57. Speech by Powell before House of Representatives, January 24, 1956.
58. Letter from Clarence Mitchell to Congressman Powell, April 18, 1956. NAACP Washington Bureau Papers, Box 71, Library of Congress.
59. Remarks of Honorable T. Millet Hand before the House of Representatives, July 5, 1956. *Congressional Record*, 84th Congress, Second Session.
60. Press release. UAW, Detroit and Washington, D.C., January 26, 1956.
61. Letter from Mrs. Franklin D. Roosevelt and Walter P. Reuther to Roy Wilkins, April 22, 1955. NAACP Papers, Group II, A-267, Library of Congress.
62. *Ibid.*
63. Interview with Joseph Rauh. Washington, D.C., November 8, 1989. In fact, Rauh revealed that Adam Powell wanted to be invited to be a member of the board of the ADA, but the board never acted on his request because of Powell's questionable Communist affiliations.
64. Letter from Roy Wilkins to Frederick F. Greenman, New York State Committee for the White House Conference on Education, November 15, 1955. NAACP Papers, Group II, A-267, Library of Congress.
65. Letter from Clarence Mitchell to Charles Abrams, July 29, 1955. NAACP Washington Bureau Papers, Box 91, Library of Congress. Also in this folder: correspondence from Abrams to Mitchell, July 21, 1955, and a copy of the Fisk University speech by Abrams, June 29, 1955.
66. Letter from Congressman Stewart L. Udall to Clarence Mitchell, July 1, 1955. NAACP Washington Bureau Papers, Box 71, Library of Congress.
67. Remarks by Representative Stewart L. Udall on introducing federal aid bill to implement the school integration decision of the United States Supreme Court, before the House of Representatives, June 14, 1955. NAACP Papers, Group II, A-267, Library of Congress.
68. Letter from Clarence Mitchell to Congressman Stewart L. Udall, July 7, 1955. NAACP Papers, Group II, A-267, Library of Congress.
69. Letter to the *Greenwich Time* from Alfred Baker Lewis, July 1955. NAACP Papers, Group II, A-267, Library of Congress.

70. Memorandum on the Powell Amendment, n.d. (ca. 1956), by Alfred Baker Lewis. NAACP Washington Bureau Papers, Box 71, Library of Congress.
71. Telegram to Congressman Adam Clayton Powell from J. H. White, President, Mississippi Vocational College, July 6, 1956. NAACP Washington Bureau Papers, Box 71, Library of Congress.
72. Letter from Clarence Mitchell to J. H. White, July 10, 1956. NAACP Washington Bureau Papers, Box 71, Library of Congress.
73. Quoted in James L. Sundquist, *Politics and Policy, The Eisenhower, Kennedy, and Johnson Years* (Washington, D.C.: The Brookings Institution, 1968), p. 166.
74. *New York Times*, July 21, 1955, p. 1.

Chapter 11

1. Stephen E. Ambrose, *Eisenhower, The President*, Vol. II (New York: Simon & Schuster, 1984), p. 241.
2. *Congressional Record*, House of Representatives, January 26, 1955.
3. Letter from Powell to Rabb, February 2, 1955. DDE Library.
4. Memo from W. K. Scott to Rabb, February 16, 1955. DDE Library.
5. Memo, February 23, 1955, from Rabb to Walter K. Scott, Department of State. DDE Library.
6. Unsigned memo. Tuesday, March 2, 1955. DDE Library.
7. Press Release No. 105. Statement on Asian-African Meeting, Issued by the Council of the Southeast Asia Collective Defense Treaty, Bangkok, Thailand, February 25, 1955. DDE Library.
8. Statement (Confidential) by Secretary of State John Foster Dulles, n.d. DDE Library.
9. Memorandum for Sherman Adams from John Foster Dulles. Subject: Proposed Presidential Speech Before the Bandung Conference. March 31, 1955. (Italics added.) DDE Library.
10. Telegram from Powell to Eisenhower. April 6, 1955. DDE Library.
11. Telegram from Powell to Thruston B. Morton. April 7, 1955. DDE Library.
12. Homer Bigart, "Powell Tells Asia About U.S. Negro; Red Newsmen Find Him Off the 'Line,'" *New York Herald Tribune*, April 18, 1955.
13. These quotes taken from "Interview with Adam Clayton Powell, Jr.—Red China Exposed—Not Dominant in Asia," *U.S. News & World Report*, April 29, 1955, pp. 42–44.
14. "Madden Praises Powell, Representative Says Colleague Upset Red's Bandung Plans," *New York Times*, April 27, 1955.

15. Telegram from Powell to President Eisenhower, May 1, 1955. DDE Library.
16. Series of memos: May 2, 4, 5, 9, 1955. DDE Library.
17. *New York Daily News*, May 9, 1955.
18. Notes by Maxwell Rabb of meeting between Powell and Eisenhower, May 11, 1955. Powell left with Rabb some comments on note cards for further consideration by the President, one item pertaining to an ambiguously worded White House letter to Congressman Zelenko on the school construction bill. Powell suggested, on his note card, that Eisenhower clear up the confusion (which was not stipulated) in another letter. And Powell urged more stringent enforcement of integration in the armed forces.
19. P. L. Prattis, "Horizon—Letter to Adam Powell," *Pittsburgh Courier*, n.d. DDE Library.
20. Abner W. Berry, "On the Way—Come Back Congressman, You're Over Your Head," *Daily Worker*, April 26, 1955, p. 10.
21. *Washington Afro-American*, May 14, 1955, p. 2.
22. J. A. Rogers, "Powell Off Pitch," n.d. DDE Library.
23. "Powell's Asia Reports are Criticized," *Amsterdam News*, May 21, 1955, p. 1.
24. "Adam Powell at Bandung," *New York Mirror*, April 20, 1955.
25. Editorial: "The New Cong. Powell," *Pittsburgh Courier*, June 4, 1955.
26. *New Republic*, May 2, 1955.
27. *Dayton Daily News*, April 22, 1955.

Chapter 12

1. Memo. FBI Files. No. HQ 100-51230-192X16. July 3, 1953.
2. *Ibid.*
3. Memo to Drew Pearson from Jack Anderson. Drew Pearson Papers, Box 18, G-260, LBJ Library. October 19, 1956.
4. Affidavit filed in United States District Court, Southern District of New York, re *United States of America* v. *Hattie Freeman Dodson and Howard T. Dodson.* Index No. C146-82. May 31, 1955. DDE Library.
5. *Ibid.*
6. *Ibid.*
7. *New York Herald Tribune*, May 9, 1956.
8. *New York Times*, May 18, 1956.
9. *Washington Star*, May 15, 1956.

10. *New York Times*, May 18, 1956.
11. *New York Post*, June 4, 1956.
12. *New York Times*, May 21, 1956.
13. *Washington Evening Star*, July 17, 1956.
14. Interview with Mrs. Hattie Freeman Dodson, 1989, New York City. Conducted by Richard Kilberg and Yvonne Smith, R.K.B. Productions.
15. *New York Post*, March 29, 1956.

Chapter 13

1. Minutes of Cabinet Meeting, March 9, 1956. Dwight D. Eisenhower Library, Abilene, Kansas.
2. Cabinet Paper. *The Civil Rights Program—Proposed Statement of the Attorney General.* Memorandum for the Attorney General. Subject: The President's Views on the Proposed Civil Rights Program. Maxwell Rabb. March 7, 1956. DDE Library.
3. *New York Times*, March 3, 1956.
4. *Greensboro Daily News*, March 16, 1956.
5. "Powell Weighing Bigger Bias Fight. Considers Resigning Pulpit and Possibly Congress to Spur Integration Drive," *New York Times*, March 4, 1956.
6. White House Memorandum to Governor Adams from E. Frederick Morrow. OF 102-B-3. December 16, 1955. DDE Library.
7. E. Frederick Morrow, *Black Man in the White House* (New York: Coward-McCann, Inc., 1963), p. 46.
8. *Ibid.*, pp. 47–48.
9. Memorandum to Gov. Sherman Adams from Val J. Washington, Republican National Committee. OF 142-A. Subject: The Gallup Poll Among Negroes. January 4, 1956. DDE Library.
10. *Ibid.*
11. Memorandum to Governor Adams from E. Frederick Morrow. OF 72-A2. February 27, 1956.
12. *Ibid.*
13. *Ibid.*
14. Morrow, *Black Man . . .*, pp. 51–52.
15. *Ibid*, p. 52.
16. "Adam Clayton Powell, Jr.: A Post Portrait," *New York Post*, March 30, 1956 (last in a series of five articles beginning March 26, 1956).
17. *The Afro-American*, June 30, 1956. The two Negro delegates were

Hulan E. Jack, president of the Borough of Manhattan, and Mrs. Thurgood Marshall. The two alternate Negro delegates were councilman Earl Brown and Mrs. Bessie A. Buchanan, wife of Powell's former business partner at *The People's Voice*. Jack and Brown would figure prominently in an election fight against Powell two years hence.

18. Notes by Ann Whitman: Telephone Calls, August 19, 1956. DDE Library.
19. *Newsweek*, October 1, 1956.
20. Unpublished memo-notes from Frederick S. Weaver to Drew Pearson, April 11, 1959. Drew Pearson Papers, Box 18, G-260, LBJ Library.
21. Memo to DP from JA. October 19, 1956. Drew Pearson Papers, Box 18, G-260, LBJ Library.
22. Drew Pearson, "Merry-Go-Round" (written by Jack Anderson in Pearson's overseas absence), *Greensboro Daily News*, September 5, 1956.
23. Letter from Powell to Drew Pearson, September 19, 1956. Drew Pearson Papers, Box 18, G-260, LBJ Library.
24. Such a Powell letter may have been written and turned over to Willis, but it was not, as of December 1989, among the papers in the Charles Willis File at the DDE Library.
25. In his 1959 memo to Pearson, Weaver wrote: "I asked only that I be placed on a salary for the duration of the campaign and continue thereon thereafter until a suitable job, better than the one I vacated, was made available to me, together with all expenses incurred in the campaign."
26. Oral History Interview with James C. Hagerty. Columbia University Oral History Project. Conducted by Herbert Parmet, April 9 & 11, 1969. Columbia University Library, New York City.
27. Diary, Ann Whitman, October 11, 1956. DDE Library.
28. Memorandum Covering Appointment of Congressman Adam Clayton Powell with the President on October 11, 1956. 3:02–3:27 P.M. Bernard M. Shanley. DDE Library.
29. *New York Mirror*. October 16, 1956. Fifteen years later in his autobiography, Powell gave a different version of the meeting. He indicated that he clearly noted the differences between himself and the President on civil rights, but put specific proposals before Eisenhower. These included a major civil rights bill that would be drawn up by his administration, and a promise that he would get his "lieutenants" in Congress to push it. Eisenhower, according to Powell, agreed to do so, and Powell then agreed to endorse him for reelection. Powell, *Adam by Adam*, p. 130.

30. President's Press Conference, September 11, 1956. Transcript in Presidential Files. OF 142-A-5. DDE Library.
31. Statement of Congressman Adam Clayton Powell, Jr., released by James C. Hagerty, Press Secretary to the President. October 23, 1956. OF 142-A-5. DDE Library.
32. *New York Herald Tribune,* October 24, 1956, p. 1.
33. *New York Times,* October 25, 1956.
34. *New York Daily News,* October 13, 1956.
35. *New York Post,* October 14, 1956.
36. *New York Times,* October 29, 1956.
37. Newsletter. Notes from COPE, AFL-CIO Committee on Political Education, Washington, D.C., October 26, 1956. NAACP Papers, Group III, B-309, Library of Congress.
38. Letter from Leo Fox to Marty Snyder, November 2, 1956. GF 109-A-2. DDE Library.
39. Letter from Samuel W. Witwer to Hon. Adam Clayton Powell, October 31, 1956. GF 109-A-2. DDE Library.
40. Letter from Rabb to Senator Everett M. Dirksen, October 26, 1956. OF 138-A-6. DDE Library. In this letter, Rabb also noted: "Such figures as Branch Rickey, so highly regarded by negroes [as the owner of the Brooklyn Dodgers who hired Jackie Robinson], will be sent out to do their part. We are also giving attention to those of the Jewish faith on the South side."
41. *New York Times,* October 26, 1956.
42. Max Lerner, "The Negroes and the Election," *New York Post,* October 17, 1956, p. 48.
43. Letter from Marty Snyder to Governor Sherman Adams, November 20, 1956. GF 109-A-2. DDE Library.
44. Jacob K. Javits, *Javits, The Autobiography of a Public Man* (Boston: Houghton Mifflin Company, 1981), p. 251.
45. Murray Kempton, "Runaway Slave," *New York Post,* November 9, 1956.
46. *New York Times,* November 17, 1956.
47. Letter from Roy Wilkins to Hon. Sam Rayburn, November 15, 1956. NAACP Papers, Group III, B-309, Library of Congress.
48. Letter from Sam Rayburn to Roy Wilkins, December 3, 1956. NAACP Papers, Group III, B-309, Library of Congress.
49. Press Release. Americans for Democratic Action, November 18, 1956. Washington, D.C. NAACP Papers, Group III, B-309, Library of Congress.
50. *Amsterdam News,* November 17, 1956.
51. *Daily Worker,* December 5, 1956.
52. Letter from Congressman Emanuel Celler to Roy Wilkins, Decem-

ber 26, 1956. NAACP Papers, Group III, B-309, Library of Congress.

53. *Ibid.*
54. Memo from Max Rabb to Sherman Adams, January 24, 1957. GF 3-A. DDE Library.
55. Letter from Clarence Mitchell to Roy Wilkins, January 23, 1957. NAACP Papers, Group III, B-309, Library of Congress.
56. Press Release, Washington Bureau NAACP, February 4, 1957. NAACP Papers, Group III, B-309, Library of Congress.
57. "Death of an Investigation: The Wheels of Justice Stop for Adam Clayton Powell, Jr.," *National Review*, December 14, 1957, pp. 537–41.
58. Irwin Ross, "Powell and the Polls," *New York Post*, October 25, 1956, p. 41.
59. Memo from Rabb to Sherman Adams, February 4, 1957. GF 122. DDE Library.
60. Memo from Rabb to Adams, February 8, 1957. GF 122. DDE Library.
61. David Garrow, *Bearing the Cross* (New York: William Morrow and Company, Inc., 1986), p. 90.
62. *Adam by Adam*, p. 136.
63. Memo from Janey to Adams, April 2, 1957. OF 142-A. Box 731. DDE Library.
64. Memo from Rabb to Adams, April 3, 1957. OF 142-A. Box 731. DDE Library.
65. *Ibid.*
66. Memo from Rabb to Adams, April 17, 1957. OF 142-A. Box 731. DDE Library.
67. Garrow, *Bearing the Cross*, p. 92.
68. Letter from Powell to Adams, March 28, 1957. OF 142-A. Box 731. DDE Library.
69. Memo from E. Frederick Morrow to Sherman Adams, June 4, 1957. OF 142-A. DDE Library.
70. Memo from Rabb to Adams, June 5, 1957. OF 142-A. DDE Library.
71. Memo from Rabb to Adams, June 24, 1957. OF 142-A. DDE Library.
72. Telegram to James Hagerty from Powell, September 19, 1957. DDE Library.
73. Letter from Louis Lautier to Rabb, September 20, 1957. DDE Library.
74. Letter from Robert C. Durham to Rabb, September 24, 1957. DDE Library.
75. Memo from Rabb to Adams, September 27, 1957. DDE Library.

76. Letter from Powell to Sherman Adams, September 27, 1957. DDE Library.
77. *Adam by Adam*, pp. 131–32.
78. Memo to the President from Arthur Larson, November 14, 1957. DDE Library. The quotes are Larson's words.
79. Memo note: Bryce to Rabb to Harlow, November 16, 1957. OF 151-A. DDE Library.
80. Memo from Morrow to Harlow, November 19, 1957. OF 151-A. DDE Library.
81. Memo to Adams from Harlow, November 25, 1957. OF 151-A. DDE Library.
82. Memorandum from Harry Tyson Carter, Deputy General Counsel, USIA, to Maxwell Rabb, January 6, 1958. OF 151-A. DDE Library.
83. Telegram from Powell to Eisenhower, January 28, 1958. DDE Library.
84. Letter from Rabb to Powell, February 3, 1958. DDE Library.
85. Letter from Powell to Rabb, February 7, 1958. DDE Library.
86. Memo from Rabb "To File," February 12, 1958. DDE Library.
87. Memo from Rocco C. Siciliano to Sherman Adams, June 10, 1958. DDE Library.
88. *Ibid.*
89. *Adam by Adam*, p. 138.
90. See Charles V. Hamilton, *Minority Politics in Black Belt Alabama* (Eagleton Institute Case Studies No. 19, McGraw-Hill Book Company, 1960).
91. This conversation was between Powell and Charles V. Hamilton, then an instructor at Tuskegee Institute, and chairman of the Political Education Committee of TCA.
92. Telegrams to Eisenhower from Powell: February 17, 1959; March 1, 1959. OF 171. DDE Library.
93. Telegram to Eisenhower from Powell, March 4, 1959. OF 171. DDE Library.
94. Letter from Jack Z. Anderson to Powell, March 9, 1959. OF 171. DDE Library.
95. Letter from William P. Rogers to Paul W. Williams, May 23, 1957. DDE Library.
96. Interview with Edward Dudley, November 18, 1989.

Chapter 14

1. "Powell Dares Democrats to Drop Him," *New York Post*, February 10, 1958, p. 18.

2. "Powell Demands Aid of Democrats," *New York Times*, February 25, 1958.
3. "Harlem Leaders May Drop Powell," *New York Times*, May 8, 1958.
4. Arthur Massolo and Oliver Pilat, "In the Backrooms," *New York Post*, March 2, 1958.
5. Quoted in David Hapgood, *The Purge That Failed: Tammany v. Powell* (Eagleton Institute Case Studies, McGraw-Hill Book Company, 1960), p. 12.
6. *Ibid.*, p. 13.
7. *New York Times*, May 18, 1958, p. 27.
8. Letter from John C. Williams, Pres., to Mr. Roy Wilkins, June 4, 1958. NAACP Papers, Group III, B-309, Library of Congress. Wilkins's reply iterated his earlier statement.
9. *New York Times*, June 18, 1958.
10. *Ibid.*
11. *New York Post*, June 18, 1958.
12. John C. Walter, *The Harlem Fox: J. Raymond Jones and Tammany, 1920–1970* (Albany: State University of New York Press, 1989), p. 129.
13. Interview with J. Raymond Jones, St. Thomas, Virgin Islands, December 2, 1972.
14. Interview with Ed Dudley, New York City, November 18, 1989.
15. Hapgood, *The Purge* . . ., p. 15.
16. Letter from Stewart L. Udall to Earl Brown, July 16, 1958. Drew Pearson Papers, Box 18, G-260, LBJ Library.
17. Alfred T. Hendricks and Ted Poston, "Post Survey in Harlem: Heavy Support for Powell in Tammany Row," *New York Post*, May 23, 1958.
18. *New York Times*, July 29, 1958.
19. *New York Times*, August 13, 1958.
20. *New York Post*, August 14, 1958.
21. Notes to Drew Pearson from Fred Weaver, n.d. Drew Pearson Papers, LBJ Library.
22. *New York Post*, November 3, 1958; *New York Times*, October 21, 1958.
23. *New York Times*, November 3, 1958.
24. *New York Times*, October 8, 1958.
25. *New York Times*, October 29, 1958.

Chapter 15

1. "Death of an Investigation: The Wheels of Justice Stop for Adam Clayton Powell, Jr.," *National Review*, December 14, 1957, pp. 537–41.

2. Oliver Pilat, "Powell's Political Aide Sees Tammany Hand in New Tax Inquiry," *New York Post*, April 24, 1958.
3. Don Hogan, "Powell Tells Flock He Is Persecuted," *New York Herald Tribune*, April 28, 1958.
4. *New York Times*, May 12, 1958.
5. *New York Herald Tribune*, May 14, 1958.
6. Letter from the Rev. Ernest Hutcheson, Jr., to Powell, May 12, 1958. NAACP Papers, Group III, B-309, Library of Congress.
7. Letter from the Rev. Hutcheson to Wilkins, May 12, 1958. NAACP Papers, Group III, B-309, Library of Congress.
8. Letter from Wilkins to Hutcheson, May 23, 1958. NAACP Papers, Group III, B-309, Library of Congress.
9. Layhmond Robinson, "Powell's Career—Tied to Race Issue," *New York Times*, May 16, 1958.
10. *New York Post*, March 9, 1960.
11. *New York Times*, April 20, 1960.
12. *New York Times*, April 21, 1960.
13. *New York Post*, April 21, 1960.
14. *New York Post*, April 24, 1960.
15. *Ibid.*
16. *New York Post*, May 23, 1960.

Chapter 16

1. *New York Times*, January 23, 1960.
2. *New York Times*, January 26, 1960.
3. *New York Times*, January 29, 1960.
4. Letter to the editor from John Young III, *New York Times*, January 29, 1960. In 1966 this same supporter would unsuccessfully challenge Powell in a primary election.
5. *U.S. News & World Report*, February 19, 1960.
6. *New York Times*, February 19, 1960.
7. *New York Post*, February 3, 1960.
8. "The Presidential Elections of 1960." Press release from the office of Congressman Adam Clayton Powell, June 25, 1960.
9. Walter, *The Harlem Fox*, pp. 139–44.
10. Interview with J. Raymond Jones, December 2, 1972, St. Thomas, Virgin Islands. Jones humorously summed up his difficulties with Robert Kennedy by saying: "We had the misfortune of being born on the same day, November 19th. Plus, we were two arrogant people. He because of his wealth and family. I because I'm West Indian."

11. Adam Clayton Powell, Jr., *Keep The Faith, Baby!* (New York: Trident Press, 1967), pp. 78–79.
12. *Ibid.*, p. 85.
13. *New York Times*, November 2, 1960.
14. Memorandum to Roy Wilkins from Clarence Mitchell re conversation with Adam Clayton Powell, December 7, 1960. NAACP Papers, Group III, B-435, Library of Congress.
15. Mitchell sent a detailed memo to Powell describing the segregated and discriminatory use of the barber shop and cafeteria in Capitol Hill buildings. NAACP Papers, Group III, B-309, Library of Congress. These were the same conditions that prevailed fifteen years earlier when Powell first got to Congress and personally challenged the traditional practices of segregation. Apparently, he was able to gain access for himself and his staff, but little else had changed.
16. Frederick W. Roevekamp, "Storms Weathered, Harlem's Powell Garners Tributes," *Christian Science Monitor*, January 31, 1960.
17. *New York Times*, April 14, 1961.
18. Theodore C. Sorensen, *Kennedy* (New York: Harper & Row, Publishers, 1965), p. 475.
19. *Ibid.*
20. Roy Wilkins with Tom Mathews, *Standing Fast: The Autobiography of Roy Wilkins* (New York: The Viking Press, 1982), p. 282.
21. *Ibid.*, p. 279.
22. *Ibid.*, p. 285.
23. Murray Kempton, "The Payoff," *New York Post*, June 20, 1960.
24. Interview with Dr. Deborah Partridge Wolfe, January 23, 1990, Princeton, New Jersey.
25. Interview with John Brademas. Conducted by R.K.B. Productions, 1989, New York City.
26. Ludwig Teller. Columbia University Oral History Interview, p. 516.
27. Memorandum from Claude Desautels to Larry O'Brien, March 8, 1961. John F. Kennedy Library, Boston, Massachusetts.
28. Letter from John A. Davis, Commissioner, New York State Commission Against Discrimination, to Clarence Mitchell, May 4, 1961. NAACP Washington Bureau Papers, Box 115, Library of Congress.
29. Sorensen, *Kennedy*, p. 352.
30. Letter from Adam C. Powell to President Kennedy, April 27, 1961. JFKL, Box 2227.
31. Letter from Powell to President Kennedy, July 21, 1961. JFKL, Box 2227.
32. Letter from Powell to President Kennedy, January 17, 1962. JFKL, Box 2227.

33. *New York Times*, January 30, 1962.
34. Letter from Powell to Congressman Carroll D. Kearns, September 14, 1961. JFKL, Box 2227. He sent a copy of the letter to the Secretary of Defense and to Larry O'Brien at the White House.
35. Letter from Alfred B. Fitt, Deputy Under Secretary, Department of Defense, to Honorable Adam C. Powell, Jr., December 13, 1961. JFKL, Box 2227.
36. Letter from Adam Yarmolinsky to Adam Powell, September 27, 1961. JFKL, Box 2227.
37. Press release, July 12, 1961, Committee on Education and Labor. Speech delivered by Chairman Adam C. Powell at Labor Banquet of National Convention of the National Association for the Advancement of Colored People, on Friday, July 14, 1961, at the Sheraton Hotel, Philadelphia, Pennsylvania. NAACP Papers, Group III, B-309, Library of Congress.
38. Memo for "Mr. Donahue," March 16, 1961. JFKL, Box 2227.
39. Interview with Justin Feldman, November 14, 1989, New York City.
40. These data are from the *Congressional Quarterly*, October 6, 1961, pp. 1690–1701.
41. *Congressional Quarterly*, June 23, 1961, p. 1032.
42. There were times, of course, when Powell would be "paired" with another absent member who planned to vote the opposite way. Thus their votes would, if they were present, cancel each other out.
43. Press release from the Office of Congressman Adam C. Powell, February 14, 1962. NAACP Washington Bureau Papers, Box 115, Library of Congress.
44. Letter from Lee C. White, Assistant Special Counsel to the President, to Honorable Adam C. Powell, May 27, 1963. JFKL, Box 2227.
45. *Newsweek*, April 1, 1963, p. 21.
46. Handwritten four-page memorandum (Powell). NAACP Papers, Group III, B-309, Library of Congress.
47. Press release. "Wilkins Denounces Powell's Call for Boycott of NAACP," March 30, 1963. NAACP Papers, Group III, B-309, Library of Congress.
48. *. . . Adam . . . Where Art Thou?: The NAACP and Adam Clayton Powell.* National Association for the Advancement of Colored People, New York, April 1963.
49. Letter from Donald P. McCullum to Roy Wilkins, April 29, 1963. Telegram from Wilkins to McCullum, President, Oakland Branch NAACP, May 3, 1963. NAACP Papers, Group III, B-309, Library of Congress.

50. Transcript of WNEW news interview with Representative Adam Clayton Powell, broadcast on April 3, 1963, 6:00 P.M. NAACP Papers, Group III, B-309, Library of Congress.
51. Adam Clayton Powell, Jr., *Marching Blacks* (New York: The Dial Press, 1945). He kept this passage in the revised edition published shortly before his death in 1972.
52. Letter from Buell G. Gallagher to Powell, April 9, 1963. NAACP Papers, Group III, B-309, Library of Congress.
53. Letter from Mike Masaoka to Roy Wilkins, April 19, 1963. He attached an editorial from the weekly *Pacific Citizen*, April 5, 1963. NAACP Papers, Group III, B-309, Library of Congress.
54. "The United Nations in 1963," speech by Ralph Bunche, Tougaloo Southern Christian College, Tougaloo, Mississippi, October 23, 1963. Ralph Bunche Papers, UCLA Archives, Los Angeles, California.
55. "Adam Powell and Roy Wilkins." Editorial, *Washington Afro-American*, March 30, 1963. NAACP Papers, Group III, B-309, Library of Congress.
56. Clarence Mitchell. Columbia University Oral History Interview.
57. Reported in Neil Hickey and Ed Edwin, *Adam Clayton Powell and the Politics of Race* (New York: Fleet Publishing Company, 1965), p. 248.
58. Letter from Lawrence O'Brien to Senator Strom Thurmond, July 9, 1963. JFKL, Box 2227.

Chapter 17

1. *New York Times*, December 11, 1963, pp. 1, 33.
2. Telegram from Adam Clayton Powell, Jr., Chairman, House Education and Labor Committee, to President Lyndon B. Johnson, December 11, 1963. Box 280, LBJL, Austin, Texas.
3. Memorandum from Lawrence F. O'Brien to the President, the White House, January 31, 1964. Adam Clayton Powell Name File, LBJL.
4. *Ibid.*
5. Letter from Speaker John W. McCormack to Adam Powell, January 30, 1964. *Congressional Record*. Appendix, A5212, October 10, 1966.
6. See James L. Sundquist, *Politics and Policy, The Eisenhower, Kennedy, and Johnson Years* (Washington, D.C.: The Brookings Institution, 1968); John C. Donovan, *The Politics of Poverty* (New York: Pegasus, 1967).

7. Memo from Charles L. Schultze to Henry Wilson, the White House, January 31, 1964. Adam Clayton Powell Name File, LBJL.
8. Memo from Henry H. Wilson, Jr., to Lawrence F. O'Brien, February 4, 1964. Adam Clayton Powell Name File, LBJL.
9. Transcript of WMAC interview with Congressman Adam Clayton Powell, March 19, 1964. PR 18-1, LBJL.
10. Memo from JV to Mr. President, April 24, 1964. PR 18-1, LBJL.
11. Letter from Adam C. Powell to the Honorable Anthony J. Celebrezze, Secretary of Health, Education and Welfare, December 2, 1963. Adam Clayton Powell Name File, LBJL.
12. Letter from Powell to Ralph Dungan, the White House, regarding promotion of Negroes and Puerto Ricans in the New York Post Office, April 17, 1964. HU Z-1/st 31, LBJL.
13. Letter from Powell to President Johnson, with attached four-page memorandum, December 18, 1964. Office Files of John Macy, LBJL.
14. Memo from Larry O'Brien to John Macy (with attached correspondence from Powell to the President), March 4, 1965. Office Files of John Macy, LBJL.
15. Letter from John W. Macy, Jr., to Congressman Powell, March 15, 1965. Office File of Lawrence F. O'Brien, Box 19, LBJL.
16. Letter from C. Sumner Stone to John W. Macy, Jr., March 29, 1965. Office Files of John Macy, Box 870, LBJL.
17. Letter from Adam C. Powell to President Johnson, March 11, 1964. FG 999, Box 430, LBJL.
18. Memorandum from Burke Marshall to Lee C. White, Assistant Special Counsel to the President re Congressman A. C. Powell's Proposed Fact Finding Commission to Investigate Possible Civil Rights Trouble Areas, April 2, 1964. FG 999, Box 430, LBJL.
19. Interview with Roger Wilkins by R.K.B. Productions, 1989.
20. Every definitive account highlights the role of that group. See Charles and Barbara Whalen, *The Longest Debate, A Legislative History of the 1964 Civil Rights Act* (New York: New American Library, 1985); Robert D. Loevy, "Lobbyists for Civil Rights: Clarence Mitchell, Joseph Rauh, and the Civil Rights Act of 1964" (unpublished paper presented at the annual convention of the American Political Science Association, Atlanta, Georgia, September 1989).
21. Interview with Joseph Rauh, Washington, D.C., November 8, 1989.
22. Memo, "Battle to Renew NDEA," Maurice Rosenblatt to Drew Pearson, October 23, 1964. Drew Pearson Papers, LBJL.
23. *Ibid.*
24. Letter to Adam Powell from Wayne Morse, October 5, 1964. *Congressional Record*, Appendix 5212, October 10, 1966.

25. *Congressional Quarterly*, week ending October 30, 1964, p. 2597.
26. Goldwater won Arizona, Louisiana, Alabama, Georgia, South Carolina and Mississippi.
27. Memorandum from Hobart Taylor, Jr. for the President, November 27, 1964. PL HU2 MC, LBJL.
28. Memo from Chuck Daly to Larry O'Brien, April 13, 1964. Office Files of Lawrence F. O'Brien, Box 19, LBJL.
29. *1965 Congressional Quarterly Almanac*, p. 65.
30. *Ibid.*
31. Lyndon B. Johnson, *The Vantage Point, Perspectives of the Presidency, 1963–1969* (New York: Holt, Rinehart, 1971), pp. 210–11. This is the only mention of Powell in the President's memoirs.
32. Memo from Jack Valenti to the President, February 24, 1965. Executive FG 411 F, Box 334, LBJL.
33. Memo from Larry O'Brien to President Johnson, March 8, 1965. Executive LE/FAZ, LBJL.
34. Memo from Douglass Cater to President Johnson, March 30, 1965. Box 280, Adam Clayton Powell Name File, LBJL.
35. Memo from Lawrence O'Brien to President Johnson, April 13, 1965. Executive LE/FA2, LBJL.
36. Memorandum from Ralph K. Huitt, Assistant Secretary for Legislation, to Douglass Cater and Henry Wilson, February 24, 1966. Executive FA2, LBJL.
37. The proposed legislation—and the general, popular language—had not yet adopted the term "black" or "African-American." This would begin the following year, late 1966, with the development of the Black Power movement.
38. Press release: "Powell Convenes Ad Hoc Sub-Committee on De Facto School Segregation; Announces Investigation," March 7, 1966. Executive HU 2, LBJL.
39. *Ibid.*
40. Memorandum from Douglass Cater to the President, May 13, 1966. Executive FG 165-4-A-2, LBJL.
41. Memorandum from Ervin Duggan to Douglass Cater, July 7, 1966. WHCF (Sam Gibbons), LBJL.
42. Memo for the President from Henry H. Wilson, Jr., July 13, 1966. Executive LE/FA2, LBJL.
43. *Daily Worker*, April 18, 1965, p. 2.
44. Memo to Lawrence O'Brien from Gillis Long, Congressional Affairs, OEO, April 26, 1965. Henry Wilson Files, Box 9, LBJL.
45. Memo to Larry O'Brien from Claude Desautels, June 8, 1965. O'Brien Office Files, LBJL.
46. Memo from Claude Desautels to Larry O'Brien, July 22, 1965. O'Brien Office Files, LBJL.

47. *New York Times*, December 10, 1965, p. 32.
48. *Ibid.*
49. Memo to President Johnson from Marvin Watson, December 21, 1965. President's Appointment File, Box 27, LBJL.
50. *Muhammad Speaks*, April 8, 1966, p. 12.
51. *New York Times*, March 23, 1966, p. 29.
52. *1966 Congressional Quarterly Almanac*, p. 237.
53. *Ibid.*
54. *Ibid.*
55. James Farmer, *Lay Bare the Heart* (New York: Arbor House, 1985), pp. 294–305.
56. *Ibid.*, p. 304.
57. *New York Times*, July 6, 1966, p. 11.
58. Memo for Bill Moyers from Henry H. Wilson, Jr., February 21, 1966. Office Files of Charles Roche, Box 8, LBJL.
59. Interview with James Farmer, 1989. Conducted by R.K.B. Productions.
60. Letter to Sargent Shriver from Adam Clayton Powell, August 24, 1966. *Administrative History of the OEO*. OEO, Vol. II, Documentary Supplement, LBJL.
61. Memo from Douglass Cater to the President, January 12, 1966. President's Appointment File (Diary Backup) 1/1/66–1/24/66, Box 27, LBJL.
62. Letter from Adam C. Powell to John Macy, Jr., Chairman, U.S. Civil Service Commission, August 5, 1965. General HU 2-1, LBJL.
63. Memo from Henry H. Wilson, Jr. to John Macy, September 8, 1966. Office Files of Henry H. Wilson, Jr., Box 28, LBJL.
64. "Johnson—A Friend," *The Voice* (San Diego), March 24, 1966, p. A-9.
65. Memo for the President from John W. Macy, Jr., April 12, 1966. Executive PE 2, LBJL.
66. Memo, July 29, 1965. Box 280, LBJL.
67. Memo from Marvin Watson to the President, July 20, 1965. Box 280, LBJL. In this same memo, Watson said that Powell "stated that the Jewish community was concerned about Justice Goldberg's going off the Supreme Court."
68. Memo for John Macy from Joe Califano, May 11, 1966. Box 280, LBJL.
69. Memo for the President from Jack Valenti, March 29, 1965. Box 280, LBJL.
70. Memo from Henry H. Wilson, Jr., to the President, February 17, 1966. Executive LE/LA, LBJL.

71. Memo from Henry H. Wilson, Jr., to the President, July 18, 1966. Executive FI 4/FG 11-15, LBJL.
72. Memo from Henry H. Wilson, Jr., to the President, May 13, 1966. Executive FI 4/FG 11-15, LBJL.

Chapter 18

1. *Congressional Quarterly*, week ending March 1, 1963, p. 241.
2. *Congressional Record* (House), February 26, 1963, p. 2857.
3. *Ibid.*
4. Copy of cable in Drew Pearson Papers, Box 18, G260, LBJL.
5. *Ibid.*
6. Mrs. Adam Clayton Powell, "My Life with Adam Clayton Powell," *Ladies' Home Journal*, May 1967.
7. *Ibid.*
8. *Adam By Adam*, p. 234.
9. James L. Hicks, "I Traveled in Europe with Congressman Powell," *Amsterdam News*, September 22, 1962.
10. "The Washington Merry-Go-Round: Negroes Found Ashamed of Powell," *Washington Post*, September 22, 1966, p. F-17.
11. Letter from Ralph Winkler to Drew Pearson, September 22, 1966. Drew Pearson Papers, LBJL. Pearson responded: "I appreciate your letter. I confess that I was very thoughtless and I am sorry. I'll bear in mind your kind advice the next time."
12. Letter from Tamara J. Wall to Drew Pearson, September 23, 1966. Drew Pearson Papers, LBJL.
13. Letter from Drew Pearson to Mrs. Tamara J. Wall, October 3, 1966. Drew Pearson Papers, LBJL.
14. "The Absentee Secretary," *New York Times*, April 5, 1962.
15. Cecil Holland, "Peace Corps in Harlem Toils to Get Off Ground," *Washington Star*, February 17, 1963.
16. FBI Files. March 28, 1963, No. HG 139-17-1-A.
17. "Clip His Money Wings," *Tampa* (Florida) *Tribune*, February 19, 1963.
18. *New York World-Telegram*, April 2, 1963.
19. *New York Herald Tribune*, May 20, 1963.
20. "Adam Powell in Congress," *Amsterdam News*, September 22, 1962, p. 1.
21. *Congressional Record* (House), February 26, 1963, p. 2856.
22. *Congressional Record*, week ending March 8, 1963, p. 291.
23. FBI Files. April 28, 1963, No. HG 100-51230-A.
24. *New York Herald Tribune*, March 1, 1963.

25. Letter from John A. Morsell, Assistant to the Executive Secretary, NAACP, to Mr. J. Blecheisen, March 15, 1963. NAACP Papers, Group III, B-309, Library of Congress.
26. FBI Files. No. HG 58-4552, July 14, 1959; July 15, 1959.
27. This story told by Justin Feldman in an interview, November 14, 1989, New York City.
28. Walter, *The Harlem Fox,* p. 170.
29. *New York Times*, March 17, 1964, p. 1.
30. Memo from Chuck Daly to Larry O'Brien, April 13, 1964. Office Files of Lawrence F. O'Brien, Box 19, LBJL.
31. Walter, *The Harlem Fox,* p. 176.
32. *Narrative History of the OEO*, Vol. I, Part I: "HARYOU-ACT," pp. 103–15, LBJL.
33. Interview with Dr. Kenneth Clark. Conducted by RKB Productions, 1989, New York City.
34. *Narrative History of the OEO*, p. 104.
35. Memo from Lee C. White to Jack Valenti, May 12, 1964. Box 280, LBJL.

Chapter 19

1. *New York Times*, January 4, 1960.
2. *Congressional Record*, January 27, 1960.
3. Letter from Shirley Washington to Roy Wilkins, January 14, 1960. NAACP Papers, Group III, B-309, Library of Congress.
4. Letter from Roy Wilkins to Shirley Washington, February 1, 1960. NAACP Papers, Group III, B-309, Library of Congress.
5. *New York Post*, January 18, 1960, p. 20; *New York Times*, January 18, 1960.
6. Speech by Congressman Adam Clayton Powell, Jr., on the floor of the House of Representatives. *Congressional Record*, February 25, 1960.
7. *Ibid.*
8. The letter (from Harleston Patterson to Mr. John Walsh, Supervising Assistant Chief Inspector) of September 9, 1959, read in part: ". . . The people who have complained against this woman, and many others who would like to complain against her, do not profess to be angels. They are gamblers and they admit it. All of them, at one time or another, have been arrested, arraigned, and convicted for the crime of policy. This, however, does not give anyone the right to extort money from them. Esther James found that gamblers were easy prey, because of their willingness to pay

to avoid being exposed. Their crime, under the law, is a misdemeanor, but extorting money under threat of exposure is a felony."

9. *Adam by Adam*, p. 157.
10. Interview with Charles McKinney, January 8, 1990, New York City.
11. *New York World-Telegram*, April 5, 1963, p. 3.
12. *San Juan Star*, December 29, 1963.
13. Memorandum for Mike Feldman, May 11, 1964. Adam Clayton Powell File, FG 170-5, LBJL.
14. Memorandum. Office Files of Lawrence O'Brien, Box 19, LBJL.
15. Letter from Nicholas Katzenbach to Honorable Adam C. Powell, October 23, 1964. Office Files of Lawrence O'Brien, Box 19, LBJL.
16. Letter from Powell to Katzenbach, October 26, 1964. Office Files of Lawrence O'Brien, Box 19, LBJL.
17. *New York Times*, May 11, 1965, p. C-27. The group's account was in the Freedom National Bank in Harlem, and Mrs. James's attorney sought to have this account frozen.
18. Memo in FBI Files, January 26, 1965. Subject: Allegation re Attempted Bribery—Congressman Adam C. Powell (D.-N.Y.)—Complainant. 58-5832.
19. Memorandum, FBI Files, May 4, 1964: Congressman Adam C. Powell Inquiry re Flickering Lights, No. HG 100-51230-264; May 11, 1964: Congressman Adam Clayton Powell Report of Suspicious Person, No. HG 100-51230-265.
20. *Congressional Record*, February 18, 1965, p. 3006.
21. Drew Pearson, "Who Is Mrs. James?," *New York Post*, February 14, 1967, p. 34.
22. *Congressional Record*, February 18, 1965, p. 3038.
23. *New York Times*, November 29, 1966, p. 46.
24. *New York Times*, December 3, 1966, p. 28.
25. "Mr. Powell Defaults,"*New York Times*, December 10, 1966, p. 36.

Chapter 20

1. Letter from Powell to all members of the House Education and Labor Committee, May 5, 1966. Adam Clayton Powell File, LBJL.
2. *1967 Congressional Quarterly*, p. 535.
3. Memorandum for the President, from Henry H. Wilson, Jr., July 18, 1966. LE/FA 2, LBJL.
4. Letter from Adam Clayton Powell to Hon. Wayne L. Hays, December 17, 1966. Report of Committee on House Administra-

tion, Special Subcommittee on Contracts. House Report N. 2349. 89th Congress, 2d Session, 1967.

5. Bayard Rustin, Columbia University Oral History Interview.
6. "15 Facts," statement issued January 5, 1967, by the Office of Adam Clayton Powell. *1967 Congressional Quarterly Almanac*, pp. 536–37. The statement was reproduced in the press across the country.
7. *New York Post*, January 9, 1967.
8. Memo in Office Files of Henry H. Wilson, Jr., January 9, 1967. Box 28, LBJL.
9. *New York Times*, January 19, 1967.
10. Statement on Adam Clayton Powell, January 23, 1967, by Dr. Martin Luther King, Jr., A. Philip Randolph, Bayard Rustin, Roy Wilkins, and Whitney M. Young. NAACP Papers, Group III, B-378, Library of Congress.
11. *New York Post*, January 25, 1967.
12. *New York Post*, January 12, 1967.
13. "In Defense of Powell," *Pittsburgh Courier*, January 21, 1967.
14. *National Guardian*, January 21, 1967.
15. *New York Times*, January 16, 1967.
16. *New York Times*, January 21, 1967.
17. *Ibid.*
18. *Daily Worker*, January 17, 1967.
19. "Disciplining of Powell," *New York Times*, January 13, 1967, p. 12.
20. "Wilkins Accuses Powell of Apathy," *New York Times*, January 14, 1967.
21. "Rebuke for Powell," *New York Times*, January 10, 1967, p. 42.
22. *Life*, January 13, 1967.
23. Memo from Henry Wilson, Jr., to the President, January 3, 1967. EX LE/LI, Box 51, LBJL.
24. Memo from Henry H. Wilson, Jr., to the President, January 24, 1967. PE I, LBJL. Wilson's apparent conclusion about the Speaker came from McCormack's inability to work out a compromise before the vote, perhaps even his inability to get Powell to cooperate in the first place.
25. The most authoritative firsthand account of the committee's deliberations was made by one of its members. See Andy Jacobs, *The Powell Affair: Freedom Minus One* (New York: Bobbs-Merrill Company, Inc., 1973).
26. *New York Post*, January 19, 1967.
27. Jacobs, *The Powell Affair*, p. 2.
28. Interview with Joseph Rauh, November 8, 1989, Washington, D.C.
29. Jacobs, p. 140.
30. *Ibid.*, p. 143.
31. *Congressional Quarterly*, February 17, 1967, p. 246.

32. Jacobs, p. 219.
33. Quoted in Kent M. Weeks, *Adam Clayton Powell and the Supreme Court* (New York: Dunellen Publishing Company, Inc., 1971).
34. *Congressional Quarterly*, January 12, 1968, p. 71.
35. FBI Files. No. HG 100-51230-A, January 24, 1968.
36. FBI Files. Logs, No. HG 100-111180-9-155, January 16, 1968.
37. "Anti-Powell Forces Are Gaining in Harlem," *New York Times*, December 5, 1969, p. 47.
38. *Ibid.* Later Rangel would often say that, in effect, he ran for a "vacant seat."
39. Interview with Charles Rangel, January 22, 1990, New York City.
40. *New York Times*, January 20, 1970, p. 18.
41. *New York Times*, February 1, 1970, p. 44.
42. *Amsterdam News*, January 10, 1970.
43. Informal discussion with Adam Clayton Powell, February 15, 1970, Cleveland, Ohio. I told him of a telephone conversation I had with him eleven years earlier over a bill he introduced on voting rights for our civil rights group in Tuskegee, Alabama. Obviously he did not remember, and we jokingly alluded to his fading memory, but he proceeded to discuss the years of the 1950s when he kept introducing the Powell Amendment. He was proud of those struggles, he said. He kept repeating, "Good fight, good fight. Tough times, tough times. But I finally got it passed in the '64 bill. That's what people won't forget. Win? Of course, I'll win."
44. FBI Files. March 10, 1970, No. HG 100-51230, Sub A, Section 9.
45. Press release, May 22, 1970: "Assemblyman Charles Rangel Blasts Congressman Adam Powell's Visit to Vietnam."
46. Press release, June 17, 1970, from "Rangel for Congress."
47. Press release, June 17, 1970.
48. FBI Files. No. HG 100-51230-423. Transcript of speech by Powell on February 26, 1970, at Chicago State College.
49. *Amsterdam News*, "Our Choice," June 20, 1970.
50. *Amsterdam News*, July 4, 1970, p. 10.
51. FBI Files. June 25, 1970, No. HG 100-51230, Section 19.
52. At the time of his death, Powell was living with Darlene Expose Hine, who was caring for him in his illness. A dispute arose between Ms. Hine and Powell's wife in Puerto Rico over Powell's marital status and custody of the body. A Miami circuit court ruled that Ms. Hine should take the body to Abyssinian Baptist Church for a funeral and, according to Powell's will, have it cremated. Ms. Hine made no claim of being Powell's lawful wife. See *New York Times*, April 5, 1972, pp. 1, 30.

Chapter 21

1. Editorial, "King vs. Powell," *New York Times*, April 6, 1972, p. 42.
2. *New York Times*, April 6, 1972, p. 32.
3. *New York Times*, April 10, 1972, p. 1.
4. James Q. Wilson, "Two Negro Politicians: An Interpretation," *The Midwest Journal of Political Science*, Vol. IV, No. 4 (November 1960), pp. 346–69.
5. Clarence M. Mitchell interview, Columbia University Oral History Records, July 24, 1981.
6. Bayard Rustin interview, Columbia University Oral History Records.
7. Gordon Parks, "The Violent End of the Man Called Malcolm X," *Life*, March 5, 1965.
8. Interview with John A. Davis, New Rochelle, New York, November 29, 1989.
9. "The Life and Times of Adam Clayton Powell," WNBC-TV, New York, Gus Heningberg, producer, April 1, 1990.
10. *New York Times*, November 15, 1989, p. C-24.

Index

Charles V. Hamilton is the Wallace S. Sayre Professor of Government at Columbia University. He received his Ph.D. from the University of Chicago and has taught at several universities, including Tuskegee, Rutgers, Lincoln (Pa.), and Roosevelt, his undergraduate alma mater. In addition to a Guggenheim Fellowship and alumni awards from Roosevelt University and the University of Chicago, he has received the Mark Van Doren Teacher Award from Columbia College; the Great Teaching Award from the Society of Columbia Graduates; and the Lindback Distinguished Teaching Award at Lincoln University.

OTHER COOPER SQUARE PRESS TITLES OF INTEREST

AFRICA EXPLORED
Europeans on the Dark Continent, 1769–1889
Christopher Hibbert
344 pp., 54 b/w illustrations, 16 maps
0-8154-1193-6
$18.95

A NEGRO EXPLORER AT THE NORTH POLE
Matthew A. Henson
Preface by Booker T. Washington
Foreword by Robert E. Peary, Rear Admiral, U.S.N.
New introduction by Robert A. Bryce
232 pp., 6 b/w photos
0-8154-1125-1
$15.95

BLACKFACE
Reflections on African Americans in the Movies
Expanded Edition
Nelson George
330 pp., 23 b/w photos
0-8154-1194-4
$16.95

JUST FOR A THRILL
Lil Hardin Armstrong, First Lady of Jazz
James L. Dickerson
350 pp., 15 b/w photos
0-8154-1195-2
$28.95

WESTSIDE
The Coast-to-Coast Explosion of Hip Hop
William Shaw
334 pp.
0-8154-1196-0
$16.95

WAITING FOR DIZZY
Fourteen Jazz Portraits
Gene Lees
Foreword by Terry Teachout
272 pp.
0-8154-1037-9
$17.95

OSCAR PETERSON
The Will to Swing
Updated Edition
Gene Lees
328 pp., 15 b/w photos
0-8154-1021-2
$18.95

REMINISCING WITH NOBLE SISSLE AND EUBIE BLAKE
Robert Kimball and William Bolcom
256 pp., 244 b/w photos
0-8154-1045-X
$24.95

JOSEPHINE BAKER
The Hungry Heart
Jean-Claude Baker & Chris Chase
592 pp., 84 b/w photos
0-8154-1149-9
$18.95